Contents

KU-629-929

Introduction

These are testing times for hotels. The recession has hit them with a double whammy: banks, once so profligate in their lending, have cracked down on credit for small businesses, while potential guests are being much more careful about their spending. Some weaker hotels have fallen by the wayside. Each week brings a new advertisement in the trade press for the sale of a hotel on the instructions of an administrator. There are other equally troubling threats to the kind of small, owner-managed hotel that the *Guide* has long championed. Despite the fluctuations in the property market, prospective buyers of existing hotels believe that they will get a better financial return by converting the buildings into apartment blocks. The *Gara Rock Hotel* in Devon, a popular *Guide* entry for several years, has been torn down and is being replaced by 'self-catering holiday apartments' with an attached restaurant. Two hotels on the Isles of Scilly are set to be converted into 'serviced apartments': *St Martin's on the Isle*, St Martin's, was due to close in October 2009; *The Island Hotel*, Tresco, will continue to operate for the 2010 season, but planning permission has been granted for the building to be replaced by apartments and a new restaurant.

Another threat to the hard-pressed independent hotelier is what the *Guide*'s founding editor, Hilary Rubinstein, called 'the formidable opposition of the big battalions with all the resources and economies of scale which they are able to deploy'. He was writing in the first edition in 1977, but the message is just as valid today. Then, the threat was led by the remorseless growth of the Trusthouse chain (later owned by Forte). Today's threat comes with a fierce discounting campaign by budget hotel groups offering rooms from £29 a night. This is targeted at guests who would otherwise choose a three- or four-star hotel. At the higher end of the hotel spectrum, we have watched as the von Essen group has bought up a significant number of owner-managed hotels long liked by readers. We bear von Essen no ill will, but the experience of our correspondents and inspectors bears out our preference for individually managed establishments. It is instructive that the two von Essen properties which we continue to include are those where the managers are still evidently in charge (Joan Reen who has remained as hands-on manager at *Ynyshir Hall*, Eglwysfach, and Jason Hornbuckle, the chef/*patron* at *Lewtrenchard Manor*, Lewdown).

Happily, the vast majority of the hotels favoured by the *Guide* are weathering the storms: as ever, we salute these dedicated hoteliers who provide the comfort, character and service that our readers enjoy. And we welcome those enterprising newcomers to hotel-keeping who bring fresh ideas and enthusiasm without stinting on the old-fashioned values of care.

When is a hotel not a hotel?

'It's not a hotel, yet this is the sort of place I buy the *Guide* for.' This comment from a reader catches the spirit that informs the *Guide*'s selection. There is something for every taste and budget in our choices, which explains the variety. We are sometimes asked why bed-and-breakfast establishments are included alongside more traditional hotels. A simple B&B or guest house might not provide all the facilities of a full-service hotel, but those which we have selected offer good value as well as a warm welcome and a concern for the welfare of the visitor from hands-on owners. Often the breakfast at a B&B is considerably better than the offerings from some larger hotels which ought to know better.

Perhaps the biggest change in recent times on the British and Irish hospitality scene is in the much-improved quality of the cooking. A recurring theme in our entries this year has been praise for chefs who make skilful use of fresh local produce, often with vegetables from their own garden, top-drawer meat from nearby butchers, fish straight from the quay. When bright young chefs look to start their own business, they are more likely to open a restaurant with rooms attached than a hotel. This explains the increasing number of restaurants-with-rooms within these pages. The quality of the cooking is considered by many readers to be as important as the ambience of the bedroom. The *Guide*'s editors maintain an eagle eye on the comfort of the facilities, and whether breakfast is given as much thought as dinner, when assessing restaurants-with-rooms. Many pass the test with flying colours: *Morston Hall* in north Norfolk, and the *Kilberry Inn* on the Kintyre peninsula each receive a *César* award this year.

Likes and dislikes

In a report this year, a *Guide* inspector identified the special quality that can define a good hotel. 'What made all the difference were the things that cost relatively little but need thought: gorgeous fresh flowers; a roaring log fire though the evening wasn't that cold; intelligent use of space.' She was writing about *Heasley House*, North Molton, another of this year's *César* winners, but the accolade applies to many of our favourite hotels. We do not inspect hotels with a checklist or a set of boxes to tick (we are not looking for a trouser press or 24-hour room service). Little details help us separate the good from the bad. Here, in no particular order, are some of the things we like, and some that we don't:

We like

• Good bedside lighting • Proper hangers in the wardrobe • Fresh milk with the tea tray in the bedroom • A choice between blankets and sheets and a duvet • Fresh bread and home-made preserves at breakfast.

We don't like

• Bossy notices in the bedrooms and bathroom • Intrusive background music • Hidden service charges • Restricted breakfast times • Stuffy dress codes.

New GHG website wins praise

One asset welcomed by readers and hoteliers and the media is the *Guide*'s newly designed website, which is attracting up to 15,000 unique visitors every month. Described by the *Sunday Times* as 'fiercely independent', www.goodhotelguide.com has been selected by *The Times* as one of its top 100 travel websites. We believe that it is an excellent complement to the printed guide.

Thank you

The reports on hotels by readers are what give the *Guide* its edge. Every comment, positive or negative, is considered before the entries are written. All reports are carefully monitored and filtered to detect the sort of collusive praise (usually encouraged by the hotelier) that can be found on TripAdvisor. The editing process is crucial: the editors are not frightened to take the occasional risk in the search for a good hotel. Our thanks go to all the correspondents who take such trouble to update us on *Guide* entries and recommend new ones. And we are hugely grateful to our experienced inspectors who travel long distances at their own expense to check hotels.

DESMOND BALMER AND ADAM RAPHAEL
July 2009

The 2010 César Awards

Our *César* award, named after César Ritz, the most celebrated of all hoteliers, is the accolade that hoteliers most want to win. Every year we nominate ten places that stand out for their excellence. Our laurel wreaths are not given for grandeur: we champion independent hotels of all types and sizes. The following special places caught our eye this year. Each has a distinct character; what they have in common is an attitude to service that puts the customer first. Previous *César* winners, provided that they are still in the same hands and as good as ever, are indicated in the text by the symbol of a small laurel leaf.

LONDON HOTEL OF THE YEAR

Durrants

A traditional British atmosphere is maintained at the Miller family's discreet Georgian building. One of London's oldest privately owned hotels, it is liked for the old-fashioned values and service. The staff are attentive but never stuffy.

CUMBRIAN INN OF THE YEAR

The Punch Bowl Inn, Crosthwaite

In the lovely Lyth valley, this old inn has been sympathetically restored by Paul Spencer and Richard Rose, combining history with contemporary taste. Visitors are well looked after while village needs are fulfilled.

RESTAURANT-WITH-ROOMS OF THE YEAR

Morston Hall, Morston

The exceptional cooking of Galton Blackiston and his chefs has long attracted food lovers to this Jacobean mansion on the north Norfolk coast. Bedrooms are well thought out, and breakfast is up to the standards of dinner.

DEVON HOTEL OF THE YEAR

Heasley House, North Molton

Hospitality and attention to detail make all the difference at Jan and Paul Gambrill's Georgian dower house on the southern edge of Exmoor national park: gorgeous flowers, a roaring fire, a warm welcome. His uncomplicated modern cooking is much liked.

NEWCOMER OF THE YEAR

The Elephant at Pangbourne

In a 'characterful' village on the Thames, Christoph Brooke has restored this 19th-century hotel with flair and style. It scores in all departments: the staff are warm, the accommodation is attractive, and Douglas Lindsay's cooking is skilful.

CORNISH HOTEL OF THE YEAR
driftwood hotel, Porthscatho

Paul and Fiona Robinson keep a close eye on every aspect of their contemporary hotel in an idyllic spot on the Roseland peninsula. The style is elegant and understated, the staff are anxious to please. Chris Eden's modern European dishes are delicious.

ROMANTIC HOTEL OF THE YEAR
Howard's House, Teffont Evias

In a quiet English village with the little River Teff running through, this wisteria-clad dower house is managed with courtesy and skill by Noële Thompson. It has the feel of a country home; the hillside garden is a place to relax, and the food is enjoyed.

INN OF THE YEAR
Kilberry Inn, Kilberry

In a glorious setting on the remote Kintyre peninsula, this unpretentious inn is run with friendly efficiency by Clare Johnson and David Wilson. The atmosphere is happy, and the food is sublime. The modern bedrooms are simple but stylish.

WELSH COUNTRY HOUSE OF THE YEAR
Neuadd Lwyd, Penmynydd

Susannah and Peter Woods are proud of the Welsh atmosphere at their immaculate early Victorian rectory in farmland with splendid views of the mountains of Snowdonia. They look after visitors well. She uses local ingredients for her excellent dinners.

IRISH HOTEL OF THE YEAR
Rosleague Manor, Letterfrack

Guests are made to feel special at the Foyle family's Georgian manor house on Connemara's Atlantic coast. Mark Foyle is a personable manager, involved in all aspects of the hotel. The freshest fish is featured in Pascal Marinot's uncomplicated menus.

Readers' Club and Report of the Year

Send us a review of your favourite hotel.
As a member of the club, you will be entitled to:
1. A pre-publication discount offer
2. Personal advice on hotels
3. Advice if you are in dispute with a hotel

Send your review via:
our website: www.goodhotelguide.com
or email: editor@goodhotelguide.com
or fax: 020-7602 4182
or write to:
Good Hotel Guide, Freepost PAM 2931, London W11 4BR
(no stamp is needed in the UK)
or, from outside the UK:
Good Hotel Guide, 50 Addison Avenue, London W11 4QP,
England

Readers' contributions are the lifeblood of the *Good Hotel Guide*. Everyone who writes to the *Guide* is a potential winner of the Report of the Year competition. Each year a dozen correspondents are singled out for the helpfulness and generosity of their reports. They win a copy of the *Guide*, and an invitation to our annual launch party in October. The following generous readers are winners this year.

Janet and Dennis Allom of Cawsand
David Berry of London
Brian and Mary Blaxall of Chelmsford
Jane and Tony Cowan of Oulston
Josephine and Tony Green of Leeds
Jean and Richard Green of Ambaston
Jim Grover of London
Max Lickfold of Olney
Susan and Colin Raymond of Pulborough
Angela Thomason of Glenfield
Michael Wace of London
Mrs G Wolstenhome of Bucks Green

Hotelfinder

A visit to a hotel should be a special occasion. This section will help you find a good hotel that matches your mood, whether for romance or sport, or to entertain the children. Don't forget to turn to the full entry for the bigger picture.

DISCOVERIES

There are 55 new hotels in the *Guide* this year. Here are some of the most interesting finds

The Marquis at Alkham, Alkham

In a pretty village on the Kent Downs, this 200-year-old inn was given a thorough makeover before reopening as a restaurant-with-rooms. It has a white-painted brick exterior. The interior is contemporary, with oak flooring, exposed brickwork, pale grey walls. Charles Lakin's three-course menu is a well-balanced 'celebration of English produce' with local wines; breakfast includes kippers from Whitstable.
Read more: page 73.

whitehouse, Chillington

In 'charming' gardens on the edge of a South Hams village, this Georgian house has been given a modern interior by Tamara Costin, Matthew Hall and Ally Wray (the chef). They run it in 'an unfussy way', creating 'a country house atmosphere without pretension'. In the conservatory restaurant, local and organic ingredients are used. The Aga-cooked breakfast is served until '11-ish'.
Read more: page 130.

Shakespeare House, Grendon Underwood

Property developers Nick Hunter and Roy Elsbury have renovated, 'with a sense of theatre', this half-timbered, mullion-windowed Elizabethan coaching inn (Grade II listed) in a village near Bicester. The 'exquisite' lounge and 'opulent' dining room have a dramatic decor; bedrooms have elaborate fittings, a modern bathroom. The high-quality breakfast has fresh fruit salad, home-made jams.
Read more: page 164.

Charles Cotton Hotel, Hartington

In an attractive Peak District village, Ray and Carolyn Cook have renovated this stone-built 17th-century coaching inn, creating a 'happy buzz'. Imaginative meals are served in the simple dining room. Bedrooms, in the main house and a converted stable block, have original beams, pine furnishings.
Read more: page 170.

Verzon House, Ledbury

Experienced hoteliers Peter and Audrey Marks, with their

daughter, Jane (the manager), have renovated this handsome Georgian farmhouse (1790) which has uninterrupted views to the Malvern hills. Inside are original cornices, open fires. Each bedroom has its own style. Chef Ian Howell cooks 'first-class' modern American and European dishes.
Read more: page 194.

The Anchor Inn, Lower Froyle

In a prosperous village on the edge of the South Downs, this handsome old inn has been given the 'relaxed, understated look of a bygone England'. Public rooms have low beams, open fires, an 'amiable clutter of bygones'. Bedrooms have generous bedlinen, earthy fabrics, lots of pictures. Kevin Chandler's modern cooking is 'inventive but unpretentious'.
Read more: page 206.

Three Choirs Vineyard, Newent

There are hints of Tuscany in the views across vines from the restaurant and rooms of the Three Choirs estate, one of Britain's best-regarded vineyards. French windows open on to a terrace from the large bedrooms: eight are in a single-storey building beside the restaurant; three lodges are among the vines. Excellent estate wines are served at dinner.
Read more: page 231.

Lovat Arms, Fort Augustus

On the southern shore of Loch Ness, this former railway hotel has been thoughtfully renovated by experienced hoteliers David and Geraldine Gregory (who ran *The Torridon* for ten years) and their daughter, Caroline, the managing partner. The decor is a mix of the traditional and the modern. Guests can choose between a brasserie menu and more formal dishes.
Read more: page 337.

Bryniau Golau, Bala

Katrina Le Saux and Peter Cottee are 'welcoming, personal and natural' hosts at their Victorian house which has wonderful views on the eastern edge of Snowdonia national park. Bedrooms are impeccably furnished; bathrooms have state-of-the-art fittings. Visitors share a long table for the excellent breakfast that uses local produce.
Read more: page 382.

Cairn Bay Lodge, Bangor

The white pebble-dashed home of Chris and Jenny Mullen (and their daughters, Poppy and Daisy) overlooks a bay on the outskirts of a seaside resort on the Belfast Lough. They run it as a 'tranquil' B&B. Breakfast is 'exceptional', with interesting variations of the traditional Ulster fry.
Read more: page 430.

VALUE

Limit the damage to your
wallet at these hotels;
each offers value in its
own category

Abbey House, Abbotsbury

In a lovely, large garden next to a
fragment of an 11th-century
abbey, this 15th-century building
is run 'with kindness and
friendliness' by Jonathan and
Maureen Cooke. There are flagstoned floors, panelled doors,
original windows; lots of chintz
and knick-knacks in the cosy
lounge and cottagey bedrooms.
Breakfast, served on damask, has
a cold buffet and wide choice of
cooked dishes. B&B £35–£50 per
person. Evening meals for house
parties only.
Read more: page 72.

The Old Store, Halnaker

This inexpensive B&B is an
18th-century red brick and flint
house, once the village store and
bakery. Patrick and Heather
Birchenough are the 'model'
hosts. There are beamed
ceilings, a small lounge. Some
bedrooms look across fields to
Chichester cathedral. Breakfast
has free-range eggs, local
sausages. There is a pub across
the road for evening meals. B&B
£30–£47.50 per person.
Read more: page 166.

Charles Cotton Hotel, Hartington

In an attractive Peak District
village, this stone-built 17th-
century coaching inn with 'a
happy buzz' provides 'excellent
value, good food'. Imaginative
food with generous portions in
the simple dining room; equally
good breakfasts. B&B £30–£55
per person, D,B&B £48.75–
£67.50.
Read more: page 172.

Dalegarth House, Keswick

'One of the best bargains
around', this Edwardian guest
house overlooks Derwentwater.
The bedrooms have flowers from
the garden. The owners, Bruce
and Pauline Jackson, are locals.
He cooks an 'excellent, sensible
menu', with mainly local
produce, some of it home grown.
D,B&B £55–£65 per person.
Read more: page 185.

Molesworth Manor, Little Petherick

Complimentary tea greets
arriving guests at Jessica and
Geoff French's B&B in a village
near Padstow. The 17th-century
former rectory has 'plenty of

sitting room and bedroom space'. The 'superb' breakfast includes freshly baked muffins and a daily special. B&B £29–£50 per person. *Read more: page 199.*

The Chaff House, Littlebury Green

Diana Duke is 'exceptionally hospitable, and a brilliant cook' at her delightful barn conversion in a quiet village near Saffron Walden. The bedrooms are 'relaxing and comfortable'; no baths but 'super power showers'. On weekdays she cooks a 'delicious' farmhouse meal by arrangement, using local produce. B&B £35–£50 per person; set dinner £25. *Read more: page 200.*

The Black Swan, Ravenstonedale

In a conservation village in the Eden valley, Alan and Louise Dinnes, 'likeable and friendly', have renovated this Victorian inn, incorporating a village shop. Real ales are served in the bar. An extensive menu of 'generous portions of straightforward food', much of it sourced locally, is taken in two dining rooms. Bedrooms are well equipped; two have direct outdoor access. B&B £37.50–£55 per person, dinner £33. *Read more: page 254.*

Bealach House, Duror

The only dwelling in 'stunning scenery', Jim and Hilary

McFadyen's small guest house is surrounded by woods and mountains (much wildlife). The bedrooms, though not large, are warmly furnished; beds have a thick mattress, 'gorgeous soft pillows'. She is a 'superb' cook. A complimentary glass or two of 'very drinkable' wine is offered at dinner. B&B £40–£55 per person, dinner £28. *Read more: page 333.*

The Steam Packet Inn, Whithorn

This 'delightful' inn stands on the quayside of a pretty sea-faring village on the tip of the Machars peninsula. It is run by Alastair Scoular, who promises 'no TV, fruit machines or piped music'. Fresh fish (landed at the doorstep) and local lamb are served in a cheerful dining room. Seven of the rooms are in the family's neighbouring pub. B&B £30–£55 per person, dinner £20. *Read more: page 377.*

The Hand at Llanarmon, Llanarmon Dyffryn Ceiriog

'*The Hand* is part of the community, popular with locals and visitors alike,' say visitors to Martin and Gaynor De Luchi's old inn at the head of a pretty valley. 'Comfortable' bedrooms, housekeeping 'immaculate'. Large restaurant, serving 'straightforward, hearty' food. D,B&B £60–£87.50 per person. *Read more: page 397.*

GREEN

Enjoy a guilt-free stay at
these places which take
active measures to protect
the environment

Paskins Town House, Brighton

Soap and shampoo are synthetic-free, animal-free at Susan and Roger Marlowe's 'quirky' B&B in a conservation area near the sea. They hold a Green Business Tourism Gold Award. Breakfast has organic local ingredients, Fairtrade tea and coffee; vegetarian dishes are a speciality. *Read more: page 111.*

Treglos Hotel, Constantine Bay

The Barlow family 'are doing their best to become greener' at their traditional hotel on the north Cornish coast. Two new condenser boilers have reduced oil consumption by 50 per cent; they have installed new shower heads, 'hippos' in the loos to reduce water consumption, and low-energy light bulbs. Chemical usage on their golf course has been reduced by 60 per cent. *Read more: page 134.*

Overwater Hall, Ireby

At their castellated Grade II listed Georgian mansion, owners Stephen Bore and Adrian and Angela Hyde are 'committed to being considerate, not only to their guests and staff, but also towards the environment'. They avoid products imported by aircraft, and food items packaged in polystyrene or plastic. A biomass boiler that burns environmentally friendly fuel has been installed. *Read more: page 184.*

Augill Castle, Kirkby Stephen

'Not quite the good life, but it's a good life,' say Simon and Wendy Bennett who run their Victorian fantasy-Gothic castle in informal style. 'From recycling to investing in new technology, nothing is overlooked.' Heating stoves use fuel from managed local woods; low-energy light bulbs are used; bathrobes are made from a special eco-weave. *Read more: page 187.*

Bedruthan Steps Hotel, Mawgan Porth

'Going green is no longer an option, it's a necessity,' says Ellie Dyer, the sustainability manager at this large hotel above a sandy beach in north Cornwall. She oversees environmental practices that include recycling, and efficient water and energy

consumption. The hotel staff are encouraged to join a green team to discuss new initiatives.
Read more: page 217.

Strattons, Swaffham

Vanessa and Les Scott 'passionately believe in ethical business systems' at their Palladian-style villa in a Norfolk market town. Their environmental policy covers practical things (recycling, etc) and broader issues (a discount of 10 per cent on the B&B rate is given to visitors who arrive by public transport). She leads a team of chefs who use local ingredients for 'interesting, tasty' dishes. Four eco-lodges are being built.
Read more: page 285.

Lovat Arms, Fort Augustus

Caroline Gregory follows a green policy at this former railway hotel on the southern shore of Loch Ness. A biomass woodchip burner provides heating and hot water; eco-friendly cleaning products are used, as are energy-saving lamps. The decor mixes traditional with modern; the staff, mainly female, are 'attentive'.
Read more: page 337.

Argyll Hotel, Iona

'A delightful hotel on a magical island': it is a short walk from the jetty where the ferry from Mull docks. Owners Daniel Morgan and Claire Bachellerie have a strong ecological ethos: most of their produce is organically home grown, local or Fairtrade. They are committed recyclers and users of environmentally friendly products. Corridor lights are dimmed in the evening.
Read more: page 346.

Y Goeden Eirin, Dolydd

'Green doesn't have to be spartan; it's simply a natural way of living,' says John Rowlands who runs this small guest house near Caernarfon with his wife, Eluned. They follow recycling and composting policies, serve locally sourced organic food, Fairtrade tea and coffee, and have installed solar panels. Guests arriving by train are met at Bangor, and advice is given about the 'excellent local transport'.
Read more: page 392.

Hafod Elwy Hall, Pentrefoelas

At their 'characterful house with an Edwardian feel' on a working farm on the Denbighshire mountains, Roger and Wendy Charles-Warner have won awards for sustainability. The cooking is 'country style, authentic'; everything is home made: they produce their own lamb, pork and beef; eggs come from the farm's hens; vegetables and fruit are organically grown.
Read more: page 410.

FAVOURITE B&Bs

Breakfast is often better than at a five-star hotel at these homely B&Bs

The Kennard, Bath

The Anglo-Italian owners, Giovanni and Mary Baiano, are 'most helpful' at their Georgian town house just over the Pulteney Bridge. They have decorated the house in flamboyant style: a golden urn on the landing is flanked by a pair of *chaise longues*. Bedrooms have swagged pelmets, heavy drapes and colourful cushions. Breakfast ingredients come from local farms.
Read more: page 87.

The Mount, Bideford

Andrew and Heather Laugharne are the 'warm and accommodating' owners of this imposing Georgian house near the town centre and quay. 'Charming, and airy', it is decorated in bright colours. 'Everything is spotless' in the bedrooms. Guests have access to the pretty, partly walled garden.
Read more: page 94.

The Old Rectory, Boscastle

Guests are encouraged to 'come and go throughout the day' by Sally and Chris Searle at their historic rectory (immortalised by Thomas Hardy) near the north Cornish coast. The comfortable guests' sitting room looks over terrace and garden. Breakfast, with organic ingredients, and 'the best produce we have in the garden' served until 10 am.
Read more: page 100.

Orchard Barn, Bradpole

Nigel and Margaret Corbett (formerly owners of *Summer Lodge*, Evershot) receive B&B guests 'with genuine warmth' at their home on the site of an old Dorset farm. Simple but comfortable bedrooms have fine linen, good lighting. 'Unbelievable quality and choice' (free-range eggs cooked many ways, local bacon and sausages) at breakfast.
Read more, page 105.

Parford Well, Chagford

Tim Daniel, for many years manager and co-owner of the elegant *Number Sixteen* in London, runs this smart little B&B in a village in the Dartmoor national park. The house, in a pretty walled garden, has three 'immaculate' small bedrooms

with 'everything you might possibly expect'. Breakfast, taken communally around a farmhouse table, has fresh local produce.
Read more: page 125.

Timberstone, Clee Stanton

In a hamlet in the hills above Ludlow, Alex Read and Tracey Baylis follow a green agenda at their 'charming' house. Bedrooms in the original house have beams, old pine furnishings. Those in an extension have crafted oak fittings. Breakfast, served communally in a lovely linking room, has chunky toast, local bacon and sausages, eggs from their own hens.
Read more, page 131.

Swan House, Hastings

By a charming church on a narrow street of medieval houses in the old town, this 15th-century cottage has been given a 'restful, pleasing' look by the owners, Brendan McDonagh and Lionel Copley. They have furnished it with an eclectic mix of paintings, antiques and bric-a-brac from their online design shop. The large lounge has a beamed ceiling and huge fireplace; bedrooms have original wood beams, white walls and floorboards. Breakfast includes freshly squeezed orange juice, bread from a nearby bakery.
Read more, page 172.

The Lynch Country House, Somerton

'Always worth a detour when in the West Country', Roy Copeland's Grade II listed Regency house stands in extensive grounds in a small town above the Cary valley. In his absence Dave Williamson looks after guests with 'trust and hospitality'. Breakfast is served in an orangery overlooking a lake with black swans, exotic ducks.
Read more, page 278.

Thomas Luny House, Teignmouth

Long liked for its high standards and good value, this Georgian house is run by its 'charming' owners, John and Alison Allan. The bedrooms have tea-making kit with fresh milk, mineral water, books and magazines, bathrobes and flowers. 'Delicious' cake with afternoon tea, taken in a walled garden in summer.
Read more, page 288.

The Grange, Fort William

With 'stunning views over Loch Linnhe', Joan and John Campbell's Victorian Gothic house stands in a 'peaceful' garden on the outskirts of this popular west Highland town. There are fresh flowers from the garden, a decanter of sherry in the bedrooms. Porridge at breakfast comes with whisky, cream, brown sugar and honey.
Read more, page 338.

FAMILY

Parents can relax knowing that their children are welcomed at these family-friendly hotels

The Blakeney Hotel, Blakeney

There is much to occupy young people at Michael Stannard's large, traditional hotel in a village facing the tidal estuary and salt marshes. During school holidays children stay free if sharing an adult's room. There are children's channels on digital TV, an indoor swimming pool, a games room with table tennis, pool and darts, board games. Nearby are good beaches, sailing, fishing water sports, golf and tennis.
Read more: page 105.

The Trout at Tadpole Bridge, Buckland Marsh

In a large garden that slopes down to the Thames, Gareth and Helen Pugh's 17th-century Cotswold pub welcomes children of all ages. Parents themselves, they have made it 'as child-friendly as possible', with games and toys, plenty of space in the garden, 'decent children's menus (no nuggets)'. The atmosphere is informal, the decor contemporary, unfussy. Guests can hire a small electric punt.
Read more: page 118.

The Evesham Hotel, Evesham

Young guests have play areas (with swings, trampoline, slides, etc) in the grounds at John and Sue Jenkinson's quirky, informal hotel. There's a games room and indoor swimming pool. Children have a jokey high tea menu and are charged according to age and the amount eaten. A family suite is among the beams.
Read more: page 151.

Moonfleet Manor, Fleet

In large grounds above the Fleet lagoon, this sprawling Georgian manor house is part of the von Essen group. 'Still excellent' (according to a visitor returning this year), it has two swimming pools, play areas, swings and a slide. There is a supervised nursery for the very small; older siblings can be left at the Four Bears' Den. Children sharing their parents' room stay free.
Read more: page 154.

Augill Castle, Kirkby Stephen

'A family home that welcomes guests', Simon and Wendy Bennett's Victorian Gothic folly is run in informal house-party

style. Their children welcome
visiting young as 'special
friends'; there are cats and dogs,
a playground, a fort in the forest.
Bedrooms are big enough to
take extra beds; some are
interconnecting. Cots and high
chairs are provided.
Read more: page 187.

Swinton Park, Masham

'A good balance is struck
between being child friendly and
offering adults space to get away
from the little monsters,' says a
parent visiting Mark and Felicity
Cunliffe-Lister's creeper-clad
17th-century castle. Family
activity days include treasure
hunts, pony rides, feeding the
ducks. There are 'half-term
heaven' packages and children's
cookery courses.
Read more: page 214.

Bedruthan Steps, Mawgan Porth

Above a golden, sandy beach in
north Cornwall, this large,
purpose-built family hotel has
much for children: an indoor play
area, an Ofsted-registered
nursery, a soft play and ball pool
for toddlers, a junior assault
course, and a teenagers' room. A
family dining option has special
menus for adults and children.
Read more: page 217.

The Seaview, Seaview

A teddy bear is left on the pillow
during the evening turn-down
at this hotel/restaurant near the

sea in a village on the Solent.
Families are actively welcomed:
children's teas are served in
the bar, and there is a child-
friendly brunch. The staff
showed 'unruffled calm', says a
parent. Beaches with rock pools
are nearby.
Read more: page 273.

Calcot Manor, Tetbury

Run by Richard Ball, this
Cotswold hotel combines a
genuine welcome for children
with extensive facilities for
adults. Suites have a bedroom for
parents and a sitting room with
bunk beds or sofa beds for the
young. Older children have an
unsupervised play area; there's
a Playzone for their younger
siblings; for the youngest an
Ofsted-registered crèche. Adults
enjoy the spa (where special
times are allocated for children).
Read more: page 289.

Porth Tocyn Hotel, Abersoch

'Some mothers who come with
children came here as children
themselves,' say the Fletcher-
Brewer family. Their hotel faces
Cardigan Bay and the Snowdonia
mountains on the Lleyn
peninsula. Children have a
dedicated area with a cosy 'snug'
(TV and DVDs) and a games
room with table tennis. High
chairs, cots and baby-listening
devices are available. Excellent
beaches close by.
Read more: page 381.

SEASIDE

Pack your buckets and spades and be ready to get sand in your shoes at these coastal places

Burgh Island Hotel, Bigbury-on-Sea

On a private tidal island in sandy Bigbury Bay, this Art Deco hotel is reached by a specially built sea tractor at high tide. Everything is in period style; mementos of the Jazz Age; 1920s cocktails; diners in full evening dress. There is a natural swimming pool in the rocks; one of the suites is on stilts above a private beach.
Read more: page 94.

Hell Bay Hotel, Bryher

A fine sandy beach lies at the bottom of the garden of this contemporary hotel on the western side of an island reached only by boat; other good beaches can be found around the island. Accommodation is mainly in suites, decorated in appropriate seaside colours (each has a terrace or a balcony); huge seascapes are hung in the restaurant.
Read more: page 116.

Bedruthan Steps Hotel, Mawgan Porth

On a cliffside in a seaside village between Newquay and Padstow, this large, purpose-built hotel stands above a golden, sandy beach with rock pools for young explorers. Atlantic breakers make this surfing territory and there are many good beaches nearby. There is much for children to do beyond the beach: play areas, indoor and outdoor swimming pools, children's clubs, and 'water fun sessions'.
Read more: page 217.

driftwood hotel, Portscatho

A private path down steep steps leads to a quiet beach below this contemporary hotel in an idyllic setting on the Roseland peninsula. There is good walking in both directions along the Cornish coastal paths. The seaside theme is echoed in the interiors; colours are white with shades of blue; driftwood tables and lamps. Almost all the bedrooms face the sea.
Read more: page 251.

The Tides Reach, Salcombe

On a tree-fringed sandy cove inside the Salcombe estuary, the Edwards family's traditional hotel has its own boathouse on South Sands beach. There is safe bathing and many water sports at this sailing resort. Guests can catch a ferry to Salcombe or across the bay to other fine beaches. For damp days, there is a swimming pool in an 'exotic' conservatory.
Read more: page 271.

Soar Mill Cove Hotel, Soar Mill Cove

In grounds that slope down to an isolated cove with a beautiful beach, this single-storey stone and slate hotel is surrounded by National Trust land. Sea-facing rooms have a patio which catches the afternoon sun. It is popular with families: children are warmly welcomed with small swimming pools, a play area, activity packs.
Read more: page 277.

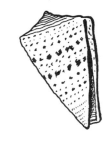

Island Hotel, Tresco

'We could lie in bed looking over a small garden to the sea and other islands,' say visitors to Robert Dorrien-Smith's 'splendid' single-storey hotel on a promontory by a large sandy beach. Most of the bedrooms have a sea view. There are other beaches within easy reach on this small private island.
Read more: page 292.

The Colonsay, Colonsay

Just eight miles long, this idyllic Hebridean island has a dozen white sandy beaches; at low tide a mile-long strip of sand connects Colonsay with the neighbouring island of Oransay. Grey seals, otters, dolphins, even whales can be spotted. Visitors are 'well looked after' at this unpretentious inn, the social hub of the island
Read more: page 327.

Ceol na Mara, Tarbert

The Gaelic name of this renovated stone house above a rocky tidal loch translates as 'music of the sea'. The Isle of Harris is noted for its broad, long white sandy beaches. The hosts, John and Marlene Mitchell, earn 'full marks for everything' at their B&B. For evening meals the *Hotel Hebrides* in Tarbert (see Shortlist) is recommended .
Read more: page 371.

The Druidstone, Broadhaven

On a cliff-top above a huge sandy beach (safe for swimming), this 'family holiday centre' is liked by families for its relaxed, informal welcome for children. Regulars like the 'rough around the edges' feel. Surfing, sailing, windsurfing and canoeing are all available on the beach or nearby.
Read more: page 386.

COUNTRY HOUSE

These bastions of old-fashioned service provide plenty of pampering

Hartwell House, Aylesbury

Owned by the National Trust (and managed by Historic House Hotels), this stately home with a Jacobean front and a Georgian rear is 'exquisite in 18th-century pastoral style'. It is beautifully restored but has all mod cons (air conditioning, flat screen TV in bedrooms). The elegant public rooms are furnished with antiques 'to be used, not just admired'.
Read more: page 81.

Farlam Hall, Brampton

A sense of humour 'abounds alongside proper service' at this manorial house run by the Quinion and Stevenson families since 1975. Approached up a sweeping drive, it stands in an 'immaculate' landscaped garden with a large ornamental lake. Public rooms are ornate, with patterned wallpaper, open fires; bedrooms are traditionally furnished. Barry Quinion cooks 'delicious' country house meals.
Read more: page 107.

Gravetye Manor, East Grinstead

'A lovely place to stay', this creeper-covered Elizabethan manor stands amid woodland in grounds designed by William Robinson, pioneer of the English natural garden. Owners Andrew Russell and Mark Raffan promise 'never to be modern and trendy'; readers agree that it might be 'a little stuck in a time warp, but none the worse for that'.
Read more: page 146.

Summer Lodge, Evershot

Built as a retreat for the earls of Ilchester and enlarged by Thomas Hardy, this country house stands in large grounds in an attractive Dorset village. The staff are 'friendly and helpful'. The pretty bedrooms are traditionally furnished with fine fabrics, heavy drapes. In an 'elegant' dining room, Steven Titman serves 'excellent' modern dishes with French influences.
Read more: page 150.

Stock Hill House, Gillingham

The friendly atmosphere ('guests get to know each other quickly,' says a reader) is liked at this late Victorian mansion, once the country home of the cartoonist Osbert Lancaster. Peter and Nita Hauser are the 'hospitable' owners. Service is formal in the restaurant where his classic cooking sometimes reflects his Austrian heritage. *Read more: page 158.*

Hambleton Hall, Hambleton

The staff at Tim Hart's Victorian mansion balance 'professionalism with relaxed friendliness'. It has an 'idyllic' setting on a peninsula jutting into Rutland Water. His wife, Stefa, designed the classic interiors with Nina Campbell: fine fabrics, antiques, 'traditional but sumptuous and comfortable'. Aaron Patterson has a *Michelin* star for his seasonal cooking. *Read more: page 167.*

Hotel Endsleigh, Milton Abbot

The 'historic feeling' of this luxurious Regency shooting and fishing lodge has been retained in Olga Polizzi's imaginative restoration. It stands in beautiful gardens on an estate running down to the River Tamar. The house has Regency panelling, original artefacts, contemporary paintings; candles provide much of the lighting at night. *Read more: page 222.*

Gilpin Lodge, Windermere

Two generations of the Cunliffe family provide hands-on owner management at their Edwardian country house in woodland and gardens within the Lake District national park. They combine informality with 'exceptional' service. Chef Russell Plowman is 'passionate about using local and organic ingredients'. *Read more: page 305.*

Glenapp Castle, Ballantrae

'Highly recommended as a place of peace and privacy', this 19th-century Scottish baronial castle was restored from near ruin by Graham and Fay Cowan. They have furnished it 'beautifully with antiques lovingly collected during the restoration. The large wooded grounds have a lake, a walled garden, and a Victorian glasshouse. *Read more: page 320.*

Kinnaird, Dunkeld

'Each morning a chambermaid brings tea on a tray and lights the gas log fire.' This creeper-covered Victorian stone mansion in a wooded sporting estate is liked for the discreet service. It is sumptuously furnished; family portraits, a grand piano, antiques, flowers, billiards. Most bedrooms are large, with a view of the valley. Men wear a jacket at dinner in the elegant restaurant (frescoes and ornate ceiling) where Jean-Baptiste Bady uses home-produced or local ingredients for his three-course dinner menu. *Read more: page 331.*

CITY CHIC

Expect cutting-edge urban style and high-tech fittings at these contemporary city hotels

One Aldwych, London

Gordon Campbell Gray's 'wonderfully ultra-modern' conversion of the Edwardian offices of the *Morning Post* has a collection of 400 pieces of contemporary art. Bedrooms have a 'clever, thoughtful' design; all the latest technology.
Read more: page 66.

The rockwell, London

Architect Michael Squire and Tony Bartlett have given two Victorian terrace houses on the Cromwell Road a sharp, modern feel. The bright facade has pea-green highlights; interiors have interesting wallpaper, patterns and colours. Contemporary dishes are served in a restaurant overlooking a courtyard garden.
Read more: page 67.

The Zetter, London

In Clerkenwell, this converted 19th-century warehouse is stylish and comfortable. It has a striking contemporary decor throughout; bright colours; raindance showers in bathrooms. All the bedrooms have been redecorated with neutral colours enlivened by bright splashes of colour. Roof studios have a patio with a panoramic view. Mediterranean dishes are served in the informal restaurant.
Read more: page 70.

The Queensberry, Bath

John Wood designed these four adjoining town houses for the Marquis of Queensberry in 1771. Laurence and Helen Beere have given the interior a 'cool, contemporary' look. A glass roof contributes to a light feel. Public rooms are elegant. Well-designed and furnished bedrooms have neutral colours, modern technology; some have a roll-top bath; suites have a wet room.
Read more: page 89.

drakes, Brighton

You can enjoy the sea views from your bath in more than half the bedrooms at Andy Shearer's modern conversion of two 19th-century town houses on the seafront in sight of the pier. Front rooms have a standalone double-ended bath by the bay window; there are hand-made beds, contemporary ceiling mouldings, natural wood; colours are cream and brown.
Read more: page 110.

Hotel du Vin, Bristol

An imaginative conversion of a group of Grade II listed buildings in the city centre, the Bristol branch of the du Vin chain is liked for the friendly welcome, and the buzzy atmosphere in the bistro. A

glassed canopy entrance opens to a reception desk beside a 100-foot chimney. In the bathrooms there are king-sized beds, stand-alone baths, a walk-in shower.
Read more: page 112.

Hope Street Hotel, Liverpool

A striking modern conversion of a 19th-century carriage works (built in the style of an Italian *palazzo*). It doubled in size in summer 2009 with new bedrooms in a linked adjacent building rebuilt in similar contemporary style. Leather sofas and pop music in the bar; dramatic floor-to-ceiling glass sculptures in the restaurant where chef Paul Askew serves modern dishes.
Read more: page 200.

Hart's Hotel, Nottingham

In a quiet cul-de-sac on the site of the city's medieval castle, Tim Hart's purpose-built hotel has striking lines; curved buttresses; lots of glass. Inside are contemporary artwork and furniture, limestone floors; well-equipped bedrooms (most have 'breathtaking' views); 'efficient'

bathrooms. Light meals, and wine and champagne by the glass are served in the bar; excellent meals in the associated *Hart's* restaurant.
Read more: page 236.

Malmaison, Oxford

Oxford's Victorian castle jail has been imaginatively converted into a modern hotel. Metal walkways, cell doors, keys, spyholes (reversed) have been retained. The lack of light can be seen as dramatic or 'stygian, if deeply trendy'. 'Not a bit stuffy': the young staff are 'professional, welcoming'. Bistro meals in the underground brasserie.
Read more: page 240.

Old Bank, Oxford

'Modern but relaxing', Jeremy Mogford's hotel, centrally located opposite All Souls, is an elegant conversion of three buildings, one a former bank. His abundant collection of modern art is displayed in the public rooms and bedrooms. Most of the rooms face the dreaming spires. The old banking hall houses *Quod*, a lively bar/restaurant.
Read more: page 241.

ROMANCE

Get in the mood for love by spiriting your chosen one away to one of these romantic hotels

Linthwaite House, Bowness-on-Windermere

Sleep under the stars in a new luxury suite at this creeper-covered hotel overlooking Lake Windermere. The loft suite has a sliding glass panel in the ceiling that opens up to allow star-gazing; a telescope is provided. The suite, with its own entrance, has an open-plan design; the highlight in the bathroom is a huge freestanding Italian bath. The house itself has 'amazing views' over the landscaped gardens to the lake.
Read more: page 104.

Hell Bay Hotel, Bryher

You can walk straight to the beach from the terrace of a ground-floor suite at this contemporary hotel on the smallest of the inhabited Scilly islands (no made-up roads, few inhabitants). It is on an isolated bay on the island's wilder western coast, next stop America. The bedrooms are decorated in seaside colours and many face the bay; some have a balcony. Cornish artworks hang in the spacious lounge.
Read more: page 116.

The Abbey Inn, Byland

English Heritage has refurbished this 12th-century inn by the ruins of Byland Abbey, 'one of the most romantic settings in England'. The abbey, floodlit at night, can be seen through the windows of the Byland suite which has a four-poster bed, a seating area, and a modern bathroom with a roll-top bath.
Read more: page 120.

whitehouse, Chillington

Backed by a charming garden, this Georgian house on the edge of a South Hams village has been given a funky modern look. The bedrooms are 'good fun'; lots of natural wood, big handmade beds; one has a rocking chair in the bathroom, a freestanding bath big enough for two, and a separate shower. Breakfast is served until '11-ish'.
Read more: page 130.

The New Inn, Coln St Aldwyns

In a pretty Cotswold village, this 400-year-old inn has been given a make-over by the quirky Hillbrooke group. The bedrooms

are decorated in bold colours: Room 3 has a bright red carpet and back wall, a black bedcover and furnishings. A romantic package promises rose petals on the bed, with chilled bubbly in the room.
Read more: page 132.

Lavenham Priory, Lavenham

Step back into an earlier age at Tim and Gilli Pitt's beautiful Grade I listed building (formerly a priory, later an Elizabethan merchant's mansion). The 13th-century Great Hall has a beamed ceiling, huge inglenook fireplace. The five bedchambers, reached by an oak Jacobean staircase, are spacious; unusual beds (four-poster, polonaise, or sleigh), creaking floorboards.
Read more: page 193.

The Old Railway Station, Petworth

'A unique and nostalgic experience', this B&B by a disused Victorian railway line has been restored with flair. The biggest bedrooms are in the former station building; the most romantic are in converted Pullman railway cars. They have a comfortable bed, and a surprising amount of furniture.
Read more: page 246.

Howard's House, Teffont Evias

In a peaceful English village, this wisteria-clad, mellow stone dower house has a charming hillside garden. It is managed as a small hotel with 'courtesy and skill' by Noële Thompson. Bedrooms have pastel colours, floral prints; some look over a pond to a church steeple. There are tables, parasols, a pergola in the garden; cows in the field opposite.
Read more: page 287.

Holbeck Ghyll, Windermere

In large grounds which slope down to Lake Windermere, this former Victorian hunting lodge is run as a luxurious hotel by David and Patricia Nicholson. Public rooms have 'a baronial feel', with open fires, panelling, antiques. An 'ultimate romantic package' has a mini-facial, red roses, a box of chocolates and champagne. Book this with a room in the main house with a four-poster bed and double spa bath.
Read more: page 306.

Toravaig House, Sleat

In a lovely position on a coast road on the Isle of Skye, this handsome white-painted 1930s building has been renovated by Anne Gracie and Kenneth Gunn. They offer to tailor-make a romantic package for visitors. A former captain of a cruise ship, he takes guests on trips on his 42-foot yacht; you might even get married on board.
Read more: page 369.

GOURMET

Savour the pleasures of the table at these hotels and restaurants-with-rooms without having to drive home

Blagdon Manor, Ashwater

'The south-west has such a larder of ingredients, we need look no further,' says Steve Morey who with his wife, Liz, runs this 17th-century manor house in a 'friendly, easy manner'. His cooking 'never ceases to amaze'. Typical dishes: tempura of skate, mushy peas, onion gravy; slow-cooked Devon beef, scrumpled streaky bacon, corned beef mash, baby onions.
Read more: page 79.

Little Barwick House, Barwick

Tim and Emma Ford's restaurant-with-rooms near the Somerset/Dorset border continues to impress as an 'exceptional all-round experience'. His modern English menu is 'beautifully prepared and presented'. Highlights for a visitor this year were 'scallops; saddle of wild venison; rhubarb and ginger tart'.
Read more: page 82.

Read's, Faversham

David Pitchford sources local produce (fish from the quay at Whitstable, fruit and vegetables from the garden) for his seasonal menus at his Georgian manor house. He has a *Michelin* star for his classic dishes, perhaps smoked eel on a salad of celeriac and potato; Coopers Farm lamb three ways, Puy lentils, Savoy cabbage.
Read more: page 154.

The Star Inn, Harome

A 'proud' Yorkshireman, Andrew Pern 'pays homage to his roots' at his restaurant-with-rooms (*Michelin* star), a thatched medieval longhouse. He gives local ingredients a fresh, modern twist in dishes like 'posh' prawn cocktail, marinated tomatoes, whisky Marie-Rose; belly pork with a warm black pudding; Ampleforth apple salad, fried village duck egg, devilled sauce.
Read more: page 169.

Mr Underhill's, Ludlow

Christopher Bradley's *Michelin*-starred cooking is a high point at his restaurant-with-rooms in gardens by the River Teme below Ludlow Castle. His menu has no choice (alternatives are offered). Dinner starts with 'hobbit-sized tasters'; a visitor this year enjoyed 'stunning' pavé of brill; slow-roasted fillet of

Marches beef 'with a doll's house-sized lasagne'; a tiny cherry sponge before a choice of seven desserts.
Read more: page 208.

Morston Hall, Morston

Tracy and Galton Blackiston's hotel/restaurant in an area of outstanding natural beauty on the north Norfolk coast 'lived up to its reputation for exceptional food' when an inspector called. The four-course dinner (no choice) has 'a sublime balance of ingredients, each flavour distinct': perhaps seared scallop, Alsace bacon, sautéed horse mushrooms, Madeira shallot reduction.
Read more: page 226.

The Neptune, Old Hunstanton

The 'excellent' cooking and 'attractive' presentation of chef Kevin Mangeolles were admired by inspectors at this restaurant-with-rooms, an ivy-clad, red brick coaching inn near the north Norfolk coast. He was awarded a *Michelin* star in 2009 for 'unfussy, flavoursome' dishes, perhaps seared tuna, black olive dressing; English rose veal, cauliflower purée, deep-fried veal tongue, wild mushroom sauce.
Read more: page 237.

The Three Chimneys, Dunvegan

In a remote setting by Loch Dunvegan in north-west Skye, Eddie and Shirley Spear's restaurant-with-rooms, is 'worth every penny', say visitors this year. She is *patronne*/director; Michael Smith the acclaimed chef, uses local meat and fish in dishes like Glenhinnisdale lamb haggis, croft kale, neep purée; roast Mallaig hake and Sconser scallops, parsley mash.
Read more: page 332.

Plas Bodegroes, Pwllheli

A self-taught chef, Chris Chown is passionate about local ingredients for his classically based dishes at the Georgian manor house he runs as a restaurant-with-rooms with his wife, Gunna. 'Pre-starters are served in the bar; Welsh Black beef and mountain lamb, and seafood from the Lleyn peninsula, appear on the dining room menus.
Read more: page 413.

The Crown at Whitebrook, Whitebrook

Inspired by the traditional Welsh cooking of his mother and grandmother, James Sommerin has developed his own style, combining British modernism with French influences, at this 17th-century inn in a village near Monmouth. He has a *Michelin* star for dishes like caramelised pork belly with peanut-encrusted langoustines. One visitor appreciated his under-standing of vegetarian cooking.
Read more: page 418.

GASTROPUBS

Interesting cooking and a lively atmosphere can be expected at these revitalised old inns and pubs

The Devonshire Arms at Beeley, Beeley

'Good fun provided you recognise it's a pub', this 17th-century coaching inn on the Chatsworth estate has been renovated by the Duke and Duchess of Devonshire. The young staff 'take their cooking and serving seriously' in the contemporary brasserie: an inspector this year enjoyed 'superb local sausages, beautifully cooked sea bass, and battered haddock with skinny chips'.
Read more: page 92.

The Horse and Groom, Bourton-on-the-Hill

Brothers Tom and Will (the chef) Greenstock are the hands-on owners of this Georgian coaching inn at the top of the hill in a Cotswold village. It has ancient beams, wooden floors and tables, sisal matting. Local ingredients (vegetables from the garden, eggs from the brothers' chickens) are cooked 'with passion' on a modern menu, perhaps crispy duck salad, oriental dressing; roasted turbot, sautéed samphire.
Read more: page 102.

The Royal Oak, East Lavant

Chef Simon Haynes serves modern European and English dishes in this listed Georgian flintstone inn in an attractive village near Chichester. The seasonal menu might include chicken liver parfait with toasted cep brioche; beer-battered fish, minted pea purée. Guests returning after the theatre when dinner was over were given a 'lavish cheeseboard'.
Read more: page 147.

The Griffin Inn, Fletching

'A civilised place', the Pullan family's 16th-century Grade II listed coaching inn is in a pretty village overlooking the Ouse valley. Chef Andrew Billings uses local produce (fresh fish from Rye) for his daily-changing menu with dishes like peppered beef carpaccio; black bream, chorizo, chickpeas.
Read more: page 155.

The Chequers Inn, Froggatt Edge

Amid some of the Peak District's finest scenery, this 17th-century inn is 'popular yet calm'. Phil

Ball's cooking, served in an attractive bar/restaurant (dark beams, library chairs), is much admired. He combines pub favourites (lamb shank, winter vegetables) with more modern dishes (garlic prawns, plum sauce, guacamole).
Read more: page 156.

The Angel Inn, Hetton

One of the early inns to take food seriously (moving on from chips with everything), this old drovers' inn in the Yorkshire Dales is liked for the friendly atmosphere and 'impeccable food and service'. Guests can choose from a bar menu with blackboard specials, and a *carte* (try free-range black pudding Scotch egg; organic sea trout ballotine, garden herbs).
Read more: page 175.

The Anchor Inn, Lower Froyle

In a village on the edge of the South Downs, this handsome old inn has the 'relaxed, understated look of a bygone England'. In the dining room, chef Kevin Chandler serves 'inventive but unpretentious' modern dishes (eg, pork, apple and black pudding terrine; lemon sole, whole burnt butter).
Read more: page 206.

The Gurnard's Head, Zennor

Local farmers deliver vegetables and herbs to this yellow-painted inn, 'a laid-back, right-on kind of place' on the north Cornish coast. Chef Robin Wright's menu might include fish soup, rouille, crostini; duck breast, confit leg, boulangère potatoes, red cabbage. 'Nothing fancy' in the bedrooms.
Read more: page 315.

The Felin Fach Griffin, Felin Fach

'Everyone is friendly and knowledgeable about food' at this old inn between the Brecon Beacons and Black Mountains. In the popular restaurant, chef Ricardo Van Ede uses home-grown organic ingredients in dishes like local smoked salmon tartare, watercress panna cotta; wild venison, butternut squash, roasted carrots. The simple bedrooms have luxurious bedlinen.
Read more: page 394.

The Bell at Skenfrith, Skenfrith

In a beautiful setting deep in the Welsh Marches, Janet and William Hutchings's 17th-century coaching inn has flagstone floors, an inglenook fireplace, 'simple yet sophisticated' bedrooms. The restaurant serves elaborate modern British dishes, perhaps seared foie gras, glazed chicory, orange syrup; caramelised loin of Welsh lamb, braised sweetbreads; fondant potato.
Read more: page 415.

GARDENS

Glorious gardens and beguiling landscapes make each of these hotels a destination in its own right

Lindeth Fell, Bowness-on-Windermere

Laid out by Thomas Mawson (a renowned Windermere landscape gardener), the gardens at Pat and Diana Kennedy's Edwardian house above Lake Windermere are filled with rhododendrons, azaleas and specimen trees. When at its best, in spring and early summer, it is open to the public. A small lake is a haunt for wildlife.
Read more: page 103.

Gravetye Manor, East Grinstead

The gardens are filled with bulbs, wild flowers and indigenous varieties at this luxurious hotel, a 16th-century manor house, once the home of William Robinson, the father of the English natural garden. He was helped by his close friend, Gertrude Jekyll, in the planting of a naturalistic garden. Only hotel guests have access to the gardens.
Read more: page 146.

Lewtrenchard Manor, Lewdown

The gardens at this manor house (mentioned in the Domesday Book) have walkways, an avenue of beech trees, fountains, statuary and sunken lawns. They were designed by Walter Sorel and Gertrude Jekyll. It is now run as a small hotel/restaurant by chef/*patron* Jason Hornbuckle for the von Essen group. There's a large rustic dovecot and a restored walled garden.
Read more: page 196.

Hob Green, Markington

Walkways and paths lead through extensive herbaceous borders to feature lawns in the 800-acre grounds of the Hutchinson family's traditional hotel. There are award-winning gardens, a rockery and a pergola; a large greenhouse and a walled kitchen garden. Beyond are woodlands and a farm.
Read more: page 212.

Meudon, Mawnan Smith

Rare shrubs, plants and trees abound in the grounds of the Pilgrim family's traditional hotel which stands at the head of a wooded valley leading to a private beach. A fine example of a Cornish 'hanging garden' (designed by Robert Were Fox *c.* 1800), it has specimens from early RHS expeditions to the Yangtze and the Himalayas. Giant Australian tree ferns were brought as ballast by packet ships to Falmouth, and thrown overboard in the bay.
Read more: page 219.

Hotel Endsleigh, Milton Abbot

The Duchess of Bedford commissioned Humphry Repton to design the gardens for her shooting and fishing lodge in an extensive wooded estate running down to the River Tamar. It is now run by Olga Polizzi as a luxury hotel. Repton created forested walks, wild meadows, a rose and jasmine walkway. There are rare and grand trees, a parterre beside the veranda, and a shell-covered summer house.
Read more: page 222.

Millgate House, Richmond

Above the River Swale in the pretty town of Richmond, this Georgian house has a much-admired sheltered walled garden. Owners Austin Lynch and Tim Culkin open it to the public from April to October. Meandering paths lead through luxuriant planting; two of the three bedrooms overlook the garden.
Read more: page 256.

Stone House, Rushlake Green

The huge grounds of Jane and Peter Dunn's 15th-century house (with 18th-century modifications) have an ornamental lake, gazebos, a rose garden, a 100-foot herbaceous border, a walled herb, vegetable and fruit garden. Visitors are encouraged to relax in the summer house, explore the gardens, and visit the greenhouses.
Read more: page 262.

Ladyburn, Maybole

Surrounded by woods and fields, Jane Hepburn's former dower house has a luxurious feel. Its large wild and formal gardens, part of Scotland's Garden Scheme, have several authenticated national rose collections. Rhododendrons, bluebells and azaleas flower in spring. Guests may also walk in the grounds of the 'magnificent' neighbouring Kilkerran estate.
Read more: page 358.

Bodysgallen Hall & Spa, Llandudno

Now owned by the National Trust, this Grade I listed 17th-century mansion is 'beautifully situated' in parkland and gardens with views of Snowdonia and Conwy. A rare parterre of box hedges is filled with sweet-scented herbs; there's a walled rose garden; interesting trees including medlar and mulberry; a rockery with a cascade.
Read more: page 400.

FISHING

No need to cast around for
the best beats; these hotels
all have private access to
rivers and lakes

The Arundell Arms, Lifton

Anne Voss-Bark's creeper-
covered sporting hotel has
20 miles of its own water on the
Tamar and six of its tributaries,
and a three-acre stocked lake.
'Spate' rivers rising on the
moors, they have long, slow
pools, gravelly runs, fast shallows
and open glides. Fishing courses
are run for all levels, tackle is
sold and maps provided. The
hotel is liked for its 'immaculate
service' and good food.
Read more: page 197.

The Peat Spade Inn, Longstock

Popular with locals, this old
inn and 'rooming house' has
a tranquil setting in the Test
valley, 'fly-fishing capital of the
world'. Fly-fishing can be
arranged with professional
guides at several of the chalk
stream rivers (including the
Test, Itchen and Dever) within
a few miles of the inn. Guests
also have access to a spring-fed
private estate, good for beginners
and improvers alike. 'Full of
character', the inn has 'charming'
bedrooms, admired cooking.
Read more: page 203.

Hotel Endsleigh, Milton Abbot

A member of the Endsleigh
fishing club, this luxurious hotel
has seven rods on eight miles
of the River Tamar; the club's
ghillie is available to assist
guests fishing for salmon and sea
trout. Built in the early 19th
century as a shooting and fishing
lodge by Georgina, Duchess of
Bedford, the *Endsleigh* has been
restored with style by Olga
Polizzi.
Read more: page 222.

The Inn at Whitewell, Whitewell

High above the River Hodder,
this 300-year-old inn has seven
miles of river with 14 pools and
'lots of interesting runs'. It has
four rods on the Hodder for
trout, sea-trout, and salmon in
season. The inn is filled with
family antiques, old paintings,
oriental rugs. 'Excellent' food is
served in the busy bar and the
more formal dining room.
Read more: page 301.

Kinnaird, Dunkeld

A 'cast and curl up' break at this
luxurious hotel includes fishing
with ghillies for brown trout on

the River Tay, which runs through the 7,000-acre sporting estate. There are two beats on a five-mile stretch of Scotland's largest fishing river, famous for salmon, brown trout and grayling. The listed Victorian stone mansion is sumptuously furnished.
Read more: page 331.

Tomdoun Hotel, Invergarry

Mike Pearson's simple sporting hotel off a single-track drovers' road to Skye has 25,000 acres of water for fishermen on the Upper Garry river and six hill lochs. Ghillie Peter Thomas can supply tackle as well as local knowledge; a three-day course for beginners covers both loch and river fishing. *Tomdoun*, with its roaring log fires and squashy sofas, is recommended as an 'unreconstructed hideaway with old-world charm'.
Read more: page 345.

Gliffaes, Crickhowell

In wooded grounds on a broad sweep of the Usk ('possibly the best brown trout river in England and Wales'), this smart sporting hotel arranges fishing courses. It has a private stretch on the trout- and salmon-laden river whose spawning grounds have been revitalised by a European-funded programme. The best bedrooms have a river view and balcony.
Read more: page 390.

Ballyvolane House, Castlelyons

In glorious grounds with woodland and three trout lakes, Justin and Jenny Green's Georgian home is run on house party lines. They have four beats on a 24-mile stretch of the Blackwater, the finest salmon fishing river in Ireland; these are available at all times in season, others can be arranged.
Read more: page 436.

Newport House, Newport

'All our fish are wild; we do not stock or ranch the system,' say Thelma and Kieran Thompson who hold the fishing rights to eight miles of the River Newport and also have fishing on Lough Beltra West, one of the few fisheries in Ireland where salmon can be fished from a boat. They run their Georgian mansion 'like a large private home'.
Read more: page 454.

Currarevagh House, Oughterard

The fishing is a major draw at the Hodgson family's early Victorian manor house in beautiful parkland and woodland on Lough Corrib, an important wild brown trout lake. They have their own boats and ghillies on the lake, which also has pike, perch, and a small run of salmon from May to July. The family are 'as attentive as one could wish'.
Read more: page 455.

WALKING

Your boots are meant for walking at these hotels which cater for ramblers and casual walkers alike

Biggin Hall, Biggin-by-Hartington

Liked for its 'good value and good food at the price', this small hotel, high in the Peak District, has long been popular with walkers. The style is 'simple, unfussy'. Footpaths lead in all directions over beautiful countryside; nearby disused railway tracks provide flat walking. Rooms in a barn conversion have a porch.
Read more: page 96.

Seatoller House, Borrowdale

At the head of the beautiful Borrowdale valley, this unpretentious guest house has received walkers and climbers for more than a century. The welcome is warm, the atmosphere homely; it is free of 'modern intrusions' like television and radio. Meals are interesting and suitably hearty; there is non-stop coffee and an honesty bar.
Read more: page 99.

Underleigh House, Hope

'Our waterproofs were taken away to be dried.' Philip and Vivienne Taylor, 'generous' hosts, provide maps and packed lunches for walkers at their barn and cottage conversion in the Hope valley in the Peak District national park. There is good walking from the door.
Read more: page 178.

Overwater Hall, Ireby

Ordnance Survey maps are available to guests at this castellated Georgian mansion beside Overwater Tarn, close to Bassenthwaite Lake. There is good walking from the door, from a lakeside ramble to a more demanding mountain climb. Because this is the quieter, northern Lakes, 'you often have it all to yourself'.
Read more: page 184.

Lastingham Grange, Lastingham

On the edge of the North Yorkshire Moors national park, this traditional hotel is run by Bertie Wood, helped by his mother, Jane, and brother, Tom. There is excellent walking in the moors and dales. A guide is supplied for a dawn safari through the local forest and woodland: this two-hour walk returns in time for breakfast. *Read more: page 191.*

Heddon's Gate Hotel, Martinhoe

'A walkers' paradise', this former Victorian hunting lodge has a 'splendid' position on the wooded slopes of the Heddon valley. Walks begin at the door, or you can venture out to explore Exmoor. Return in time for an 'excellent' afternoon tea. The traditional hotel is 'comfortable and quiet' (no mobile phone signal; poor TV reception). *Read more: page 213.*

Hazel Bank, Rosthwaite

New owners Rob van der Palen and Anton Renac (the chef) have created 'a warm, professional atmosphere' at this small hotel in Borrowdale. There is immediate access from the grounds to many well-known peaks; for easier days there are pleasant walks along the River Derwent, up the Langstrath or over to Watendlath. The dinners, served at flexible times, are admired. Packed lunches are available. *Read more: page 261.*

Howtown Hotel, Ullswater

'We love the scope for walking from the door, which allowed us to be carless in Cumbria,' say visitors to this simple guest house on the quiet eastern shores of Lake Ullswater. Walkers can ask for a substantial picnic before heading out along the shores of the lake, or on to the wooded hillside. Traditional cooking. Generous breakfasts. *Read more: page 294.*

Deeside Hotel, Ballater

Set back among trees on the road to Braemar, this Victorian house is owned and run by Gordon Waddell (the chef) and Penella Price ('unfailingly pleasant'). They promise 'great walks for all ages and of varying degrees of exertion': three start from the back gate. Drying facilities and packed lunches are available. *Read more: page 321.*

Pen-y-Gwryd Hotel, Nant Gwynant

Popular with walkers and climbers, this eccentric old inn is now run by the third generation of the Pullee family, brothers Rupert and Nicolas. Any child under 13 who climbs Snowdon is inducted in the Snowdon Club. Substantial packed lunches. *Read more: page 405.*

GOLF

Golfers and golf widows alike can enjoy these hotels, well placed for some of the best courses on these islands

The Mount, Bideford

Discounts at the Royal North Devon course at Westward Ho are available for guests at Andrew and Heather Laugharne's B&B, an imposing Georgian house. The fast greens at the course, the oldest links in England, are at their most testing when the wind blows. The second green, shaped like a small upturned saucer, is especially hard to hold. *Read more: page 94.*

Treglos Hotel, Constantine Bay

Guests at Jim and Rose Barlow's traditional hotel on the north Cornwall coast have access in early and late season to the family-owned Merlin Golf and Country Club nearby (half-price in summer). A golfing package includes two group tuition sessions. Other excellent courses are within easy driving distance. *Read more: page 134.*

Budock Vean, Mawnan Smith

The attractive nine-hole parkland course at Martin and Amanda Barlow's traditional hotel is a good place to sharpen up your game. PGA professional David Short offers three-day golf schools and a free winter workshop, and he organises competition weeks played over four local courses. Hotel guests also qualify for reduced green fees at several nearby clubs. *Read more: page 218.*

The Cleeve House, Mortehoe

Golfers can choose between the challenges of links or parkland courses at this small, unpretentious hotel in a village above Woolacombe. For a full day's golf, play the two championship links courses (East and West) at nearby Saunton; parkland courses include Ilfracombe, a relatively short but testing layout with spectacular views over the Bristol Channel. *Read more: page 227.*

Gilpin Lodge, Windermere

The entrance to Windermere golf club is almost opposite this Edwardian country house hotel. Golfing breaks with tuition are offered at the undulating course – 'Gleneagles in miniature'. It may appear short, but it is challenging, with narrow fairways,

natural water hazards and blind second shots into greens.
Read more: page 305.

Glenapp Castle, Ballantrae

Four championship courses are within an hour's drive of this 19th-century baronial castle (now a luxury hotel) in Ayrshire. They include Turnberry, which hosted the Open championship in 2009. Tee times can be arranged here and at Royal Troon, another historic Open venue. Guests have access to the private course at nearby Caley Palace.
Read more: page 320.

Castleton House, Glamis

'We are always happy to help with golf arrangements,' say David and Verity Webster. Their Edwardian stone house has 'good relations' with local courses, including Alyth and Blairgowrie. 'We have our own well-kept putting green, and plenty of space to practise longer shots.'
Read more: page 340.

The Dower House, Muir of Ord

Robyn Aitchison, the host at this gabled *cottage-orné* in a large garden bordered by two rivers, is a keen golfer and can advise on the 25 courses within an hour's drive. Try the championship links at Nairn, which has hosted the Walker Cup: you can see the Moray Firth from every hole, and

it is possible to strike the ball into the sea on the first seven.
Read more: page 359.

Castle Cottage, Harlech

Guests at this restaurant-with-rooms (run by Glyn and Jacqueline Roberts) receive a ten per cent discount at six nearby golf courses. These include the championship links at Royal St David's, on the dune land between Harlech Castle and the sea.
Read more: page 395.

Stella Maris, Ballycastle

Each bedroom at this converted 19th-century coastguard station in north Mayo is named after a golf course, and there are golfing books aplenty in the 100-foot conservatory that runs the length of the building. Terence McSweeney, who runs it with his wife, Frances Kelly, works for the US PGA in Florida during the winter. He can guide golfers to the world-class links at Carne, Enniscrone and, further afield, Rosses Point and Westport.
Read more: page 427.

DOGS

Your best friend can expect a five-star welcome at these hotels where dogs command special treatment

The Regent by the Lake, Ambleside

Visiting dogs can run 'tail-waggingly free' on Borrans Park and Bird House Meadow, a short stroll from the door at Christine Hewitt's white-fronted hotel opposite a slipway on Lake Windermere. 'We are a family of dog lovers and we welcome dogs,' she says. Dog owners can come and go as they please from courtyard rooms. 'We can prepare food for dogs the same as their owners; special requests and diets are no problem.'
Read more: page 75.

Blagdon Manor, Ashwater

Dogs are 'positively welcomed' at Liz and Steve Morey's rambling 17th-century manor house. The resident chocolate Labradors, Nutmeg and Cassia, 'always look forward to meeting new friends'. Canine visitors are given a fleece blanket, towel, dog bowl and treats 'to make sure their stay is as comfortable as yours'. Good walking in 17 acres of open fields leading from the garden.
Read more: page 79.

Knocklayd, Dartmouth

Susan and Jonathan Cardale's two aged Labradors may 'have gone to doggy heaven', but Molly, their little woolly white hearing dog for the deaf (retired), 'is all the keener to welcome visiting dogs for some company'. The large, rambling house stands at the highest point of Kingswear village. Visiting canines must sleep in the doggie dormitory near the Aga.
Read more: page 142.

Overwater Hall, Ireby

'Perfect for dogs on or off the leash', this castellated Georgian mansion welcomes dogs in the bedrooms and one of the lounges (but no sitting on chairs). They are allowed to enjoy unleashed the 18-acre grounds, including a woodland boardwalk. A dog-sitting service is offered for 'those rainy days when you want to visit an art gallery'.
Read more: page 184.

The Boar's Head, Ripley

Dogs are welcomed 'providing they bring with them well-trained owners' at Sir Thomas and Lady Ingilby's 'elegant but

not stuffy' old inn in a model village on their castle estate. Dogs are allowed (£10 charge) in two courtyard rooms, which may be smallish, but a 'turn-down Bonio is placed in their basket, and water bowls are provided'.
Read more: page 257.

Plumber Manor, Sturminster Newton

'Dogs will love it here,' say the Prideaux-Brune family at their 17th-century manor house in well-kept gardens. Dogs are not allowed in the main house but are encouraged to stay in dog-friendly courtyard bedrooms which have direct access to the gardens where they can join the two resident black Labradors.
Read more: page 284.

Holbeck Ghyll, Windermere

Treat your pooch to a designer doggy break at this luxurious Lakeland hotel where dogs are welcomed in the bedrooms and the grounds for £8 a night. Guests can upgrade this to a £15 package that includes a *Michelin*-star menu; a doggy bag with treats, chews and a toy; a blanket for bedtime and a special dog bowl.
Read more: page 306.

Coul House, Contin

'Our Labrador was made very welcome; she was allowed to join us in the lounge after dinner,' say visitors to this listed Regency hunting lodge outside a Highland village. Dogs (£5 a night) can enjoy the large grounds and walks in the Achilty forest (which has miles of trails). There are views over the Strathconon valley from the terrace.
Read more: page 328.

Kilcamb Lodge, Strontian

You might find some doggy treats in your bedroom at Sally and David Fox's old stone lodge 'in a lovely situation' on the shores of Loch Sunart. 'The natural beauty and outdoor life of the Highlands have to be shared with your best pal,' they say. Dogs benefit from the 'wonderful freedom' in the grounds and on the shore. Towels are provided for drying after swimming.
Read more: page 370.

Rathmullan House, Rathmullan

Dogs have an outdoor area to run around in at the Wheeler family's handsome white 19th-century mansion by a two-mile sandy beach on Lough Swilly (pooper-scoopers provided). The superior doggy room is in a courtyard extension with a patio door leading to the garden. It has a canine 'room within a room', with a bed and toys, and a doormat decorated with patterns of paws.
Read more: page 456.

LAKE DISTRICT

In the magnificent setting of lakes and mountains, these are some of the *Guide*'s favourite hotels

Rothay Manor, Ambleside

Near the head of Lake Windermere (which can be reached through fields), Nigel Nixon's white Regency house is 'a lovely, civilised' hotel. Delightful gardens insulate the building from daytime traffic noise; they are overlooked by the quietest bedrooms. The staff are 'experienced, helpful'. Jane Binns cooks traditional dishes with a slight French influence. *Read more: page 76.*

The Pheasant, Bassenthwaite Lake

In gardens and woodland between lakes and fells in the quieter northern Lake District, this 400-year-old inn is managed by Matthew Wylie for the trustees of the Inglewood estate. The lounges and bar have oak beams, log fires, antiques, old prints and paintings. Most bed-rooms are large and comfortable. Good walking in all directions. *Read more: page 85.*

Lindeth Fell, Bowness-on-Windermere

On the hills above Lake Windermere ('fantastic views'), Pat and Diana Kennedy's traditional hotel is liked for its 'old-world charm'. Beds are turned down during dinner, made during breakfast. Hearty meals are served in the dining room, which has conservatory-style extensions. *Read more: page 103.*

Linthwaite House, Bowness-on-Windermere

In a 'great location', Mike Bevans's timbered, creeper-covered mansion stands in landscaped gardens with 'amazing' views over Lake Windermere. An enclosed veranda faces the water. In the restaurant, chef Richard Kearsley serves modern dishes. 'Delicious' scones with afternoon tea. *Read more: page 104.*

The Cottage in the Wood, Braithwaite

The 'excellent' service and 'superb' cooking are admired at Liam and Kath Berney's restaurant-with-rooms. Their 17th-century Lakeland inn on Whinlatter Pass looks down the valley to the Skiddaw mountain range. He uses local produce for

his modern European dishes. Guests have a sitting room with walking magazines, books and games; in summer they can sit in the small garden.
Read more: page 106.

Aynsome Manor, Cartmel

A member of the Varley family is always on hand at the traditional Lakeland hotel between the fells and the sea which they have run for 30 years. Many of their visitors are regulars. Smart casual dress is required in the evening in the oak-panelled restaurant where ingredients are sourced within Cumbria for Gordon Topp's five-course dinner.
Read more: page 122.

Overwater Hall, Ireby

Two miles from Bassenthwaite Lake, the most northerly of the lakes, this castellated Georgian mansion stands in large grounds below Skiddaw and Uldale Fells. The public rooms have bold colours, an opulent style. Bathrooms have a double-ended bath and walk-in shower. Stephen Bore is the friendly front-of-house. Adrian Hyde cooks 'well-balanced' modern dishes. Children and dogs are welcomed.
Read more: page 184.

Ees Wyke Country House, Near Sawrey

Once the Lake District retreat of Beatrix Potter, this attractive Georgian house has panoramic views over Esthwaite Water and the fells beyond. It is run by Richard (the chef) and Margaret Lee who greet visitors with their friendly Old English sheepdogs, Harry and Teddy. His imaginative, daily-changing dinner menu is served in a dining room facing the lake.
Read more: page 227.

Howtown Hotel, Ullswater

On the quiet eastern shore of Lake Ullswater, this guest house has a loyal following drawn by its simplicity and quirkiness. It is run by owners Jacquie Baldry and her son, David; their multi-national staff are 'pleasant and efficient'. House routines include a gong summoning guests to dinner. No frills (like phones, TV, radio) in bedrooms, but many have lake views.
Read more: page 294.

Holbeck Ghyll, Windermere

Built as a hunting lodge by Lord Lonsdale in 1888, David and Patricia Nicholson's luxurious hotel stands in large grounds that slope down to the lake. Visitors praise the 'good food, helpful staff, lovely location, and pampering'. Public rooms have a 'baronial feel': stained glass, open fires, wood panelling, antiques. David McLaughlin has a *Michelin* star for his refined cooking.
Read more: page 306.

COTSWOLDS

Enjoy the rolling hills and explore towns and villages whose wealth was built on the wool trade

The Horse and Groom, Bourton-on-the-Hill

At the top of a steep hill in a pretty, honey-stone village, this old coaching inn is run by 'engaging' brothers Tom (front-of-house) and Will (the chef) Greenstock. Good-sized bedrooms have been refurbished in modern style; bathrooms are well equipped. Modern meals on a blackboard menu are served by enthusiastic young staff. Breakfasts are generous.
Read more: page 102.

The Malt House, Broad Campden

Judi Wilkes runs her acclaimed B&B in a beautiful old building in Cotswold vernacular style (a converted malt house with two adjacent cottages) in a hamlet near Chipping Campden. The well-furnished and equipped bedrooms face the pretty garden. Generous breakfasts have a vast choice. From the gate you can walk on to the Cotswold Way.
Read more: page 113.

Russell's Restaurant, Broadway

Barry Hancox and Andrew Riley's restaurant-with-rooms is on the main street of a celebrated Cotswolds village. They have given the listed building a contemporary look, combining modern gadgets and paintings with original features (inglenook fireplaces, an oak staircase). Matthew Laughton serves a seasonal menu of modern dishes.
Read more: page 114.

The New Inn, Coln St Aldwyns

In a quiet Cotswold village near Cirencester, this 400-year-old inn has been given a make-over by the small Hillbrooke group. They kept original features in the bar and restaurant (flagstone floors, oak beams, etc), while giving the accommodation a quirky look (dramatic use of red and black in themed bedrooms). Oliver Addis's seasonal dinner menu has interesting daily specials.
Read more: page 132.

The Rectory Hotel, Crudwell

In stone-walled gardens in a village near Malmesbury, this 16th-century former rectory has been given a contemporary feel by Julian Muggridge and Jonathan Barry. All bedrooms overlook the gardens; there are sprung mattresses, Egyptian linen, deep baths, power showers. Peter Fairclough, the chef, serves classic British dishes on a seasonal menu in the panelled restaurant, and meals can be taken in the garden in summer. *Read more: page 141.*

At the Sign of the Angel, Lacock

In an ancient National Trust village on the southern edge of the Cotswolds, this 15th-century half-timbered inn has oak panels, creaking doors, low ceilings, beams and ancient steps. Rooms in the old house, if small, have 'great character'; bathrooms are 'excellent'. Four newer rooms are in a cottage across a garden. 'Delicious' English dishes in the candlelit medieval dining rooms. *Read more: page 188.*

The Grey Cottage, Leonard Stanley

'It just gets better and better.' Visitors return to Rosemary Reeves's little stone guest house near Stroud to enjoy 'incomparable cosseting'. Extra touches include help with luggage, leaf tea and biscuits on arrival; fruit, fresh milk, a clothes brush in the immaculate bedrooms. Bring your own bottle (no corkage charge) for the 'wonderful' no-choice dinners. *Read more: page 195.*

The Fox Inn, Lower Oddington

In a quiet village near Stow-on-the-Wold, Ian MacKenzie's creeper-clad 16th-century pub has flagstone floors, beams and old fireplaces. Guests are looked after 'with great care'. The three bedrooms are stylish and well equipped. In the inviting dining room (slate floors, wooden tables and chairs) chef Raymond Pearce's cooking is admired. Good value for the Cotswolds. *Read more: page 207.*

The Redesdale Arms, Moreton-in-Marsh

With a honey-coloured Georgian facade, Robert Smith's centuries-old coaching inn stands on the wide main street of an attractive market town. He is a 'most engaging host'. Bedrooms (some in a stable block a short walk outside) are of a high standard. Craig Mallins's cooking is praised. *Read more: page 225.*

Calcot Manor, Tetbury

In countryside west of Tetbury, this 'civilised' hotel is a stylish renovation of a 14th-century farmhouse and its surrounding cottages and outbuildings. Children are well catered for; facilities for adults include a spa with a large swimming pool. Michael Croft cooks good modern dishes in the *Conservatory* restaurant; the food is also enjoyed in the *Gumstool* pub. *Read more: page 289.*

EAST ANGLIA

Whether you are seeking a seascape or a country hideaway, the *Guide* has a wide choice in East Anglia

The Wentworth, Aldeburgh

Facing fishing huts, boats and Aldeburgh's shingle beach, the Pritt family's traditional seaside hotel is popular with musicians, actors and writers. There are antiques, books, plants; Russell Flint prints in the lounges; sea views (binoculars provided) from the best bedrooms. Chef Graham Reid serves generous dishes ('fish supremely fresh') in the conservatory restaurant.
Read more: page 73.

The Blakeney Hotel, Blakeney

Michael Stannard's large, traditional hotel has 'inspiring' views across the tidal estuary and salt marshes to Blakeney Point. The public rooms face the estuary as do many of the bedrooms (others overlook the garden). The dining room has a relaxed feel; well-presented dishes are not 'showy'. Local

kippers for breakfast. A good base for walking.
Read more: page 97.

The White Horse, Brancaster Staithe

Looking over the sea and salt marshes of Brancaster Bay, Cliff Nye's informal inn is liked for its 'relaxed' style. The open-plan interior has a contemporary rustic feel: Lloyd Loom chairs in the lounge, scrubbed pine wooden tables and chairs in the restaurant.
Read more: page 108.

Byfords, Holt

On the main square of a charming little Norfolk town, Iain and Clair Wilson's unusual venture combines a 'posh' B&B, an all-day continental-style café/bistro, and a delicatessen. There are tables and chairs on the pavement; old beams and exposed brickwork in a series of eating rooms. Seven bedrooms and a new reception have been added this year.
Read more: page 177.

Morston Hall, Morston

Chef/*patron* Galton Blackiston's restaurant-with-rooms 'lived up to its reputation for exceptional

food' when visited by inspectors this year. It stands in lovely gardens in a designated area of outstanding natural beauty on the north Norfolk coast. The restaurant and older bedrooms are in a Jacobean flint-and-brick mansion; newer rooms are in a discreet single-storey modern building.
Read more: page 226.

Beechwood, North Walsham

Once Agatha Christie's Norfolk hideaway, this creeper-clad Georgian house (with Victorian character) is run as a small hotel by owner/managers Lindsay Spalding and the 'ebullient' Don Birch. Bedrooms are well proportioned; there's a turn-down service at night. Chef Steven Norgate sometimes serves a 'Ten Mile Dinner' with all ingredients sourced within a 10-mile radius.
Read more: page 233.

By Appointment, Norwich

Robert Culyer presides like an impresario at his restaurant-with-rooms in three merchants' dwellings in the centre of Norwich. Full of character, it is filled with antiques and artefacts, masses of pictures and curios in the public rooms and bedrooms. Ellery Powell's cooking is 'excellent'; good ingredients well presented; robust sauces.
Read more: page 235.

The Neptune, Old Hunstanton

Kevin Mangeolles was awarded a *Michelin* star in 2009 for his refined, flavoursome cooking at the restaurant-with-rooms he runs with his wife, Jacki, in an 18th-century coaching inn a short walk from the sea. The centre of the action is the dining room.
Read more: page 237.

The Crown and Castle, Orford

In a peaceful Suffolk village, this old red brick inn is owned and run by cookery writer/TV presenter Ruth Watson and her husband, David. Bedrooms in the house are furnished in minimalist style; each of the garden rooms has a terrace. In the bistro-style restaurant, Ruth Watson and David Williams have a *Michelin Bib Gourmand* for their unfussy seasonal cooking.
Read more: page 238.

The Rose & Crown, Snettisham

'The welcome is warm' at Jeannette and Anthony Goodrich's old (14th-century) country pub opposite the cricket pitch in a pleasant Norfolk village. Popular with locals, it has twisting passages, hidden corners, low ceilings and old beams. Residents have their own lounge. Chef Keith McDowell mixes pub favourites with contemporary dishes.
Read more: page 276.

WEST COUNTRY

The biggest concentration of *Guide* hotels is found in England's West Country

Blagdon Manor, Ashwater

'Every visit is a joy' at Liz and Steve Morey's 17th-century manor house in rolling country with panoramic views towards Dartmoor. They maintain high standards 'without ever appearing harassed'. She is a 'friendly' front-of-house; his 'imaginative' cooking is much enjoyed. Fresh flowers and open fires in the bar and lounge.
Read more: page 79.

Bridge House, Beaminster

'Welcoming and comfortable', Mark and Joanna Donovan's small hotel/restaurant is a former priest's house with thick walls, mullioned windows and beams. The quietest rooms overlook the large walled garden. The staff are 'friendly', the atmosphere 'relaxed'. In a dining room with conservatory extension, chef Linda Paget's dishes emphasise local organic produce.
Read more: page 90.

The Henley, Bigbury-on-Sea

Martyn Scarterfield and his wife, Petra Lampe, are 'energetic, conscientious' hosts at their small, unpretentious hotel on a cliff above the Avon estuary. In the evening in the lounge, she recites the short menu; his cooking is much admired. 'An enjoyable place for quiet, wonderful food, marvellous views.'
Read more: page 95.

The New Angel, Dartmouth

John Burton-Race's 'superb' cooking attracts visitors to Dartmouth's delightful waterfront. Now they can stay in six smart bedrooms in a house on a side street a short walk away. They are bright by day, quiet at night; a top-floor suite is reached by a private staircase. There is a small lounge. Breakfast is a leisurely affair.
Read more: page 143.

The Crown, Exford

On the green of a picturesque village in Exmoor national park, this much-extended 17th-century inn has been upgraded by owners Chris Kirkbride and Sara and Dan Whittaker. In the attractive restaurant, the cooking of chef Darren Edwards is 'seriously good'. The original stabling is available for visitors who arrive on horseback.
Read more: page 152.

Combe House, Gittisham

'A magnificent building in a beautiful setting', Ken and Ruth

Hunt's Elizabethan manor house stands on a vast country estate of woodland, meadows and pastures. They preside informally; their staff are 'attentive and knowledgeable'. Grand public rooms have oak panelling, antiques, fresh flowers. Vegetables come from a new kitchen garden for the modern dishes of chefs Hadleigh Barratt and Stuart Brown.
Read more: page 159.

Molesworth Manor, Little Petherick

Jessica and Geoff French's B&B in a 17th-century rectory is in attractive gardens in a tiny village near Padstow (reached by a riverside footpath). It has an elaborate carved staircase, stained glass, good artwork. 'Plenty of sitting room and bedroom space', 'a friendly atmosphere'. The 'superb' breakfast has organic ingredients, freshly baked muffins and a daily special.
Read more: page 199.

Meudon, Mawnan Smith

Mark Pilgrim, a fifth-generation hotelier, runs this traditional red-brick hotel with his father, Harry. Old-fashioned values include turn-down service at night, shoe cleaning. A dress code of jacket and tie is encouraged in the restaurant where chef Alan Webb's cooking uses local produce, including fish

from Newlyn, for his daily-changing menus.
Read more: page 219.

Yeoldon House, Northam

'Very much a family affair', this 19th-century gabled house is run by owners Jennifer and Brian (the chef) Steele. There are suitcases on the stairs, old stained glass, teddy bears everywhere. His traditional cooking, served in a room facing the River Torridge, is 'the main reason for coming'. He says guests will 'feel comfortable in any attire'. Breakfast is plentiful.
Read more: page 234.

Ennys, St Hilary

The door to the big farmhouse kitchen is always open at Gill Charlton's creeper-covered 17th-century manor house surrounded by fields that lead to the River Hayle. She runs it as a B&B (with self-catering apartments). She is a travel writer, which shows in 'the little comforts in the bedrooms' (big waffle bathrobes, books and magazines, good toiletries, as well as flat-screen TV and free Wi-Fi).
Read more: page 266.

TENNIS AND SWIMMING

Each of these hotels has a tennis court (T) and/or a swimming pool (S)

London
One Aldwych (S)

England
Regent by the Lake, Ambleside (S)
Hartwell House, Aylesbury (T,S)
Bath Priory, Bath (S)
West Coates, Berwick-upon-Tweed (S)
Burgh Island, Bigbury-on-Sea (T,S)
Blakeney, Blakeney (S)
Frogg Manor, Broxton (T)
Hell Bay, Bryer (S)
Brockencote Hall, Chaddesley Corbett (T)
Tor Cottage, Chillaton (S)
Treglos, Constantine Bay (S)
Corse Lawn House, Corse Lawn (T,S)
Cloth Hall Oast, Cranbrook (S)
Rectory, Crudwell (S)
Summer Lodge, Evershot (T,S)
Evesham, Evesham (S)
Moonfleet Manor, Fleet (T,S)
Stock Hill House, Gillingham (T)
Hambleton Hall, Hambleton (T,S)
Pheasant, Harome (S)

Feversham Arms, Helmsley (S)
Esseborne Manor, Hurstbourne Tarrant (T)
Ilsington Country House, Ilsington (S)
Lyzzick Hall, Keswick (S)
Augill Castle, Kirkby Stephen (T)
Feathers, Ledbury (S)
Bedruthan Steps, Mawgan Porth (T,S)
Budock Vean, Mawnan Smith (T,S)
TerraVina, Netley Marsh (S)
Penzance, Penzance (S)
Ennys, St Hilary (T,S)
Star Castle, St Mary's (S)
Tides Reach, Salcombe (S)
Soar Mill Cove, Soar Mill Cove (T,S)
Stoke Lodge, Stoke Fleming (T,S)
Plumber Manor, Sturminster (T)
Calcot Manor, Tetbury (T,S)
Island, Tresco (T,S)
Nare, Veryan-in-Roseland (T,S)
Gilpin Lodge, Windermere (S)
Holbeck Ghyll, Windermere (T)
Watersmeet, Woolacombe (S)
Broad Hs, Wroxham (S)
Middlethorpe Hall, York (S)

Scotland

Glenapp Castle, Ballantrae (T)
Kinloch Hs, Blairgowrie (S)
Kinnaird, Dunkeld (T)
Greshornish Hs, Edinbane (T)
Isle of Eriska, Eriska (T,S)
Eaglescairnie Mains, Gifford (T)
Ardanaiseig, Kilchrenan (T)
New Lanark Mill, Lanark (S)
Kirroughtree Hs, Newton Stewart (T)
Skirling Hs, Skirling (T).

Wales

Porth Tocyn, Abersoch (T,S)
Sychnant Pass Hs, Conwy (S)
Glangrwyney Ct, Crickhowell (T)
Gliffaes, Crickhowell (T)
Bodysgallen Hall and Spa, Llandudno (T,S)
St Tudno, Llandudno (S)
Lake, Llangammarch Wells (T,S)
Portmeirion, Portmeirion (S)

Channel Islands

White House, Herm (T,S)
Atlantic, St Brelade (T,S)
St Brelade's Bay, St Brelade (T,S)
Longueville Manor, St Saviour (T,S)

Ireland

Cashel House, Cashel Bay (T)
Glin Castle, Glin (T)
Marlfield House, Gorey (T)
Shelburne Lodge, Kenmare (T)
Rosleague Manor, Letterfrack (T)
Currarevagh House, Oughterard (T)
Rathmullan House, Rathmullan (T,S)
Coopershill, Riverstown (T)
Ballymaloe House, Shanagarry (T,S)

DISABLED FACILITIES

Each of these hotels has at least one bedroom equipped for a visitor in a wheelchair

We advise phoning to discuss individual requirements.

London
One Aldwych; Goring; Zetter

England
Wentworth, Aldeburgh
Rothay Manor, Ambleside
Hartwell House, Aylesbury
Bath Priory, Bath
Leathes Head, Borrowdale
Millstream, Bosham
White Horse, Brancaster Staithe
Frogg Manor, Broxton
Hell Bay, Bryher
Blackmore Farm, Cannington
Brockencote Hall, Chaddesley Corbett
Beech House & Olive Branch, Clipsham
Treglos, Constantine Bay
Clow Beck House, Croft-on-Tees
Coach House at Crookham, Crookham
Summer Lodge, Evershot
Evesham, Evesham
Angel Inn, Hetton
Byfords, Holt
Bath Arms, Horningsham
Northcote Manor, Langho
Lewtrenchard Manor, Lewdown

Cottage in the Wood, Malvern Wells
Swinton Park, Masham
Meaburn Hill Farmhouse, Maulds Meaburn
Bedruthan Steps, Mawgan Porth
Meudon, Mawnan Smith
Redesdale Arms, Moreton-in-Marsh
Cleeve House, Mortehoe
Jesmond Dene House, Newcastle upon Tyne
Three Choirs Vineyard, Newent
Beechwood, North Walsham
Hart's, Nottingham
Grange at Oborne, Oborne
Malmaison, Oxford
Old Bank, Oxford
Old Parsonage, Oxford
Elephant, Pangbourne
Seafood Restaurant, Padstow
Old Railway Station, Petworth
Black Swan, Ravenstonedale
Bourgoyne, Reeth
Seaview, Seaview
Rose & Crown, Snettisham
Titchwell Manor, Titchwell
Mannings, Truro
Nare, Veryan-in-Roseland
Windy Ridge, Whitstable
Holbeck Ghyll, Windermere

Watersmeet, Woolacombe
Old Vicarage, Worfield
Dean Court, York
Middlethorpe Hall, York

Scotland
Loch Ness Lodge, Brachla
Dunvalanree in Carradale,
   Carradale
Three Chimneys, Dunvegan
Lovat Arms, Fort Augustus
Corsewall Lighthouse,
   Kirkcolm
Lynnfield, Kirkwall
New Lanark Mill, Lanark
Langass Lodge, Locheport
Viewfield House, Portree
Skirling House, Skirling
Torridon, Torridon

Wales
Harbourmaster, Aberaeron
Olde Bulls Head, Beaumaris
Hand at Llanarmon,
   Llanarmon Dyffryn Ceiriog
Bodysgallen Hall, Llandudno
Lake, Llangammarch Wells
Hafod Elwy Hall, Pentrefoelas
Portmeirion, Portmeirion

Ireland
Stella Maris, Ballycastle
Seaview House, Ballylickey
Quay House, Clifden
Rayanne House, Holywood
Sheedy's, Lisdoonvarna
Rathmullan House,
   Rathmullan
Barberstown Castle, Straffan

How to use the *Good Hotel Guide*

Hotelfinder is for those looking for ideas: we suggest hotels to match your mood or interests, perhaps romance or sport, for a family or for gourmets. We highlight hotels in a wide range of categories, giving a short profile and a cross-reference to the main entry.

Main entries carry our considered judgment, based on anonymous inspections and reader reports, of those hotels that we consider to be the best of their type. Hotels are listed alphabetically by country, under the name of the town or village. If you remember a hotel's name but not where it is, consult the alphabetical hotel list at the end of the book.

The Shortlist suggests alternatives, especially in areas where we have a limited choice. We also include some potential main entries which have not yet been checked, and hotels which have recently changed hands. These short entries have not been subjected to the same rigorous tests as the main entries; standards may be variable.

The maps Each hotel's location is marked. A small house indicates a main entry, a triangle a Shortlist one. We give the map number and grid reference at the top of the entry.

Reading the entries

Information panels We give the number of bedrooms without detailing the type of room (the distinction between a single room and a small double for single use, a standard or a superior double, a junior or a senior suite varies widely between hotels). We give the geographical location, but not detailed driving directions. As with room types, these are best discussed with the hotel when booking; directions are usually found on a hotel's website.

Prices We give each place's estimated prices for 2010, or the 2009 prices, which applied when the *Guide* went to press. The figures indicate the range of prices per person from off-season to high season. A 'set lunch/dinner' can be no-choice or *table d'hôte*. The 'full alc' price is the cost per person of a three-course meal with a half bottle of wine; 'alc' indicates the price excluding wine. These figures cannot be guaranteed. *You should always check prices when booking.*

Symbols The label 'New' at the top of an entry identifies a hotel making its first appearance in the *Guide*, or one returning after an absence. We say 'Unsuitable for &' when a hotel tells us that it cannot accommodate wheelchair-users. We do not have the resources to inspect such facilities or to assess the even more complicated matter of facilities for the partially disabled. Please discuss such details directly with the hotel.

Names We give the names of the readers who have nominated or endorsed a hotel in brackets at the end of each entry. We do not name inspectors, correspondents who ask to remain anonymous, or those who have written critical reports.

Facilities We give an outline of the facilities offered by each hotel. We suggest that you check in advance if specific items (tea-making equipment, trouser press, sheets and blankets instead of a duvet, etc) are important to you.

Changes We try to ensure that the details we provide are correct, but inevitably they are subject to change. Small places sometimes close at short notice off-season. Some hotels change hands after we have gone to press.

Vouchers Hotels which join our voucher scheme – identified by a *V* – have agreed to give readers a discount of 25% off their normal bed-and-breakfast rate for one night only. You will be expected to pay the full price for other meals and all other services. *You should request a voucher reservation at the time of booking.* A hotel may refuse to accept it at busy times. The six vouchers in the centre of the book are valid until the publication of the next edition of the *Guide*.

Hotel reports

The report forms on pages 571–6 may be used to endorse or criticise an existing entry or to nominate a hotel for inclusion in the *Guide*. But it is not essential that you use our forms or restrict yourself to the space available. Many readers email their reports to us.

All reports (*each on a separate piece of paper, please*) should include your name and address, the name and location of the hotel, and the date and length of your stay. Please nominate only places that you have visited in the past 12 months, unless friends tell you that standards have been maintained. Please be as specific as possible, and critical where appropriate, about the building, the public rooms and bedrooms, the meals, the service, the nightlife, the grounds.

If you describe the location as well as the hotel, particularly in less familiar regions, that is helpful. In the case of B&B hotels it is useful if you can recommend any restaurants.

We want the *Guide* to convey the special flavour of its hotels, and any details that you provide will give life to the description. If the report is too brief we may not be able to follow it up. You need not give prices and routine information about number of rooms and facilities; we get such details from the hotels. We want readers to supply information that is not accessible elsewhere. In the case of a new nomination, it helps if you include a brochure or mention a website.

Please never tell a hotel that you intend to file a report. Anonymity is essential to objectivity.

The 2011 edition of the *Guide* will be written between mid-March and the end of May 2010, and published in early October 2010. Nominations should reach us not later than 15 May 2010. The latest date for comments on existing entries is 1 June 2010.

We have space for only three report forms this year; please let us know if you would like us to send you more report forms. Our address for UK correspondents (no stamp needed) is: *Good Hotel Guide*, Freepost PAM 2931, London W11 4BR.

Reports can be emailed to editor@goodhotelguide.com or faxed to us on 020-7602 4182.

Reports posted outside the UK should be stamped normally and addressed to: *Good Hotel Guide*, 50 Addison Avenue, London W11 4QP, England.

LONDON

Large chain hotels, efficient but often faceless, continue to dominate the London scene. Fortunately, it is still possible to find hotels of character in family ownership. A classic example, *Durrants*, owned by the Miller family for 90 years, is awarded a 2010 *César* for its old-fashioned values and service that is attentive but never stuffy.

Durrants, London

LONDON   Map 2:D4

The Capital   *Tel* 020-7589 5171
22–24 Basil Street   *Fax* 020-7225 0011
London SW3 1AT   *Email* reservations@capitalhotel.co.uk
                            Website www.capitalhotel.co.uk

🏆 *César award in 2008*

'An oasis of civilised calm', David Levin's 'grand hotel in miniature' is hidden away in a side street near Harrods. The ambience is luxurious, discreet and traditional. Visitors write of 'seriously high standards', and praise the staff ('attentive without obsequiousness'). The comfortable bedrooms have heavy fabrics, flowers, double glazing, air conditioning, marble bathroom. 'Big, firm' beds have Egyptian cotton sheets and duvet. In the compact restaurant, 'service is efficient', and Eric Chavot has a *Michelin* star for his 'superb' Franco-fusion cooking, eg, roasted lobster with chilli and coconut broth; fillet of lamb with cumin jus and spicy couscous. There is an 'extensive wine list' (some wines from Mr Levin's vineyard in the Loire). 'Good breakfasts' and 'afternoon tea of impeccable country house standard'. Guests can also eat at the basement brasserie, *Le Metro*, in *The Levin* (*qv*), the sister hotel next door, and they have access to a nearby health club (£10 per person).

Bedrooms: 49. *Open*: all year. *Facilities*: lift, sitting room, bar, restaurant, brasserie/bar nearby, 2 private dining rooms, business facilities, only restaurant suitable for ♿. *Background music*: 'modern' in bar. *Location*: central, under-ground Knightsbridge, private car park (£6 an hour, £30 a day). *Smoking*: not allowed. *Children*: all ages welcomed. *Dogs*: not allowed. *Credit cards*: all major cards. *Prices*: [2009] room £230–£455, breakfast £16–£19.50, set dinner £55–£70 (*plus 12½% discretionary service charge*), various packages – see website.

Charlotte Street Hotel   *Tel* 020-7806 2000
15 Charlotte Street   *Fax* 020-7806 2002
London W1T 1RJ   *Email* reservations@charlottestreethotel.com
                       Website www.charlottestreethotel.com

The spirit of Bloomsbury artists Vanessa Bell and Duncan Grant inspired the decor of this member of Tim and Kit Kemp's small Firmdale group (see also Shortlist) just north of Soho. Kit Kemp has followed the theme in her interiors using original art from the period. The entrance lobby is 'elegant but not pompous'; the lounges are 'comfortable, quite large', and the bar/restaurant, *Oscar*, has a mural of contemporary London. Its open-plan kitchen serves a short menu of modern dishes (eg, crispy chicken, mango and macadamia salad; steamed steak and ale pudding). 'A lovely hotel, though expensive,' said recent visitors. 'Staff attentive and friendly. Our quiet, air-conditioned bedroom had sitting area, good storage, beautiful, well-heated bathroom.' The 'excellent' buffet breakfast has fresh fruit, cereals, etc, cooked English. There is a 64-seat screening room. The manager is Jakob Hansen. More reports, please.

Bedrooms: 52. *Open*: all year, restaurant closed Sun noon–5 pm. *Facilities*: lift, ramps, drawing room, library, bar/restaurant, 3 private dining/meeting rooms, screening room, limited access for ♿. *Background music*: none. *Location*: West End, N of Soho, underground Goodge Street. *Smoking*: allowed in all bedrooms. *Children*: all ages welcomed. *Dogs*: not allowed. *Credit cards*: all major cards. *Prices*: [2009] room (*excluding VAT*) £220–£1,150, breakfast £19, set dinner £21.50, full alc £45, special breaks, Christmas/New Year packages.

Church Street Hotel   NEW

29–33 Camberwell Church Street
London SE5 8TR

Tel 020-7703 5984
Fax 020-7358-4110
Email info@churchstreethotel.com
Website www.churchstreethotel.com

In a 'busy and far from glamorous' street by Camberwell Green, this grey-fronted building has been decorated in flamboyant style by Greek/Spanish brothers José and Mel Raido. 'A lovely, unusual place to stay,' say inspectors. 'A wonderful painted altar serves as reception desk: bright reds, ochres and Mediterranean blues create the feel of a Spanish or Cuban *casita*.' There are 'colourful paintings and kitsch ornaments' in the winding corridors. The bedrooms vary in size; eight small (cheaper) rooms have shared bathrooms. 'Our room, simply furnished, had good bedding and lovely details: a single rose in a Cuba Havana bottle, a hand-written welcome note, chocolate, and a jar of hot sauce made by the owners' father. The bathroom was a riot of coloured tiles. Generous organic bath products, but a shower attachment, not a proper shower.' Some walls are thin: 'We heard some corridor noise.' There is an honesty bar and free tea and coffee in the lounge/breakfast room downstairs. A restaurant was due to open as we went to press. The area has 'good gastropubs, we liked the *Dark Horse*'. Breakfast includes organic ingredients, perhaps muesli with Tibetan goji berries and watermelon smoothies.

Bedrooms: 28. *Open*: all year. *Facilities*: lounge/breakfast room, unsuitable for ♿. *Background music*: in public areas. *Location*: Camberwell Green, underground Oval. *Smoking*: not allowed. *Children*: all ages welcomed. *Dogs*: not allowed. *Credit cards*: Amex, MasterCard, Visa. *Prices*: B&B £35–£85 per person, weekend deals, Christmas/New Year packages. *V*

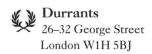

Durrants
26–32 George Street
London W1H 5BJ

Tel 020-7935 8131
Fax 020-7487 3510
Email enquiries@durrantshotel.co.uk
Website www.durrantshotel.co.uk

César award: London hotel of the year

The 'traditional British atmosphere' is much liked by regular visitors to the Miller family's 'old-fashioned' and 'discreet' hotel, a conversion of four terraced houses with a Georgian facade, just north of Oxford Street and near the Wallace Collection. 'So much better than the ultra-boring modern look,' says a visitor this year. Ian McIntosh is the manager; the staff are 'attentive, but not stuffy'. 'Porters take your luggage from the taxi direct to your room.' There are small panelled lounges with leather settees and chairs; original paintings, prints and engravings; antique furniture; a 'cosy', wood-panelled bar. 'The brass at the front is polished every day; public areas are well kept.' Renovation of the bedrooms continues. The larger rooms at the front may get some traffic noise; rooms at the back might sometimes hear early-morning deliveries. 'Our very nice room in the older part of the building had antique-style furniture, effective air conditioning.' Beds are 'comfy'; some bathrooms may be small. The restaurant serves 'generous portions' of international dishes, eg, grilled goat's cheese, endive and walnut salad; grilled sea bass with confit fennel. 'Crisp white linen, shiny glasses.' 'The cooked breakfast was first rate' (continental may be 'a bit unimaginative'). (*Wolfgang Stroebe, AJ Moore, and others*)

Bedrooms: 92, 7 on ground floor. *Open*: all year, restaurant closed 25 Dec evening. *Facilities*: lifts, ramp, bar, restaurant, lounge, 5 function rooms. *Background music*: none. *Location*: off Oxford Street, underground Bond Street, Baker Street. *Smoking*: not allowed. *Children*: all ages welcomed. *Dogs*: only guide dogs allowed. *Credit cards*: Amex, MasterCard, Visa. *Prices*: [2009] room £125– £425, breakfast £13.50–£17, full alc £50 (*excluding 'optional' 12½% service charge*), weekend offers.

How to contact the *Guide*
By mail: From anywhere in the UK, write to Freepost PAM 2931, London W11 4BR (no stamp is needed)
From outside the UK: *Good Hotel Guide*, 50 Addison Avenue, London W11 4QP, England
By telephone or fax: 020-7602 4182
By email: editor@goodhotelguide.com
Via our website: www.goodhotelguide.com

Egerton House   *Tel* 020-7589 2412
17–19 Egerton Terrace   *Fax* 020-7584 6540
London SW3 2BX   *Email* bookeg@rchmail.com
                                 Website www.egertonhousehotel.com

Guests are greeted with a glass of chilled champagne or a pot of tea at
this conversion of two Victorian town houses in Knightsbridge. It is
owned by the Red Carnation group; Sandra Anido is the manager.
Returning visitors were 'warmly welcomed' and found 'front desk
impressive; all staff helpful; housekeeping spot on'. Original artworks
abound. Traditional afternoon tea (with freshly baked scones with
clotted cream and fruit preserves) is taken in the drawing room. The
'skilful' bartender, Antonio (famed for his Martinis), presides in the
bar. The bedrooms are 'attractive and outstandingly well equipped',
with iPod docking station and cable TV, though 'one doesn't get a lot
of square footage for the money'. At the evening turn-down,
chocolates are provided and a scented candle is lit in the bathroom.
Breakfast is available round the clock: between 7 and 11 am it is served
in a pretty room where there is a large buffet (fruit, ham, 'excellent'
bread rolls, pastries and fresh orange juice) and cooked dishes. Snacks
and meals are available all day. There is free Wi-Fi throughout, and
'many good restaurants are nearby'. More reports, please.

Bedrooms: 28, some on ground floor, all air conditioned. *Open*: all year. *Facilities*:
lift, drawing room, bar, breakfast room, private dining/meeting room, 24-hour
butler service. *Background music*: 'soft classical' in bar in evening. *Location*:
central, valet parking, underground Knightsbridge, South Kensington. *Smoking*:
not allowed. *Children*: all ages welcomed (must be accompanied by an adult).
Dogs: allowed. *Credit cards*: Amex, MasterCard, Visa. *Prices*: [2009] room (*excluding
VAT*) £255–£695, breakfast £17–£24.50, Christmas/New Year packages.

The Goring   *Tel* 020-7396 9000
Beeston Place   *Fax* 020-7834 4393
Grosvenor Gardens   *Email* reception@goringhotel.co.uk
London SW1W 0JW   *Website* www.goringhotel.co.uk

❦ *César award in 1994*

'Wonderful as ever, worth every pound; professional in all respects.' A
returning visitor again praises the Goring family's traditional city hotel
near Victoria Station and Buckingham Palace. Jeremy Goring is the
fourth generation to be in charge; the manager, David Morgan-Hewitt,
leads a long-serving staff. They create an atmosphere like that of 'a
large family welcoming guests into their home, almost apologetic at

having to charge', says a trusted reporter. The lounge bar and terrace room (which faces a private garden open to residents) have been refurbished this year. The spacious dining room (with glass chandeliers by David Linley) is 'well organised: comfortable chairs, attractive table settings'. Chef Derek Quelch's cooking is thought 'excellent': 'A very good free-range chicken salad; a superb omelette crammed with chunks of lobster; perfectly steamed sea bass. Delicious puddings included lavender panna cotta with thyme ice cream. Service was friendly without being familiar.' Many of the 'very comfortable' bedrooms face the garden; some have a private terrace. All have Internet access. Breakfast has an extensive selection of fruit; kippers and venison kidneys among the cooked dishes. An 'endearingly eccentric' touch is added by the large replica sheep which migrate round the building. (*Brian Pullee, PH, David Carment*)

Bedrooms: 71, 2 suitable for &. *Open*: all year. *Facilities*: lift, ramps, lounge bar (pianist in evening), terrace room, restaurant, function facilities, civil wedding licence. *Background music*: none. *Location*: near Victoria Station, garage, mews parking, underground Victoria. *Smoking*: allowed in some bedrooms. *Children*: all ages welcomed. *Dogs*: not allowed. *Credit cards*: all major cards. *Prices*: [2009] room (*excluding VAT*) £199–£790, breakfast £23, set dinner £47.50, Christmas/New Year packages.

Hazlitt's
6 Frith Street
London W1D 3JA

Tel 020-7434 1771
Fax 020-7439 1524
Email reservations@hazlitts.co.uk
Website www.hazlittshotel.com

Q *César award in 2002*

'Charming and interesting', this stylish B&B hotel, owned by Peter McKay, is named after the essayist who lived in this building, now listed. In 2009, eight new bedrooms were added in a conversion of an adjacent building linked by a corridor: unlike the original building, it has a lift. The bedrooms vary in size: all are traditional in style, furnished with antiques; many have original panelling and a four-poster or half-tester bed; some have a freestanding Victorian bath. Plumbing and other facilities are modern: there is air conditioning, Wi-Fi and flat-screen LCD television. Visitors liked their 'small but opulent and quirky room with an illuminated bust in the fireplace. The bed was very comfortable.' The quietest rooms are at the back; those overlooking Frith Street, which is busy with revellers especially at weekends, have triple glazing. A continental breakfast (freshly baked bread, freshly squeezed juice, etc) is brought to the bedroom on a tray. Light refreshments may be served in the lounge (no dining room), and a room-service menu is available from 11 am to 10.30 pm. *Hazlitt's* is popular with people in film, fashion, music and publishing: writers who stay here leave a signed copy of their book. (*PR, JA*)

Bedrooms: 30, 2 on ground floor. *Open*: all year. *Facilities*: lift, sitting room, 3 small courtyard gardens, unsuitable for &. *Background music*: none. *Location*: Soho (front windows triple glazed, rear rooms quietest), NCP nearby, underground Tottenham Court Road, Leicester Square. *Smoking*: allowed in 7 bedrooms. *Children*: all ages welcomed. *Dogs*: not allowed. *Credit cards*: all major cards. *Prices*: room (*excluding VAT*) £175–£750, breakfast £10.95, special breaks.

The Levin
28 Basil Street
London SW3 1AS

Tel 020-7589 6286
Fax 020-7823 7826
Email reservations@thelevinhotel.co.uk
Website www.thelevinhotel.co.uk

'What a great place to stay.' Praise in 2009 for this luxurious small Knightsbridge hotel. Named after its owner, David Levin, it is next door to its bigger sister, *The Capital* (*qv*). 'Our higher grade room had a large seating area. Lovely, comfortable, large, well-equipped bathroom.' 'It couldn't be faulted for service, room, facilities and location,' said an inspector, 'but prices are high.' The decor takes inspiration from the 1930s, but the bedrooms are sophisticated; instead of a minibar they have a champagne bar. There is air conditioning, Wi-Fi Internet access, 'state-of-the-art audio and video system', 24-hour room service. 'The welcome was charming: luggage carried into the pistachio-green lobby, elegant with easy chairs, tables, long windows, formal flower arrangements. Our large room overlooking Basil Street had a huge bed with massive headboard, deliciously soft pillows and duvet.' Continental breakfast, with 'high-quality leaf tea', is included in the room rate (cooked dishes cost extra). It is available between 7.30 and 11.30 am in the basement brasserie, *Le Metro*, which is open to the public. Lunch and dinner are served here from noon to 9.30 pm. The menu includes salads, sandwiches, cottage pie. 'Good house wines from David Levin's French vineyard.' (*Tony and Marlene Hall, and others*)

Bedrooms: 12. *Open*: all year, restaurant closed Sun night and 24–26 Dec, 1 Jan. *Facilities*: lobby, library, honesty bar, bar/brasserie (*Le Metro*), access to nearby health club/spa, unsuitable for &. *Background music*: none. *Location*: central, underground Knightsbridge (Harrods exit), private car park (£30 a night). *Smoking*: not allowed. *Children*: all ages welcomed, under-12s must be accompanied by an adult, cot £30 per night. *Dogs*: not allowed. *Credit cards*: all major cards. *Prices*: [2009] B&B (*excluding VAT*) £125–£152.50 per person, full alc £30, seasonal offers, Christmas/New Year packages.

One Aldwych

Tel 020-7300 1000
Fax 020-7300 1001
Email reservations@onealdwych.com
Website www.onealdwych.com

1 Aldwych
London WC2B 4RH

❧ *César award in 2005*

The 'friendly young staff' are praised again this year at Gordon Campbell Gray's 'wonderfully ultra-modern' hotel, originally the Edwardian offices of the *Morning Post*. Stefan Soennichsen was appointed manager in 2009. 'As enjoyable a stay as we had six years ago,' say returning visitors, who appreciated 'the quality of everything, the bustling, vibrant bar/cocktail area, the excellent basement swimming pool'. The ground-floor public areas have a double-height lobby, large flower arrangements, a giant statue of an oarsman. The bedrooms have a 'clever, thoughtful design', 'fantastic pillows' on the luxurious beds; the latest technology; granite surfaces, environmentally friendly toiletries, a vacuum-based waste water system in the bathroom. Triple glazing gives 'absolute peace and quiet at night' (the road outside is busy). There are two restaurants: the 'relaxed' *Indigo*, on a balcony, has a contemporary European menu using organic ingredients (eg, pan-roasted monkfish cheeks, white beans, chorizo). Dishes served in the more formal *Axis*, on the lower ground floor, include smoked salmon fishcakes; grilled calf's liver with pancetta. Breakfast has 'delicious handmade conserves, nothing from a packet'. A visitor who complained of cold plates at breakfast received a letter of apology from the restaurant manager. Children are welcomed. *Dukes Hotel*, St James, is under the same ownership (see Shortlist). (*John and Ann Smith, Nigel Mackintosh, RG*)

Bedrooms: 105, 6 suitable for &. *Open*: all year. *Facilities*: lifts, 2 bars (live DJ Sat evening), 2 restaurants, private dining rooms, function facilities, civil wedding licence, screening room, newsagent, florist, health club (18-metre swimming pool, spa, sauna, gym). *Background music*: in lobby bar. *Location*: Strand (windows triple glazed), valet parking, underground Covent Garden, Charing Cross, Waterloo. *Smoking*: allowed in 16 bedrooms. *Children*: all ages welcomed (some interconnecting rooms). *Dogs*: only guide dogs allowed. *Credit cards*: all major cards. *Prices*: [2009] room/suite (*excluding VAT*) £195–£1,195, breakfast £16.75–£24.75, pre- and post-theatre menu (*Indigo*) £16.75–£19.75, full alc (*Axis*) £40, promotional offers, New Year package.

The Portobello
22 Stanley Gardens
London W11 2NG

Tel 020-7727 2777
Fax 020-7792 9641
Email info@portobellohotel.com
Website www.portobellohotel.com

'Changing fashions in hotels may have passed *The Portobello* by, but it is redeemed by a sense of character, nothing anonymous here.' Praise from an inspector for this bohemian little hotel, long popular with A-list celebrities, in a Victorian terrace on a Notting Hill residential street. It is owned by Tim and Cathy Herring with partner Johnny Ekperigin (who manages it with Hanna Turner). The bedrooms vary considerably in size ('cabin' rooms have a small bathroom); the 'special rooms' are recommended. 'Discuss your choice before booking, preferably with Gloria, who is often on hand; she will describe all the features and/or drawbacks.' A third-floor room had a 'supremely comfortable four-poster bed, quality bedlinen and towels, large bathroom with dressing area; small balcony over the peaceful garden'. A simple continental breakfast is included in the room rate ('freshly squeezed juice, slabs of butter, excellent tea and coffee, but tiny pots of preserves'). It can be taken in the bedroom or the 'charming' garden-facing drawing room, which has gilt mirrors, military pictures, potted palms, Edwardiana. Cooked breakfast dishes are available *à la carte*; a 24-hour room service menu has snacks and light meals. *The Portobello*'s residents get a discount at *Julie's*, the owners' restaurant/bar/café in nearby Clarendon Cross.

Bedrooms: 21. *Open*: all year. *Facilities*: lift, small bar, foyer/lounge, access to nearby health club, unsuitable for &. *Background music*: none. *Location*: Notting Hill, meter parking, underground Notting Hill Gate. *Smoking*: allowed in 6 bedrooms. *Children*: all ages welcomed. *Dogs*: allowed by prior arrangement, not in public rooms. *Credit cards*: Amex, MasterCard, Visa. *Prices*: B&B (continental) £100–£150 per person.

The rockwell
181 Cromwell Road
London SW5 0SF

Tel 020-7244 2000
Fax 020-7244 2001
Email enquiries@therockwell.com
Website www.therockwell.com

Two Victorian terrace houses on the busy Cromwell Road have been turned into a hotel with a 'bright, modern' feel by owners Michael Squire (architect) and Tony Bartlett. Ocky Paller is the manager. 'Our emphasis is on understated contemporary style, crafted to create a relaxed atmosphere,' they say. The 'fine, high-ceilinged' lounge has an open fire; the small bar opens on to a garden with plants in huge pots, where drinks and meals can be served. There are 'interesting' wall-papers, bright patterns and colour. The bedrooms vary considerably in size. The biggest mezzanine suites have a lounge and sleeping area down a curved staircase; two garden rooms have a patio; smaller rooms make 'good use of space' with built-in light oak furnishings. All rooms have flat-screen TV, free broadband Internet access, a minibar. 'Double glazing kept out road noise.' Bathrooms are well lit and have a powerful shower. In the restaurant, overlooking the courtyard garden, chef Stephan Preda serves contemporary dishes, perhaps Cajun chicken skewer; cod with a Brazilian coconut and palm oil sauce. There is 24-hour room service. Breakfast, served until 10 am, has a buffet and various cooked dishes. 'Reasonable prices for central London.' More reports, please.

Bedrooms: 40, some on ground floor. *Open*: all year. *Facilities*: lift, ramps, lobby, lounge, bar, restaurant, conference room, garden. *Background music*: in lobby and library area. *Location*: 1 mile W of West End, opposite Cromwell Hospital, underground Earls Court. *Smoking*: not allowed. *Children*: all ages welcomed. *Dogs*: not allowed. *Credit cards*: Amex, MasterCard, Visa. *Prices*: room £117–£176, breakfast £9.50–£12.50, full alc £28.

Twenty Nevern Square

20 Nevern Square
London SW5 9PD

Tel 020-7565 9555
Fax 020-7565 9444
Email hotel@twentynevernsquare.co.uk
Website www.twentynevernsquare.co.uk

Facing a garden square, this converted red brick Victorian town house (owned by the Mayflower group) is 'surprisingly peaceful', yet only a few minutes' walk from Earls Court underground station. 'Exotic' bedrooms have 'a mix of European and Asian influences'. The Sleigh Double has a mahogany sleigh bed and silk-draped canopy; the Pasha Suite, which faces the square, has gold silk curtains framing large balcony windows; the Four Poster room has a small private staircase and a carved, canopied bed. Some rooms are small, but all are well equipped, with free Wi-Fi, CD-player, widescreen TV and safe. Complimentary afternoon tea is served in a small lounge with armchairs. In the conservatory-style *Café Twenty*, a 'generous' continental breakfast has cold meats, fruit salad, etc. This is included in the room price; cooked costs extra. A 'South African-style' barbecue is sometimes held. Leisure facilities are available at a nearby gym.

Bedrooms: 20. *Open*: all year. *Facilities*: lounge, restaurant, small garden, unsuitable for &. *Background music*: in public rooms. *Location*: central, underground Earls Court. *Smoking*: not allowed. *Children*: all ages welcomed (under-2s accommodated free). *Dogs*: not allowed. *Credit cards*: Amex, MasterCard, Visa. *Prices*: B&B £49.50–£119 per person, cooked breakfast £9, barbecue from £18, Christmas/New Year packages.

The Victoria   NEW

10 West Temple Sheen
London SW14 7RT

Tel 020-8876 4238
Fax 020-8878 3464
Email bookings@thevictoria.net
Website www.thevictoria.net

In a leafy residential area, this unpretentious gastropub is just 25 minutes by train from Waterloo station. In May 2008, it was bought by celebrity chef Paul Merrett and his business partner, Greg Bellamy. Inspectors, who revisited in 2009, wrote of a 'relaxed neighbourhood feel' and 'good value in an agreeable area of London'. The simple bedrooms are in an annexe at the back: 'We had a warm welcome from a young Frenchman who carried our bag to one of the two large rooms. It had a medium-sized bed with a thick duvet; no wardrobe, but a dress rack with hanging shelves; the small shower room was efficient. All was quiet at night, but in the early morning we heard trains.' The 'charming' conservatory restaurant has wooden floor, big hanging lights (dim at night). Adjacent is a large and pretty terrace, with wisteria and fruit trees, for drinks and summer meals. The menu is based on seasonal ingredients, from small producers when possible. 'We enjoyed the bistro-style cooking: chicory and pear salad; trout with asparagus. Breakfast has good cereals and orange juice, DIY toast from good bread, delicious chunky marmalade. The bacon was disappointing, and tea was brought in the cup with a tea bag in: time they bought some teapots.' Popular with locals for a morning coffee or an evening drink.

Bedrooms: 7, 3 on ground floor. *Open*: all year. *Facilities*: bar, restaurant, garden, unsuitable for &. *Background music*: in bar and restaurant. *Location*: Mortlake (5 mins' walk) to Waterloo/Clapham Jct, car park. *Smoking*: not allowed. *Children*: all ages welcomed. *Dogs*: allowed in bar and garden. *Credit cards*: MasterCard, Visa. *Prices*: [2009] B&B (continental) £52.50–£67.50 per person, cooked breakfast £6.50, full alc £50, tailor-made breaks, Christmas/New Year packages. *V*

The *V* sign at the end of an entry indicates a hotel that has agreed to take part in our Voucher scheme (see page 57).

The Zetter	*Tel* 020-7324 4444
86–88 Clerkenwell Road	*Fax* 020-7324 4445
London EC1M 5RJ	*Email* info@thezetter.com
	Website www.thezetter.com

'Comfortable, stylish, romantic yet anonymous. Lovely beds and pillows; adequate food.' In design-conscious Clerkenwell, this 19th-century warehouse (for many years the home of Zetters football pools) was converted to a hotel five years ago by owners Mark Sainsbury and Michael Benyan and given a contemporary look. Justin Pinchbeck is manager; the staff are 'exceptionally friendly'. The crescent-shaped restaurant has floor-to-ceiling windows, tables well spaced, 'good atmosphere'. The Mediterranean menu of chef Diego Jacquet might include tuna and seared scallops with chive, lemon and ginger. 'Good puddings. Portions not over-large; reasonable prices.' On Sunday there is a brunch menu and a short *carte*, accompanied by live jazz. The bedrooms have been redecorated this year, neutrally with bright splashes of colour. There are comfortable beds with duck-down duvet, modern bathrooms with raindance shower, free Wi-Fi. There are interconnecting rooms for visitors with children. Breakfast can be continental, classic English, vegetarian, or *à la carte* (including porridge with apple compote and maple syrup). Vending machines on each floor produce drinks, disposable cameras, champagne, etc. *The Zetter* 'has an environmental conscience' (sustainable materials, energy-efficient technology; they pump and bottle their own water from a well almost a mile below the building).

Bedrooms: 59, 1 suitable for &. *Open*: all year. *Facilities*: 2 lifts, ramps, cocktail bar/lounge, restaurant, 2 function/meeting rooms. *Background music*: modern eclectic mix. *Location*: Clerkenwell, by St John's Sq, NCP garage 5 mins' walk, underground Farringdon. *Smoking*: allowed in 12 bedrooms. *Children*: all ages welcomed. *Dogs*: only guide dogs allowed. *Credit cards*: Amex, MasterCard, Visa. *Prices*: [2009] room £195.50–£396.75, breakfast £6.50–£16.50, full alc £40.

See also Shortlist

ENGLAND

The breadth and variety of the *Guide*'s selection of
hotels in England are illustrated by our choices for
the 2010 *César* awards. They range from a
sympathetic conversion of an old Cumbrian inn to a
Georgian dower house on the edge of Exmoor where
the hospitality 'makes all the difference'; from a
Jacobean mansion in north Norfolk where the
cooking is exceptional, to an elegant, modern hotel
on the Cornish coast; from a small hotel with the feel
of a country home in a quintessential Wiltshire
village, to a hotel that has been restored with flair and
style in a Thames-side village. The common
denominator in these and our other entries
is hands-on ownership (sometimes executed
by a good manager) with an overriding concern
for the well-being of the guest.

Morston Hall, Morston

ABBOTSBURY Dorset   Map 1:D6

Abbey House   *Tel* 01305-871330
Church Street   *Fax* 01305-871088
Abbotsbury DT3 4JJ   *Email* info@theabbeyhouse.co.uk
                          Website www.theabbeyhouse.co.uk

'Strongly recommended' again in 2009, this 15th-century building is
'beautifully situated' next to a remaining fragment of an 11th-century
abbey. 'A warm welcome, comfortable stay and excellent breakfast,'
say visitors. The owners, Jonathan and Maureen Cooke, are regularly
praised for their 'kindness and friendliness'. They run their guest
house 'impeccably', yet 'find time to chat'. There are flagstone floors,
panelled doors, original windows; a 'cosy lounge with plenty of books';
'lots of chintz and knick-knacks'. Light lunches and cream teas are
served in summer in the 'lovely large garden'; it has flowerbeds in
wide lawns that slope down to a millpond. Beyond is Abbotsbury's
huge, ancient tithe barn. The 'cottagey' bedrooms vary in size and
style: 'Ours, inside the main roof gable on the second floor, had a
sitting area and a big brass bed; good, modern TV.' 'Views from the
rooms were over rolling countryside towards the sea.' 'Watch your
head in an attic room.' Breakfast, served with damask tablecloths, has
a cold buffet, 'croissants worth a mention', and a wide choice of
cooked dishes using local produce. Evening meals are available only
for house parties, but *Abbey House* has a comprehensive list of local
eating places. The village is famed for its ancient swannery and its
subtropical gardens. (*Christopher Haddock, Catherine Held, Derek French*)

Bedrooms: 5. *Open*: all year, tea room open for lunches Apr–Oct, dinners for
house parties only. *Facilities*: reception, lounge, breakfast/tea room, 1½-acre
garden (stage for opera), sea 15 mins' walk, unsuitable for &. *Background music*:
sometimes. *Location*: village centre. *Smoking*: not allowed. *Children*: not under
12. *Dogs*: not allowed. *Credit cards*: none. *Prices*: [2009] B&B £35–£50 per person,
New Year package, 1-night bookings sometimes refused.

ABINGDON Oxfordshire   *See Shortlist*

ALDEBURGH Suffolk   Map 2:C6

The Wentworth   *Tel* 01728-452312
Wentworth Road   *Fax* 01728-454343
Aldeburgh IP15 5BD   *Email* stay@wentworth-aldeburgh.co.uk
                          Website www.wentworth-aldeburgh.com

Owned for 90 years by one family, this traditional seaside hotel faces
fishing huts and boats on Aldeburgh's shingle beach. The 'hands-on'
Michael Pritt, the third generation, runs it. 'He seems omnipresent,'
says a visitor in 2009. 'The hotel is frozen in a time when good service
was guaranteed, but it has all mod cons.' There is 'a relaxed feel; three
wonderful seating areas to enjoy coffee or a reasonably priced lunch
(one has a blazing log fire, another sumptuous sofas)'. In the conservatory restaurant (recently refurbished), chef Graham Reid serves
generous dishes from a daily-changing menu. 'Fish supremely fresh,
vegetables *al dente*, cardamom brûlée very moreish.' Sea-facing
bedrooms have binoculars. 'Ours, on the second floor, up 39 narrow
steps, was not large but nicely furnished; a well-equipped modern
bathroom.' The annexe, *Darfield House*, has large rooms and a garden,
but no sea view. Each room has a copy of Kathleen Hale's *Orlando the
Marmalade Cat* (her 'Owlbarrow' is Aldeburgh). Musicians and actors
stay here during the Aldeburgh Festival, as do writers during the
literary festival. (*Sue McNally, Sir John Hall, Robert Gower*)

Bedrooms: 35, 7 in *Darfield House* opposite, 5 on ground floor, 1 suitable for &.
Open: all year. *Facilities*: ramps, 2 lounges, bar, restaurant, private dining room,
conference room, 2 terrace gardens, shingle beach 200 yds. *Background music*:
none. *Location*: seafront, 5 mins' walk from centre, car park, train Saxmundham
8 miles. *Smoking*: not allowed. *Children*: all ages welcomed. *Dogs*: not allowed
in restaurant. *Credit cards*: all major cards. *Prices*: [2009] B&B £47.50–£116
per person, D,B&B £52.50–£126, set dinner £19.95, weekend/midweek
breaks, Christmas/New Year packages, 1-night bookings refused Sat. *V*
(midweek only)

ALKHAM Kent   Map 2:D5

The Marquis at Alkham   NEW   *Tel* 01304-873410
Alkham Valley Road   *Fax* 01304-873418
Alkham   *Email* info@themarquisatalkham.co.uk
CT15 7DF   *Website* www.themarquisatalkham.co.uk

In a pretty village at the southern end of the Kent Downs, this 200-
year-old inn was given a thorough make-over by Hugh Oxborrow and

his business partner, Tony Marsden. It reopened as a restaurant-with-rooms in November 2008: Ben Walton is the manager. The white-painted brick exterior, with Kentish clapboard additions, is 'strikingly lit at night'. Inside, it is 'immediately inviting' (says an inspector), with a contemporary look: wide-beam oak flooring, dark wood tables, exposed brickwork, pale grey walls. 'On a quiet evening, we were upgraded to a huge suite with a large bedroom and sitting area; dark wood, contemporary furniture; imaginatively decorated in co-ordinated green and brown. Good equipment, plenty of storage. The bed could have been bigger. In the well-designed bathroom you needed a step to enter the deep bath.' The restaurant was busy with locals: chef Charles Lakin's three-course menu was a well-balanced 'celebration of English produce', with local wines. 'Fresh home-made bread came with the carrot and orange soup; a perfect trio of corn-fed chicken; a superb platter of 18 English cheeses.' A 'lovely' breakfast has a buffet with croissants, home-made preserves; 'good cooked choices included Whitstable kippers; full English, up to scratch'. The road in front is busy 'but inside you are not aware of noise'. Close to the ferries to France, 'this is a good example of English hospitality and food'.

Bedrooms: 8, 3 in cottages 3 mins' drive away. *Open*: all year, restaurant closed Sun evening/Mon (bar snacks). *Facilities*: bar, lounge, dining room, small garden, unsuitable for &. *Background music*: 'refined' in public areas. *Location*: 4 miles W of Dover. *Smoking*: not allowed. *Children*: all ages welcomed. *Dogs*: allowed in cottages. *Credit cards*: all major cards. *Prices*: [2009] B&B £37.50–£97.50 per person, D,B&B £55–£132.50, set meals £15.50–£25, full alc £44, special breaks, Christmas/New Year packages. *V*

ALSTON Cumbria   Map 4:B3

Lovelady Shield
Nenthead Road
nr Alston CA9 3LF

Tel 01434-381203
Fax 01434-381515
Email enquiries@lovelady.co.uk
Website www.lovelady.co.uk

Set peacefully among trees on the banks of the River Nent, this 'grand old house' (white-fronted and Georgian) stands on the site of a 13th-century convent. It has long been run as a small hotel/restaurant by owners Peter and Marie Haynes, who live in a cottage in the grounds. Visitors like the silence, both in the grounds (no traffic noise) and the house, which is 'blissfully free of muzak'. 'Service is eager but relaxed,' say visitors this year. Guests have the use of a sitting room with open fire, and a small library 'full of books and games for rainy days'. Bedrooms are 'comfortably furnished'; Room 9 has a four-poster bed and a separate seating area with a settee. Some rooms are small. Barrie Garton, the chef for almost 20 years, describes his style as 'British with continental excursions'. His daily-changing four-course *table d'hôte* menu might include tiger prawn wonton, avocado purée; slow-braised blade of beef, reversed cauliflower cheese. An 'excellent' breakfast has 'lots of choice'. There is good walking from the door. Guests at three self-catering cottages in the grounds can use the hotel facilities. (*Claire and David Stevens*)

Bedrooms: 12. *Open*: all year. *Facilities*: 2 lounges, bar, restaurant, conference facilities, civil wedding licence, 2-acre grounds (river, fishing, croquet, woodland walks), unsuitable for &. *Background music*: none. *Location*: 2 miles N of Alston on A689. *Smoking*: not allowed. *Children*: all ages welcomed. *Dogs*: not allowed in public rooms. *Credit cards*: Amex, MasterCard, Visa. *Prices*: B&B £80–£150 per person, D,B&B £100–£170, set dinner £41.50, special breaks, Christmas/New Year packages. *V*

AMBLESIDE Cumbria   Map 4: inset C2

The Regent by the Lake
Waterhead Bay
Ambleside LA22 0ES

Tel 015394-32254
Fax 015394-31474
Email info@regentlakes.co.uk
Website www.regentlakes.co.uk

'We enjoyed being made to feel like part of a family.' 'A thoroughly reliable, reasonably priced hotel.' Praise this year for this white-fronted building opposite a slipway on to Lake Windermere, near this picturesque village. Owned by Christine Hewitt, it is managed by her son, Andrew. The public rooms have a modern decor of pale browns and cream. Bedrooms 'come in all shapes and sizes'. 'Our sail loft room had a wonderful view of the lake from its own private terrace, and a secluded feeling.' Some rooms, if 'fairly small', are 'comfortable and well equipped'. A courtyard room was 'packed with wonderful features including music centre and DVD-player; its modern bathroom had a spa bath'. These rooms are recommended for children (near the swimming pool) and for dogs: both are welcomed ('special requests and diets no problem'). In the split-level restaurant, the daily-changing menus of chef John Mathers are commended: 'Our favourite dish was frittata of Mediterranean vegetables, roast garlic and cherry tomato, served with mixed leaves.' Breakfast, served until midday, is 'varied and innovative: notable scrambled egg laced with bacon; wide choice of omelettes'. 'By jingo, the kippers were good.' (*Frank G Millen, Simon Rodway, David EW Jervois, GM*)

Bedrooms: 30, 10 in courtyard, 5 in garden, 7 on ground floor. *Open*: all year, except 20–27 Dec. *Facilities*: ramp, lounge, sun lounge, bar, restaurant, 17-metre indoor swimming pool, courtyard, ¼-acre garden, on Lake Windermere (sailing, waterskiing, fishing). *Background music*: classical/jazz in public rooms in evening. *Location*: on A591, S of centre, at Waterhead Bay. *Smoking*: not allowed. *Children*: all ages welcomed. *Dogs*: not allowed in public rooms, some bedrooms. *Credit cards*: Amex, MasterCard, Visa. *Prices*: [2009] B&B £42.50–£80 per person, D,B&B £60–£97.50, full alc £35, New Year package, 1-night bookings sometimes refused Sat. *V*

Rothay Manor
Rothay Bridge
Ambleside LA22 0EH

Tel 015394-33605
Fax 015394-33607
Email hotel@rothaymanor.co.uk
Website www.rothaymanor.co.uk

César award in 1992

'A lovely, civilised hotel', this white Regency house near the head of Lake Windermere has been run by the Nixon family for over 40 years. Nigel Nixon is at the helm; Peter Sinclair, the manager, 'fits in well in the Nixon tradition of being around much of the time and waiting at dinner' (say returning visitors). The 'quality, experience and helpfulness of the staff' continue to stand out. The lounges are 'light and comfortable'. The bedrooms are 'well furnished, with good bedlinen, impeccable housekeeping'; many are large. 'Ours had a comfortable sofa.' The quietest rooms overlook the 'well laid-out' garden. The chef, Jane Binns, provides 'traditional English food with a slight French influence', which is 'quite simply cooked, but beautifully presented'. An 'excellent and very filling afternoon tea' and a children's menu are available. One visitor 'attempted the Lakeland cooked breakfast, but had to admit defeat before the end'. A family group with eight children was 'well looked after; croquet much enjoyed'. Study courses – bridge, Scrabble, antiques, etc – 'look interesting' and are booked early. The 'delightful garden insulated the hotel from daytime traffic' and 'the roads are quiet at night'. You can walk across fields to the lake. (*Margaret H Box, Anthony Bradbury, Jane Petrie*)

Bedrooms: 19, 2 in annexe, 2 suitable for ♿. *Open*: all year except 3–28 Jan. *Facilities*: ramp, 2 lounges, bar, 2 dining rooms, meeting/conference facilities, 1-acre garden (croquet), free access to local leisure centre. *Background music*: none. *Location*: ¼ mile SW of Ambleside. *Smoking*: not allowed. *Children*: all

ages welcomed. *Dogs*: not allowed. *Credit cards*: all major cards. *Prices*: [2009]
B&B £72.50–£110 per person, D,B&B £102.50–£147.50, set dinner £34–£46,
special breaks (antiques, bridge, Scrabble, walking, etc), Christmas/New Year
packages, 1-night bookings refused Sat.

AMPLEFORTH North Yorkshire   Map 4:D4

Shallowdale House
West End, Ampleforth
nr York, YO62 4DY

Tel 01439-788325
Fax 01439-788885
Email stay@shallowdalehouse.co.uk
Website www.shallowdalehouse.co.uk

❦ *César award in 2005*

'I can't stay away. What wonderful hosts; everyone is treated with
impeccable kindness.' Praise from a regular visitor, returning this year
to Phillip Gill and Anton van der Horst's 1960s architect-designed
house on the edge of the North York Moors national park. 'As you drive
through the gates you begin to relax,' says another report. 'They make
a point of coming out to welcome guests and help with luggage; tea
and home-made cakes are quickly produced in the ground-floor
drawing room with its lovely view over the valley.' The accommodation
'is a joy': 'extremely comfortable' bedrooms have 'huge bed, capacious
chest of drawers and wardrobe'; 'delightful views' ('binoculars
thoughtfully provided'). Bathrooms have 'piping hot water and lots of
goodies'. Two bedrooms are large; the third, slightly smaller, has a
private bathroom across a corridor. A four-course set meal is served by
arrangement (48 hours' notice) at separate candlelit tables; the food is
variously described as 'delicious' and 'homely', in dishes like guineafowl breasts in prosciutto, rosemary and mascarpone. No choice but
'preferences are discussed beforehand'. Breakfast includes dry-cured
bacon, Whitby kippers, home-made preserves. There is a 'restful'
hillside garden, and 'the area is full of interest'. (*Richard Creed, Mary
Hewson, Christine Moore, John Tovey*)

Bedrooms: 3. *Open*: all year except Christmas/New Year, occasionally at other
times. *Facilities*: drawing room, sitting room, dining room, 2½-acre grounds,
unsuitable for &. *Background music*: none. *Location*: edge of village. *Smoking*:
not allowed. *Children*: not under 12. *Dogs*: not allowed. *Credit cards*: MasterCard,
Visa. *Prices*: [2009] B&B £47.50–£85 per person, set dinner £35, 1-night
bookings occasionally refused weekends.

Report forms (Freepost in UK) are at the end of the *Guide*.

ARUNDEL West Sussex   Map 2:E3

Arundel House
11 High Street
Arundel BN18 9AD

Tel 01903-882136
Fax 01903-881179
Website www.arundelhouseonline.com

'Food, service and ambience are excellent' at this 'comfortable' restaurant-with-rooms owned by Luke Hackman (the chef) and Billy Lewis-Bowker. The bow-windowed 19th-century merchant's house stands opposite the castle, at the foot of the steep High Street of this attractive town. The 'pleasing' decor is by Mr Lewis-Bowker's wife, Emma, whose paintings hang throughout. Meals are served in two rooms, one on each side of the entrance hall. 'Wild, local and seasonal' ingredients are used in the British-led, modern cuisine, eg, layered spicy crab and aubergine on a rich tomato sauce; confit belly of Sussex pork with bubble and squeak rösti. 'They took in good spirit my complaint about the music ("Mack the Knife" twice during dinner).' No residents' lounge; bedrooms have flat-screen TV, free Wi-Fi and power shower ('but only liquid soap'). There is a choice between duvet and blankets (best specify when you book). Free tea or coffee is delivered to rooms on request, but not before 8 am. The house is on a short one-way system: no car park, but you can draw up outside to unload, and vouchers are given for the large, safe municipal car park close by. (*Richard Creed, and others*)

Bedrooms: 5. *Open*: all year except 23–27 Dec, restaurant closed Sun except Mothering Sunday. *Facilities*: restaurant, unsuitable for &. *Background music*: in restaurant. *Location*: town centre. *Smoking*: not allowed. *Children*: not under 16. *Dogs*: only assistance dogs allowed. *Credit cards*: Amex, MasterCard, Visa. *Prices*: B&B £40–£80 per person, D,B&B £20 added, full alc £33. *V*

The Town House
65 High Street
Arundel BN18 9AJ

Tel 01903-883847
Email enquiries@thetownhouse.co.uk
Website www.thetownhouse.co.uk

Everyone agrees that the food is 'fabulous' at this restaurant-with-rooms in a Grade II listed Regency building. It stands at the top of the steep High Street (some traffic noise by day), opposite the castle. The owners, Lee Williams (the chef) and his wife, Katie, 'aim to attract a relaxed clientele'; children are welcomed. 'Like being looked after by friends,' writes a visitor in 2009. 'The owner greeted us warmly and carried our cases,' add inspectors. 'Our suite (with balcony and four-poster) had an open fireplace with marble surround,

19th-century moulded plaster panels, furniture from a junk shop (needed replacing), efficient radiators. Housekeeping was good.' A second-floor room (no lift) was 'modest in size, perfectly adequate with ample storage space'. 'Excellent meals with well-chosen wines.' Modern dishes use seasonal local produce: perhaps Jerusalem artichoke soup with artichoke crisps; noisette of lamb, spinach, caramelised shallots, confit potatoes. Bread is home baked. 'Service from the French waitress could not be faulted.' Breakfast is continental or 'full English with additions'. The dining room's intricately carved and gilded 16th-century Florentine ceiling was brought to England by Lord Maltravers, son of an earl of Arundel (he once lived here). No lounge or grounds, so 'best for a short stay'. On Sunday, when the restaurant is closed, guests are asked to check in before 1 o'clock (they are then given a key). (*Joe Ross, and others*)

Bedrooms: 4. *Open*: all year except 25/26 Dec, 2 weeks Feb, 2 weeks Oct, restaurant closed Sun/Mon. *Facilities*: restaurant, unsuitable for &. *Background music*: in restaurant. *Location*: top end of High Street. *Smoking*: not allowed. *Children*: all ages welcomed. *Dogs*: not allowed. *Credit cards*: Diners, MasterCard, Visa. *Prices*: [2009] B&B £42.50–£62.50 per person, D,B&B (midweek) £60–£75, set dinner £22–£27.50, 1-night bookings refused weekends in high season. *V*

ASHWATER Devon   Map 1:C3

Blagdon Manor   *Tel* 01409-211224
Ashwater EX21 5DF   *Fax* 01409-211634
                                            Email stay@blagdon.com
                                            Website www.blagdon.com

🔱 *César award in 2006*

'We never cease to be amazed by the quality of Steve's cooking – deserving of a *Michelin* star. Every visit is a joy.' 'They keep their high standards year after year without appearing harassed.' Fresh praise for Liz and Steve Morey's rambling, 17th-century manor house (Grade II listed), in rolling countryside with panoramic views towards Dartmoor. 'No noise, no traffic, only ducks and tame pheasants demanding food.' 'Furnished traditionally', it is run in a 'friendly, easy manner', said an earlier visitor. 'Our comfortable room had some surprises – a box of home-made chocolates, complimentary sherry.' Fresh flowers and open fires are in the bar and lounge. Books, ornaments and striped fabrics abound. In the bright dining room, the menu offers six choices each of starter, main course and dessert.

Ingredients are locally sourced, often from the Moreys' garden, and imaginatively transformed. 'A most wonderful dish, with lamb cooked in four different ways, the most exquisite being shoulder stuffed with haggis.' The Cornish slate terrace outside the conservatory allows alfresco dining. The 'delightful' Moreys have two 'gorgeous' chocolate Labradors, and guests' dogs 'are positively welcomed'. (*John and Ann Smith, B Emberson, GC*)

Bedrooms: 8. *Open*: all year except Jan. *Facilities*: ramps, lounge, library, snug, bar, conservatory, restaurant, private dining room, 20-acre grounds (3-acre gardens, croquet, giant chess, gazebo, pond), unsuitable for &. *Background music*: none. *Location*: 8 miles NE of Launceston. *Smoking*: not allowed. *Children*: not under 12. *Dogs*: not allowed in restaurant, conservatory. *Credit cards*: MasterCard, Visa. *Prices*: B&B £67.50–£90 per person, set lunch £20, dinner £35, midweek winter breaks, 1-night bookings refused Christmas. *V*

AUSTWICK North Yorkshire   Map 4:D3

The Austwick Traddock
Austwick, via Lancaster
LA2 8BY

Tel 01524-251224
Fax 01524-251796
Email info@austwicktraddock.co.uk
Website www.austwicktraddock.co.uk

In a pretty village in the Yorkshire Dales national park, this substantial stone-built Georgian house is run by two generations of the Reynolds family. Bruce and Jane Reynolds are gradually handing over to their son, Paul, and his wife, Jenny. A programme of 'rolling redecoration' has seen the addition of two bedrooms this year; some older bathrooms have been upgraded. One visitor wrote of 'blazing log fires in the public rooms' and a 'cosy, welcoming feel'. The bedrooms are 'comfortably furnished in restrained country style' (patterned wallpaper, plain fitted carpets, 'fine country antiques'), and have magazines, fresh milk, home-made biscuits. 'Ours had pleasantly faded elegance, comfort married to good taste.' The food, 'wherever possible' organic, is sourced locally, almost all from within a 50-mile radius. There were mixed reports on dinner: 'A really good venison pudding but an over-sweet white chocolate and raspberry soufflé.' Breakfasts, however, were 'outstanding': a 'wide and lavish choice' (porridge, eggs Benedict, kippers, smoothies and much else). 'Great walking from the door' – this is Wainwright country.

Bedrooms: 12, 1 on ground floor. *Open*: all year. *Facilities*: 3 lounges, 2 dining areas, function facilities, 1-acre grounds (sun deck), only public rooms accessible to &. *Background music*: 'if needed' in lounge and dining room.

Location: 4 miles NW of Settle, train Settle, bus. *Smoking*: not allowed. *Children*: all ages welcomed. *Dogs*: not allowed in public rooms. *Credit cards*: MasterCard, Visa. *Prices*: [2009] B&B £45–£90 per person, D,B&B £75–£120, full alc £51, Christmas/New Year packages, 1-night bookings refused weekends in season. *V*

AYLESBURY Buckinghamshire   Map 2:C3

Hartwell House
Oxford Road
nr Aylesbury HP17 8NR

Tel 01296-747444
Fax 01296-747450
Email info@hartwell-house.com
Website www.hartwell-house.com

♕ *César award in 1997*

'Exquisite in 18th-century pastoral style', this magnificent stately home is run as a luxury hotel by Richard Broyd's Historic House Hotels on behalf of the National Trust, which acquired it in autumn 2008 (see also *Middlethorpe Hall & Spa*, York, *Bodysgallen Hall & Spa*, Llandudno, Wales). The Trust will receive all profits. The long-serving, 'charming' director/general manager, Jonathan Thompson, continues to 'keep an eagle eye on everything'. 'Service just right: you are a welcome guest in their country house which they treasure.' Another comment: 'The place is stunning, the food wonderful.' The house is 'beautifully restored', and has 'all mod cons'. The four 'elegant' drawing rooms are furnished with 'priceless antiques, there to be used, not just admired'. There are 'roaring log fires' and 'friendly staff'. Air conditioning has been installed in many bedrooms, and all have a flat-screen TV. The rooms in the main house are large and 'well furnished', and have 'wonderful views'. Those in a converted stable block are 'attractively decorated' (some are split-level). The dress code for the 'excellent' dinner, provided by Daniel Richardson and served by candlelight with silver and damask, is smart casual (jacket and tie not obligatory). There is a café and bar in the spa. (*William Pedder, Hugo Peate*)

Bedrooms: 46, 16 in stable block, some on ground floor, 2 suitable for &. *Open*: all year. *Facilities*: lift, ramps, 4 drawing rooms, bar, 3 dining rooms, pianist in vestibule Fri/Sat evening, conference facilities, civil wedding licence, spa (swimming pool (8 by 16 metres), whirlpool, sauna, beauty salon, café/bar), 90-acre grounds (tennis, croquet, lake, fishing, jogging track, woodlands). *Background music*: none. *Location*: 2 miles W of Aylesbury. *Smoking*: not allowed. *Children*: not under 6. *Dogs*: allowed in ground-floor suites and *Hartwell Court*. *Credit cards*: Amex, MasterCard, Visa. *Prices*: [2009] B&B (continental breakfast) £92.50–£325 per person, D,B&B from £130, cooked breakfast £7, set dinner from £29.95, full alc £46, special breaks, Christmas/New Year packages. *V* (Sun–Thurs)

BAMPTON Devon   *See Shortlist*

BARWICK Somerset   Map 1:C6

Little Barwick House   *Tel* 01935-423902
Barwick, nr Yeovil   *Fax* 01935-420908
BA22 9TD   *Email* reservations@barwick7.fsnet.co.uk
                     Website www.littlebarwickhouse.co.uk

♛ *César award in 2002*

An 'exceptional all-round experience' was enjoyed this year at Tim
and Emma Ford's ever-popular restaurant-with-rooms in a Georgian
dower house in lovely countryside near the Somerset/Dorset border.
She is 'unfailingly smiling, attentive and efficient'. 'We were greeted
with complimentary tea and banana cake in front of a log fire in the
comfortable drawing room.' His 'superb' cooking continues to impress:
the 'delightful modern English' menu has 'plenty of options, and a
couple of changing dishes per course each night'. 'Highlights were
scallops; saddle of wild venison; rhubarb and ginger tart. 'Beautifully
prepared and presented. The service was immaculate, unhurried;
table spacing is good.' 'Emma was spot-on with her advice on wine';
'the list is a thing of beauty'. Bedrooms vary in size (some are small).
'Our large room had king-size bed, turned down during dinner;
functional bathroom with good power shower.' 'Our high-ceilinged
room was tastefully decorated; we liked the fresh milk and home-
made shortbread.' Housekeeping is 'impeccable' and guests appreciate
being offered a choice between duvet and blankets and sheets.
Breakfast was 'first class, with good choice'. 'Just how a restaurant-
with-rooms should be run.' The house has been freshly rendered this
year, and the car park re-gravelled. (*Richard Barrett, Bryan and Mary
Blaxall, Alan and Audrey Moulds, Simon Willbourn*).

Bedrooms: 6. *Open*: all year except Christmas, 2 weeks Jan, restaurant closed
Sun evenings, midday on Mon and Tues. *Facilities*: ramp, 2 lounges, restaurant,
conservatory, 3½-acre garden (terrace, paddock), unsuitable for &. *Background
music*: none. *Location*: ¾ mile outside Yeovil. *Smoking*: not allowed. *Children*: not
under 5. *Dogs*: not allowed in public rooms. *Credit cards*: MasterCard, Visa.
Prices: [2009] B&B £69–£100 per person, D,B&B £80–£110, set dinner £37.95,
2-night breaks, 1-night bookings sometimes refused.

New reports help us keep the *Guide* up to date.

BASLOW Derbyshire   Map 3:A6

The Cavendish
Church Lane
Baslow DE45 1SP

Tel 01246-582311
Fax 01246-582312
Email info@cavendish-hotel.net
Website www.cavendish-hotel.net

🏆 *César award in 2002*

In September 2008, Eric March's tenancy of this much-admired hotel on the edge of the Chatsworth estate reverted to the estate trustees. *Plus ça change*, a company headed by Mr Marsh and his manager, Philip Joseph, was appointed to run *The Cavendish*. Almost all of the long-serving staff, most of whom live nearby, have stayed on: 'They are a delight, treating young and old in a kind, thoughtful manner,' says a returning visitor. New investment by the estate includes the refurbishment of six superior rooms and the suite (which is ten minutes' walk away) in early 2009. Traditionally styled, furnished with 'well-cared-for' antiques, large sofa, original artwork, they are 'unashamedly luxurious. We were wrapped in sybaritic comfort. Bathrooms are modern, white, attractive.' The hotel is on a busy road, but the bedrooms are at the back, and quiet at night. Martin Clayton, the chef, serves modern dishes in the *Gallery* restaurant and the 'more casual' *Garden Room*. 'We were impressed: a refreshing, tangy citrus-covered salmon; tender pink Goosenargh duck breast with a basil and orange salad; heavenly bread-and-butter pudding.' The 'excellent' breakfast, served until midday, is not included in the room price. Philip Joseph also manages Mr Marsh's other hotel, *The George*, in nearby Hathersage (*qv*). (*Padi Howard, and others*)

Bedrooms: 24, 2 on ground floor. *Open*: all year. *Facilities*: lounge, bar, 2 restaurants, 2 private dining rooms, ½-acre grounds (putting), river fishing nearby. *Background music*: classical CDs in *Gallery*. *Location*: on A619, in Chatsworth grounds. *Smoking*: not allowed. *Children*: all ages welcomed. *Dogs*: not allowed. *Credit cards*: all major cards. *Prices*: [2009] room £125–£210, breakfast £17.95, set meals £29.50–£47.50 (5% '*service levy*' *added to all accounts*), midweek breaks, 1-night bookings sometimes refused. *V*

The *V* sign at the end of an entry indicates that a hotel has agreed to take part in our Voucher scheme and to give *Guide* readers a 25% discount on their bed-and-breakfast rates for a one-night stay, subject to the conditions on the back of the voucher and explained in 'How to use the *Good Hotel Guide*' (page 57).

Fischer's Baslow Hall

Calver Road
Baslow DE45 1RR

Tel 01246-583259
Fax 01246-583818
Email reservations@fischers-baslowhall.co.uk
Website www.fischers-baslowhall.co.uk

♦ *César award in 1998*

At their restaurant-with-rooms near the Chatsworth estate, Max
Fischer is 'a cheerful soul, very much a hands-on owner/chef'. His wife,
Susan, is front-of-house. The 1907 building is styled as a 17th-century
Derbyshire manor house, and service in the elegant dining room is
formal. 'Correct but friendly,' is one comment: a visitor this year found
it 'reverential; our water was poured as though it was vintage champagne'. The absence of background music is appreciated, and the
cooking is always acclaimed: 'Food, accommodation and efficiency of
the staff are truly exceptional.' Mr Fischer and Rupert Rowley, the
head chef, have a *Michelin* star for dishes like textures of foie gras (pan-
fried, cured and warm); roast turbot, carrot and orange reduction. There
is a standard dinner menu, a three-course *menu du jour*, and a 'Prestige'
tasting menu (served to a whole table). 'Max was very understanding
when we found the food too rich: he allowed us to create our own
menu.' The garden rooms are 'the best', 'no frills but plenty of space
and a good bathroom'. The 'bakery' breakfast has freshly squeezed
juice, a wide range of teas, and 'good fruit salad'; cooked dishes cost
extra. The gastropub, *Rowley's Restaurant & Bar*, down the road and
under the same ownership, is 'good fun'. (*RW, A and DT, and others*)

Bedrooms: 11, 5 in *Garden House. Open*: all year except 25/26 and 31 Dec,
restaurant closed to non-residents Sun night/Mon lunch. *Facilities*: lounge/bar,
breakfast room, 3 dining rooms, function facilities, civil wedding licence,
5-acre grounds, unsuitable for &. *Background music*: none. *Location*: edge of
village. *Smoking*: not allowed. *Children*: no under-12s in restaurant after 7 pm.
Dogs: not allowed. *Credit cards*: Amex, MasterCard, Visa. *Prices*: [2009] B&B
£70–£140 per person, English breakfast from £6, set dinner £43–£68, 1-night
bookings refused at weekends in season.

Readers' contributions, written on the forms at the back of the
book or sent by email, are the lifeblood of the *Good Hotel Guide*.
Our readers play a crucial role by reporting on existing entries
as well as recommending new discoveries. Everyone who writes
to the *Guide* is a potential winner of the Report of the Year
competition (page 10) in which a dozen correspondents each
year win a copy of the *Guide* and an invitation to our annual
launch party in October.

BASSENTHWAITE LAKE   Map 4: inset C2
Cumbria

The Pheasant
Bassenthwaite Lake
nr Cockermouth
CA13 9YE

Tel 017687-76234
Fax 017687-76002
Email info@the-pheasant.co.uk
Website www.the-pheasant.co.uk

Set in gardens and woodland between the lakes and fells at the unspoilt northern end of the Lake District, this long, low, L-shaped inn is managed by Matthew Wylie for the trustees of the Inglewood estate. It is endorsed again this year by the original nominator: 'Our favourite Lakeland hotel, it exudes warmth, comfort and an air of confidence.' There are antiques, old prints and paintings, open log fires, and a 'most attractive', 'deliciously old-fashioned', oak-panelled bar with oak settles. The lounges, where afternoon teas are served, have parquet flooring and potted plants. No background music ('to our delight'). Most bedrooms are 'large and comfortable'. 'Ours had a roomy, quite modern, bathroom. Good to excellent food, welcoming service.' Chef Malcolm Ennis serves modern dishes in the beamed dining room, eg, ham hock terrine with pan-fried quail's egg; grilled sea bass with wilted spinach and crisp pancetta. The four-course menu changes daily. The wine list, though not vast, is 'well thought out', and has good choice by the glass. Lighter meals are served in the lounges and bar. Good walking in all directions. (*Robert Cooper, A and PG*)

Bedrooms: 15, 2 on ground floor in lodge. *Open*: all year except 25 Dec. *Facilities*: 3 lounges, bar, dining room, 10-acre grounds, lake 200 yds (fishing), unsuitable for &. *Background music*: none. *Location*: 5 miles E of Cockermouth, ¼ mile off A66 to Keswick. *Smoking*: not allowed. *Children*: not under 8. *Dogs*: allowed in lodge bedrooms and public rooms. *Credit cards*: MasterCard, Visa. *Prices*: [2009] B&B £83–£103 per person, D,B&B £88–£133, set dinner £33.25–£37, full alc £45, midweek breaks, New Year package, 1-night bookings refused Fri and Sat.

BATH Somerset   Map 2:D1

Apsley House
141 Newbridge Hill
Bath BA1 3PT

Tel 01225-336966
Fax 01225-425462
Email info@apsley-house.co.uk
Website www.apsley-house.co.uk

'From the moment we walked through the door (held open for us), we knew that *Apsley House* was special.' More praise this year for this 'elegant' Georgian house, built by the Duke of Wellington in 1830 for his mistress. 'Charming, with the luxurious feel of a hotel,' said earlier visitors. Owned by Nicholas and Claire Potts, the guest house is managed by the 'smart, friendly' Duncan and Anél Neville. Furnished with fine antiques and paintings, it is a 'pleasant 20-minute walk in to town'. The 'delightful' lounge has 'a coal fire that is hard to resist', and an honesty bar. 'We stayed in the Wellington room, slightly more expensive but worth it for the beautiful views of Bath from our window and the luxurious super-king-size bed.' Two rooms can make a family suite. On the ground floor, a newly redecorated four-poster room with walk-in shower is suitable for visitors with limited mobility. A coach house has been turned into an apartment for families. Breakfast has fresh fruit, marmalade in a jar, and 'Duncan's cooked feasts' (eg, pancakes with maple syrup). Soup and sandwiches can be provided, and a light supper is available by arrangement during the week in the quieter months. (*Tricia and Neil Clark, and others*)

Bedrooms: 11, 1 on ground floor, 1 self-contained apartment. *Open*: all year except 24/25/26 Dec. *Facilities*: drawing room, bar, dining room, ¼-acre garden. *Background music*: Classic FM in dining room. *Location*: 1¼ miles W of city centre. *Smoking*: not allowed. *Children*: all ages welcomed (under-2s free). *Dogs*: only guide dogs allowed. *Credit cards*: Amex, MasterCard, Visa. *Prices*: [2009] B&B £35–£95 per person, 1-night bookings refused Sat and bank holidays. *V* (not weekends or Valentine's)

Small hotels will often try to persuade you to stay for two nights at the weekend. We ask all the hotels in the *Guide* whether they ever refuse a one-night booking, and indicate those that won't take them. It is worth asking about this, especially off-season or when booking late.

BATH   87

The Bath Priory
Weston Road
Bath BA1 2XT

Tel 01225-331922
Fax 01225-448276
Email mail@thebathpriory.co.uk
Website www.thebathpriory.co.uk

There are changes this year at Andrew and Christina Brownsword's luxurious hotel, a listed mansion in landscaped grounds (Sue Williams is the manager). The public areas were refurbished in early 2009, and the kitchen was rebuilt for the new executive chef, Michael Caines, who holds two *Michelin* stars at the sister hotel, *Gidleigh Park*, Chagford (*qv*). The spa, also being renovated, was due to reopen as the *Guide* went to press. The opulent public areas have arches, gargoyles, French chandeliers, *objets d'art*, plush sofas, early 20th-century and contemporary paintings; a lounge bar is new in 2009. The modern European menus might include ravioli of quail; John Dory, crispy pork belly, apple and ginger purée, crab cannelloni. A 'grazing menu' offers 'small plates of our *à la carte* dishes'. Children are welcomed; they have a toy box, polka-dot dressing gown, personalised toothbrush holder; high chairs and cots are provided. Four suites in *The Lindens*, adjacent, are suitable for a family. Under-eights may not join their parents in the restaurant in the evening (high tea is available between 5 and 6.30 pm). Dogs are now welcomed in some bedrooms. The city centre is reached by a short walk through Royal Victoria Park. More reports, please.

Bedrooms: 27, 3 on ground floor, 1 suitable for &. *Open*: all year. *Facilities*: ramps, lounge bar, library, drawing room, 2 dining rooms, private dining rooms, wine room, conference facilities, civil wedding licence, spa (indoor heated swimming pool (9 by 5 metres), gym, sauna, beauty treatments), 4-acre grounds (heated outdoor pool (11 by 4 metres), croquet). *Background music*: none. *Location*: 1½ miles W of centre. *Smoking*: not allowed. *Children*: no under-8s in restaurant at night. *Dogs*: allowed in 5 bedrooms, not in public rooms. *Credit cards*: all major cards. *Prices*: [2009] B&B £130–£380 per person, set dinner £65, full alc £88, special breaks, Christmas/New Year packages, 1-night bookings refused weekends.

The Kennard   **NEW**
11 Henrietta Street
Bath BA2 6LL

Tel 01225-310472
Fax 01225-460054
Email reception@kennard.co.uk
Website www.kennard.co.uk

Just over Pulteney Bridge, in a location 'perfect for walking everywhere', this Georgian town house is run as a B&B by its 'most helpful' Anglo-Italian owners, Giovanni and Mary Baiano. 'Everything is clean and comfortable,' say visitors. The building is decorated in flamboyant style: on the landing a golden urn stands on a Corinthian column flanked by a pair of *chaises longues*. There are swagged pelmets, heavy drapes and colourful cushions in the bedrooms; 'excellent mattresses, fine bedlinen'. Two single rooms share a bathroom. The high-ceilinged, green-walled breakfast room (the original Georgian kitchen) has a huge gilded mirror and Venetian chandeliers. Breakfast can be continental or English; ingredients come from local farms. There is a wide selection of leaf teas, speciality fruit and scented teas, and a choice of coffees. The Baianos have created a 'charming' garden, 'inspired by Jane Austen', where guests may sit in summer. A free parking permit can be provided for those who arrive by car. (*MW*)

Bedrooms: 12, 2 on ground floor. *Open*: all year except 25 Dec. *Facilities*: 2 sitting areas, breakfast room, courtyard garden. *Background music*: none. *Location*: near Pulteney Bridge. *Smoking*: not allowed. *Children*: not under 8. *Dogs*: not allowed. *Credit cards*: Amex, MasterCard, Visa. *Prices*: B&B £49–£70 per person, 1-night bookings refused Sat.

Number 30

30 Crescent Gardens
Bath BA1 2NB

Tel/Fax 01225-337393
Email david.greenwood12@btinternet.com
Website www.numberthirty.com

'Recommended without reservation', this 'spotless and comfortable' B&B is a short walk from Bath's historic centre. The owners, David and Caroline Greenwood, say fans, are 'friendly, helpful, recommending restaurants and places to visit'. The house is decorated in pastel colours (much blue and white). 'Our bedroom had crisp cotton sheets, blankets (we hate duvets but they are also available), flat-screen TV, CD-player, free Wi-Fi connection, natural toiletries from New Zealand.' Bathrooms are 'impeccable'. Three rooms have facilities *en suite*; the fourth has an adjacent private bathroom. The 'beautifully cooked and presented' breakfast has an 'amazing range', including fresh fruit, fruit compote, leaf tea, home-made muesli, organic toast, full English. 'A vegetarian option was a sumptuous English muffin spread with pesto, topped with avocado, tomato, mozzarella, then grilled. All this, and home-made marmalade and hedgerow jam.' Help is given with luggage. Car parking is available by arrangement. (*Ad van Tiggelen, Kevin and Sabina Connell-Moore, and others*)

Bedrooms: 4. *Open*: all year except Christmas/New Year. *Facilities*: dining room, patio garden, unsuitable for &. *Background music*: none. *Location*: 5 mins' walk from centre, parking. *Smoking*: not allowed. *Children*: not under 12. *Dogs*: not allowed. *Credit cards*: MasterCard, Visa. *Prices*: B&B £42.50–£67.50 per person, 1-night bookings refused weekends.

The Queensberry

4–7 Russel Street
Bath BA1 2QF

Tel 01225-447928
Fax 01225-446065
Email reservations@thequeensberry.co.uk
Website www.thequeensberry.co.uk

In a quiet residential street just off the Circus, this boutique hotel is owned by Laurence and Helen Beere and managed by Lauren McCann. It is a conversion of four adjoining town houses designed by John Wood for the Marquis of Queensberry in 1771. The service is 'good to excellent', writes an inspector this year, 'everything professional; the food is good'. The public rooms are 'elegant, well kept'; a glass roof contributes to a light feel. The bedrooms are reached off a series of stairs and corridors. 'Ours, well designed and furnished, had a spacious, well-appointed bathroom. The cool contemporary style was almost taken too far; I yearned for a dash of colour, even in bad taste.' All rooms have flat-screen TV, DAB radio and CD-player; the suites have an iPod docking station and a wet room; there are roll-top baths and huge shower heads. In the smart *Olive Tree* restaurant, in three rooms below stairs, chef Nick Brodie's modern menu might include seared scallops with Jerusalem artichoke confit; duo of beef, creamed potato, glazed root vegetables. Breakfast, served here, in the bedrooms, or in one of the four 'charming' terraced gardens, 'was good, especially the bread and patisserie'. Other visitors this year found 'little to criticise' except for a request for a tip on the credit card slip.

Bedrooms: 29, some on ground floor. *Open*: all year, restaurant closed Mon lunch. *Facilities*: lift, 2 drawing rooms, bar, restaurant, meeting room, 4 linked courtyard gardens, unsuitable for &. *Background music*: in restaurant. *Location*: near Assembly Rooms. *Smoking*: not allowed. *Children*: all ages welcomed. *Dogs*: not allowed. *Credit cards*: Amex (*2% handling charge*), MasterCard, Visa. *Prices*: [2009] B&B £75–£130 per person, D,B&B £112.50–£167.50, full alc £47, 1-night bookings refused Sat. *V*

Tasburgh House

Warminster Road
Bath BA2 6SH

Tel 01225-425096
Fax 01225-463842
Email hotel@bathtasburgh.co.uk
Website www.bathtasburgh.co.uk

The 'elegant and kind hostess', Sue Keeling, is 'very much around' at her red brick Victorian house in 'lovely', large grounds that slope down to the Kennet and Avon canal. She 'presides at breakfast with her girls (who wear white gloves)'. The bedrooms, each named after an English author, vary in size: Charles Dickens can accommodate one person, John Keats three, Percy Shelley five. The house faces a busy road: 'But it is in a dip,' says an inspector, 'I wasn't bothered by traffic noise in my immaculate small front room.' Sheets and blankets can be provided instead of a duvet. Restaurant lists are available but, should you wish to stay in, drinks and a 'simple supper' can be provided from Monday to Thursday. Breakfast, served in a 'pretty conservatory with a chandelier', has a 'small buffet of cereals, croissants, fruit and jams in little jars'; cooked costs extra. 'There is a nice sitting room.' Mrs Keeling tells us that the background music can be 'muted or turned off if a guest prefers peace and quiet'. The house is a three-minute taxi ride from the city centre. 'In good weather you can walk along the canal past fields with sheep.' Hen parties and small wedding receptions are catered for. 'A parrot whistles musically at Reception.'

Bedrooms: 12, 2 on ground floor. *Open*: 14 Jan–21 Dec. *Facilities*: drawing room, dining room, conservatory, terrace, 7-acre grounds (canal walks, mooring), unsuitable for &. *Background music*: Classic FM at breakfast, jazz in the evening. *Location*: on A36 to Warminster, ½ mile E of centre. *Smoking*: not allowed. *Children*: all ages welcomed ('well-behaved, with well-behaved parents'). *Dogs*: only guide dogs allowed. *Credit cards*: MasterCard, Visa. *Prices*: B&B (continental breakfast) £47.50–£70 per person, D,B&B £57.50–£82.50, cooked breakfast £7.50, full alc £32, special breaks, 1-night bookings refused Sat.

See also Shortlist

BATHFORD Somerset   *See Shortlist*

BEAMINSTER Dorset   Map 1:C6

Bridge House   *Tel* 01308-862200
3 Prout Bridge   *Fax* 01308-863700
Beaminster DT8 3AY   *Email* enquiries@bridge-house.co.uk
                    Website www.bridge-house.co.uk

'Absolutely charming. Excellent cuisine.' 'Welcoming and comfortable. Two very good meals.' This former priest's house, by a bridge in this pretty old market town, dates back to the 13th century. Visitors write of the 'relaxed' atmosphere created by owners Mark and Joanna Donovan and their 'very friendly staff', the 'high standards', and the 'unusual, pleasing' interior. There are thick walls, mullioned windows, fresh flowers, candles, old beams, open fires in inglenook fireplaces, and a priest's hole. The quietest bedrooms face the large walled garden at the back; front ones face a road that is busy by day. 'Our room was bright, well furnished, spacious.' Some small rooms and a family suite are in a coach house at the rear (baby-listening, cots, etc, provided). In the brasserie, Steve Pielesz offers a reasonably priced *carte* (eg, daily terrine, home-made chutney; beer-battered pollack, rustic chips). In the candlelit, oak-beamed dining room with conservatory extension, Linda Paget provides modern dishes using Dorset produce, perhaps linguine of Lyme Bay crab and clams with coriander. Summer meals can be served in the garden. Tea is taken by a fire in winter. Nearby are Abbotsbury (with its famous swannery), the Jurassic Coast, Mapperton Gardens. (*Ken Stanhope, MM-D*)

Bedrooms: 14, 5 in coach house, 4 on ground floor. *Open*: all year. *Facilities*: hall/reception, lounge, bar, conservatory, brasserie, restaurant, civil wedding licence, ¼-acre walled garden. *Background music*: classical/orchestral in bar and dining areas, jazz in brasserie. *Location*: 100 yards from centre. *Smoking*: not allowed. *Children*: all ages welcomed. *Dogs*: allowed in coach house (not unattended), in bar except during service. *Credit cards*: Amex, MasterCard, Visa. *Prices*: [2009] B&B £58–£100 per person, D,B&B £94–£130, full alc £30 (brasserie)–£50 (restaurant), special breaks, Christmas/New Year packages, 1-night bookings refused weekends and bank holidays. *V*

BEAULIEU Hampshire   Map 2:E2

Montagu Arms   *Tel* 01590-612324
Palace Lane   *Fax* 01590-612188
Beaulieu SO42 7ZL   *Email* reservations@montaguarmshotel.co.uk
                     Website www.montaguarmshotel.co.uk

'Elegantly restored', this much-extended 18th-century building in a famous New Forest riverside village is managed by Philip Archer. 'A good welcome, rooms and ambience,' is this year's comment. An earlier guest, who appreciated luggage being taken 'without our asking', had 'a pleasant, quiet garden-facing room'. The *Terrace* restaurant has 'beautiful views of the formal garden', a 'smart dress code (no trainers or denim)'. Its chef, Matthew Tomkinson, was awarded a *Michelin* star in 2009 for his 'classical' cuisine, eg, slow-cooked oxtail and celeriac lasagne; sea bass with Jerusalem artichoke purée. *Monty's*, the informal bar/brasserie, serves 'home-cooked classics' (like sausage and mash); children under eight have supper here. Lavish afternoon teas include Fairtrade teas, and scones with clotted cream. The bedrooms vary greatly: 'Ours was a little dark but well furnished.' Many suites have a four-poster. 'Excellent breakfasts' have 'a wide choice of home-made pastries, etc, and well-cooked hot dishes'. (*EJT Palmer, I and BD*)

Bedrooms: 22. *Open*: all year, *Terrace* restaurant occasionally closed Mon. *Facilities*: lounge, conservatory, bar/brasserie, restaurant, conference/function facilities, civil wedding licence, garden, access to nearby spa, only public rooms suitable for &. *Background music*: none. *Location*: village centre. *Smoking*: not allowed. *Children*: all ages welcomed (under-3s stay free). *Dogs*: not allowed. *Credit cards*: Amex, MasterCard, Visa. *Prices*: B&B £89–£169 per person, D,B&B £129–£209, full alc £57, special breaks, Christmas/New Year packages, 1-night bookings refused Sat. *V*

BEELEY Derbyshire   Map 3:A6

The Devonshire Arms at Beeley   *Tel/Fax* 01629-733259
Devonshire Square   *Email* enquiries@devonshirebeeley.co.uk
Beeley, nr Matlock   *Website* www.devonshirebeeley.co.uk
DE4 2NR

In a village on the Chatsworth estate, this 17th-century coaching inn has been given a thorough make-over by the Duke and Duchess of Devonshire. It is run by chef/*patron* Alan Hill. The original bar has oak beams, stone crannies, flagged floors, log fires; the brasserie extension and the bedrooms are more contemporary, with lots of colour. 'It is friendly, informal, but efficient,' say inspectors. 'Good fun provided you recognise that it's a pub. The enthusiastic young staff take their cooking and serving seriously. We enjoyed the most enormous prawn cocktail, very 1960s; superb local sausages; beautifully cooked sea bass and battered haddock with skinny chips. Excellent wine by the glass: try the Viognier.' The bedrooms are in the main building and in *Brookside House*, next door. Peak Dale, in the inn, in rich pink with beige fabrics, has a freestanding bath and washbasin in the room, and a separate loo; a family suite has a white and turquoise bedroom, and a pink sitting room with sofa bed. 'Exquisite botanical watercolours' by the duke's sister, Emma Tennant, hang throughout. Breakfast has fresh and stewed fruit, home-made muesli, yogurt, local breads; cooked choices include fried Derbyshire oatcakes with bacon and cheese.

Bedrooms: 8, 4 in annexe, 2 on ground floor. *Open*: all year. *Facilities*: bar, brasserie, malt vault. *Background music*: light jazz/classical in brasserie. *Location*:

5 miles N of Matlock, off B6012. *Smoking*: not allowed. *Children*: all ages welcomed. *Dogs*: allowed in *Brookside* bedrooms, not in public rooms. *Credit cards*: all major cards. *Prices*: [2009] B&B £61–£95.50 per person, full alc £37, special breaks, Christmas/New Year packages.

BELFORD Northumberland   *See Shortlist*

BERWICK-UPON-TWEED   Map 4:A3
Northumberland

West Coates   *Tel/Fax* 01289-309666
30 Castle Terrace   *Email* karenbrownwestcoates@yahoo.com
Berwick-upon-Tweed TD15 1NZ   *Website* www.westcoates.co.uk

'Wonderfully comfortable', this Georgian house is close to the centre of this historic border town. Set in an attractive, mature garden, it has a pool house with large heated swimming pool and a hot tub. 'Welcoming; excellent food,' writes a returning visitor. The bedrooms are 'beautifully furnished, and have everything one could want, including home-made cake on the hospitality tray each day'. 'My room had a spacious dressing room/bathroom.' The owner, Karen Brown, who runs a cookery school, uses local ingredients for her 'fabulous' no-choice three-course dinners, served by candlelight. Sample dishes: organic asparagus from the garden; Burnside duck breast with Calvados apples on Puy lentils. The 'wonderful' breakfast has smoked salmon and scrambled eggs, porridge, yogurt, home-made preserves, etc. (*Dr JT Roberts*)

Bedrooms: 3. *Open*: all year except Christmas/New Year. *Facilities*: sitting/dining room, 2½-acre garden, 12-metre indoor swimming pool, hot tub, croquet, unsuitable for ♿. *Background music*: 'varied'. *Location*: 10 mins' walk from centre. *Smoking*: not allowed. *Children*: not allowed. *Dogs*: not allowed. *Credit cards*: MasterCard, Visa. *Prices*: [2009] B&B £45–£60 per person, D,B&B £62.50–£77.50, special breaks, 1-night bookings sometimes refused weekends.

> We say 'Unsuitable for ♿' when a hotel tells us that it cannot accommodate wheelchair-users. We do not have the resources to inspect such facilities or to assess the even more complicated matter of facilities for the partially disabled. We suggest that you discuss such details with the hotel.

BIDEFORD Devon   Map 1:C4

The Mount   *Tel* 01237-473748
Northdown Road   *Fax* 01271-373813
Bideford EX39 3LP   *Email* andrew@themountbideford.co.uk
                              Website www.themountbideford.co.uk

In a 'great location' near the town centre and the quay where fishing
boats unload their catches by the medieval bridge, this B&B is
owned and run by Andrew and Heather Laugharne. 'They are warm
and accommodating,' says a visitor this year. The imposing Georgian
house is 'charming, light and airy; lovely decorative touches make it
feel homely and welcoming', writes another. The public areas have
bright colours; red walls to the white-painted, winding staircase, pink
in the lounge (which has an open fire and a licence to sell alcohol),
blue in the room where the 'fantastic' breakfasts 'using lots of local
produce' are served ('the bacon and sausages are particularly good').
'Everything is spotlessly clean' in the spacious bedrooms (two have
been redecorated this year). 'The bed in my room was so comfortable, it was difficult to leave.' Guests have access to the pretty,
partly walled garden. Discounts are available at the Royal North
Devon Golf Club. Guests arriving by train can be met at Barnstaple.
(*Cynthia Ritchie, J Rixson*)

Bedrooms: 8, some family, 1 on ground floor. *Open*: all year. *Facilities*: ramp,
lounge, breakfast room, ½-acre garden. *Background music*: none. *Location*: town
centre. *Smoking*: not allowed. *Children*: all ages welcomed. *Dogs*: not allowed.
Credit cards: MasterCard, Visa. *Prices*: B&B £33–£38 per person, 1-night
bookings may be refused.

BIGBURY-ON-SEA Devon   Map 1:D4

Burgh Island Hotel   *Tel* 01548-810514
Burgh Island   *Fax* 01548-810243
Bigbury-on-Sea TQ7 4BG   *Email* reception@burghisland.com
                              Website www.burghisland.com

Like a great white Art Deco liner, this hotel has dominated its private
tidal island in Bigbury Bay since its opening in 1929. Early guests
included Edward and Mrs Simpson, Agatha Christie, Noël Coward.
Visitors admire the 'fabulous location', 'great atmosphere, good food'.
At high tide, they arrive on a sea tractor; at low tide by a four-wheel-
drive vehicle. The owners, Tony Orchard and Deborah Clark, have

completed a full refurbishment with the addition of a new room (Miss Button). Everything is in period style; mementos of the Jazz Age; 1920s cocktails are served in the Palm Court bar (with magnificent peacock dome). Meals are taken in the Ganges Room, decorated in black and white; dinner dances are held in the ballroom (diners in full evening dress). Chef Conor Heneghan serves modern, seasonal dishes, eg, mussel, scallop, razor clam, oyster leaf soup; slow-roast beef fillet, veal sweetbread, beetroot purée. Vegetarian options are available. There is an all-day menu of sandwiches and 'plates' (eg, grilled mackerel fillets; local oysters). Many bedrooms have a sea view: most have a balcony. The ten suites include one on stilts above the beach, one above the *Pilchard Inn* on the seafront. There is a natural swimming pool in the rocks, and a private beach. Non-residents are not admitted unless they have booked lunch or dinner. More reports, please.

Bedrooms: 25, 1 suite in beach house, apartment above *Pilchard Inn*. *Open*: all year. *Facilities*: lift, sun lounge, Palm Court bar, dining room, ballroom (live 1930s music Wed and Sat nights), children's games room, spa (treatment room, gym, sauna), dinner/dance Wed and Sat, civil wedding licence, 12-acre grounds on 26-acre island (30-metre natural sea swimming pool, beach, water sports, tennis, helipad). *Background music*: 1920s and 1930s music in bar. *Location*: 5 miles S of Modbury, private garages on mainland. *Smoking*: not allowed. *Children*: not under 5, no under-13s at dinner. *Dogs*: not allowed. *Credit cards*: MasterCard, Visa. *Prices*: D,B&B £192.50–£300 per person, set dinner £55, special events, Christmas/New Year packages, 1-night bookings sometimes refused Sat.

The Henley

Folly Hill
Bigbury-on-Sea TQ7 4AR

Tel/Fax 01548-810240
Email thehenleyhotel@btconnect.com
Website www.thehenleyhotel.co.uk

🏆 *César award in 2003*

In an 'idyllic spot' on a cliff above the tidal Avon estuary, this small, unpretentious Edwardian villa has many fans. Its owners, Martyn Scarterfield and his wife, Petra Lampe, are 'energetic, conscientious hosts'. 'It is an enjoyable place for quiet, wonderful food, marvellous views,' says a visitor in 2009 who had been unwell and was told to 'come down for breakfast when you like'. The public rooms have dark red walls, well-polished old furniture, Lloyd Loom chairs, books and magazines; binoculars are provided for enjoyment of the 'magnificent' views. The bedrooms have been upgraded (two smaller rooms were amalgamated). They are relatively simple, 'always clean'.

'Our room, the largest, was as warm and friendly as the owners; a beautiful bunch of flowers on the table.' Guests gather in the lounge at 7 pm for drinks before dinner: 'Petra recites the short menu with a twinkle in her eye; Martyn's cooking is very good.' 'Unusual and delicious' dishes might include cream of parsnip, apple and potato soup; Gruyère-glazed fillet beef, Provençal sauce. Breakfast is 'tasty, unhurried'. The garden, 'spectacularly precipitous', has 'many sheltered nooks with seating'. 'The entrance hall has a wooden sign: "We welcome dogs" – and they do.' The 'lovely' resident Labrador, Kasper, has been joined by a new member of the family, the couple's baby daughter, Marika. (*AE Silver, Jennifer and Colin Beales, Simon Rodway, Christine Moore*)

Bedrooms: 5. *Open*: Mar–Oct. *Facilities*: 2 lounges, bar, conservatory dining room, small garden (steps to beach, golf, sailing, fishing), Coast Path nearby, unsuitable for &. *Background music*: jazz, classical in the evenings in lounge, dining room. *Location*: 5 miles S of Modbury. *Smoking*: not allowed. *Children*: not under 12. *Dogs*: not allowed in public rooms. *Credit cards*: Amex, MasterCard, Visa. *Prices*: [2009] B&B £55–£71 per person, D,B&B (3 nights min.) £77–£92, set dinner £33, 1-night bookings sometimes refused weekends.

BIGGIN-BY-HARTINGTON   Map 3:B6
Derbyshire

Biggin Hall
Biggin-by-Hartington
Buxton SK17 0DH

Tel 01298-84451
Fax 01298-84681
Email enquiries@bigginhall.co.uk
Website www.bigginhall.co.uk

Offering 'remarkably good value' and 'good food at the price', this Grade II* listed 17th-century building in a small Peak District village is popular with walkers for its simple, unfussy style. Close by are 'footpaths in all directions over beautiful countryside': one starts from the grounds, and disused railway tracks nearby provide flat walking and cycling. The house has antiques, narrow mullioned windows, and 'warm and inviting' public rooms. The lounge, with its massive stone fireplace, can get crowded when guests gather at 6.30 for drinks before dinner which is served at 7 pm in the chintzy dining room. 'There are no table reservations, so when dinner is announced, we all troupe off to grab a good one without looking too competitive.' Mark Wilton's 'traditional English' dishes are hearty and 'well cooked', eg, baked Scottish salmon with chive sauce; apple and cinnamon crumble with custard. Breakfast is a 'comprehensive hot and cold buffet'. Packed lunches are available. The master suite (beamed, with four-poster) is in the main house. Some rooms are in buildings in the courtyard or across the lawn. 'Mine needed a make-over,' one guest thought. The owner, James Moffett, is 'semi-retired'; his manager is Steven Williams. (*Max Lickfold, Rex Bellamy, and others*)

Bedrooms: 20, 12 in annexes, some on ground floor. *Open*: all year. *Facilities*: sitting room, library, dining room, meeting room, civil wedding licence, 8-acre grounds (croquet), River Dove 1½ miles, unsuitable for &. *Background music*: none. *Location*: 8 miles N of Ashbourne. *Smoking*: not allowed. *Children*: not under 12. *Dogs*: allowed in some bedrooms, not in public rooms. *Credit cards*: MasterCard, Visa. *Prices*: [2009] B&B £39–£68 per person, D,B&B £53–£82, full alc £25, Christmas/New Year packages, 1-night bookings sometimes refused. *V*

BIRMINGHAM West Midlands   *See Shortlist*

BLACKBURN Lancashire   *See Shortlist*

BLACKPOOL Lancashire   *See Shortlist*

BLAKENEY Norfolk   Map 2:A5

The Blakeney Hotel
Blakeney
nr Holt NR25 7NE

Tel 01263-740797
Fax 01263-740795
Email reception@blakeney-hotel.co.uk
Website www.blakeney-hotel.co.uk

'One of our regular haunts where a pleasant stay is assured,' say fans of this large, traditional hotel, which has 'inspiring' views across the tidal estuary and salt marshes to Blakeney Point. Owned by Michael Stannard, it is managed by Anne Thornalley; their staff are 'friendly, reliable, unobtrusive'. The public rooms overlook the estuary, so do many bedrooms: others face the garden (some have a patio). One couple who 'have tried many of the rooms' find them all 'adequately appointed and maintained, with first-class housekeeping'. 'We treated ourselves to a second-floor room with balcony and enjoyed the luxury of a panoramic view.' The cooking in the 'well-appointed' dining room may not be 'showy', but 'high standards of presentation and service are maintained' along with 'a relaxed feeling'. The daily-changing menu might include cream of mushroom soup with croutons; braised lamb shank with fondant potato. There are light lunches on weekdays; a choice of roasts on Sunday. 'All you could want for breakfast' (including local smoked kippers). *The Blakeney* is busy with families at weekends and in school holidays – there is much for children to do (see below). It makes 'a good base for walking in all directions'; in winter you can 'watch the changing Norfolk skies'. (*Bryan and Mary Blaxall, Anthony Bradbury, Betty Carr*)

Bedrooms: 64, 16 in *Granary* annexe opposite, some on ground floor. *Open*: all year. *Facilities*: lift, ramps, lounge, sun lounge, bar, restaurant, function facilities, indoor heated swimming pool (12 by 5 metres), spa bath (steam room), mini-gym, games room (table tennis, pool, darts), ¼-acre garden, sailing, fishing, water sports, golf, tennis nearby. *Background music*: none. *Location*: on quay. *Smoking*: not allowed. *Children*: all ages welcomed. *Dogs*: allowed in some bedrooms, not in public rooms. *Credit cards*: all major cards. *Prices*: [2009] B&B £70–£132 per person, D,B&B £82–£150, set dinner £27.50, full alc £56.50, activity breaks, Christmas/New Year packages, 1-night bookings sometimes refused Fri/Sat, bank holidays.

BLOCKLEY Gloucestershire   *See Shortlist*

BONCHURCH Isle of Wight   *See Shortlist*

BORROWDALE Cumbria   Map 4: inset C2

The Leathes Head Hotel
Borrowdale
Keswick CA12 5UY

Tel 017687-77247
Fax 017687-77363
Email enq@leatheshead.co.uk
Website www.leatheshead.co.uk

Popular with serious walkers and climbers, this gabled Edwardian house, built of local slate, is run as a traditional hotel by its 'amenable and helpful' owners, Roy and Janice Smith. 'The food is a strong point,' say visitors this year. The chef, David Jackson, serves a daily-changing four-course modern menu, including a 'much-appreciated' fish course. Typical dishes: salad of herbed smoked chicken, pear and dried fruit chutney; seared tuna, pickled sweet peppers. Arriving visitors are served complimentary tea and coffee in a sunroom. Free Wi-Fi throughout the house is new in 2009; all bedrooms have been given digital TV and DVD-player (a free DVD library is available), and all have bathrobes. Readers again recommend the double-aspect superior rooms: 'Ours was spacious, with glorious views to Cat Bells.' A smaller bedroom had a 'very small bathroom with a tiny basin'. 'Excellent access for the slightly disabled; pretty good, too, if you are in a wheelchair.' The house is in extensive wooded grounds, high above Borrowdale. 'There is a pleasant spot with wooden seats, nice for an evening drink, though it hears a kitchen extractor fan.' A regular bus service passes the entrance. 'Good packed lunches.' (*John Barnes, PE Carter, and others*)

Bedrooms: 12, 3 on ground floor, 1 suitable for &. *Open*: Mar–Nov. *Facilities*: ramp, lounge, sun lounge, bar lounge, restaurant, sun terrace, 3-acre grounds (woodland). *Background music*: none. *Location*: 3½ miles S of Keswick. *Smoking*: not allowed. *Children*: not under 15. *Dogs*: not allowed. *Credit cards*: MasterCard, Visa. *Prices*: [2009] D,B&B £80–£105 per person, set dinner £31.50, special breaks, 1-night bookings refused at weekends. *V*

Seatoller House

Borrowdale
Keswick CA12 5XN

Tel 017687-77218
Fax 017687-77189
Email seatollerhouse@btconnect.com
Website www.seatollerhouse.co.uk

'The setting is superb and the welcome is warm' at this popular, unpretentious guest house at the head of the beautiful Borrowdale valley. It has received walkers and ramblers for more than a century. Owned by a private company, The Lake Hunts Ltd, it is managed by 'the ebullient' Daniel Potts and Lynne Moorehouse. There are no 'modern intrusions' like television and radio, and guests love its 'homely atmosphere'. It has creaky floorboards, an oak-panelled sitting room, cosy chairs, cushioned window seats and a piano. 'The furniture still has a shabby and dependable air,' say visitors who returned after 20 years. In the tea bar, non-stop coffee is available (it can be taken out in flasks); there is an honesty bar, and a self-help fridge. The simple bedrooms have private facilities, though six are not *en suite*. Lynne Moorehouse serves a no-choice, daily-changing menu at 7 pm, 'providing the hungry walker with an interesting menu and large portions if desired'. Her style is traditional 'with a twist', eg, stuffed flat mushrooms with goat's cheese; Aga-baked trout fillet with herb crust. 'The traditional serving of Stilton makes for good entertainment.' On Tuesday, there is a light supper of soup, bread and cheese. Breakfast, between 8 and 8.30 am, is hearty. 'Many of the guests have been going for years; I'm sure we will be joining the ranks of Seatollerholics,' say first-timers. (*Yvonne McKeown, GC, Tom and Sarah Mann*)

Bedrooms: 10, 2 on ground floor, 1 in garden bungalow, all with shower. *Open*: 12 Mar–22 Nov, dining room closed midday, Tues night (light supper available). *Facilities*: lounge, library, tea bar, dining room, drying room, 1-acre grounds (beck), unsuitable for &. *Background music*: none. *Location*: on B5289, 7 miles S of Keswick. *Smoking*: not allowed. *Children*: not under 5 (unless in a private group). *Dogs*: not allowed in public rooms. *Credit cards*: MasterCard, Visa. *Prices*: B&B £45–£54 per person, D,B&B £55–£64, set dinner £19, reductions for longer stays, 1-night bookings sometimes refused weekends.

BOSCASTLE Cornwall   Map 1:C3

The Old Rectory
St Juliot, nr Boscastle
PL35 0BT

Tel/Fax 01840-250225
Email sally@stjuliot.com
Website www.stjuliot.com

Thomas Hardy met his future wife Emma Gifford, the rector's sister-in-law, here in 1870. It appears as Endelstow Vicarage in his novel *A Pair of Blue Eyes*. Now it is a B&B, run by the 'welcoming' owners, Chris and Sally Searle, who stress that (unlike in some B&Bs) visitors may come and go throughout the day. Its comfortable guests' sitting room, with fireplace, looks over the terrace and the attractive south-facing garden. Three bedrooms are in the main house. The Rector's has a super-king-size bed, 'luxury' whirlpool bath and views of the garden, Mr Hardy's has an antique carved double bed and a power shower, Emma's has a large shower and the original thunderbox loo. The fourth room, Old Stables, has its own entrance and is linked to the main house by a conservatory; it has a wood-burning stove, a sofa bed, and both bath and shower. Breakfast, served until 10 am (or in bed until midday), has fresh fruit from the garden, local apple juice, free-range chicken and duck eggs, bacon and sausages from Tintagel; other cooked dishes include Cornish rarebit; kippers; French toast with fruit compote. More reports, please.

Bedrooms: 4, 1 in stables (linked to house). *Open*: mid-Feb–mid-Nov, Christmas, New Year. *Facilities*: sitting room, breakfast room, 3-acre garden (croquet lawn, 'lookout'), unsuitable for &. *Background music*: none. *Location*: 2 miles NE of Boscastle. *Smoking*: not allowed. *Children*: not under 12. *Dogs*: only allowed in stables. *Credit cards*: MasterCard, Visa. *Prices*: [2009] B&B £39–£57 per person, 1-night bookings sometimes refused weekends, bank holidays.

See also Shortlist

BOSHAM West Sussex   Map 2:E3

The Millstream   *Tel* 01243-573234
Bosham Lane   *Fax* 01243-573459
Bosham, nr Chichester   *Email* info@millstream-hotel.co.uk
PO18 8HL   *Website* www.millstream-hotel.co.uk

'Well run, with enthusiastic staff; the welcome was warm,' writes an inspector in 2009. On the road leading to the harbour in a 'delightful' village on the West Sussex coast, this converted manor house has a manicured garden with millstream and gazebo. Long managed by the 'ever-present' Antony Wallace, it has many fans. 'We were impressed with the service,' one wrote. 'A happy weekend,' said another. The bedrooms, with conventional decor, vary in size: all have a fridge with fresh milk and bottled water. 'Ours had a four-poster, lots of space, comfortable chairs.' 'Our small room had patterned wallpaper and carpet, curtains heavily draped. Its small bathroom was fresh and clean.' A wheelchair-dependent visitor found the garden room 'ideal'. The bar area and large lounge, 'if old-fashioned, have comfortable settees and chairs'. The cooking is generally thought 'good, if not exceptional; well presented. Waiting staff, a mix of British and East European, were unfailingly smiling and keen. Wines reasonably priced.' A pianist accompanies dinner on Friday and Saturday. The 'excellent' breakfast includes wide choice of fruit, cereals, kippers, comb honey. Bar lunches are available. Guests attending the Chichester theatre can have an early supper. (*Ann Morrison, Zara Elliott, Brian and Gwen Thomas, John and Valerie Fleming, and others*)

Bedrooms: 35, 2 in cottage, 7 on ground floor, 1 suitable for &. *Open*: all year. *Facilities*: lounge, bar, restaurant (pianist Fri and Sat), conference room, civil wedding licence, 1½-acre garden (stream, gazebo), Chichester Harbour (sailing, fishing) 300 yards. *Background music*: classical 10.30 am–10.30 pm. *Location*: 4 miles W of Chichester. *Smoking*: not allowed. *Children*: all ages welcomed. *Dogs*: only guide dogs allowed. *Credit cards*: all major cards. *Prices*: [2009] B&B £71–£91 per person, D,B&B (min. 2 nights) £74–£109, set dinner £29, full alc £37, Christmas/New Year packages, 1-night bookings refused Sat.

BOURNEMOUTH Dorset   *See Shortlist*

The terms printed in the *Guide* are only an indication of the size of the bill to be expected at the end of your stay. It is wise to check the tariffs when booking.

BOURTON-ON-THE-HILL
Gloucestershire

Map 3:D6

The Horse and Groom

Bourton-on-the-Hill
nr Moreton-in-Marsh
GL56 9AQ

Tel/Fax 01386-700413
Email greenstocks@horseandgroom.info
Website www.horseandgroom.info

'Just how an old inn should be', this Grade II listed Georgian building stands atop a hill in a honey-stone Cotswold village. It is run as a dining pub by brothers Will (chef) and Tom (front-of-house) Greenstock; Richard Tustin is the manager. These 'engaging hosts' are 'in evidence throughout the evening'; their staff are 'young, enthusiastic'. 'We were addressed by name from the moment we checked in.' The bedrooms, in modern style, are good sized, with a well-equipped bathroom, but light sleepers may hear traffic. An inspector's room at the back was 'lovely, light; well thought out: good storage; a most comfortable bed; glazed doors opened on to the garden'. Downstairs, there are ancient beams, wooden floors and tables, sisal matting, stools by the bar. Modern dishes on a blackboard menu use local ingredients, eg, fennel risotto, crumbled goat's cheese; rack of lamb, mustard greens. Vegetables are home grown, and eggs come from the brothers' chickens. Following a comment in last year's *Guide*, they have introduced freshly squeezed orange juice for breakfast, which has 'excellent preserves, good toast, tea and coffee'. 'We loved our stay; they made us feel at home,' say visitors in 2009. (*Jennifer Kipphut, Jane and Stephen Marshalt*)

Bedrooms: 5. *Open*: all year except 25/31 Dec, 1 Jan, restaurant closed Sun eve. *Facilities*: bar/restaurant, 1-acre garden, unsuitable for ঙ. *Background music*: none. *Location*: village centre. *Smoking*: not allowed. *Children*: all ages welcomed. *Dogs*: allowed in garden only. *Credit cards*: MasterCard, Visa. *Prices*: [2009] B&B £52.50–£75 per person, D,B&B (min. 2 nights) £75–£95, full alc £35, 1-night bookings refused weekends.

BOVEY TRACEY Devon

See Shortlist

The *Guide*'s website can be used alongside the printed edition. It has photographs of nearly all of the hotels, with a direct link to its website. It also has a Special Offers section with some excellent deals exclusively for *Guide* readers. See www.goodhotelguide.com.

BOWNESS-ON-WINDERMERE Map 4: inset C2
Cumbria

Fayrer Garden House Hotel
Lyth Valley Road
Bowness-on-Windermere
LA23 3JP

Tel 015394-88195
Fax 015394-45986
Email lakescene@fayrergarden.com
Website www.fayrergarden.com

In large grounds with award-winning gardens, this former Edwardian gentleman's residence faces, through trees, Lake Windermere and the surrounding countryside. Owned by Claire and Eric Wildsmith, it is managed by the 'very helpful' Mark Jones. Visitors find it 'well run', 'comfortable, friendly'. There are original oil paintings and flowers in the lounge which faces the water, as do the *Terrace Restaurant* and some bedrooms. Other rooms have a garden view (the ground-floor ones are good for people with a 'mobility problem'). 'Service is excellent all round,' one guest wrote. 'The *maitre d'* knew our names within minutes of our appearance; though we stayed only two nights, he called us by our names unfailingly thereafter.' 'I've never had such a luxurious single room,' says another. She appreciated 'being given a table with a view, not hidden behind a pillar'. Head chef Eddie Wilkinson serves a daily-changing menu of modern dishes, using local produce, eg, leek and black pudding quiche with apple coleslaw; Cartmel Valley venison on braised red cabbage with redcurrant sauce. Vegetarian options available. Small weddings are a speciality. (*Dorothy Brining, SD*)

Bedrooms: 29, 5 in cottage in grounds, 7 on ground floor. *Open*: all year except first 2 weeks Jan. *Facilities*: 2 lounges, lounge bar, restaurant, civil wedding licence, 5-acre grounds. *Background music*: classical, 'easy listening'. *Location*: 1 mile S of Bowness on A5074. *Smoking*: not allowed. *Children*: not under 5. *Dogs*: allowed in cottage rooms only. *Credit cards*: MasterCard, Visa. *Prices*: B&B £53–£110 per person, D,B&B £62–£140, set dinner £40, Christmas/New Year packages, 1-night bookings sometimes refused Sat.

Lindeth Fell
Lyth Valley Road
Bowness-on-Windermere
LA23 3JP

Tel 015394-43286
Fax 015394-47455
Email kennedy@lindethfell.co.uk
Website www.lindethfell.co.uk

♛ *César award in 2009*

'Friendly, welcoming, relaxed', Pat and Diana Kennedy's Edwardian gentleman's residence has 'fantastic views' over Lake Windermere.

'The atmosphere is settled, homey rather than elegant, despite the plutocratic architecture,' says a reporter this year. Another comment: 'The staff make you feel at home; there are delicious scones if you arrive in time for tea.' The 'old-world charm' is liked. Mrs Kennedy is supported by Linda Hartill, the 'delightful, long-standing' manageress; service is 'painstaking and kind'. Bedrooms vary in size: 'Ours was large, airy, with gorgeous views; good king-size bed, chair and sofa.' A smaller room was 'clean, comfortably furnished, though a bit flowery'. Housekeeping is praised (beds turned down during dinner, made during breakfast). 'We never saw anyone cleaning.' There are two spacious lounges: deep sofas in the main one; books and memorabilia from Mr Kennedy's time in the RAF in the blue one. The dining room, with conservatory-style extensions, faces the view. Chefs Philip Taylor and Harry Coates serve a 'hearty' daily-changing menu: 'Delicious soups; sirloin steak cooked rare to perfection; lamb as it used to taste. No music; bliss.' Breakfast has a self-service buffet; cooked dishes brought to the table. (*Jill and Mike Bennett, Peter Buckley, S and CR*)

Bedrooms: 14, 1 on ground floor. *Open*: 30 Jan–2 Jan. *Facilities*: ramp, hall, 2 lounges, dispense bar, 3 dining rooms, 7-acre grounds (gardens, croquet, putting, bowls, tarn, fishing permits). *Background music*: none. *Location*: 1 mile S of Bowness on A5074. *Smoking*: not allowed. *Children*: all ages welcomed. *Dogs*: only assistance dogs allowed. *Credit cards*: MasterCard, Visa. *Prices*: [to spring 2010] B&B £50–£85 per person, D,B&B £82–£121, set dinner £35, Christmas/New Year packages, special breaks, 1-night bookings sometimes refused Sat, bank holidays. *V*

Linthwaite House

Crook Road
Bowness-on-Windermere
LA23 3JA

Tel 015394-88600
Fax 015394-88601
Email stay@linthwaite.com
Website www.linthwaite.com

In a 'great location', this timbered, creeper-covered, white and stone house has 'amazing views' over landscaped gardens to Lake Windermere. Public rooms have oriental rugs, potted plants, cabin trunks, memorabilia, and an enclosed veranda faces the water. The owner, Mike Bevans, tells us that five new bedrooms have been added, including a suite which has a sliding roof 'for stargazing'. This year's praise: 'As good as ever.' 'Friendly staff provided excellent service throughout. Our room, which overlooked the garden, was large, with a comfortable bed, good sitting space and well-equipped bathroom.' Rooms 14 and 15 (each with king-size bed and lake views) are liked. The cooking of chef Richard Kearsley, who arrived in late 2008, is liked too. His modern dishes might include crispy ravioli of rabbit confit; steamed fillet of sea bream, caramelised chicory, orange and star anise sauce. One guest found the restaurant service 'very formal'. 'Delicious scones at teatime.' (*John and Jean Saul, Nigel Davies, Gordon Hands*)

Bedrooms: 32, some on ground floor. *Open*: all year. *Facilities*: ramp, lounge/bar, conservatory, 3 dining rooms, function facilities, civil wedding licence, 14-acre grounds (croquet, tarn, fly-fishing). *Background music*: in bar all day, dining room during meals. *Location*: ¾ mile S of Bowness off B5284. *Smoking*: not allowed. *Children*: no under-7s in dining rooms after 7 pm. *Dogs*: allowed in grounds only. *Credit cards*: Amex, MasterCard, Visa. *Prices*: [2009] B&B £95–£260 per person, D,B&B £110–£239, full alc £65, special breaks, Christmas/New Year packages, 1-night bookings refused weekends, bank holidays, in season. *V*

See also Shortlist

BRADFORD-ON-AVON Wiltshire *See Shortlist*

BRADPOLE Dorset   **Map 1:C6**

Orchard Barn   *Tel/Fax* 01308-455655
Bradpole   *Email* enquiries@lodgeatorchardbarn.co.uk
nr Bridport DT6 4AR   *Website* www.lodgeatorchardbarn.co.uk

On the site of an old Dorset farm, with a river at the bottom of the garden, Nigel and Margaret Corbett run their B&B 'with genuine warmth', according to their many fans. 'It is a delight, Nigel is so warm,' says one this year. Their collection of cheese dishes has come with them from their earlier, much-loved hotel, *Summer Lodge* at Evershot (*qv*). 'Attention to our needs was exemplary,' wrote an earlier guest. 'Nigel ushered us into a large, vaulted, high-ceilinged lounge with an open log fire burning on a deep bed of ashes; tea quickly arrived with home-made cake and shortbread.' The comfortable bedrooms 'are simple, but have fine linen, good lighting, free-range coat-hangers and individual temperature control'. One bedroom has a private bathroom adjacent. The ground-floor room has a separate entrance. Guests can be provided with a snack in the evening (soups, quiches, salads) given 24 hours' notice. Breakfast, in a room with a log fire or on the patio, has 'unbelievable quality and choice'; it includes free-range eggs cooked in many ways, local bacon and sausages, 'delicious, unusual yogurts', organic wholemeal toast, home-made marmalade and jams. (*Mick Keates, and others*)

Bedrooms: 3, 1 on ground floor. *Open*: all year except Christmas/New Year. *Facilities*: lounge, dining room. *Background music*: none. *Location*: off A35, via Lee Lane, in village adjoining Bridport, train Dorchester, bus to Bridport. *Smoking*: not allowed. *Children*: all ages welcomed. *Dogs*: allowed in public rooms subject to other guests' approval. *Credit cards*: none in 2009, will reconsider in 2010. *Prices*: B&B £47.50–£80 per person, snack supper £5–£15, 1-night bookings sometimes refused Sat.

BRAITHWAITE Cumbria   Map 4: inset C2

The Cottage in the Wood   *Tel* 017687-78409
Magic Hill   *Email* relax@thecottageinthewood.co.uk
Whinlatter Forest   *Website* www.thecottageinthewood.co.uk
Braithwaite CA12 5TW

The 'excellent personal service' and 'superb' cooking are liked at this restaurant-with-rooms, a 17th-century coaching inn on Whinlatter Pass. 'A lovely, lovely place to stay,' says a visitor in 2009. It is owned by Kath and Liam Berney. She runs front-of-house, he is the chef, using local produce for his modern European dishes, eg, Cumbrian charcuterie, melon and rocket salad; breast of Goosnargh chicken, bacon and colcannon. The bedrooms are decorated in cottage style: a room in the attic has a roll-top bath and separate shower; two superior rooms with views towards Skiddaw have a sleigh bed; smaller rooms have brass bed, pine furniture. Guests have a cosy sitting room with walking magazines, books and games; in summer they can sit in the small garden. Breakfast has fresh grapefruit, yogurts, fruit; a cooked platter. (*Hilary Blakemore*)

Bedrooms: 9, 1 on ground floor. *Open*: Feb–Dec, restaurant closed Sun/Mon. *Facilities*: lounge, bar, restaurant, 5-acre grounds (terraced garden). *Background music*: eclectic. *Location*: 5 miles NW of Keswick. *Smoking*: not allowed. *Children*: not under 10. *Dogs*: not allowed. *Credit cards*: MasterCard, Visa. *Prices*: B&B £45–£120 per person, D,B&B £70–£105, set dinner £28, midweek breaks, Christmas/New Year packages, 1-night bookings refused weekends.

We ask for more reports on a hotel if we haven't received feedback from readers for some time. Please send an endorsement if you think a hotel should remain in the *Guide*.

BRAMPTON Cumbria   Map 4:B3

Farlam Hall   *Tel* 01697-746234
Brampton CA8 2NG   *Fax* 01697-746683
                                    Email farlam@farlamhall.co.uk
                                Website www.farlamhall.co.uk

César award in 2001

'A sense of humour abounds alongside proper service' at this
traditional hotel (Relais & Châteaux), an old manorial house which
takes its character from a Victorian modernisation. It has been run by
the Quinion and Stevenson families since 1975; they 'clearly take
great pride in their country hotel and the service they provide', say
recent visitors. The creeper-clad building stands in an 'immaculate'
landscaped garden with a large ornamental lake, tall trees, a stream
and a paddock. The ornate public rooms, filled with knick-knacks,
fresh flowers and Victoriana, reflect its character. Drinks are served in
the lounge (there is no bar). Barry Quinion's 'delicious' country house
cooking might include dishes like sweet potato and chive soup;
medallion of local beef with horseradish mash and pink peppercorn
sauce and caramelised red onions. The 'old-fashioned way of serving
vegetables' is appreciated. Bedrooms are priced according to size (best
ones have a whirlpool bath). 'Our beautiful room had a huge new
bathroom, and an American-size bed; it couldn't have been more
comfortable. Breakfasts were lovely. Expensive, but well worth it.'
(*T and RV, MW*)

Bedrooms: 12, 1 in stables, 2 on ground floor. *Open*: all year except 24–30 Dec,
restaurant closed midday (light lunches for residents by arrangement). *Facilities*:
ramps, 2 lounges, restaurant, 10-acre grounds (croquet lawn), unsuitable for &.
Background music: none. *Location*: on A689, 2½ miles SE of Brampton (*not* in
Farlam village). *Smoking*: not allowed. *Children*: not under 5. *Dogs*: not allowed
unattended in bedrooms. *Credit cards*: Amex, MasterCard, Visa. *Prices*: [2009]
B&B £102–£127 per person, D,B&B £145–£170, set dinner £43–£45, special
breaks, New Year package. *V*

Check the Hotelfinder section (page 11) if you are looking
for a hotel for a special occasion, perhaps a memorable meal
(see Gourmet and Gastropubs); a sporting weekend (see
Golf, Fishing, Walking); somewhere that will welcome your
children – or your dog. Our editors have selected ten hotels
in each of these categories (and many more) to help you
make your choice.

BRANCASTER STAITHE Norfolk   Map 2:A5

The White Horse
Brancaster Staithe
PE31 8BY

Tel 01485-210262
Fax 01485-210930
Email reception@whitehorsebrancaster.co.uk
Website www.whitehorsebrancaster.co.uk

On the sea marsh side of a village in north Norfolk, Cliff Nye's informal inn (managed by Kevin Nobes) is liked for its 'relaxed' style. There are panoramic views across the tidal marshes from the conservatory restaurant and terrace. The open-plan interior has a contemporary rustic style; Lloyd Loom chairs in the lounges, scrubbed pine wooden tables and chairs in the restaurant. Eight of the bedrooms are in a grass-roofed annexe built into the contours of the garden; each has a terrace which provides separate access. These rooms are popular with walkers (the Coast Path runs along the bottom of the garden) and dog owners. There are spacious bedrooms upstairs in the pub; the split-level Room at the Top (£15 supplement) has a viewing balcony with telescope. Some rooms have a sofa bed; all have Wi-Fi. Rene Llupar joined as chef in 2009. His new daily-changing menu 'celebrates' local produce. Fishermen in the village deliver their catch of the day and 'Cyril's mussels' come from beds at the bottom of the garden. Dishes include medallions of monkfish with aubergine caviar; baked cod with pancetta, broad beans, peas and baby leeks. Children have their own menu (and colouring books and crayons in the lounge); there is a separate menu in the bar (frequented by locals). Breakfast is served until 11 am. (*RM, and others*)

Bedrooms: 15, 8 on ground floor in annexe, 1 suitable for &. *Open*: all year. *Facilities*: 2 lounge areas, public bar, conservatory restaurant, dining room, ½-acre garden (covered sunken garden), harbour sailing. *Background music*: 'easy listening' at quiet times. *Location*: centre of village just E of Brancaster. *Smoking*: not allowed. *Children*: all ages welcomed. *Dogs*: allowed in annexe rooms (£10) and bar. *Credit cards*: Diners, MasterCard, Visa. *Prices*: [2009] B&B £50–£93 per person, D,B&B £68–£98, full alc £36, off-season breaks, Christmas/New Year packages.

We update the *Guide* every year. Hotels are dropped or may be demoted to the Shortlist if there has been a change of owner (unless reports after the change are positive), if this year's reports are negative, or in rare cases where there has been no feedback. A lot of hotels are omitted every year, and many new ones are added.

BRANSCOMBE Devon   Map 1:C5

The Masons Arms   *Tel* 01297-680300
Branscombe EX12 3DJ   *Fax* 01297-680500
                        Email reception@masonsarms.co.uk
                        Website www.masonsarms.co.uk

'The location is a short-break dream,' write regular visitors to Carol
and Colin Slaney's creeper-covered 14th-century inn. Other praise:
'Owners very much in evidence. Staff, mainly European trainees from
a London college, attentive, polite and professional.' 'A fantastic place
to stay.' Grade II listed, in the centre of a 'lovely, peaceful' National
Trust village, it is an 'undemanding stroll' from Branscombe's shingle
beach. Many of the bedrooms (some are large) are in cottages across a
terrace set back from the pub. During the 'buzz' of the summer
season, when the inn was 'busy with diners and drinkers of all ages',
guests 'enjoyed peace and quiet' in their cottage room. 'Four-poster
bed, *chaise longue*, a table and chairs in the secluded, flower-filled
garden. Green hills with sheep and even a glimpse of the sea were in
the background.' In the restaurant (three cosy small rooms) head chef
Andrew Deam's cooking is commended. His menu might include
seared West Country scallops with port wine shallot salad; grilled
medallions of beef fillet. The extensive bar menu includes children's
meals. 'Breakfast was excellent.' Booking is advised for meals in both
restaurant and pub. Popular with dog owners. (*Lee Ely, Mary Ellin
Osmond, B and PB*)

Bedrooms: 21, 14 in cottages. *Open*: all year. *Facilities*: ramps, lounge, 2 bars,
2 dining rooms, large terraced gardens, pebble beach ½ mile, unsuitable for &.
Background music: none. *Location*: village centre. *Smoking*: not allowed. *Children*:
all ages welcomed. *Dogs*: allowed in some bedrooms, bar. *Credit cards*: Diners,
MasterCard, Visa. *Prices*: [2009] B&B £28–£85 per person, D,B&B
£48.50–£114.50, set dinner £29.95, full alc £37.50, Christmas/New Year
packages, 1-night bookings refused weekends.

BRAY Berkshire   Map 2:D3

The Waterside Inn   *Tel* 01628-620691
Ferry Road   *Fax* 01628-784710
Bray SL6 2AT   *Email* reservations@waterside-inn.co.uk
                          Website www.waterside-inn.co.uk

'Definitely a place for the special occasion,' say visitors this year
endorsing this renowned restaurant-with-rooms (Relais & Châteaux)

on the River Thames. It is owned by Alain Roux and his father, Michel. 'The setting, the cuisine, the service and the bedrooms are first class.' The restaurant (its kitchen entirely revamped this year) has held three *Michelin* stars for 24 years for its French *haute cuisine*: dishes like pan-fried lobster medallion with white port sauce; roasted Challandais duck with lightly spiced prunes and Puy lentils. There is a five-course *menu exceptionnel* (to be ordered by the whole table) at £109.50 per person. Drinks can be taken in a summer house or on an electric launch. For the 'sybaritic overnight stay', there are bedrooms upstairs and in a nearby cottage. Designed by Michel's wife, Robyn, they have an 'elegant French feel': linen sheets, Wi-Fi, flat-screen TV, flowers and access to a kitchenette. The two best rooms, La Terrasse and La Tamise, open on to a terrace with 'stunning views of the river'. 'Continental breakfast, served in one's room overlooking the water on a sunny morning, is an experience to be treasured.' Diego Masciaga is the 'dedicated', long-serving general manager. (*Bryan and Mary Blaxall, and others*)

Bedrooms: 9, 1, plus 2 apartments, in nearby cottage. *Open*: all year except 26 Dec–28 Jan, Mon/Tues (except Tues evening June–Aug). *Facilities*: restaurant, private dining room (with drawing room and courtyard garden), civil wedding licence, riverside terrace (launch for drinks/coffee), unsuitable for &. *Background music*: none. *Location*: 3 miles SE of Maidenhead. *Smoking*: not allowed. *Children*: not under 12. *Dogs*: not allowed. *Credit cards*: all major cards. *Prices*: [2009] B&B £90–£145 per person, apartment £420–£675, set dinner £54–£109.50.

BRIDPORT Dorset   *See Shortlist*

BRIGHTON East Sussex   Map 2:E4

drakes   *Tel* 01273-696934
43/44 Marine Parade   *Fax* 01273-684805
Brighton BN2 1PE   *Email* info@drakesofbrighton.com
                    Website www.drakesofbrighton.com

On the seafront, in sight of the pier and a few minutes' walk from The Lanes and the Pavilion, this 'wonderful' design hotel with 'very helpful staff' is a conversion of two 19th-century town houses. Owned by Andy Shearer and managed by Richard Hayes, it has 'expensive, lovely bedrooms': the better ones face the sea; others have a 'city view', mainly of the back gardens of other houses. A circular suite has a freestanding bath in front of floor-to-ceiling windows. A second-floor room, up a steep hanging staircase, was 'smallish, well designed, done in cream, shades of brown and natural wood; it had air conditioning, flat-screen TV, DVD-player, Internet access, etc. Excellent lighting; but not much storage space.' Our inspector's 'wardrobe' was a hanging space with electrically operated curtains. There are 'very comfortable beds, good linen; water everywhere in the wet room'. Breakfast has fruit, yogurt, porridge, kippers, etc. There is 24-hour service in the ground-floor lounge bar. Hotel guests should reserve a table for the basement *Gingerman* restaurant, 'perhaps the best in Sussex', which is separately owned by Ben McKellar. The head chef, Andrew MacKenzie, offers a five-course tasting menu as well as a *carte*.

Bedrooms: 20, 2 on ground floor. *Open*: all year, restaurant closed midday. *Facilities*: ramp, lounge/bar/reception, restaurant (separately owned), meeting room, civil wedding/partnership licence, unsuitable for &. *Background music*: 'easy listening' in bar and restaurant. *Location*: ½ mile from centre, station 20 mins' walk. *Smoking*: not allowed. *Children*: not under 10, except young babies. *Dogs*: only guide dogs allowed. *Credit cards*: Amex, MasterCard, Visa. *Prices*: [2009] room £100–£325, breakfast £5–£12.50, full alc £50, midweek packages, 3-night min. stay bank holidays, Christmas/New Year packages, 1-night bookings refused Sat.

Paskins Town House

18–19 Charlotte Street
Brighton BN2 1AG

Tel 01273-601203
Fax 01273-621973
Email welcome@paskins.co.uk
Website www.paskins.co.uk

'A positive, fun experience,' says an endorsement this year. Holders of a gold award from the Green Business Tourism Scheme, Susan and Roger Marlowe run their B&B in two Grade II listed buildings in a conservation area near the sea. Proud of their 'quirky' style, they and their staff 'genuinely care for their guests'. A visitor in 2009 was 'warmly greeted by a young Hungarian receptionist who carried my luggage to a very small room dominated by overpowering black-and-white wallpaper which made me feel dizzy. Quiet at night, it had comfortable bed, excellent information folder.' The bedrooms, all different, include a spacious family room. They have a modern Japanese-style decor; bathrooms have synthetic-free, animal produce-free soap and shampoo. There is an Art Nouveau theme in Reception, the 'comfortable small sitting room with a splendid 1920s/30s gramophone', and the breakfast room (this year's visitors had no complaints about the Rennie Mackintosh chairs). 'The interesting breakfast menu, generous, thoughtfully presented, caters for all tastes.' There are organic muesli, jams and peanut butter, bread from a local independent baker, and the host's cooked dishes include 'full Sussex', 'Hove' ('quieter and more refined'); and a special of mushrooms, chorizo, walnuts and blue cheese. His wife is a 'friendly presence, waiting at table'. Tea and coffee are Fairtrade. Sandwiches and local beers are served in the lounge or bedroom. (*Rosemary Reeves, A and VG*)

Bedrooms: 19. *Open*: all year. *Facilities*: lounge, breakfast room. *Background music*: none. *Location*: 10 mins' walk from centre. *Smoking*: not allowed. *Children*: all ages welcomed. *Dogs*: not in public rooms. *Credit cards*: all major cards. *Prices*: B&B £40–£70 per person, 3-night breaks, 1-night bookings refused weekends, bank holidays.

See also Shortlist

BRISTOL   Map 1:B6

Hotel du Vin Bristol   NEW   *Tel* 0117-925 5577
The Sugar House   *Fax* 0117-925 1199
Narrow Lewins Mead   *Email* info@bristol.hotelduvin.com
Bristol BS1 2NU   *Website* www.hotelduvin.com

The Bristol branch of the growing Hotel du Vin chain (fourteen and counting) is an imaginative conversion of a group of Grade II listed buildings in the city centre. Managed by Lorraine Jarvie, it returns to a full *Guide* entry on the 2009 recommendation of a regular reader who praised the 'friendly, informative welcome', and enjoyed the 'buzzy atmosphere' in the bistro. A glassed canopy entrance opens to a Reception desk beside a 100-foot chimney. Spacious public areas have tables and potted plants, and a sweeping steel and oak staircase. 'Our large room had a king-sized bed with high-quality linen; fresh milk in the fridge (what a joy). Housekeeping was good, though bedside lighting was poor (you couldn't read a book in bed); in the bathroom a stand-alone roll-top bath and terrific walk-in monsoon shower. The room was at the front, but secondary double glazing cut out the traffic noise. A very good dinner, especially the rib-eye steak, served by friendly young staff. A long wine list: house wine good value at £14.75.' The 'extensive, imaginative' breakfast (charged extra) is 'a great start to the day'. It has home-made smoothies, fresh juices, cereals, 'lovely'

French yogurts, full English, but 'poor toast'. The hotel has a secure car park, but space is limited and cannot be reserved; other parking spaces are outside the building. (*Ian Malone, Helen Carless*)

Bedrooms: 40. *Open*: all year. *Facilities*: lift, ramp, lounge, library/billiard room, 2 bars, bistro, 3 private dining rooms, civil wedding licence. *Background music*: none. *Location*: city centre. *Smoking*: not allowed. *Children*: all ages welcomed. *Dogs*: allowed. *Credit cards*: Amex, MasterCard, Visa. *Prices*: [2009] room £145–£215, breakfast £9.95–£13.50, set meals £25–£35, full alc £60, special breaks, Christmas/New Year packages. *V*

BROAD CAMPDEN Gloucestershire   Map 3:D6

The Malt House
Broad Campden
nr Chipping Campden
GL55 6UU

Tel 01386-840295
Fax 01386-841334
Email info@malt-house.co.uk
Website www.malt-house.co.uk

'A lovely house to sit around in, with open fires and lots of welcoming armchairs, sofas, newspapers and magazines.' This 'beautiful old building' in Cotswold vernacular style (a conversion of a Grade II listed malt house with two adjacent cottages) is a 'pleasant B&B', run by the 'charming' owner, Judi Wilkes, and her 'helpful and efficient' staff. The bedrooms are 'beautifully furnished' and well equipped, with umbrella, spare toothbrush, torch, and fresh milk for tea-making. All overlook the large, pretty garden which has 'lovely countryside views'; three have a private entrance, one a fireplace, one a small sitting room. 'Ours was cosy on a cold evening; cottagey furnishings, big soft bed, huge bathroom.' Breakfasts are 'generous', and in warm weather, tea (with home-made biscuits) and evening drinks are served in the summer house in the garden. Meals may be provided, by arrangement, for groups of 12 or more, and house parties are catered for. 'There are lots of excellent gastropubs within a short drive' (coming by car is advised), and a map with recommendations is in each room. From the gate you can walk on to the Cotswold Way. (*ANR, EA and G Smith, and others*)

Bedrooms: 7, 2 on ground floor, 3 with own entrance. *Open*: all year except Christmas. *Facilities*: 2 lounges, dining room, 3-acre garden (croquet, orchard, stream), unsuitable for &. *Background music*: none. *Location*: 1 mile S of Chipping Campden. *Smoking*: not allowed. *Children*: all ages welcomed. *Dogs*: allowed in 1 bedroom only. *Credit cards*: MasterCard, Visa. *Prices*: [2009] B&B £65–£85 per person, special breaks, 1-night bookings sometimes refused weekends high season. *V*

BROADWAY Worcestershire   Map 3:D6

Russell's Restaurant
The Green, 20 High Street
Broadway WR12 7DT

Tel 01386-853555
Fax 01386-853964
Email info@russellsofbroadway.co.uk
Website www.russellsofbroadway.co.uk

♉ *César award in 2006*

Named after Gordon Russell, the celebrated furniture designer who once used it as his headquarters, this restaurant-with-rooms is on the wide main street of this honey-stoned Cotswold village. The owners, Barry Hancox and Andrew Riley, have given it a chic, contemporary look: original features (beams, inglenook fireplaces, an oak staircase) were retained while modern gadgets and paintings were added. The L-shaped bistro-style dining room is 'stylish; china, glass, all top quality, modern cutlery', wooden tables with grey slate mats. A visitor returning in 2009 was again enthusiastic about the 'high standards of service, comfort and food'. Earlier comments: 'Our beautiful bedroom (No. 4), on two levels, was exciting and comfortable. Plenty of space and colour, large double bed, two comfortable armchairs, a window on almost every wall: light flooded in during the day.' Some rooms face the village, but windows are double glazed, and 'all is quiet at night'; a supermarket car park is visible from the rear windows and patio. 'Dinners were first class.' Matthew Laughton serves a seasonal set menu at midday and from 6 to 7 pm; later, guests eat *à la carte*. The style is modern, eg, crispy fishcake with a cress salad; spiced lamb meatball, with chorizo, spinach and artichoke pizza. Staff are 'friendly, efficient'. There is a 'parasol-covered patio with metal chairs and tables'. (*Tom Mann*)

Bedrooms: 7, 3 in adjoining building, 2 on ground floor. *Open*: all year, restaurant closed Sun night. *Facilities*: ramp, residents' lobby, bar, restaurant, private dining room, patio (heating, meal service). *Background music*: 'ambient', in restaurant. *Location*: village centre. *Smoking*: not allowed. *Children*: all ages welcomed. *Dogs*: not allowed. *Credit cards*: all major cards. *Prices*: [2009] B&B £60–£162.50 per person, full alc £40, seasonal breaks on website, 1-night bookings refused weekends. *V*

BROCKENHURST Hampshire   *See Shortlist*

For details of the Voucher scheme see page 57.

BROXTON Cheshire   Map 3:A5

Frogg Manor   *Tel* 01829-782629
Nantwich Road (A594)   *Fax* 01829-782459
Broxton, Chester CH3 9JH   *Email* info@froggmanorhotel.co.uk
                                  Website www.froggmanorhotel.co.uk

César award in 1997

'This must rank as one of the most unusual hotels in the *Guide*, but it
is high on the list of those we have enjoyed most.' Long-standing
correspondents were 'not disappointed' this year by John Sykes's
Georgian manor house hotel dedicated to frogs (he has around 300 of
them, ceramic, brass, straw, etc). It may be eccentric (you might be
welcomed by the host in his dressing gown) 'but it exudes a wonderful
generosity of spirit which puts host and guests alike in a good mood'.
There is 'a hint of an Agatha Christie whodunit' in the 'cluttered'
public rooms, with their antique furniture and frogs. Background
music is from the 1930s/40s. Well-equipped, if 'quirky', bedrooms are
themed (Mountbatten, Brontë, Wellington, etc). 'We were upgraded
to a suite; if it was over the top it was in a thoroughly tasteful way.
Every possible contingency had been provided for.' The Lady
Guinevere tree house in the garden has Arthurian murals. There can
be noise from traffic on the Nantwich road. James Powell and Sion
Newton cook 'superb, beautifully presented' food on an extensive
menu (but no frogs' legs) between 7 and 10 pm in the conservatory
restaurant. Continental breakfast is included in the price ('a delicious
porridge with maple syrup'); other breakfast dishes are *à la carte* (up
to £15 for full English). (*Sarah and Tony Thomas, and others*)

Bedrooms: 8, 1 in tree house, 1 suitable for &. *Open*: all year. *Facilities*: ramp,
lounge, bar lounge, restaurant, private dining room, conference/function
facilities, civil wedding licence, 12-acre grounds (tennis). *Background music*:
1930s/40s CDs in lounge, restaurant and bar lounge. *Location*: 12 miles SE of
Chester. *Smoking*: allowed in 2 bedrooms. *Children*: all ages welcomed. *Dogs*:
allowed in bedrooms, bar lounge. *Credit cards*: all major cards. *Prices*: [2009]
B&B (continental) £49–£135 per person, D,B&B £86–£172, set dinner
£37–£42, full alc £51, midweek discounts. ***V***

When you make a booking you enter into a contract with a
hotel. Most hotels explain their cancellation policies, which
vary widely, in a letter of confirmation. You may lose your
deposit or be charged at the full rate for the room if you cancel
at short notice. A travel insurance policy can provide protection.

BRYHER Isles of Scilly   Map 1: inset C1

Hell Bay Hotel	*Tel* 01720-422947
Bryher, Isles of Scilly	*Fax* 01720-423004
Cornwall TR23 0PR	*Email* contactus@hellbay.co.uk
	Website www.hellbay.co.uk

Robert Dorrien-Smith, who has the lease for Tresco, also owns this hotel on the 'wilder, less manicured' neighbouring island of Bryher (the smallest of the inhabited Scilly Isles). It is built in the style of cottages, on an isolated bay facing jagged rocks on the western shore. Inspectors found the style and colours of bedrooms and public areas 'appropriately seaside'. Accommodation is in suites, some with two bedrooms and a lounge, in buildings around a courtyard and in the garden. Many face the bay; some first-floor rooms have a private balcony. 'Our corner-facing studio was light, bright; a huge bathroom (with notes about the conservation policy). A door led on to a decking patio; you can walk straight to the beach.' Mainly Cornish artworks (by Barbara Hepworth, Ivon Hitchens and others) are displayed in the large lounge. Huge paintings by local artist Richard Pearce are in the panoramic dining room where Glenn Gatland serves a 'well-balanced' daily-changing menu of modern dishes, eg, cauliflower and cumin soup; beer-battered haddock, Parmentier potatoes. Breakfast has a 'superior' buffet; cooked dishes include three kinds of fish. 'Lovely, relaxed, relaxing.' *Hell Bay* has facilities for disabled visitors but 'Bryher has no made-up roads and no dedicated transport system'.

Bedrooms: 25 suites, in 5 buildings, some on ground floor, 1 suitable for &. *Open*: Mar–Nov. *Facilities*: lounge, games room, bar, 2 dining rooms, gym, sauna, large grounds (heated swimming pool, 15 by 10 metres, giant chess, *boules*, croquet, children's playground, par 3 golf course), beach 75 yds. *Background music*: none. *Location*: W coast of island, boat from Tresco (reached by boat/helicopter from Penzance) or St Mary's, hotel will make travel arrangements. *Smoking*: not allowed. *Children*: all ages welcomed (high tea at 5.30). *Dogs*: not allowed in public rooms. *Credit cards*: MasterCard, Visa. *Prices*: [2009] D,B&B £155–£300 per person, 4-night breaks.

> Check the Hotelfinder section (page 11) if you are looking for a hotel for a special occasion, perhaps a memorable meal (see Gourmet and Gastropubs); a sporting weekend (see Golf, Fishing, Walking); somewhere that will welcome your children – or your dog. Our editors have selected ten hotels in each of these categories (and many more) to help you make your choice.

BUCKDEN Cambridgeshire   Map 2:B4

The George
High Street
Buckden PE19 5XA

Tel 01480-812300
Fax 01480-813920
Email manager@thegeorgebuckden.com
Website www.thegeorgebuckden.com

On the main street of a historic village between the market towns of
Huntingdon and St Neots, this 19th-century coaching inn is 'strongly
commended'. Owners Anne, Richard and Becky Furbank have
created a 'fashionably stylish' look with neutral colours (taupe,
chocolate, grey-green), leather tub chairs and sofas. 'Furnishings are
well chosen, comfortable and eye-catching,' say guests. The bedrooms are all named after famous Georges; Hanover and Gershwin
(premier rooms) have mahogany furniture and a 'very comfortable'
bed with brass bedhead. A standard room (Mallory, 'perhaps because
of the climb') has a patchwork counterpane. Handel is twin bedded.
The bustling ground-floor brasserie, where breakfast, light lunch and
dinner are served, has 'chic night-light holders, quirky prints',
wooden tables and an 'orangerie' extension. Summer meals can be
taken on the terrace. The chef, Ray Smikle, serves modern dishes, eg,
stuffed leg of rabbit wrapped in pancetta with mustard mash. The
wine list is well priced ('plenty in the £15–£16 range'). Waiters wear
grey shirt and tie. Breakfast includes brown bread toast, croissants,
fruit, cheese, etc, and any variation of a standard fry-up. 'Good coffee.
Plenty of free newspapers.' Anne Furbank runs a smart clothing
boutique next door. (*KS*)

Bedrooms: 12. *Open*: all year. *Facilities*: lift, bar, lounge, restaurant, private dining
room, civil wedding licence, courtyard. *Background music*: jazz/contemporary in
all public areas. *Location*: village centre. *Smoking*: not allowed. *Children*: all ages
welcomed, baby-changing facilities. *Dogs*: allowed in bedrooms and foyer.
Credit cards: all major cards. *Prices*: [2009] B&B £50–£80 per person, D,B&B
£72.50–£115, full alc £50, Christmas package.

BUCKLAND Gloucestershire   *See Shortlist*

Small hotels will often try to persuade you to stay for two nights
at the weekend. We ask all the hotels in the *Guide* whether they
ever refuse a one-night booking, and indicate those that won't
take them. It is worth asking about this, especially off-season or
when booking late.

BUCKLAND MARSH Oxfordshire   Map 2:C2

The Trout at Tadpole Bridge
Buckland Marsh
SN7 8RF

Tel 01367-870382
Fax 01367-870912
Email info@trout-inn.co.uk
Website www.trout-inn.co.uk

'Idyllically located', by a bridge, on the Thames as it meanders through the Cotswolds, this 17th-century stone inn is run as an informal pub-with-rooms by its 'efficient, friendly' owners, Gareth and Helen Pugh. Its bar is popular with locals and boating visitors; six private moorings are free if you dine in the restaurant. The atmosphere is informal and the decor is 'unfussy': contemporary colour schemes combined with traditional materials. Parents of young children themselves, the Pughs welcome families of all ages, with games and toys, and a children's menu. The 'immaculate' bedrooms (all different) have flat-screen digital TV, DVD/CD-player and quality toiletries, and there is free Wi-Fi throughout. Pascal Clavaud is now the chef: his seasonal menu includes locally sourced produce, perhaps salad of smoked eel, Noilly Prat jelly; Kelmscott fillet of pork, parsnip purée, black pudding. 'Excellent breakfast': fresh orange juice, home-made bread, a 'well-stocked' sideboard; kippers and haddock among the cooked choice. Guests can hire a small electric punt for picnics on the river. Check in before 3 pm or after 6 pm. More reports, please.

Bedrooms: 6, 3 in courtyard. *Open*: all year except 25/26 Dec, restaurant closed Sun night in winter. *Facilities*: bar, dining area, breakfast area, 2-acre garden (river, moorings), unsuitable for &. *Background music*: none. *Location*: 2 miles N of A420, halfway between Oxford and Swindon. *Smoking*: not allowed. *Children*: all ages welcomed. *Dogs*: allowed. *Credit cards*: MasterCard, Visa. *Prices*: [2009] B&B £55–£75 per person, D,B&B £85–£105, full alc £33, New Year package, 1-night bookings refused weekends.

BUDE Cornwall   *See Shortlist*

How to contact the *Guide*
By mail: From anywhere in the UK, write to Freepost PAM 2931, London W11 4BR (no stamp is needed)
From outside the UK: *Good Hotel Guide*, 50 Addison Avenue, London W11 4QP, England
By telephone or fax: 020-7602 4182
By email: editor@goodhotelguide.com
Via our website: www.goodhotelguide.com

BUDLEIGH SALTERTON Devon   Map 1:D5

Downderry House   `NEW`   *Tel* 01395-442663
10 Exmouth Road   *Email* info@downderryhouse.co.uk
Budleigh Salterton EX9 6AQ   *Website* www.downderryhouse.co.uk

On the outskirts of a seaside resort in an area of outstanding natural
beauty, this detached 1920s house has been renovated as a luxury
B&B by Don and Amanda Clarke. 'They are friendly but not intrusive
hosts,' say visitors this year. 'It is more like a boutique hotel than a
B&B.' The drawing room, for the exclusive use of guests, has an
honesty bar; no background music. 'Our large top-floor bedroom,
Tipton, had a king-size bed, a bathroom with a separate shower; extras
included a decanter of sherry.' Sidbury, a ground-floor room, has a
sitting area with a leather sofa, a bathroom with a walk-in deluge
shower, and a private terrace. 'A top-class breakfast is taken at separate
tables in the lovely dining room overlooking the garden.' On warm
days, guests are encouraged to sit in the garden or play croquet. A
room-service supper menu is available. (*Tracy Hoggarth*)

Bedrooms: 5, 1 on ground floor. *Open*: all year. *Facilities*: drawing room, dining
room, 1-acre garden, croquet. *Background music*: none. *Location*: edge of town,
5 miles E of Exmouth. *Smoking*: not allowed. *Children*: not under 10. *Dogs*:
allowed in ground-floor room only. *Credit cards*: MasterCard, Visa. *Prices*: [2009]
B&B £42.50–£89 per person, 1-night bookings refused high season weekends,
public holidays.

BUNGAY Suffolk   *See Shortlist*

BURFORD Oxfordshire   *See Shortlist*

BURY ST EDMUNDS Suffolk   *See Shortlist*

BUXTON Derbyshire   *See Shortlist*

We asked hotels to quote their 2010 tariffs. Many had yet to fix
these rates as we went to press. Prices should always be
checked on booking.

BYLAND North Yorkshire   Map 4:D4

The Abbey Inn
Byland Abbey, nr Coxwold
YO61 4BD

Tel 01347-868204
Fax 01347-868678
Email abbey.inn@english-heritage.org.uk
Website www.bylandabbeyinn.com

By the ruins of Byland Abbey, this 12th-century inn has been given an elaborate make-over by English Heritage, 'without losing its intrinsic history'. Much of the furniture is 'Mouseman', made in the nearby village of Kilburn. Inspectors enjoyed their stay. 'The setting is beautiful, isolated; the accommodation very comfortable.' The three bedrooms, Byland and Mouseman (abbey view) and Kilburn (which faces the 'lovely garden with trees, shrubs and a patio for outside eating'), are done 'with great attention to detail'. 'Excellent information folder, lots of extras (sherry, sweets, flowers), lovely old wardrobe with proper hangers; well-lit bathroom, white and blue, with window. Access from outside: umbrellas and torches provided.' Paul Tatham is the manager; Wayne Rogers has joined this year as chef. He uses local ingredients for modern dishes like nettle and watercress soup; roast rack of Philip Trevelyan's Shearling with a little pan of mutton and turnip stew. These are served in *The Piggery* (main dining area) and two smaller rooms, *Coxwold* and *Wass* ('slate floors, plain wood tables, views of the abbey, floodlit at night'). Breakfast, ordered at dinner, has freshly squeezed orange juice, smoked salmon with scrambled eggs. We would welcome reports on the cooking.

Bedrooms: 3. *Open*: all year except Christmas/New Year, closed Sun night/Mon/Tues. *Facilities*: 3 dining rooms, patio, 1-acre grounds, unsuitable for &. *Background music*: soft jazz in dining rooms. *Location*: 2 miles W of Ampleforth. *Smoking*: not allowed. *Children*: in restaurant only. *Dogs*: not allowed. *Credit cards*: MasterCard, Visa. *Prices*: [2009] B&B £34.50–£99.50 per person, set dinner £15.95, full alc £22.

CAMBER East Sussex   *See Shortlist*

CAMBRIDGE Cambridgeshire   *See Shortlist*

CAMPSEA ASHE Suffolk   *See Shortlist*

CANNINGTON Somerset   Map 1:B5

Blackmore Farm   *Tel* 01278-653442
Blackmore Lane   *Fax* 01278-653427
Cannington   *Email* dyerfarm@aol.com
nr Bridgwater TA5 2NE   *Website* www.dyerfarm.co.uk

'Great for lovers of historic buildings, and for children', Ann and Ian Dyer's large 15th-century, Grade I listed manor house is on their working dairy farm. It has views to the Quantock hills. 'Younger visitors,' said inspectors, 'will love the quirky rooms, the nooks and crannies, the lack of formality and the farm animals (there is even a special room from which to see the cows being milked).' Entry is through the Great Hall with its long oak refectory table, large open fireplace and full suit of armour. The small sitting room has books, board games and brochures. One bedroom, The Gallery, has original wall panelling, wide, comfortable bed, sitting room up a steep flight of steps, small bathroom (lavatory in a medieval garderobe). A family room, The Solar, has a large double bedroom, a single bed in a closet leading off it, and bathroom. Tea and 'delicious home-made cake' are served free to arriving guests. They take breakfast ('lovely'; 'lots of local ingredients') together around a refectory table: fresh fruit salad, cereals, toast, croissants and any combination of full English. The *Maltshovel* pub nearby has a friendly atmosphere and 'basic pub grub'; there are plenty of restaurants within easy driving distance. (*AC, and others*)

Bedrooms: 6, 3 in ground-floor barn, suitable for ♿. *Open*: all year. *Facilities*: lounge/TV room, hall/breakfast room, 2-acre garden (stream, coarse fishing). *Background music*: none. *Location*: 4 miles NW of Bridgwater. *Smoking*: not allowed. *Children*: all ages welcomed. *Dogs*: not allowed. *Credit cards*: all major cards. *Prices*: B&B £37.50–£55 per person, 1-night bookings refused bank holiday weekends.

CANTERBURY Kent   *See Shortlist*

We update the *Guide* every year. Hotels are dropped or may be demoted to the Shortlist if there has been a change of owner (unless reports after the change are positive), if this year's reports are negative, or in rare cases where there has been no feedback. A lot of hotels are omitted every year, and many new ones are added.

CARTMEL Cumbria   Map 4: inset C2

Aynsome Manor   *Tel* 01539-536653
Cartmel   *Fax* 01539-536016
nr Grange-over-Sands   *Email* aynsomemanor@btconnect.com
LA11 6HH   *Website* www.aynsomemanorhotel.co.uk

❦ *César award in 1998*

Two generations of one family have run this traditional Lakeland
hotel for 30 years; Christopher and Andrea Varley are in charge, helped
by his parents, Tony and Margaret. One of them is always on hand.
'Everything is as it should be; food, service, management, value,
faultless as ever,' is a comment from a regular visitor. Dog owners
thought the hotel 'an excellent place'. The Varleys have a loyal
following (readers staying for the fourth time were 'positively the
junior veterans; others were on their 20th-plus visit'). Bedrooms vary
in size; some are suitable for a family, two are in a cottage across the
cobbled courtyard. A smaller room at the top was 'comfortable, with a
good view across rolling fields'. This year, two of the bathrooms have
been revamped, and the boiler has been upgraded to a pressurised
system; both lounges have had their sofas and chairs replaced. 'Smart
casual' dress is required in the oak-panelled restaurant where
ingredients are sourced within Cumbria for Gordon Topp's 'very
pleasing', daily-changing five-course dinner menu. Typical dishes:
terrine of pheasant studded with pistachio; pan-fried breast of
guineafowl. Lighter options are always available. At busy times there
are two sittings for dinner. (*CB, DR*)

Bedrooms: 12, 2 in cottage (with lounge) across courtyard. *Open*: 29 Jan–2 Jan,
lunch served Sun only, Sun dinner for residents only. *Facilities*: 2 lounges, bar,
dining room, ½-acre garden, unsuitable for ♿. *Background music*: none. *Location*:
½ mile outside village. *Smoking*: not allowed. *Children*: no under-5s at dinner.
Dogs: not allowed in public rooms. *Credit cards*: Amex, MasterCard, Visa. *Prices*:
B&B £49.50–£63 per person, D,B&B £65–£87, set dinner £26, New Year
package, 1-night bookings sometimes refused Sat, bank holidays. ***V***

CASTLE COMBE Wiltshire   *See Shortlist*

Most hotels have reduced rates out of season, and offer special
breaks throughout the year. It is worth checking the hotel's
website for special offers and late deals. Always ask about deals
when booking by telephone.

CHADDESLEY CORBETT   Map 3:C5
Worcestershire

Brockencote Hall

Chaddesley Corbett
nr Kidderminster DY10 4PY

Tel 01562-777876
Fax 01562-777872
Email info@brockencotehall.com
Website www.brockencotehall.com

'Truly wonderful. It is run just as a hotel should be.' Praise in 2009 from a frequent visitor to this 19th-century, white-fronted mansion in 'glorious' parkland south-west of Birmingham. The staff, led by owners Joseph and Alison Petitjean, are 'without exception excellent; they treat you as someone special'. Visitors commend the bedrooms: 'Ours was spacious and slightly eccentric.' 'Our superior room had a huge four-poster and a double-aspect view over the lawns. Its bathroom had a shower cabinet and a good-sized bath.' The attractive restaurant is now in two rooms with high ceiling and fine oak panelling. Tables are 'well spaced, each with a nice flower arrangement'. Head chef Didier Philipot's 'exceptional' *table d'hôte* dinner menu might include rillettes of free-range woodland pork with pickled vegetables; fillet of Brixham line-caught brill, mussel and saffron sauce. A six-course *dégustation* menu suggests a wine for each course, and there are separate menus for vegetarians and for children. One visitor could have done without the piped music. The landscaped grounds have a lake, a historic dovecote and some fine trees; all-weather tennis courts and a croquet lawn. (*Gordon Hands, Jonathan Rose, and others*)

Bedrooms: 17, some on ground floor, 1 suitable for &. *Open*: all year, restaurant closed Sat midday. *Facilities*: lift, ramp, hall, 3 lounges, bar, conservatory, restaurant, function facilities, civil wedding licence, 70-acre grounds (gardens, lake, fishing, croquet, tennis). *Background music*: in restaurant, lounges. *Location*: 3 miles SE of Kidderminster. *Smoking*: not allowed. *Children*: all ages welcomed. *Dogs*: not allowed. *Credit cards*: all major cards. *Prices*: [2009] B&B £60–£96 per person, D,B&B £97.50–£133.50, set dinner £37.50, full alc £50–£60, short breaks, midweek discounts, Christmas/New Year packages. *V*

The *V* sign at the end of an entry indicates that a hotel has agreed to take part in our Voucher scheme and to give *Guide* readers a 25% discount on their bed-and-breakfast rates for a one-night stay, subject to the conditions on the back of the voucher and explained in 'How to use the *Good Hotel Guide*' (page 57).

CHAGFORD Devon   Map 1:C4

Gidleigh Park   *Tel* 01647-432367
Chagford TQ13 8HH   *Fax* 01647-432574
Email gidleighpark@gidleigh.co.uk
Website www.gidleigh.com

'The approach along a narrow lane is quite lovely; in the grounds you are greeted by the tame and formal alongside the wild.' Dramatically contrasting with the surrounding Dartmoor national park, this luxurious country house hotel (Relais & Châteaux) is owned by Andrew and Christina Brownsword (who also own *The Bath Priory*, Bath, *qv*) and managed by Sue Williams. The Tudor-style building stands in a large estate with marked walks, bridges over the River Teign (narrow at this point), an 'interesting' kitchen garden, and plenty of activities (see below). The 'very comfortable' bedrooms have 'superb beds, quality furniture, and welcoming touches (fresh fruit, mineral water, a decanter of Madeira),' says a visitor in 2009. 'Service is welcoming, a balance of formality and friendliness. The two-*Michelin*-starred food is accomplished.' Head chef Michael Caines's modern dishes include sea bass with shellfish mousse, roast lobster, gazpacho sauce; partridge, quince purée, braised chicory. The bedrooms, all different, contain antiques, paintings, prints, flowers. Earlier comments: 'Attention to detail is impeccable.' 'Prices are high, on the edge in terms of value for money.' 'Our splendid suite, the most expensive, had two big sofas, desk, wide balcony with armchairs facing the garden and the moor beyond.' Two rooms have a sauna, one a hot tub on the roof. The thatched two-bedroom pavilion in the garden is good for a family: young guests are welcomed; babysitting can be arranged. (*Steven Parsons, CD, and others*)

Bedrooms: 24, 2 in annexe, 75 yds, 2 in cottage, some, on ground floor, suitable for &. *Open*: all year. *Facilities*: ramps, drawing room, hall, bar, loggia, conservatory, 2 dining rooms, civil wedding licence, 54-acre grounds (gardens, croquet, bowling, tennis, 18-hole putting course, river, fishing). *Background music*: none. *Location*: 2 miles from Chagford. *Smoking*: only allowed in covered seated area overlooking gardens. *Children*: no under-8s at dinner. *Dogs*: allowed in 3 bedrooms, not in public rooms. *Credit cards*: all major cards. *Prices*: B&B £155–£225 per person, D,B&B £250–£320, set meals £36–£85, full alc £95, special breaks, Christmas/New Year packages, 1-night bookings refused at weekends.

Hotels do not pay to be included in the *Guide*.

Mill End Hotel   *Tel* 01647-432282
Sandy Park   *Fax* 01647-433106
nr Chagford TQ13 8JN   *Email* info@millendhotel.com
                                        Website www.millendhotel.com

'Peace and quiet and a blanket of stars at night was what we wanted,
and what we got,' writes a visitor to this white-walled former corn mill
in the Dartmoor national park, by a bridge over the River Teign.
'Lovely accommodation in beautiful grounds, good hospitality.' The
owner, Keith Green, when present, 'keeps everyone happy, lighting
fires, delivering drinks, mowing the lawn'. The lounges, with log fires,
'have a homely feel rather than a smart country house look'. The
bedrooms vary from a large first-floor suite to standard ones that face
the road; there are three south-facing ground-floor rooms, each with
private patio. 'Our pretty, light room, in the extension, had large
bathroom, lots of hot water. No turn-down service or bathrobes. The
window alcove faced a rather scruffy back garden, but there is a nice
front garden on the river. You can walk upstream to Chagford and
downstream to a wooded gorge below Castle Drogo.' Non-residents
and walkers frequent the bar. The mill wheel, which 'revolves with
much splashing at the back of the building', is visible from the
restaurant. There's a new chef this year, Jay Allen, who uses local
ingredients for his modern dishes: we would welcome reports on his
cooking. (*Cynthia Ritchie, and others*)

Bedrooms: 14, 3 on ground floor. *Open*: all year. *Facilities*: 3 lounges, bar,
restaurant, 15-acre grounds (river, fishing, bathing), unsuitable for &.
Background music: none. *Location*: village on A382, 1½ miles NE of Chagford.
Smoking: not allowed. *Children*: all ages welcomed, no under-12s in restaurant
in evening. *Dogs*: not allowed in public rooms. *Credit cards*: MasterCard, Visa.
Prices: B&B £45–£110 per person, D,B&B £75–£140, set dinner £42, full alc
£60, Christmas/New Year packages, 1-night bookings sometimes refused. ***V***

Parford Well   *Tel* 01647-433353
Sandy Park   *Email* tim@parfordwell.co.uk
nr Chagford TQ13 8JW   *Website* www.parfordwell.co.uk

'Each time, something good gets better,' wrote one frequent visitor
to this smart little B&B in a village in the Dartmoor national park.
Owner Tim Daniel, once co-owner of *Number Sixteen* in South
Kensington, London (see Shortlist), lives in an adjoining cottage.
Named after the village well, and set in a walled garden, the house
overlooks meadows. It has a comfortable lounge with original

paintings, sculptures, fresh flowers, books and a fire. The 'immaculate' small bedrooms upstairs 'have everything you might expect'. One has its bathroom across the hall. Breakfast is 'varied, cooked to order, nothing packaged, all fresh local produce', and with blue-and-white china. It is normally served communally, round a farmhouse table, but guests wanting privacy may eat at a table for two across the hall, in a small room hung with luxurious drapes that once belonged to the late Queen Mother. There are good walks from the door, on the moor and in the wooded Teign valley. 'A hidden gem,' says a visitor in 2009. (*David Charlesworth*))

Bedrooms: 3. *Open*: all year except Christmas. *Facilities*: sitting room, 2 breakfast rooms, ⅓-acre garden, unsuitable for &. *Background music*: none. *Location*: in hamlet 1 mile N of Chagford. *Smoking*: not allowed. *Children*: not under 8. *Dogs*: not allowed. *Credit cards*: none. *Prices*: B&B £37.50–£55 per person, 1-night bookings sometimes refused weekends in season. *V*

CHARMOUTH Dorset   *See Shortlist*

CHELTENHAM Gloucestershire   *See Shortlist*

CHESTER Cheshire   Map 3:A4

Green Bough   *Tel* 01244-326241
60 Hoole Road   *Fax* 01244-326265
Chester CH2 3NL   *Email* luxury@greenbough.co.uk
                            Website www.greenbough.co.uk

Owned by Janice and Philip Martin, this 'well-run' conversion of two Victorian town houses stands a mile from Chester's historic centre. 'I would not hesitate to recommend it for a short stay,' says a visitor who came for a celebration weekend. Bedrooms vary. 'Ours, overlooking the rooftop garden, was spacious, meticulously clean, and with comfortable furniture including a king-size bed.' Earlier visitors had a 'large, light' deluxe room with 'antique brass bed, two armchairs, squashy sofa, luxurious fabrics'. A card offers a choice of pillows and type of bedding. Muzak plays all day in the public rooms. Traditional afternoon tea is served in the lounge. In the *Olive Tree* restaurant, 'the food was well cooked and presented; starters particularly good. Accompanying portions of vegetables with the main courses were rather small. Service by the all-English staff was excellent. Proper linen napkins and tablecloths, a treat, but the menu didn't change in two days.' Head chef Tim Seddon's modern European menu might include bouillabaisse; twice-roasted leg of Welsh salt marsh lamb. Breakfast has 'a wonderful buffet of fruit compotes, salads, yogurt and comb honey'. The rooftop garden has a water feature. Buses can be taken into the centre from the busy, tree-lined street. (*Neil Butler*)

Bedrooms: 15, 8 in lodge linked by 'feature bridge'. *Open*: all year except 25 Dec–2 Jan. *Facilities*: ramp, lounge, champagne bar, 2 dining rooms, banqueting room, theatre/conference room, rooftop garden, small front garden. *Background music*: classical/jazz in public rooms. *Location*: 1 mile from centre. *Smoking*: not allowed. *Children*: not under 14. *Dogs*: only guide dogs allowed. *Credit cards*: Amex, MasterCard, Visa. *Prices*: [2009] B&B £87.50–£172.50 per person, D,B&B £97.50–£195, full alc £55, special breaks.

See also Shortlist

CHESTERFIELD Derbyshire   Map 4:E4

Buckingham's Hotel

85–87 Newbold Road, Newbold
Chesterfield S41 7PU

Tel 01246-201041
Fax 01246-550059
Email info@buckinghams-table.com
Website www.buckinghams-table.com

In the city known for its crooked spire, Nick and Tina Buckingham have created an unusual hotel/restaurant. It is managed by their daughters, Vicci and Emma; son Will is co-chef. Mr Buckingham, once chef at *The Cavendish*, Baslow (*qv*), has created two restaurants. *The Restaurant with One Table* has no menu: ten guests (a group or unconnected visitors) eat together having indicated their likes and dislikes, and selected the level of meal (Bronze, Silver, Gold or Platinum). 'I will create a meal unique to you, making the most of the market that day.' *Clowns* conservatory restaurant, open all day, has separate tables; again menus are created after discussion; dishes might include lobster fish sausage with black noodles; chicken with wild mushroom sauce, mustard mashed potatoes. The lounge is papered in lemons and deeper yellows; white dado rails. The bedrooms vary in size: 'Ours was generously proportioned, thoughtfully furnished,' said a recent visitor. There are 'stunning afternoon teas', award-winning breakfasts and Wi-Fi. Children are welcomed. More reports, please.

Bedrooms: 10. *Open*: all year except Christmas/New Year. *Facilities*: stair lift, 2 lounges, bar, 2 restaurants, small conference facilities, courtyard, small Japanese garden. *Background music*: none. *Location*: 1 mile NW of centre. *Smoking*: not allowed. *Children*: all ages welcomed (under supervision). *Dogs*: only guide dogs allowed in public rooms. *Credit cards*: Amex (*5% surcharge*), MasterCard, Visa (*3% surcharge*). *Prices*: B&B £47.50–£70 per person, set meals £26.50–£130 (*plus 10% 'discretionary' service charge*), special breaks. *V*

CHETTLE Dorset   Map 2:E1

Castleman   *Tel* 01258-830096
Chettle   *Fax* 01258-830051
nr Blandford Forum   *Email* enquiry@castlemanhotel.co.uk
DT11 8DB   *Website* www.castlemanhotel.co.uk

'Unpretentious, charming and friendly', this Queen Anne dower house is run as an informal restaurant-with-rooms by Barbara Garnsworthy and Edward Bourke. His family has owned the estate, which includes the village of Cranbourne Chase, for over 150 years. She says: 'They are hands-on proprietors of several businesses, including the hotel and the village shop, which employ local people as much as possible.' The building, enlarged and remodelled in Victorian days, has a porticoed doorway, galleried hall, carved staircase, plasterwork ceilings, Jacobean fireplace, 'much dark wood'. 'Slightly faded gentility; haphazard decor.' 'Both lounges have deep armchairs and sofas, plenty of reading matter.' In the 'softly elegant', yellow-walled dining room, Mrs Garnsworthy and Richard Morris serve 'excellent' dinners, from a daily-changing menu: 'Halibut, king prawn, and potted crab were notable starters; medallions of venison, whole plaice, and duck breast were significant main courses. The puddings enchanted us.' 'Like being in one's own home. The comfort and charm of the place is delightfully understated.' 'Our room, with four-poster bed, was very comfortable.' There is free Wi-Fi throughout, and bedrooms have a digital TV/DVD-player. Breakfast is cooked to order: 'Faultless scrambled eggs.' 'Staff universally helpful (but don't expect hotel service).' (*BR, and others*)

Bedrooms: 8 (1 family). *Open*: Mar–Jan, except 25/26 Dec, 31 Dec, restaurant closed midday except Sun. *Facilities*: 2 drawing rooms, bar, restaurant, 1½-acre grounds (stables for visiting horses), riding, fishing, shooting, cycling nearby, only restaurant suitable for &. *Background music*: none. *Location*: village, 1 mile off A354 Salisbury–Blandford, hotel signposted. *Smoking*: not allowed. *Children*: all ages welcomed. *Dogs*: not allowed. *Credit cards*: MasterCard, Visa. *Prices*: [2009] B&B £40–£55, full alc £31.50, discount for 3 or more nights.

CHICHESTER West Sussex   *See Shortlist*

CHIDDINGFOLD Surrey   *See Shortlist*

CHILLATON Devon   Map 1:D3

Tor Cottage   *Tel* 01822-860248
Chillaton, nr Lifton   *Fax* 01822-860126
PL16 0JE   *Email* info@torcottage.co.uk
          Website www.torcottage.co.uk

'The hospitality is second to none' at Maureen Rowlatt's upmarket
B&B up a bridle path in a private and secluded mid-Devon valley.
The cottage stands in large wooded grounds with abundant flowers
and wildlife; badgers and deer enjoy the cover of the gorse on the
hillside beyond the garden. Visitors are welcomed with a trug
containing sparkling wine, home-made truffles, fresh fruit. Four
bedrooms, each with private terrace, are in the garden. 'We had Deco,
a museum of Art Deco, with a cabinet full of collectibles to which
many guests have contributed, and a splendid tiled fireplace.'
Laughing Waters has Shaker furniture, a gypsy caravan, a hammock
and a barbecue. All rooms have CD- and DVD-player. 'We enjoyed
lazy days by the glorious swimming pool', which is available for the
use of guests, 'even for those who want a midnight swim'. 'Wonderful'
breakfasts, ordered the evening before, are taken in the conservatory
or on a terrace. 'We asked for a modest portion of smoked salmon and
scrambled eggs. I hate to think what a full portion must do to your
figure.' A light supper tray can be ordered in advance (soup and pasty,
salads, etc). (*Louise Neesham, and others*)

Bedrooms: 5, 4 in garden. *Open*: mid-Jan–mid-Dec, do not arrive before 4 pm.
Facilities: sitting room, large conservatory, breakfast room, 28-acre grounds
(2-acre garden, heated swimming pool (13 by 6 metres), barbecue, stream,
bridleway, walks), river (fishing ½ mile), unsuitable for &. *Background music*: in
breakfast room. *Location*: ½ mile S of Chillaton. *Smoking*: not allowed. *Children*:
not under 14. *Dogs*: only guide dogs allowed. *Credit cards*: MasterCard, Visa.
Prices: B&B (min. 2 nights) £70–£98 per person, tray supper £24, autumn and
spring breaks, 1-night bookings sometimes refused.

All our inspections are paid for, and carried out, anonymously.

CHILLINGTON Devon   Map 1:D4

whitehouse   **NEW**   *Tel* 01584-580505
Chillington   *Email* frontofhouse@whitehousedevon.com
TQ7 2JX   *Website* www.whitehousedevon.com

'What a surprise to find, on the edge of a staid village in the South
Hams, such a funky place,' comment inspectors. Backed by a
'charming' garden, this Georgian house stands on the road to
Dartmouth. It has been given a modern look by three friends who met
while studying hospitality at Plymouth University: Tamara Costin,
Matthew Hall ('charming, relaxed') and Ally Wray (the chef) 'pamper
their guests in an unfussy way', creating 'a country house atmosphere
without pretension'. The lounges have wooden floors, log fires, large
leather chairs and sofas, books and games, 'soft muzak'. The
bedrooms, all different, are 'good fun'; lots of natural wood, big
handmade bed, plasma TV, DVD-player, Wi-Fi access. One room has
an 'Egg'-chair swing, another a rocking chair in its bathroom, also a
freestanding bath and separate shower. Quietest rooms face the
garden. In the conservatory restaurant, local and organic ingredients
are used in dishes like wild mushroom raviolini with thyme butter;
sea bass with fennel mayonnaise. 'Excellent steak; delicious crème
brûlée.' The Aga-cooked breakfast, served until '11-ish', has freshly
squeezed juices, spicy fruit compote; cooked dishes, which change
daily, include wild mushroom and potato frittata with scrambled egg.
'On a sunny day, we took tea in the garden; delicious warm scones
with excellent local jam and cream, served on white Royal Doulton
china.' Children are welcomed; so are dogs. (*Gill Thomas, and others*)

Bedrooms: 6. *Open*: all year. *Facilities*: bar, sitting room, study, dining room,
restaurant, meeting room, civil wedding licence, terrace, garden, unsuitable
for &. *Background music*: 'chill out' in public areas. *Location*: on edge of village,
4 miles E of Kingsbridge. *Smoking*: not allowed. *Children*: all ages welcomed.
Dogs: allowed, must be on a lead in public rooms. *Credit cards*: all major cards.
Prices: [2009] B&B £90–£115 per person, full alc £45, Christmas/New Year
packages, 1-night bookings refused Thurs–Sat.

CHIPPING CAMPDEN   *See Shortlist*
Gloucestershire

CHRISTCHURCH Dorset   *See Shortlist*

CLEE STANTON Shropshire   Map 3:C5

Timberstone   *Tel* 01584-823519
Clee Stanton   *Email* enquiry@timberstoneludlow.co.uk
Ludlow SY8 3EL   *Website* www.timberstoneludlow.co.uk

At their 'charming house', in a hamlet reached down narrow lanes in
the hills above Ludlow, Alex Read and Tracey Baylis (a 'delightful'
couple) follow a green agenda. An underground heat pump, solar
panels and wood burners provide much of the energy; organic and
Fairtrade produce is used where possible for meals. Two of the
bedrooms are in the old house, two in an extension connected by a
'lovely, light room' with comfy sofas and chairs, and a large dining
table; kilim rugs on oak floorboards. 'We loved our large bedroom in
the main house, with its original beams, old pine furniture, sofa,
window seat, attractive bathroom.' The bedrooms in the extension
have 'beautifully crafted oak fittings'; one has a freestanding bath in
the room. Breakfast, served communally, includes 'big jars of organic
cereals and muesli, fresh fruit, yogurt, home-made preserves. Lovely
chunky toast, tasty bacon and sausages, eggs from their own hens.'
The hostess, who once worked with the chef Shaun Hill in Ludlow,
cooks dinner by arrangement: 'Good country dishes, local pork and
lamb, delicious summer pudding'. Children and dogs are welcomed;
the owners have two young sons and two outdoor dogs.

Bedrooms: 4 (plus summer house retreat in summer). *Open*: all year except
25 Dec. *Facilities*: lounge/dining room, ½-acre garden, treatment room,
unsuitable for &. *Background music*: in lounge/dining room ('but guests may
turn it off'). *Location*: 5 miles NE of Ludlow. *Smoking*: not allowed. *Children*: all
ages welcomed. *Dogs*: allowed (£4). *Credit cards*: MasterCard, Visa. *Prices*: [2009]
B&B £44–£50 per person, full alc £31.

CLIPSHAM Rutland   Map 2:A3

Beech House & Olive Branch   *Tel* 01780-410355
Main Street   *Fax* 01780-410000
Clipsham LE15 7SH   *Email* beechhouse@theolivebranchpub.com
                    Website www.theolivebranchpub.com

In an attractive village near Stamford, Sean Hope (chef) and Ben
Jones, formerly of *Hambleton Hall*, Hambleton (*qv*), have a *Michelin*
star for their informal pub/restaurant with a rustic feel (old pews and
wooden tables on stone-flagged floors). The bedrooms are in a
Georgian house opposite, which faces rolling fields. It has a 'cheerful'

hall with a checked carpet and contemporary hunting prints. The colourful rooms combine antiques with a contemporary bathroom. Berry, on the ground floor, has a separate dressing room and a power shower over a double-ended bath; Double Cream has 'a stunning bathroom, claw-footed bath positioned so you get nice views while soaking'. Aubergine has an Art Deco theme. The only public area is the landing, which has a fridge, CDs, DVDs, magazines, books and local information. 'I use the best of local food, and cook it simply with minimum fuss,' says Sean Hope, who seeks his ingredients from as close to the pub as possible. 'Excellent' dishes might include brawn terrine with grape and apple chutney; roast halibut, fennel and mixed bean cassoulet. Breakfast, in the *Barn*, adjacent, has fresh juice, a buffet of fresh fruit, muesli, yogurt, smoothies, etc; cooked dishes include boiled eggs with soldiers, and kippers. (*Gordon Murray, MBG*)

Bedrooms: 6, 2 on ground floor, family room (also suitable for &) in annexe. *Open*: all year except 25/26 Dec, 1 Jan. *Facilities*: ramps, pub, dining room, breakfast room, small front garden. *Background music*: in pub. *Location*: in village 7 miles NW of Stamford. *Smoking*: not allowed. *Children*: all ages welcomed. *Dogs*: allowed in downstairs bedrooms and bar. *Credit cards*: MasterCard, Visa. *Prices*: [2009] B&B £50–£85 per person, D,B&B £72.50–£87.50, set meals £16.50–£25, full alc £39, seasonal breaks.

COLCHESTER Essex   *See Shortlist*

COLN ST ALDWYNS   Map 3:E6
Gloucestershire

The New Inn   NEW   *Tel* 01285-750651
nr Cirencester   *Fax* 01285-750657
GL7 5AN   *Email* info@thenewinnatcoln.co.uk
                 Website www.new-inn.co.uk

In a pretty and quiet Cotswold village, this 400-year-old inn is now owned by the small Hillbrooke group (see also *The Bath Arms*, Horningsham, *The Elephant*, Pangbourne, *qqv*). They have refurbished throughout, retaining many original features (flagstone and wooden floors, oak beams, etc). The manager is Stuart Hodges. The bar has wooden tables and chairs, black leather sofas (background pop music); the dining room, with brick red and cream walls, has three eating areas. The chef, Oliver Addis, serves a seasonally changing dinner menu with daily specials. 'These were the pick of an excellent meal,' said an inspector. 'A tasty ham hock terrine with pear chutney; the freshest pollack on a leek risotto; a wonderful apple and pear crumble with a tiny baked Alaska. The Italian house wines were especially good; service was well paced.' The bedrooms vary in size and style. 'Our spacious first-floor room had a bright red carpet and back wall, a black bedcover and furniture; proper hangers in the good cupboards. The well-fitted bathroom was down a short internal corridor.' Breakfast 'was a slight step down from dinner; a small buffet with a fruit salad; decent butter but weak coffee and sliced toast, no sign of last night's bread'. The four-mile walk along the river to Bibury is 'delightful'.

Bedrooms: 13, 1 on ground floor. *Open*: all year. *Facilities*: bar, restaurant, terrace, unsuitable for &. *Background music*: in public areas. *Location*: in village 8 miles E of Cirencester. *Smoking*: not allowed. *Children*: all ages welcomed. *Dogs*: allowed in 1 bedroom, not in restaurant. *Credit cards*: Diners, MasterCard, Visa. *Prices*: B&B £35–£75 per person, D,B&B £65–£105, full alc £40, special breaks on website, Christmas/New Year packages, 1-night bookings sometimes refused. *V*

COLWALL Worcestershire   Map 3:D5

Colwall Park Hotel
Colwall, nr Malvern
WR13 6QG

Tel 01684-540000
Fax 01684-540847
Email hotel@colwall.com
Website www.colwall.co.uk

'Excellent food and friendly service' were enjoyed this year at Iain and Sarah Nesbitt's 'traditional hotel with high standards'. It stands on a road in the middle of a pretty village below the western slopes of the Malvern hills. The Edwardian house 'has a warm and welcoming feeling, thanks to the caring and efficient staff'. It is 'far removed from the world of chain hotels'. Its *Lantern* bar, which serves real ales, is popular with locals; snacks can be taken here. In the oak-panelled *Seasons* restaurant, James Garth's modern cooking is again praised: 'He coped with my special medical diet without fuss; everything of high quality; pea and mint soup tasted like liquid velvet.' Local suppliers are named on a menu that might include warm goat's cheese fritters with pine nut and chive dressing; seared fillet of sea bream with buttered spinach and asparagus. The bedrooms vary in size: 'Everything we needed; reading lamps that worked; power points for the hairdryer within distance of the mirror; plenty of hot water.'

'Proper bedding, home-made biscuits.' Some visitors find the decor 'dated, flowered curtains, etc'. 'Breakfast lived up to the standard of dinner.' There is good walking nearby. (*Claire Heizler, Ian Malone, Alison Pitman*)

Bedrooms: 22. *Open*: all year. *Facilities*: ramp, 2 lounges (1 with TV), library, bar, restaurant, ballroom, business facilities, 1½-acre garden (croquet, *boules*), only public rooms suitable for &. *Background music*: blues in bar, jazz in restaurant. *Location*: halfway between Malvern and Ledbury on B4218, train Colwall. *Smoking*: not allowed. *Children*: all ages welcomed. *Dogs*: only guide dogs allowed. *Credit cards*: MasterCard, Visa. *Prices*: [2009] B&B £44.50–£79 per person, D,B&B £90, full alc £40, gourmet breaks, Christmas/New Year packages, 1-night bookings refused weekends. *V*

CONSTANTINE BAY Cornwall   Map 1:D2

Treglos Hotel   *Tel* 01841-520727
Constantine Bay   *Fax* 01841-521163
Padstow PL28 8JH   *Email* stay@tregloshotel.com
                                 Website www.tregloshotel.com

The old-fashioned extras (early-morning tea brought to the room, nocturnal shoe cleaning) are welcomed by the many regular visitors to Jim and Rose Barlow's traditional hotel. It stands in landscaped gardens with fine views over Constantine Bay's shining beach. 'Charming, beautifully trained staff, excellent food, comfortable bedrooms,' is a recent comment. 'They have the continuing ingredients of a good hotel, with further upgrades and nice added touches each year,' say other returning guests. Jonathan Summerfield is now the restaurant manager; men are asked to wear a jacket or tie at dinner. Chef Paul Becker serves a daily-changing four-course menu with plenty of choice, eg, local fish and shellfish bisque; grilled Dover sole with sea salt, lime and garden peas. Families are welcomed, but not children under seven in the restaurant in the evening (they have supper at 5.30 pm). Breakfasts are 'commendable': hot dishes cooked to order include smoked haddock and kippers. The garden has secluded sitting places and a children's play area. The Barlows also own Merlin Golf and Country Club (ten minutes' drive). The beach, with access to the Coast Path, is five minutes' walk away. (*JS-M, and others*)

Bedrooms: 42, some on ground floor, 2 suitable for &. *Open*: Mar–Nov. *Facilities*: ramps, 2 lounges (pianist twice weekly), bar, restaurant, children's den, snooker room, beauty treatments, indoor swimming pool (10 by 5 metres), whirlpool, treatment rooms, 3-acre grounds (croquet, badminton, children's play area), sandy beach 5 mins' walk. *Background music*: piano, Tues and Thurs nights in restaurant. *Location*: 3 miles W of Padstow. *Smoking*: not allowed. *Children*: no under-7s in restaurant after 6.30 pm. *Dogs*: not allowed in public rooms. *Credit cards*: MasterCard, Visa. *Prices*: [2009] B&B £61.95–£124.90 per person, D,B&B £76.65–£142.50, full alc £40, 4 nights for the price of 3 Mar, Apr, May, Oct, 1-night bookings sometimes refused.

COOKHAM DEAN Berkshire   *See Shortlist*

CORSE LAWN Gloucestershire   Map 3:D5

Corse Lawn House   *Tel* 01452-780771
Corse Lawn GL19 4LZ   *Fax* 01452-780840
                          Email enquiries@corselawn.com
                          Website www.corselawn.com

♥ *César award in 2005*

'A home from home, with personal attention, excellent food, polite and efficient staff, delightful situation and grounds.' 'Most efficiently run, most reasonably priced.' Praise again this year for this red brick Queen Anne Grade II listed building. Another comment: 'We had the last available room and even the rather noisy late-night party in a function room next door did not spoil our enjoyment.' The house, set back from the village green and a busy road near Tewkesbury, is fronted by a large pond. Its owner, Baba Hine, is 'charming and front-of-house'. Traditionally furnished bedrooms, 'like a comfortable spare room in someone's country house', have a fridge with fresh milk, a teapot, biscuits and fruit. 'Our ground-floor room was spacious.' Chef Andrew Poole is now in his twelfth year. His robust Franco-British cooking remains 'first class' in dishes like chicken liver parfait with apple chutney; slow-cooked belly of pork with grain mustard mash. A full vegetarian menu is always available. Smart casual dress is 'preferred' in the restaurant; T-shirt and jeans may be worn in the bistro. Visiting dogs are welcomed. (*Alan Langton, Joanna Russell, Jenny Dawe*)

Bedrooms: 19, 5 on ground floor. *Open*: all year except 24–26 Dec. *Facilities*: lounge, bar lounge, bistro/bar, restaurant, 2 conference/private dining rooms, civil wedding licence, 12-acre grounds (croquet, tennis, covered heated swimming pool, 20 by 10 metres). *Background music*: none. *Location*: 5 miles SW of Tewkesbury on B4211. *Smoking*: not allowed. *Children*: all ages welcomed. *Dogs*: allowed in bedrooms, drawing rooms. *Credit cards*: all major cards. *Prices*: B&B £80–£100 per person, D,B&B £100–£120, set dinner £21.50–£32.50, short breaks, New Year package. *V*

COVERACK Cornwall   Map 1:E2

The Bay Hotel   *Tel* 01326-280464
North Corner, Coverack   *Email* enquiries@thebayhotel.co.uk
nr Helston TR12 6TF   *Website* www.thebayhotel.co.uk

'If you want a simple, well-run small hotel in a charming place, you
can't do much better than this,' says a visitor who returned in 2009.
The white-painted building is in a 'delightfully unspoilt fishing village
with a welcoming local community' on the Lizard peninsula. Since
buying it in 2006, the 'delightful' House family have completely
refurbished in 'mellow coastal tones'. 'Friendly, bright and clean', it
has a 'lovely position looking straight out to sea'; the dining room and
conservatory restaurant have unobstructed views over Coverack Bay.
Gina House is the 'tireless' front-of-house; her husband, Ric, is the
chef. 'His daily-changing menu has plenty of delicious fresh fish', eg,
local sea bass with julienne of vegetables; whole Cornish sole with
anchovy butter. A Cornish cream tea can be taken on the garden
terrace. The bedrooms have full or partial views across the sea: 'We
loved watching the tide, ships, and shoals of mackerel.' 'Our room had
fresh furnishings and comfy seating.' The beach is nearby. 'There is
no through traffic in the village, guaranteeing peace,' we are told.
(*Mrs CR Austin, Mrs A Persson, Chris Hutt*)

Bedrooms: 13, some on ground floor. *Open*: Mar–Nov, Christmas/New Year.
Facilities: reception lounge, lounge, bar lounge, restaurant, 1-acre garden.
Background music: none. *Location*: village centre, 10 miles SE of Helston.
Smoking: not allowed. *Children*: not under 8. *Dogs*: not allowed in public rooms.
Credit cards: MasterCard, Visa. *Prices*: B&B £59–£95 per person, D,B&B
£69–£115, set dinner £25.95, full alc £33, special offers, Christmas/New Year
house parties. ***V***

COWAN BRIDGE Lancashire   Map 4: inset D2

Hipping Hall   *Tel* 015242-71187
Cowan Bridge   *Email* info@hippinghall.com
nr Kirkby Lonsdale LA6 2JJ   *Website* www.hippinghall.com

♻ *César award in 2008*

In a village near Kirkby Lonsdale, this 17th-century house (with other
stone buildings) stands amid mature trees in 'immaculate' gardens.
They have been turned by Andrew Wildsmith into a small
hotel/restaurant that is much admired. He is 'hard-working, always

present at mealtimes', say trusted correspondents on a return visit in 2009. 'The staff are without exception well trained and cheerful.' The bedrooms are individually decorated in contemporary style. 'Our room was given lightness and space by white walls, white rustic furniture and white carpet. Light poured in through the three windows. A well-sprung bed; smart bathroom.' A room which faces the back of the kitchen might get cooking smells. The lounge, in contrast to the bedrooms, has 'patterned wallpaper, large framed pictures, over-stuffed sofas and chairs, and a stone fireplace with open fire'. Michael Wilson is the new chef: the double-height 15th-century Great Hall, with tapestries and minstrels' gallery, is a 'remarkable setting for his accomplished cooking. Oxtail cannelloni, with a restrained addition of truffle oil, was followed by pink slices of lamb fillet and a ravioli of shoulder meat; artisan cheeses in good condition.' Breakfast 'is taken seriously: a selection of freshly squeezed juices, tea and coffee freshly made; eggs, bacon and sausages carefully sourced and cooked to order'. (*David and Kate Wooff; also Gordon Murray*)

Bedrooms: 9, 3 in cottage, 8 on ground floor. *Open*: all year except 3–8 Jan. *Facilities*: lounge, bar, restaurant, civil wedding licence. *Background music*: classical in restaurant, jazz in lounge and bar. *Location*: 2 miles SE of Kirkby Lonsdale, on A65. *Smoking*: not allowed. *Children*: no under-12s. *Dogs*: allowed in Room 7 only. *Credit cards*: Amex, MasterCard, Visa. *Prices*: [2009] B&B £77.50–£137.50 per person, D,B&B £107.50–£167.50, set dinner £49.50–£60, Christmas/New Year packages, 1-night bookings normally refused Sat.

CRANBROOK Kent   Map 2:E4

Cloth Hall Oast   *Tel/Fax* 01580-712220
Coursehorn Lane   *Email* clothhalloast@aol.com
Cranbrook TN17 3NR

'You feel like an honoured guest in an aristocratic home,' say American visitors to this 'decidedly upmarket' guest house. An 'impeccable' conversion of an oast house, barn and stables, it stands amid fields in the Kentish Weald. 'The grounds are spectacular, with a terrace, gardens and a heated swimming pool. Katherine Morgan is a gracious and sensitive hostess who welcomes you with sincerity and charm.' A Cordon Bleu cook, she presides at the communal dinner, which might include home-made pâté or soup; stuffed leg of lamb with apricots. 'Lovely meals in a wonderful setting.' No licence: bring your own wine. 'Fine china, home-made jams and good coffee made breakfast a pleasure.' The building is filled with Persian rugs, 'beautiful porcelain and silverware and delicate paintings'. 'The spaces are open, warm, lovely.' Sofas and armchairs face a deep carved stone fireplace in the elegant lounge where 'expanses of glass look over the garden'. Two bedrooms are in the oast house, the third is off a galleried landing; one room is triple-bedded; bathrooms are 'state-of-the-art'. Mrs Morgan is 'informative about local attractions' (Sissinghurst, Chartwell, Bodiam Castle, etc). (*William and Andrea Clarkson, and others*)

Bedrooms: 3. *Open*: all year except Christmas. *Facilities*: sitting room, dining room, 5-acre garden (croquet, fishpond, heated swimming pool, 5 by 10 metres), unsuitable for &. *Background music*: none. *Location*: 1 mile SE of Cranbrook. *Smoking*: not allowed. *Children*: by arrangement. *Dogs*: not allowed. *Credit cards*: none. *Prices*: [2009] B&B £45–£62.50 per person, evening meal £25, 1-night bookings sometimes refused Sat, bank holidays.

CROFT-ON-TEES Co. Durham   Map 4:C4

Clow Beck House   *Tel* 01325-721075
Monk End Farm   *Fax* 01325-720419
Croft-on-Tees   *Email* david@clowbeckhouse.co.uk
nr Darlington DL2 2SW   *Website* www.clowbeckhouse.co.uk

&& *César award in 2007*

The 'friendly welcome and high level of personalised service' make this a 'very special, superior place', say visitors this year to David and Heather Armstrong's small hotel. 'We felt thoroughly pampered.' In award-winning gardens in open countryside on the outskirts of Croft-on-Tees, the house has a touch of eccentricity (giant pigs in the flowerbeds, a miniature cricket game on the lawn, 'ornaments everywhere indoors and out'). One visitor found this 'amusing', another 'an assault for those of an aesthetic sensibility'. The large, comfortable bedrooms are in stone-built outbuildings around a landscaped garden. Some have their own small garden. One room has 'sparkly chandeliers and carved wooden ceiling roses'. Wi-Fi is free. The 'most attractive', large restaurant, on two levels, with beams, arched windows and tiled floor, leads to a terrace. David Armstrong serves 'good, large, rustic portions' of food, perhaps pork loin fried with apples, cider and honey; cod chunk roasted with crayfish, Mediterranean tomato sauce. 'Those with moderate appetite would do well to go for a starter and dessert, which will keep you going until it's time to tackle the huge breakfast.' Vegetarians are catered for. Children have their own menu. Difficult to find: you approach via an unmade road (follow the brown signs). (*Ann Morrison, and others*)

Bedrooms: 13, 12 in garden buildings, 1 suitable for &. *Open*: all year except Christmas, New Year, restaurant closed midday. *Facilities*: ramps, lounge, restaurant, small conference facilities, 2-acre grounds in 100-acre farm. *Background music*: classical in restaurant. *Location*: 3 miles SE of Darlington. *Smoking*: not allowed. *Children*: all ages welcomed. *Dogs*: not allowed. *Credit cards*: Amex, MasterCard, Visa. *Prices*: B&B £67.50–£85 per person, full alc £32–£37.

CROOKHAM Northumberland   Map 4:A3

The Coach House at Crookham
Crookham
Cornhill-on-Tweed
TD12 4TD

Tel 01890-820293
Fax 01890-820284
Email stay@coachhousecrookham.com
Website www.coachhousecrookham.com

'A well-run guest house rather than a posh hotel. The welcome is warm, and great consideration is given to guests.' Praise in 2009 from regular correspondents for Toby and Leona Rutter's listed 17th-century dower house. Some critics find the decor old-fashioned, but fans write of the 'high standards of housekeeping', the service by 'well-trained local women', the 'remarkable value'. Most of the bedrooms are in single-storey buildings linked by paved paths around a courtyard. Eight have facilities *en suite* (the others each have a private bathroom). The bigger rooms have large-screen TV and DVD/CD-player. Adjoining rooms are good for a family (children are welcomed, and so are dogs). A wheelchair-dependent visitor praised the facilities (three bedrooms are adapted for disabled guests). All rooms have a fridge with fresh milk and mineral water. The vaulted residents' lounge, with open fire, faces an orchard; drinks are taken here from a 'well-stocked' honesty bar, before dinner at 7.30 pm. 'Good home cooking: choice of starters but a set main course including wild salmon one evening. No repetition over nine days.' Vegans and vegetarians are catered for. Breakfast has a large selection of fruits, yogurt and cereals; kedgeree, haddock and kippers, full English. The house is set back from the road near Flodden Field: 'a lovely setting': good views of the Cheviot hills. (*Dr JMR Irving, Tony Betts, and others*)

Bedrooms: 11, 7 around courtyard, 3 suitable for &. *Open*: all year except Christmas/New Year. *Facilities*: lounge, 2 dining rooms, terrace, orchard. *Background music*: none. *Location*: On A697, 3 miles N of Milfield. *Smoking*: not allowed. *Children*: all ages welcomed. *Dogs*: not allowed in public rooms or main house bedrooms. *Credit cards*: MasterCard, Visa (*2% surcharge*). *Prices*: [2009] B&B £39–£64 per person, set dinner £22.95.

CROSBY RAVENSWORTH   *See Shortlist*
Cumbria

CROSTHWAITE Cumbria   Map 4: inset C2

 The Punch Bowl Inn   *Tel* 01539-568237
Crosthwaite, Lyth Valley   *Fax* 01539-568875
LA8 8HR   *Email* info@the-punchbowl.co.uk
Website www.the-punchbowl.co.uk

César award: Cumbrian inn of the year

The 'special touches', 'unfailingly helpful, good-humoured, mostly
local staff', and 'old-fashioned (in the best sense) ethos' are praised by
visitors in 2009 to this 300-year-old inn in a 'straggling village' in the
unspoilt Lyth valley. 'One of the nicest places we have stayed at for a
long time,' add inspectors. Owners Paul Spencer and Richard Rose
have sympathetically restored the 'charming' building, 'combining
history with contemporary taste. Muted colours; furniture eclectic,
well chosen. They could have created a boutique hotel; they've
chosen to fulfil a local need.' In the bar, with slate-flagged floor and
traditional furniture, 'no one need be embarrassed about muddy boots
or a wet collie'. The lounge has open fires, leather sofas. A free cream
tea is served between 3 and 6 pm. Of the 'lovely' bedrooms, even the
smaller ones 'have ample space'; 'splendid' bathrooms are well
equipped (though 'lighting made shaving difficult'). 'Our large,
stylishly designed room had striking wallpaper and unusual furniture.
It was very comfortable.' In the 'smartly set' restaurant (leather chairs,
polished floorboards), chef Jonny Watson serves a modern *carte*, eg,
cottage pie in miniature, pickled beetroot salad; sea bass, marinated
tomatoes. 'Wholesome and filling.' 'Satisfying local ingredients.'
'Terrific breakfast: freshly baked bread and croissants; local honey,
jam and cheese; Manx kippers; freshly squeezed orange juice.' The
village post office is operated from Reception. (*Josephine and Tony
Green, and others*)

Bedrooms: 9. *Open*: all year. *Facilities*: lounge, 2 bar rooms, restaurant, civil
wedding licence, 2 terraces, only restaurant suitable for &. *Background music*:
none. *Location*: 5 miles W of Kendal, via A591. *Smoking*: not allowed. *Children*:
all ages welcomed. *Dogs*: not allowed in bedrooms. *Credit cards*: Amex,
MasterCard, Visa. *Prices*: B&B £62.50–£155 per person, full alc £35,
Christmas/New Year packages.

CRUDWELL Wiltshire   Map 3:E5

The Rectory Hotel
Crudwell, nr Malmesbury
SN16 9EP

Tel 01666-577194
Fax 01666-577853
Email info@therectoryhotel.com
Website www.therectoryhotel.com

Given a contemporary feel by owners Julian Muggridge (antique dealer) and Jonathan Barry (ex-Hotel du Vin group), this 16th-century former rectory stands in stone-walled gardens in a village near Malmesbury. The manager is Lee Mitchell. All the bedrooms overlook the gardens: they have a 'miscellany of furniture', sprung mattress, Egyptian linen, deep bath and power shower. There are soft chairs and magazines in the large hall/sitting room. The high-ceilinged bar lounge (plastic side tables, glass-shelved alcoves) has a 'well-displayed' collection of ornamental glass. In the wood-panelled restaurant, which looks over a sunken Victorian pool, chef Peter Fairclough serves classic British dishes on a seasonal menu: perhaps confit of duck leg, hazelnut and chorizo sausage; seared sea bass, king prawns, linguini. Guests can also eat at *The Potting Shed*, a pub opposite under the same ownership ('it provides lollies for children and dog biscuits for visiting hounds'). At breakfast, the English platter was 'copious and tasty'. In summer, meals can be taken in the garden, and there is an outdoor swimming pool. (*NB, and others*)

Bedrooms: 12. *Open*: all year. *Facilities*: lounge, bar, dining room, civil wedding licence, 3-acre garden (heated 20-metre swimming pool), unsuitable for &. *Background music*: 'light jazz' in dining room, evenings. *Location*: 4 miles N of Malmesbury. *Smoking*: not allowed. *Children*: all ages welcomed. *Dogs*: not allowed in dining room. *Credit cards*: MasterCard, Visa. *Prices*: B&B £52.50–£107.50 per person, full alc £43, midweek breaks, Christmas/New Year packages, 1-night bookings refused bank holidays.

DARLINGTON Co. Durham   *See Shortlist*

Readers' contributions, written on the forms at the back of the book or sent by email, are the lifeblood of the *Good Hotel Guide*. Our readers play a crucial role by reporting on existing entries as well as recommending new discoveries. Everyone who writes to the *Guide* is a potential winner of the Report of the Year competition (page 10) in which a dozen correspondents each year win a copy of the *Guide* and an invitation to our annual launch party in October.

DARTMOUTH Devon   Map 1:D4

Knocklayd
Redoubt Hill, Kingswear
Dartmouth TQ6 0DA

Tel/Fax 01803-752873
Email stay@knocklayd.com
Website www.knocklayd.com

'Elegant and smart', Susan and Jonathan Cardale's 'delightful' small guest house stands at the highest point in Kingswear village, and has panoramic views over the estuary to Dartmouth. All the bedrooms have the views: they are 'stylish', well appointed; there are fluffy towels and abundant hot water in the bathrooms, and 'an excellent shower'. On cold days, guests can sit by an Edwardian fireplace in the sitting room. The Garden Room (with TV/DVD) has French windows on to the lawn, and a huge picture window facing the river. Mrs Cardale, a Cordon Bleu cook, will provide an evening meal by arrangement: 'We enjoyed a fishy feast.' Breakfast, taken at a table with white linen and silverware, has fruit, 'excellent' coffee, full English, smoked haddock or French toast with maple syrup. The Cardales' dog Molly, a bichon frise, is a retired hearing dog for the deaf. Visiting canines are welcomed; they are encouraged to sleep in the 'doggie dormitory' (the utility room) or by the Aga in the kitchen. (*S and PW*)

Bedrooms: 3. *Open*: all year, except Christmas/New Year. *Facilities*: lounge, garden room, dining room, garden, rock beach 300 yds, sailing nearby, unsuitable for &. *Background music*: none. *Location*: 5 mins' walk from ferry to Dartmouth. *Smoking*: not allowed. *Children*: all ages welcomed (under-12s in room with parents). *Dogs*: not allowed in bedrooms, except by negotiation. *Credit cards*: MasterCard, Visa. *Prices*: [2009] B&B £50–£60 per person, D,B&B £80–£90, set dinner £30, reductions for 3 nights out of season.

Nonsuch House
Church Hill, Kingswear
Dartmouth TQ6 0BX

Tel 01803-752829
Fax 01803-752357
Email enquiries@nonsuch-house.co.uk
Website www.nonsuch-house.co.uk

César award in 2000

'Kit and Penny Noble are perfect hosts, paying great attention to the needs of visitors without intruding on their privacy.' Praise this year for this upmarket guest house in an Edwardian villa high on the south-facing Kingswear side of the Dart estuary. Another comment: 'From the warm welcome with tea and home-made cakes in the conservatory to the excellent breakfast and perfect dinners, we don't think it could be better.' The bedrooms have 'everything you need'. 'Housekeeping is faultless; fittings are of the highest standard; the bed in our room was the most comfortable we have ever slept in. We had a bay window, with two armchairs offering views across the river to Dartmouth.' The public rooms have canary-yellow walls, royal-blue carpets, 'interesting ornaments and books'. Dinner is available four nights a week. 'Kit, a talented cook, discusses the menu beforehand'; his blackboard menu depends on local produce, eg, salad of Dartmouth crab; Blackawton lamb, pistachio and Parmesan crust. No liquor licence – bring your own wine ('a real cost-saver'). Breakfast has 'proper bread', fresh orange juice, home-made muesli. The house 'is on a steep hill, good exercise for the reasonably fit'. (*Bill Bennett, Christine Hastings*)

Bedrooms: 4. *Open*: all year, dining room closed midday, evening Tues/Wed/Sat. *Facilities*: ramps, lounge, dining room/conservatory, ¼-acre garden (sun terrace), rock beach 300 yds (sailing nearby), membership of local gym and spa. *Background music*: none. *Location*: 5 mins' walk from ferry to Dartmouth. *Smoking*: not allowed. *Children*: not under 10. *Dogs*: not allowed. *Credit cards*: MasterCard, Visa. *Prices*: [2009] B&B £52.50–£72.50 per person, set dinner £35, Christmas/New Year packages, special breaks, 1-night bookings sometimes refused weekends.

The New Angel   NEW

51 Victoria Road
Dartmouth
TQ6 9RT

Tel 01803-839425
Fax 01803-839505
Email info@thenewangel.co.uk
Website www.thenewangel.co.uk

In a 'delightful' setting facing the estuary, *The New Angel* restaurant (owned by Clive Jacobs and managed by Fabrice Hequet) has a *Michelin* star for John Burton-Race's 'superb' cooking. Six 'smart, modern' bedrooms (and a small lounge) have been added in a house on a side street a short walk away. Inspectors report: 'Our high-ceilinged room, Old Mill Creek, was bright by day, quiet at night; it had a big wardrobe (only three hangers), a sofa, two cane chairs, large TV, lots of lights. A noisy fridge held a half bottle of white wine and mineral water; red wine, nuts and shortbread were on the tea tray. A very fine shower room (with window).' A suite on the top floor, Mount Boone, is reached by a private staircase. The restaurant has an open kitchen adjacent to the downstairs dining area; upstairs is a 'more sedate' dining room, and there is a cocktail lounge on the top floor. 'Our meal was superb; mussel and saffron soup, guineafowl cottage pie; red mullet on butter beans and chorizo. The unpretentious atmosphere matched the quality of the food; service was prompt but not rushed. The set menu was good value.' Breakfast (in the restaurant) was 'leisurely, no buffet; nice fruit salad with honey and yogurt; a good cooked platter; no fresh orange juice, however'. A voucher is provided for one of the town's car parks.

Bedrooms: 6. *Open*: 1 Feb–31 Dec, restaurant closed Sun night/Mon except bank holidays. *Facilities*: lounge, dining room, unsuitable for ♿. *Background music*: none. *Location*: central. *Smoking*: not allowed. *Children*: all ages welcomed. *Dogs*: not allowed. *Credit cards*: Diners, MasterCard, Visa. *Prices*: [2009] B&B £37.50–£75 per person, D,B&B £79, set meals £24.50–£29.50 (*12½ per cent service charge added*), Christmas/New Year packages.

See also Shortlist

DEDHAM Essex   Map 2:C5

Dedham Hall & Fountain House	*Tel* 01206-323027
Restaurant NEW	*Fax* 01206-323293
Brook Street, Dedham	*Email* sarton@dedhamhall.demon.co.uk
nr Colchester CO7 6AD	*Website* www.dedhamhall.demon.co.uk

On the edge of this pretty village in Constable country, this cluster of buildings stands down a bumpy lane by a pond. A 15th-century cottage, an 18th-century house and an old Dutch barn, now a studio, constitute this informal guest house/restaurant/art school run by its owners, Jim and Wendy Sarton. 'I enjoyed my stay: a good dinner and a fine bedroom,' says a visitor this year, restoring it to a full *Guide* entry after a period without reports. Another guest liked the 'family feel'. In the 'cosy' lounges are log fires, oak beams and art books; walls are crammed with paintings by local artists (and guests). Artists attending the painting courses (February to November) are accommodated in large rooms around the barn. Other guests stay in bedrooms in the house (no keys given). Tables should be reserved when booking for the restaurant which is popular locally (typical dishes: mushrooms stuffed with bacon and cheese; peppered sirloin steak, herb and garlic butter). The Vale of Dedham is an area of outstanding beauty: Flatford Mill is a two-mile walk away, on a footpath by the River Stour. (*Colin W McKerrow, and others*)

Bedrooms: 20, 16 in annexe, some on ground floor. *Open*: all year except Christmas/New Year, restaurant closed Sun/Mon. *Facilities*: ramps, 2 lounges,

2 bars, dining room, restaurant, studio, 6-acre grounds (pond, gardens). *Background music*: none. *Location*: end of High Street. *Smoking*: not allowed. *Children*: all ages welcomed. *Dogs*: not allowed. *Credit cards*: MasterCard, Visa. *Prices*: B&B £55–£60 per person, D,B&B £85–£90, set dinner £32.50, painting holidays (Feb–Nov).

The Sun Inn

High Street, Dedham
nr Colchester CO7 6DF

Tel 01206-323351
Email office@thesuninndedham.com
Website www.thesuninndedham.com

Discreetly restored by owner Piers Baker, this 15th-century yellow-painted inn stands opposite Dedham's church. In the bar (also painted yellow) are old oak floorboards and beams, log fires, window seats, sofas, club chairs, board games, books, lots of local information. The drawing room, with its large fireplace, is in country-house style ('much preferable to the favoured minimalist style'). Jessica Savill is now the manager; the young staff were praised by readers: 'They insisted on carrying upstairs our numerous pieces of luggage.' In the bedrooms, furniture is a mix of antique and repro; beds are large, with 'divinely comfortable mattress'; there are neutral fabrics, 'great' showers, and quirky touches (old packing cases for bedside tables). The chef, Ugo Simonelli, provides 'inventive' dishes with an Italian influence, eg, carpaccio di manzo; arrosto pollo (roasted farmyard chicken, panzanella tomato and bread salad). Breakfast has orange juice ('squeezed by our own hands'); hand-cut wholemeal and soda bread toast; fresh and dried fruit from Victoria's Plums (*The Sun*'s own deli); and a choice of dishes including farmyard egg frittate. Children are welcomed (special menus; games, books; slide, swing, etc, in the large walled garden). There is a covered terrace with heaters. Background music plays all day, but at night 'only church bells might disturb the peace'. (*KA*)

Bedrooms: 5. *Open*: all year except 25/26 Dec. *Facilities*: lounge, bar, dining room, ½-acre garden (covered terrace, children's play area), unsuitable for &. *Background music*: jazz/Latin/blues throughout. *Location*: central, 5 miles NE of Colchester. *Smoking*: not allowed. *Children*: all ages welcomed. *Dogs*: not allowed in bedrooms. *Credit cards*: all major cards. *Prices*: B&B £40–£75 per person, D,B&B £50–£100, set meals £10.50–£13.50, full alc £25, see website for special offers.

See also Shortlist

Prices may change – always check them when booking.

DERBY Derbyshire   *See Shortlist*

DODDISCOMBSLEIGH Devon   *See Shortlist*

DONCASTER South Yorkshire   *See Shortlist*

DORCHESTER Dorset   *See Shortlist*

DOVER Kent   *See Shortlist*

DULVERTON Somerset   *See Shortlist*

DURHAM   *See Shortlist*

EAST GRINSTEAD West Sussex   Map 2:D4

Gravetye Manor   *Tel* 01342-810567
Vowels Lane   *Fax* 01342-810080
East Grinstead RH19 4LJ   *Email* info@gravetyemanor.co.uk
                              Website www.gravetyemanor.co.uk

'A lovely place to stay.' This creeper-clad Elizabethan manor house (Relais & Châteaux) stands amid woodland in grounds (open only to hotel guests) designed by William Robinson, pioneer of the English natural garden. It is owned and run by Andrew Russell (manager) and Mark Raffan (head chef), who worked for many years with the founders, Peter and Sue Herbert. 'The decor and furnishings in the public rooms and bedrooms are high grade, but a little stuck in a time warp: none the worse for that,' say visitors in 2009. Mr Russell tells us he has updated five bedrooms, but '*Gravetye* is never going to be modern or trendy; most important, we do not intend to become a spa hotel'. Another guest this year praised the 'warmth of welcome, charming staff, and pleasing attention to detail'. Bedrooms (the best are large) have fruit, magazines and books; 'large and comfy bed'. The quality of the cooking in the oak-panelled restaurant (with open fire and patterned carpet) is 'extremely high'. The style is eclectic modern English, eg, gratin of lemon sole and lobster; slow-braised cheek of veal with a herb crust. 'Expensive, but achievable when you can get a special rate.' (*Tony and Marlene Hall, Janine Roebuck*)

Bedrooms: 18. *Open*: all year. *Facilities*: 3 lounges, bar, restaurant, private dining room, civil wedding licence, 35-acre grounds (gardens, croquet, trout lake, fishing), only restaurant suitable for &. *Background music*: none. *Location*: 5 miles SW of East Grinstead. *Smoking*: not allowed. *Children*: not under 7. *Dogs*: not allowed. *Credit cards*: Amex, MasterCard, Visa. *Prices*: [2009] room £110–£345, breakfast £13–£18, set dinner £37, full alc £75 (*12½% discretionary service charge on food and drink*), off-season rates, New Year package, special breaks, 1-night bookings refused Sat. *V*

EAST LAVANT West Sussex   Map 2:E3

The Royal Oak   *Tel* 01243-527434
Pook Lane   *Email* rooms@royaloakeastlavant.co.uk
East Lavant PO18 0AX   *Website* www.royaloakeastlavant.co.uk

'We really enjoyed our few days,' says a visitor to this listed Georgian flint-stone inn in an attractive village near the South Downs, just north of Chichester. 'All the staff were helpful: twice, when we came back after the theatre when dinner was over, they were happy to give us a snack (a lavish cheeseboard).' The owner is Charles Ullmann, his manager is Karen Wright. The bedrooms, in a converted barn and cottage, combine old features (inglenook fireplace, beams, flagstones) with contemporary furniture, modern comforts ('excellent bathroom with under-floor heating and strong shower') and 'nice touches': flowers, flat-screen TV, CD/DVD-player, discs and films. 'Very comfortable bed.' Some rooms are 'small, with a small bathroom'. The chef, Simon Haynes, serves a modern menu which might include red onion and goat's cheese tarte Tatin with pesto; seared fillet of sea bass with Selsey crab. One guest thought that though 'staff were enthusiastic, there seemed to be a lack of hands-on management'. Breakfast has 'plenty of fresh fruit'; 'cooked dishes well up to standard'. Children are warmly welcomed (cots, high chairs provided). Alfresco meals are served on the front terrace, which has country views; a small garden is at the side. (*Sara Price, Richard Creed, and others*)

Bedrooms: 6, 3 in adjacent barn and cottage, 2 self-catering cottages nearby. *Open*: all year except nights of 25 Dec, 1 Jan. *Facilities*: bar/restaurant, terrace (outside meals), small garden, unsuitable for &. *Background music*: jazz in restaurant. *Location*: 2 miles N of Chichester. *Smoking*: not allowed. *Children*: all ages welcomed. *Dogs*: allowed in bar area only. *Credit cards*: all major cards. *Prices*: [2009] B&B £47.50–£80, full alc £33, winter breaks, Christmas/New Year packages, 1-night bookings refused weekends.

EASTBOURNE East Sussex   *See Shortlist*

EMSWORTH Hampshire   Map 2:E3

Restaurant 36 on the Quay
47 South Street
Emsworth PO10 7EG

Tel 01243-375592
Email 36@onthequay.plus.com
Website www.36onthequay.co.uk

With views over the harbour of a pretty fishing village, this 17th-century building is now a smart restaurant-with-rooms run by owners Ramon and Karen Farthing. He is the *Michelin*-starred chef, she is front-of-house. Five bedrooms are above the restaurant, including a new family suite which was due to open as the *Guide* went to press. The biggest room, Vanilla, which overlooks the harbour, has a separate sitting area with a large sofa. Nutmeg, though small, 'is tastefully decorated' and faces the quay and harbour. Clove faces the Emsworth Sailing Club boatyard. Cinnamon has a sitting area looking onto South Street's old fishermen's cottages, and a bathroom with walk-in shower. Cardamom Cottage, across the road, has a double bedroom, lounge (with sofa bed) and kitchen. There is a courtyard where aperitifs and after-dinner coffee are served in fine weather. In the restaurant, decorated in pastel colours, fish is a speciality. Modern English/French dishes include monkfish marinated in a spicy lemon marinade; sea bass poached in light thyme stock on fondant potato with asparagus spears. A 'superb' continental breakfast is served in the rooms or the lounge area on the landing. More reports, please.

Bedrooms: 6, 1 in cottage (with lounge) across road (can be let weekly). *Open*: all year except 3 weeks Jan, 1 week May, 1 week Oct, restaurant closed Sun/Mon. *Facilities*: lounge area, bar area, restaurant, terrace, only restaurant suitable for &. *Background music*: none. *Location*: on harbour. *Smoking*: not allowed. *Children*: all ages welcomed. *Dogs*: only allowed in cottage, by arrangement. *Credit cards*: Diners, MasterCard, Visa. *Prices*: [2009] B&B £47.50–£100 per person, set dinner £46.95, full alc £63.

Report forms (Freepost in UK) are at the end of the *Guide*.

ERMINGTON Devon   Map 1:D4

Plantation House   *Tel* 01548-831100
Totnes Road   *Email* info@plantationhousehotel.co.uk
Ermington, nr Plymouth   *Website* www.plantationhousehotel.co.uk
PL21 9NS

'Everything is delivered with effortless panache' at this small hotel, a cream-painted former rectory (Grade II listed) on the sunny side of the River Erme valley. The welcome from the 'enthusiastic' owners, Richard and Magdalena Hendey, 'is warm; they deserve continuing success', says a visitor in 2009. They have renovated much of the house; the hall, stairs and landings have been renewed; all but two bedrooms ('which we offer to budget-conscious guests') have been updated. 'The decor is light and modern: Matisse prints on pale pastel walls, beautiful fresh flowers, striking chandeliers and artefacts,' wrote inspectors. 'Our spacious bedroom overlooked the walled garden. Furnished with flair, it had TV, plants, fresh fruit, chocolates, a well-appointed, if slightly dark, bathroom. The lounge is pleasing, and has a well-stocked bar.' Mr Hendey, 'a talented chef', serves a fixed-price five-course dinner menu: 'Delicious scallops; well-flavoured venison stew; desserts as good as the rest. Service was attentive and effective.' Midweek visitors can choose from a *carte*: 'He provided a simple two-course meal, perfectly cooked and presented.' Breakfast has a buffet with squeezed juices, 'excellent fruit salad; delicious smoked haddock; well-judged scrambled eggs with smoked salmon'. (*Alan W Moulds, and others*)

Bedrooms: 9. *Open*: all year, restaurant closed midday, generally closed Sun. *Facilities*: lounge/bar, 2 dining rooms, terrace, garden, unsuitable for ♿. *Background music*: if required. *Location*: 10 miles E of Plymouth. *Smoking*: not allowed. *Children*: 'well-behaved' children welcomed. *Dogs*: allowed in 1 bedroom, not in public rooms. *Credit cards*: Amex, MasterCard, Visa. *Prices*: B&B £55–£75 per person, set dinner £36, New Year package, 1-night bookings occasionally refused.

How to contact the *Guide*
By mail: From anywhere in the UK, write to Freepost PAM 2931, London W11 4BR (no stamp is needed)
From outside the UK: *Good Hotel Guide*, 50 Addison Avenue, London W11 4QP, England
By telephone or fax: 020-7602 4182
By email: editor@goodhotelguide.com
Via our website: www.goodhotelguide.com

EVERSHOT Dorset   Map 1:C6

Summer Lodge   *Tel* 01935-482000
9 Fore Street   *Fax* 01935-482040
Evershot DT2 0JR   *Email* summer@relaischateaux.com
                          Website www.summerlodgehotel.com

'An exceptional hotel, well maintained throughout, with very nice
gardens and comfortable bedrooms.' 'Well up to standard (high).'
More praise this year for this luxury hotel (Relais & Châteaux)
managed by Charles Lötter for the Red Carnation group. 'The service
was outstanding from all staff; they were friendly and helpful.' In large
grounds in a pretty Dorset village, the house was built as a retreat for
the earls of Ilchester; it was enlarged in 1893 by Thomas Hardy. One
of his original rooms is now a suite with an open fireplace, rich fabrics
and antiques. The chef, Steven Titman, serves modern British dishes
with French influences, eg, trio of foie gras with Yorkshire rhubarb,
warm brioche; roast loin of Dorset lamb, braised shoulder shepherd's
pie, savoy cabbage. One visitor encountered 'occasional confusion' in
the elegant dining room, from a staff member with little English. The
spa has a 'very good' swimming pool, aromatherapy and reflexology.
'Not cheap but good value,' and 'Will return when feeling wealthier,'
are two comments. Red Carnation also owns the less expensive
Acorn Inn in the village, and the little local shop. (*Michael and Eithne
Dandy, EJT Palmer*)

Bedrooms: 24, 9 in coach house and courtyard house, 4 in lane, 1 on ground
floor suitable for &. *Open*: all year. *Facilities*: ramps, drawing room, lounge/bar,
restaurant, indoor swimming pool (11 by 6 metres), civil wedding licence,
4-acre grounds (garden, croquet, tennis). *Background music*: 'contemporary' in
lounge/bar. *Location*: 10 miles NW of Dorchester, train Yeovil/Dorchester
(they will fetch). *Smoking*: allowed in 1 bedroom. *Children*: all ages welcomed.
Dogs: allowed in some bedrooms, some public rooms. *Credit cards*: all major
cards. *Prices*: [2009] B&B £112.50–£257.50 per person, D,B&B £172.50–
£317.50, full alc £75, Christmas/New Year packages, 1-night bookings refused
weekends July–Oct.

Check the Hotelfinder section (page 11) if you are looking
for a hotel for a special occasion, perhaps a memorable meal
(see Gourmet and Gastropubs); a sporting weekend (see
Golf, Fishing, Walking); somewhere that will welcome your
children – or your dog. Our editors have selected ten hotels
in each of these categories (and many more) to help you
make your choice.

EVESHAM Worcestershire   Map 3:D6

The Evesham Hotel
Cooper's Lane, off Waterside
Evesham
WR11 1DA

Tel 01386-765566
Fax 01386-765443
Freephone 0800-716969 (reservations only)
Email reception@eveshamhotel.com
Website www.eveshamhotel.com

♕ *César award in 1990*

John and Sue Jenkinson have run their family-friendly, quirky,
informal hotel since 1975. He is a man of strong opinions: 'Is there
background music?' we asked. 'Only over my dead body,' he replied.
A wearer of loud ties, he is proud of the hotel's eccentricity, reflected
in 'smile-enforcing loos' and a wine list that has no French or German
bottles. A 'caring owner', he is supported by senior staff whose average
length of service is 25 years. A visitor who has stayed many times
confirms that 'standards are as good as ever'. Another wrote of 'a
feeling of relaxation and humour'. The themed bedrooms, designed
by Mrs Jenkinson, include Alice in Wonderland, a family suite among
the beams; Apologies to Gaudí, dedicated to the equally quirky
architect. All rooms have a silent fridge with soft drinks, milk and a
half bottle of wine; bathroom fans are quiet; rooms in the extension
have double doors to reduce corridor noise. Children are charged
according to age and amount eaten. They can enjoy the indoor
swimming pool ('none of this serious spa stuff here') and play areas in
the grounds. They have a jokey high tea menu ('a junior *à la carte*').
For adults, chef Adam Talbot offers a wide choice of international
dishes, eg, Thai chicken soup; rosemary-braised lamb shank. A vegetarian menu is available. (*T Lee, Frank G Millen*)

Bedrooms: 40, 11 on ground floor, 2 suitable for &. *Open*: all year except 25/26
Dec. *Facilities*: 2 lounges, bar, restaurant, private dining room, indoor swimming
pool (5 by 12 metres), 2½-acre grounds (croquet, putting, swings, trampoline).
Background music: none. *Location*: 5 mins' walk from centre, across river.
Smoking: allowed in 2 bedrooms. *Children*: all ages welcomed. *Dogs*: only guide
dogs allowed in public rooms. *Credit cards*: all major cards. *Prices*: [2009] B&B
£61.50–£87 per person, full alc £37.50, New Year package, 1-night bookings
refused Sat, for Cheltenham Gold Cup, New Year.

EXETER Devon   *See Shortlist*

New reports help us keep the *Guide* up to date.

EXFORD Somerset   Map 1:B4

The Crown   *Tel* 01643-831554
Exford   *Fax* 01643-831665
Exmoor National Park   *Email* info@crownhotelexmoor.co.uk
TA24 7PP   *Website* www.crownhotelexmoor.co.uk

'Everything a small, privately owned country hotel should be,' say
American visitors in 2009. A *Guide* inspector agreed: 'A real winner: an
unpretentious inn with a remarkably sophisticated restaurant.' The
owners, Chris Kirkbride and Sara and Dan Whittaker, have upgraded
their much-extended 17th-century coaching inn, on the green of a
picturesque village in Exmoor national park. 'We were warmly
greeted; luggage carried to our large, double-aspect second-floor room,
which had two armchairs, lots of storage; good shower over the bath.'
The L-shaped lounge has plenty of armchairs and settees: 'Bland
decor enlivened by large framed prints; leading off it is a pleasant
cocktail bar.' The attractive restaurant (dark red walls, full-length
cream curtains) has 'eye-catching' table settings, crisp white cloths,
black napkins and glass tableware. The 'seriously good' cooking of
chef Darren Edwards 'matches the promise of his enticing modern
menu. Highlights were a duo of tempura langoustines with crushed
basil, minted peas and lemon olive oil; halibut on garlic violet potatoes
in a mussel broth; blackcurrant soufflé. Good wines by the glass.'
There are blackboard specials on a bar menu; also curry nights. A
stream runs through the large grounds. The original stabling is
available for visitors on horseback ('it does happen in this hunting
community'). (*Steven M Schick Jr, and others*)

Bedrooms: 17. *Open*: all year. *Facilities*: lounge, cocktail bar, public bar,
restaurant, meeting room, 3½-acre grounds (trout stream, water garden, terrace
garden), stabling for visiting horses, unsuitable for &. *Background music*: in bar
and restaurant. *Location*: on village green. *Smoking*: not allowed. *Children*: all
ages welcomed. *Dogs*: not allowed in restaurant. *Credit cards*: MasterCard, Visa.
Prices: [2009] B&B £45–£70 per person, D,B&B £62.50–£95, full alc £40, special
breaks, Christmas/New Year packages, 1-night bookings refused holiday
weekends.

We say 'Unsuitable for &' when a hotel tells us that it cannot
accommodate wheelchair-users. We do not have the resources
to inspect such facilities or to assess the even more complicated
matter of facilities for the partially disabled. We suggest that
you discuss such details with the hotel.

FALMOUTH Cornwall   Map 1:E2

The Rosemary
22 Gyllyngvase Terrace
Falmouth TR11 4DL

Tel 01326-314669
Email therosemary@tiscali.co.uk
Website www.therosemary.co.uk

On a quiet residential road in this Cornish port, this traditional B&B
is run by 'hard-working' owners Suzanne and Geoff Warring. 'Like a
family home where we were invited guests,' wrote one of many fans.
'Our room was large, clean and very attractive,' said others. 'Squashy
sofa and slimline TV.' The white-walled, grey-roofed Victorian house
is a short walk from the town centre, and close to the South West
Coast Path. It contains a collection of paintings by contemporary
Cornish artists; there is Wi-Fi access throughout, a small bar, and a
pretty south-facing garden with a sun deck. The 'very comfortable
lounge' looks over the garden to the sea. There are good sea views too
from the room where the Warrings serve 'wonderful breakfasts using
local produce'. They 'have extensive local knowledge' and advise on
excursions, eateries, etc. 'Excellent value for money.' (*Harold Wood
and Neil Lucas, Pauline Foster, and others*)

Bedrooms: 10 (two 2-bedroom suites). *Open*: Feb–Oct. *Facilities*: lounge, bar,
dining room, small garden (sun deck), unsuitable for &. *Background music*:
none. *Location*: 10 mins' walk from centre. *Smoking*: not allowed. *Children*:
all ages welcomed. *Dogs*: not allowed in dining room. *Credit cards*:
MasterCard, Visa. *Prices*: [2009] B&B £34–£45 per person, 1-night bookings
sometimes refused.

See also Shortlist

FAVERSHAM Kent   Map 2:D5

Read's
Macknade Manor
Canterbury Road
Faversham ME13 8XE

Tel 01795-535344
Fax 01795-591200
Email enquiries@reads.com
Website www.reads.com

♥ *César award in 2005*

In immaculate gardens near this old market town, this *Michelin*-starred
restaurant-with-rooms 'fully lives up to its reputation', say guests this
year. An earlier visitor arrived 'weary, at a busy lunchtime, to the

warmest welcome; someone unpacked our car and we were immediately given restorative tea with shortbread'. The 'spacious, comfortable, well-equipped' bedrooms in the handsome Georgian building have rich fabrics, a sherry decanter. They are 'complemented by first-class cooking'. Chef/*patron* David Pitchford sources local produce (fish from Whitstable, vegetables and herbs from the manor's walled garden) for his seasonal menus, eg, smoked eel on a salad of new potatoes and chives; roasted Kentish lamb, buttered black cabbage with celeriac purée. His wife, Rona, leads the 'friendly, disarming' staff; service is 'attentive, unfussy'. Vegetarian options are offered verbally; the wine list has a 'reasonably priced' best buys section. Guests have access, on an honesty basis, to the Pantry, which has a well-stocked fridge: this 'promotes the feeling of being in someone's home despite the distinctly professional approach to running the hotel. All the staff inconspicuously ensured our comfort.' Breakfast has croissants, 'delicious' home-made jams; 'excellent' cooked dishes. Don't miss the farm shop behind the manor. (*Bryan and Mary Blaxall, EB*)

Bedrooms: 6. *Open*: all year except 25/26 Dec, 1 Jan, restaurant closed Sun/Mon. *Facilities*: sitting room/bar, restaurant, private dining room, civil wedding licence, 3-acre garden (terrace, outdoor dining), only restaurant suitable for &. *Location*: ½ mile SE of Faversham. *Smoking*: not allowed. *Children*: all ages welcomed. *Dogs*: not allowed. *Credit cards*: all major cards. *Rates*: B&B £82.50–£185 per person, D,B&B £130–£230, set dinner £52.

FLEET Dorset   Map 1:D6

Moonfleet Manor   *Tel* 01305-786948
Fleet Road, Fleet   *Fax* 01305-774395
nr Weymouth DT3 4ED   *Email* info@moonfleetmanorhotel.co.uk
                  Website www.moonfleetmanorhotel.co.uk

A visitor returning this year found this sprawling Georgian manor house 'still excellent'. Managed by Neil Carter for von Essen's Luxury Family Hotels group, it stands in large grounds above the Fleet lagoon and Chesil Beach. Activities for children include computer games, ping-pong, indoor tennis, two indoor swimming pools (refurbished this year), a supervised nursery, the Four Bears' Den (where small children can be left). In the grounds are play areas, swings, slide, sandpit. Adults can retreat to the spa, which offers various treatments. Children sharing their parents' room stay free of charge; cots and Z-beds are available. They have high tea at 5 pm (fish pie; bangers and mash). The large public rooms have a colonial feel. The long-serving chef, Tony Smith, cooks British/French dishes, eg, smooth duck liver parfait, apple and shallot chutney; crayfish and leek lasagne with king prawns. Spicer, the hotel's dog, died in April 2009; a descendant, Snoopy, has taken his place. Family pets are welcomed. Strong currents rule out sea bathing, but there are good walks along the Coast Path, and the lagoon has a 'fantastic variety of birdlife'. (*Dr Margaret West*)

Bedrooms: 36, 6 in 2 annexes, 3 on ground floor. *Open*: all year. *Facilities*: lift, 2 lounges with dispense bar, restaurant, meeting room, games room/nursery, disco, indoor 10-metre swimming pool, sauna, solarium, sunbed, aroma therapy, snooker, 5-acre grounds (children's play areas, tennis, bowls, squash, badminton), riding, golf, sailing, windsurfing nearby. *Background music*: none. *Location*: 7 miles W of Weymouth. *Smoking*: not allowed. *Children*: all ages welcomed. *Dogs*: not allowed in restaurant. *Credit cards*: all major cards. *Prices*: [2009] B&B £80–£205 per person, D,B&B £87.50–£232.50, special offers, Christmas/New Year packages, 1-night bookings refused weekends, bank holidays.

FLETCHING East Sussex   Map 2:E4

The Griffin Inn
Fletching, nr Uckfield
TN22 3SS

Tel 01825-722890
Fax 01825-722810
Email info@thegriffininn.co.uk
Website www.thegriffininn.co.uk

'A pub, but also a civilised place to spend a night or two.' Owned by the Pullan family, this 16th-century Grade II listed coaching inn, with its beams, horse brasses and 'homely bedrooms', is in a pretty village overlooking the Ouse valley. 'The staff are friendly, helpful, if sometimes a little disorganised, which probably comes from being busy.' Meals are served in the panelled bar (with its own menu) and the 'very good' restaurant. Chef Andrew Billings uses local produce (fresh fish from Rye) for his daily-changing menu, which might include grilled rock oysters, Cashel Blue cheese; monkfish, butter beans, pancetta. 'Excellent' sprats were enjoyed this year. Five of the bedrooms are in *Griffin House* next door: 'Ours was spacious and comfortable; bathroom done out in modern retro style (plentiful hot water).' Four 'quirky' rooms are in the main building; others (with four-poster) in a renovated coach house where 'best use possible has been made of the space available'. The Pullans have improved lighting in all rooms this year. The wine list is 'extensive and interesting'. Children are welcomed: there is a large rear garden (with a 'stunning outlook'), and a 'healthy' children's menu. Four golf courses are nearby, and *The Griffin* has its own cricket team. (*Richard and Catriona Smith, and others*)

Bedrooms: 13, 4 in coach house, 5 in *Griffin House* next door, 4 on ground floor. *Open*: all year except 25 Dec, hotel closed 24 Dec, restaurant closed Sun evening, 1 Jan evening. *Facilities*: ramps, 2 lounge bars (1 with TV), restaurant, occasional live music Sun lunch, terrace (1-acre garden). *Background music*: none. *Location*: 3 miles NW of Uckfield. *Smoking*: not allowed. *Children*: all ages welcomed. *Dogs*: allowed in bar only. *Credit cards*: all major cards. *Prices*: [2009] B&B £42.50–£80 per person, set Sun lunch £30, full alc £32–£40, inclusive breaks, 1-night bookings refused bank holidays. *V* (not Sat)

FOLKESTONE Kent   *See Shortlist*

FOWEY Cornwall   *See Shortlist*

FROGGATT EDGE Derbyshire   Map 3:A6

The Chequers Inn
Froggatt Edge
Hope Valley S32 3ZJ

Tel 01433-630231
Fax 01433-631072
Email info@chequers-froggatt.com
Website www.chequers-froggatt.com

Below rugged Froggatt Edge, in some of the Peak District's best scenery, Joanne and Jonathan Tindall's Grade II listed 16th-century inn is 'popular yet calm', say visitors this year (most reports continue to be positive). 'More like a restaurant-with-rooms than a pub', it has 'smart hanging flower baskets and troughs by the entrance'. The elevated 'secret' garden at the back has panoramic views to the west. The 'very attractive' bar/restaurant has original heavy lintels, dark beams, library chairs, high-backed settees, countless knick-knacks. 'The food was better than in many hotels.' Chef Phil Ball blends modern dishes (eg, belly pork with saffron and red peppers) with traditional pub favourites like steak and ale pie. Wines ('good quality, sensibly chosen') and dishes of the day are listed on blackboards. 'The service is professional.' The bedrooms are simple but thoughtfully furnished (pine furniture, country-style decor; bathroom with roll-top bath). 'Ours, recently refurbished, had a four-poster bed.' Rear bedrooms, away from the busy road adjacent, are quietest. At breakfast

GALMPTON   157

('very good'), a buffet is followed by cooked dishes (including vegetarian sausages). 'We were given our own door key so that we could come and go as we wished.' Good walking and climbing. (*Stephen and Pauline Glover, P and JH*)

Bedrooms: 5. *Open*: all year except 25 Dec. *Facilities*: bar, 2 eating areas, terrace with seating, large garden, unsuitable for &. *Background music*: 'easy listening' all the time, radio at breakfast. *Location*: On A625, near Calver village. *Smoking*: not allowed. *Children*: all ages welcomed. *Dogs*: not allowed. *Credit cards*: Amex, MasterCard, Visa. *Prices*: [2009] B&B £35–£50 per person, full alc £35–£40, special weekend breaks, 1-night bookings refused weekends.

GALMPTON Devon   Map 1:D4

Old Mill Farm   NEW   *Tel* 01803-842344
Greenway, Galmpton   *Fax* 01803-843750
Brixham   *Email* enquiries@oldmillfarm-dart.co.uk
TQ5 0ER   *Website* www.oldmillfarm-dart.co.uk

'A wonderful waterside retreat', this old mill stands where the Dart estuary is at its widest: 'The only sound is of the lapping river and birdsong.' It has been sympathetically converted, using natural materials (slate and stone), by Robert and Kate Chaston, the 'warmly welcoming' owners. Three of the bedrooms have 'spellbinding' views of the river. 'Kingfisher has a huge bed with sumptuous bedlinen, two stylish chairs by the windows; off-white carpet, aquamarine curtains, fresh flowers; glorious views, too, from the oversized bath tub; a large walk-in shower. Good lighting.' Breakfast in the River Room (wisteria wallpaper, 'beautiful' furnishings) is a 'relaxed affair; delicious house apple juice, excellent fruit salad, home-baked croissants, yogurts and cereals, home-made marmalade and jam. The cooked selection includes kippers and scrambled eggs and smoked salmon.' The hot dish of the day might be eggs Benedict. Greenway House and gardens, Agatha Christie's home now owned by the National Trust, is close by (a 20-minute walk, an advantage as car parking is restricted). (*Wendy Ashworth*)

Bedrooms: 4, on ground floor. *Open*: all year except Jan, 2 weeks Feb. *Facilities*: 2 sitting rooms, river room, 'natural swimming pond' (45 by 15 metres), unsuitable for &. *Background music*: none. *Location*: 3 miles S of Paignton. *Smoking*: not allowed. *Children*: all ages welcomed. *Dogs*: not allowed. *Credit cards*: none. *Prices*: [2009] B&B £40–£65 per person, midweek off-season rates.

Hotels do not pay to be included in the *Guide*.

GATESHEAD Tyne and Wear   Map 4:B4

Eslington Villa
8 Station Road, Low Fell
Gateshead NE9 6DR

Tel 0191-487 6017
Fax 0191-420 0667
Email home@eslingtonvilla.co.uk
Website www.eslingtonvilla.co.uk

With its 'gorgeous gardens' in a leafy suburb of Gateshead, Nick and Melanie Tulip's substantial Victorian villa is thought 'excellent all round'. It is 'within easy distance of the many attractions of the area'. 'Good value, with friendly staff,' is another comment. The attractive restaurant, with its conservatory extension, is a 'buzzy place', popular with local diners (the 'nice' lounge can get crowded). Chef Andy Moore serves modern dishes, eg, crispy duck confit; cassoulet of beans, smoked bacon and parsley. Bedrooms in the extension have a contemporary feel; those in the main house are more traditional, perhaps 'sombre' ('reading was difficult'); three rooms have a separate entrance off the car park. Breakfast has a wide choice including smoked haddock risotto and 'tasty' kippers. The only drawback is the 'intrusive' background music. Seminars, private meetings and functions are often held. (*JB*)

Bedrooms: 18, 3 with separate entrance on ground floor. *Open*: all year except Christmas, restaurant closed Sun night. *Facilities*: ramp, lounge/bar, conservatory, restaurant, private dining room, conference/function facilities, 2-acre garden (patio). *Background music*: jazz/modern throughout. *Location*: 2 miles from centre, off A1. *Smoking*: not allowed. *Children*: all ages welcomed. *Dogs*: not allowed. *Credit cards*: Amex, MasterCard, Visa. *Prices*: B&B [2009] £69.50–£79.50 per person, D,B&B £95–£115, set dinner £22.50. *V*

GATWICK West Sussex   *See Shortlist*

GILLINGHAM Dorset   Map 2:D1

Stock Hill House
Stock Hill
Gillingham SP8 5NR

Tel 01747-823626
Fax 01747-825628
Email reception@stockhillhouse.co.uk
Website www.stockhillhouse.co.uk

Once the summer home of the cartoonist Osbert Lancaster, this late Victorian mansion, now a small hotel/restaurant, is run by its 'hospitable' owners, Peter and Nita Hauser. It stands in 'delightfully landscaped' grounds with terraced lawns, herbaceous borders, a small lake with wildlife, and a walled vegetable garden. 'The atmosphere is friendly; guests got to know each other quickly,' said a visitor at Christmas. The 'quiet, relaxation, fresh air and superb food' are also mentioned. One of the two lounges is decorated in period style (striped fabrics, mirror and china figurines); the other is 'cosy', with a log fire. Service is 'formal' in the restaurant: Mr Hauser's extensive daily-changing menu of classic/French dishes with 'Austrian and British undertones' might include cream of sweet potato soup, pumpkin seed oil; seared pork tenderloin, Bohemian bread dumpling. The wine list is 'good but not cheap'. The bedrooms, which have antiques and curios, vary greatly in size; two have been refurbished this year. One reader found his room 'quirky, individual, supremely comfortable'. Opinions of the coach-house rooms varied from 'pleasant' to 'old-fashioned, cold'. A 'fine' breakfast is taken in the Lancaster room (with an original print): it has freshly squeezed orange juice, home-made jams, etc. 'Well-behaved' children are welcomed. (*John Wilkinson, Ralph Kenber, Hugo Peate, and others*)

Bedrooms: 9, 3 in coach house. *Open*: all year, restaurant closed Mon lunch. *Facilities*: ramp, 2 lounges, restaurant, breakfast room, private dining room, 11-acre grounds (tennis, croquet, small lake), unsuitable for &. *Background music*: none. *Location*: On B3081, 1½ miles W of Gillingham. *Smoking*: not allowed. *Children*: not under 7. *Dogs*: not allowed. *Credit cards*: MasterCard, Visa. *Prices*: [2009] D,B&B £115–£160 per person, set lunch £17.50–£30, dinner £45, Christmas/New Year packages, 1-night bookings refused bank holidays.

GITTISHAM Devon   Map 1:C5

Combe House   *Tel* 01404-540400
Gittisham   *Fax* 01404-46004
nr Honiton EX14 3AD   *Email* stay@thishotel.com
                                 Website www.thishotel.com

❦ *César award in 2007*

'Beautiful setting, magnificent building, memorable food.' With the feel of 'a true country house', this extended Grade I listed Elizabethan building stands up a mile-long drive in a huge estate of woodland, meadows and pastures. The owners, Ken and Ruth Hunt, 'preside informally', supported by 'attentive and knowledgeable' staff. The public rooms (refurbished this year) have carved oak panelling, antiques, fresh flowers, 18th-century portraits. The master bedrooms and suites, in similar style, have also had a make-over. The Linen

Suite (the former laundry room) has a six-foot circular copper bath.
Bedrooms in the former servants' wing have a country look (floral
prints and stripes). In the restaurant, chefs Hadleigh Barratt and Stuart
Brown use local ingredients in modern dishes on a seasonal menu, eg,
marinated red mullet, celeriac remoulade; roast loin of venison with
parsnip purée and Puy lentils. Vegetables come from a new kitchen
garden. Breakfast, served until 10 am, has 'toast from three types of
home-baked bread, thickly cut and served hot when required'.
Children and dogs are welcomed (the latter stay in rooms with a secure
walled garden). There is an 'African writers' camp' in an arboretum.
(*Christopher and Felicity Smith, PEC*)

Bedrooms: 16, 1 in cottage. *Open*: all year. *Facilities*: ramp, sitting room, Great
Hall, bar, restaurant, private dining rooms, civil wedding licence, 10-acre
garden in 3,500-acre estate (helipad), coast 9 miles, only public rooms suitable
for &. *Background music*: in hall and bar 'when requested'. *Location*: 2 miles SW
of Honiton. *Smoking*: not allowed. *Children*: all ages welcomed. *Dogs*: allowed in
public rooms except restaurant, some bedrooms. *Credit cards*: MasterCard, Visa.
Prices: [2009] B&B £87.50–£185 per person, D,B&B £125–£218, set dinner
£25–£29, full alc £55, Christmas/New Year packages, 1-night bookings
sometimes refused Fri/Sat. *V* (Sun–Thurs, depending on season)

GLASTONBURY Somerset   Map 1:B6

Number Three   NEW   *Tel* 01458-832129
3 Magdalene Street   *Fax* 01458-834227
Glastonbury BA6 9EW   *Email* info@numberthree.co.uk
                                Website www.numberthree.co.uk

Beside the 'superb' ruins of Glastonbury Abbey, this 'pleasant'
Georgian house is run as a B&B by its 'welcoming' owner, Patricia
Redmond. 'A housekeeper greeted us and showed us to our bedroom
in the annexe in the pretty walled garden,' says an inspector in 2009.
'Mrs Redmond phoned when she returned to check that all was OK.'
No guest lounge, but all bedrooms have a sofa and tea/coffee-making
tray with fresh milk in a Thermos flask. 'Our first-floor Blue Room
looked over the abbey orchard; it had a sideboard, large wardrobe and
slightly dated TV (good reception). The lighting was good. The
reasonable bathroom had a cascade shower over the bath. All was
quiet, and we slept well.' Breakfast is taken in an attractive room in
the main house: 'No cooked dishes, but a superb selection of cereals,
fresh fruit (strawberries, melon, grapes, apple), cheeses, ham, toast
and croissants; excellent coffee.' Free Wi-Fi is available. A private car

park is behind the house (guests are given a key). Glastonbury is short of interesting places to eat in the evening: 'inexpensive pub food with good service' was enjoyed at the *Who'd A Thought It* inn, a ten-minute walk away.

Bedrooms: 5, 3 in annexe, 1 on ground floor. *Open*: all year. *Facilities*: entrance hall, dining room, walled garden. *Background music*: none. *Location*: central, by abbey ruins. *Smoking*: not allowed. *Children*: all ages welcomed. *Dogs*: not allowed in main house. *Credit cards*: Amex, MasterCard, Visa. *Prices*: [2009] B&B £60–£105 per person.

GOLANT-BY-FOWEY Cornwall   *See Shortlist*

GORING-ON-THAMES   *See Shortlist*
Oxfordshire

GRANGE-OVER-SANDS   *See Shortlist*
Cumbria

GRASMERE Cumbria   Map 4: inset C2

White Moss House   *Tel* 015394-35295
Rydal Water   *Fax* 015394-35516
Grasmere LA22 9SE   *Email* sue@whitemoss.com
    Website www.whitemoss.com

'An excellent, small, personal place.' Home to the William Wordsworth family for more than a century, this grey stone creeper-covered house has been owned by Peter and Sue Dixon since 1981. It stands at the northern end of Rydal Water, between Grasmere and Windermere, a good location for exploring the Lakeland countryside. The oak-panelled lounge has a wood-burning fire, flowers, books, games and sofas, and there is a terrace with seating for warm days. Room and breakfast only is offered, except for five 'dinner club' weekends and for house parties (when 'the food was excellent, waiting attentive, portions well balanced'), but drinks and wines are available and there are plenty of eating places nearby. A busy road is close by, but windows are double glazed, and there is little traffic at night. In the main house, the small bedrooms have a tiny bathroom and many extras (herbal bathsalts, fresh flowers, books, etc). Breakfast includes Cumberland organic muesli, leaf tea, Cartmel valley sausages, home-made marmalade. *Brockstone*, the cottage up the hill, is available for self-catering (a minimum stay of three nights). (*Stephen and Pauline Glover*)

Bedrooms: 5, 1 self-catering cottage. *Open*: Mar–Nov. *Facilities*: lounge, restaurant, terrace, 1-acre garden/woodland, free use of indoor pool at local leisure club, unsuitable for &. *Background music*: none. *Location*: 1 mile S of Grasmere on A591. *Smoking*: not allowed. *Children*: all ages welcomed. *Dogs*: allowed in cottage downstairs only. *Credit cards*: MasterCard, Visa. *Prices*: B&B £39–£69 per person, set dinner £39.50, special breaks, 1-night bookings refused weekends, bank holidays.

See also Shortlist

GREAT BIRCHAM Norfolk   *See Shortlist*

GREAT DUNMOW Essex   Map 2:C4

Starr Restaurant with Rooms
Market Place
Great Dunmow
CM6 1AX

Tel 01371-874321
Fax 01371-876642
Email starrrestaurant@btinternet.com
Website www.the-starr.co.uk

On the market place of a busy little town, this timber-framed 15th-century former inn is run as a restaurant-with-rooms by owners Terence and Louise George. Stephanie Etienne is the manager; the East European staff are helpful, we are told. An inspector was given a 'perfect' welcome: bags carried, tea served in the bar. The bedrooms are in a stable block in the rear courtyard. The Pine Room has a corner bath, marble 'his and hers' washbasins; a four-poster bed and Victorian freestanding bath are in the Oak Room. A smaller room 'had no great character but was immaculate'; a green-patterned carpet, orange checked bedspread (blankets not duvet); a large bath and separate shower cubicle in the 'neat' bathroom. The restaurant, 'smart and colourful', has a peaceful atmosphere (free of muzak and mobile phones). It is in two parts, one with old beams stripped blond, the other a bright conservatory extension. Chef Mark Pearson's three-course menu ('good if pricey') has seven choices for each course, perhaps seared scallops and ham hock croquette; pork belly in paella flavours, calamari. There is yogurt with fruit compote, freshly squeezed orange juice, a fry-up, 'good croissants', and leaf tea at breakfast. A busy road runs alongside, 'but it was quiet at night'. Stansted airport is 15 minutes' drive away.

Bedrooms: 8, in stable block in courtyard, 2 on ground floor. *Open*: all year except 26 Dec–5 Jan, restaurant closed Sun night/Mon. *Facilities*: bar/lounge, restaurant, 2 private dining rooms, unsuitable for &. *Background music*: none. *Location*: central. *Smoking*: not allowed. *Children*: all ages welcomed. *Dogs*: not allowed. *Credit cards*: all major cards. *Prices*: B&B £65–£90 per person, set dinner £48.75, full alc £70. *V*

GREAT LANGDALE Cumbria   *See Shortlist*

GREAT MILTON Oxfordshire   Map 2:C3

Le Manoir aux Quat'Saisons
Church Road
Great Milton OX44 7PD

Tel 01844-278881
Fax 01844-278847
Email lemanoir@blanc.co.uk
Website www.manoir.com

César award in 1985

Endorsed in 2009 'with confidence', by the *Guide*'s founding editor, Raymond Blanc's hotel (Relais & Châteaux), which he co-owns with Orient Express Hotels, stands in 'immaculate and beautiful' grounds in a pretty Oxfordshire village. 'The feel is exemplary: our meal was outstanding at every course; the staff were wholly professional, cordial and welcoming.' A porter meets visitors in the car park; luggage is delivered to the bedrooms, which are supplied with fresh fruit and a decanter of Madeira. Many are in garden buildings; each has a theme: Lalique has a bathroom finished in dark marble with 'silhouettes of unclad ladies decorating the walls'; Lemongrass is inspired by South-East Asia and has a bathroom with a 'vast' walk-in shower and a steam room with stone relaxation beds. There is a choice of menus in the famous conservatory restaurant (two *Michelin* stars for 24 years). The short *carte* might include risotto of spring vegetables; slow-roasted aromatic Cornish turbot. There is lunchtime *Menu du Jour*; a five-course *Les Classiques* ('best-loved' dishes) and a ten-course *Menu Découverte*. 'When we found the main course too large, our hosts asked for a doggy bag which was instantly supplied; not every luxury hotel would be as helpful.' (*Hilary and Helge Rubinstein*)

Bedrooms: 32, 22 in garden buildings, some on ground floor. *Open*: all year. *Facilities*: ramps, 2 lounges, champagne bar, restaurant, private dining room, cookery school, civil wedding licence, 27-acre grounds (gardens, croquet, lake). *Background music*: in the lounges. *Location*: 8 miles SE of Oxford. *Smoking*: not allowed. *Children*: all ages welcomed. *Dogs*: not allowed in house (free kennels). *Credit cards*: all major cards. *Prices*: [2009] B&B (French breakfast) £205–£510 per person, set lunch £49, *Les Classiques* £95, *Menu Découverte* £116, full alc £90, special breaks, cookery courses, Christmas/New Year packages, 1-night bookings refused Sat June/July.

GREAT TEW Oxfordshire   *See Shortlist*

GRENDON UNDERWOOD   Map 2:C3
Buckinghamshire

Shakespeare House   `NEW`   *Tel* 01296-770776
Main Street   *Fax* 01296-770670
Grendon Underwood   *Email* enquiries@shakespeare-house.co.uk
nr Bicester HP18 0ST   *Website* www.shakespeare-house.co.uk

Renovated with 'panache' by property developers Nick Hunter and Roy Elsbury, this half-timbered, mullion-windowed Elizabethan coaching inn (Grade II listed), in a village near Bicester, hosted William Shakespeare on his journeys to London. The style is theatrical: 'The drama begins in the dining area with its opulent black-and-white curtains and co-ordinated tableware,' said an inspector, 'and continues in the exquisite drawing room which has patterned sofas and a log fire blazing in the inglenook fireplace.' The bedrooms (each named after a character in *A Midsummer Night's Dream*) vary in size; some have a private bathroom across the hall (robes supplied). 'Oberon was a decent size and had panelled walls painted grey, elaborate gold-framed mirrors, pretty lamps, antiques. The modern black-tiled bathroom opposite had a spa bath and shower with water jets.' The Shakespeare suite has a queen-size bed and a walk-in shower room. A set dinner is cooked on request. 'Nick chatted about the area as he served us. We enjoyed a wonderful combination of soft goat's cheese with apple; superb lamb shank; hot chocolate pudding. The wine came from an honesty bar. Breakfast is also good-quality fare: fresh fruit salad, yogurt and cereal from a buffet; wholemeal toast in a covered basket, home-made jams, lovely pot of coffee.'

Bedrooms: 5. *Open*: all year, except 19 Dec–1 Jan. *Facilities*: drawing room, 2 dining rooms, ½-acre garden, unsuitable for ♿. *Background music*: light classical and jazz in drawing room and 1 dining room ('at guests' discretion'). *Location*: in village, 8 miles E of Bicester. *Smoking*: not allowed. *Children*: all ages welcomed. *Dogs*: allowed in bedrooms and drawing room. *Credit cards*: Amex, MasterCard, Visa. *Prices*: B&B £42.50–£107.50 per person, D,B&B £77.50–£142.50, full alc £45–£55. *V*

GULWORTHY Devon   Map 1:D3

The Horn of Plenty   NEW
Gulworthy
nr Tavistock PL19 8JD

Tel 01822-832528
Fax 01822-834390
Email enquiries@thehornofplenty.co.uk
Website www.thehornofplenty.co.uk

In peaceful countryside near Tavistock, this wisteria-covered stone Georgian house has wide views over the Tamar valley. It is run as a restaurant-with-rooms by the chef, Peter Gorton, who owns it with Paul Roston. 'The food is good,' says a visitor this year. 'Peter Gorton's friendliness must rub off on the staff; they are superb.' In the L-shaped, glass-fronted dining room, with its contemporary decor, he serves international dishes, eg, scallops and king prawns in prosciutto with an oriental dressing; roast duck breast, rösti, Madeira sauce. On Monday evening there is a shorter, reduced-price menu. There are fresh flowers, and a log fire in the drawing room. The most expensive bedrooms are in the main house. Others, each with a balcony (where breakfast can be served) and a small bathroom, are in a converted coach house. 'Ours was large, well set out, good bed, fluffy towels always heated in the bathroom. A beautiful outlook on to a walled garden.' Breakfast is 'a lovely start to the day; fresh fruit, excellent scrambled eggs and smoked salmon, fishcakes'. Cookery courses and weddings are held. (*John Ford*)

Bedrooms: 10, 6 in stables (20 yds). 4 on ground floor. *Open*: all year except 24–26 Dec. *Facilities*: bar, library, drawing room, restaurant, civil wedding licence, 4½-acre grounds. *Background music*: classical. *Location*: 3 miles SW of Tavistock. *Smoking*: not allowed. *Children*: not under 10 in restaurant, unless residents. *Dogs*: allowed in garden rooms, guide dogs only in public rooms. *Credit cards*: Amex, MasterCard, Visa. *Prices*: [2009] B&B £60–£100 per person, D,B&B £30 added, set dinner £47, cookery courses, New Year package. *V*

HALIFAX West Yorkshire   *See Shortlist*

HALNAKER West Sussex   Map 2:E3

The Old Store   *Tel* 01243-531977
Stane Street, Halnaker, nr Chichester   *Email* theoldstore4@aol.com
PO18 0QL   *Website* www.theoldstoreguesthouse.com

'First class. Excellent service. Good value. We were made most welcome,' says a visitor in 2009 to this inexpensive B&B. The Georgian Grade II listed building, once the village store and bakery, is near the Goodwood estate and within easy reach of Chichester. It is owned by 'model hosts' Patrick and Heather Birchenough. Downstairs, there are beamed ceilings, a small lounge and a breakfast room. Bedrooms are on two floors: some look across fields to the cathedral spire (and as far as the Isle of Wight on a clear day); some are suitable for a family. The shower rooms have been refitted this year. Tea/coffee-making facilities are available, with fresh milk. Wi-Fi is available free of charge. Breakfast has fresh fruit salad, yogurts, muesli, home-made jams; award-winning sausages, local free-range eggs; American pancakes with bacon and maple syrup. There is a pub, *The Anglesey Arms*, for evening meals, almost opposite, and the Birchenoughs are 'helpful about other places to eat and details of walks'; they offer a laundry service and will make a packed lunch. Plenty of interesting sightseeing: Arundel, Petworth, Uppark, Fishbourne Roman palace; walks through woods to the South Downs. The village name is pronounced 'Hannaka'. (*David Voller, AJWH*)

Bedrooms: 7, 1 on ground floor. *Open*: all year except Christmas, Jan, Feb. *Facilities*: lounge, breakfast room, ¼-acre garden with seating, unsuitable for &. *Background music*: none. *Location*: 3 miles NE of Chichester. *Smoking*: not allowed. *Children*: all ages welcomed (under-5s free). *Dogs*: not allowed. *Credit cards*: MasterCard, Visa. *Prices*: B&B £30–£47.50 per person (higher for Goodwood 'Festival of Speed' and 'Revival' meetings), 1-night bookings sometimes refused weekends.

HAMBLETON Rutland   Map 2:B3

Hambleton Hall
Hambleton
Oakham LE15 8TH

Tel 01572-756991
Fax 01572-724721
Email hotel@hambletonhall.com
Website www.hambletonhall.com

🏆 *César award in 1985*

'Nothing much changes here, thank goodness,' say trusted *Guide* reporters returning this year to Tim and Stefa Hart's 'splendid' country house hotel (Relais & Châteaux). The setting is 'memorable', on a peninsula jutting into Rutland Water. 'The staff balance professionalism with relaxed friendliness. The decor, which some might find a little traditional, is sumptuous and comfortable.' Other praise in 2009: 'Simply a league above the competition: service, cooking, wine list, ambience, value are exceptional.' Stefa Hart designed the classic interiors (fine fabrics, antiques, good paintings, open fires, flowers) with Nina Campbell. 'Excellent' bedrooms have 'nice small touches like a Roberts radio'. The Croquet Pavilion suite is good for a family (children are welcomed; the very young get an early supper). Chef Aaron Patterson has long held a *Michelin* star for his seasonal cooking ('it never disappoints'), eg, sautéed scallops with onions and lemon grass sauce; loin of rabbit with pearl barley risotto. Continental breakfast, included in the price, is 'generous: a cornucopia of fruits and cereals; hot toast and croissants just when you want them'. The bread comes from Mr Hart's new bakery. 'The gardens have matured and are suitably manicured, the views down to the water are superb.' Tim Hart also owns *Hart's Hotel*, Nottingham (*qv*). (*Kate and David Wooff, Robert Gower*)

Bedrooms: 17, 2-bedroomed suite in pavilion. *Open*: all year. *Facilities*: lift, ramps, hall, drawing room, bar, restaurant, 2 private dining rooms, small conference facilities, civil wedding licence, 17-acre grounds (swimming pool, heated May–Sept, tennis, cycling, lake with fishing, windsurfing, sailing). *Background music*: none. *Location*: 3 miles SE of Oakham, train Peterborough/ Kettering/Oakham (branch line), helipad. *Smoking*: not allowed. *Children*: only children 'of a grown-up age' in restaurant, except at breakfast. *Dogs*: not allowed in public rooms, nor unattended in bedrooms. *Credit cards*: all major cards. *Prices*: [2009] B&B (continental) £100–£300 per person, set dinner from £40, full alc £85, seasonal breaks, Christmas/New Year packages, 1-night bookings sometimes refused.

HARDWICK Cambridgeshire   Map 2:B4

Wallis Farmhouse   NEW   *Tel* 01954-210347
98 Main Street   *Fax* 01954-210988
Hardwick   *Email* enquiries@wallisfarmhouse.co.uk
Cambridge CB23 7QU   *Website* www.wallisfarmhouse.co.uk

'Everything is immaculate' at this B&B, a late Georgian farmhouse in large grounds in a village near Cambridge. Owners Linda and Peter Sadler are 'relaxed, friendly' hosts. He tends arable fields and sheep. The bedrooms, all on the ground floor of a 'clever' conversion of a barn, are 'full of character and charm'. They have wooden beams, original features, pine furniture, 'comfortable bedding', tea/coffee-making equipment, and Wi-Fi access; 'interconnecting doors when required'. A 'great' breakfast is served in the farmhouse. 'The formal gardens are well tended and interesting, with specimen trees, shrubs and an orchard.' The *Black Lion Inn*, close by, is recommended for meals: 'It is very special.' (*Malcolm Turner*)

Bedrooms: 6, all on ground floor. *Open*: all year. *Facilities*: ramp, dining room, 2-acre garden. *Background music*: none. *Location*: 5 miles W of Cambridge. *Smoking*: not allowed. *Children*: all ages welcomed. *Dogs*: by arrangement. *Credit cards*: Amex, MasterCard, Visa. *Prices*: [2009] B&B £32.50–£37.50 per person. *V*

HARMONDSWORTH Middlesex   *See Shortlist*

HAROME North Yorkshire   Map 4:D4

The Pheasant   *Tel* 01439-771241
Harome, nr Helmsley   *Fax* 01439-771744
YO62 5JG   *Email* reservations@thepheasanthotel.com
                      Website www.thepheasanthotel.com

Composed of the village smithy and other buildings, this small hotel has been 'radically renovated', since they bought it, by Andrew and

Jacquie Pern, owners of the popular *Star Inn* 'a few steps away' (see next entry). Their former head chef, Peter Neville, has returned from the *Michelin*-two-starred *Hibiscus* in London as their working partner; many of the staff have remained from the previous regime. Inspectors were impressed: 'A friendly welcome from a receptionist who showed us the smart public areas. Our bedroom had a warm, bright feel; a modern four-poster without drapes, clean beige and cream tones, Shaker-style furnishings. Everything was comfortable and convenient; the small bathroom was well thought out, with space for personal clutter.' The oak-beamed bar and lobby, decorated in country style, have exposed stone work, tartan wall coverings. The large lounge opens on to a stone-flagged terrace. Local, seasonal ingredients are 'sensitively handled' in the 'elegant' restaurant (with 'subdued lighting'). 'Gratin of mussels redolent of the sea; best end of lamb, pink and juicy, with a perfect wild garlic risotto, pickled clam. Service was friendly; piped music not overly intrusive.' Breakfast in a conservatory has a buffet of juices, fruit salads and compotes; 'good full English; interesting egg dishes'. There is a kidney-shaped indoor swimming pool. (*Endorsed by Gordon Murray*)

Bedrooms: 12, 2 courtyard suites. *Open*: all year except 24–26 Dec, 1 Jan. *Facilities*: lounge, bar, dining room, conservatory, indoor swimming pool, courtyard, garden, 10-acre deer park. *Background music*: in bar and restaurant. *Location*: village centre. *Smoking*: not allowed. *Children*: all ages welcomed. *Dogs*: not allowed. *Credit cards*: MasterCard, Visa. *Prices*: [to 31 March 2010] B&B £75–£85 per person, D,B&B £95–£105, set dinner £30.

The Star Inn
Harome, nr Helmsley
YO62 5JE

Tel 01439-770397
Fax 01439-771833
Email jpern@thestaratharome.co.uk
Website www.thestaratharome.co.uk

❦ *César award in 2004*

A 'proud' Yorkshireman (he grew up in Whitby), Andrew Pern 'pays homage to his roots' at this thatched medieval longhouse in a village near Helmsley. He runs it as a restaurant-with-rooms (*Michelin*-starred) with his wife, Jacquie (front-of-house). 'A truly superb evening' was enjoyed by visitors this year. The 'excellent' seasonal menu, served in the restaurant, bar or alfresco in the garden, identifies the suppliers for dishes like risotto of wild mushrooms, Hawes Wensleydale salad; loin of Leckenby's lamb, creamed Lowna goat's cheese, Sand Hutton asparagus. Many vegetables and herbs come from the garden; fish is from Whitby. There is an open-plan, split-level lounge. The decor is rustic/modern in the bedrooms in *Cross House Lodge* opposite (which has an 'opulent' sitting room with honesty bar). All rooms have TV, CD/DVD-player, home-made biscuits, fruit and fudge; one has a bath in the bedroom, several have a shower big enough for two. Breakfast can be taken round a huge table in the *Wheelhouse* below, or as a 'picnic' in the bedroom. Other accommodation is in a four-bedroom farmhouse and in *Black Eagle Cottage*: 'beautifully furnished', this has three interconnected suites. 'We cooked breakfast ourselves from an amazing supply of *Star*/Yorkshire produce; we were also given a tuck-shop basket.' (*Jon Hughes, and others*)

Bedrooms: 14, 8 in *Cross House Lodge* opposite, others in separate buildings. *Open*: all year except 24–26 Dec, 1 Jan. *Facilities*: 2 lounges, coffee loft, bar, breakfast room, restaurant, private dining room, civil wedding licence, 2-acre garden, unsuitable for &. *Background music*: varied CDs. *Location*: village centre. *Smoking*: not allowed. *Children*: all ages welcomed (children's menu). *Dogs*: not allowed. *Credit cards*: MasterCard, Visa. *Prices*: [2009] B&B £70–£115 per person, full alc £45.

HARROGATE North Yorkshire   *See Shortlist*

HARTINGTON Derbyshire   Map 2:A2

Charles Cotton Hotel   **NEW**   *Tel* 01298-84229
Hartington   *Fax* 01298-84301
SK17 0AL   *Email* info@charlescotton.co.uk
                            Website www.charlescotton.co.uk

In an attractive Peak District village, this four-square, stone-built 17th-century coaching inn has been renovated by Ray and Carolyn Cook, who bought it in 2006. It is 'strongly recommended' by regular *Guide* readers for its 'happy buzz, excellent value and very good food'. Clive and Tracy Watson are the resident managers. 'The service from the pleasant local staff was impeccable.' The bedrooms, in the main house and a converted stable block, have original beams, white-painted walls, pine furnishings. 'Our small room at the front of the house had a fine view of the square, a comfortable bed, plenty of storage (though small drawers), a wall-mounted flat-screen television. Some noise from quarry lorries in the early morning. Housekeeping was good.' Downstairs is a small residents' lounge, a tea room (which serves sandwiches and light meals during the day), and a large bar, busy with locals. In the simple dining room, 'food is imaginative, portions generous: delicious smoked haddock and mussel pie with sautéed smoked bacon and savoy cabbage; sticky toffee pudding; a short but good-value wine list. Breakfast, served in the tea room, was equally good.' Children are welcomed (family rooms have bunk beds), as are dogs and walkers, 'their boots, maps, and tales of blisters'. (*Richard and Jean Green*)

Bedrooms: 17, 3 on ground floor. *Open*: all year. *Facilities*: lounge, bar, restaurant, tea room. *Background music*: 'soft' in bar. *Location*: centre of village, 9 miles N of Ashbourne. *Smoking*: not allowed. *Children*: all ages welcomed. *Dogs*: allowed in 6 bedrooms, bar. *Credit cards*: MasterCard, Visa. *Prices*: [2009] B&B £30–£55 per person, D,B&B (min. 2 nights) £49–£67.50, full alc £32.50, special breaks.

HARWICH Essex   Map 2:C5

The Pier at Harwich
The Quay
Harwich CO12 3HH

Tel 01255-241212
Fax 01255-551922
Email pier@milsomhotels.com
Website www.milsomhotels.com

'A stylish hotel in a wonderful position overlooking the water, by the pier in this forgotten corner of Essex.' A returning visitor this year watched passing ferries and container ships from Paul Milsom's hotel/restaurant on the quayside of old Harwich (Nick Chambers is the manager). The two restaurants, and most bedrooms, are in the larger of two historic buildings. Other rooms, and the beamed lounge, are in a former pub. In the first-floor *Harbourside* restaurant, with its 'minimalist' decor, 'theatrical' lighting and polished pewter cham-pagne bar, chef Chris Oakley specialises in seafood (fish comes daily from the harbour), eg, home-smoked salmon with peeled brown shrimps; grilled sea bass on braised red cabbage. Informal meals are served in the ground-floor *Ha'Penny Bistro*. 'One slight niggle: a few stools would be welcome in the ground-floor bar.' Bedrooms have minibar, satellite TV and a hospitality tray; many face the harbour (the Mayflower suite has a telescope). 'Our room had views through three windows, a comfortable sofa and bed, a good bathroom.' Breakfast includes freshly squeezed juice, 'thick slices of ham and cheese'. Paul Milsom also owns *Le Talbooth* restaurant in Dedham and two hotels: *milsoms*, a 'stylish gastropub with rooms', and *Maison Talbooth*, Dedham (see Shortlist). (*Lynn Wildgoose*)

Bedrooms: 14, 7 in annexe, 1 on ground floor. *Open*: all year. *Facilities*: ramps, lounge (in annexe), restaurant, bistro, civil wedding licence, small front terrace. *Background music*: in bar. *Location*: on quay. *Smoking*: not allowed. *Children*: all ages welcomed. *Dogs*: only guide dogs allowed. *Credit cards*: all major cards. *Prices*: [2009] B&B £52.50–£95 per person, full alc £38.65, special breaks, Christmas package, 1-night bookings sometimes refused weekends. ***V***

HASTINGS Sussex   Map 2:E5

Swan House   NEW   *Tel* 01424-430014
1 Hill Street   *Email* res@swanhousehastings.co.uk
Hastings TN34 3HU   *Website* www.swanhousehastings.co.uk

On a narrow street of medieval houses in the old town, this 15th-century cottage stands by a 'charming' church. It has been given a 'restful, pleasing' look (say inspectors in 2009) by owners Brendan McDonagh and Lionel Copley, who run it as a B&B. The large lounge has a beamed ceiling, white walls, a huge stone fireplace; two long linen-covered settees, 'an eclectic mix of paintings, antique furniture and bric-a-brac from the owners' other business, an online design shop'. The bedrooms have original wood beams, white walls and floorboards, 'simple, fresh' furnishings. 'We were given one of the two rooms in the Renaissance suite: large and sunny, it had windows to two sides, a wardrobe painted in a distinctive black-and-white pattern; a small balcony above the garden. This suite would be ideal for a family: it has a second smaller bedroom connected to a shower room.' The 'excellent' breakfast can be served in the lounge or the bedroom: 'freshly squeezed orange juice, superb bacon, bread from a neighbouring bakery'. Hastings is 'delightful', away from the candy floss and carousel strip. *Swan House* is on a narrow street: 'Don't take a large car; Brendon took our luggage, then hopped in to help me find parking (permit provided).'

Bedrooms: 4, 1 on ground floor. *Open*: all year except Christmas. *Facilities*: lounge/breakfast room, courtyard garden, civil wedding licence. *Background music*: none. *Location*: in old town, near seafront. *Smoking*: not allowed. *Children*: not under 5. *Dogs*: not allowed. *Credit cards*: all major cards. *Prices*: B&B £57.50–£95 per person, website offers, 1-night bookings refused weekends.

The 'New' label indicates hotels which are appearing in the *Guide* for the first time or which have been readmitted after an absence.

HATHERSAGE Derbyshire   Map 3:A6

The George Hotel   *Tel* 01433-650436
Main Road   *Fax* 01433-650099
Hathersage S32 1BB   *Email* info@george-hotel.net
                                      Website www.george-hotel.net

In the Peak District village that inspired Charlotte Brontë when she
wrote *Jane Eyre*, this 'welcoming' 600-year-old grey stone inn is owned
by Eric Marsh, who also runs *The Cavendish* at nearby Baslow (*qv*), and
managed by Philip Joseph: he and some of the 'helpful' staff work at
both. The large lounge and bar have a 'rich brown carpet, dramatic
fabrics, modern tables; seating in hospitable groups', one couple wrote.
'We loved it.' The bedrooms, 'beautifully decorated in neutral
colours', have high headboard, ceiling spotlights, comfortable chairs,
plain white walls, 'attractive, unfussy' drapes. 'Our spacious back
room, thoughtfully equipped, had decent sheets on bed, a small but
well-thought-out bathroom.' One couple disliked the bedside lighting
in their otherwise 'pleasant' room. Front bedrooms face a busy road
and have double glazing. In the dining room, Helen Heywood's
modern menus might include duck and sour cherry rillettes, wasabi
dressing; red pepper crusted cod steak, warm chorizo and chickpea
salad. 'Excellent breakfast: a beautifully laid buffet with delicious
muesli, fresh fruit, creamy yogurt but commercial juices; a perfect Full
Monty, toast in relays.' 'Helen's home-made marmalade' is commended. (*H and HR, and others*)

Bedrooms: 22. *Open*: all year. *Facilities*: lounge/bar, restaurant, 2 function rooms,
civil wedding licence, courtyard, only restaurant suitable for &. *Background
music*: light jazz in restaurant. *Location*: in village centre, parking. *Smoking*: not
allowed. *Children*: all ages welcomed. *Dogs*: not allowed. *Credit cards*: all major
cards. *Prices*: B&B £65–£105 per person, set dinner £28–£35, full alc £45, special
breaks, Christmas/New Year packages, 1-night bookings occasionally refused
weekends. *V*

HAWORTH West Yorkshire   *See Shortlist*

HAY-ON-WYE Herefordshire   *See Shortlist*

> The *V* sign at the end of an entry indicates a hotel that has
> agreed to take part in our Voucher scheme (see page 57).

HELMSLEY North Yorkshire   Map 4:C4

The Feversham Arms	*Tel* 01439-770766
1 High Street	*Fax* 01439-770346
Helmsley YO62 5AG	*Email* info@fevershamarmshotel.com
	Website www.fevershamarmshotel.com

Owned by Simon and Jill Rhatigan, this former coaching inn (Small Luxury Hotels of the World) stands on the main street of a 'delightful' town ('with some wonderful pastry shops') on the edge of the North Yorkshire moors. This year, they have opened the Verbena Spa in a new poolside wing. The bedrooms in the main house vary greatly; the larger ones are much liked: 'Ours was well equipped; enormous bed, divine bedlinen.' 'Suite the best we've seen in the UK; beautifully appointed, with flat-screen TV in both rooms, and wood-burning stove in its lounge.' For families, some rooms have a sofa bed and some are interconnecting. There are 'relaxing' sitting areas and 'punctilious staff', though during a Christmas break service was 'a bit patchy'. In the high-ceilinged conservatory restaurant, chef Simon Kelly uses local produce in his modern dishes, eg, pan-roast halibut, scallops, citrus salsify. Breakfast is 'exceptional'. (*BE, J and AL*)

Bedrooms: 33, 5 in garden, 12 by pool, 8 on ground floor. *Open*: all year. *Facilities*: 2 lounges, bar, conservatory restaurant, private dining room, library, boardroom, terrace (outside dining), civil wedding licence, 1-acre garden (heated 13-metre swimming pool, spa). *Background music*: in restaurant, private dining room, boardroom. *Location*: central, safe parking. *Smoking*: not allowed. *Children*: all ages welcomed. *Dogs*: not allowed in public rooms. *Credit cards*: Amex, MasterCard, Visa. *Prices*: [2009] B&B £75–£187.50 per person, D,B&B £105–£222.50, set dinner £33, full alc £50, special breaks, Christmas/New Year packages, 1-night bookings sometimes refused on Sat.

See also Shortlist

HENLEY-ON-THAMES   *See Shortlist*
Oxfordshire

HEREFORD Herefordshire   *See Shortlist*

HETTON North Yorkshire   Map 4:D3

The Angel Inn	
The Angel Inn	*Tel* 01756-730263
Hetton, nr Skipton	*Fax* 01756-730363
BD23 6LT	*Email* info@angelhetton.co.uk
	Website www.angelhetton.co.uk

One of the first inns in England to break away from the traditional 'chips with everything' approach to food, this old drovers' inn in the Yorkshire Dales has been run as a fine-dining pub since 1983. It is owned by Juliet Watkins; Bruce Elsworth is the chef director, Simon Farrimond the manager. This year's praise: 'Friendly, relaxed; food and service impeccable.' 'It was a pleasure to be looked after so well.' Mrs Watkins's son, Pascal, runs a wine 'cave' (which contributes to an interesting wine list) in a converted barn opposite. Above are two studio bedrooms and three 'lovely' suites. These have brass bed fittings and bright fabrics, and are 'thoughtfully equipped' (tea-making equipment, honesty bar, well-lit, modern bathroom). The wide-ranging bar menu includes a page of vegetarian options, and there are daily blackboard specials. Head chef Mark Taft uses local produce for a *carte* of dishes like ballottine of Goosnargh duck leg; chargrilled rib of Waterford House beef, curly kale, boulangère potatoes. Summer meals can be taken on a flagged forecourt overlooking Cracoe Fell. Breakfast, served until 10 am, has 'very good' fresh juices, big bowls of cereals and fruit, an 'immense' Yorkshire platter. (*Claire Burton, Jennifer Davis, RL*)

Bedrooms: 5 in barn across road, 1, on ground floor, suitable for &. *Open*: all year except 25 Dec, 1 week Jan. *Facilities*: bar/brasserie, restaurant (2 rooms), civil wedding licence, terrace (outside dining), wine shop. *Background music*: none. *Location*: off B6265, 5 miles N of Skipton, car park. *Smoking*: not allowed. *Children*: all ages welcomed. *Dogs*: not allowed in public rooms. *Credit cards*: Amex, MasterCard, Visa. *Prices*: [2009] B&B £65–£90 per person, D,B&B £90–£117.50, set Sat dinner £36.50, full alc £40, midweek breaks, New Year package. *V*

HEXHAM Northumberland   *See Shortlist*

> Always discuss accommodation in detail when making a booking, and don't hesitate to ask for an upgrade on arrival if a hotel is obviously not full. If you don't like the room you are shown, ask for another one.

HINTON ST GEORGE Somerset   Map 1:C6

The Lord Poulett Arms
High Street
Hinton St George
TA17 8SE

Tel 01460-73149
Email steveandmichelle@lordpoulettarms.com
Website www.lordpoulettarms.com

Ω *César award in 2008*

In a 'lovely' village of stone houses and thatched roofs, this 'very attractive' 17th-century inn is run as restaurant/pub-with-rooms by owners Steve Hill and Michelle Paynton. A Dutch visitor this year found it 'charming: beautifully decorated; log fires; excellent food'. The 'quirky' old building has 'floors of bare flags or boards, tables of old oak or elm, antique chairs, open fires, numerous pictures'. In the bar, 'busy in a relaxed way', 'dogs sleep on the hearth, and interesting local conversations can be overheard'. The bedrooms have a 'considerable wow factor, and a touch of eccentricity': two have a slipper bath in the room; two have a bathroom across the corridor. 'We loved the no-television policy, and the bath.' 'Lighting a bit dim, and only one chair.' Gary Coughlan, the head chef, uses local, mainly organic produce, for dishes like goat's cheese and walnut salad; cumin and apple-glazed belly pork. 'Superb service; staff dressed in black; a good, buzzy atmosphere.' Breakfast, served until 9 am, has fresh juices, fruit compote, leaf tea, toasted home-made bread, 'perfectly poached eggs', local marmalade. Behind the building is a 'French-style' garden with a *boules* piste edged by lavender. (*Quirine Hammerstein, Barbara Garnsworthy*)

Bedrooms: 4. *Open*: all year except 26 Dec, 1 Jan, check-in 12 noon–3 pm, 6.30–11 pm. *Facilities*: bar, restaurant, private dining room, 1-acre grounds, unsuitable for &. *Background music*: none. *Location*: village centre. *Smoking*: not allowed. *Children*: all ages welcomed. *Dogs*: not allowed in bedrooms. *Credit cards*: MasterCard, Visa. *Prices*: B&B £44–£59 per person, full alc £30, 1-night bookings refused Sat.

HOARWITHY Herefordshire   *See Shortlist*

HOLKHAM Norfolk   *See Shortlist*

HOLMFIRTH West Yorkshire   *See Shortlist*

HOLT Norfolk   Map 2:A5

Byfords   *Tel* 01263-711400
1–3 Shirehall Plain   *Fax* 01263-714815
Holt NR25 6BG   *Email* queries@byfords.org.uk
                                          Website www.byfords.org.uk

Seven bedrooms, including one for disabled guests and one (with an
adjacent room) suitable for a family, and a new reception area have
been added to Iain and Clair Wilson's unusual venture, a combination
of 'posh B&B', continental-style café/bistro and delicatessen. The
'higgledy-piggledy' conversion of old houses (Grade II listed) is on
the main square of a charming little Norfolk town. Tables and chairs
stand on the pavement outside; inside is a series of eating rooms with
old beams, exposed bricks, wooden tables. A self-confessed 'fussy'
visitor thought 'the staff delightful, the welcome excellent'. Free tea
on arrival might include 'delicious ginger cake'. The 'charming' older
bedrooms ('one of the nicest we have ever stayed in,' wrote inspectors)
are decorated in 'North Norfolk style' with flint, exposed brickwork,
oak floorboards, slate. But a visitor on a three-night stay complained
of lack of drawer storage. Café-style meals are served all day; in the
evening there is bistro food like 'posh pizza'; classic paella, or dishes
from the vegetarian, gluten-free, dairy-free and 'small people' menus.
Breakfast in a large, light room 'could not be better': freshly squeezed
juices, cereals, croissants, fruit compote, etc, on a central table; cooked
dishes brought with thick toast. Visitors are given a comprehensive
handbook of information on the area. (*BAJ, and others*)

Bedrooms: 16, 3 on ground floor, 1 suitable for &. *Open*: all year. *Facilities*: ramps,
5 internal eating areas, deli. *Background music*: jazz/'easy listening', live jazz on
last Wed of every month. *Location*: central, private secure parking. *Smoking*: not
allowed. *Children*: all ages welcomed. *Dogs*: only guide dogs allowed. *Credit
cards*: MasterCard, Visa. *Prices*: [2009] B&B £47.50–£90 per person, D,B&B
£50–£107.50, full alc £35, winter offers, Christmas/New Year packages, 1-night
bookings usually refused Sat.

HOPE Derbyshire   Map 3:A6

Underleigh House	*Tel* 01433-621372
off Edale Road	*Fax* 01433-621324
Hope S33 6RF	*Email* info@underleighhouse.co.uk
	Website www.underleighhouse.co.uk

Set peacefully amid 'idyllic' scenery outside a village in the Hope valley (within the Peak District national park), this extended barn and cottage conversion, now a B&B, provides 'amazing value'. The owners, Vivienne Taylor ('delightful, warm') and her husband, Philip, will provide maps and packed lunches for walkers. 'Their generous hospitality never failed. Each afternoon, when we returned from walking, we were greeted with a tray of tea and cakes, and our waterproofs were taken away to be dried.' All the bedrooms have tea/coffee-making equipment, hairdryer, TV with DVD- and CD-player. 'Our small room had lots of patterns, views on both sides of fields with sheep, everything one could want, even bathrobes (nice lightweight ones); small bathroom with a bath; a comprehensive information pack.' The 'superb' breakfast is taken around a large oak table in the flagstoned hall. Lots of choice: jugs of orange juice, eight types of home-made jam, own-recipe muesli, fresh and dried fruits from the buffet; porridge and croissants from the Aga; home-made bread, local oatcakes, sausages and black pudding from the Hope butcher. Drinks are served in a large lounge with a log fire, or on a terrace; recommendations are given on local eating places. (*HP, and others*)

Bedrooms: 5. *Open*: Feb–Dec, except Christmas/New Year. *Facilities*: lounge, breakfast room, ⅓-acre garden, unsuitable for &. *Background music*: none. *Location*: 1 mile N of Hope. *Smoking*: not allowed. *Children*: not under 12. *Dogs*: allowed by arrangement. *Credit cards*: MasterCard, Visa (*both 3% surcharge*). *Prices*: [2009] B&B £40–£80 per person, 3-night rates, 1-night bookings refused Fri/Sat.

See also Shortlist

When you make a booking you enter into a contract with a hotel. Most hotels explain their cancellation policies, which vary widely, in a letter of confirmation. You may lose your deposit or be charged at the full rate for the room if you cancel at short notice. A travel insurance policy can provide protection.

HORDLE Hampshire   Map 2:E2

The Mill at Gordleton   *Tel* 01590-682219
Silver Street   *Fax* 01590-683073
Hordle, nr Lymington   *Email* info@themillatgordleton.co.uk
SO41 6DJ   *Website* www.themillatgordleton.co.uk

There has been a mill at Gordleton, on the edge of the New Forest, since the Domesday survey: the present building dates from the 17th century and is run as a restaurant-with-rooms by owner Elizabeth Cottingham; Terri Seabright is the manager. 'We try not to be pretentious,' they say. Guests write of a 'warm welcome' and 'uniformly friendly, efficient staff'. The decor is traditional. 'Our room, furnished in artistic fawn and blue, had a large, comfortable bed, and a nice terrace where we sat in the sun; a very modern bathroom with an intricate shower.' Outside are 'beautifully sculpted' gardens by a river with ducks and sometimes a heron. Service in the bustling restaurant, which faces the river, was 'friendly, measured and accurate'. The cooking of chef Karl Wiggins has 'a contemporary twist', perhaps tiger prawns and scampi in garlic and parsley butter; honey-glazed breast of corn-fed duck with rösti potatoes. There is always a vegetarian dish of the day. A busy road is nearby, but 'our mini-suite was well positioned and insulated so there was no trace of noise'. A useful base for visiting Beaulieu, Buckler's Hard, the Isle of Wight, etc. More reports, please.

Bedrooms: 7. *Open*: all year except 25 Dec, restaurant closed Sun night. *Facilities*: lounge, 2 bars, restaurant, private dining room, 2-acre grounds on river (fishing rights), only restaurant suitable for &. *Background music*: in restaurant and bar. *Location*: 3 miles W of Lymington. *Smoking*: not allowed. *Children*: all ages welcomed. *Dogs*: allowed in front bar, terrace and gardens only. *Credit cards*: Amex, MasterCard, Visa. *Prices*: [2009] B&B £65–£105 per person, set dinner £19.50–£34.50, full alc £45, phone for special breaks, 1-night bookings sometimes refused Sat in season.

HORNINGSHAM Wiltshire   Map 2:D1

The Bath Arms   *Tel* 01985-844308
Longleat   *Fax* 01985-845187
Horningsham BA12 7LY   *Email* enquiries@batharms.co.uk
                            Website www.batharms.co.uk

Near the entrance to the Longleat estate, on the Wiltshire/Somerset border, this creeper-clad old inn is leased from the Marquis of Bath by the 'affable' Christoph Brooke. It is managed by Sara Elston. The 'handsome', square grey stone building, filled with Indian furniture and fabrics, has a 'happy, informal atmosphere' (said inspectors). The bedrooms, created by interior designer Miv Watts, also have an oriental theme. One, upstairs, is called Kama Sutra ('may be a little risqué for some'). There are exotic wallpapers, bright colours. 'Our garden room had quirky decor, carved Buddhas, delightful terrace, view of rolling fields, evening turn-down service.' Rooms in the stables were less liked. There is a traditional pub (packed with locals at night) and a dining bar that serves simple meals (eg, meatballs, tomatoes and garlic). In the spacious restaurant (oak floorboards, colourful rugs, a splendid stone fireplace, three massive gilded chandeliers), the chef Frank Bailey promises simple, local food: 'We don't do towers and drizzles.' Typical dishes: Parma ham, garden pea salad; chump of Dorset lamb, roast shallot purée. Families are encouraged. Two sister hotels, *The Elephant*, Pangbourne, and *The New Inn*, Coln St Aldwyns, enter the *Guide* this year. We'd welcome reports on the other newcomer to the group, *The Master Builder's House* at Buckler's Hard.

Bedrooms: 16, 6 in stables, 1 suitable for &. *Open*: all year. *Facilities*: ramp, lounge, bar, 2 dining rooms, Hip Bath (beauty treatments/therapies), 2 patios, lawn. *Background music*: in bar and restaurant. *Location*: Longleat estate, 4 miles W of Warminster. *Smoking*: not allowed. *Children*: all ages welcomed. *Dogs*: allowed in 3 bedrooms, bar and lounge. *Credit cards*: MasterCard, Visa. *Prices*: B&B £70–£140 per person, D,B&B £99.50–£209, full alc £43, website offers, Christmas/New Year packages, 1-night bookings refused Fri.

HUDDERSFIELD West Yorkshire   *See Shortlist*

HULL East Yorkshire   *See Shortlist*

HUNGERFORD Berkshire   *See Shortlist*

Check the Hotelfinder section (page 11) if you are looking for a hotel for a special occasion, perhaps a memorable meal (see Gourmet and Gastropubs); a sporting weekend (see Golf, Fishing, Walking); somewhere that will welcome your children – or your dog. Our editors have selected ten hotels in each of these categories (and many more) to help you make your choice.

HUNTINGDON Cambridgeshire   Map 2:B4

The Old Bridge   *Tel* 01480-424300
1 High Street   *Fax* 01480-411017
Huntingdon PE29 3TQ   *Email* oldbridge@huntsbridge.co.uk
                           Website www.huntsbridge.com

'An excellent, friendly place; they were not at all put out by our appearing at 11.30 pm.' This year's praise for John Hoskins's handsome, creeper-clad 18th-century building, once a private bank, by a medieval bridge over the River Ouse. Nina Beamond is the manager. 'Even the smallest double room was impeccably kitted out and had a very good bathroom.' Earlier visitors liked their 'wonderfully comfortable, spacious, well-thought-out bedroom and bathroom'. Mr Hoskins, a Master of Wine, has opened a wine shop in the hotel: not surprisingly, the wine list in the restaurant ('with lovely large oval cupola') is 'outstanding, mark-ups reasonable or non-existent'. The chef, Simon Cadge, serves a monthly-changing menu of modern dishes, perhaps tortellini of Portland crab with leeks; rump of lamb, potato and celeriac boulangère. The building is hedged in by a busy traffic system but has triple glazing and air conditioning, and the small riverside garden is relatively peaceful. The bedrooms are themed: there are mosaic tiles, *chaises longues*, an up-to-date music system, a smart bathroom (some have a claw-footed bath). Early morning tea and a free newspaper are delivered to the room; shoes are shined; there is free Wi-Fi. Breakfast includes scrambled eggs with smoked salmon. (*Richard Baker, and others*)

Bedrooms: 24, 2 on ground floor. *Open*: all year. *Facilities*: ramps, lounge, bar, restaurant, private dining room, wine shop, business centre, civil wedding licence, 1-acre grounds (terrace, garden), river (fishing, jetty, boat trips), unsuitable for &. *Background music*: none. *Location*: 500 yds from centre, parking, station 10 mins' walk. *Smoking*: not allowed. *Children*: all ages welcomed. *Dogs*: allowed. *Credit cards*: all major cards. *Prices*: [2009] B&B £60–£95 per person, full alc £35, Christmas/New Year packages.

How to contact the *Guide*
By mail: From anywhere in the UK, write to Freepost PAM 2931, London W11 4BR (no stamp is needed)
From outside the UK: *Good Hotel Guide*, 50 Addison Avenue, London W11 4QP, England
By telephone or fax: 020-7602 4182
By email: editor@goodhotelguide.com
Via our website: www.goodhotelguide.com

HURSTBOURNE TARRANT
Hampshire
Map 2:D2

Esseborne Manor
Hurstbourne Tarrant, nr Andover
SP11 0ER

Tel 01264-736444
Fax 01264-736725
Email info@esseborne-manor.co.uk
Website www.esseborne-manor.co.uk

Near the Bourne valley, in an area of outstanding natural beauty, this traditional hotel has a 'family-run atmosphere' and 'most helpful staff'. The late Victorian house has been sympathetically extended by its owners, Lucilla and Ian Hamilton; their son, Mark, is the manager. It is approached up a long drive flanked by fields with sheep grazing, off a busy road (traffic noise audible in the garden). There is an abundance of fresh flowers in the two lounges. Some bedrooms in the main house have a spa bath, some a four-poster; six rooms around a courtyard are good for families (children are welcomed, though there are no special facilities for them). Three small rooms are in cottages. A premier deluxe room with private patio overlooks the pretty herb garden. 'Very comfortable bed, huge open bathroom/dressing area with spa bath, separate multi-jet shower; lots of storage, good lighting apart from bedside lights. In the dining room (red-patterned wallpaper, blue carpet, big windows), the Slovenian chef, Anton Babarovic, offers 'very good, straightforward dishes', eg, chicken livers with mashed potato; sticky toffee pudding. 'Excellent value.' Weddings (marquee on the lawn) and meetings are catered for. (*A and CR, and others*)

Bedrooms: 20, 6 in courtyard, 3 in cottages. *Open*: all year. *Facilities*: 2 lounges, bar, restaurant, function room, civil wedding licence, 3-acre grounds (formal gardens, tennis, croquet), arrangements with nearby golf club and fitness centre. *Background music*: in bar. *Location*: on A343, 7 miles N of Andover. *Smoking*: not allowed. *Children*: all ages welcomed. *Dogs*: not allowed in public rooms. *Credit cards*: all major cards. *Prices*: [2009] B&B £62.50–£125 per person, D,B&B £30 added, set meals £15–£18, full alc £35, special breaks, Christmas package. *V*

ILMINGTON Warwickshire
See Shortlist

Deadlines: nominations for the 2011 edition of this volume should reach us no later than 15 May 2010. Latest date for comments on existing entries: 1 June 2010.

ILSINGTON Devon   Map 1:D4

Ilsington Country House   `NEW`   *Tel* 01364-661452
Ilsington   *Fax* 01364-661307
nr Newton Abbot   *Email* hotel@ilsington.co.uk
Dartmoor TQ13 9RR   *Website* www.ilsington.co.uk

In a 'stunning' setting below Haytor within Dartmoor national park, this traditional hotel is owned by the Hassell family; brothers Tim and Richard are the managers. It is 'highly recommended' in 2009 by a returning visitor, a long-time *Guide* reader. 'The rooms are comfortable, the food is superb; we were particularly pleased with the friendly, helpful staff.' Cream teas are served in a south-facing conservatory; the lounges have comfortable seating. A smart casual dress code is required in the recently rebuilt restaurant which has 'semi-circular windows with beautiful views across the country below the moor'. Chef Mike O'Donnell serves a 'modern eclectic' menu, perhaps sautéed chicken livers, remoulade of celeriac; pavé of halibut, butternut squash fondant. 'Two plus points: I am poorly sighted and was given my own large-type menu; we found breakfast coffee a little weak, and were given our own cafetières thereafter.' Weddings and conferences are held. The many activities in the area include fly- and sea fishing, mountain biking, and walking on the moors. (*Gurnos Jones*)

Bedrooms: 25, 8 on ground floor. *Open*: all year. *Facilities*: ramp, lift, bar, lounge, library, conservatory, 3 conference rooms, indoor swimming pool (4 by 11 metres), 10-acre grounds. *Background music*: in evening in bar and restaurant. *Location*: in village 4 miles NE of Ashburton. *Smoking*: not allowed. *Children*: all ages welcomed. *Dogs*: allowed in ground-floor rooms (£8 per night), not in public rooms. *Credit cards*: all major cards. *Prices*: [2009] B&B £77–£105 per person, D,B&B (min. 2 nights) £102–£126, set dinner £34, full alc £55, special offers, Christmas/New Year packages, 1-night bookings sometimes refused weekends and in season.

IPSWICH Suffolk   *See Shortlist*

The *Guide*'s website can be used alongside the printed edition. It has photographs of nearly all of the hotels, with a direct link to its website. It also has a Special Offers section with some excellent deals exclusively for *Guide* readers. See www.goodhotelguide.com.

IREBY Cumbria   Map 4: inset B2

Overwater Hall   *Tel* 017687-76566
Overwater, nr Ireby   *Fax* 017687-76921
CA7 1HH   *Email* welcome@overwaterhall.co.uk
                        Website www.overwaterhall.co.uk

'Location, house and food are excellent reasons for returning for another relaxing stay,' said a visitor to this castellated Grade II listed Georgian mansion in the Lake District national park. The owner/managers, Stephen Bore and Adrian and Angela Hyde, welcome children: there is high tea for under-fives at 5.30 pm. Dogs may sit with their owners in one of the lounges, and they have the run of the large grounds. This did not disturb a dog-free visitor: 'They and their owners were responsible guests.' The public rooms have a bold decor: 'audacious' wallpaper, contrasting panelling and lights. 'Their opulence and individuality suit the house. Our lovely bedroom had a blue-and-beige colour scheme.' Bathrooms have a double-ended bath and a separate walk-in shower; extras include bathrobes, flowers, fruit. Smart casual dress is expected in the dining room where Adrian Hyde's four-course menus are thought 'well balanced'. The cooking is modern, eg, Orkney scallops on fondant sweet potato with sautéed king prawns, crab risotto and saffron velouté. Breakfast, 'a full Cumbrian affair', is served at table on linen cloths. Good walking from the door; red squirrels, deer and woodpeckers can be seen, and osprey nest nearby. (*JC, and others*)

Bedrooms: 11, 1 on ground floor. *Open*: all year. *Facilities*: drawing room, lounge, bar area, restaurant, civil wedding licence pending, 18-acre grounds, Overwater tarn 1 mile. *Background music*: classical in restaurant. *Location*: 2 miles NE of Bassenthwaite Lake. *Smoking*: not allowed. *Children*: not under 5 in restaurant (high tea at 5.30 pm). *Dogs*: allowed except in one lounge. *Credit cards*: MasterCard, Visa. *Prices*: [2009] B&B £70–£115 per person, D,B&B £20 added, set dinner £40, full alc £50, 4-night breaks all year, Christmas/New Year packages, 1-night bookings refused. *V*

IRONBRIDGE Shropshire   *See Shortlist*

Every year we give a free copy of the *Guide* to each of the 12 readers who send us the best reports. Every report received is considered in this competition.

KESWICK Cumbria   Map 4: inset C2

Dalegarth House   `NEW`   *Tel* 017687-72817
Portinscale, Keswick   *Email* allerdalechef@aol.com
CA12 5RQ   *Website* www.dalegarth-house.co.uk

In an attractive Lakeland village, this traditional guest house is recommended as 'one of the best bargains around'. Its elevated position gives it 'superb views' over Derwentwater. The owners, Bruce and Pauline Jackson, proud of having been born locally, are keen to advise visitors about the area. The decor in the Edwardian house is traditional and 'the rooms are spotlessly clean'. The garden has 'a profusion of flowers, which appear on the tables'. Mr Jackson, the chef, serves 'a sensible menu of excellent food, mainly with local produce', some of it home-grown, eg, black pudding salad, poached egg, baby beetroot; smoked haddock, broad beans, pancetta and butter sauce. Guests are asked at breakfast to choose their dishes for dinner at 7 pm. 'In a week's stay nothing was repeated.' Breakfast has fruit compotes and cereals; full English and lighter options. There is good walking all around. (*R Postlethwaite, Peter R Appleyard*)

Bedrooms: 10, 2 on ground floor. *Open*: Mar–Dec. *Facilities*: lounge, bar, dining room, garden, unsuitable for &. *Background music*: in public rooms. *Location*: 1½ miles W of Keswick. *Smoking*: not allowed. *Children*: not under 10. *Dogs*: not allowed. *Credit cards*: MasterCard, Visa. *Prices*: B&B £35–£45 per person, D,B&B £55–£65, set dinner £22, special breaks, 1-night bookings sometimes refused.

Lyzzick Hall   `NEW`   *Tel* 017687-72277
Underskiddaw, Keswick   *Fax* 017687-80618
CA12 4PY   *Email* info@lyzzickhall.co.uk
                          Website www.lyzzickhall.co.uk

In 'small but pretty' grounds in a 'glorious' position on the lower slopes of Skiddaw, this former gentleman's residence is run as a hotel by the Fernandez and Lake families. It is recommended by a regular *Guide* reader for the 'charm of the owners and the attentiveness of the staff'. The manager is David Lake, son-in-law of the 'genial' Alfredo Fernandez. 'We were helped with luggage to our comfortable bedroom; decorated in neutral colours, clean; towels were provided daily for the swimming pool.' Soundproofing 'might not be perfect'. The daily-changing menu reflects Mr Fernandez's heritage 'fusing traditional English with a decidedly Spanish accent: we enjoyed black pudding and chorizo with Puy lentil salad; braised ox cheek; Eton mess. The wine waiter's recommendations were good. We were impressed that a full menu was available when we ate early before a theatre visit.' Background music 'was not too intrusive'. (*Sara Hollowell*)

Bedrooms: 31, 1 on ground floor. *Open*: Feb–Dec except 24–26 Dec. *Facilities*: bar, 2 lounges, indoor swimming pool (10 by 5 metres), 4-acre grounds. *Background music*: in public rooms. *Location*: 2 miles N of Keswick. *Smoking*: not allowed. *Children*: all ages welcomed. *Dogs*: not allowed. *Credit cards*: MasterCard, Visa. *Prices*: [2009] B&B £58–£90 per person, D,B&B £76–£110, set dinner £29.50, full alc £40, spring/winter breaks, New Year package, 1-night bookings sometimes refused.

KINGHAM Oxfordshire   *See Shortlist*

KING'S LYNN Norfolk   *See Shortlist*

KINGSBRIDGE Devon   *See Shortlist*

KIRKBY LONSDALE Cumbria   *See Shortlist*

KIRKBY STEPHEN Cumbria   Map 4:C3

A Corner of Eden   NEW   *Tel* 015396-23370
Low Stennerskeugh   *Email* enquiries@acornerofeden.co.uk
Ravenstonedale   *Website* www.acornerofeden.co.uk
Kirkby Stephen CA17 4LL

'Romantic and charming', this Grade II listed farmhouse has been 'painstakingly restored' by owners Debbie and Richard Temple. It stands in 'beautiful farmland surrounded by dramatic countryside', between the Yorkshire dales and the Lake District. The 'helpful but not intrusive' hosts follow a green policy (they will meet visitors who travel by bus or train to Kirkby Stephen). Because of planning restrictions, none of the four bedrooms has facilities *en suite*: 'Thick towelling robes are provided for visits to the lovely bathroom and the shower room.' Some noise may be heard from other bedrooms, but they have no television or radio. 'There was always a fire in the welcoming lounge; lots of books and magazines.' A butler's pantry has 'a fresh supply of Debbie's amazing home-made cakes; bread, crackers, cheese and fruit, all included in the price'. There is a 'well-stocked' honesty bar, and 'complimentary blackcurrant vodka in the room'. The 'very good breakfast', served until 9.30 am, has home-made muesli, a wide choice of cooked dishes. A no-choice dinner is served ('generally at weekends') by arrangement: it might include a trio of pâtés with Richard's chutney; slow-cooked beef and apricot casserole. House-party bookings are taken. (*Olivia Howes*)

Bedrooms: 4. *Open*: all year except 1 week at Christmas, house party only at New Year. *Facilities*: lounge, dining room, pantry, 5-acre grounds, unsuitable for &. *Background music*: none. *Location*: 4 miles S of Kirkby Stephen. *Smoking*: not allowed. *Children*: not under 12 except for house parties. *Dogs*: not allowed in dining room, 1 bedroom (£5 per night charge). *Credit cards*: none. *Prices*: [2009] B&B £65–£85 per person, set dinner £30.

Augill Castle

South Stainmore
nr Kirkby Stephen CA17 4DE

Tel 01768-341937
Email enquiries@stayinacastle.com
Website www.stayinacastle.com

'Not a hotel, but a family home which welcomes guests', this early Victorian fantasy-Gothic castle is in the upper Eden valley. 'You may find a piano in the bathroom, a church pew next to the loo, or an African tribal hanging above your bed,' write the owners, Simon and Wendy Bennett, who run it in informal style. Their children welcome young visitors as 'special friends': there are cats and dogs, a playground, a fort in the forest, a tree house, toys. Early suppers, baby monitors and cots are available, and there is a children's cookery school. Visitors write of the 'happy atmosphere'. 'We were invited to treat the place as our own.' It has a panelled hall, vaulted ceilings, turrets, leaded or stained-glass windows. Many bedrooms are big enough for a family, some are interconnecting. A four-poster room 'had enough space to swing several tigers; sherry and flapjacks replenished daily'. An evening meal is available by arrangement: a two-course supper is often served during the week; at weekends there is a four-course house-party-style dinner. Dishes might include prawn cocktail with mango and crevettes; Cumbrian lamb chump, rosemary roasties, buttered spinach. Breakfast, which 'seldom kicks off before 9 am', is leisurely; it has freshly squeezed orange juice, home-made bread, real tea, eggs from the castle's resident hens. 'Great walking' from the door. (*JA, PH, and others*)

Bedrooms: 11, 2 on ground floor, 2 in stable block (*Little Castle*). *Open*: all year, dinner by arrangement, lunch for groups, by arrangement. *Facilities*: hall, drawing room, library (honesty bar), music (sitting) room, dining room, civil wedding licence, 15-acre grounds (landscaped garden, tennis). *Background music*: none. *Location*: 3 miles W of Kirkby Stephen. *Smoking*: not allowed. *Children*: all ages welcomed. *Dogs*: not allowed. *Credit cards*: Amex, MasterCard, Visa. *Prices*: B&B £80 per person, supper £20, dinner £35, Christmas/New Year packages, 2-night bookings preferred weekends. *V*

KIRTLINGTON Oxfordshire   *See Shortlist*

KNUTSFORD Cheshire   *See Shortlist*

LACOCK Wiltshire   Map 2:D1

At the Sign of the Angel   *Tel* 01249-730230
6 Church Street   *Fax* 01249-730527
Lacock, nr Chippenham SN15 2LB   *Email* angel@lacock.co.uk
          Website www.lacock.co.uk

César award in 1989

'An enchanting period inn of great character', this 15th-century half-timbered building is one of the oldest in an 'atmospheric' National Trust village much favoured by film-makers. With oak panels, creaking doors, low ceilings, beams and ancient steps, it has long been run by owners Lorna and George Hardy. The bedrooms reflect the age: most are small, but the bathrooms are 'magnificent'. 'My ground-floor room, cramped but nicely decorated, had white walls and attractive floral curtains.' Four other bedrooms ('quiet and comfortable') are in a cottage 'through the garden and over a brook', 'a delightful walk'. They have under-floor heating. There is a first-floor lounge with deep leather chairs, flowers and books. 'I was cheerfully served a drink under the fruit trees in the garden.' The dining rooms have low ceilings, uneven floors and doors, old mellow tables laid with silverware. 'The food was delicious: a hearty helping of Cornish crab soup; succulent shin of beef braised in beer, with an equally tender Yorkshire pudding, topped up with an exceptional gooseberry and rhubarb sorbet. Full marks.' 'Good breakfast': it has stewed fruit, home-made bread and marmalade, 'tasty local produce'. (*Roland Cassam, Bryan and Mary Blaxall, PJK*)

Bedrooms: 10, 3 on ground floor, 4 in cottage. *Open*: all year except 23–31 Dec (open for dinner 31 Dec), restaurant closed Mon except bank holidays. *Facilities*: ramps, lounge, bar, restaurant, civil wedding licence, unsuitable for &. *Background music*: none. *Location*: village centre. *Smoking*: not allowed. *Children*: all ages welcomed. *Dogs*: not allowed in public rooms. *Credit cards*: all major cards. *Prices*: [2009] B&B £60–£82 per person, set lunch £12.95, dinner (2 courses) £16.95, full alc £40.

LANGAR Nottinghamshire   Map 2:A3

Langar Hall
Langar NG13 9HG

Tel 01949-860559
Fax 01949-861045
Email info@langarhall.co.uk
Website www.langarhall.co.uk

♔ *César award in 2000*

'I would return again and again,' says one of the many fans. After a short time away, Imogen Skirving is back at the helm of her informal hotel, a honey-stone Georgian mansion which has been owned by her family since the mid-19th century. She tells us: 'I have come out of retirement (temporarily) to work with Pascal, our party/wedding organiser, restaurant manager, waiter, pot-washer, etc.' Many of her staff 'have been here for years'. Regular visitors (who include barristers attending Nottingham Crown Court and cricket commentators broadcasting at Trent Bridge) love the 'flexible' atmosphere, the 'elegant but homely' feel and characterful decor. Family portraits line the stairs that lead from the flagstoned hall to themed bedrooms, all different. They include Bohemia (honeymoon superior, 'one of the most romantic'), once an artist's studio, with poetry on the bathroom walls; Cartland, dedicated to the romantic novelist (another visitor); Barristers, 'masculine, with painted panelling'. The drawing room has a club fender, and paintings by and of the Bloomsbury group. The small bar has cartoons, and photographs taken by designer Paul Smith, also a frequent guest. 'Gorgeous food': in the candlelit dining room, chef Gary Booth offers a daily-changing menu which might include grilled Scottish langoustines and scallops with garlic butter; chargrilled fillet of local beef with truffle mash. Light meals are served all day in a conservatory. There is a chapel in the 'lovely' grounds: this is a popular wedding venue. (*David Berry*)

Bedrooms: 12, 1 on ground floor, 1 garden chalet. *Open*: all year. *Facilities*: ramps, sitting room, study, library, bar, garden room, restaurant, private dining room, small conference/function facilities, civil wedding licence, 20-acre grounds (gardens, children's play area, croquet, ponds, fishing), unsuitable for &. *Background music*: none. *Location*: 12 miles SE of Nottingham. *Smoking*: not allowed. *Children*: all ages welcomed. *Dogs*: small dogs on a lead allowed by arrangement, in chalet only. *Credit cards*: MasterCard, Visa. *Prices*: [2009] B&B £37.50–£92.50 per person, D,B&B (Mon–Thurs, winter) from £80, set dinner £20, full alc £35, special offers, Christmas/New Year packages. *V*

LANGHO Lancashire   Map 4:D3

Northcote
Northcote Road, Langho
nr Blackburn BB6 8BE

Tel 01254-240555
Fax 01254-246568
Email reservations@northcote.com
Website www.northcote.com

Chef/*patron* Nigel Haworth and his business partner, Craig Bancroft, run this red brick, late Victorian/Edwardian residence as an informal restaurant-with-rooms (*Michelin* star). It stands in wooded grounds with views of the Ribble valley, near the busy A59 (windows are double glazed). It has been renovated, with original features retained (beautiful wooden doors and windows); there are brown leather armchairs and sofas in the sitting rooms. Inspectors liked their refurbished bedroom: 'Comfortable rather than stylish, it had a magnificent Victorian wardrobe, large bed, *chaise longue*, games, magazines, CD-player, flat-screen TV, fridge; well-equipped, efficient bathroom. Gold wallpaper added to the sombre ambience, but the huge bay window, with view of fields, brought light and colour.' A dissenter this year thought that the bedrooms did not live up to the food, and complained of long delays at breakfast. Everyone admires the restaurant (the window tables are recommended and service is 'good humoured, attentive'). The tasting menu was 'impressive and well balanced', with dishes like Jerusalem artichoke soup, artichoke carpaccio; beef cannon, smoked marrowbone. More reports, please.

Bedrooms: 14, 4 on ground floor, 1 suitable for &. *Open*: all year except 25 Dec. *Facilities*: ramp, lounge, drawing room, cocktail bar, restaurant, private dining/meeting room, civil wedding licence, 2-acre garden. *Background music*: jazz in restaurant. *Location*: 4½ miles N of Blackburn, on A59. *Smoking*: not allowed. *Children*: all ages welcomed. *Dogs*: not allowed. *Credit cards*: Amex, MasterCard, Visa. *Prices*: B&B [2009] £100–£125 per person, set dinner £50–£70, full alc £75, gourmet breaks.

Please always send a report if you stay at a *Guide* hotel, even if it's only to endorse the existing entry.

LASTINGHAM North Yorkshire   Map 4:C4

Lastingham Grange   *Tel* 01751-417345
Lastingham YO62 6TH   *Fax* 01751-417358
                    Email reservations@lastinghamgrange.com
                    Website www.lastinghamgrange.com

 César award in 1991

For a regular visitor from America, this is 'one of our favourite
places'. Other returning visitors are equally enthusiastic: 'As good as
ever.' 'Truly family-run.' 'Like a second home.' This traditional
hotel on the edge of the North Yorkshire Moors national park is run
by Bertie Wood, helped by his mother, Jane, and brother, Tom. One
of them is 'always on hand to attend to the residents during pre-
dinner drinks'. The converted 17th-century farmhouse stands in
large gardens with an adventure playground for children, and good
walking from the door. The decor is traditional. 'Bedrooms are very
comfortable, particularly the beds.' There are 'real cotton sheets
and blankets, rather than the dreaded duvet', and 'excellent
lighting; sheer bliss'. The 'good, plain English cooking' of Paul
Cattaneo and Sandra Thurlow, on a daily-changing menu, might
include game terrine with home-made chutney; roast Yorkshire
goose with sage and onion stuffing. 'Good breakfasts' have
'excellent kippers'. Rates include newspaper, morning coffee and
afternoon tea ('good as ever, hot scones, jam and cream'). (*RL, Anne
and Denis Tate, and many others*)

Bedrooms: 11, also cottage in village. *Open*: all year except Dec, Jan, Feb.
Facilities: ramps, hall, lounge, dining room, laundry facilities, 12-acre grounds
(terrace, garden, adventure playground, croquet, *boules*), limited assistance
for &. *Background music*: none. *Location*: 5 miles NE of Kirkbymoorside.
Smoking: not allowed. *Children*: all ages welcomed. *Dogs*: not allowed in public
rooms. *Credit cards*: Diners, MasterCard, Visa. *Prices*: [2009] B&B £62.50–£105
per person, D,B&B £75–£145, set dinner £37.50. *V*

Readers' contributions, written on the forms at the back of the
book or sent by email, are the lifeblood of the *Good Hotel Guide*.
Our readers play a crucial role by reporting on existing entries
as well as recommending new discoveries. Everyone who writes
to the *Guide* is a potential winner of the Report of the Year
competition (page 10) in which a dozen correspondents each
year win a copy of the *Guide* and an invitation to our annual
launch party in October.

LAVENHAM Suffolk   Map 2:C5

The Great House
Market Place
Lavenham CO10 9QZ

Tel 01787-247431
Fax 01787-248007
Email info@greathouse.co.uk
Website www.greathouse.co.uk

♛ *César award in 2009*

On the marketplace of this 'most English of towns', this 'impressive half-timbered corner house' is run in true Gallic style as a restaurant-with-rooms by its 'amiable' owners, Régis and Martine Crépy. 'Our welcome by a charming young Frenchman was perfect,' wrote inspectors. The candlelit dining room, with its contemporary decor, is 'bare boarded, spotlessly clean; each table with spring flowers', said a visitor in 2009. The chef, Enrique Bilbault, serves modern dishes combined with French classics. 'We enjoyed red pepper soup with goat's cheese ravioli; creamy vegetable risotto; Shetland salmon with parsnip purée; smiling service from the manager and his attentive staff.' Four of the five bedrooms have a sitting room; there are king-size beds (one is a Jacobean four-poster), rich fabrics and antiques, old beams, a marble bathroom; also sherry and fresh flowers. All are decorated in sophisticated style. 'Ours had large windows, smart bathroom with window and under-floor heating.' Breakfast has 'delicious croissants, fruit, but packets of cereals and jam in little jars'; cooked dishes cost extra unless you are on a two-night half-board rate. The set lunch is 'outstanding value'. (*Robert Gower, and others*)

Bedrooms: 5. *Open*: Feb–Dec, restaurant closed Sun night, Mon, Tues midday. *Facilities*: lounge/bar, restaurant, ½-acre garden (patio, swings), unsuitable for &. *Background music*: French. *Location*: by Market Cross, near Guildhall, public car park. *Smoking*: not allowed. *Children*: all ages welcomed. *Dogs*: not allowed in public rooms. *Credit cards*: MasterCard, Visa. *Prices*: [2009] room £110–£195, D,B&B £100 per person, breakfast continental £8.50, English £12.50, set lunch £18.95, dinner £28.95, full alc £48, midweek breaks, 1-night bookings refused Sat.

Lavenham Priory
Water Street
Lavenham CO10 9RW

Tel 01787-247404
Fax 01787-248472
Email mail@lavenhampriory.co.uk
Website www.lavenhampriory.co.uk

'If only it could talk, this wonderful old building would surely have many fascinating tales to tell.' The 'stunningly beautiful' Grade I listed former Benedictine priory, later an Elizabethan merchant's mansion, has been sympathetically restored and 'furnished with imagination' by owners Tim and Gilli Pitt. It stands in 'lovely' gardens, with lawns, shrubs, flagged paths and benches. Inside, 'comfort is timeless, the plumbing modern'. There are comfortable sofas and chairs in the 13th-century Great Hall with its beamed ceiling, huge inglenook fireplace and antique furniture. The 'snug' has TV, books and an honesty bar. The spacious 'bed chambers', reached up an oak Jacobean staircase, have sloping beamed ceilings, mullioned windows, 'authentically creaking' old oak floorboards. There are unusual beds (four-poster, sleigh or polonaise). The 'good-sized' Gallery Chamber has a 'comfortable sleigh bed'. 'Our large room had a high bed, tea/coffee-making facilities, and TV.' The 'excellent' breakfast is communally served around a large table in the Merchants Room or sometimes, in summer, in the herb garden. 'You squeeze your own orange juice, and make your own toast', and there are kippers, smoked haddock, scrambled eggs, 'superb sausages', three types of bread. The Pitts have a licence to sell alcohol, and they help with bookings in local restaurants. (*Ken and Priscilla Winslow, Mary Hewson, Anthony Meakin*)

Bedrooms: 6. *Open*: all year except Christmas/New Year. *Facilities*: Great Hall/sitting room, snug, breakfast room, 3-acre garden (medieval courtyard, herb garden), unsuitable for &. *Background music*: none. *Location*: central. *Smoking*: not allowed. *Children*: not under 10. *Dogs*: not allowed. *Credit cards*: MasterCard, Visa. *Prices*: [2009] B&B £50–£85 per person, winter midweek discount for 2 nights or more, 1-night bookings refused Sat, some holidays.

See also Shortlist

LEDBURY Herefordshire   Map 3:D5

The Feathers   *Tel* 01531-635266
High Street   *Fax* 01531-638955
Ledbury HR8 1DS   *Email* mary@feathers-ledbury.co.uk
                          Website www.feathers-ledbury.co.uk

Owned by David Elliston and managed by Mary Diggins, this 'fascinating' half-timbered 16th-century inn is 'part of the social scene' of this historic market town. Its car park is reached through a narrow alleyway from the High Street. It has a 'nice, old-fashioned' Reception area, and a beamed lounge. Guests' bags are carried to their bedroom.

Some rooms are on the second floor, reached up a 'characterful' staircase (no lift). 'Ours had beamed walls washed in yellow. Period charm meant uneven floors and one step up to and then down into a large bathroom whose floor had clearly never seen a spirit level. Everything was well kept.' Double glazing keeps out exterior noise. Of the two eating places, *Fuggles* brasserie has a 'varied and well-executed menu' including perhaps casserole of local game. *Quills*, the restaurant, which looks over the town, serves more sophisticated dishes like duck breast with girolles and red wine jus. Meals are accompanied by 'excellent, not overpriced wines'. Service is 'extremely friendly'. 'Well-presented' breakfasts include 'good full English'. Summer meals can be served in the garden. Also liked: the absence of muzak, and the leisure centre. (*RC, and others*)

Bedrooms: 22, 1 suite in cottage, also self-catering apartments. *Open*: all year. *Facilities*: lounge, bar, brasserie, restaurant, function/conference/wedding facilities, spa (swimming pool, whirlpool, gym), civil wedding licence, courtyard garden (fountain, alfresco eating), unsuitable for &. *Background music*: none. *Location*: town centre, parking. *Smoking*: not allowed. *Children*: all ages welcomed. *Dogs*: allowed, only guide dogs in restaurant and brasserie. *Credit cards*: all major cards. *Prices*: [2009] B&B £65–£125 per person, full alc £45, New Year package, 1-night bookings refused weekends in season. *V*

Verzon House   NEW

Hereford Road, Trumpet
Ledbury
HR8 2PZ

Tel 01531-670381
Fax 01531-670830
Email info@verzonhouse.com
Website www.verzonhouse.com

In a hamlet outside the market town, this handsome Georgian farmhouse (1790) stands in large grounds with uninterrupted views to the Malvern hills. It has been refurbished by Peter and Audrey Marks, experienced hoteliers; their daughter, Jane, is the manageress. 'No expense has been spared on the furnishings and rooms; they are modern, not traditional, no sign of chintz,' says a regular *Guide* reporter. 'All very comfortable; staff were attentive.' The building has original cornices, an inlaid staircase, open fires. Each bedroom is named after a local apple variety; each has its own style; all have fruit, sweets, and a fridge with water, apple juice and fresh milk. On fine days, lunch, afternoon tea and dinner can be taken on the brasserie terrace. Chef Ian Howell cooks 'first-class' modern American and European dishes, eg, corned beef hash, poached free-range egg; sweet herb marinated lamb chops, 'gone wrong' potatoes. Breakfast has 'the best' scrambled eggs. Weddings and parties are catered for. (*Richard Baker*)

Bedrooms: 8. *Open*: all year except 2 weeks Jan. *Facilities*: bar, lounge, dining room, civil wedding licence, terrace, 5-acre grounds, only public areas suitable for &. *Background music*: 'occasionally' in bar. *Location*: 2 miles W of Ledbury. *Smoking*: not allowed. *Children*: not under 7. *Dogs*: only guide dogs allowed. *Credit cards*: Amex, MasterCard, Visa. *Prices*: [2009] B&B £57.50–£92.50 per person, full alc £39.50, winter breaks, Christmas/New Year packages, 1-night bookings refused summer weekends. *V*

LEEDS West Yorkshire

See Shortlist

LEONARD STANLEY
Gloucestershire

Map 3:E5

The Grey Cottage

Tel/Fax 01453-822515

Bath Road
Leonard Stanley
Stonehouse GL10 3LU

Email rosemary.reeves@btopenworld.com
Website www.greycottage.ik.com

🏆 *César award in 1999*

'You can arrive stressed, but after an hour or two you feel completely relaxed,' say visitors returning in 2009 to this little stone Cotswolds guest house. 'It just gets better and better, you cannot fault it.' Others write of the 'incomparable cosseting' by the 'perfectionist', 'always cheerful' owner, Rosemary Reeves. 'Such an enthusiastic welcome; tea and cake with time for a catch-up.' 'Our room, as always, was clean and fresh; fruit and bottled water provided. The large bathroom had lovely new shower, luxury soaps, large fluffy towels.' Other touches include fresh milk in a flask for the tea tray, clothes brush, torch, and 'a hand bell to summon Rosie in an emergency'. There is an honesty bar, and guests can bring their own wine (no corkage charge). Dinner is by arrangement; no choice: preferences discussed at the time of booking. 'Beautifully laid tables' have 'candles and proper linen napkins'. 'A wonderful meal: baked organic breast of chicken with a creamy herb sauce and dauphinoise potatoes, followed by Bramley apple crumble with organic vanilla ice cream.' Breakfast includes freshly squeezed orange juice, smoked salmon with scrambled eggs, home-made jams, loaves of home-made bread for DIY toasting, 'butter balls, loads of cereals'. In the garden is a yew hedge planted in 1840. (*Sue and Colin Raymond, BJ Brooke-Smith, RGS*)

Bedrooms: 3. *Open*: all year except Christmas/New Year, occasional holidays. *Facilities*: sitting room with TV, conservatory, dining room, ¼-acre garden, unsuitable for ♿. *Background music*: 'no, never!' *Location*: 3 miles SW of Stroud. *Smoking*: not allowed. *Children*: not under 10. *Dogs*: not allowed. *Credit cards*: none. *Prices*: B&B £30–£55 per person, set dinner £23–£25, discount for 3-night stays.

LEWDOWN Devon   Map 1:C3

Lewtrenchard Manor   *Tel* 01566-783222
Lewdown   *Fax* 01566-783332
nr Okehampton EX20 4PN   *Email* info@lewtrenchard.co.uk
                                 Website www.lewtrenchard.co.uk

Chef/*patron* Jason Hornbuckle has introduced a private dining room, the *Purple Carrot*, at this 17th-century stone manor house which he manages for the von Essen group. Guests will watch the kitchen activity on screens (one of the eight courses will be cooked in the dining room). He says he has chosen the name to emphasise his 'back to nature policy': 80 per cent of the vegetables and fruit are grown in the grounds. His standard three-course dinner menu might include chicken and nutmeg *boudin blanc*; pan-fried John Dory, curried apple, cauliflower bhaji. In extensive, peaceful grounds (a dovecote, sunken garden and lake with swans), the 'romantic' house is a 'Victorian/ Elizabethan fantasy'. Once the home of the Revd Sabine Baring Gould, who wrote 'Onward Christian Soldiers', it has ornaments and carvings, stained glass, huge fireplaces, family portraits and antiques. Most bedrooms (two can be interconnecting) are off a music gallery, reached by a fine wooden staircase; the bridal suite is in a tower, overlooking the garden. There are fine fabrics, four-poster and sleigh beds, flowers, fruit, etc. More reports, please.

Bedrooms: 14, 1 suitable for ♿. *Open*: all year. *Facilities*: 2 lounges, bar, restaurant, 2 dining rooms, beauty treatments, function facilities, civil wedding licence, 12-acre garden. *Background music*: classical/'easy listening' in bar, restaurant. *Location*: 10 miles N of Tavistock town centre. *Smoking*: not allowed. *Children*: not under 8 at dinner. *Dogs*: allowed in bedrooms, and lounge areas on a lead 'if no one objects'. *Credit cards*: all major cards. *Prices*: [2009] B&B £67.50–£182.50, D,B&B £116.50–£237.50, full alc £65, special breaks, Christmas/New Year packages, 1-night bookings sometimes refused weekends. *V*

New reports help us keep the *Guide* up to date.

LEWES East Sussex   *See Shortlist*

LIFTON Devon   Map 1:C3

The Arundell Arms   *Tel* 01566-784666
Fore Street   *Fax* 01566-784494
Lifton PL16 0AA   *Email* reservations@arundellarms.com
                         Website www.arundellarms.com

💮 *César award in 2006*

'A lovely place. Immaculate yet friendly service.' Praise in 2009 for
this creeper-covered sporting hotel which its owner, Anne Voss-Bark,
has run for over 40 years. 'A discreet presence in the evening, she
greeted us warmly.' Her manager, James Storey, is 'a delight to deal
with', said another couple who took over the hotel for their daughter's
wedding. 'Outstanding staff, food and atmosphere.' Bedrooms are
'very comfortable'; the best are in a rear extension (front ones face a
road). All have flat-screen TV, a modern bathroom. There are 'antique
dressers, desks and chairs; pictures of country pursuits'. Dogs are
welcomed, as are children: this 'adds to the unstuffy atmosphere' in
the lounge, which has slate floors, rugs, large, comfortable sofas and
chairs. Chef Steven Pidgeon's cooking is admired: 'A sumptuous meal
with leek, potato and bacon soup; medallions of wild venison with
rösti. Coffee and truffles beside the log fire, a perfect way to end a day
on snow-clad Dartmoor.' Breakfast 'reflected the high standard of the
evening; poached eggs and bacon as perfect as can be'. Fisherfolk
come for the 20 miles of fishing on the Tamar, its six tributaries, and
a three-acre stocked lake; courses offer instruction at all levels. Non-
sporting visitors are equally welcomed. (*Trevor Lockwood, Graham and
Barbara Stradling, Max Lickfold*)

Bedrooms: 21, 4 on ground floor. *Open*: all year except evenings of 24–26 Dec,
27 Dec. *Facilities*: ramp, lounge, cocktail bar, public bar, 2 dining rooms,
conference/meeting rooms, games room, skittle alley, civil wedding licence,
½-acre garden, 20 miles fishing rights on River Tamar and tributaries (3-acre
stocked lake, fishing school). *Background music*: classical in restaurant,
classical/jazz in bar. *Location*: ½ mile off A30, 3 miles E of Launceston. *Smoking*:
not allowed. *Children*: all ages welcomed. *Dogs*: not allowed in restaurant. *Credit
cards*: all major cards. *Prices*: [2009] B&B £47.50–£97.50 per person, D,B&B
£30 added, full alc £50, off-season breaks, sporting, gourmet, etc, New Year
package. *V*

LINCOLN Lincolnshire   *See Shortlist*

LITTLE EASTON Essex   Map 2:C4

Roslyns
Duck Street
Little Easton, nr Great Dunmow
CM6 2JF

Tel 01371-852177
Fax 08715-036768
Email clare@roslynsbandb.co.uk
Website www.roslynsbandb.co.uk

In a village near Great Dunmow, a Victorian school house has been turned into this small B&B. Owner Clare Taege provides a 'friendly "home from home" atmosphere'. Only three bedrooms: a ground-floor room has direct access to the garden; the family room, with king-size bed and sofa, is 'quiet, simply furnished' and provided with shortbread, flowers, fluffy bath towels, constant hot water. There is no residents' lounge, but guests are given 'excellent' information on where to dine, and local attractions. Breakfast (continental or full English) is taken around a large table in a 'modern, airy' kitchen/ dining area, or on fine days by a fishpond overlooking farmland, in the 'well-maintained' garden. Hot dishes, cooked to order, include local sausages, 'sumptuous' scrambled eggs, and 'excellent toast'. A good overnight stop, handy for Stansted airport (limited parking is available and transfers can be arranged). The 'forgotten gardens' of Easton Lodge are close by. (*RR*)

Bedrooms: 3. *Open*: all year. *Facilities*: breakfast room, small garden, unsuitable for &. *Background music*: 'easy listening' at breakfast. *Location*: 2 miles N of Great Dunmow. *Smoking*: not allowed. *Children*: all ages welcomed. *Dogs*: not allowed. *Credit cards*: MasterCard, Visa. *Prices*: B&B £37.50–£65 per person.

How to contact the *Guide*
By mail: From anywhere in the UK, write to Freepost PAM 2931, London W11 4BR (no stamp is needed)
From outside the UK: *Good Hotel Guide*, 50 Addison Avenue, London W11 4QP, England
By telephone or fax: 020-7602 4182
By email: editor@goodhotelguide.com
Via our website: www.goodhotelguide.com

LITTLE PETHERICK Cornwall   Map 1:D2

Molesworth Manor   *Tel* 01841-540292
Little Petherick   *Email* molesworthmanor@aol.com
nr Padstow PL27 7QT   *Website* www.molesworthmanor.co.uk

Jessica and Geoff French run their B&B in a tiny village near Padstow
(which can be reached by a riverside footpath). The 17th-century
former rectory has 'comfortable accommodation, plenty of sitting
room and bedroom space'. There is an elaborately carved staircase,
stained glass, 'nice artwork'. Complimentary tea greets arriving
guests: on fine days, it can be taken on a terrace, and they can listen
to music and have a drink in the lounges (redecorated this year):
wines are taken seriously here. The bedrooms, named according to
their earlier use or position, vary in size and grandeur: His Lordship's
(large double, 'refined, classic'), Seigneur-de-la-Trinité, Cook's, etc.
'My top-floor room had far-reaching views, attractive period
furniture.' The 'superb' breakfast has fresh fruit salads and compotes,
freshly baked muffins and a 'daily special' as well as full English. The
Frenches are participants in the Green Tourism Business Scheme
and, where possible, all food is organic and locally sourced. Many
pubs, bistros and restaurants are near: a list is provided. The whole
house can be booked for a conference, wedding, etc. Newquay airport
is nine miles away.

Bedrooms: 9, plus 3 in self-catering cottage in grounds. *Open*: Feb–Oct. *Facilities*:
3 lounges, 1 with home cinema, breakfast conservatory, terrace, garden
(children's play area), unsuitable for &. *Background music*: none. *Location*:
1½ miles SE of Padstow off A389 to Wadebridge. *Smoking*: not allowed.
Children: all ages welcomed. *Dogs*: not allowed. *Credit cards*: none. *Prices*: [2009]
B&B £29–£50 per person, 1-night bookings sometimes refused. *V*

LITTLE SHELFORD   *See Shortlist*
Cambridgeshire

The *V* sign at the end of an entry indicates that a hotel has
agreed to take part in our Voucher scheme and to give *Guide*
readers a 25% discount on their bed-and-breakfast rates for a
one-night stay, subject to the conditions on the back of the
voucher and explained in 'How to use the *Good Hotel Guide*'
(page 57).

LITTLEBURY GREEN Essex   Map 2:C4

The Chaff House
Ash Grove Barns
Littlebury Green
nr Saffron Walden CB11 4XB

Tel 01763-836278
Email thechaffhouse@googlemail.com

In a quiet village near Saffron Walden, this picturesque and 'delightful' barn conversion stands on a large estate. The owner, Diana Duke, is 'exceptionally hospitable, and a brilliant cook', say visitors in 2009. The bedrooms are 'relaxing and comfortable': one is in the *Chaff House*, where the owner lives; the other two are in the *Dairy* and the *Log Shed* ('king-size bed, limited storage; small but adequate bathroom'). 'No baths, but super power showers.' Guests can sit on a patio with plants in tubs. On weekdays Mrs Duke serves, by arrangement, 'delicious' farmhouse meals using local produce. The short menu might include tomato and red pepper soup followed by duck breast with cherry sauce. Some good local pubs are nearby, including *Cricketers* at Clavering, run by Jamie Oliver's parents. 'Lovely walks around; totally rural', apart from 'occasional plane noise, barely noticeable'. Stansted airport and Cambridge are about 30 minutes' drive. (*John Jenkinson, T and RV*)

Bedrooms: 3, 2 in annexe on ground floor. *Open*: all year except Christmas/New Year, dining room closed midday and Sat/Sun. *Facilities*: lounge, dining room, kitchen for guests' use in annexe, small courtyard garden, in 900-acre estate, unsuitable for &. *Background music*: none. *Location*: 5 miles W of Saffron Walden. *Smoking*: not allowed. *Children*: not allowed. *Dogs*: not allowed. *Credit cards*: MasterCard, Visa. *Prices*: [2009] B&B £35–£50 per person, set dinner £25 (*not VAT-rated*).

LIVERPOOL Merseyside   Map 4:E2

Hope Street Hotel
40 Hope Street
Liverpool L1 9DA

Tel 0151-709 3000
Fax 0151-709 2454
Email sleep@hopestreethotel.co.uk
Website www.hopestreethotel.co.uk

Opposite the Philharmonic Hall in Liverpool's cultural centre, this striking modern conversion of a 19th-century carriage works is owned and managed by David Brewitt. It doubled in size during the summer of 2009, with the addition of 41 bedrooms in a linked adjacent building, reconstructed in modern style. This has sixth-floor conference facilities with panoramic views over the city. The earlier conversion, liked by *Guide* readers (and inspectors), has original iron columns, beams and exposed brickwork: 'It must be the best place to stay in Liverpool.' Bedrooms have solid wood floor, cherry wood furniture, Egyptian cotton sheets, goose-down pillows. 'Boys' toys' include LCD TV screens, DVD/CD-players, suites have a sophisticated entertainment system. The wooden corridor floors have under-laid sea-grass matting to combat noise. The trendy bar, *The Residents' Lounge*, has leather sofas and pop music. There are dramatic floor-to-ceiling glass sculptures, bare oak and yellow brickwork in the restaurant, *The London Carriage Works*. Chef Paul Askew's *prix fixe* dinner menu has modern dishes, perhaps Southport potted shrimps, with warm onion bread; Leahurst Farm organic smoked pork loin with whole-grain mustard sauce. A light menu of sandwiches, soups and salads is also available. Breakfast can be *à la carte*, continental or a 'super' cooked affair. (*PB, MP*)

Bedrooms: 89, some suitable for &. *Open*: all year. *Facilities*: lift, ramps, lobby, reading room, bar, restaurant, conference facilities, gym, treatment rooms. *Background music*: 'eclectic jazz' in bar and restaurant, live music weekends in lounge. *Location*: opposite Philharmonic Hall. *Smoking*: not allowed. *Children*: all ages welcomed. *Dogs*: only guide dogs allowed in restaurants. *Credit cards*: Amex, MasterCard, Visa. *Prices*: [2009] room £110–£350, breakfast £15.50 (full English), set dinner £18.95–£23.95, full alc £39, Christmas/New Year, 1-night bookings sometimes refused.

See also Shortlist

LODDISWELL Devon   Map 1:D4

Hazelwood House
Loddiswell
nr Kingsbridge TQ7 4EB

Tel 01548-821232
Fax 01548-821318
Email info@hazelwoodhouse.com
Website www.hazelwoodhouse.com

'The sort of hotel the *GHG* is all about: personally run, giving excellent value, and with very good food.' Inspectors returning to this early Victorian house found 'the welcome as charming as ever' and were 'impressed by the improvements' (spruced-up public rooms and heating in all bedrooms). Accommodation ranges from 'simple to gracious', say the 'wonderfully friendly' owners, Jane Bowman, Gillian Kean and Anabel Farnell-Watson. It stands 'idyllically' above the River

Avon in unspoilt woodland, rich in wildlife. Log fires burn in the public rooms, which have brightly coloured walls, antiques and local paintings. 'It felt like a private house.' The larger bedrooms on the first floor have a bathroom *en suite*; those on the second floor are simpler, and have bathrooms nearby. In the candlelit dining room, Kevin Wrigley offers a shortish menu of imaginative dishes. 'Delicious starters (crab risotto; aubergine salad); good main courses (bouillabaisse; lemon sole). The organic wines were good, too (no headache in the morning). No background music, such bliss.' Weddings, cultural courses, concerts and weekends with entertainments are held. Children are welcomed. A non-refundable deposit of the cost of a night's stay is requested on booking. The sea is six miles away.

Bedrooms: 14, 7 with facilities *en suite*. *Open*: all year. *Facilities*: hall with piano, drawing room, study/TV room, dining room, function/conference facilities, civil wedding licence, 67-acre grounds (river, boathouse, chapel), only restaurant suitable for &. *Background music*: on request. *Location*: 2 miles N of Loddiswell. *Smoking*: not allowed. *Children*: all ages welcomed. *Dogs*: not in dining room, on leads elsewhere. *Credit cards*: MasterCard, Visa. *Prices*: [2009] B&B £45–£80 per person, D,B&B £63–£108, set dinner £28, full alc £35, Christmas/New Year packages, special breaks. *V*

LONGHORSLEY Northumberland   Map 4:B3

Thistleyhaugh Farm
Longhorsley, nr Morpeth
NE65 8RG

Tel 01665-570629
Email thistleyhaugh@hotmail.com
Website www.thistleyhaugh.co.uk

'Not easy to find, but much harder to leave,' says a visitor this year to this 'combination of busy working farm and delightful country hotel' in an 'utterly remote corner of rural Northumberland'. A couple returning after two years to the Georgian house found it 'if anything better than before'. 'A real haven', set by the River Coquet, it is run 'with friendly skill' by Enid Nelless with daughters-in-law Zoë and Janice; her husband, Henry, with their two sons, runs a large organic cattle and sheep farm. The public rooms are 'beautifully furnished', with comfortable chairs and sofas, antique cupboards and grandfather clocks. The five bedrooms, priced according to size, are 'spotless', 'decorated to a high standard'. Bedlinen is 'of unusually high quality'. You can choose between duvet and blankets and sheets. There is a small refrigerator with milk and bottled water. Complimentary pre-dinner sherry is served in the garden room; the meal is taken communally at 7 pm around a huge oval oak table. Four courses, no choice, 'all superbly cooked from prime ingredients'. 'Home-fed lamb on the first night, ham on the second, both enhanced by the quality and variety of the vegetables.' Wine is available at £9 per bottle from 'a surprisingly good list'. The 'sumptuous' breakfast has porridge, cereals, sausages, eggs, bacon from the farm or locally cured. (*Mary Hewson, David and Joan Marston, Gordon Murray*)

Bedrooms: 5. *Open*: all year except Christmas, Jan. *Facilities*: 2 lounges, dining room, 720-acre farm, ¾-acre garden (summer house), fishing, shooting, golf, riding nearby, unsuitable for &. *Background music*: on request. *Location*: 10 miles N of Morpeth, W of A697. *Smoking*: not allowed. *Children*: all ages welcomed. *Dogs*: not allowed (kennels nearby). *Credit cards*: MasterCard, Visa. *Prices*: B&B £40–£80 per person, D,B&B £20 added, 1 night bookings often refused.

LONGSTOCK Hampshire   Map 2:D2

The Peat Spade Inn
Village Street
Longstock SO20 6DR

Tel 01264-810612
Fax 01264-811078
Email info@peatspadeinn.co.uk
Website www.peatspadeinn.co.uk

In a tranquil rural setting in the Test valley ('fly-fishing capital of the world'), this old inn and 'rooming house', 'full of character', is owned by Lucy Townsend (front-of-house) and Andy Clark (chef). Popular with locals, it gets very busy at the weekend. It caters for country pursuits, having a wet-gear drying room, and a safe for guns when shooting parties come. Recent praise: 'Very good. Nice room; delicious dinner and breakfast.' Accommodation is in the main building and in the red brick *Peat House* behind, where inspectors had a 'charming room, up a flight of steps; it had steeply sloping ceiling, olive-green walls, pale carpet, fridge with fresh milk, modem point. Beautiful shower room (skylight, large cabinet, huge shower head).' A new bedroom has been added this year. Andy Clark was joined in the kitchen in January 2009 by Chris Mackett. The seasonal menu might include Stilton and onion pasty with home-made pickle; beer-battered fish and chips. 'Wines chosen with care; real ales stocked.' Breakfast (no menu) includes eggs as you like, 'delicious fresh fruit salad, chunky toast'. There is a residents' lounge with fire, books and games, and a 'delightful rear patio'. The *Anchor Inn* at Lower Froyle, under the same ownership, enters the *Guide* this year. (*BR, and others*)

Bedrooms: 7, 5 in *Peat House* at rear. *Open*: all year except 25/26 Dec, restaurant closed Sun night. *Facilities*: ramps, lounge, bar, restaurant, private dining room, patio, garden. *Background music*: in restaurant. *Location*: centre of village, 1 mile

N of Stockbridge. *Smoking*: not allowed. *Children*: all ages welcomed. *Dogs*: allowed in public rooms and some bedrooms. *Credit cards*: all major cards. *Prices*: B&B £65 per person, set meal £34, full alc £40.

LOOE Cornwall   Map 1:D3

The Beach House
Marine Drive, Hannafore
Looe PL13 2DH

Tel 01503-262598
Fax 01503-262298
Email enquiries@thebeachhouselooe.co.uk
Website www.thebeachhouselooe.co.uk

'Everything is still of a high standard,' writes a visitor who returned in 2009 to this B&B in this popular Cornish resort. White-walled and gabled, the detached house stands across a road from the sea, and has panoramic views of Whitsand Bay, Looe Island and the coastline. The South West Coast Path runs past the front gate. The 'dedicated' owners, Rosie and David Reeve, provide 'a warm welcome': 'tea, delicious home-made cake and a chat'. Three bedrooms face the sea. 'Ours, Fistral, was perfect, so clean and fresh, with wonderful white bedlinen and a small balcony. An amazing view from French windows.' Rear rooms are 'decent sized' too: from Mullion, the cheapest, 'you have only to cross a corridor to sit in the tiny garden room and enjoy the view'. All bedrooms have been given a new carpet and colour scheme this year. Wi-Fi is available. The 'superb' breakfast is taken in a sea-facing room. You order the evening before, to coordinate at 15-minute intervals with other guests. Cooked dishes included 'cheese omelette one day, pancakes the next: we couldn't eat lunch after such a feast'. A non-refundable deposit of one night's tariff is required to confirm a booking. The private parking 'is a blessing in Looe'. (*Pam Adams, Sue and Colin Raymond, MB*)

Bedrooms: 5. *Open*: all year except Christmas. *Facilities*: garden room, breakfast room, terrace, garden, beach opposite, unsuitable for &. *Background music*: in breakfast room. *Location*: ½ mile from centre. *Smoking*: not allowed. *Children*: not under 16. *Dogs*: dogs not allowed. *Credit cards*: MasterCard, Visa. *Prices*: [2009] B&B £50–£65 per person, New Year package, 1-night bookings refused high season.

See also Shortlist

Report forms (Freepost in UK) are at the end of the *Guide*.

LORTON Cumbria   Map 4: inset C2

New House Farm
Lorton
nr Cockermouth CA13 9UU

Tel 01900-85404
Fax 01900-85478
Email hazel@newhouse-farm.co.uk
Website www.newhouse-farm.com

With views over lakeside fells in the Lorton/Buttermere valley, this Grade II listed 17th-century, whitewashed farmhouse is 'attractive and well maintained'. Owner Hazel Thompson is 'a friendly hostess', say visitors in 2009. Period features include oak beams, flagged floors and stone open fireplaces. The small lounges have bright colours, silver and antiques; there is Wi-Fi but no television (reception is poor). Two of the bedrooms are on the ground floor in converted outbuildings. Low Fell, in the oldest part of the old house, has a large slipper bath (water pressure may be variable). 'I enjoy providing traditional English home cooking, nothing fancy,' says Mrs Thompson, whose dinner menu (guests are asked to register likes and dislikes in advance) might include Solway potted shrimps; Herdwick lamb in a red wine casserole. Breakfast has freshly squeezed orange juice, fruit, porridge, croissants ('straight from the Aga'); sausage, bacon, mushrooms and eggs cooked to order, home-made marmalade. Lunches and teas are served in the café in a converted barn. Riders may bring their own horses. Traffic passes on the country road in front of the house, but the two rear bedrooms are 'perfectly quiet'. (*SW, and others*)

Bedrooms: 5, 1 in stable, 1 in old dairy. *Open*: all year. *Facilities*: 3 lounges, dining room, 17-acre grounds (garden, hot tub, streams, woods, field, lake and river, safe bathing, 2 miles), unsuitable for &. *Background music*: none. *Location*: on B5289, 2 miles S of Lorton. *Smoking*: not allowed. *Children*: not under 6. *Dogs*: not allowed in public rooms. *Credit cards*: MasterCard, Visa. *Prices*: B&B £70–£85 per person, D,B&B £28 added, Christmas/New Year packages, 1-night bookings sometimes refused. *V*

LOWER BOCKHAMPTON Dorset   Map 1:C6

Yalbury Cottage   NEW
Lower Bockhampton
nr Dorchester DT2 8PZ

Tel 01305-262382
Email enquiries@yalburycottage.com
Website www.yalburycottage.com

In early 2008, Jamie and Ariane Jones, who have a combined 45 years of experience in hotels, acquired this small hotel/restaurant, a conversion of four thatched cottages in peaceful Hardy country. 'They are friendly and helpful, and are working very hard,' says a visitor this year restoring it to the *Guide*. 'Everything is well maintained.' 'A very enjoyable stay,' others wrote. 'She is the cheerful front-of-house, he the excellent chef.' The restaurant and lounge are in the 300-year-old thatched cottage, the bedrooms are in more modern buildings. They are 'fresh, clean, well appointed; good bathrooms'. 'Our downstairs room was slightly small and dark, but comfortable.' In the 'stylish' dining room, Jamie Jones sources local produce for his modern dishes on a 'short, well-chosen' menu, eg, Portland crab and smoked salmon roll; braised shoulder of Westfield mutton and roast loin, butter crushed potatoes, swede cream. 'Excellent and well presented. Breakfast was wonderful, too, especially the smoked haddock with poached egg and lightly creamed sauce, and the home-made croissants.' 'The silence was palpable at night.' Children are welcomed, and *Yalbury Cottage* is dog-friendly. (*Veronica Murray, Lesley and Denis Paiba, Bryan and Mary Blaxall*)

Bedrooms: 8, 6 on ground floor. *Open*: all year except 22–29 Dec, 4–25 Jan. *Facilities*: lounge, restaurant, unsuitable for &. *Background music*: 'easy listening' in lounge. *Location*: 2 miles E of Dorchester. *Smoking*: not allowed. *Children*: welcomed on request. *Dogs*: allowed in lounge, some bedrooms. *Credit cards*: Amex, MasterCard, Visa. *Prices*: [2009] B&B £44–£80 per person, D,B&B £77.50–£110, set meals £29–£34, full alc £45. *V*

LOWER FROYLE Hampshire   Map 2:D3

The Anchor Inn   NEW

Lower Froyle
GU34 4NA

Tel 01420-23261
Fax 01420-520467
Email info@anchorinnatlowerfroyle.co.uk
Website www.anchorinnatlowerfroyle.co.uk

In a prosperous village on the edge of the South Downs, this handsome old inn has been given the 'relaxed, understated look of a bygone England' by Miller's Collection, a small group which includes *The Peat Spade Inn* at Longstock (*qv*). It is managed by Steven Liston with 'a capable young team' who 'gallantly' greeted *Guide* inspectors. Public rooms have 'low-flying beams (thoughtfully padded), open fires, an amiable clutter of bygones that coalesce into a theme of imperial nostalgia (rifle cases, helmets, bugles, etc)'. Bedrooms are named after First World War poets. 'Wilfred Owen was a pleasing double-aspect room, attractively done in duck-egg blue with white woodwork. Generous bedlinen, earthy fabrics, lots of pictures, well-chosen furnishings and fittings. Champagne and fresh milk were in a discreet mini-fridge; the galley bathroom was slightly cramped, but the walk-in shower worked well.' In the 'pleasantly proportioned' main dining room, chef Kevin Chandler serves 'inventive but unpretentious' modern dishes: 'We thoroughly enjoyed pork and sage pâté; smoked haddock with Welsh rarebit; café liégeoise. Service was well paced, unstarchy.' Breakfast is an informal affair in the bar: 'No menu, you have to ask if you want cooked dishes (good local sausage, bacon and black pudding); nice fresh berries and cereals; decent coffee, lots of toast, a bit short on jam.' Shooting and fly-fishing can be arranged locally.

Bedrooms: 5. *Open*: all year except 25 Dec. *Facilities*: bar, lounge, dining room, courtyard garden. *Background music*: 'soft' in public areas. *Location*: centre of village, 4 miles NE of Alton. *Smoking*: not allowed. *Children*: not under 10 in bedrooms. *Dogs*: allowed. *Credit cards*: all major cards. *Prices*: [2009] B&B £65–£85 per person, full alc £35, special breaks.

LOWER ODDINGTON
Gloucestershire

Map 3:D6

The Fox Inn   NEW

Lower Oddington
nr Stow-on-the-Wold
GL56 0UR

Tel 01451-870555
Fax 01451-870666
Email info@foxinn.net
Website www.foxinn.net

Creeper-clad, with flagstone floors, beams and old fireplaces, this 16th-century pub ('We are not a hotel,' says its owner, Ian MacKenzie) is in a quiet Cotswold village near Stow-on-the-Wold. 'He looked after us with great care,' says the nominator. 'Our room was stylish, well equipped, good value. A lovely place.' The 'high standards without formality' were admired by an inspector. The greeting is friendly, bags carried to the bedrooms – only three, reached by a staircase from the entrance hall. The Garden Room is the largest, 'spacious, with double aspect, sloping ceilings; well coordinated with wallpaper in winter berry tones, and checked tweedy curtains; antique furnishings: handsome carved bed ends, chest of drawers, dressing table; two leather armchairs, a table with books and magazines. A Victorian-style bathroom.' The Courtyard room has a private bathroom opposite. In the 'inviting' dining room (slate floors, old beams, wooden tables and chairs) the Australian chef, Raymond Pearce, provides 'excellent food, with sensible portions'. 'All perfect: starters of steamed mussels, and goat's cheese, roasted pepper and pesto tart; steak and ale pie, and scallops to follow. Service by the charming staff was well coordinated.' Summer meals can be taken in the garden. Only continental breakfast is served: 'Delicious croissants, home-made marmalade and jam; help-yourself muesli and cereals, do-it-yourself toast; a large pot of excellent coffee.' (*James Moy, and others*)

Bedrooms: 3. *Open*: all year except 25 Dec. *Facilities*: bar, 2 dining rooms, ¼-acre garden, unsuitable for &. *Background music*: none. *Location*: 3 miles E of Stow-on-the-Wold. *Smoking*: not allowed. *Children*: all ages welcomed. *Dogs*: not allowed in bedrooms. *Credit cards*: MasterCard, Visa. *Prices*: [2009] B&B £34–£47.50 per person, full alc £30, 1-night booking usually refused Sat.

LOWESTOFT Suffolk   *See Shortlist*

LUDLOW Shropshire   Map 3:C4

Mr Underhill's   *Tel* 01584-874431
Dinham Weir   *Website* www.mr-underhills.co.uk
Ludlow SY8 1EH

♧ *César award in 2000*

In gardens by the River Teme below Ludlow Castle, Christopher and Judy Bradley's restaurant-with-rooms is a 'welcoming place', say fans returning in 2009. 'There is always someone to greet you, help with luggage, explain how the room works.' Christopher Bradley's *Michelin*-starred cooking remains the 'high point'; the menu has no choice until dessert, but alternatives are offered. Dinner starts with 'hobbit-sized tasters' (eg, cornets of smoked salmon; a 'stunning' butternut squash soup; duck liver custard). 'Pavé of brill was stunning, with the refreshing flavours of lime, coriander and ginger; slow-roasted fillet of Marches beef came with a doll's house-sized lasagne; a tiny cherry sponge is served before the desserts. Service by a well-trained young team is almost balletic.' *Miller's House* (which had two suites) has been sold; a new suite, with a sitting room and two bathrooms, has been created in the main house. The *Shed* suite, in the garden, is liked. Other bedrooms are small but 'well thought out; the bed is high, wide, blissfully comfortable; two bucket chairs, a decent wardrobe with plenty of hangers, a tea and coffee tray with good china, fresh milk; compact bathroom well fitted'. Accommodation is also available in the *Old School* (breakfast, afternoon tea and pasta suppers stocked in kitchen). Guests are asked not to arrive before 3 pm except by arrangement. (*Padi Howard*)

Bedrooms: 6, 1 in annexe. *Open*: all year except Christmas, 10 days June, 10 days Nov, restaurant closed Mon/Tues. *Facilities*: small lounge, restaurant, function facilities, ½-acre courtyard, riverside garden (fishing, swimming), unsuitable for &. *Background music*: none. *Location*: below castle, on River Teme, station ½ mile, parking. *Smoking*: not allowed. *Children*: not 2–8. *Dogs*: not allowed. *Credit cards*: MasterCard, Visa. *Prices*: [2009] B&B £65–£150 per person, set dinner £47.50–£55, New Year packages, 1-night bookings sometimes refused Sat.

See also Shortlist

LYDFORD Devon   Map 1:C4

The Dartmoor Inn   *Tel* 01822-820221
Moorside   *Fax* 01822-820494
Lydford, nr Okehampton   *Email* info@dartmoorinn.co.uk
EX20 4AY   *Website* www.dartmoorinn.com

Q *César award in 2007*

'Charm without chintz' is the style at Karen and Philip Burgess's restaurant-with-rooms on a busy road west of Dartmoor. In two ground-floor rooms of this small inn, Mrs Burgess runs a boutique selling Swedish linen and glassware, French quilts and locally designed jewellery. The other ground-floor rooms form a series of dining areas, some formal, with wood-burning stove, others more casual. The modern cooking of Philip Burgess and Andrew Honey is thought 'very good'. They use local, seasonal ingredients in dishes like Falmouth Bay scallops, bacon and cauliflower purée; roast fillet of wild black bream, almonds and coriander; home-made biscuits with the farmhouse cheeses. 'A separate vegetarian menu was produced at one hour's notice when we stayed.' The bedrooms are 'spacious, comfortable, warm, and pleasantly decorated in pale colours'; bathrooms are 'of good size and well equipped'. A Roberts radio is provided; TV is available on request, but no tea/coffee-making facilities. 'One of the best breakfasts we have been offered anywhere.' Unusual items include corned beef hash; fillet of beef; caramel-glazed bananas and sugared blood oranges. (*Jeanette Bloor, DT, and others*)

Bedrooms: 3. *Open*: all year, restaurant closed Sun evening, Mon lunch. *Facilities*: 2 bars, restaurant, small sunken garden, unsuitable for &. *Background music*: none.

Location: 6 miles E of Tavistock on A386 to Okehampton, train Exeter/Plymouth, parking. *Smoking*: not allowed. *Children*: not really suitable for small children. *Dogs*: not allowed in bedrooms. *Credit cards*: Amex, MasterCard, Visa. *Prices*: B&B from £62.50 per person, set dinner £22.50, full alc £38, special breaks.

LYME REGIS Dorset   *See Shortlist*

LYMINGTON Hampshire   Map 2:E2

Britannia House   *Tel* 01590-672091
Station Street   *Email* enquiries@britannia-house.com
Lymington SO41 3BA   *Website* www.britannia-house.com

'Wonderfully positioned', a short stroll from the marina, cobbled streets and smart shops, Tobias Feilke's B&B consists of two houses opposite each other. 'An enthusiastic and charming host. The material put together for visitors was as good as any we have seen,' says a visitor in 2009. 'The decor in the very comfortable, large sitting room, the "farmhouse" kitchen and our room were planned by someone with a discerning eye for design.' The sitting room, in the older building (which dates from 1865), has wide views (harbour and marina) and 'a lovely ambience'. Decorated in dramatic blue and yellow, it contains 'large, enveloping sofas, good lighting, plenty of books (lots in German), and magazines'. The bedrooms here have plain walls, Berber carpet, patterned curtains, bedcovers and cushions. 'Ours, at the top, was decent sized, very pleasant, with adjacent romantic, spacious bathroom.' Three bedrooms in the more modern (2003) three-storey town house on the quayside have a plainer style: check fabrics, pine and painted furniture. Mr Feilke cooks a good breakfast, served at a 'convivial' communal table in the large pine kitchen: 'Delicious mushrooms, non-meat sausages for vegetarians.' 'Excellent value for money.' (*Mrs MJ Hall*)

Bedrooms: 6. *Open*: all year. *Facilities*: lounge, kitchen/breakfast room, courtyard garden, unsuitable for &. *Background music*: none. *Location*: 2 mins' walk from High Street/quayside, parking. *Smoking*: not allowed. *Children*: not under 12. *Dogs*: not allowed. *Credit cards*: MasterCard, Visa. *Prices*: B&B £37.50–£45 per person, midweek discount, 1-night bookings refused weekends.

LYNMOUTH Devon   *See Shortlist*

LYNTON Devon   *See Shortlist*

LYTHAM Lancashire   *See Shortlist*

MALVERN WELLS Worcestershire   Map 3:D5

The Cottage in the Wood	*Tel* 01684-588860
Holywell Road	*Fax* 01684-560662
Malvern Wells	*Email* reception@cottageinthewood.co.uk
WR14 4LG	*Website* www.cottageinthewood.co.uk

The views from this traditional hotel, high on the wooded eastern slopes of the Malvern hills, are 'reason enough to go': on a clear day you can see the spire of Gloucester cathedral, some 30 miles away. Owners John and Sue Pattin run it with son Dominick (chef) and son-in-law Nick Webb (manager). They and their staff are 'friendly, welcoming'. Seven bedrooms 'with a country feel' are in the main house ('ours was large and comfortable'). The newer bedrooms are in the purpose-built *Pinnacles* 100 yards away: they are 'pleasant, well equipped' (free Wi-Fi, tea-making kit, home-made shortbread, a 'comprehensive information guide'). One visitor found the decor 'dated'. In the panoramic restaurant, the food is generally admired: 'Competent and beautifully presented' is a comment this year. The menus might include tian of crayfish with a roasted red pepper dressing; chicken supreme with chorizo, ratatouille. 'A wonderful selection of wines.' You can walk from the door to the top of the hills. (*Chris and Liz Blount, John Moy, and others*)

Bedrooms: 30, 4 in *Beech Cottage*, 70 yds, 19 (1 suitable for ♿) in *The Pinnacles*, 100 yds. *Open*: all year. *Facilities*: lounge, bar, restaurant, function facilities, 7-acre grounds (terrace), leisure facilities nearby. *Background music*: none. *Location*: 3 miles S of Great Malvern. *Smoking*: not allowed. *Children*: all ages welcomed. *Dogs*: Guide dogs welcomed, other dogs in *The Pinnacles* only. *Credit cards*: Amex, MasterCard, Visa. *Prices*: [2009] B&B £39.50–£92.50 per person, D,B&B £72–£114.50, full alc £35, Christmas/New Year packages. *V*

MANCHESTER   *See Shortlist*

For details of the Voucher scheme see page 57.

MARAZION Cornwall   Map 1:E1

Mount Haven Hotel & Restaurant	*Tel* 01736-710249
Turnpike Road	*Fax* 01736-711658
Marazion TR17 0DQ	*Email* reception@mounthaven.co.uk
	Website www.mounthaven.co.uk

The smell of incense greets visitors to Mike and Orange Trevillion's contemporary hotel on the edge of a village overlooking St Michael's Mount. They have given it an Asian aspect: a Buddha over the entrance; silks from Mumbai, tapestries from Jaipur. 'A friendly place, personally run,' say inspectors this year. 'We couldn't have been more warmly welcomed.' Originally a coach house, much altered in 1970, it is 'immaculate'; it has long wood-lined, carpeted corridors, original paintings. There are leather sofas and bold floral decorations in the large lounge/bar, which has a picture window leading to a terrace with smart steel and slatted furniture and views of Mount's Bay. The young staff 'are genuinely interested in visitors, but not over-familiar'. 'Our attractive bedroom, in cream and beige, had a small balcony with a view of the mount across an old stone building; good storage.' There is a new chef, Bruce Rennie, who uses local, organic ingredients for a short seasonally-changing menu (with daily specials): dishes might include crab and avocado salad; shin of beef, crisped celeriac. We'd welcome reports on his cooking. A team of holistic therapists comes to give treatment to guests (Indian head massage, etc).

Bedrooms: 18, some on ground floor. *Open*: mid-Feb–mid-Dec. *Facilities*: lounge/bar, restaurant, healing room (holistic treatments), sun terrace, ½-acre grounds (rock/sand beaches 100 yds), unsuitable for &. *Background music*: 'chill-out' music all day, bar, lounge. *Location*: 4 miles E of Penzance, car park. *Smoking*: not allowed. *Children*: all ages welcomed. *Dogs*: allowed in public rooms. *Credit cards*: MasterCard, Visa. *Prices*: [2009] B&B £50–£100 per person, D,B&B £77–£112, full alc from £40, 3-night breaks spring/autumn, min. 2 nights on bank holidays.

MARKINGTON North Yorkshire   Map 4:D4

Hob Green	*Tel* 01423-770031
Markington	*Fax* 01423-771589
nr Harrogate HG3 3PJ	*Email* info@hobgreen.com
	Website www.hobgreen.com

The Hutchinson family have been 'actively involved' in running this 18th-century house as a 'most comfortable' traditional hotel since 1982; Christopher Ashby is the manager. There are extensive views across a valley and woodland walks from the award-winning gardens. A Victorian kitchen garden provides produce for long-serving chef Chris Taylor's 'professionally presented' menus (with dishes like salad Niçoise; duck confit, black cherry and red wine sauce). The Friday fish menu is 'particularly good'. All main courses come with the chef's selection of vegetables. Many original features (panelling and moulding) were retained in the restoration of the house. The sitting rooms have 'lots of comfortable seating', curios, marquetry furniture, a log fire. In the 'exceptionally well-equipped' bedrooms are flowery fabrics, patterned wallpaper, tea/coffee-making, fresh milk in a fridge, chocolates, books; there is an evening turn-down service. One room has a four-poster, one has a private lounge. Breakfast has 'proper butter', home-made preserves; a wide choice of cooked dishes. Conferences and functions are catered for. Wi-Fi is available. Fountains Abbey is three miles away. (*Dorothy Brining*)

Bedrooms: 11. *Open*: all year. *Facilities*: hall, drawing room, sun lounge, restaurant, civil wedding licence, 2½-acre garden (children's play area), 800-acre grounds, unsuitable for &. *Background music*: classical in public rooms. *Location*: 1 mile SW of Markington, 5 miles SW of Ripon. *Smoking*: not allowed. *Children*: all ages welcomed. *Dogs*: not allowed in public rooms. *Credit cards*: all major cards. *Prices*: B&B £57.50–£95 per person, D,B&B £77.50–£120, set dinner £27.50, full alc £38, special breaks, 1-night bookings refused weekends.

MARTINHOE Devon   Map 1:B4

Heddon's Gate Hotel   *Tel* 01598-763481
Martinhoe, Parracombe   *Email* hotel@heddonsgate.co.uk
Barnstaple   *Website* www.heddonsgate.co.uk
EX31 4PZ

'Splendidly located', on the slopes of the heavily wooded Heddon valley, this small hotel is 'comfortable and quiet', say visitors this year. Its 'obliging' owners, Anne and Eddie Eyles, are 'warmly welcoming'. Formerly a Victorian hunting lodge, it has an 'amazing falling away and down garden', and an old-fashioned decor. There are stags' antlers and black leather furniture in the bar; tapestries on green walls; cases of china ornaments in the lounge. Housekeeping is 'immaculate'. A complimentary afternoon cream tea 'was very welcome after a day on Exmoor'. The daily-changing four-course menu (with limited choice) has 'mostly traditional' dishes using local produce, eg, twice-baked cheese soufflé; rib-eye of beef, roasted cherry tomatoes, whisky sauce. 'Excellent, quite sophisticated but essentially simple, and served without maddening delays.' The bedrooms vary greatly (some are large). Some are named after their original use: Grandma's ('nicely furnished', Victorian-style); Nanny's (antique stained-glass windows); Servants' Quarters (with private sitting room). Beds are turned down at night. Poor TV reception and the lack of a mobile phone signal are a 'distinct advantage' to some. A 'walker's paradise', this is 'good for dog owners'. (*John and Valerie Fleming, and others*)

Bedrooms: 10. *Open*: all year, except Christmas/New Year, dining room closed midday. *Facilities*: 2 reception halls, 2 lounges, library, bar, dining room, 2½-acre grounds, river, fishing, riding, pony trekking nearby, sea ¾ mile, unsuitable for &. *Background music*: none. *Location*: 6 miles W of Lynton. *Smoking*: not allowed. *Children*: not under 12 (except in parties taking exclusive use). *Dogs*: not allowed in dining room, not unattended in bedrooms. *Credit cards*: MasterCard, Visa. *Prices*: [2009] B&B £48–£74 per person, D,B&B £75–£101, set dinner £31.50, special breaks, 1-night bookings occasionally refused. ***V***

MASHAM North Yorkshire   Map 4:D4

Swinton Park   *Tel* 01765-680900
Masham, nr Ripon   *Fax* 01765-680901
HG4 4JH   *Email* reservations@swintonpark.com
                                  Website www.swintonpark.com

'A good balance is struck between being child friendly and offering adults the space to get away from the little monsters,' says a parent visiting this creeper-clad, 17th-century castle (Grade II* listed). 'The most amazing hotel I have stayed in,' wrote another. Set on a 'spectacular' huge estate, it is the family home of Mark and Felicity Cunliffe-Lister who run it as a luxury hotel; Andrew McPherson is the manager. 'Staff are unfailingly friendly, down to earth.' For children there is a playroom with toys, ducks to feed, a tree house. Adults can enjoy a wide range of activities in the grounds (see below), and dine alone in the evenings (babysitting provided). There is also a cookery school and a spa. The large reception rooms have antique furniture, family portraits, mirrors, rugs on polished floors. The restaurant, *Samuel's*, has a gold-leaf ceiling, mahogany panelling, an open fire. 'The food is outstanding': chef Simon Crannage serves a seasonal market menu, eg, local duck royale; estate venison with garden vegetables. There are 'stunning views' from many of the spacious bedrooms. All have Wi-Fi access; four have 'disabled-friendly fittings'. Good walking all around: 'We liked the suggested walks within the grounds.' The castle has an eco-friendly laundry and a 'carbon-neutral' wood-chip boiler. (*Matt Windsor, Anthony Bradbury, Vicky Morrison*)

Bedrooms: 30, 4 suitable for &. *Open*: all year, restaurant closed midday Mon/Tues. *Facilities*: lift, ramps, 3 lounges, library, bar, restaurant, banqueting hall, private dining room, spa, games room, snooker room, cinema, conference facilities, civil wedding licence, 200-acre grounds (grotto, orangery, deer park, 5 lakes, fishing, falconry centre, model boat racing, swings, play castle, bowls, croquet, cricket, 9-hole golf course, clay-pigeon shooting, riding, falconry, kite flying, etc). *Background music*: light jazz in bar, classical in dining room. *Location*: 1 mile SW of Masham. *Smoking*: not allowed. *Children*: all ages welcomed. *Dogs*: not allowed in public rooms, or unattended in bedrooms. *Credit cards*: all major cards (*Amex 3% service charge*). *Prices*: [2009] B&B £80–£175 per person, D,B&B £115–£210, set dinner £42–£62, full alc £51, special breaks, Christmas/New Year packages, 1-night bookings sometimes refused Sat. *V*

MATLOCK Derbyshire   *See Shortlist*

MATLOCK BATH Derbyshire   Map 3:B6

Hodgkinson's Hotel   *Tel* 01629-582170
150 South Parade   *Fax* 01629-584891
Matlock Bath, Matlock   *Email* enquiries@hodgkinsons-hotel.co.uk
DE4 3NR   *Website* www.hodgkinsons-hotel.co.uk

'Professionally' run by its 'caring' proprietor, Dianne Carrieri, with a small staff, this small hotel provides 'excellent-value rooms and food', writes a regular visitor in 2009. 'Very much a family place, where the friendly owners make all the difference.' The Victorian building, cut into the cliff face, stands on the busy Matlock–Derby road, the A6 (rear rooms are quietest). The 'quirky ambience' is liked: it is dedicated to Victoriana. There are original fittings (stained glass, etc), combined with antiques plus 'esoteric items' (old books and prints, fox furs, hats, Staffordshire china). Chef Krisztian Hadszala's Mediterranean-style dishes are 'good, fairly simple': perhaps herb- and nut-crusted salmon with baby spinach, basil and lime juice. The 'clean and comfortable' bedrooms, which have 'real character', are on four floors, no lift. Most are a good size, but the single is small. Three bathrooms have been renovated this year. The 'memorable', award-winning breakfast includes porridge, freshly squeezed orange juice, non-packaged butter and conserves. There are books and games in the lounge. The small rear garden has roses and a pergola built of brick, old chimney pots and timber. The town is a tourist centre for the Derbyshire dales and the Peak District, and is popular with bikers on Saturday morning, but despite amusement arcades and take-away food outlets, it 'retains some charm'. (*David Verney, EC*)

Bedrooms: 8. *Open*: all year except 25/26 Dec. *Facilities*: lounge, bar, restaurant, meeting/private dining room, 1-acre garden (opposite River Derwent, fishing, day ticket), unsuitable for &. *Background music*: in restaurant, blues/jazz, classical. *Location*: central, parking for 5 cars. *Smoking*: not allowed. *Children*: all ages welcomed. *Dogs*: not allowed in restaurant. *Credit cards*: Amex, MasterCard, Visa. *Prices*: [to Mar 2010] B&B £45–£90, set dinner £26.50–£29.50, full alc £40, 2-night breaks, New Year package, 1-night bookings refused Sat July–Oct. *V*

MAULDS MEABURN
Cumbria

Map 4: inset C2

Meaburn Hill Farmhouse   NEW

Tel 01931-715168
Email kindleysides@btinternet.com
Website www.cumbria-bed-and-breakfast.co.uk

Maulds Meaburn, Penrith
CA10 3HN

On the edge of a village near Penrith, this 'welcoming, relaxing' 16th-century farmhouse returns to the *Guide* after a period without reports. 'We were cosseted and spoilt rotten; we enjoyed browsing through newspapers and magazines in front of a roaring fire,' says a visitor in 2009. Run by 'chatty but never intrusive' hosts, Annie Kindleysides (whose parents farmed here) and Brian Morris, the house has oak beams, knick-knacks everywhere. The bedrooms are up 14 steps. 'Newly baked brownies or flapjacks would appear in our room around teatime; there was always a bowl of fresh fruit.' Mrs Kindleysides will serve a three-course supper by arrangement. She uses home-grown or locally sourced (within six miles) produce for her dishes, eg, warm salad of leaves with dry-cured ham; hotpot roast of Herdwick hogget, Jerusalem artichoke gratin. 'Exquisite kedgeree; delicate trout.' No wine licence, bring your own. Breakfast has freshly baked bread, potato cakes, fruit salad, eggs cooked to order. Packed lunches can be provided. Afternoon tea can be taken on the lawn. Dogs are welcomed. (*Margaret Meacher, and others*)

Bedrooms: 4, 1 in adjoining farmhouse suitable for &. *Open*: all year, dining room closed Mon/Fri, B&B only at Christmas/New Year. *Facilities*: library, dining room, lounge, 2-acre garden (tea/picnic area, dog-walking area). *Background music*: on request. *Location*: 1 mile N of Crosby Ravensworth. *Smoking*: not allowed. *Children*: all ages welcomed. *Dogs*: allowed 'if fully vaccinated and acceptable to other guests'. *Credit cards*: none. *Prices*: [2009] B&B £37.50–£60 per person, set dinner £16, 1-night bookings sometimes refused at peak times.

MAWGAN PORTH Cornwall   Map 1:D2

Bedruthan Steps Hotel
Mawgan Porth
TR8 4BU

Tel 01637-860555
Fax 01637-860714
E.mail stay@bedruthan.com
Website www.bedruthan.com

In a spectacular setting above a golden, sandy beach in north Cornwall, this large hotel has welcomed families for over 40 years. Owner/manager sisters Emma Stratton, Deborah Wakefield and Rebecca Whittington have won awards for their committed green agenda: this year's initiatives include the installation of a recapture system to harness waste heat from fridges. A 'real nappy kit' is being tested. 'A most enjoyable stay: lovely staff, excellent food, attractive decor,' one visitor wrote. The public areas are 'relatively glamorous', with slate flooring, neutral colours, lots of oak. The bedrooms range from larger suites for families, to cheaper rooms without the sea view. There is much for children to do beyond the beach: they have clubs, indoor and outdoor play areas, daily entertainment; an Ofsted-registered nursery. The Ocean Spa has an indoor pool, an adult-only thermal suite, a hammam, and treatments. The chef, Adam Clark, serves *table d'hôte* menus in two dining rooms: he tries to source 70 per cent of the ingredients from Cornwall for his dishes (eg, roasted butternut squash, spinach and Cornish Blue cheese tart; rump of spring lamb, Cornish asparagus). A family dining option has special menus for adults and children. Lighter lunches are served in the *Café Indigo*. A sister hotel, *The Scarlet*, was due to open close by as the *Guide* went to press. (*DM, PF*)

Bedrooms: 101, 1 suitable for &. *Open*: all year except 22–29 Dec. *Facilities*: lift, 2 lounges, 2 bars, 3 dining rooms, ballroom (live music 2/3 times a week), 4 children's clubs, spa (indoor swimming pool), civil wedding licence, 5-acre grounds (heated swimming pools, tennis, playing field). *Background music*: occasional. *Location*: 4 miles NE of Newquay. *Smoking*: not allowed. *Children*: all ages welcomed. *Dogs*: only guide dogs allowed. *Credit cards*: MasterCard, Visa. *Prices*: [2009] B&B £65–£130 per person, D,B&B £77–£142, set dinner £29.95, special breaks, Christmas/New Year packages, 1-night bookings sometimes refused.

MAWNAN SMITH Cornwall   Map 1:E2

Budock Vean   *Tel* 01326-252100
Helford Passage, Mawnan Smith   *Fax* 01326-250892
nr Falmouth TR11 5LG   *Email* reservations@budockvean.co.uk
                                    Website www.budockvean.co.uk

'Full marks yet again; I don't know why I bother going anywhere else.'
Praise in 2009 from a fan on her 'umpteenth' visit to Martin and
Amanda Barlow's traditional hotel in large grounds above the River
Helford. Other visitors, returning after some years, were impressed: 'It
has the buzz of a good family hotel; good value, too.' The manager,
Vicky Harrison, is 'charming, efficient'; the staff, many long serving,
are 'excellent in their various roles'. The enlargement of the terrace for
drinks, meals and sunbathing is 'a great benefit'. 'Superior' bedrooms
are recommended as 'standard ones can be basic'. 'Our large room was
perfectly prepared, squeaky clean, everything worked; a dazzling
white bathroom with generous towels.' Men must wear jacket and tie
after 7 pm in the bar and the main restaurant, where chef Darren
Kelly's traditional cooking was again admired: 'Scallops with king
prawns; tasty soups; delicious Bodmin venison; main courses are
accompanied by a generous dish of vegetables; puddings are
imaginative.' Breakfast ('as good as it gets') has fresh fruit salad,
tempting cooked dishes; a supplement of £2 for freshly squeezed
orange juice. A country club in the large grounds has a nine-hole golf
course, tennis and croquet. The garden leads down past terraced
ponds and waterfalls to a secluded creek. (*Mary Woods, Ian and
Barbara Dewey, also PW Townend*)

Bedrooms: 57, 4 self-catering cottages. *Open*: all year except 2–22 Jan (for
refurbishment). *Facilities*: lift, ramps, 3 lounges, conservatory, 2 bars, restaurant,
snooker room, civil wedding licence, 65-acre grounds (covered heated
swimming pool (15 by 8 metres), hot tub, health spa, country club with bar,
restaurant, 9-hole golf course, tennis, croquet, archery), river frontage (water
sports, boat trips), unsuitable for ♿. *Background music*: live in restaurant.
Location: 6 miles SW of Falmouth. *Smoking*: not allowed. *Children*: no under-7s
on ground floor after 7 pm. *Dogs*: allowed in some bedrooms, not in public
rooms. *Credit cards*: Diners, MasterCard, Visa. *Prices*: [2009] B&B £53–£111 per
person, D,B&B £65–£123, set dinner £33.50, full alc £50, themed breaks,
Christmas/New Year/Easter packages.

We ask for more reports on a hotel if we haven't received
feedback from readers for some time. Please send an
endorsement if you think a hotel should remain in the *Guide*.

Meudon
Mawnan Smith
nr Falmouth TR11 5HT

Tel 01326-250541
Fax 01326-250543
Email wecare@meudon.co.uk
Website www.meudon.co.uk

'Splendid location in lovely grounds. Impeccable service and attention.' This year's praise for this red brick building with a large 1960s extension and a decor of 'patterned carpets and chintz'. Its subtropical 'hanging gardens' with rare shrubs, plants and trees lead down a valley to a private beach. The veteran Harry Pilgrim is chairman; his son, Mark, the fifth hotelier generation, is managing director. The traditional values include turn-down service at night and shoe cleaning. An earlier endorsement: 'Staff, rooms, and variety and quality of food, all excellent.' All bedrooms have double-glazed windows. Suites have a patio or balcony; one has an adjoining room for children. The comfortable main lounge has open fire, flowers and 'lovely garden views'. A 'dress code of jacket and tie' is encouraged for evening dining: 'As a tie-wearer, perhaps a dying breed, I found this pleasing,' one correspondent tells us. In the restaurant, chef Alan Webb uses local produce, including fresh fish from Newlyn, for his daily-changing menus, eg, smoked salmon and crab roulade; roast noisettes of Cornish lamb. 'The cooking is never repetitive.' A yacht is available for skippered charter; garden packages, creative writing weekends, etc, are offered. (*Philip Quick, K and ME*)

Bedrooms: 29, 16 on ground floor, 2 suitable for &, self-catering cottage. *Open*: all year except Jan. *Facilities*: lift, ramps, 3 lounges, bar, restaurant, 10-acre grounds (gardens, private beach, yacht), golf, riding, windsurfing nearby. *Background music*: none. *Location*: 4 miles SW of Falmouth. *Smoking*: not allowed. *Children*: all ages welcomed. *Dogs*: not allowed in public rooms. *Credit cards*: all major cards. *Prices*: [2009] B&B £75–£100 per person, set dinner £39, full alc £46.50, special breaks, Christmas package.

MELTON MOWBRAY Leicestershire Map 2:A3

Sysonby Knoll
Asfordby Road
Melton Mowbray LE13 0HP

Tel 01664-563563
Fax 01664-410364
Email reception@sysonby.com
Website www.sysonby.com

In a market town famous for pork pies and Stilton cheese, this traditional hotel stands in large grounds with a river frontage. Owners Jenny and Gavin Howling, with manager Wayne Jenson, provide 'fantastic accommodation and superb food', says a visitor in 2009.

'Good value; clean, well cared for', the red brick Edwardian house has a 'magical' garden with a pond, manicured lawns in front, trees on either side. Windows that face the road are double or triple glazed. Most bedrooms overlook a quadrangle around a central courtyard. They vary greatly in size and shape; two four-poster rooms look over the garden and river to cattle in fields. Rooms at the back are 'quiet, but slightly anonymous'. One couple found their room above the kitchen noisy and uncomfortable. The restaurant has recently been extended, and there is a new conservatory/coffee lounge area. Chef Susan Meakin's *à la carte* menu might include potted crab and prawns with cayenne, lemon and dill; venison stroganoff, basmati rice. Meals can also be taken in the bar. 'Interesting food, with an emphasis on local produce; cooking of an excellent standard.' 'Staff are very willing.' Children are not specifically catered for, but 'well-behaved ones are welcome', say the Howlings, parents of young children themselves, and there is a family room. The hotel is dog friendly, too. (*Loren Swan, and others*)

Bedrooms: 30, 6 in annexe (30 yds), some on ground floor. *Open*: all year, except Christmas/New Year. *Facilities*: ramps, reception/lounge, upstairs lounge, coffee lounge, bar, restaurant, function room, 5-acre grounds on river (fishing), unsuitable for &. *Background music*: restaurant and bar. *Location*: On A6006, ¾ mile from town centre. *Smoking*: not allowed. *Children*: all ages welcomed. *Dogs*: not allowed in restaurant. *Credit cards*: all major cards. *Prices*: [2009] B&B £42.50–£93 per person, D,B&B £55.50–£72.50, set dinner £21, full alc £35. *V*

MIDDLEHAM North Yorkshire   Map 4:C3

Waterford House

19 Kirkgate
Middleham DL8 4PG

Tel 01969-622090
Fax 01969-624020
Email info@waterfordhousehotel.co.uk
Website www.waterfordhousehotel.co.uk

'Our third visit to Martin and Anne Cade's lovely little guest house; what a treat,' writes a fan. The Grade II listed Georgian stone house overlooks the main square of this unspoilt little town, noted for its racehorses. Earlier visitors 'were made to feel so welcome by our hosts, who provided tea and delicious home-made tea bread'. The house has an 'intensely Victorian feel: thick fringed curtains, tassels, dark William Morris wallpaper'. It is 'chock-full' of antiques, *objets d'art* and bric-a-brac 'on the theme of horses, hunting and country pursuits'. 'The whole place is spotless, quality of fittings above average.' The residents' lounge has a baby grand piano and log fire. A 'lovely' first-floor bedroom had 'supremely comfortable bed, nice extras (sherry, home made cakes and chocolates)'. Several bedrooms have been refurbished this year, and public rooms recarpeted. The 'striking' dining room has 'burgundy-coloured walls, well-spaced tables, red bows on chair backs, candles'. 'The food is outstanding, a credit to Anne, an enthusiastic cook. Starters included a retro king prawn cocktail, better than anything we remember from the 1960s. Martin served attentively.' 'We walked up to the gallops to watch the horses training, then back to breakfast', 'a fried feast'. (*Gail Thorpe, and others*)

Bedrooms: 5. *Open*: all year except Christmas/New Year, restaurant closed Sun night. *Facilities*: drawing room, TV room, restaurant, walled garden, patio, unsuitable for &. *Background music*: none. *Location*: village centre. *Smoking*: not allowed. *Children*: not under 12. *Dogs*: not allowed. *Credit cards*: MasterCard, Visa. *Prices*: [2009] B&B £45–£75 per person, set dinner £35, 1-night bookings occasionally refused at weekends.

MIDHURST West Sussex   *See Shortlist*

MIDSOMER NORTON Somerset   Map 2:D1

The Moody Goose at The Old Priory
Church Square
Midsomer Norton
nr Bath BA3 2HX

Tel 01761-416784
Fax 01761-417851
Email info@theoldpriory.co.uk
Website www.theoldpriory.co.uk

Said to be one of the oldest houses in Somerset (it dates back to 1152), this handsome Grade II listed building stands by a church in a peaceful walled garden. 'An oasis', in a village which 'reflects its Victorian mining past', it is run as a restaurant-with-rooms by proprietor/chef Stephen Shore. It has inglenook fireplaces, flagged floors, artefacts and antiques in the hall. 'Wonderful. Good value. They were very welcoming, especially to our young boy,' says a visitor in 2009. The bedrooms vary in size and style: 'Ours was small but comfortable, especially the bed.' Others liked their four-poster room; 'towelling robes and decent soaps in the bathroom; only downside the view of a neighbouring house'. In the bright restaurant, the modern cooking is 'exceptional; attention to detail and freshness lived up to expectations'; 'everything was delicious'. The set dinner menu has three choices for each course (typical dishes: double-baked Roquefort soufflé and tomato fondue; pan-fried breast of poussin, borlotti beans with truffle oil). Breakfast in the 'cosy' rear dining room has croissants, toasted brioches, freshly squeezed juice, full English, cheese, ham and smoked haddock. 'Superb: it made lunch redundant.' (*Sian Esner, J and AL*)

Bedrooms: 6. *Open*: all year, except Christmas/New Year, restaurant closed Sun night, Mon. *Facilities*: 2 lounges, 2 dining rooms, private dining/function room, ¼-acre garden, unsuitable for &. *Background music*: classical in restaurants. *Location*: 9 miles SW of Bath. *Smoking*: not allowed. *Children*: all ages welcomed. *Dogs*: not allowed. *Credit cards*: MasterCard, Visa. *Prices*: [2009] B&B £55–£95 per person, set dinner £30, full alc £40–£45.

MILDEN Suffolk   *See Shortlist*

MILLOM Cumbria   *See Shortlist*

MILTON ABBOT Devon   Map 1:D3

Hotel Endsleigh   *Tel* 01822-870000
Milton Abbot   *Fax* 01822-870578
nr Tavistock PL19 0PQ   *Email* mail@hotelendsleigh.com
                                      Website www.hotelendsleigh.com

In an 'incomparable setting' in 'beautiful gardens' running down to the River Tamar, this luxurious Regency shooting and fishing lodge is owned by Olga Polizzi of *Hotel Tresanton*, St Mawes (*qv*). Stuart MacLeod is the manager. Mrs Polizzi oversaw the restoration of the house (designed by the eccentric Jeffry Wyattville), retaining the 'historic feeling'. The interior has regency panelling, contemporary paintings, original artefacts (fire buckets for the 'superb' log fires); candles provide much of the lighting at night. The bedrooms are 'beautifully kept'; a smaller room was 'slightly disappointing'; a suite had 'beautiful views'. Room 17 is the former gatekeeper's lodge at the top of the drive. Paul Crawford is the new chef in 2009, and we would welcome reports on his modern European cooking (typical dishes: wild garlic risotto; honey-glazed pork belly, pak choi and mustard velouté). Georgina, Duchess of Bedford, who built the lodge, was a passionate gardener; she commissioned Humphry Repton to design the gardens, which are also Grade I listed. The *Endsleigh* owns seven rods for guests to fish along 'eight miles of the best salmon and sea trout river in England'. (*AF, and others*)

Bedrooms: 16, 1 on ground floor, 1 in lodge. *Open*: all year. *Facilities*: drawing room, library, card room, bar, 2 dining rooms, civil wedding licence, terraces, 108-acre estate (fishing, ghillie available). *Background music*: none. *Location*: 7 miles NW of Tavistock, train/plane Plymouth. *Smoking*: not allowed. *Children*: all ages welcomed. *Dogs*: not allowed in restaurant. *Credit cards*: Amex, MasterCard, Visa. *Prices*: [2009] B&B £90–£180 per person, D,B&B £110–£200, set dinner £40, full alc £55, Christmas/New Year packages, 1-night bookings refused weekends.

MISTLEY Essex   Map 2:C5

The Mistley Thorn

High Street	*Tel* 01206-392821
Mistley, nr Manningtree	*Fax* 01206-390122
CO11 1HE	*Email* info@mistleythorn.co.uk
	Website www.mistleythorn.com

'Comfortable, with good food, welcoming staff, in a lovely, unspoilt area. Good value.' In a historic coastal village, Sherri Singleton and her husband, David McKay, run this restaurant-with-rooms in a yellow-painted old inn. She and Chris Pritchard have a *Michelin Bib Gourmand* for their cooking, specialising in local seafood. 'Rock oysters the best we have had. There was a real buzz about the restaurant, busy on both nights.' They were also voted 'best steak joint in the UK' by *The Times*. Their vegetarian options (perhaps aubergine rollatini) are praised: 'Such a change from the standard vegetable lasagne or stir fry.' The 'uncluttered' bedrooms are decorated in taupe and cream; beds are large, there is 'plenty of cupboard space', organic tea and coffee. All bathrooms have a double-ended bath and a shower. Wi-Fi Internet access is available throughout. For breakfast ('good, and freshly cooked'), you can have a Bloody Mary with pepper vodka; a continental selection; smoked kipper; Lowestoft haddock with poached egg; full English. There is a small sitting area for residents. Sherri Singleton runs cookery workshops and owns an Italian restaurant, *Lucca Enoteca*, in nearby Manningtree. (*Sara Price, Jeanette Bloor, GM*)

Bedrooms: 5. *Open*: all year. *Facilities*: ramp, small sitting area, bar, restaurant, bedrooms unsuitable for &. *Background music*: light jazz in restaurant. *Location*: village centre, 9 miles W of Harwich. *Smoking*: not allowed. *Children*: all ages welcomed. *Dogs*: allowed, if small and well behaved. *Credit cards*: MasterCard, Visa. *Prices*: [2009] B&B £45–£60 per person, D,B&B £60–£77.50, cookery courses, Christmas/New Year packages, 1-night bookings refused bank holidays.

MOCCAS Herefordshire   Map 3:D4

Moccas Court   *Tel* 01981-500019
Moccas, nr Hereford   *Fax* 01981-500095
HR2 9LH   *Email* info@moccas-court.co.uk
                             Website www.moccas-court.co.uk

César award in 2008

'An exceptional experience, a cross between being a guest in someone's home and staying in a hotel with personal service.' 'A wonderful place.' High praise comes again this year for Ben and Mimi Chester-Master, who welcome visitors to their family home, a Grade I listed Georgian house (original designs by the Adam brothers). It stands by the River Wye in a park designed by Capability Brown and Humphry Repton, and with a 12th-century church. 'Ben and Mimi are courteous, friendly'; they join guests, who are 'immediately on first-name terms', for pre-dinner drinks in the library hung with family portraits. Dinner, by arrangement and cooked by the host, is taken around a communal table in an 'exquisite circular room'. 'Excellent food, locally sourced; we had exceptional duck and beautiful lamb.' A stone-floored hall leads to a magnificent cantilevered staircase below a glass dome. A spacious first-floor bedroom ('best ever') had 'fabulous fabrics and decor; big bathroom, piping hot water'. Upper rooms are smaller. Breakfast has hot croissants, good preserves and cooked dishes. Zulu, the black Labrador, 'took us for a walk along the Wye'. (*David Birnie, Ursula Mackenzie, Tessa Harris*)

Bedrooms: 5. *Open*: 1 Apr–31 Jan, closed Sun/Mon, Christmas. *Facilities*: 2 lounges, music room, library, dining room, civil wedding licence, 75-acre grounds (river, fishing), unsuitable for &. *Background music*: none. *Location*: 10 miles W of Hereford. *Smoking*: not allowed. *Children*: not under 16 except by arrangement. *Dogs*: not allowed in house. *Credit cards*: Amex, MasterCard, Visa. *Prices*: B&B £68.50–£137 per person, set dinner £45.

How to contact the *Guide*
By mail: From anywhere in the UK, write to Freepost PAM 2931, London W11 4BR (no stamp is needed)
From outside the UK: *Good Hotel Guide*, 50 Addison Avenue, London W11 4QP, England
By telephone or fax: 020-7602 4182
By email: editor@goodhotelguide.com
Via our website: www.goodhotelguide.com

MORETON-IN-MARSH
Gloucestershire

Map 3:D6

The Redesdale Arms

High Street
Moreton-in-Marsh
GL56 0AW

Tel 01608-650308
Fax 01608-651843
Email info@redesdalearms.com
Website www.redesdalearms.com

'Our room was beautifully appointed and clean. Little touches like the generous carafe of sherry and the selection of expensive toiletries made the visit seem special.' A guest this year at this centuries-old coaching inn felt 'well looked after'. With its honey-coloured Georgian facade, it stands on the main street of this attractive market town. Co-owner Robert Smith is a 'most engaging host'. Other praise: 'Quick and courteous service.' 'Bedrooms of a high standard' (a suite was greatly admired). Some rooms are in the converted stable block which means a short walk outside, but umbrellas are located at strategic points. One room is equipped for disabled visitors; two have a whirlpool bath. Front ones have double glazing, but when windows are open in hot weather there can be noise from the street and from the oak-panelled bar below (a popular local). One visitor felt housekeeping could have been better, but everyone praises the standards in the dining room, especially the traditional Redesdale beef Wellington. Chef Craig Mallins also offers a short list of daily specials. The 'splendid and abundant' breakfast is a buffet for both hot and cold dishes. (*David Brindley, and others*)

Bedrooms: 24, 10 in annexe across courtyard, 1 suitable for &. *Open*: all year. *Facilities*: 3 lounge bars, 2 restaurants, heated open dining area. *Background music*: in all public areas. *Location*: town centre. *Smoking*: not allowed. *Children*: all ages welcomed. *Dogs*: allowed in public rooms only. *Credit cards*: MasterCard, Visa. *Prices*: B&B £32.50–£70 per person, D,B&B £47.50–£87.50, full alc £38, special breaks, Christmas/New Year packages, 1-night bookings refused Sat Apr–Nov. *V*

See also Shortlist

MORPETH Northumberland

See Shortlist

Prices may change – always check them when booking.

MORSTON Norfolk   Map 2:A5

 **Morston Hall**
Morston, Holt
NR25 7AA

Tel 01263-741041
Fax 01263-740419
Email reception@morstonhall.com
Website www.morstonhall.com

César award: Restaurant-with-rooms of the year

In an area of outstanding natural beauty on the north Norfolk coast, this Jacobean flint-and-brick mansion 'lived up to its reputation for exceptional food' when inspectors called. Owners Tracy (front-of-house) and Galton Blackiston, chef/*patron* (who appears on television), are sometimes away. 'In their absence, service by the attentive young British staff was excellent, and the cooking of head chef Samantha Wegg was impeccable.' Guests gather at 7.30 pm for aperitifs and canapés in two lounges with log fires and candles. In the dining room and conservatory, the four-course dinner menu changes daily: no choice until dessert or cheese; menus discussed in advance ('dislikes easily dealt with'). 'A sublime balance of ingredients, each flavour distinct. A highlight was a single seared scallop with a sliver of crisp Alsace bacon and sautéed horse mushrooms.' Bedrooms are in the main house and in a 'discreet' single-storey villa in the gardens. 'Ours was huge, on two levels, with an enormous bed; patio doors opened on to a terrace overlooking fields; the hi-tech bathroom had a built-in TV.' Tables are laid with blue gingham for breakfast: 'superb fruit salad, a warm blueberry muffin, toast from decent bread'; 'fantastic, creamy scrambled eggs'. (*Ken and Priscilla Winslow, Anne and Denis Tate, and others*)

Bedrooms: 13, 6 in garden pavilion on ground floor. *Open*: all year except Christmas, 3 weeks Jan, restaurant closed midday. *Facilities*: hall, lounge, conservatory, restaurant, 3½-acre garden (pond, croquet). *Background music*: none. *Location*: 2 miles W of Blakeney. *Smoking*: not allowed. *Children*: all ages welcomed. *Dogs*: not allowed in public rooms. *Credit cards*: all major cards. *Prices*: [2009] D,B&B £150–£170 per person, set dinner £55, New Year package, 1-night bookings sometimes refused Sat.

We update the *Guide* every year. Hotels are dropped or may be demoted to the Shortlist if there has been a change of owner (unless reports after the change are positive), if this year's reports are negative, or in rare cases where there has been no feedback. A lot of hotels are omitted every year, and many new ones are added.

MORTEHOE Devon   Map 1:B4

The Cleeve House
North Morte Road
Mortehoe, nr Woolacombe
EX34 7ED

Tel 01271-870719
Email info@cleevehouse.co.uk
Website www.cleevehouse.co.uk

Recommended again in 2009 for its 'good value', this small, unpretentious and 'welcoming' hotel is run by owners David and Anne Strobel, 'such helpful hosts'. 'We were greeted like old friends,' say a couple on their sixth visit. It stands in a village above Woolacombe and its three-mile Blue Flag beach. The bedrooms, with their pine furniture, 'are fairly small, but have everything you might need'. Rear rooms have country views. The Strobels share the cooking (he does the main course, she the puddings). 'We endeavour to support our local suppliers,' they say. Bread, cakes, jam, sauces, chocolate truffles are all home made. 'David's dishes are imaginative', eg, 'excellent crab salad'; supreme of free-range chicken with mushroom and ginger sauce. There is a range of vegetarian alternatives. The dining room closes during the school summer holidays, when 'most guests prefer B&B'. Breakfast can be continental or full English. There is a 'comfortable' lounge. The South West Coast Path is nearby. (*Christine Moore*)

Bedrooms: 6, 1, on ground floor, suitable for &. *Open*: Apr–Sept, restaurant closed Wed, and evenings 21 July–31 Aug. *Facilities*: ramp, lounge, bar area, dining room, ½-acre garden (patio), golf nearby, Woolacombe beach 1½ miles. *Background music*: none. *Location*: 4 miles W of Ilfracombe, train/coach Barnstaple. *Smoking*: not allowed. *Children*: not under 12. *Dogs*: not allowed. *Credit cards*: MasterCard, Visa (*both 1% charge*). *Prices*: B&B £41–£46 per person, D,B&B £22 added, full alc £30, 1-night bookings sometimes refused Sat.

MUCH WENLOCK Shropshire   *See Shortlist*

NEAR SAWREY Cumbria   Map 4: inset C2

Ees Wyke Country House
Near Sawrey
Ambleside LA22 0JZ

Tel 015394-36393
Email mail@eeswyke.co.uk
Website www.eeswyke.co.uk

Once the Lake District retreat of Beatrix Potter, this 'most attractive' Georgian building is endorsed this year for its 'friendly country house atmosphere and high standard of food and service'. Set in pretty gardens, it has panoramic views of Esthwaite Water and the fells beyond. Inspectors were greeted by chef/proprietor, Richard Lee (who runs it with his wife, Margaret), in his 'whites', and supported by friendly sheepdogs Harry and Teddy. The two 'nicely decorated' lounges have 'comfortable sofas, good pictures and ornaments'. 'The good accommodation has wonderful views.' Two bedrooms have their private bathroom across a landing (dressing gown provided). The 'excellent' dinner is at 7.30, in a 'lovely room with super views, well-spaced tables nicely laid'. Guests choose at 6.30 from a daily-changing five-course menu (three choices for each course); perhaps seared scallops with salad, rocket and basil dressing; roast breast of duckling with red onion and juniper marmalade. 'Well presented, varied, prepared with imagination.' There is a well-detailed wine list, 'reasonably priced'. Breakfast has a buffet (cereals, yogurts, freshly squeezed orange juice, etc); 'scrambled eggs the best of our trip; honey in the comb'. 'Ees Wyke' means east area. (*Mr and Mrs GE Goodbody, ET, and others*)

Bedrooms: 8, 1 on ground floor. *Open*: all year. *Facilities*: 2 lounges, restaurant, veranda, 1-acre garden, unsuitable for &. *Background music*: none. *Location*: edge of village 2½ miles SE of Hawkshead on B5286. *Smoking*: not allowed. *Children*: not under 12. *Dogs*: not allowed. *Credit cards*: MasterCard, Visa. *Prices*: B&B £50–£65 per person, D,B&B £83–£98, set dinner £33, full alc £49, New Year package.

NETLEY MARSH Hampshire   Map 2:E2

Hotel TerraVina
174 Woodlands Road
Netley Marsh
nr Southampton SO40 7GL

Tel 02380-293784
Fax 02380-293627
Email info@hotelterravina.co.uk
Website www.hotelterravina.co.uk

❦ *César award in 2009*

'We were wrapped up in a blanket of charm,' says a visitor who arrived with a young baby (and 'frayed nerves') at Nina and Gérard Basset's 'stylish contemporary hotel' in the New Forest. They are hands-on owners who 'made great efforts to give us a pleasant stay', said inspectors on an earlier visit. 'No stuffiness; the staff are enthusiastic.' Baby bathrobes, rubber ducks, baby-listening monitors and a children's menu are provided. The interior of the 'not particularly distinguished' building is 'open, modern; everything tastefully done:

top-quality fittings, glass panels, natural wood or slate flooring'. 'Our room, on two levels in the new extension, had state-of-the-art fittings, including soundproofed doors and a mini-espresso machine.' 'Our spacious room had desk, free Wi-Fi, TV/DVD-player, minibar, etc, but could have benefited from a chest of drawers. Bathroom well equipped.' Most rooms have a patio or terrace. There is a 'lovely sitting room', a 'nicely lit bar area', and a colonial-style roofed terrace overlooking the large garden. The cooking of David Giles, the head chef, is 'delicious, refined, using organically grown local produce; portions just right; imaginative combinations'. The eclectic wine list has 'surprisingly reasonable prices' (M. Basset is a distinguished *sommelier*). Breakfast has a buffet, and cooked dishes to order.

Bedrooms: 11, some on ground floor, 1 suitable for &. *Open*: all year, except 2 days between Christmas/New Year. *Facilities*: ramp, lounge, bar, restaurant, private dining room, civil wedding licence, 1-acre grounds (heated swimming pool in summer). *Background music*: none. *Location*: NW of Southampton, 2 miles W of Totton. *Smoking*: not allowed. *Children*: all ages welcomed. *Dogs*: not allowed. *Credit cards*: all major cards. *Prices*: [2009] room £140–£230, breakfast £9.50–£12.50, full alc £50, 2-night bookings preferred at weekends (check with hotel).

NEW ROMNEY Kent   Map 2:E5

Romney Bay House
Coast Road, Littlestone
New Romney TN28 8QY

Tel 01797-364747
Fax 01797-367156

Designed by Sir Clough Williams-Ellis of Portmeirion fame in the late 1920s for the American actress/journalist Hedda Hopper, this red-roofed, white-fronted house is reached by a 'bumpy', private road along the sea wall. Owners Clinton and Lisa Lovell, who live here with their young family, advise guests to ask them for directions, rather than rely on 'outdated' satnav information. They run it 'professionally, in friendly, personal fashion', say returning visitors. The 'feel of a home, rather than a hotel' is liked. Everyone is 'courteous, smiling and helpful'. 'Full of character', the house is filled with antiques, pictures and knick-knacks; at night, candles burn, and there is a log fire. The first-floor 'lookout' has a telescope, books and games. Drinks at 7.30 can be taken on the terrace before dining at 8, in the conservatory, which has 'a lovely seaside atmosphere'. An 'excellent' four-course no-choice dinner is cooked by the host on four days of the week (dishes like pan-fried local turbot with wilted spinach; rump of Romney Marsh lamb, roasted fennel and baby parsnips), 'portions not too large'. The 'colourful and airy' bedrooms have nearly floor-length windows with views of sea or golf course, plain carpet, light colours, four-poster or half-tester bed, armchairs. Breakfast is full English, or continental (cold meats, cheese, fruits, croissants, toast). Cream teas are served. (*B and PO, and others*)

Bedrooms: 10. *Open*: all year except 1 week Christmas, 1 week early Jan, dining room closed midday, Sun/Mon/Thurs evenings. *Facilities*: 2 lounges, bar, conservatory, dining room, small function facilities, 1-acre garden (croquet, *boules*), opposite sea (sand/pebble beach, safe bathing, fishing), unsuitable for &. *Background music*: none. *Location*: 1½ miles from New Romney. *Smoking*: not allowed. *Children*: not under 14. *Dogs*: not allowed. *Credit cards*: Amex, MasterCard, Visa. *Prices*: B&B £46–£95 per person, set menu £45 ('*optional*' *5% service charge added to bill*), New Year package, 1-night advance bookings refused weekends.

NEWBURY Berkshire   *See Shortlist*

NEWBY BRIDGE Cumbria   *See Shortlist*

NEWCASTLE UPON TYNE   Map 4:B4
Tyne and Wear

Jesmond Dene House	*Tel* 0191-212 3000
Jesmond Dene Road	*Fax* 0191-212 3001
Newcastle upon Tyne	*Email* info@jesmonddenehouse.co.uk
NE2 2EY	*Website* www.jesmonddenehouse.co.uk

In a wooded valley in Newcastle's north suburbs, this Arts and Crafts mansion is run as a boutique hotel by Terry Laybourne (Newcastle restaurateur) and Peter Candler. 'No gimmicks, no fuss,' they promise. 'A haven of calm and excellence,' say visitors. 'Service, always by name, was friendly.' There are inglenook fireplaces, stained-glass windows, a wood-panelled Great Hall with a minstrels' gallery, and two 'elegant' lounges (one the former billiard room). Bedrooms, 'fitted to the highest quality', have flat-screen TV, digital radio, 'smartly designed furniture; a commodious bath and double basin'. Some rooms are high-ceilinged, others 'cosy'. The spacious suites in the *New House* have a sitting room, big bed, bold wallpaper. There are two dining areas, one the former music room (with delicate plasterwork), the other the 'light and leafy' oak-floored garden room. Head chef Pierre Rigothier's modern dishes include wild sea bass carpaccio with clementine and fresh coriander; fillet of Northumbrian beef, glazed Swiss chard and mashed potatoes. 'Exquisite scrambled egg and bacon for breakfast.' Conferences, weddings and other celebrations are catered for. The house stands in a 'contemporary-style' garden; next door is a larger, wooded, Victorian garden with exotic trees, waterfalls and a pets' corner for children. (*RG, and others*)

Bedrooms: 40, 8 in adjacent annexe, 2 suitable for &. *Open*: all year. *Facilities*: lift, 2 lounges, cocktail bar, restaurant, conference/function facilities, civil wedding licence, 2-acre garden. *Background music*: in public areas. *Location*: 5 mins' drive from centre via A167. *Smoking*: not allowed. *Children*: all ages welcomed. *Dogs*: only guide dogs allowed. *Credit cards*: all major cards. *Prices*: [2009] room £165–£450, breakfast £13.50–£16.50, set dinner from £25, Christmas/New Year packages.

See also Shortlist

NEWENT Gloucestershire   Map 3:D5

Three Choirs Vineyard   NEW   *Tel* 01531-890223
Newent   *Email* info@threechoirs.com
GL18 1LS   *Website* www.three-choirs-vineyards.co.uk

On the crest of a hill with views over vines as far as the Malvern hills, the restaurant and rooms on the Three Choirs estate are 'a feast for the eye, with a suggestion of Tuscany'. A visit was 'greatly enjoyed' this year: 'Reception, in the bar, was friendly, the bedroom was excellent, the food magnificent.' Eight of the rooms are in a single-storey building beside the restaurant. 'Ours was large with a king-size bed, wardrobe, dressing table, two good chairs; French windows opened on to a terrace overlooking the vines. There was a good shower over the bath, but no handrail.' Three newer, Scandinavian-style lodge rooms stand among the vines; they have private parking. In the restaurant (the chef is Darren Leonard), a small lounge area has a log fire, comfortable chairs. 'The tables were large (hurray) and the service well paced. A good tian of crevettes and avocado; my bream fillet was perfectly cooked with interesting garnishes; good bread and local butter. An estate wine, Siegerrebe, was so good we bought some in the shop in the morning. Breakfast had crisp toast, lovely scrambled eggs and smoked salmon, but, alas, marmalade in small jars. We would definitely go again.' (*LM Mayer-Jones, and others*)

Bedrooms: 11, 3 in lodges 500 yds from restaurant, all on ground floor, 1 suitable for &. *Open*: all year, except Christmas. *Facilities*: lounge, restaurant, 100-acre grounds. *Background music*: none. *Location*: 3 miles W of Newent. *Smoking*: not allowed. *Children*: all ages welcomed. *Dogs*: not allowed. *Credit cards*: MasterCard, Visa. *Prices*: [2009] B&B £42.50–£87.50 per person, D,B&B £92.50–£130, full alc £40, wine-tasting breaks, 1-night bookings sometimes refused. *V*

NEWLANDS Cumbria   *See Shortlist*

NEWMARKET Suffolk   *See Shortlist*

NEWQUAY Cornwall   *See Shortlist*

NORTH MOLTON Devon   Map 1:B4

 Heasley House   *Tel* 01598-740213
Heasley Mill   *Fax* 01598-740677
North Molton   *Email* enquiries@heasley-house.co.uk
EX36 3LE   *Website* www.heasley-house.co.uk

César award: Devon hotel of the year

'Hospitality is what it is all about,' says an enthusiastic inspector of this hotel/restaurant in a hamlet on the southern edge of Exmoor national park. 'What made all the difference were the things that cost relatively little but need thought: gorgeous fresh flowers; a roaring log fire though the evening wasn't that cold; intelligent use of space.' Visitors are 'warmly welcomed', with tea and fruitcake, by owners Jan and Paul (the chef) Gambrill. Original features of their Georgian dower house include the fireplace and ceiling hooks for hanging game in the dining room (formerly the kitchen). The individually styled bedrooms have king-size or super-king-size bed, Egyptian cotton linen; there are extra-wide baths, and power showers. Wireless broadband is available. The public rooms have deep leather sofas and chairs, stripped wooden floors, original artwork. 'The food is fab' on a daily-changing three-course menu of 'uncomplicated' modern dishes.

'Delicious green soup; quail with perfect roast potatoes; sea bream had us purring. Paul has natural talent. Wine list not too long, well balanced, modest mark-up. Great breakfast: freshly squeezed orange juice, really good porridge, perfect poached egg, variety of breads. The prices for this quality make it a bargain.' This is a dog-friendly place: a lobby links to the garden; ground-floor rooms have direct access to the car park. Around are wooded slopes and water meadows running down to the tiny River Mole.

Bedrooms: 8, some on ground floor. *Open*: all year except Christmas, Feb (private parties only at New Year). *Facilities*: 2 lounges, bar, restaurant, ¼-acre garden, unsuitable for ♿. *Background music*: in bar on request. *Location*: N of N Molton. *Smoking*: not allowed. *Children*: all ages welcomed. *Dogs*: not allowed in restaurant. *Credit cards*: MasterCard, Visa. *Prices*: [2009] B&B £65 per person, D,B,&B £28 added, full alc £35, New Year package (private parties). *V*

NORTH WALSHAM Norfolk   Map 2:A6

Beechwood	*Tel* 01692-403231
20 Cromer Road	*Fax* 01692-407284
North Walsham	*Email* enquiries@beechwood-hotel.co.uk
NR28 0HD	*Website* www.beechwood-hotel.co.uk

'Good value.' 'Accommodation, welcome and service excellent.' More acclaim for this part 19th-century, creeper-clad Georgian house in a market town near the north Norfolk coast. 'Friendly staff carried our baggage to our room; we were given complimentary tea and cake though we didn't arrive until 6 pm.' Owner/managers Lindsay Spalding and the 'ebullient' Don Birch write: 'We guarantee a restful stay because we don't take large groups, wedding parties or conferences. We make guests travelling alone particularly welcome.' Some bedrooms have a half-tester or four-poster bed; all have traditional and antique furniture, bathrobes, flat-screen TV, CD-player; Wi-Fi is available. 'Our large ground-floor room had a superb bathroom, a very good shower.' 'The most comfortable bed ever.' There is a turn-down service at night. Steven Norgate, the long-serving chef, is praised, though portions may be too large for some. A 'Ten Mile Dinner' is sometimes served: all ingredients from within a ten-mile radius (Cromer crab, Morston mussels, Sheringham lobster). Breakfast 'could not be faulted; lots of fruit, good scrambled eggs'. In the large garden are shrubs, a long lawn and a sunken area. The resident Airedale terriers, Harry and Emily, appear in the lounge after their evening walk; visiting dogs are welcomed. (*Zara Elliott, and others*)

Bedrooms: 17, some on ground floor, 1 suitable for ♿. *Open*: all year, except Christmas, restaurant closed midday Mon–Sat. *Facilities*: 2 lounges, bar, restaurant, 1-acre garden (croquet). *Background music*: none. *Location*: near town centre. *Smoking*: not allowed. *Children*: not under 10. *Dogs*: allowed (3 'dog' bedrooms). *Credit cards*: MasterCard, Visa. *Prices*: B&B £45–£75 per person, D,B&B £55–£90, set dinner £34, short breaks, New Year package, 1-night bookings sometimes refused Sat. *V*

NORTHAM Devon   Map 1:B4

Yeoldon House
Durrant Lane
Northam, nr Bideford
EX39 2RL

Tel 01237-474400
Fax 01237-476618
Email yeoldonhouse@aol.com
Website www.yeoldonhousehotel.co.uk

Inspectors in 2009 had an enjoyable stay at this 19th-century gabled house. 'Very much a family affair', it stands at the end of a private drive; its lawns slope down towards the River Torridge. It is managed by owners Jennifer and Brian Steele (he is the chef). He says that guests will 'feel comfortable in any attire' in the river-facing restaurant. His three-course dinner menu has a choice of traditional dishes. 'The main reason for coming is the food: guineafowl with orange and ginger stuffing was interesting; sea bass was wonderful, so fresh and perfectly baked; lemon tart was tangy. Breakfast was plentiful; poached eggs were perfect; my husband loved the porridge and smoked haddock.' Bedrooms vary: one has a four-poster, another is decorated in country style. Lundy has paintings of the island by a local artist, the split-level Hubbastone has its own balcony, the popular Crow's Nest overlooks the estuary and has a battlemented balcony. 'Our pretty room had rather a lot of furniture and a smallish bathroom. Teddy bears are everywhere.' There are suitcases on the stairs, old stained glass, a large lounge. Books and games are provided. Donkeys graze in a meadow up the drive. Nearby are Rosemoor Garden and the delightful fishing town of Appledore.

Bedrooms: 10. *Open*: all year except 21–26 Dec, restaurant closed midday and Sun evening. *Facilities*: lounge/bar, restaurant, civil wedding licence, 2-acre grounds, beach 5 mins' drive, unsuitable for ♿. *Background music*: classical evenings in public rooms. *Location*: 1 mile N of Bideford. *Smoking*: not allowed. *Children*: all ages welcomed. *Dogs*: allowed, but not left unattended and not in restaurant. *Credit cards*: Amex, MasterCard, Visa. *Prices*: B&B £55–£82.50 per person, D,B&B £85–£102.50, set menu £35, short breaks, New Year package, 1-night bookings sometimes refused. *V*

NORWICH Norfolk   Map 2:B5

By Appointment   *Tel/Fax* 01603-630730
25–29 St George's Street   *Email* puttii@tiscali.co.uk
Norwich NR3 1AB   *Website* www.byappointmentnorwich.co.uk

♙ *César award in 1999*

With 'bags of character', this restaurant-with-rooms is spread through
a labyrinth of rooms in three 15th-century merchants' dwellings in the
centre of Norwich. Guests arrive by a side gate that leads into the
kitchen. Inspectors 'were greeted by a chef who carried our bags to
our room and brought us a tray of tea'. The owner Robert Culyer
(Timothy Brown has retired) is 'the main presence, cooking and
serving breakfast and presiding over dinner like an impresario'.
Twisting staircases lead to the bedrooms: 'Ours, Queen Elizabeth, in
the eaves, was gloriously furnished with antiques and artefacts, sheets
and blankets on the bed, a proper dressing table, masses of pictures
and curios. The spacious bathroom had a claw-footed bath and
separate power shower.' The Queen Consort is 'a delightful room with
high ceilings, two huge chandeliers and a coal fire'. In the 'exotic'
dining rooms, 'Robert recites the menu, part of the operatic
experience'. The chef, Ellery Powell, joined in late 2008. 'His cooking
is excellent: good ingredients, well presented; robust sauces, a
delicious selection of roasted winter vegetables.' Breakfast, ordered
before dinner, 'is as good; leaf tea in a silver pot, four home-made
jams, croissants and good breads; generous cooked dishes'.

Bedrooms: 5. *Open*: all year except 25 Dec/1 Jan, restaurant closed midday, and
Sun and Mon evenings. *Facilities*: 2 lounges, restaurant, small courtyard,
unsuitable for &. *Background music*: classical/jazz in restaurant. *Location*: city
centre. *Smoking*: not allowed. *Children*: not under 12. *Dogs*: not allowed. *Credit
cards*: MasterCard, Visa. *Prices*: B&B £60–£80 per person, full alc £40.

See also Shortlist

Check the Hotelfinder section (page 11) if you are looking
for a hotel for a special occasion, perhaps a memorable meal
(see Gourmet and Gastropubs); a sporting weekend (see
Golf, Fishing, Walking); somewhere that will welcome your
children – or your dog. Our editors have selected ten hotels
in each of these categories (and many more) to help you
make your choice.

NOTTINGHAM Nottinghamshire   Map 2:A3

Hart's Hotel
Standard Hill, Park Row
Nottingham NG1 6GN

Tel 0115-988 1900
Fax 0115-947 7600
Email reception@hartshotel.co.uk
Website www.hartsnottingham.co.uk

Ϙ *César award in 2007*

Built on the site of Nottingham's medieval castle, Tim Hart's purpose-built hotel has striking modern lines, with curved buttresses, lots of glass. Paul Fearon is its manager. Standing quietly in a cul-de-sac, it has wide views over the city. Visitors admire the 'well-thought-out' building, and praise the staff ('young, bright, enthusiastic'). Inside, there is contemporary furniture and artwork, limestone floors. Bedrooms are 'well equipped, and naturally ventilated through louvred shutters, giving pleasant air quality without dryness or noise'. All have Internet access and voicemail, and 24-hour room service. Each of the six garden rooms has a private terrace. Light meals (Spanish omelette; spiced chicken salad, etc) are served all day in *Park's Bar*. Breakfast, which costs extra, can be continental (freshly squeezed orange juice, the 'freshest' fruit salad, etc), or cooked ('fine local pork sausages and free-range eggs'). 'Perfectly prepared coffee by the cup.' Booking is required for *Hart's*, the adjacent restaurant in the former radiology department of Nottingham's general hospital. Gareth Ward, the chef, serves modern dishes like sea bass, broccoli purée, confit tomatoes; roast venison with red cabbage, parsnip, pear and chocolate. We would welcome reports on his cooking. Mr Hart also owns *Hambleton Hall*, Hambleton (*qv*). (*RN, and others*)

Bedrooms: 32, 2 suitable for &. *Open*: all year, restaurant closed 26 Dec and 1 Jan. *Facilities*: lift, ramps, reception/lobby, bar, restaurant (30 yds), conference/banqueting facilities, small exercise room, civil wedding licence, small garden, private car park with CCTV. *Background music*: light jazz in bar. *Location*: city centre. *Smoking*: not allowed. *Children*: all ages welcomed. *Dogs*: not allowed in public rooms, or unattended in bedrooms. *Credit cards*: Amex, MasterCard, Visa. *Prices*: [2009] room £120–£260, breakfast £8.50–£13.50, set dinner £25, full alc £50, Christmas/New Year packages. *V*

See also Shortlist

The *V* sign at the end of an entry indicates a hotel that has agreed to take part in our Voucher scheme (see page 57).

OBORNE Dorset

Map 1:C6

The Grange at Oborne
Oborne, nr Sherborne
DT9 4LA

Tel 01935-813463
Fax 01935-817464
Email reception@thegrange.co.uk
Website www.thegrangeatoborne.co.uk

Reached by a quiet country lane with a notice warning of 'ducks crossing', this 'trim' 200-year-old stone-built country house is within easy reach of Sherborne. Managed by Jennifer and Jon Fletcher, it is owned by her parents, Ken and Karenza Mathews. Visitors this year praised the 'excellent' service: 'The owners and staff were very friendly.' 'When my husband took ill, they were helpful and sympathetic.' Bedrooms are a mix of modern and traditional; some have a patio and direct garden access; two have a balcony. 'Ours was spacious, and had a large and impressive bathroom.' Traditional bedding is available, and there is a choice of pillows. In the 'pleasant' candlelit dining room, chef Nick Holt's dinner menu might include smoked haddock chowder, poached quail's egg; roasted breast of Gressingham duck with honey roast parsnips. 'On four successive nights the same vegetables were served, which was boring, but the highlight of the dinner was that increasing rarity, a dessert trolley.' Vegetarians were 'not treated like pariahs; not a pasta in sight'. 'Breakfast was fine, including a generous plateful of scrambled eggs and bacon' – but little pots of preserves. There is a large room for functions, weddings, etc. (*AJ Gillingwater, Kathryn Colgrave*)

Bedrooms: 18, 1 suitable for &. *Open*: all year, restaurant closed Sun evenings. *Facilities*: lounge, bar, restaurant, 2 function rooms, civil wedding licence, ¾-acre garden. *Background music*: 'easy listening' all day, in public rooms. *Location*: 2 miles NE of Sherborne by A30. *Smoking*: not allowed. *Children*: all ages welcomed. *Dogs*: only guide dogs allowed. *Credit cards*: all major cards. *Prices*: B&B £54.50–£90 per person, D,B&B (min. 2 nights) £81.50–£112, set dinner £26–£32, full alc £40, hibernation breaks Oct–Mar, Christmas/New Year packages, 1-night bookings refused Sat in summer. *V*

OLD HUNSTANTON Norfolk

Map 2:A5

The Neptune
85 Old Hunstanton Road
Old Hunstanton PE36 6HZ

Tel 01485-532122
Email reservations@theneptune.co.uk
Website www.theneptune.co.uk

Chef Kevin Mangeolles was awarded a *Michelin* star in 2009 for his restaurant-with-rooms, an ivy-clad, red brick, 18th-century coaching inn near the north Norfolk coast. He runs it with his wife, Jacki. *Guide* inspectors (visiting before the award) were impressed by the 'excellent' cooking and 'careful and attractive' presentation. The residents' lounge and the bar (with a nautical feel) may be small, but the 'centre of the action' is the 'smart' restaurant (well-spaced tables, parquet floor, high-backed Lloyd Loom chairs). 'Interesting' starters, like Thornham mussel risotto; basil and pine kernel caramel, might be followed by Gressingham duck with praline, butternut squash purée; sea bass, braised fennel and orange, almond cream. Bedrooms are 'thoughtfully equipped'; all have a shower (no baths). 'Our small room, No. 7, had a sitting area with a Lloyd Loom-style sofa, white walls and furniture, pale blue carpet; very small shower room, like a ship's galley.' 'Good breakfast': freshly squeezed orange juice, fruit yogurt, two types of toast, home-made croissants, 'delicious scrambled eggs'. The sea is a short walk away.

Bedrooms: 6, all with shower. *Open*: all year, except 26 Dec, 2 weeks Jan, 2 weeks Nov, Mon off-season. *Facilities*: residents' lounge, bar, restaurant, unsuitable for &. *Background music*: jazz in bar. *Location*: village centre, on A149. *Smoking*: not allowed. *Children*: not under 10. *Dogs*: not allowed. *Credit cards*: MasterCard, Visa. *Prices*: [2009] B&B £47.50–£55, full alc £46, New Year package, 1-night bookings refused Sat in season.

ORFORD Suffolk   Map 2:C6

The Crown and Castle   *Tel* 01394-450205
Orford, nr Woodbridge   *Email* info@crownandcastle.co.uk
IP12 2LJ   *Website* www.crownandcastle.co.uk

In a peaceful Suffolk village, this old red brick inn is owned and run by Ruth Watson (cookery writer and one-time TV 'hotel inspector'), with her husband, David, and Tim Sunderland (the manager). Not surprisingly, it comes under close scrutiny from visitors who can be critical as well as enthusiastic. 'As good as ever,' says a fan returning in 2009. Another reader pays tribute to the 'wonderful young staff, kind and hard-working'. Others commented on the 'number of signs and notices'. Bedrooms are in the house ('the place to stay is the sea-facing rooms on the first floor, simply furnished with modern art, minimalist style and generous bathroom, the best monsoon shower I have encountered') or in garden buildings. These have 'a fine interior – excellent, huge bed and good bathroom', but might feel 'a bit motel-like'. Public rooms have 'interesting furniture, modern chandeliers and wall lights; good art on walls'. Mrs Watson shares the cooking in the bistro-style *Trinity* restaurant (*Michelin Bib Gourmand*) with new head chef David Williams. 'Food was outstanding: fantastic prawn and chervil risotto; smoked trout and sorrel quiche.' Children over four are welcomed, 'but in limited numbers, and not in *Trinity* at dinner'. Breakfast includes 'toast straightaway or later on', cereals, yogurts, fruit, and cooked dishes including eggs Benedict. Snack lunches are served at the *King's Head*, opposite, also run by the Watsons. (*CLH, Robert Gower, and others*)

Bedrooms: 19, 10 (all on ground floor) in garden, 1 in courtyard. *Open*: all year except 4–7 Jan. *Facilities*: lounge/bar, restaurant, private dining room, gallery (with Wi-Fi), ½-acre garden. *Background music*: none. *Location*: market square. *Smoking*: not allowed. *Children*: not under 4, except babes-in-arms. *Dogs*: allowed in bar, 5 garden rooms (£10). *Credit cards*: MasterCard, Visa. *Prices*: B&B £57.50–£102.50 per person, D,B&B £77.50–£122.50, set dinner £38–£45, special breaks, Christmas/New Year packages, 1-night bookings refused Sat.

OSWESTRY Shropshire   Map 3:B4

Pen-y-Dyffryn
Rhydycroesau
Oswestry SY10 7JD

Tel 01691-653700
Fax 01978-211004
Email stay@peny.co.uk
Website www.peny.co.uk

❦ *César award in 2003*

On the last hill in Shropshire, and with uninterrupted views of the hills of North Wales, this listed Georgian rectory is run as a country hotel by Miles and Audrey Hunter. They are 'marvellous, caring' owner/managers. Even in their absence, 'standards remain high', say returning visitors this year. 'The food and service were as good as ever.' Others wrote of 'young, well-trained staff', and enjoyed the complimentary tea served on arrival. Bedrooms in the main house vary in size: the double-aspect Rector's Room is liked; Rose Room, next door, 'beautifully decorated in blue and cream', has 'just enough space'. Each of the four 'airy, well-lit' rooms in the coach house has a patio leading to the garden with its 'lovely views'; they are popular with visitors with dogs. The chef, David Morris, uses local organic ingredients for his 'excellent' daily-changing menu, eg, spiced parsnip and apple soup; rare breed pork loin with Shropshire Blue cheese sauce and quince jelly. Breakfast has DIY fresh orange juice, organic porridge, pancakes with cherries, 'excellent full English'. 'A nice touch is a daily page with the weather forecast and suggestions of things to do.' Good walking from the door. (*Dan and Beverley Allen, and others*)

Bedrooms: 12, 4, each with patio, in coach house, 1 on ground floor. *Open*: all year except Christmas. *Facilities*: 2 lounges, bar, restaurant, 5-acre grounds, unsuitable for &. *Background music*: light classical in evening. *Location*: 3 miles W of Oswestry off B4580. *Smoking*: not allowed. *Children*: not under 3. *Dogs*: not allowed in public rooms after 6 pm. *Credit cards*: Diners, MasterCard, Visa. *Prices*: [2009] B&B £56–£81 per person, D,B&B £78–£112, set dinner £30–£35, full alc £50, New Year package, 1-night bookings sometimes refused Sat. *V*

OTLEY West Yorkshire   *See Shortlist*

OTTERBURN Northumberland   *See Shortlist*

OXFORD Oxfordshire   Map 2:C2

Malmaison   *Tel* 01865-268400
3 Oxford Castle   *Email* oxford@malmaison.com
New Road   *Website* www.malmaison.com
Oxford OX1 1AY

Liked for its 'sheer drama', this unusual hotel is an imaginative conversion of Oxford's Victorian castle gaol (Grade I listed). Take a lift from the modern Reception area and 'you come out in prison'. 'Clever use has been made of the difficult layout of the small cells,' says a visitor this year. 'Our bedroom was formed from two, with a third for a bathroom.' Original features (metal walkways, cell doors, keys, spyholes – reversed) have been retained. The Governor's Suite is 'a spacious open-plan room with fabulous bathroom; dark brown walls, furniture and floors. The effect was a little stygian, if deeply trendy.' Other visitors found the 'lack of light because of the small, high-up windows and inadequate lighting' unappealing: 'I had to read by torchlight.' Meals are served in a 'gloomy' below-ground brasserie. 'Breakfast had plenty of choice and was good, apart from Radio 2 playing in the background.' The young staff, dressed in black, were 'very professional, but welcoming too – not a bit stuffy'. (*AC, and others*)

Bedrooms: 94, 16 in *House of Correction*, some in *Governor's House*, 3 suitable for &. *Open*: all year. *Facilities*: ramps, *Visitors' Room* lounge, 2 bars, brasserie, 2 private dining rooms, gym, free Wi-Fi, outside seating. *Background music*: in public areas. *Location*: central, pre-booked parking (£20 a night). *Smoking*: not allowed. *Children*: all ages welcomed. *Dogs*: allowed. *Credit cards*: all major cards. *Prices*: [2009] room £180–£395, breakfast from £11.95, full alc £35.

Old Bank

92–94 High Street
Oxford OX1 4BN

Tel 01865-799599
Fax 01865-799598
Email info@oldbank-hotel.co.uk
Website www.oldbank-hotel.co.uk

'Service is helpful and friendly throughout,' say returning visitors to this 'very good hotel', an elegant conversion of three buildings, one a former bank, opposite All Souls. 'A fantastic, central location, and it has its own dinky on-site car park.' The decor is 'stylish without being too cutting-edge; mushroom cream and muted red, modern but relaxing'. Most of the bedrooms, 'nicely finished, and with good facilities', face the 'dreaming spires'. 'Our comfortable attic room had armchairs, desk, a pleasingly spacious bathroom with powerful shower, dressing gowns, slippers.' An earlier visitor wrote: 'Thought has been applied to "what guests want": firm, large bed, good bath products, Wi-Fi and, bliss, a quiet room when asked for.' Owner Jeremy Mogford's collection of modern art ('a delight') is displayed in the old banking hall which also houses *Quod*, the 'always busy' bar/restaurant. It provides a 'good choice of pizzas, pastas, bistro favourites (eg, braised lamb shanks) and robust daily specials (fish and chips with mushy peas on Friday)'. 'Dinner and breakfast were excellent.' Breakfast (7 to 11 am, charged extra) can be English, continental or vegetarian; there is a children's menu, and teas are served between 3 and 5 pm. (*Michael and Eithne Dandy, SH*)

Bedrooms: 42, 1 suitable for &. *Open*: all year. *Facilities*: lift, residents' lounge/bar, bar/grill, dining terrace, 2 meeting/private dining rooms, small garden. *Background music*: jazz in library/bar. *Location*: central (windows facing High St double glazed), access to rear car park. *Smoking*: not allowed. *Children*: all ages welcomed. *Dogs*: not in bedrooms. *Credit cards*: Amex, MasterCard, Visa. *Prices*: room £185–£250, breakfast £11.95–£12.95, set dinner £29.50, Christmas/New Year package.

Old Parsonage

1 Banbury Road
Oxford OX2 6NN

Tel 01865-310210
Fax 01865-311262
Email reception@oldparsonage-hotel.co.uk
Website www.oldparsonage-hotel.co.uk

A popular meeting place for town and gown, this wisteria-covered 17th-century building is owned, like *Old Bank* (above), by Jeremy Mogford. Deniz Bostanci is the manager. Despite its location, between Keble and Somerville colleges on the busy Banbury Road, it has the 'ambience of a small country house'. A massive oak door opens into the bar/restaurant with its year-round log fire and Russian red walls covered with original cartoons and portraits. 'All very congenial, and diners seemed not to notice guests tramping through to get to their rooms.' A ground-floor bedroom was 'characterful and comfortable, more spacious than some of the first-floor rooms'. 'The evening turn-down was as efficient and comprehensive as ever.' Some bedrooms are small, and traffic noise may be a nuisance. Head chef Simon Cottrell was appointed in November 2008. His dinner menu has 'classic British dishes with a modern interpretation', eg, warm bacon and scallop salad; Old Parsonage hamburger. We would welcome reports on his cooking. A 'very high' tea (wide range of sandwiches) is also available. 'Cooked breakfast [charged extra] full and satisfying.' In fine weather, the 'pretty walled front terrace' is 'a chic spot for drinks or a meal'. (*CF, PJ, and others*)

Bedrooms: 30, 10 on ground floor, 1 suitable for &. *Open*: all year. *Facilities*: lounge, bar/restaurant, civil wedding licence, terrace, roof garden, small walled garden. *Background music*: jazz in bar/restaurant area. *Location*: NE end of St Giles, some traffic noise, windows double glazed, small car park. *Smoking*: not allowed. *Children*: all ages welcomed. *Dogs*: not allowed in restaurant. *Credit cards*: Amex, MasterCard, Visa. *Prices*: room £175–£230, breakfast £12.95–£14, set dinner £32, full alc £40, special breaks, Christmas package.

See also Shortlist

PADSTOW Cornwall   Map 1:D2

The Seafood Restaurant
Riverside
Padstow PL28 8BY

Tel 01841-532700
Fax 01841-532942
Email reservations@rickstein.com
Website www.rickstein.com

Celebrity chef Rick Stein may not often be seen at this north Cornish port, but his ex-wife Jill, who continues to be his business partner, is based here. She is responsible for the design of the bedrooms in six separate buildings across the town. The most expensive are in *St Edmund's House* (two open on to the private garden) and the one-bedroom *Bryn Cottage*; the cheapest are above the *Middle Street Café*. The decor is 'modern, but not aggressively so' in the rooms above the flagship *Seafood Restaurant* (which has a lift). A visitor this year reported that the food here and at *St Petroc's Bistro* was 'excellent', but felt that the hotel service 'needed attention'. David Sharland is the executive chef for the waterfront restaurant whose menu might include crab, ginger and coriander broth; skate with black butter and capers. *St Petroc's* (wooden floors, tables and chairs; bold artwork on white walls) has a shorter menu of 'unfussy' dishes (eg, haddock with beer, bacon and savoy cabbage). The *Café* offers an 'interesting' lunch, and an evening set menu. For a change try the fish-and-chip shop: eat battered or grilled fish in a cardboard container at a communal wooden table.

Bedrooms: 40, in 6 buildings, some on ground floor, 2 suitable for ♿. *Open*: all year except 24–26 Dec, restaurants also closed 1 May. *Facilities*: ramps, *Seafood*: lift, conservatory bar, restaurant, *St Petroc's*: lounge, reading room, bar, bistro, courtyard, *Café* unsuitable for ♿. *Background music*: St Petroc's and Café. *Location*: *Seafood Restaurant* on harbour, other buildings nearby. *Smoking*: not allowed. *Children*: all ages welcomed, but no under-4s in restaurant. *Dogs*: allowed in public rooms except restaurants, most bedrooms. *Credit cards*: MasterCard, Visa. *Prices*: [2009] B&B £45–£150 per person, *Restaurant* tasting menu £64, full alc £60, *St Petroc's Bistro* winter set meal £17.50, full alc £40, *Café* set dinner £21.50, full alc £30, special breaks, New Year package, 1-night bookings refused Sat.

PANGBOURNE Berkshire   Map 2:D3

 The Elephant at   NEW   *Tel* 01189-842244
Pangbourne   *Fax* 01189-767346
Church Road   *Email* reception@elephanthotel.co.uk
Pangbourne RG8 7AR   *Website* www.elephanthotel.co.uk

César award: Newcomer of the year

In a 'characterful' village on the Thames (rewarding tow-path walks), this 19th-century hotel has been modernised by Christoph Brooke's small Hillbrooke group, which has restored the original name (abandoned in the 1960s). Managed by Annica Eskelius, 'it scores in all departments,' said an inspector in 2009, 'warmth of the staff, attractive accommodation, seriously good cooking, reasonable prices.' The decor and furnishings have oriental references ('elephant theme played up in the public rooms'). The public bar, *Bulls and Cows*, is 'clearly popular' with locals. 'Our bedroom, in an annexe to the side, overlooked an attractive garden; it was so immaculate we might have been the first users: a spotless bathroom; appropriate accessories included ironing board and hairdryer. Inadequate bedside lighting was the only let-down.' Rooms at the front face the main crossroads in the village. Service was 'admirable' in the large dining room where Douglas Lindsay's cooking 'exceeded expectations: not a bit precious, skilfully using good produce. A generous plate of smoked salmon and grapefruit; belly of pork with bubble and squeak; vanilla panna cotta with rhubarb. Breakfast continued to impress: unusually good coffee, three versions of eggs Benedict, smoked haddock.' Two of *The Elephant*'s sister hotels have a *Guide* entry: *The Bath Arms*, Horningsham, and *The New Inn*, Coln St Aldwyns.

Bedrooms: 22, 8 in annexe, 4 on ground floor, 1 suitable for ♿. *Open*: all year. *Facilities*: bar, 2 lounges, restaurant, conference rooms, civil wedding licence. *Background music*: 'soft'. *Location*: in village, 6 miles NW of Reading. *Smoking*: not allowed. *Children*: all ages welcomed. *Dogs*: allowed in 1 bedroom, not in restaurant. *Credit cards*: Amex, MasterCard, Visa. *Prices*: [2009] B&B £70–£100 per person, D,B&B from £100, full alc £37.50, website offers, Christmas/New Year packages. *V*

PENRITH Cumbria   *See Shortlist*

PENZANCE Cornwall   Map 1:E1

The Abbey Hotel
Abbey Street
Penzance TR18 4AR

Tel 01736-366906
Fax 01736-351163
Email hotel@theabbeyonline.co.uk
Website www.theabbeyonline.co.uk

César award in 1985

'Comfortable, beautiful, interesting.' On a narrow street leading down to the harbour, this blue-painted listed building (part 17th-century), owned by Jean Shrimpton, is run by her son, Thaddeus Cox. A visitor who arrived after a stormy crossing from the Scilly Isles was transported 'from hell to heaven; Thad was waiting for us, took our luggage, looked after us'. Inspectors were equally taken: 'Decorated with character and attitude: scarlet walls and carpets in hall and corridors, a wonderful collection of original paintings.' The 'inviting' drawing room is 'full of curios; huge arched windows open on to the exotically planted walled garden, where tea and breakfast are served in summer'. A top-floor bedroom had 'massive wooden headboard, huge bedside tables, big ceramic reading lights; fluffy towels in the private shower room across the corridor'. Five rooms have been given a new bathroom; all have flat-screen TV, free Wi-Fi. In 2009, the dining room ('very attractive; antique dresser, ancient fireplace, posies of flowers on wooden tables') reopened in the evening after an eight-year gap: Chef Adam Cain cooks modern dishes, eg, Dover sole with mussel tortellini, ginger foam. Breakfast has 'freshly squeezed orange juice, a silver pot of tea, home-made marmalade, good cooked dishes'. (*Chris Matcham, and others*)

Bedrooms: 6, also 2 apartments in adjoining building. *Open*: Feb–Dec, restaurant closed Sun and Mon. *Facilities*: drawing room, dining room, garden, unsuitable for &. *Background music*: none. *Location*: 300 yds from centre, parking. *Smoking*: not allowed. *Children*: all ages welcomed. *Dogs*: allowed. *Credit cards*: Amex, MasterCard, Visa. *Prices*: [2009] B&B £52.50–£130 per person, set dinner £25–£30, midweek offers. *V*

Hotel Penzance   NEW

Britons Hill
Penzance TR18 3AE

Tel 01736-363117
Fax 01736-350970
Email enquiries@hotelpenzance.com
Website www.hotelpenzance.com

In a quiet residential area near the harbour, and with 'wonderful' views over Mount's Bay to St Michael's Mount, owners Stephen and Yvonne Hill have turned two 1920s houses into this 'attractive' small hotel. Andrew Griffiths, the manager, leads a 'very helpful staff', say regular *Guide* correspondents in 2009. The *Bay Restaurant* (with modern decor, sliding glass doors, well-spaced tables, local artwork and a bar) is popular with outside diners. The chef, Ben Reeves, who has worked with Anton Mosimann, uses Cornish produce (especially seafood) for his 'imaginative' modern dishes, eg, pickled tuna loin with fennel and radish salad; oven-baked hake, saffron bisque, white crabmeat, watercress pesto. The 'charming' bedrooms are decorated in bright colours; many have the view. There is a heated swimming pool in the small subtropical garden. The heliport to the Isles of Scilly is five minutes' drive away; two-centre breaks with *Island Hotel*, Tresco (*qv*), are among the special offers. (*John and Theresa Stewart*)

Bedrooms: 25, 2 on ground floor. *Open*: all year. *Facilities*: ramps, 3 lounges, bar/restaurant, ½-acre garden, terrace, 15-metre swimming pool, rock beach, safe bathing nearby. *Background music*: soft jazz in restaurant. *Location*: on hill, 550 yds from centre. *Smoking*: not allowed. *Children*: all ages welcomed. *Dogs*: not allowed in restaurant. *Credit cards*: Amex (*2½% surcharge*), MasterCard, Visa. *Prices*: [2009] B&B £60–£90 per person, D,B&B £85–£115, set dinner £24–£30, full alc £40, special breaks, Christmas/New Year packages, 1-night bookings refused Christmas/Easter. *V*

Smaller hotels, especially in remote areas, may close at short notice off-season. Check before travelling that a hotel is open.

PETERSFIELD Hampshire   Map 2:E3

JSW   NEW   *Tel* 01730-262030
20 Dragon Street   *Email* jsw.restaurant@btinternet.com
Petersfield GU31 4JJ   *Website* www.jswrestaurant.com

In this busy but attractive Hampshire town, Jake (Saul) Watkins runs
this old coaching inn as a restaurant-with-rooms (*Michelin* star). An
inspector in 2009 found 'superb food, excellent staff', and 'reasonably
comfortable' accommodation. 'Our bedroom, off a wide landing, was
small, fresh and light, decorated in cream and brown. Heating was super-
efficient; there was a comfortable bed with a duvet, a desk, a wardrobe,
a large flat-screen TV, Wi-Fi. The modern bathroom had a glass shower
cabinet, no bath.' In the 'welcoming' restaurant, with subdued lighting,
well-spaced tables, pristine linen and settings, 'the cooking was sublime:
scallops with butternut squash purée; an outstanding dish of venison
with Jerusalem artichoke; a delicious chocolate délice with malt ice
cream. Superb home-made truffles with coffee.' A breakfast tray is
brought to the bedroom: 'It had orange juice, muesli, crème fraîche with
mango, toast, home-made marmalade and lemon curd. The croissants
and pains au raisin came from Rungis market in Paris. No guest lounge,
but this is fine for a one-night gastronomic experience.'

Bedrooms: 3. *Open*: all year except 2 weeks Jan, 2 weeks June. *Facilities*:
restaurant, courtyard. *Background music*: none. *Location*: town centre. *Smoking*:
not allowed. *Children*: not under 7. *Dogs*: not allowed. *Credit cards*: MasterCard,
Visa. *Prices*: [2009] B&B £42.50–£55 per person, set meals £19.50–£50.

PETWORTH West Sussex   Map 2:E3

The Old Railway Station   *Tel* 01798-342346
Petworth GU28 0JF   *Fax* 01798-343066
                                Email info@old-station.co.uk
                               Website www.old-station.co.uk

'A unique and nostalgic experience', a Victorian railway station, listed
Grade II*, and three Pullman carriages house this 'tranquil' and
'romantic' B&B beside a disused railway line. 'We love it,' said a
visitor on her fourth visit. Restored 'with flair', it is owned by
Gudmund Olafsson (Icelandic) and Catherine Stormont. He is 'always
on hand to talk about the refurbishment, and clearly has a great
relationship with his staff'. The biggest bedrooms (one up a spiral
staircase and through a library) are in the station building. Those in the

Pullman cars (of the type used for the original Orient Express) are, inevitably, narrow, but are 'beautifully restored, well designed, with comfortable bed and a surprising amount of furniture'. A 'first-class' breakfast is taken in the waiting room (with 20-foot vaulted ceiling and original ticket-office windows), on the platform or in the carriages. 'Served in a leisurely fashion, it uses the best local ingredients.' The pretty garden has ancient trees, a sunken lawn, and steep banks covered with shrubs. 'The surrounding area offers a variety of good gastropubs': menus of local eating places are in the information folders. Convenient for Goodwood, the Weald and Downland Museum, Chichester. (*SM*)

Bedrooms: 10, 8 in Pullman carriages, 1 suitable for &. *Open*: all year except Christmas/New Year. *Facilities*: lounge/bar/breakfast room, platform/terrace, 2-acre garden. *Background music*: classical/soft 1940s in waiting room. *Location*: 1½ miles S of Petworth. *Smoking*: not allowed. *Children*: not under 10. *Dogs*: not allowed. *Credit cards*: Amex, MasterCard, Visa. *Prices*: [2009] B&B £41.50–£97 per person, special breaks, 1-night bookings refused weekends and during Goodwood events.

PICKERING North Yorkshire   Map 4:D4

The White Swan Inn
Market Place
Pickering YO18 7AA

Tel 01751-472288
Fax 01751-475554
Email welcome@white-swan.co.uk
Website www.white-swan.co.uk

Built in 1532, this old inn is in the centre of a pretty market town. Once a four-room cottage, it was later extended, and became a coaching stop for the York to Whitby stagecoach. It has been updated by Victor and Marion Buchanan, the second generation of the family who have owned it for more than 25 years. Alison Dunning is the manageress. The staff (most are locals) are 'always friendly and helpful', said regular visitors. There is an open fire, complimentary tea and coffee, an honesty bar, a pool table, newspapers and magazines in the residents' lounge (and no muzak). The bar has leather banquettes. The 'traditional' bedrooms in the main building, off a winding corridor, were refurbished this year. The newer, contemporary rooms, in an annexe, are 'exceptionally good, and free of traffic noise'. Jokey information packs provide entertainment, as do large plasma television sets. There are flagstones, an open fire, low ceiling and Gothic screens in the restaurant where Chef Darren Clemmit's 'country cooking' is thought 'excellent, with high-quality ingredients, large portions, good daily specials'. Typical dishes: moules marinière; Holme Farm venison haunch with dauphinoise potatoes. 'An impressive wine list.' Children have their own menu, games and baby-listening. 'Delicious breakfast: home-made breads and jams, first-rate Whitby kippers and haddock.' The Buchanans also own *tutti*, the pizzeria/wine bar next door, and the *Ginger Pig* farm shop close by. (*J and MW, CG, and others*)

Bedrooms: 21, 9 in annexe. *Open*: all year. *Facilities*: ramps to ground-floor facilities, lounge, bar, Club Room, restaurant, private dining room, conference/meeting facilities, civil wedding licence, small terrace (alfresco meals), 1½-acre grounds. *Background music*: none. *Location*: central. *Smoking*: not allowed. *Children*: all ages welcomed. *Dogs*: not allowed in restaurant. *Credit cards*: Amex, MasterCard, Visa. *Prices*: [2009] B&B £72.50–£125 per person, D,B&B £100–£150, full alc £35, Christmas/New Year packages, 1-night bookings sometimes refused weekends. *V*

PICKHILL North Yorkshire   Map 4:C4

The Nag's Head
Pickhill, nr Thirsk
YO7 4JG

Tel 01845-567391
Fax 01845-567212
Email enquiries@nagsheadpickhill.co.uk
Website www.nagsheadpickhill.co.uk

The bedrooms are 'not luxurious, but perfectly adequate', and the food is 'very good' at this 200-year-old former coaching inn in an ancient village in Herriot country. Owned and managed by one family since 1972, it is now run ('impeccably') by Edward and Janet Boynton. A visitor returning this year enjoyed 'a warm welcome, excellent dinner and breakfast'. Everyone agrees about the 'good value', and the quality of Mark Harris's cooking. Dishes from an extensive menu ('three boards of starters and two of main courses') can be ordered in both the bar (where a large collection of ties is displayed) and the busy restaurant (where booking is essential). Typical offerings: game broth, herb dumpling; smoked haddock, mashed potato, Béarnaise sauce. In the 'large, pleasant' breakfast room (oak bookshelves, plants and traditional ornaments), smoked haddock and poached egg were 'excellent once again'. Some bedrooms are in an annexe, a converted Victorian house. Some rooms might be 'somewhat noisy (thin walls)'. Children 'with well-behaved parents' are welcomed, and pets 'must be properly controlled'. (*Ann Duncan, Sir John B Hall, and others*)

Bedrooms: 14, 6 in annexe, 2 in cottage, 3 on ground floor. *Open*: all year except 25 Dec. *Facilities*: ramps, lounge, bar, restaurant, meeting facilities, lawn (croquet, putting). *Background music*: in lounge, bar and restaurant. *Location*: 5 miles SE of Leeming. *Smoking*: not allowed. *Children*: all ages welcomed. *Dogs*: in 2 bedrooms, not unattended. *Credit cards*: MasterCard, Visa. *Prices*: [2009] B&B £47.50–£80 per person, full alc £33, themed breaks, New Year package.

PLYMOUTH Devon   *See Shortlist*

POOLE Dorset   *See Shortlist*

PORLOCK Somerset   Map 1:B5

The Oaks   *Tel* 01643-862265
Porlock TA24 8ES   *Fax* 01643-863131
                    Email info@oakshotel.co.uk
                    Website www.oakshotel.co.uk

In an elevated position on the edge of a village where the Exmoor national park meets the sea, this gabled Edwardian country house has pretty gardens with wide lawns and oak trees. It has long been run, 'almost single-handed', by its 'very nice' owners, Tim and Anne Riley, 'with quiet efficiency'. Guests love its traditional style and 'old-fashioned courtesy'. Cases are carried, and tea, coffee and shortbread are served free of charge to arriving visitors. The main lounge has an open fire, chintzes, oil paintings and prints. All bedrooms have sea views, fresh flowers and Egyptian cotton bedlinen. 'Ours was beautifully kept, and had comfortable easy chairs,' said a recent guest. The extras like fresh milk and fruit are appreciated. Tables are arranged around the panoramic windows of the restaurant to take advantage of the views of Porlock and the Bristol Channel. Anne Riley's four-course dinner menu changes daily. Dishes might include cream of pear and watercress soup; guineafowl breast in Parma ham with prunes and Armagnac. Service, by Tim Riley, is 'superb'. A warning: 'The hotel's entrance is at a sharp angle of the main road.' (*Michael and Jenifer Price, DS*)

Bedrooms: 8. *Open*: Apr–Nov, Christmas/New Year. *Facilities*: 2 lounges, bar, restaurant, 2-acre garden, pebble beach 1 mile, unsuitable for &. *Background music*: classical during dinner. *Location*: edge of village. *Smoking*: not allowed. *Children*: not under 8. *Dogs*: not allowed. *Credit cards*: MasterCard, Visa. *Prices*: [2009] B&B £72.50–£102.50 per person, D,B&B £32.50 added, special breaks, Christmas/New Year packages.

PORT ISAAC Cornwall   Map 1:D2

Port Gaverne Hotel   *Tel* 01208-880244
Port Gaverne   *Freephone* 0500 657867
nr Port Isaac   *Fax* 01208-880151
PL29 3SQ   *Email* graham@port-gaverne-hotel.co.uk
                            Website www.port-gaverne-hotel.co.uk

'Friendly, welcoming and easy-going', this unpretentious inn stands 'idyllically' in a secluded cove near the fishing village of Port Isaac. 'Every member of staff was helpful,' says a visitor with mobility problems, who stayed in one of the inn's cottages. Another comment: 'It's a pub at heart, quite basic, but friendly. I liked it very much.' Owned by Graham and Annabelle Sylvester, it is 'the hub of the village'; the bar, with slate floors, wooden beams, Cornish artwork (for sale) and log fire, is popular with locals. The cooking of Ian Brodey and Tristan Halliday was greatly enjoyed: their short, daily-changing menu might include warm sun-blushed tomato and Cornish cheese tart; whole grilled lemon sole with anchovy butter. The wine list is 'surprisingly short'. The simple bedrooms are up steep steps; sound insulation may not be perfect. 'Our first-floor room was large, comfortable, well equipped; a powerful shower over the bath.' An attic room was also liked. Breakfast has a buffet for cereals, packaged juices, cooked dishes brought to the table; pats of butter. 'Very dog friendly' (the owners' dogs often sit under tables in the bar). (*Helen Anthony, Josie Mayers*)

Bedrooms: 14. *Open*: all year except Christmas, 1–8 Feb. *Facilities*: lounge, 2 bars, restaurant, beer garden, rock cove 60 yds, golf, fishing, surfing, sailing, riding nearby, unsuitable for &. *Background music*: none. *Location*: ½ mile N of Port Isaac. *Smoking*: not allowed. *Children*: all ages welcomed. *Dogs*: allowed throughout. *Credit cards*: MasterCard, Visa. *Prices*: [2009] B&B £45–£65 per person, set dinner £27, New Year package.

Readers' contributions, written on the forms at the back of the book or sent by email, are the lifeblood of the *Good Hotel Guide*. Our readers play a crucial role by reporting on existing entries as well as recommending new discoveries. Everyone who writes to the *Guide* is a potential winner of the Report of the Year competition (page 10) in which a dozen correspondents each year win a copy of the *Guide* and an invitation to our annual launch party in October.

PORTSCATHO Cornwall   Map 1:E2

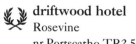 **driftwood hotel**
Rosevine
nr Portscatho TR2 5EW

Tel 01872-580644
Fax 01872-580801
Email info@driftwoodhotel.co.uk
Website www.driftwoodhotel.co.uk

César award: Cornish hotel of the year

Down a private lane with 'beautiful sea views' over the Roseland peninsula, this 'happy place to stay' is owned and managed by Paul and Fiona Robinson. They keep 'a close eye on every aspect', says a visitor this year; their staff are 'anxious to please'. 'An idyllic spot. Most guests are on a return visit.' The interiors are contemporary: colours are white with shades of blue; there are rugs on bare floorboards, driftwood table lamps and mirrors. 'The theme and style are consistent throughout; it is elegant and understated.' Almost all the bedrooms face the sea; ground-floor rooms have their own decked terrace. Even a small room 'was perfectly adequate; it had the view'. Summer lunches can be taken on a large decked terrace. In the evening, in the candlelit dining room, the chef, Chris Eden, serves modern European dishes, including a tasting menu which might include red mullet and mackerel tartare, oyster beignet; sirloin of beef, shallot purée, beer-pickled onions, rösti, port jus. 'Dinner was delicious, with home-made bread, good local fish; they were especially helpful over a no-fat diet.' The 'lavish' breakfast is liked. Steep steps lead through woodland down to a beach (picnics are available). The Eden Project and the 'Lost' Gardens of Heligan are within a half-hour drive. (*Dr and Mrs Peter Partner, Claire Haigh*)

Bedrooms: 15, 4 in courtyard, also 2 in Cabin (2 mins' walk). *Open*: 6 Feb–6 Dec. *Facilities*: 2 lounges, bar, restaurant, children's games room, 7-acre grounds (terraced gardens, private beach, safe bathing), unsuitable for &. *Background music*: jazz in restaurant and bar. *Location*: N side of Portscatho. *Smoking*: not allowed. *Children*: all ages welcomed. *Dogs*: not allowed. *Credit cards*: Amex, MasterCard, Visa. *Prices*: B&B £72.50–£120 per person, D,B&B (Nov–Mar) £97.50–£125, set dinner £40, tasting menu £55, website offers, 1-night bookings sometimes refused weekends.

The *Guide*'s website can be used alongside the printed edition. It has photographs of nearly all of the hotels, with a direct link to its website. It also has a Special Offers section with some excellent deals exclusively for *Guide* readers. See www.goodhotelguide.com.

POSTBRIDGE Devon   Map 1:D4

Lydgate House   `NEW`
Postbridge, Dartmoor
PL20 6TJ

Tel 01822-880209
Fax 01822-880360
Email lydgatehouse@email.com
Website www.lydgatehouse.co.uk

In May 2008, this late Victorian country house in Dartmoor national park was bought by Douglas and Anna Geikie. It returns to the *Guide* after enthusiastic reports from visitors who remember the previous regime. The setting ('in the middle of nowhere', near the village's famous clapper bridge over the River Dart) is 'wonderful', it is 'still excellent value for money', and 'the Geikies are delightful. Their two very nice young daughters and shy dog, Mossy, create an atmosphere of relaxation and warmth.' An inspector agreed: 'When we telephoned to say we might be early, Anna, an exuberant personality, set the tone by saying, "Come whenever you like, I'll put a fresh batch of mince pies in the oven."' There are 'superb' views from the sitting room, the conservatory dining room and most bedrooms. 'The sound of the river' is another attraction. '*Lydgate* is emphatically not smart; log fires make for a cheerful atmosphere. Our large bedroom had red chintz, toning red-check tie-back curtains, a huge, blissfully comfortable bed; a bathroom big enough to swing many cats, a freestanding red-painted bath.' The 'excellent' chef, Philip Davies-Russell, cooks a simple supper: 'Anna, who grew up on the moor, knows all the suppliers' for the short menu: perhaps watercress and potato soup; Dartmoor beef braised in Jail Ale (from nearby Princetown). 'First-class ingredients and presentation.' Breakfast has locally made granola, compote of berries, 'a lavish cooked choice'. 'For walkers this would be bliss.' (*Jennifer Harte, Helen Anthony, and others*)

Bedrooms: 7, 1 on ground floor. *Open*: all year, dining room closed Sun/Mon evenings. *Facilities*: lounge/bar, snug, dining room, terrace, 36-acre grounds (moorland, paddock, river, private access for guests), fishing, swimming, unsuitable for &. *Background music*: jazz/classical in bar in evening. *Location*: on edge of hamlet, 500 yds off B3212. *Smoking*: not allowed. *Children*: not under 16. *Dogs*: not allowed in public rooms. *Credit cards*: MasterCard, Visa. *Prices*: [2009] B&B £40–£60 per person, D,B&B £67.50–£87.50, full alc £31, special rates for 3 nights or more, New Year package, 1-night bookings refused bank holidays. *V*

The 'New' label indicates hotels which are appearing in the *Guide* for the first time or which have been readmitted after an absence.

PURTON Wiltshire   Map 3:E5

The Pear Tree at Purton
Church End
Purton, nr Swindon SN5 4ED

Tel 01793-772100
Fax 01793-772369
Email stay@peartreepurton.co.uk
Website www.peartreepurton.co.uk

In 'lovely' gardens, on the edge of a Saxon village in the Vale of the White Horse, this Cotswold stone former vicarage is run as a country hotel (Pride of Britain) by owners Francis and Anne Young. 'They are outstanding hosts,' say inspectors in 2009. 'We were struck by the courtesy of all their staff.' In the bedrooms (each named after a village character), fresh flowers match the colour scheme. A four-poster room had 'bottled water, fruit, a decanter of sherry, but no tea/coffee-making; nice spa bath, fluffy towels, and robes'. Some rooms may feel 'a bit old-fashioned', and one visitor found lighting 'rather dim', but 'housekeeping was immaculate; beds turned down in the evening'. In the candlelit green-and-white restaurant, the modern cooking of Alan Postill is enjoyed: 'Excellent lamb and venison, good beef and duck' in dishes like pressed duck confit; rib-eye steak, garlic, shallot and Dijon sauce. The vegetarian dishes are also praised. 'The impressive wine list has house wines under £20.' Breakfast is 'a good start to the day: fresh juices, grapefruit segments, croissants, home-made jams, rounds of butter and good full English'. The Youngs say they are 'consciously green': 'We have a wild-flower meadow, a vineyard and a beehive.' All uncooked kitchen waste is processed by an accelerated composter. (*IM, and others*)

Bedrooms: 17, some on ground floor. *Open*: all year except 26–30 Dec. *Facilities*: ramps, lounge/bar, library, restaurant, function/conference facilities, civil wedding licence, 7½-acre grounds (vineyard, croquet, pond, jogging route). *Background music*: none. *Location*: 5 miles NW of Swindon. *Smoking*: not allowed. *Children*: all ages welcomed. *Dogs*: not unattended in bedrooms, not in public rooms. *Credit cards*: all major cards. *Prices*: B&B £60–£140 per person, set dinner £34.50, full alc £45, special breaks. *V*

RAMSGATE Kent   *See Shortlist*

'Set meal' indicates a fixed-price meal, with ample, limited or no choice. 'Full alc' is the hotel's estimated price per person of a three-course *à la carte* meal, with a half bottle of house wine. 'Alc' is the price of an *à la carte* meal excluding the cost of wine.

RAMSGILL-IN-NIDDERDALE   Map 4:D3
North Yorkshire

The Yorke Arms   *Tel* 01423-755243
Ramsgill-in-Nidderdale   *Fax* 01423-755330
nr Harrogate HG3 5RL   *Email* enquiries@yorke-arms.co.uk
                              Website www.yorke-arms.co.uk

♥ *César award in 2000*

'Unconditionally recommended' by a gourmet reader this year, this creeper-covered rural inn has a timeless setting on the green of a hamlet in a beautiful Yorkshire dale. Bill Atkins is the 'amiable' host in the busy flagstoned bar; the dales are the larder for the *Michelin*-starred cooking of his wife, Frances. Herbs and vegetables come from a cultivated field behind the inn for her innovative dishes, eg, rabbit, leek and carrot terrine; saddle of venison, wild mushroom, tournegas, braised celery. Service is 'excellent'. The bar has old beams, log fires, wooden tables and settles; lunches here (or outside in good weather) include toasted sandwiches, salads, fish and chips, mutton with spiced lentils. The 'well-furnished' bedrooms have high-tech fittings (LCD TV and DVD-player) and an 'ultra-modern' bathroom, but some rooms are small. Breakfast, between 8 and 9 am, has fresh juices, home-made marmalade; strong-cured bacon. Good walking from the door; the Gouthwaite Reservoir bird sanctuary is nearby. (*David Hampshire, and others*)

Bedrooms: 12. *Open*: all year, Sun dinner for residents only. *Facilities*: ramp, lounge, bar, 2 dining rooms, function facilities, 2-acre grounds, unsuitable for &. *Background music*: classical in dining rooms. *Location*: centre of village, train from Harrogate. *Smoking*: not allowed. *Children*: not under 12. *Dogs*: allowed by arrangement in 1 bedroom, not in restaurant. *Credit cards*: Diners, MasterCard, Visa. *Prices*: [2009] B&B £75–£120 per person, D,B&B £150–£190, tasting menu £75, full alc £75, winter offers, Christmas/New Year packages.

RAVENSTONEDALE Cumbria   Map 4:C3

The Black Swan   NEW   *Tel/Fax* 015396-23204
Ravenstonedale   *Email* enquiries@blackswanhotel.com
Kirkby Stephen CA17 4NG   *Website* www.blackswanhotel.com

In a conservation village in a 'lovely, hilly setting' in the Eden valley, this once run-down Victorian inn has been renovated by its 'likeable and friendly' owners, Alan and Louise Dinnes. 'They seem determined to inject new life into the village,' say inspectors. Mrs Dinnes has reopened (after 20 years) the village shop in a converted downstairs bedroom. There is a 'comfortable' bar area (which serves real ales), and two 'attractive' dining rooms. 'Our pleasant bedroom was well equipped; it had new carpets, curtains and lamps, a comfortable seating area with armchairs; the compact bathroom had good storage and lots of hot water.' Two bedrooms in a ground-floor annexe with direct outdoor access are equipped for disabled visitors; dogs are also welcomed here. There are family rooms, and games and DVDs for children. 'A well-written information pack.' Chef Tim Stephenson's extensive menu offers 'generous portions of straight-forward food', as much as possible sourced locally: 'My haddock came in a crispy beer batter with good mushy peas, and a mountain of thick chips.' Breakfast has a 'well-executed' cooked English, kippers; 'four generous slices of cheese, chorizo and Serrano ham'; packaged juice. 'Good value.' Musical events are held.

Bedrooms: 11, 2 in ground-floor annexe suitable for &. *Open*: all year except 25 Dec, 1st week in Jan. *Facilities*: bar, 2 dining rooms, beer garden, tennis and golf in village. *Background music*: optional 'easy listening'. *Location*: in village 5 miles SW of Kirkby Stephen. *Smoking*: not allowed. *Children*: all ages welcomed. *Dogs*: allowed in 2 bedrooms, not in restaurant. *Credit cards*: MasterCard, Visa. *Prices*: [2009] B&B £37.50–£55 per person, full alc £27, New Year package. *V*

REETH North Yorkshire   Map 4:C3

The Burgoyne Hotel   *Tel/Fax* 01748-884292
On the Green   *Email* enquiries@theburgoyne.co.uk
Reeth, nr Richmond   *Website* www.theburgoyne.co.uk
DL11 6SN

❧ *César award in 2002*

Visitors on a 'happy return' after five years to this late Georgian Grade II listed country house found the owner, Derek Hickson, 'as charming as ever'. 'He works tirelessly to keep up the standards,' said other guests. In a commanding position above the green of an attractive village in the Yorkshire Dales national park, the house is traditionally furnished. Two 'comfortable' sitting rooms have 'squashy sofas and armchairs', and a 'good supply of up-to-date magazines'. Mr Hickson takes orders here for dinner, served at 8 pm in the green-walled restaurant. Paul Salonga and Chris Harker's daily-changing four-course dinner menu (six choices for each course) is 'very good:

traditional dishes using top ingredients from local suppliers'. 'We enjoyed best end of lamb and guineafowl with orange and sherry sauce. Portions were generous but this is Yorkshire.' Bedrooms are 'tasteful and well equipped': those at the front have 'lovely views over Swallowdale'. 'Our twin room was beautifully furnished, and provided with all kinds of extras, even a hot-water bottle.' A comfortable rear room had antique pine furniture which matched the panelling around the large sash windows. Breakfast has a 'generous selection of fruit and good muesli'; 'nicely presented dishes, kippers, eggs Benedict; delicious jams'. (*Karina Spero, Peter and Maggie Scott, and others*)

Bedrooms: 8, 1 suite, 1 suitable for &. *Open*: 10 Feb–2 Jan, restaurant closed midday. *Facilities*: ramp, 2 lounges, dining room, ½-acre garden. *Background music*: jazz/classical in dining room 'when required'. *Location*: village centre. *Smoking*: not allowed. *Children*: not under 10. *Dogs*: not allowed in 1 lounge, dining room, or unattended in other lounge, bedrooms. *Credit cards*: MasterCard, Visa. *Prices*: [2009] B&B £66–£97.50 per person, set dinner £33, midweek/Christmas/New Year packages, 1-night bookings sometimes refused Sat.

RICHMOND North Yorkshire   Map 4:C3

Millgate House   *Tel* 01748-823571
Richmond DL10 4JN   *Fax* 01748-850701
                              Email oztim@millgatehouse.demon.co.uk
                              Website www.millgatehouse.com

Near the market place of this 'delightful' town, this early Georgian stone house has an award-winning walled garden (open to the public from April to October). The owners, Austin Lynch and Tim Culkin, who emphasise that 'we are not a restaurant/hotel, this is our home', tell us that they have redecorated throughout, replacing windows, refreshing bathrooms (and renewing towels). Two of the three bedrooms overlook the garden. A recent visitor had 'a large, light room with fabulous views over the dales; bed nicely dressed; thoughtful extras'. The 'charming' public rooms are 'filled with delightful objects': antiques, pictures, books, etc. One couple described the style as 'shabby chic'. Breakfast, now served until 9.45 am in the elegant green-walled dining room, has a 'bountiful' buffet (fresh fruit, 'perfect' croissants), 'good cooked dishes', 'excellent coffee'. 'Thankfully, no background music.' A set, pre-selected six-course dinner (£60–£65) is available for groups of 16 or more (a performance by a magician can be arranged). Dogs are welcomed. (*WA, and others*)

Bedrooms: 3, also self-catering facilities for 12. *Open*: all year. *Facilities*: hall, drawing room, dining room, ½-acre garden, unsuitable for &. *Background music*: sometimes, classical in dining room. *Location*: town centre. *Smoking*: not allowed. *Children*: not under 10. *Dogs*: not in dining room. *Credit cards*: none. *Prices*: B&B £47.50–£62.50 per person, Christmas/New Year packages.

RIPLEY North Yorkshire   Map 4:D4

The Boar's Head
Ripley Castle Estate, Ripley
nr Harrogate HG3 3AY

Tel 01423-771888
Fax 01423-771509
Email reservations@boarsheadripley.co.uk
Website www.boarsheadripley.co.uk

🏆 *César award in 1999*

'Standards are just as high as on our first visit, and the food is possibly even better.' Praise from a visitor returning in 2009 to this 18th-century former coaching inn which has been renovated by Sir Thomas and Lady Ingilby. It stands within the Ripley Castle estate, his family's domain for 700 years. Steve Chesnutt is the manager. An 'agreeable' combination of pub and country hotel, it is 'elegant but not stuffy'. 'Service is uniformly excellent; the efficient young waiting staff are charming.' Lounges have antique and period furniture, portraits and pictures from the castle's attics. In the smart restaurant, Oliver Stewart is now the chef: his dishes might include cured beef carpaccio with rocket and Parmesan salad; plaice with spinach and tomato confit. 'The menu didn't change, but provided plenty of choice for a three-night stay. The *pièce de résistance* was the perfectly executed hot praline soufflé with banana ice cream.' Simpler meals are available in the bistro. Many of the bedrooms look over the cobbled market square and historic church. The 'superior' bedrooms in *Birchwood House*, across a courtyard, are 'light, airy and beautifully presented'; they have flowers, fresh fruit, bottled water, sherry. Hotel guests have access to the castle grounds. (*Jenny Buckley, and others*)

Bedrooms: 25, 10 in courtyard, 6 in *Birchwood House* adjacent, some on ground floor. *Open*: all year. *Facilities*: ramps, 2 lounges, bar/bistro, restaurant, civil wedding licence (in castle), 150-acre estate (deer park, lake, fishing, 20-acre garden). *Background music*: 'easy listening' in restaurant and bistro. *Location*: 3 miles N of Harrogate. *Smoking*: not allowed. *Children*: all ages welcomed. *Dogs*: allowed. *Credit cards*: all major cards. *Prices*: [2009] B&B £62.50–£75 per person, full alc from £30, Christmas/New Year packages.

RIPON North Yorkshire   Map 4:D4

The Old Deanery   *Tel* 01765-600003
Minster Road   *Fax* 01765-600027
Ripon HG4 1QS   *Email* reception@theolddeanery.co.uk
                              Website www.theolddeanery.co.uk

Opposite the 'awe-inspiring' cathedral, the oldest in England, this
stylishly modernised building, which dates back to 1625, is on the site
of a former monastery. Owner/manager Linda Whitehouse is around
much of the time, say enthusiastic guests this year. An earlier visitor
wrote of 'peaceful surroundings, good food, comfortable rooms with
modern bathroom'. No lift: an 18th-century oak staircase leads up to
the bedrooms. The six first-floor rooms have original pine shutters and
panelling; two have a Victorian-style slipper bath, two a four-poster.
The 'characterful' second-floor rooms have a 'splendid' shower, old
beams and sloping ceilings. But one shower may be very small. All
rooms have broadband Internet access, bathrobes, digital TV, fresh
fruit and bottled water. The bar/lounge, at the front of the house, has
leather sofas and a log fire on cold days. In the candlelit restaurant,
with 'striking' contemporary decor (bare dark floorboards, high-backed
leather chairs and crystal chandeliers), chef Barrie Higginbotham uses
local ingredients in his modern dishes, eg, pan-fried scallops with
Yorkshire rhubarb; assiette of rabbit, Chantenay carrots and new
potatoes. For breakfast there are croissants, ham, etc, and cooked
dishes. In summer, teas, drinks and meals are served in the large
secluded garden. Weddings are held. More reports, please.

Bedrooms: 11. *Open*: all year except 25 Dec, 1 Jan, restaurant closed Sun
evening. *Facilities*: lounge, bar, restaurant, conference facilities, civil wedding
licence, 1-acre garden, only restaurant suitable for &. *Background music*: in bar,
restaurant rooms. *Location*: town centre. *Smoking*: not allowed. *Children*: all ages
welcomed. *Dogs*: not allowed in public rooms. *Credit cards*: MasterCard, Visa.
Prices: [2009] B&B £60–£95 per person, set dinner £31.50, full alc £37.50,
special breaks. *V*

ROCK Cornwall   *See Shortlist*

The more reports we receive, the more accurate the *Guide*
becomes. Please don't hesitate to write again about an old
favourite, even if only to endorse the entry. New reports help
us keep the *Guide* up to date.

ROMALDKIRK Co. Durham   Map 4:C3

The Rose and Crown

Romaldkirk
nr Barnard Castle
DL12 9EB

Tel 01833-650213
Fax 01833-650828
Email hotel@rose-and-crown.co.uk
Website www.rose-and-crown.co.uk

🏆 *César award in 2003*

Beside the Saxon church opposite the green (where the stocks still stand) in a Teesdale village, this 18th-century, creeper-clad coaching inn is admired. 'We were impressed by the meals, the service and the hospitality,' say visitors in 2009, endorsing earlier praise ('excellent in every way'). It is owned and run by Alison and Christopher Davy (he is joint chef with Andrew Lee); Jenny Hollando (now married, formerly Ranner) is the manager. There are stone walls, beams and panelling; log fires, old farming implements, grandfather clocks, gleaming brass and copper and fresh flowers in the public areas. All the bedrooms, which vary in size and style, have now been refurbished. Rooms in the main house may have beams, antiques; some have a private sitting room. The five rooms in a courtyard at the back of the house are good for dog-owners and walkers, and have a more contemporary decor. The four-course menu has modern English dishes 'with a regional influence', eg, baked smoked salmon soufflé; roast Teesdale Fell lamb, confit of shoulder, Madeira jus; lemon posset with red berry compote. The bread, marmalade and jams at breakfast are home made. The Davys have written a 'very useful' guidebook to local attractions, which include High Force, England's highest waterfall. (*Dursley Stott, MA*)

Bedrooms: 12, 5 in rear courtyard, some ground floor. *Open*: all year except 24–26 Dec. *Facilities*: residents' lounge, lounge bar, Crown Room (bar meals), restaurant, fishing (grouse shooting, birdwatching) nearby. *Background music*: none. *Location*: village centre. *Smoking*: not allowed. *Children*: all ages welcomed. *Dogs*: allowed in bar, not unattended in bedrooms. *Credit cards*: MasterCard, Visa. *Prices*: [2009] B&B £70–£119 per person, D,B&B £100–£150, set dinner £30, winter discounts, New Year package, 1-night bookings refused Sat 'except quiet periods'. *V*

The *V* sign at the end of an entry indicates a hotel that has agreed to take part in our Voucher scheme and to give *Guide* readers a 25% discount on their bed-and-breakfast rates for a one-night stay, subject to the conditions explained in *How to use the Good Hotel Guide*, and given on the back of each voucher.

ROSS-ON-WYE Herefordshire   Map 3:D5

Wilton Court   *Tel* 01989-562569
Wilton Lane, Ross-on-Wye   *Fax* 01989-768460
HR9 6AQ   *Email* info@wiltoncourthotel.com
                                 Website www.wiltoncourthotel.com

'Good room, excellent food, helpful owners.' An endorsement this
year for this small hotel on the banks of the River Wye, facing the
pretty market town on the Welsh borders. The pink stone part-
Elizabethan building was once a magistrates' court (the bar is the
former courthouse). It has ancient beams, leaded windows, uneven
floors, a huge fireplace with its original iron grate. The owners, Helen
and Roger Wynn, have filled it with curios and *objets d'art* from their
time working (in hotels) in the Far East. Three of the traditionally
furnished bedrooms face the river; others overlook the garden. An
earlier visitor had an 'enchantingly pretty' room decorated in blue:
'crisp cotton sheets, striped duvet; kimonos in the wardrobe'. In the
eaves is a family suite with two bedrooms. The conservatory-style
Mulberry restaurant has beige Lloyd Loom tables and chairs. Michael
Fowler is now the chef, and we would welcome reports on his
British/European cooking (eg, carpaccio of Herefordshire beef,
pickled chicory; seared tuna, Provençal vegetables). Manager Jason
Davies leads a 'helpful' staff. *Wilton Court* has been given a gold award
by Visit Wales (a rare accolade for a hotel five miles inside the English
border). (*Jamie and Wendy Woods, MW*)

Bedrooms: 10. *Open*: all year except 3–17 Jan. *Facilities*: sitting room, bar,
restaurant, private dining room, conference facilities, civil wedding licence,
2-acre grounds (riverside garden, fishing), only restaurant suitable for &.
Background music: classical at mealtimes in restaurant. *Location*: ½ mile from
centre. *Smoking*: not allowed. *Children*: all ages welcomed. *Dogs*: not allowed in
restaurant. *Credit cards*: Amex, MasterCard, Visa. *Prices*: [to April 2010] B&B
£52.50–£135 per person, D,B&B £72.50–£155, full alc £37.50, special breaks,
Christmas/New Year packages, 1-night bookings sometimes refused Sat in
season. *V*

See also Shortlist

Report forms (Freepost in UK) are at the end of the *Guide*. If
you need more, please ask. We welcome email reports, too:
send these to editor@goodhotelguide.com.

ROSTHWAITE Cumbria   Map 4: inset C2

Hazel Bank
Rosthwaite
nr Keswick CA12 5XB

Tel 017687-77248
Fax 017687-77373
Email enquiries@hazelbankhotel.co.uk
Website www.hazelbankhotel.co.uk

In November 2008, this small hotel (a Victorian building with neo-Gothic influences) was bought by Rob van der Palen and Anton Renac. 'They have created a friendly, warm, professional atmosphere,' says a visitor in 2009. They are restyling the house, with oak flooring and William Morris wallpaper in the public rooms. Mealtimes are now more flexible. Anton Renac is the chef, serving a daily-changing no-choice menu, using local produce in dishes like smoked duck breast, raspberry sauce; fillet of sea bass, saffron sauce. Vegetarian alternatives are offered. Returning guests report: 'The food has gone up to a higher level. One evening we prized Anton out of the kitchen for a round of applause.' He 'bakes the most amazing bread', says another diner. The bedrooms vary in size from large to 'compact'. There are 'stunning views' of the surrounding fells with good walking in the area. Packed lunches are available. (*Tom and Sarah Mann, Jennifer Davis*)

Bedrooms: 8, 2 on ground floor, also self-catering cottage. *Open*: all year. *Facilities*: ramp, lounge, honesty bar, dining room, drying room, 4½-acre grounds (croquet, woods, becks). *Background music*: none. *Location*: 6 miles S of Keswick on B5289 to Borrowdale. *Smoking*: not allowed. *Children*: not under 12. *Dogs*: not allowed. *Credit cards*: MasterCard, Visa. *Prices*: D,B&B £73–£85 per person, set dinner £26, special breaks, Christmas/New Year packages, 1-night bookings sometimes refused.

ROTHBURY Northumberland   *See Shortlist*

ROWSLEY Derbyshire   Map 3:A6

The Peacock at Rowsley
Bakewell Road
Rowsley DE4 2EB

Tel 01629-733518
Fax 01629-732671
Email reception@thepeacockatrowsley.com
Website www.thepeacockatrowsley.com

Visitors this year 'almost had to beat off offers to carry our bags' into this former dower house for Haddon Hall. 'Arriving late on a freezing afternoon, we were soothed by the cosiness and the warm welcome.' The attractive building, with a stone exterior, stands in grounds that run down to the River Derwent. Owned by Lord Edward Manners, managed by Ian and Jenni MacKenzie, it is a 'wonderful mixture of ancient building with modern, classy interior', says another report. 'Our standard double bedroom, and our daughter's single, were a blend of traditional and antique furniture with some colourful design-led pieces. Bathrooms were tiny but luxuriously appointed.' The quietest rooms are at the rear; front ones face the busy A6 but have double-glazed windows. The evening turn-down service includes next day's weather forecast. In the two dining rooms, which have 'wonderful Mouseman furniture', food was 'stunning'. Chef Dan Smith serves modern dishes, perhaps Dorset crab, blood orange and radish salad; assiette of lamb, aubergine, chickpeas, moussaka. Traditional lunches and suppers are served in the bar. Breakfast has a good buffet: 'plenty of cereals, good toast, croissants, pastries, waffles'; cooked costs extra. Guests can shoot on the estate, and visit Haddon Hall (50% discount). (*Jenny Buckley, Celia and Peter Gregory*)

Bedrooms: 16. *Open*: all year except 24–26 Dec (open for lunch only), 3–11 Jan. *Facilities*: lounge, bar, dining room, live classical guitar Fri, conference rooms, civil wedding licence, ½-acre garden on river, fishing Apr–Oct, unsuitable for &. *Background music*: none. *Location*: village centre. *Smoking*: not allowed. *Children*: 'no children under 10 Fri/Sat.' *Dogs*: not allowed in public rooms. *Credit cards*: all major cards. *Prices*: [2009] B&B £72.50–£107.50 per person, D,B&B £102.50–£145, cooked breakfast £6.50, full alc £52, website offers, New Year package, 1-night bookings refused Sat.

RUSHLAKE GREEN East Sussex   Map 2:E4

Stone House
Rushlake Green
Heathfield TN21 9QJ

Tel 01435-830553
Fax 01435-830726
Website www.stonehousesussex.co.uk

'A wonderfully relaxing place', this Tudor manor house, with Georgian additions, has been owned by the Dunn family for five centuries. Peter and Jane Dunn welcome guests warmly; their staff are 'excellent and discreet', says a visitor this year. 'Within minutes, the stresses of the outside world are eased; lovely rooms, comfortable beds, exceptional meals.' The public rooms 'are a delight': a grand double staircase rises from the black-and-white marble floor of the entrance hall. The Georgian part of the house has the larger bedrooms, two with a four-poster. In the Tudor wing, rooms are smaller but 'attractive and quite adequate'; they have beams, sloping ceilings, antiques. The Dunns tell us that the water pressure has been improved after a comment last year about the showers in this part of the building. Jane Dunn has a *Michelin Bib Gourmand* for her French- and Thai-influenced cooking on a daily-changing menu (Rye scallops with chilli, grapefruit, crystallised ginger; saddle of wild rabbit, thyme and three-mustard cream sauce). The traditional breakfast has a 'superb buffet'; continental can be taken in the bedrooms. The huge grounds have a walled garden with an ornamental lake, gazebos, a 100-foot herbaceous border. A picnic can be provided for Glyndebourne, 20 minutes' drive away. (*Caroline Evans, PE Carter, and others*)

Bedrooms: 6. *Open*: all year except 21 Dec–1 Jan. *Facilities*: hall, drawing room, library, dining room, billiard room, 1,000-acre estate (5½-acre garden, farm, woodland, croquet, shooting, pheasant/clay-pigeon shooting, 2 lakes, rowing, fishing), unsuitable for &. *Background music*: none. *Location*: 4 miles SE of Heathfield, by village green. *Smoking*: not allowed. *Children*: not under 9. *Dogs*: not allowed in public rooms. *Credit cards*: MasterCard, Visa. *Prices*: [2009] B&B £62.50–£135 per person, set dinner £27.95, Glyndebourne hamper (*no VAT*) £32, weekend house parties, winter breaks, cookery courses, 1-night bookings sometimes refused Sat. *V* (1 Nov–31 Mar; not Fri/Sat)

RYE East Sussex   Map 2:E5

Durrant House   NEW   *Tel* 01797-223182
2 Market Street   *Email* info@durranthouse.com
Rye TN31 7LA   *Website* www.durranthouse.com

In the centre of historic Rye, this old house with a white-painted Georgian facade faces Market Street to the front and looks across the River Rother to Romney Marsh at the rear. It is run as a B&B by owners Jilly Mitchell and William Bilecki. 'A friendly welcome, our bags were carried to our interesting room,' say visitors this year. 'The bed was comfortable, the views were stunning. There were smiling faces, the service was personal, highly efficient.' The bedrooms vary in size: the River Room has a four-poster bed, hand-painted furniture, and two chairs; it has the views of the marsh. There is an honesty bar in the lounge. Breakfast, which can be taken in the garden in summer, has a sideboard buffet and cooked dishes to order. 'Smoked haddock and poached egg was particularly good, as was a vegetarian lentil pâté.' (*Simon Grenfell, GM Tottman, Capt and Mrs K Deverson*)

Bedrooms: 5. *Open*: all year. *Facilities*: lounge, breakfast room, small garden, unsuitable for ♿. *Background music*: classical during breakfast. *Location*: town centre. *Smoking*: not allowed. *Children*: not under 10. *Dogs*: not allowed. *Credit cards*: MasterCard, Visa. *Prices*: [2009] B&B £47.50–£78 per person, winter discounts, 1-night bookings sometimes refused.

The George in Rye

98 High Street
Rye TN31 7JT

Tel 01797-222114
Fax 01797-224065
Email stay@thegeorgeinrye.com
Website www.thegeorgeinrye.com

Rye's oldest coaching inn, established 1575 and added to until Regency times, has been given 'quirky' modern touches by owners Alex and Katie Clarke. A film set designer, she styled the bedrooms: there are tapestries, corduroy sofas, *chaises longues*, antique mirrors, roll-top baths, psychedelic prints, 'funky lighting'. 'Superb bed, nice sheets; cashmere-covered hot-water bottle.' Some rooms are in the main building, others across a courtyard. One has a shower stall in a former wig cupboard. Original features, such as beams from an Elizabethan galley, are retained. In the rambling old building 'little courtyards are hidden behind unfrequented stairs; rooms tucked in behind gables'; 'creaky corridors'. There is a 'pleasant' terrace, a 'cosy' lounge with open fire. The lively, beamed bar (which serves Sussex wines) is frequented by locals (noise could be a problem for residents). In the bistro-style restaurant (brown walls, plain wooden tables), the cooking of the chef, Rod Grossman, who worked at *Moro* in London, is modern British with Mediterranean influence, eg, scallops with quail's egg, chorizo and truffle oil; duck confit with marmalade sautéed potato. Service is by 'charming waitresses'. There is free Wi-Fi, a DVD library, bike hire; picnics can be provided. Functions are held in the 'magnificent' ballroom with its minstrels' gallery. Oliver Richards is the manager. More reports, please.

Bedrooms: 24, 6 in annexe. *Open*: all year. *Facilities*: sitting room, lounge/bar, restaurant, ballroom, civil wedding licence, terrace, courtyard garden, unsuitable for &. *Background music*: 'easy listening' in public rooms. *Location*: town centre, pay-and-display car park nearby. *Smoking*: not allowed. *Children*: all ages welcomed. *Dogs*: 'well-behaved' dogs allowed in bar/lounge/courtyard. *Credit cards*: all major cards (*3% surcharge for Amex*). *Prices*: [2009] B&B £47.50–£137.50 per person, full alc £35, special breaks, Christmas/New Year packages, supplement for 1-night bookings Sat.

Jeake's House
Mermaid Street
Rye TN31 7ET

Tel 01797-222828
Fax 01797-222623
Email stay@jeakeshouse.com
Website www.jeakeshouse.com

Ω *César award in 1992*

On one of Rye's prettiest cobbled streets, Jenny Hadfield's B&B has been created from three old buildings, one a former wool store. 'Nice and quiet', it has good views, says a visitor this year. 'Service is friendly without being fussy.' The oak-beamed parlour has an upright piano and a fireplace; the book-lined lounge has an honesty bar and sample menus from nearby restaurants. Both have Wi-Fi. All the bedrooms have been given a flat-screen TV with multiple channels this year. The larger rooms are named after writer friends of American poet Conrad Aiken, who once lived here. The top-floor suite has a window seat looking over the garden to the salt marsh. The Malcolm Lowry suite has a four-poster bed and a large bathroom with walk-in shower and roll-top bath. Housekeeping is 'of a high standard'. An 'excellent' breakfast is taken in the red-walled former chapel with its high windows, good china, plants, wooden floor. There is a self-service buffet, a choice of teas; cooked dishes include the house speciality, devilled kidneys on buttered toast. A vegetarian breakfast is also on offer. Resident cats Yum Yum and Monte are in attendance. A private car park (£3 a day) is available nearby. (*R Reynolds, and others*)

Bedrooms: 11. *Open*: all year. *Facilities*: parlour, bar/library, breakfast room, unsuitable for &. *Background music*: classical in breakfast room. *Location*: central, car park (£3 per 24 hours, advance booking needed). *Smoking*: not allowed.

Children: not under 8. *Dogs*: allowed. *Credit cards*: MasterCard, Visa. *Prices*: B&B £45–£64 per person, 2-night midweek breaks Nov–Mar, 1-night bookings sometimes refused busy weekends.

See also Shortlist

ST ALBANS Hertfordshire   *See Shortlist*

ST HILARY Cornwall   Map 1:E1

Ennys   *Tel* 01736-740262
Trewhella Lane, St Hilary   *Fax* 01736-740055
nr Penzance TR20 9BZ   *Email* ennys@ennys.co.uk
                                             Website www.ennys.co.uk

'Such a tranquil place,' said an inspector. Surrounded by fields that lead to the River Hayle, this creeper-covered Grade II listed 17th-century manor house is a 'stylish' B&B run by owner Gill Charlton, a travel writer. 'She is very welcoming; the door to the big farmhouse kitchen is always open. You can tell she is well travelled by the little comforts: big waffle bathrobes, a good selection of books and magazines, nice smellies.' The 'delightful', large sitting room has interesting artwork, a big log fire on cold days. 'Our classically fitted bedroom, in pale turquoise, had wood and cane furniture, interesting fabrics. The bed was super-comfortable, conducive to a good night's sleep.' All rooms have flat-screen TV and free Wi-Fi. There are two family suites (children must be over five) in a converted barn, each with its own entrance. 'Breakfast fuelled us for the day: freshly squeezed orange juice, stewed prunes, mini-croissants, lovely marmalade, jam and lemon curd; good toast, generous coffee in a vacuum jar, scrumptious cooked dishes. We were encouraged to feel at home.' *Ennys* has a pretty garden with exotic planting and a swimming pool (available to visitors in the morning and late afternoon).

Bedrooms: 5, 2 in barns, 3 self-catering apartments (can be B&B off-season). *Open*: 28 Mar–1 Nov. *Facilities*: sitting room, breakfast room, 3-acre grounds (tennis, 13-metre heated swimming pool, not available to residents 1–4 pm), unsuitable for &. *Background music*: none. *Location*: 5 miles E of Penzance. *Smoking*: not allowed. *Children*: not under 5. *Dogs*: not allowed. *Credit cards*: MasterCard, Visa. *Prices*: B&B £45–£67.50 per person, 1-night bookings refused high season, bank holidays.

ST IVES Cornwall   Map 1:D1

Boskerris Hotel
Boskerris Road
Carbis Bay
St Ives TR26 2NQ

Tel 01736-795295
Email reservations@boskerrishotel.co.uk
Website www.boskerrishotel.co.uk

High above sandy Carbis Bay, this 'exceptionally friendly, low-key little place' is a 30-minute coastal walk to town (five minutes by local train). 'It is everything a good hotel should be,' says a visitor this year. 'We had a lovely bedroom facing the sea; friendly staff, great breakfast.' The 1930s building has been refurbished in contemporary style by owners Jonathan and Marianne Bassett. This year they have renovated the exterior (stony cream with grey shutters), and added decking furniture to the 'lovely' terrace, which has 'splendid' views of the bay. There is new furniture in the big lounge, which has white-painted wooden floors. In the bedrooms, louvred doors to the bathroom have been replaced; all rooms have a new flat-screen TV with Freeview, and more toiletries. At breakfast 'the buffet had freshly squeezed juice, fabulous home-made muesli, a big bowl of cut fresh fruit, newspapers on a side table. A good atmosphere, guests talking to each other.' In 2009, a new, informal menu was introduced, with simple dishes using local ingredients, 'with a hint of the Med' and with a daily fish special, eg, John Dory, caramelised fennel, cherry tomato. We'd welcome reports on the meals. (*Gillian Morris, and others*)

Bedrooms: 15, 1 on ground floor. *Open*: Feb–Nov, restaurant closed Mon. *Facilities*: lounges, bar, restaurant, private dining/meeting room, decked terrace, 1½-acre garden. *Background music*: jazz/Latin. *Location*: 1½ miles from centre (5 mins by local train), car park. *Smoking*: not allowed. *Children*: not under 7. *Dogs*: not allowed. *Credit cards*: MasterCard, Visa. *Prices*: [2009] B&B £50–£105 per person, full alc £25, 1-night bookings refused bank holidays. *V* (off-season only)

See also Shortlist

The *V* sign at the end of an entry indicates that a hotel has agreed to take part in our Voucher scheme and to give *Guide* readers a 25% discount on their bed-and-breakfast rates for a one-night stay, subject to the conditions on the back of the voucher and explained in 'How to use the *Good Hotel Guide*' (page 57).

ST LEONARDS-ON-SEA   Map 2:E4
East Sussex

Zanzibar International Hotel   *Tel* 01424-460109
9 Eversfield Place   *Email* info@zanzibarhotel.co.uk
St Leonards-on-Sea   *Website* www.zanzibarhotel.co.uk
TN37 6BY

In a terrace of Victorian town houses on the seafront, this unusual
B&B has a distinctive interior. Its themed bedrooms reflect the globe-
trotting tastes of its owner, Max O'Rourke. Japan has a deep-soak
Japanese spa bath; South America has a Brazilian hand-carved bed
and a whirlpool bath for two; Bali ('bijou') has an in-room massage
shower and steam cabin. There is an honesty bar and a conservatory.
Visitors are asked to telephone 15 minutes before arriving as Mr
O'Rourke 'may not hear the bell' if he is upstairs. Parking permits
are provided for a secure underground car park nearby. Breakfast,
ordered by 9 pm the night before, is served in the bedroom or at a
large table in the Grand Salon, which has sofas, newspapers and
'extravagant flowers'. It includes champagne or Buck's Fizz, freshly
squeezed juices, fruit, cereals, a range of breads, full English and
vegetarian. 'Butter and jams in pots. Excellent coffee and tea.'
Behind the hotel is a small tropical garden, 'perfect for an afternoon
drink'. Help is given with reservations at local restaurants. Robyn
Schurr is the manager. More reports, please.

Bedrooms: 9, 1 on ground floor. *Open*: all year. *Facilities*: lounge, bar, breakfast
room, conservatory, small garden, beach across road, unsuitable for &.
Background music: radio, in lounge. *Location*: seafront, 650 yds W of Hastings
pier, free parking vouchers issued. *Smoking*: not allowed. *Children*: all ages
welcomed. *Dogs*: allowed in Bali only, not Fri–Sun, not in public rooms. *Credit
cards*: Amex, MasterCard, Visa. *Prices*: [2009] B&B £49.50–£122.50 per person,
midweek winter discounts, Christmas/New Year packages, 1-night bookings
sometimes refused weekends. *V*

See also Shortlist

We say 'Unsuitable for &' when a hotel tells us that it cannot
accommodate wheelchair-users. We do not have the resources
to inspect such facilities or to assess the even more complicated
matter of facilities for the partially disabled. We suggest that
you discuss such details with the hotel.

ST MARY'S Isles of Scilly   Map 1: inset C1

Star Castle

The Garrison, St Mary's
Isles of Scilly
Cornwall TR21 0JA

Tel 01720-422317
Fax 01720-422343
Email info@star-castle.co.uk
Website www.star-castle.co.uk

César award in 2009

'Friendly and unpretentious', 'excellent and unusual', this star-shaped Tudor fortress has a commanding position above Hugh Town. Owner Robert Francis manages it with his son, James: 'Reception service is impeccable,' say visitors this year. 'Every morning at breakfast a member of the family advises on boat trips and activities.' Other praise: 'Very welcoming; knowledgeable staff.' The building has antique furniture, tapestries and 'pictures relating to its history'; the 'slightly claustrophobic' bar is the former dungeon. Bedrooms are in the castle (an attic room had 'large bed, armchairs, adequate storage, a superb view of the harbour through a small window'), and in two single-storey garden buildings ('well furnished; thick, creamy curtains, two big armchairs, high-quality bedlinen, flat-screen TV'). Room 4 might need a facelift. The *Castle* dining room has white tablecloths, silver napkin rings, candles. Chef Gareth Stafford's 'excellent' menu might include Scillonian crab and Parmesan tart; beef Wellington, caramelised shallots, whisky jus. 'The waiting staff really knew about the food they were serving.' Alternative dining is available in warm weather in the vine-clad *Conservatory*, which specialises in fish. Breakfast has a 'well-stocked' buffet (fruit salad, yogurt, muesli, croissants); cooked options include 'quite a plateful' of kippers. (*Richard and Catriona Smith, Chris Matcham, John and Theresa Stewart, and others*)

Bedrooms: 38, 27 in 2 garden wings. *Open*: all year except 1–22 Dec, 2 Jan–14 Feb. *Facilities*: lounge, bar, 2 restaurants, 3-acre grounds (covered swimming pool, 12 by 3 metres, tennis), beach nearby, golf, bicycle hire, riding, sailing, diving, fishing available, unsuitable for &. *Background music*: none. *Location*: ¼ mile from town centre, boat (2¾ hours)/helicopter (20 mins) from Penzance, air links from Newquay, Exeter, Bristol. *Smoking*: not allowed. *Children*: not under 5 in restaurants. *Dogs*: not allowed in restaurants. *Credit cards*: Amex, MasterCard, Visa. *Prices*: [2009] B&B £65–£161 per person, D,B&B £75–£171, set dinner £28.50, Christmas/New Year packages, short breaks.

> Make sure that the hotel has included VAT in the prices which it quotes.

ST MAWES Cornwall   Map 1:E2

Tresanton   *Tel* 01326-270055
27 Lower Castle Road   *Fax* 01326-270053
St Mawes TR2 5DR   *Email* info@tresanton.com
                               Website www.tresanton.com

❧ *César award in 2009*

On a hillside amid terraced subtropical gardens, this luxurious yet
informal hotel is a cluster of old houses looking across a narrow
promenade to the Fal estuary. Owned by Olga Polizzi and managed by
Federica Bertolini, it garnered much new praise in 2009: 'Setting,
food, service and decor all faultless.' 'So thoughtfully planned and
carefully run.' 'Still our favourite hotel; pristine, very comfortable.
Attention to detail makes it special.' 'Staff were attentive, helpful;
they magically produced a waterproof to fit my diminutive partner
when she forgot hers.' Most bedrooms (the best are big) have sea
views. 'We were charmed by our room, with an adjacent bathroom and
study; though it was over the kitchens there was only the slightest
trace of noise in the morning.' Meals can be taken alfresco on the
terrace ('like being on a ship's deck') or in the restaurant (which has
an informal dress code), where white-topped tables are close together
(at busy times guests may be 'cheek by jowl'). Chef Paul Wadham's
short daily-changing menu has 'delicious' modern dishes. 'We much
enjoyed our meals; served in a friendly and professional manner: duck
with honeyed baby vegetables, tender and flavoursome; elegantly
presented brill; excellent puddings.' 'The way in which children are
made welcome gives a special holiday atmosphere to what might
otherwise be a slightly over-sophisticated seaside hotel.' 'One of those
occasions when a big bill seems good value.' Mrs Polizzi also owns
Hotel Endsleigh, Milton Abbot (*qv*). (*John Godfrey, Margaret Mallett,
David Haigh*)

Bedrooms: 29, in 4 houses. *Open*: all year. *Facilities*: 2 lounges, bar, restaurant,
cinema, playroom, conference facilities, civil wedding licence, terrace, ¼-acre
garden, by sea (shingle beach, safe bathing, 15-metre yacht), unsuitable for &.
Background music: none. *Location*: on seafront, valet parking (car park up hill).
Smoking: not allowed. *Children*: all ages welcomed. *Dogs*: allowed in 2 bedrooms,
not in public rooms. *Credit cards*: Amex, MasterCard, Visa. *Prices*: [2009] B&B
£85–£177.50 per person, set dinner £42, special breaks, Christmas/New Year
packages, 1-night bookings refused winter weekends.

New reports help us keep the *Guide* up to date.

SALCOMBE Devon   Map 1:E4

The Tides Reach   *Tel* 01548-843466
South Sands   *Fax* 01548-843954
Salcombe TQ8 8LJ   *Email* enquire@tidesreach.com
                          Website www.tidesreach.com

'On our second visit; we were again impressed by the friendliness
and attentiveness of the staff,' writes a visitor in 2009 to the
Edwards family's traditional seaside hotel on the south Devon coast
(John Edwards is the current manager). Well situated for safe
bathing and water sports, the 1960s building has angular balconies
and bright blue awnings against white-painted walls. Mainly south-
facing (some rooms face south-east), it is in a tree-fringed sandy
cove just inside the Salcombe estuary. 'My room had a nice decor
and a very comfortable, large bed.' Most bedrooms (colours are
bright) have big windows that face the sheltered garden where
summer visitors take snack lunches (soups, sandwiches, kedgeree,
etc) by a large pond which is home to ducks and fish. There is a
sea-water aquarium in the bar. In the dining room (sea views from
some tables) the chef, Finn Ibsen, serves modern and traditional
dishes 'with an emphasis on Devon meat and freshly caught fish',
eg, smoked Exmoor venison; line-caught sea bass, Béarnaise sauce.
'The evening menu was a delight.' The swimming pool is in an
'exotic conservatory' which opens to the outside on fine days. There
is easy access to the Coast Path, and the town centre can be reached
by a ferry to which passengers are transported by a sea tractor.
(*Stephen West, AN, and others*)

Bedrooms: 32. *Open*: mid-Feb–early Dec. *Facilities*: lift, ramps, 3 lounges, 2 bars,
restaurant, leisure centre (indoor swimming pool, 13 by 6 metres, gym, games
room, beauty treatments), ½-acre grounds (pond), sandy beach 10 yds,
unsuitable for &. *Background music*: none. *Location*: on Salcombe estuary, 1 mile
from town. *Smoking*: not allowed. *Children*: not under 8. *Dogs*: allowed in
bedrooms, 1 lounge. *Credit cards*: all major cards. *Prices*: B&B £56–£138 per
person, D,B&B £66–£158, set dinner £32.50, 1-night bookings sometimes
refused. *V*

SALISBURY Wiltshire   *See Shortlist*

SANDWICH Kent   *See Shortlist*

SAXMUNDHAM Suffolk   *See Shortlist*

SCARBOROUGH North Yorkshire *See Shortlist*

SCOTBY Cumbria   Map 4:B2

Willowbeck Lodge   *Tel* 01228-513607
Lambley Bank   *Fax* 01228-501053
Scotby, nr Carlisle CA4 8BX   *Email* info@willowbeck-lodge.com
                               Website www.willowbeck-lodge.com

Built in Scandinavian style, and set by a pond amid peaceful woodland
on the edge of a village near Carlisle, this architect-designed house is
popular with visitors breaking their journey to and from Scotland.
'Convenient for the M6, but it has no "motorway aura" about it,' says
one this year. Another wrote of the 'feeling of sublime comfort'. Run
by its 'warmly welcoming' owners John and Liz McGrillis, it has 'well-
appointed' bedrooms ('good storage, comfortable chairs, flat-screen
TV, Wi-Fi, etc'). 'Immaculate' bathrooms have a separate shower.
There is a large lounge with a soaring ceiling, high windows, gallery
and wood-burning stove. Mrs McGrillis cooks a 'delicious' three-
course dinner by arrangement: no choice but menus agreed in
consultation; dishes might include mussels in white wine; ginger
spiced beef with sour cream and dumplings. Mr McGrillis provides
breakfast, ordered the night before: you help yourself to fruit salad,
and muesli; cooked choices include pancakes with maple syrup and
smoked bacon. (*Joan Heath, and others*)

Bedrooms: 6, 2 in annexe. *Open*: all year except 20–28 Dec, restaurant closed
Sun. *Facilities*: lounge, lounge/dining room, conference/function facilities,
1½-acre garden (stream, pond), unsuitable for &. *Background music*: 'when
guests choose'. *Location*: 2½ miles E of Carlisle. *Smoking*: not allowed. *Children*:
not under 12. *Dogs*: not allowed. *Credit cards*: Amex, MasterCard, Visa. *Prices*:
[2009] B&B £55–£125 per person, set dinner £30.

When you make a booking you enter into a contract with a
hotel. Most hotels explain their cancellation policies, which
vary widely, in a letter of confirmation. You may lose your
deposit or be charged at the full rate for the room if you cancel
at short notice. A travel insurance policy can provide protection.

SEAVIEW Isle of Wight   Map 2:E3

The Seaview

High Street
Seaview PO34 5EX

Tel 01983-612711
Fax 01983-613729
Email reception@seaviewhotel.co.uk
Website www.seaviewhotel.co.uk

Families are actively welcomed at this 'well-run' hotel/restaurant near
the sea in a 'delightful' little village on the Solent. Owned by Brian
Gardener, it is managed by Andrew Morgan. Children's teas are
served in the bar; there is a child-friendly Sunday brunch; a teddy bear
is left on the pillow during the evening turn-down. 'The delightful
staff saw to our needs with unruffled calm,' one parent wrote. Ship's
lamps, framed photos of warships, and other seafaring memorabilia
give the 'charming' public rooms a nautical air. Meals are served in
the small Victorian dining room, the larger, blue-and-white *Sunshine*
restaurant (with a conservatory), or informally in the bars. Readers
praise chef Graham Walker's modern British cooking ('with a simple
twist'), eg, crab, lime and coriander tagliatelle; venison haunch, braised
red cabbage, sultana and thyme sauce. Vegetables and herbs come
from *The Seaview*'s own farm, which has a herd of deer. There are
seagrass carpets and luxurious fabrics in the bedrooms. A large ground-
floor room was 'spruce, quiet, light; sheets and blankets on bed;
flat-screen TV/DVD-player; table and chairs on a terrace by the pretty
garden'. 'Nothing packaged' at breakfast, which has 'succulent
kippers'. The path for a seashore walk starts at the bottom of the road.
(*FM, and others*)

Bedrooms: 28, 10 in annexe, 4 on ground floor, 1 suitable for ♿. *Open*: all year
except 21–26 Dec, restaurant closed Sun night (bar meals available). *Facilities*:
lift, ramps, lounge, 2 bars, 2 dining rooms, treatment room, function room,
patio, access to local sports club (swimming pool, gym, tennis, etc). *Background
music*: 'light and unobtrusive'. *Location*: village centre. *Smoking*: not allowed.
Children: all ages welcomed. *Dogs*: allowed in some bedrooms, not in restaurant.
Credit cards: all major cards. *Prices*: [2009] B&B £60–£199 per person, D,B&B
£90–£230, full alc £35, Christmas/New Year packages, 1-night bookings refused
weekends in summer. *V*

The *V* sign at the end of an entry indicates a hotel that has
agreed to take part in our Voucher scheme and to give *Guide*
readers a 25% discount on their bed-and-breakfast rates for a
one-night stay, subject to the conditions explained in *How to
use the Good Hotel Guide*, and given on the back of each voucher.

SHAFTESBURY Dorset   Map 2:D1

La Fleur de Lys   *Tel* 01747-853717
Bleke Street   *Fax* 01747-853130
Shaftesbury SP7 8AW   *Email* info@lafleurdelys.co.uk
                                Website www.lafleurdelys.co.uk

In one of England's oldest and highest towns in the Vale of Blackmore
(forever associated with a Hovis advertisement), David Shepherd,
Mary Griffin and Marc Preston's restaurant-with-rooms is praised
again in 2009. 'Staff are extremely pleasant,' say visitors this year,
endorsing earlier comments: 'Excellent food by David, who loves to
chat, and a warm welcome from Mary, who seems to run everything.'
She is a cat enthusiast, and cat ornaments are everywhere. There is a
comfortable lounge with sofas and armchairs. The 'immaculate'
bedrooms (each named after a wine grape: Chardonnay, Merlot, etc)
have a fridge, Internet access and 'delicious home-baked biscuits'.
One room is suitable for a family (a cot can be provided). 'Ours had
two reading chairs, a firm bed with duvet, good storage and a digital
TV.' In the smart dining room, the menu might include Cornish crab
mousse served on smoked salmon; roasted double breast of English
partridge. Breakfast has fresh orange juice, porridge, butter and
marmalade in pots. Afternoon tea and pre-dinner drinks can be served
in the courtyard. The entrance to the car park is narrow. (*Jean and
Martyn Taylor, K and PR*)

Bedrooms: 7, some on ground floor. *Open*: all year, restaurant closed Sun night,
midday Mon and Tues. *Facilities*: lounge, bar, dining room, conference room,
small courtyard. *Background music*: none. *Location*: edge of centre, car park.
Smoking: not allowed. *Children*: all ages welcomed. *Dogs*: not allowed. *Credit
cards*: Amex, MasterCard, Visa. *Prices*: [2009] B&B £50–£75 per person, set
meals £24–£29, full alc £45–£50, Christmas package, 1-night bookings refused
July–Sept.

SHANKLIN Isle of Wight   Map 2:E2

Rylstone Manor   *Tel/Fax* 01983-862806
Rylstone Gardens   *Email* rylstone.manor@btinternet.com
Popham Road, Shanklin   *Website* www.rylstone-manor.co.uk
PO37 6RG

Steep cliff steps lead down from this traditional hotel to the beaches
of Sandown Bay. Built as a Victorian gentleman's residence (with
references to neo-Tudor, Gothic and Georgian styles), it stands in

'glorious' parkland gardens ('red squirrel country'), in which visitors are encouraged to relax. The 'friendly' owners, Mike and Carole Hailston, have done much upgrading since taking over in 2006. He is the chef, cooking a daily-changing menu of 'traditional to French/ Italian' dishes, eg, butternut squash and chorizo soup; cod loin, cream and Noilly Prat sauce. This is served by candlelight in the 'intimate' dining room. 'The staff were very pleasant.' There are books and ornaments in the green-walled lounge; a Victorian-style covered patio has basket chairs and magazines. The 'well-furnished' bedrooms, named after English trees (Willow, Fir, Ash, etc), vary in size. 'Beautiful lacy linen and attractive bedding.' Shanklin is a 20-minute walk away. (*PE Carter*)

Bedrooms: 9. *Open*: all year. *Facilities*: drawing room, bar lounge, dining room, terrace, 1-acre garden in 4-acre public gardens, direct access to sand/shingle beach, unsuitable for &. *Background music*: classical, 'easy listening', in bar, restaurant. *Location*: Shanklin old village. *Smoking*: not allowed. *Children*: not allowed. *Dogs*: not allowed. *Credit cards*: Diners, MasterCard, Visa. *Prices*: [2009] B&B £60–£75 per person, D,B&B £85–£100, full alc £40, website offers, Christmas/New Year packages, 1-night bookings refused June–Aug (unless space permits). *V*

SHEFFIELD South Yorkshire   *See Shortlist*

SHREWSBURY Shropshire   *See Shortlist*

SIDLESHAM West Sussex   *See Shortlist*

SIDMOUTH Devon   *See Shortlist*

SKIPTON North Yorkshire   *See Shortlist*

Small hotels will often try to persuade you to stay for two nights at the weekend. We ask all the hotels in the *Guide* whether they ever refuse a one-night booking, and indicate those that won't take them. It is worth asking about this, especially off-season or when booking late.

SNETTISHAM Norfolk   Map 2:A4

The Rose & Crown
Old Church Road, Snettisham
nr King's Lynn
PE31 7LX

Tel 01485-541382
Fax 01485-543172
Email info@roseandcrownsnettisham.co.uk
Website www.roseandcrownsnettisham.co.uk

In a lovely Norfolk village, this much-extended inn (dating from the 14th-century) is commended this year for its 'good value'. 'The welcome is warm; all the staff are friendly, helpful.' Jeannette and Anthony Goodrich are the owners, Kim Tinkler is the 'hands-on' manageress. This is the village pub, busy with locals ('whom we treasure', writes Mrs Goodrich) as well as holidaymakers. The building has low ceilings, old beams, 'lots of corners and twisting corridors'. All bedrooms have been upgraded in contemporary style: 'Our room, Tree House, in the newest part, was a good size, brightly decorated; sufficient storage space, good lighting' though with 'a low window overlooking a car park'. Bathrooms have a power shower; the information folder is 'the best I have seen'. Residents have their own lounge with a log fire; there are three bars and three dining areas. Chef Keith McDowell uses local suppliers for a mix of pub favourites (eg, Holkham bangers and mash with onion gravy), and more contemporary dishes (black bream, baby spinach, celeriac hash). The scrambled eggs and smoked salmon at breakfast are 'particularly good'. The Goodriches also own *Bank House*, King's Lynn (see Shortlist). There is free Wi-Fi access throughout. The walled garden was once the village bowling green. (*Zara Elliott, and others*)

Bedrooms: 16, 2 suitable for &. *Open*: all year. *Facilities*: ramp, garden room with guests' seating area, lounge, 3 bars, 3 dining areas, large walled garden (play fort, barbecue, heat lamps), beaches 5 and 10 mins' drive, golf, birdwatching nearby. *Background music*: none. *Location*: village centre, 4 miles S of Hunstanton. *Smoking*: not allowed. *Children*: all ages welcomed. *Dogs*: 'well-behaved' dogs allowed (extra charge). *Credit cards*: MasterCard, Visa. *Prices*: [2009] B&B £45–£90 per person, full alc £32.50, website breaks, Christmas/New Year packages. *V*

We update the *Guide* every year. Hotels are dropped or may be demoted to the Shortlist if there has been a change of owner (unless reports after the change are positive), if this year's reports are negative, or in rare cases where there has been no feedback. A lot of hotels are omitted every year, and many new ones are added.

SOAR MILL COVE Devon   Map 1:E4

Soar Mill Cove Hotel
Soar Mill Cove
nr Salcombe TQ7 3DS

Tel 01548-561566
Fax 01548-561223
Email info@soarmillcove.co.uk
Website www.soarmillcove.co.uk

Owner Keith Makepiece 'has mastered the art of appearing to be in two places at once', says a visitor returning in 2009, for the umpteenth time, to this purpose-built, family-run stone and slate single-storey hotel. It has a lovely setting above an isolated cove surrounded by National Trust land. Other praise: 'A very efficient establishment. Excellent food; staff helpful, always courteous.' The building may be 'no beauty' but a partial revamp has been 'well executed'. All the bedrooms open on to a terrace. The lounge is 'light and bright'; the champagne bar has gold walls and black and red seats. In the formal *Serendipity* restaurant, chef Ian MacDonald's cooking is generally enjoyed. 'The menu has been simplified,' explains 2009's visitor. 'None the worse for that. Four choices for each course, including a vegetarian option; substitutes offered if requested. Soups excellent, fish attractively served, lamb especially good. The fruit flambé always attracts attention.' *Castaways*, a coffee bar, is 'for muddy paws and boots and younger guests'. Breakfast has good choice, including fruit salad and 'beautiful' marmalade. The hotel is popular with older visitors off-season: 'Couples with young children and the over-80s were equally catered for' (for children there are small swimming pools, play areas, activity packs). 'Glorious coastal walks' from the grounds. (*Margaret Box, Brian R Moate, and others*)

Bedrooms: 22, all on ground floor. *Open*: Feb–Nov. *Facilities*: lounge, 2 bars, restaurant (pianist), coffee shop, indoor swimming pool (10 by 6 metres), treatment room (hairdressing, reflexology, aromatherapy, etc), free Internet access, civil wedding licence, 10-acre grounds (swimming pool, 10 by 7 metres, tennis, putting, children's play area, jogging trail), sea, sandy beach, 600 yds. *Background music*: occasional. *Location*: 3 miles SW of Salcombe. *Smoking*: not allowed. *Children*: all ages welcomed. *Dogs*: well-behaved small dogs allowed, but not in public rooms. *Credit cards*: MasterCard, Visa. *Prices*: B&B £65–£110 per person, D,B&B £99–£145, full alc £45, Christmas/New Year packages.

If you dislike piped music, why not join Pipedown, the campaign for freedom from piped music? 1 The Row, Berwick St James, Salisbury SP3 4TP. *Tel* 01722-690622, www.pipedown.info.

SOMERTON Somerset   Map 1:C6

The Lynch Country House
4 Behind Berry
Somerton TA11 7PD

Tel 01458-272316
Fax 01458-272590
Email the_lynch@talk21.com
Website www.thelynchcountryhouse.co.uk

'One of the nicest B&Bs, always worth a detour when in the West Country.' In a small town above the Cary valley, this Grade II listed Regency house is run by its owner, Roy Copeland, a former jazz musician. In his absence, guests are welcomed by his manager, Dave Williamson. 'One feels a true house guest here, treated with trust and hospitality.' In the main house, one couple had a 'good-sized room with high ceiling, pleasant furniture, restful colour scheme, beautiful views'. Some of the 'welcoming' bedrooms have a four-poster. Smaller rooms are under the eaves. Four others are in a single-storey coach house. At the top of the house, a little observatory (with telescope) gives wide views. Breakfast is served in the 'attractive, bright' orangery whose tall windows overlook a lake with fish, black swans and exotic ducks. 'We were encouraged to explore, and could have picnicked in the garden had we wished.' 'Our small dog was made most welcome.' Advice is given, with menus, on where to dine. 2,800 trees have been planted around the house to create a wildlife sanctuary. (*John Ford, and others*)

Bedrooms: 9, 4 in coach house, 4 on ground floor. *Open*: all year except 31 Dec. *Facilities*: breakfast room, small sitting area, 2½-acre grounds (lake), unsuitable for &. *Background music*: none. *Location*: N edge of village. *Smoking*: not allowed. *Children*: all ages welcomed. *Dogs*: allowed in bedrooms by arrangement, not in public rooms. *Credit cards*: all major cards. *Prices*: B&B £35–£65 per person.

SOUTH ZEAL Devon   Map 1:C4

The Oxenham Arms
South Zeal
EX20 2JT

Tel 01837-840244
Fax 01837-840791
Email relax@theoxenhamarms.co.uk
Website www.theoxenhamarms.co.uk

A scheduled ancient monument, this ivy-clad building in a hamlet near Okehampton has been an inn for more than 500 years. The 'enthusiastic' owner/manager, Mark Payne, has refurbished it with 'remarkable attention to detail'. The bedrooms, each named after a rare-breed animal (Hereford, Rhode Island Red, etc), are 'well appointed'. All have a new bed (there are three four-posters), 'treasured' antiques, contemporary finishes (and a modem connection for 21st-century visitors). The *Ox*, as it is known locally, has a beamed and panelled bar, mullioned windows, a large granite fireplace in the main lounge, a monolith set in the wall of the smaller lounge. The restaurant, *Burgoyne's*, is in the 'great hall'. The chef, Carol Eagles, uses meat and vegetables from the hotel's own farm, its new kitchen garden, and local producers, for her daily-changing menu of modern dishes, eg, coarse pork pâté with pickles; coq au vin, roast potatoes. There are lovely views from the extensive gardens. (*JE*)

Bedrooms: 7. *Open*: all year. *Facilities*: 2 bar areas, 2 dining rooms, terrace, 3-acre garden, unsuitable for ♿. *Background music*: classical/soul/blues. *Location*: village centre, off A30 Exeter–Okehampton. *Smoking*: not allowed. *Children*: all ages welcomed. *Dogs*: not allowed in some bedrooms. *Credit cards*: Amex, MasterCard, Visa. *Prices*: [2009] B&B £42.50–£120 per person, full alc £30, Christmas/New Year packages. *V*

SOUTHAMPTON Hampshire *See Shortlist*

SOUTHPORT Merseyside *See Shortlist*

SOUTHWOLD Suffolk *See Shortlist*

SPALDING Lincolnshire *See Shortlist*

STADDLEBRIDGE North Yorkshire Map 4:C4

McCoy's at the Tontine

The Cleveland Tontine
Staddlebridge
Northallerton DL6 3JB

Tel 01609-882671
Fax 01609-882660
Email bookings@mccoystontine.co.uk
Website www.mccoystontine.co.uk

César award in 1989

Visitors returning to this 'unashamedly eccentric' restaurant-with-rooms after 18 years found it almost unchanged. 'Some of the staff were still the same. They were very understanding when we arrived late due to congestion caused by an accident on the road.' Owned by

Tom and Eugene McCoy, this northern institution has dark panelled corridors, a giant fireplace 'by Vanbrugh in his grimmest mood'; 'smiling service'. The bedrooms, 'though very eccentrically decorated, are very comfortable'. They have vibrant colours, 'junk-shop discoveries', bright soft furnishings. 'A glass of sherry greets you on arrival.' One room has dark blue William Morris-type wallpaper with iridescent pink flowers; a deep raspberry ceiling. The candlelit bistro is 'slightly subterranean', but lightened by huge mirrors. Head chef Stuart Hawkins's eclectic blackboard menu might include seafood pancake with thermidor sauce; fillet steak with watercress and chips. 'Excellent starters and main courses, but disappointing pudding.' The stone Victorian house occupies a triangular site between the A19 and a slip road on the edge of the North Yorkshire moors. 'Traffic rushes past' (windows are double glazed). (*Jackie Tunstall-Pedoe, FS, SD*)

Bedrooms: 6. *Open*: all year except 25/26 Dec, 1/2 Jan. *Facilities*: 2 lounges (residents only), breakfast room, bar, bistro, function rooms, unsuitable for &. *Background music*: 'eclectic'. *Location*: 6 miles NE of Northallerton, at junction of A19/A172. *Smoking*: not allowed. *Children*: all ages welcomed. *Dogs*: not allowed in public rooms. *Credit cards*: all major cards. *Prices*: [2009] B&B £60–£95 per person, full alc £65, 3-night D,B&B package.

STAMFORD Lincolnshire   Map 2:B3

The George
71 St Martins
Stamford
PE9 2LB

Tel 01780-750750
Fax 01780-750701
Email reservations@georgehotelofstamford.com
Website www.georgehotelofstamford.com

❦ *César award in 1986*

'Everyone is welcoming' at this busy 16th-century coaching inn in what Walter Scott called 'the finest stone town in England'. Owned by Lawrence Hoskins and managed by Chris Pitman (also executive chef), it is 'a warren of public rooms, winding corridors, nooks and crannies'. 'Room very comfy, dinner excellent,' one guest wrote. 'We were very happy when we stayed here.' An earlier visitor told of 'sterling qualities and excellent staff'. The old-style values are appreciated: nocturnal shoe clean, early morning tea delivered to the room ('what a treat these days'). The formal, oak-panelled restaurant has a dress code at night (though T-shirts have been spotted at lunchtime). The menu is 'traditional with international ideas', eg, crab and avocado salad; sirloin of beef, carved at the table; dessert from the trolley. A visitor this year thought lunch 'ordinary', the service 'eager but lacking efficiency'. Informal dining is available in the *Garden Room*, and meals are served on warm days in a 'nice courtyard with plants'. There are good flower arrangements in the lounges, which have creaking floorboards, antique panelling, log fires, mullioned windows. A courtyard bedroom was 'nicely furnished, modern; space for everything; well-equipped bathroom with power shower *and* bath'. An upstairs room had 'French-style furniture, potted plants, and a pleasing view'. (*Mary Milne-Day, and others*)

Bedrooms: 47. *Open*: all year. *Facilities*: ramps, 2 lounges, 2 bars, 2 restaurants, 4 private dining rooms, business centre, civil wedding licence, 2-acre grounds (courtyard, herb garden, monastery garden, croquet), only public areas suitable for &. *Background music*: none. *Location*: ½ mile from centre (front windows double glazed). *Smoking*: not allowed. *Children*: all ages welcomed. *Dogs*: allowed, but not unattended in bedrooms, only guide dogs in restaurant. *Credit cards*: all major cards. *Prices*: [2009] B&B £66–£127 per person, full alc £55, seasonal breaks, 1-night bookings refused Sat.

STANSTED Essex   *See Shortlist*

STANTON WICK Somerset   Map 1:B6

The Carpenters Arms   *Tel* 01761-490202
Stanton Wick, nr Pensford   *Fax* 01761-490763
BS39 4BX   *Email* carpenters@buccaneer.co.uk
                  Website www.the-carpenters-arms.co.uk

In the Chew valley eight miles south of Bristol and Bath, this small hotel/pub has been converted from a row of miners' cottages in a tranquil hamlet. It is recommended for its 'friendly' public bar and busy restaurant. The manager, Simon Pledge, is 'most attentive', said visitors who had 'an excellent night's stay'. The modern bedrooms have lights with dimmer, a large TV, Wi-Fi and a 'well-equipped bathroom'. Food was 'good and plentiful', on the traditional menu (Chris Dando is the chef), eg, duck and pistachio terrine; roast belly of pork on creamed potato. 'Wines reasonably priced and very acceptable.' Real ales are available. Generous breakfasts include fresh orange juice, fruit, full English. In fine weather, meals are served on the large landscaped patio. Guests' cars are locked in a yard at night. Children under 12 stay free in their parents' room. More reports, please.

Bedrooms: 12. *Open*: all year except 25/26 Dec, 1 Jan at night. *Facilities*: bar, 2 restaurants, function room, patio, unsuitable for &. *Background music*: none. *Location*: 8 miles S of Bristol, 8 miles W of Bath. *Smoking*: not allowed. *Children*: all ages welcomed. *Dogs*: allowed in bar and on patio only. *Credit cards*: all major cards. *Prices*: [2009] B&B £52.50–£72.50 per person, D,B&B (min. 2 nights) £22.50 added, full alc £30, New Year package.

STOKE CANON Devon   *See Shortlist*

STOKE FLEMING Devon   Map 1:D4

Stoke Lodge   *Tel* 01803-770523
Cinders Lane   *Fax* 01803-770851
Stoke Fleming   *Email* mail@stokelodge.co.uk
TQ6 0RA   *Website* www.stokelodge.co.uk

On the south Devon coast near Dartmouth, this country hotel dates back to the seventeenth century; the front was rebuilt in 1814. Further extensions over the years have added up-to-date facilities. The owners, Steven and Christine Mayer, are 'kind and helpful', said recent guests. 'Everywhere is warm, clean and cosy. Our good-sized bedroom with lovely sea view (extra charge) had ample storage space, good lighting, wide, comfortable beds (one made with duvet, the other with blankets, as we had requested).' The lounges have 'plenty of squashy sofas and chairs, plus tables for bridge, etc'. The bar is 'very elegant', in dark green. Outside are gardens, lawn, wooded areas, a pond with ducks, a swimming pool surrounded by loungers, a giant chess set and a tennis court. The chef, Paul Howard, serves a four-course daily-changing dinner menu (sample dishes: warm carpaccio of smoked salmon; Blackawton lamb casserole, crisp bacon and potato). Breakfasts have a good buffet of fruits, cereals, etc. Cream teas are served, on the lawn in fine weather. 'Staff are cheerful and anxious to please. High standards.' More reports, please.

Bedrooms: 26. *Open*: all year. *Facilities*: 2 lounges, bar, restaurant, games room, snooker room, indoor swimming pool (sauna, whirlpool), 3-acre garden (heated swimming pool, 5 by 10 metres, tennis), unsuitable for &. *Background music*: none. *Location*: 2 miles W of Stoke Fleming, on coast, 2 miles S of Dartmouth. *Smoking*: not allowed. *Children*: all ages welcomed. *Dogs*: not allowed in public rooms. *Credit cards*: MasterCard, Visa. *Prices*: [2009] B&B £46–£65 per person, D,B&B £68.50–£95, set dinner £27.50, full alc £30, special breaks, Christmas/New Year packages. *V*

STRATFORD-UPON-AVON   *See Shortlist*
Warwickshire

STUCKTON Hampshire   Map 2:E2

The Three Lions Inn
Stuckton, nr Fordingbridge
SP6 2HF

Tel 01425-652489
Fax 01425-656144
Email the3lions@btinternet.com
Website www.thethreelionsrestaurant.co.uk

In a quiet setting on the northern edge of the New Forest, this restaurant-with-rooms is run by owner/chef Mike Womersley and his wife, Jayne. He might be seen greeting guests in his chef's whites; she is the 'charming' front-of-house. Readers found it 'a most pleasant place', endorsing earlier praise by inspectors. In the main building, once a farmhouse, are a bar, small lounge area and restaurant with a conservatory. There is no menu; dishes, displayed on a portable blackboard, might include galette of smoked haddock; wood pigeon and wild mushrooms. The high-ceilinged bedrooms, in a chalet-style single-storey building, are 'light and fresh'. French doors open on to the garden (with a hot tub and sauna). Free Wi-Fi is available. The continental breakfast, included in the price, has fruit, cereals, 'good croissants, delicious coffee'; full English, 'one of the best ever', costs £7.50. Children are welcomed: there is a family room, and a play area in the garden. (*J and PW*)

Bedrooms: 7, 4 in courtyard block on ground floor. *Open*: all year except last 2 weeks Feb, restaurant closed Sun night/Mon. *Facilities*: ramps, conservatory, meeting/sitting room, public bar, restaurant, 2-acre garden (sauna, whirlpool). *Background music*: 'sometimes' in bar. *Location*: 2 miles E of Fordingbridge. *Smoking*: not allowed. *Children*: all ages welcomed, under-4s free. *Dogs*: not allowed in bar, restaurant. *Credit cards*: MasterCard, Visa. *Prices*: B&B £40–£79 per person, cooked breakfast £7.50, set lunch £19.75, set dinner £25, full alc £45, special breaks. *V*

Check the Hotelfinder section (page 11) if you are looking for a hotel for a special occasion, perhaps a memorable meal (see Gourmet and Gastropubs); a sporting weekend (see Golf, Fishing, Walking); somewhere that will welcome your children – or your dog. Our editors have selected ten hotels in each of these categories (and many more) to help you make your choice.

STURMINSTER NEWTON Dorset   Map 2:E1

Plumber Manor   *Tel* 01258-472507
Sturminster Newton DT10 2AF   *Fax* 01258-473370
                                         Email book@plumbermanor.com
                                         Website www.plumbermanor.com

♥ *César award in 1987*

'Tranquil and restful', this 'wonderful manor house' stands in
'beautiful, well-kept gardens' with a tributary of the River Stour
running through. The family home of the Prideaux-Brunes since it
was built in the early 17th century, it has long been run as a restaurant-
with-rooms by Richard Prideaux-Brune (the 'genial' front-of-house),
his wife, Alison, and brother, Brian (the chef). 'They were present
throughout our stay,' say visitors this year. 'Such a change to see all-
English, mature staff around the house, young locals serving in the
restaurant. Two elderly black Labradors in the grounds.' The
bedrooms are in the main house and (the best) a converted barn: 'Ours
was spacious, with good bathroom, piping hot water, excellent
housekeeping.' The smaller bedrooms in the main house (off a gallery
hung with family portraits) have a floral decor. Some guests find the
style dated. The public rooms have antiques, contemporary art; open
fire in winter; no background music. The restaurant, in three rooms,
has a traditional menu, eg, avocado, melon and prawns Marie Rose;
loin of pork with apples and sage jus. 'Excellent, with generous
portions and decent, piping hot vegetables; everything was home
made on the wonderful dessert trolley.' Public footpaths and the
Hardy Way lead from the door. A 'very dog-tolerant' place: pets can
stay in four courtyard rooms. (*Janice Carrera, and others*)

Bedrooms: 16, 10 on ground floor in courtyard. *Open*: all year except Feb,
restaurant closed midday except Sun. *Facilities*: lounge, bar, 3 dining rooms,
gallery, 3-acre grounds (garden, tennis, croquet, stream). *Background music*:
none. *Location*: 3 miles SW of Sturminster Newton. *Smoking*: not allowed.
Children: all ages welcomed. *Dogs*: allowed in 4 bedrooms, not in public rooms.
Credit cards: all major cards. *Prices*: [2009] B&B £60–£90 per person, set dinner
£26–£30, 1-night bookings refused Christmas, Easter, bank holidays.

The *Guide*'s website can be used alongside the printed edition.
It has photographs of nearly all of the hotels, with a direct
link to its website. It also has a Special Offers section with
some excellent deals exclusively for *Guide* readers. See
www.goodhotelguide.com.

SWAFFHAM Norfolk   Map 2:B5

Strattons   *Tel* 01760-723845
4 Ash Close   *Fax* 01760-720458
Swaffham PE37 7NH   *Email* enquiries@strattonshotel.com
                                      Website www.strattonshotel.com

♥ *César award in 2003*

'A very friendly welcome, bags carried to the bedroom,' was given this year at this Grade II listed Palladian-style villa. Though close to the old town's market place, it has a rural feel ('dodge the hens and try not to park under the trees – pigeons roosting'). Its owners, Vanessa and Les Scott, 'passionately believe in ethical business systems'. Their environmental policy covers practical things (recycling, refillable pump dispensers) and broader issues (using public transport). The information pack has several pages of advice; 'lots of notices in the bathroom about being green'. But the 'exotic' themed bedrooms are 'far from spartan': 'our pleasant room had a softish bed, two Lloyd Loom chairs, flat-screen TV and DVD; tea/coffee facilities, a carafe of Madeira, replenished daily'. The lounge, which can become crowded, has original paintings ('of varying degrees of strangeness'), sculptures and ornaments. Vanessa Scott leads a team of chefs who serve a monthly-changing menu: 'Variations and daily dishes ensured that we did not get bored: interesting, tasty cooking, with local ingredients; delicious rare breed lamb. Excellent breakfast: a buffet of cereals and fruit; unusual cooked items (mushrooms on toast; a beautiful kipper served whole).' 'Staff gave helpful information on local attractions.' Four eco-lodges are being built in an old print workshop at the entrance. (*MM-J, and others*)

Bedrooms: 10, 2 in annexe, 2 on ground floor. *Open*: all year except 1 week at Christmas. *Facilities*: drawing room, reading room, restaurant, terrace, 1-acre garden, unsuitable for ♿. *Background music*: in bar and restaurant. *Location*: central, parking. *Smoking*: not allowed. *Children*: all ages welcomed. *Dogs*: allowed in some bedrooms but not unaccompanied, not allowed in restaurant, and 'must be kept on lead' in grounds. *Credit cards*: Amex, MasterCard, Visa. *Prices*: [2009] B&B £75–£125 per person, full alc £50, special breaks, New Year package, 1-night bookings refused weekends/holidays.

SWAY Hampshire   *See Shortlist*

All our inspections are paid for, and carried out, anonymously.

SWINDON Wiltshire   *See Shortlist*

TALLAND-BY-LOOE Cornwall   *See Shortlist*

TAUNTON Somerset   Map 1:C5

The Castle at Taunton	*Tel* 01823-272671
Castle Green	*Fax* 01823-336066
Taunton TA1 1NF	*Email* reception@the-castle-hotel.com
	Website www.the-castle-hotel.com

Ω *César award in 1987*

'We are one of a kind, and remain determinedly independent,' says Kit Chapman, the owner of this wisteria-covered, castellated hotel (it has belonged to his family for over half a century). Once a Norman fortress, it has been an inn since the 12th century. The long-serving manager is Kevin McCarthy: his staff's 'kindness, skill and care' are much admired. The elegant public rooms have old oak furniture, tapestries, paintings and fresh flowers. Mr Chapman's wife, Louise, designed the bedrooms (reached up a wrought iron staircase), avoiding 'the bland, the beige and the boring'. All have flat-screen TV, free Wi-Fi, tea/coffee-making kit. Five garden rooms face the remains of the old castle keep and moat; the penthouse suite has a terrace with a roof garden. Front rooms are triple glazed against noise. There is a choice of eating styles: in the formal L-shaped restaurant the chef, Richard Guest, salutes local suppliers in his modern seasonally-changing menus, eg, warm Ogle Shield cheese and Cornish cured meats with anchovies and gherkins; braised West Country lamb with a hotpot and chop. The lively café/bistro, *Brazz*, has lighter dishes, perhaps deep-fried whitebait; smoked salmon platter. Musical weekends of a high standard are held off-season.

Bedrooms: 44. *Open*: all year, restaurant closed Sun night. *Facilities*: lift, ramps, lounge, bar, restaurant, brasserie, private dining/meeting rooms, civil wedding licence, 1-acre garden, shop. *Background music*: in bar and brasserie. *Location*: central. *Smoking*: not allowed. *Children*: all ages welcomed. *Dogs*: small 'well-behaved' dogs allowed, not in public rooms. *Credit cards*: all major cards. *Prices*: [2009] B&B £115–£162.50 per person, D,B&B £125–£177.50, full alc £57.40, special breaks, Christmas/New Year packages.

TEFFONT EVIAS Wiltshire   Map 2:D1

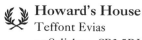 **Howard's House**
Teffont Evias
nr Salisbury SP3 5RJ

Tel 01722-716392
Fax 01722-716820
Email enq@howardshousehotel.co.uk
Website www.howardshousehotel.co.uk

César award: Romantic hotel of the year

The little River Teff, crossed by tiny bridges, runs through this 'perfect, unspoilt, English village'. Here, this 'delightful' wisteria-clad mellow stone dower house stands, backed by a 'charming' hillside garden. It is managed with 'courtesy and skill' by Noële Thompson. 'Our favourite small hotel, you feel miles from anywhere,' one returning visitor wrote. 'Beautiful, furnished in excellent taste,' said another. Inspectors were welcomed by the 'competent and experienced' young major-domo, who 'carried cases, brought tea with cakes to the lounge'. Bedrooms have pastel colours, floral prints, bathrobes. 'Ours, looking across the garden pond to the church steeple, was like a spare room in a private home; decent size, with good-sized bed, sofa, small TV, free Wi-Fi; no bossy notes, turn-down during dinner. It was beautifully quiet.' Some rooms may be small. 'The lounge, with sofas and huge fireplace, also has the feel of a country home. Noële Thompson came to take our dinner order and chat.' Chef Nick Wentworth serves 'well-presented and delicious' modern dishes: 'Chicken liver parfait; trout on a risotto with pine nuts and spinach; parfait with berries. Soft piano background music, not intrusive.' Breakfast, served at table, had 'lots of choice; good marmalade and jam; poached egg on smoked haddock'. In the garden are tables, chairs, parasols, a pergola. 'Cows in the opposite field, buzzards overhead; if you can't relax here...' (*CRH Shaw and Ann Carner, Joanna Russell, and others*)

Bedrooms: 9. *Open*: all year except Christmas week. *Facilities*: lounge, restaurant, 2-acre grounds (croquet), river, fishing nearby, unsuitable for &. *Background music*: classical/jazz in restaurant. *Location*: off B3089, 10 miles W of Salisbury. *Smoking*: not allowed. *Children*: all ages welcomed. *Dogs*: not allowed in public rooms. *Credit cards*: Amex, MasterCard, Visa. *Prices*: [2009] B&B £82.50–£105 per person, set dinner £27.95, full alc £55, winter breaks, New Year package. *V*

The *Guide* welcomes recommendations from readers for new entries. Please write or send us an email about any hotel, inn, guest house or B&B that you feel should be included.

TEIGNMOUTH Devon   Map 1:D5

Thomas Luny House   *Tel* 01626-772976
Teign Street   *Email* alisonandjohn@thomas-luny-house.co.uk
Teignmouth TQ14 8EG   *Website* www.thomas-luny-house.co.uk

Long liked by *Guide* readers for its 'high standards' and 'good value',
this white-painted Georgian house was built in 1808 by the marine
artist Thomas Luny when the town was favoured by Nelson's admirals
and captains. It is run as a B&B by its 'charming' owners, John and
Alison Allan. Of the 'well-equipped' bedrooms (mineral water, books
and magazines, tea-making with fresh milk, bathrobes and flowers),
three are spacious (the fourth is smaller). The Chinese room has hand-
painted oriental furniture, a canopy bed; the Luny room has an
appropriate nautical theme; the Bitton has a four-poster bed. Spare
blankets are kept in an old chest (which acts as luggage rack). An
'excellent' afternoon tea with 'delicious' cake is included in the price:
in summer it can be taken in a walled garden. There are antiques and
open fires in the drawing room, which runs the length of the house,
and the breakfast room; each has French windows opening on to the
garden. The 'excellent' breakfast has freshly squeezed orange juice,
compote of fruits, fresh fruit salad, local cheeses, freshly baked bread.
Cooked dishes include 'perfect' scrambled eggs. (*MF*)

Bedrooms: 4. *Open*: all year. *Facilities*: 2 lounges, breakfast room, small walled
garden, sea (sandy beach 5 mins' walk), unsuitable for &. *Background music*:
none. *Location*: town centre. *Smoking*: not allowed. *Children*: not under 12. *Dogs*:
not allowed. *Credit cards*: MasterCard, Visa. *Prices*: [2009] B&B £37.50–£70 per
person, 1-night bookings sometimes refused.

TEMPLE SOWERBY Cumbria   Map 4: inset C3

Temple Sowerby House   *Tel* 017683-61578
Temple Sowerby   *Fax* 017683-61958
Penrith CA10 1RZ   *Email* stay@templesowerby.com
                          Website www.templesowerby.com

'The rooms are comfortable, the cuisine is excellent, the welcome
warm.' In a conservation village in the Eden valley this hotel/
restaurant faces Cross Fell, the highest peak in the Pennines. Grade
II listed, the part 17th-century brick-fronted house has thick walls and
a Georgian wing. Its 'kind, enthusiastic' owners, Paul and Julie Evans,
and their staff 'create a relaxed atmosphere', say visitors this year. In

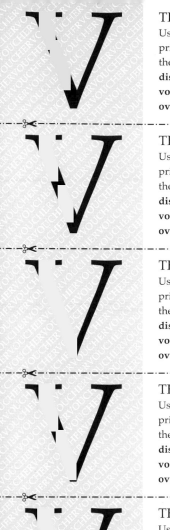

THE GOOD HOTEL GUIDE 2010

Use this voucher to claim a 25% discount off the normal price for bed and breakfast at hotels with a *V* sign at the end of their entry. **You must request a voucher discount at the time of booking and present this voucher on arrival. Further details and conditions overleaf.** Valid to 5th October 2010.

THE GOOD HOTEL GUIDE 2010

Use this voucher to claim a 25% discount off the normal price for bed and breakfast at hotels with a *V* sign at the end of their entry. **You must request a voucher discount at the time of booking and present this voucher on arrival. Further details and conditions overleaf.** Valid to 5th October 2010.

THE GOOD HOTEL GUIDE 2010

Use this voucher to claim a 25% discount off the normal price for bed and breakfast at hotels with a *V* sign at the end of their entry. **You must request a voucher discount at the time of booking and present this voucher on arrival. Further details and conditions overleaf.** Valid to 5th October 2010.

THE GOOD HOTEL GUIDE 2010

Use this voucher to claim a 25% discount off the normal price for bed and breakfast at hotels with a *V* sign at the end of their entry. **You must request a voucher discount at the time of booking and present this voucher on arrival. Further details and conditions overleaf.** Valid to 5th October 2010.

THE GOOD HOTEL GUIDE 2010

Use this voucher to claim a 25% discount off the normal price for bed and breakfast at hotels with a *V* sign at the end of their entry. **You must request a voucher discount at the time of booking and present this voucher on arrival. Further details and conditions overleaf.** Valid to 5th October 2010.

THE GOOD HOTEL GUIDE 2010

Use this voucher to claim a 25% discount off the normal price for bed and breakfast at hotels with a *V* sign at the end of their entry. **You must request a voucher discount at the time of booking and present this voucher on arrival. Further details and conditions overleaf.** Valid to 5th October 2010.

1. Hotels with a *V* have agreed to give readers a discount of 25% off their normal bed-and-breakfast rate.
2. One voucher is good for a single-night stay only, at the discounted rate for yourself alone or for you and a partner sharing a double room.
3. Hotels may decline to accept a voucher reservation if they expect to be fully booked at the full room price.

CONDITIONS

1. Hotels with a *V* have agreed to give readers a discount of 25% off their normal bed-and-breakfast rate.
2. One voucher is good for a single-night stay only, at the discounted rate for yourself alone or for you and a partner sharing a double room.
3. Hotels may decline to accept a voucher reservation if they expect to be fully booked at the full room price.

CONDITIONS

1. Hotels with a *V* have agreed to give readers a discount of 25% off their normal bed-and-breakfast rate.
2. One voucher is good for a single-night stay only, at the discounted rate for yourself alone or for you and a partner sharing a double room.
3. Hotels may decline to accept a voucher reservation if they expect to be fully booked at the full room price.

CONDITIONS

1. Hotels with a *V* have agreed to give readers a discount of 25% off their normal bed-and-breakfast rate.
2. One voucher is good for a single-night stay only, at the discounted rate for yourself alone or for you and a partner sharing a double room.
3. Hotels may decline to accept a voucher reservation if they expect to be fully booked at the full room price.

CONDITIONS

1. Hotels with a *V* have agreed to give readers a discount of 25% off their normal bed-and-breakfast rate.
2. One voucher is good for a single-night stay only, at the discounted rate for yourself alone or for you and a partner sharing a double room.
3. Hotels may decline to accept a voucher reservation if they expect to be fully booked at the full room price.

CONDITIONS

1. Hotels with a *V* have agreed to give readers a discount of 25% off their normal bed-and-breakfast rate.
2. One voucher is good for a single-night stay only, at the discounted rate for yourself alone or for you and a partner sharing a double room.
3. Hotels may decline to accept a voucher reservation if they expect to be fully booked at the full room price.

CONDITIONS

the conservatory-style dining room, which faces a walled garden and terrace (where summer drinks are served), chef Ashley Whittaker's 'imaginative' menus, with plenty of choice, feature British/French dishes, perhaps cumin-spiced scallops with cauliflower mousse; juniper-marinated haunch of venison, squash and orange purée. The wine list is 'interestingly chosen and sensibly priced'. The bedrooms, in the house or a coach house, range from 'superior' (with views) to 'classic' (smaller, many with old beams). Several of the bathrooms have aqua-spa bath and hydrotherapy shower. 'Breakfast the best we have had for choice and quality': it includes 'delicious bread and rolls', 'unwrapped butter'. Ullswater is 15 minutes' drive away. (*Tony Bryant-Fenn, Simon and Mithra Tonking, Anne Thornthwaite*)

Bedrooms: 12, 2 on ground floor, 4 in coach house (20 yds). *Open*: all year except Christmas. *Facilities*: 2 lounges, bar, restaurant, conference/function facilities, civil wedding licence, 2-acre garden (croquet). *Background music*: in restaurant at night. *Location*: village centre. *Smoking*: not allowed. *Children*: not under 12. *Dogs*: by prior arrangement, not allowed in public rooms. *Credit cards*: MasterCard, Visa. *Prices*: [2009] B&B £60–£110 per person, D,B&B £80–£130, set dinner £38.50, alc £50, special breaks, New Year package, 1-night bookings occasionally refused. *V*

TETBURY Gloucestershire   Map 3:E5

Calcot Manor   *Tel* 01666-890391
nr Tetbury GL8 8YJ   *Fax* 01666-890394
                      Email reception@calcotmanor.co.uk
                      Website www.calcotmanor.co.uk

◗ *César award in 2001*

'Fabulous: wonderful staff, lovely setting, and immaculate public rooms.' Praise from a guest who celebrated his 40th wedding anniversary at this 'civilised' hotel which combines a genuine welcome for children with extensive facilities for adults. Twenty-five years old in 2009, this 'sympathetic and stylish' renovation of a 14th-century farmhouse and its surrounding cottages and outbuildings is run by Richard Ball. His wife, Cathy, is in charge of the spa, which has a 'large, inviting' indoor swimming pool and an outside hot tub, 'with a log fire burning in the background'. Special times are allocated in the spa for children. Older children have the run of the *Mez*, an unsupervised play area ('lots of fun'); their younger siblings have a *Playzone*; for the youngest there is an Ofsted-registered crèche. Families stay in the suites in the courtyard, which have a double bedroom and a sitting room with bunks or sofa bed; also video, TV, small fridge, baby-listening. Visitors without children had 'a lovely bedroom, with huge, comfy bed, fluffy towels and robes; a top-class bathroom with a walk-in shower, good-size bath'. In the *Conservatory Restaurant*, Michael Croft's modern cooking is 'of a high standard': 'We liked the informality; the guest pack makes clear that ties and jackets are not required.' Families tend to gather in the informal *Gumstool* pub, which provides 'very good service, food and drink'. (*Ian Malone, JB*)

Bedrooms: 35, 10 (family) in cottage, 11 around courtyard, on ground floor. *Open*: all year. *Facilities*: ramps, lounge, 2 restaurants, 2 bars, private dining room, cinema, conference facilities, crèche, civil wedding licence, 220-acre grounds (tennis, heated outdoor 8-metre swimming pool, children's play area, croquet, bicycles, spa with 15-metre swimming pool, sauna, treatments, etc). *Background music*: in restaurants. *Location*: 3 miles W of Tetbury. *Smoking*: allowed in bedrooms. *Children*: all ages welcomed. *Dogs*: allowed on request in courtyard bedrooms. *Credit cards*: all major cards. *Prices*: [2009] B&B £115–£207 per person, D,B&B (min. 2 nights midweek) £146.50–£255, set dinner £40, 2-day breaks, Christmas/New Year packages, 1-night bookings sometimes refused weekends.

THIRSK North Yorkshire   *See Shortlist*

THORPE ST ANDREW Norfolk   *See Shortlist*

TISBURY Wiltshire   *See Shortlist*

TITCHWELL Norfolk   Map 2:A5

Titchwell Manor   *Tel* 01485-210221
Titchwell, nr Brancaster   *Fax* 01485-210104
PE31 8BB   *Email* margaret@titchwellmanor.com
          Website www.titchwellmanor.com

Popular with walkers and birdwatchers, Margaret and Ian Snaith's small hotel/restaurant, where their son Eric is the chef, is on the busy coastal road near the RSPB Titchwell nature reserve. Public rooms have mosaic tiled floors, dark woodwork, Lloyd Loom furniture, potted plants. The walled garden 'is a pleasant place to take a drink or a light lunch'. The 'friendly young staff' are praised this year, 'even if it was in an all-hands-to-the-pump style', but several visitors would have liked 'a more personal touch' at Reception. A Christmas guest wrote of 'excellent management'. The newest bedrooms are around a 'pretty garden square with lavender and herbs'; two are suitable for disabled visitors. 'Ours was comfortable, well equipped, with thoughtful extras; good bed, thick towels, strong shower.' The bar, with its 'feel of a gastropub', serves light meals all day. Children under 12 have their own menu. In the 'lovely' conservatory dining room (popular with non-residents), food and service were judged 'exceptionally good' by several reporters, 'OK' by another. Eric Snaith serves modern dishes, eg, soused mackerel, potato caviar; breast and loin of pork, bulgar wheat, coriander seed, chicory. 'Breakfast of a high standard: good fruit compote and fruit salad.' (*Robert Gower, Carol Jackson, Gwyn Morgan, and others*)

Bedrooms: 26, 19 on ground floor, in herb garden, 2 suitable for &. *Open*: all year. *Facilities*: 2 lounges, bar, restaurant, civil wedding licence, ½-acre garden (beaches, golf nearby). *Background music*: in bar. *Location*: on coast road, 5 miles E of Hunstanton. *Smoking*: not allowed. *Children*: all ages welcomed except under-14s at Christmas. *Dogs*: allowed in bar, some bedrooms. *Credit cards*: all major cards. *Prices*: [2009] B&B £55–£125 per person, D,B&B £25 added, full alc £40, midweek breaks, Christmas/New Year packages, 1-night bookings sometimes refused Sat. *V*

TITLEY Herefordshire   Map 3:C4

The Stagg Inn
Titley, nr Kington
HR5 3RL

Tel 01544-230221
Fax 01544-231390
Email reservations@thestagg.co.uk
Website www.thestagg.co.uk

'A warm welcome. A delightful experience. We would certainly return to this charming place,' says a report in 2009. 'Thoroughly civilised', Steve and Nicola Reynolds's white-fronted old pub stands by the road in a small village in rolling Herefordshire countryside. 'Such thoughtful people,' says another visitor. 'Very good food' (*Michelin*-starred) is served in a series of restaurant areas spread higgledy-piggledy through the building. 'We do not play background music; you can join the conversation at the bar,' say the owners. Steve Reynolds keeps his own pigs and uses vegetables from the pub's garden for his seasonally-changing menus (typical dishes: butternut squash and hazelnut risotto; slow-cooked belly pork with haricot beans and apples). Three bedrooms are above the pub. 'We were impressed by ours: bright, tastefully decorated, reasonable sized, heavily beamed; a garden-facing window. We weren't bothered by noise from passing traffic.' Three other rooms are down the road, in a listed Georgian ex-vicarage backed by a garden with stream, chickens, 'a friendly Labrador, and cats'. 'Spacious, very nice, nothing excessive.' Breakfast includes fruit, porridge with honey, 'excellent scrambled eggs, toast made from lovely bread, a large chunk of butter'. (*JA Fisher, Josie Mayers*)

Bedrooms: 6, 3 at *Old Vicarage* (300 yds). *Open*: all year except Sun night/Mon, first 2 weeks Nov, other times to be announced. *Facilities*: (*Old Vicarage*) sitting room, 1½-acre garden, (*Stagg Inn*) bar, restaurant areas, small garden, unsuitable for &. *Background music*: none. *Location*: on B4355 between Kington (3½ miles) and Presteigne. *Smoking*: not allowed. *Children*: all ages welcomed. *Dogs*: allowed in pub only. *Credit cards*: MasterCard, Visa. *Prices*: B&B £45–£65 per person, full alc £35, 1-night bookings sometimes refused. *V*

TOTNES Devon   *See Shortlist*

TRESCO Isles of Scilly   Map 1: inset C1

Island Hotel   *Tel* 01720-422883
Old Grimsby, Tresco   *Fax* 01720-423008
Isles of Scilly   *Email* islandhotel@tresco.co.uk
Cornwall TR24 0PU   *Website* www.tresco.co.uk

'A very comfortable hotel in a beautiful location', this 'splendid' single-storey hotel is by a long sandy beach on Robert Dorrien-Smith's private, car-free island. The manager is Wayne Shaw. 'It was so quiet and peaceful,' say visitors this year. 'We could lie in bed looking over a small private garden to the sea and other islands.' Guests are met at the pier or heliport and brought to the hotel by tractor and trailer. 'Reception and housekeeping staff are helpful, friendly.' Most of the 'well-planned' bedrooms have a sea view; three have a balcony overlooking the garden. The public rooms are decorated in the colours of the sea and the beach; visitors enjoy the absence of background music, and the pictures from Mr Dorrien-Smith's modern art collection, which hang throughout. In the dining room, tables are rotated so the sea views can be shared. Peter Hingston has returned to the *Island* as chef; his modern menus might include cumin-spiced butternut squash soup; roasted monkfish, pea, broad bean and crayfish risotto. Families predominate in summer (there are buckets and spades, pushchairs, a games room, high teas); also a sailing school and a heated outdoor swimming pool. Many visitors come for Tresco's famed subtropical Abbey Gardens (subject to an entry charge). Tresco Estate has been granted planning permission to replace the *Island* with self-catering apartments and a new restaurant in converted boat sheds. Mr Shaw tells us that building work will not start until at least 2011, and the hotel will continue to open as normal for the 2010 season. (*Janet Austin, and others*)

Bedrooms: 48, 8 in 2 annexes, 3 on ground floor. *Open*: early Mar–end Oct. *Facilities*: lounge, TV room, games room, bar, 2 dining rooms, civil wedding licence, 2-acre grounds (terrace, tennis, croquet, bowls, heated 15-metre swimming pool May–30 Sept), nearby beach (safe bathing, diving, snorkelling), bicycle hire (book in advance), golf buggies and wheelchairs for &. *Background music*: none. *Location*: NE side of island, boat/helicopter from Penzance (hotel will make travel arrangements). *Smoking*: not allowed. *Children*: all ages welcomed. *Dogs*: not allowed. *Credit cards*: MasterCard, Visa. *Prices*: B&B £95–£325 per person, D,B&B £130–£360, set dinner £39.50, special breaks.

TRURO Cornwall   Map 1:D2

Mannings Hotel   *Tel* 01872-270345
Lemon Street   *Fax* 01872-242453
Truro TR1 2QB   *Email* reception@manningshotels.co.uk
                                 Website www.manningshotels.co.uk

Formerly the *Royal Hotel*, this 200-year-old Grade II listed inn in the centre of the cathedral city has been renamed by its owner, Lynn Manning. It is liked for the 'relaxed atmosphere', and for the 'lively young staff who treat guests like real humans'. 'We were impressed. They coped admirably with a large family group over the Easter weekend. Our large, sensibly planned room had a large and spotless bathroom and excellent, unobtrusive housekeeping.' Each of the bedrooms is different; all beds have duck-down pillows and duvet. Free Wi-Fi is available throughout the building. Modern brasserie-style food is served from 11 am to 10 pm in the restaurant, where wooden tables are 'reasonably far apart' (some on a platform). The chef, Richard Holland, cooks modern dishes, eg, baked goat's cheese with toasted brioche and sun-dried tomatoes; pan-fried trio of sea fish. 'Good service; generous helpings.' 'At breakfast there were newspapers, a buffet with a large choice, and the food was good.' The bar, open until midnight, serves 'funky' cocktails. (*ML*)

Bedrooms: 43, 9 apartments in stable block, 1 suitable for ♿. *Open*: all year except 25/26 Dec, restaurant closed Sun midday. *Facilities*: lounge, bar, restaurant, boardroom, private dining room. *Background music*: modern in bar and restaurant. *Location*: central. *Smoking*: not allowed. *Children*: all ages welcomed. *Dogs*: only guide dogs allowed. *Credit cards*: all major cards. *Prices*: [2009] B&B £39.50–£65 per person, full alc £28. *V*

TUNBRIDGE WELLS Kent   *See Shortlist*

TWO BRIDGES Devon   *See Shortlist*

ULLSWATER Cumbria   Map 4: inset C2

Howtown Hotel   *Tel* 01768-486514
Ullswater, nr Penrith CA10 2ND

♙ *César award in 1991*

'A very special place', this guest house, run by mother and son Jacquie and David Baldry, has a loyal following among *Guide* readers, attracted by the simplicity, and the setting on the quiet eastern shore of Lake Ullswater. One wrote: 'We loved the decor, evoking memories of times past, and the scope for walking from the door, which allowed us to be carless in Cumbria. The multi-national staff were particularly pleasant and efficient.' 'The quirkiness adds to the interest,' said an earlier visitor who liked the way 'friendly returnees coach the green rookies through the house drill'. This includes the gong that announces dinner at 7 pm and breakfast at 9 am. Dinner has 'the sort of food you would like on a seven-day holiday rather than for a special occasion'; there is a set lunch and a cold supper on Sunday. No frills like phones, TV or radio in the simple bedrooms, but most have lake views; four have a bathroom across the corridor. There is turn-down in the evening, and early morning tea is brought to the room. Afternoon tea can be taken by the fire in winter, in summer in the garden facing the wooded hills. Walkers can ask for a substantial picnic. (*PE Carter, AK*)

Bedrooms: 13, 4 in annexe, 4 self-catering cottages for weekly rent. *Open*: Mar–Nov. *Facilities*: 3 lounges, TV room, 2 bars, dining room, 2-acre grounds, 200 yds from lake (private foreshore, fishing), walking, sailing, climbing, riding, golf nearby, unsuitable for ♿. *Background music*: none. *Location*: 4 miles S of

Pooley Bridge, bus from Penrith station 9 miles. *Smoking*: not allowed. *Children*: all ages welcomed (no special facilities). *Dogs*: not allowed in public rooms. *Credit cards*: none. *Prices*: [2009] D,B&B £75 per person, set dinner £22, 1-night bookings sometimes refused.

See also Shortlist

ULVERSTON Cumbria   Map 4: inset C2

The Bay Horse
Canal Foot
Ulverston
LA12 9EL

Tel 01229-583972
Fax 01229-580502
Email reservations@thebayhorsehotel.co.uk
Website www.thebayhorsehotel.co.uk

♥ *César award in 2009*

In a 'stunning position' on Morecambe Bay, where 'the tides race in and out', this old inn was once a staging post for coaches crossing the sands. It has many devotees, who admire the 'effortless charm' of owner/chef Robert Lyons and manageress Lesley Wheeler: they 'care for their guests in a no-fuss way'. Inspectors agreed: 'Exemplary welcome; help with luggage, offer of tea.' The small, simple bedrooms might be 'in the best of time warps' (chintzy curtains, etc), but 'why change what you do well?' Other visitors were less tolerant ('over-priced and over-fussy'). 'The staff and service were excellent,' said another reader. 'They didn't mind bringing tea to the bedroom, though we would prefer to have tea/coffee-making in the room.' Drinks in the bar (a popular local) at 7.30 pm precede dinner at 8 in the panoramic conservatory restaurant. Ms Wheeler tells us that they have introduced a fixed-price menu (£22 for two courses, £28 for three) alongside the seasonal *carte*. Sample dishes: butter mushrooms, tomato, cream and brandy sauce; smoked haddock, prawn and leek pie. 'Watching the tide as you dine is such fun.' Breakfast (no buffet) has fruit, good cooked dishes, leaf tea, 'nothing packaged'. (*Lynn Wildgoose, and others*)

Bedrooms: 9. *Open*: all year, restaurant closed Mon midday (light bar meals available). *Facilities*: bar lounge, restaurant, picnic area, unsuitable for &. *Background music*: classical/'easy listening'. *Location*: 8 miles NE of Barrow-in-Furness. *Smoking*: not allowed. *Children*: not under 10. *Dogs*: not allowed in restaurant. *Credit cards*: Amex, MasterCard, Visa. *Prices*: [until 31 Mar 2010] B&B £45–£60 per person, full alc £45, bargain breaks, cookery courses, Christmas/New Year packages. *V*

UPPINGHAM Rutland   *See Shortlist*

VENTNOR Isle of Wight   *See Shortlist*

VERYAN-IN-ROSELAND Cornwall Map 1:D2

The Nare   *Tel* 01872-501111
Carne Beach   *Fax* 01872-501856
Veryan-in-Roseland   *Email* stay@narehotel.co.uk
nr Truro TR2 5PF   *Website* www.narehotel.co.uk

♥ *César award in 2003*

'Wonderfully old-fashioned, family run, in a beautiful location.'
'Very comfortable; a nice place to stay.' 'The staff are quite
exceptional. We always get a huge welcome.' Owned by Toby
Ashworth, this luxury hotel (Pride of Britain) stands in large grounds
above Carne Beach, and has wide sea views of Gerrans Bay. 'We
were met with a brolly at the door by charming staff on what must
have been the wettest July day for years.' The bedrooms vary. 'We
were upgraded to a lovely room, much better than we had booked.
It had balcony and vast telly, huge bathroom with massive shower
and endless comforts.' The 'ecological sensibility' (liquid soaps in
refillable bottles) is applauded. Cream tea is served at 4 pm: 'There
is something very comforting about this calorific institution.' Dinner
in the main restaurant is a formal affair, jacket and tie 'preferred' for
men. 'The food has gone up a level, fish particularly delicious.' 'Hors
d'oeuvre trolley very 1950s; our main course of lamb was copious
and tender; puds the usual traditional temptations with lots of cream,
but also a delicious fruit and champagne jelly.' Suppers and light
lunches are recommended in the less formal *Quarterdeck* restaurant
(alfresco in summer). Breakfast was 'excellent, with masses of
choice; a succulent kipper'. Popular out of season with older guests,
many of whom have been coming for years. (*AS, Carie Roots, Joanna
Russell, and others*)

Bedrooms: 37, some on ground floor, 1 in adjoining cottage, 1 suitable for ♿.
Open: all year. *Facilities*: lift, ramps, lounge, drawing room, sun lounge, bar,
billiard room, light lunch/supper room, 2 restaurants, conservatory, indoor
swimming pool (hot tub, sauna), gym, 5-acre grounds (garden, heated
swimming pool, tennis, croquet, children's play area, safe sandy beach),

concessionary golf at Truro golf club. *Background music*: none. *Location*: S of Veryan, on coast. *Smoking*: not allowed. *Children*: all ages welcomed. *Dogs*: not allowed in public rooms. *Credit cards*: Amex, MasterCard, Visa. *Prices*: [2009] B&B £115–£330 per person, D,B&B £123–£345, set dinner £45, special breaks, Christmas/New Year packages.

WAREHAM Dorset   Map 2:E1

The Priory
Church Green
Wareham
BH20 4ND

Tel 01929-551666
Fax 01929-554519
Email reservations@theprioryhotel.co.uk
Website www.theprioryhotel.co.uk

❦ *César award in 1996*

'Service, from the moment we arrived, was superb. The staff couldn't have been more helpful.' A devotee of this luxurious hotel in a 'delightful small town' admires the 'high standards; lovely public rooms and bedrooms'. 'Up to the usual levels,' says another regular visitor this year. It is owned by Anne Turner with brother-in-law Stuart, and managed by her son, Jeremy Merchant. Approached across a green with coloured Georgian houses, and a flagstoned courtyard, the 16th-century former priory has a 'charming quirkiness'. 'The garden is beautifully maintained, terrace in front, lawn sloping down to the River Frome.' The bedrooms vary in size and aspect. 'Our recently renovated large room had a huge double bed, and a fabulous marble-tiled bathroom with a Victorian-style copper bath and an amazing, high-quality walk-through shower.' Public rooms are in 'country house style'. Drinks by a fire in the beamed drawing room precede dinner in the stone-vaulted Abbots' Cellar. Lunch is served in the Garden Room, or alfresco in fine weather. The modern cooking of chef Jon Newing is 'superb' in dishes like salmon, prawn and scallop mousse; roast breast of guineafowl, pine nut and chorizo risotto. 'Good breakfast': freshly squeezed orange juice, a 'proper full English'. (*Ian Malone, EJT Palmer, HJ Martin Tucker*)

Bedrooms: 18, some on ground floor (in courtyard), 4 suites in Boathouse. *Open*: all year. *Facilities*: ramps, lounge, drawing room (pianist Sat evening), bar, 2 dining rooms, 4-acre gardens (croquet, river frontage, moorings, fishing), bicycle hire, unsuitable for ♿. *Background music*: pianist in drawing room Sat night. *Location*: town centre. *Smoking*: not allowed. *Children*: not under 14. *Dogs*: only guide dogs allowed. *Credit cards*: all major cards. *Prices*: [2009] B&B £112.50–£172.50 per person, D,B&B £137.50–£197.50, set dinner £39.95, off-season breaks, Christmas/New Year packages.

WARMINSTER Wiltshire   Map 2:D1

Crockerton House
Crockerton Green
Warminster BA12 8AY

Tel 01985-216631
Email stay@crockertonhouse.co.uk
Website www.crockertonhouse.co.uk

'Painstakingly restored' and 'tastefully decorated' by owners
Christopher and Enid Richmond, this 'gorgeous' Grade II listed
Georgian house was once part of the Longleat estate. Old features
have been preserved. 'Inherited antiques and new furnishings are in
keeping,' said inspectors. 'All is fresh and clean.' Two of the bedrooms
have a bathroom *en suite*; the Officer's Room has an adjacent bathroom
with bath and walk-in shower, and a separate lavatory. The
Heytesbury Suite 'was a pleasant place to sit and read; a large, light
room, with king-size bed, and big windows overlooking the gardens'.
The Silk Room overlooks a lane running down to an old mill. All
rooms have flat-screen TV and Wi-Fi. Visitors who arrive before 5 pm
are given free tea, at a large table under a tree in the garden if weather
permits. Mr Richmond 'is a pleasant front-of-house'. An Aga-cooked
dinner, at 8, is served by arrangement (main courses like slow-cooked
organic beef in red wine); no licence; bring your own wine. 'Breakfast
was elegantly presented. Excellent bread, home-made preserves'; also
freshly squeezed juice, organic cereals, eggs, bacon, etc. The grounds,
with hedges, herbaceous borders, orchard and kitchen garden, face
meadows that lead down to the River Wylye, in a designated area of
outstanding natural beauty. More reports, please.

Bedrooms: 3. *Open*: all year except Christmas. *Facilities*: drawing room, dining
room, 1¼-acre garden, unsuitable for &. *Background music*: none. *Location*:
2 miles S of Warminster. *Smoking*: not allowed. *Children*: not under 12. *Dogs*:
not allowed. *Credit cards*: MasterCard, Visa. *Prices*: [2009] B&B £36–£79.50
per person, set dinner £30, reduced rates for longer stays, 1-night bookings
refused weekends.

WARTLING East Sussex   Map 2:E4

Wartling Place
Wartling, Herstmonceux
nr Eastbourne
BN27 1RY

Tel 01323-832590
Email accom@wartlingplace.prestel.co.uk
Website www.countryhouseaccommodation.co.uk

'Charming, spacious and light', this white-painted early 18th-century
Grade II listed former rectory stands on a hill near Wartling's church.
It is run as a B&B by owners Barry and Rowena Gittoes. 'All is spick

and span, lots of white paint, interesting objects, big windows,' say
inspectors. Staircases have short, wide flights; prints and pictures hang
on walls. Visitors are told not to check in before 4 pm: 'Rowena
showed us to a lovely, large room. Overlooking the garden, it had a
four-poster and nice bits and pieces; heavy curtains, plenty of chairs;
immaculate bathroom.' Wi-Fi is available. 'There was a tea-making
kit but, when asked, she served us tea in the pretty garden.' Breakfast
is at a long table 'elegantly laid, in a charming room: nice yogurt,
canned apricots, cereals, etc, on the buffet'. Cooked dishes include
kedgeree, omelettes, waffles with maple syrup, good scrambled eggs.
'Classical music played softly.' An evening meal is available by
arrangement; for dining out, *The Lamb*, an 'excellent' gastropub almost
opposite, is recommended; so is the *Sundial* in Herstmonceux.

Bedrooms: 4, also self-catering cottage. *Open*: all year. *Facilities*: lounge/dining
room with honesty bar and CD-player, 3-acre garden, unsuitable for &, except
ground floor of cottage. *Background music*: none. *Location*: 3 miles N of
Pevensey. *Smoking*: not allowed. *Children*: all ages welcomed. *Dogs*: allowed in
cottage only. *Credit cards*: Amex, MasterCard, Visa. *Prices*: B&B £65–£125 per
person, set dinner £37.50, Christmas/New Year packages, 1-night bookings
sometimes refused weekends.

WARWICK Warwickshire   *See Shortlist*

WATERMILLOCK Cumbria   Map 4: inset C2

Rampsbeck
Watermillock on Ullswater
nr Penrith CA11 0LP

Tel 01768-486442
Fax 01768-486688
Email enquiries@rampsbeck.co.uk
Website www.rampsbeck.co.uk

In 'lovely gardens with unusual plants' on the shores of Lake
Ullswater, this elegant, white, 18th-century country house is run as a
hotel by Marion Gibb, the 'hands-on' manageress. She is 'ever-
present, serving at table, answering phones, meeting guests'. This year
the bar, the lounges and six of the bedrooms have been refurbished.
The rooms vary in size and aspect. The larger ones, which look over
fields to the lake, have a sitting area; all have 'fresh water and fruit,
replenished daily'. Housekeeping is 'excellent', and the bathrooms
are modern and well lit. Andrew McGeorge, the long-serving chef,
uses local ingredients for dishes like steamed sea bass with a brochette

of langoustines, pimento sauce. Vegetarian options are available. 'Outstanding' desserts include hot plum soufflé with cinnamon milkshake and green apple sorbet. Breakfast, fully served, 'has comprehensive choice; extra helpings of juice'. Conferences, weddings, etc, are held. (*EP, and others*)

Bedrooms: 19. *Open*: all year except 4–25 Jan. *Facilities*: 2 lounges, bar, restaurant, civil wedding licence, 18-acre grounds (croquet), lake frontage (fishing, sailing, windsurfing, etc), unsuitable for &. *Background music*: occasional 'easy listening'. *Location*: 5½ miles SW of Penrith. *Smoking*: not allowed. *Children*: young children not allowed in restaurant at night. *Dogs*: allowed in 3 bedrooms, hall lounge. *Credit cards*: MasterCard, Visa. *Prices*: B&B £70–£145 per person, D,B&B £90–£185, set dinner £43–£49.50, special breaks, Christmas/New Year packages, 1-night bookings occasionally refused weekends.

WEM Shropshire   *See Shortlist*

WEST STOKE West Sussex   Map 2:E3

West Stoke House
West Stoke, nr Chichester
PO18 9BN

Tel 01243-575226
Fax 01243-574655
Email info@weststokehouse.co.uk
Website www.weststokehouse.co.uk

♥ *César award in 2008*

'A little difficult to find, but well worth the effort,' says a visitor in 2009. On the edge of the South Downs, Rowland and Mary Leach run their 'beautiful' Georgian house ('sympathetically restored') as an informal restaurant-with-rooms. 'Rowland Leach,' said an inspector, 'is sociable, unpretentious, charmingly eccentric, with out-of-control hair, and wearing baggy shorts all year round.' The 'professional' manager, Richard Macadam, has 'a warm, easy manner'. 'Guests are made to feel comfortable, whether formally or casually dressed.' In the blue-walled dining room, with musicians' gallery, chef Darren Brown has a *Michelin* star for his 'superb' modern British, French-influenced cooking (eg, pressed terrine of rabbit, truffled fine bean salad; baked hake, white bean stew, baby fennel and confit lemon). The public rooms have antiques on polished floors, plenty of seating, modern art (for sale). Drinks are taken in the large lounge (with red walls and chairs, yellow curtains). 'Everything exudes quality' in the bedrooms, which have French antiques, big bed, modern fabrics.

'Cedar, recently refurbished, was in excellent order; its spacious bathroom has an actual bath.' 'Our large room was thoughtfully furnished; trendy fittings; flat-screen TV/DVD; powerful shower (no bath); superb views; sheets and blankets as we requested.' English breakfast has fruit, cereals, yogurts, croissants, 'excellent' coffee, 'thick-cut bacon', but one reader found service 'erratic'. Weddings and other celebrations are held. (*J Rochelle, and others*)

Bedrooms: 8. *Open*: all year except Christmas, restaurant closed Sun evening/ Mon/Tues. *Facilities*: lounge, restaurant, civil wedding licence, 4-acre grounds (garden games), only restaurant suitable for &. *Background music*: soft, in restaurant. *Location*: 3 miles NW of Chichester. *Smoking*: not allowed. *Children*: all ages welcomed. *Dogs*: not allowed in public rooms. *Credit cards*: Amex, MasterCard, Visa. *Prices*: [2009] B&B £70–£112.50 per person, set dinner £45, full alc £60, see website for special breaks, 1-night bookings refused weekends.

WESTON-SUPER-MARE Somerset *See Shortlist*

WEYMOUTH Dorset   *See Shortlist*

WHITBY North Yorkshire   *See Shortlist*

WHITEWELL Lancashire   Map 4:D3

The Inn at Whitewell
Whitewell, Forest of Bowland
nr Clitheroe BB7 3AT

Tel 01200-448222
Fax 01200-448298
Email reception@innatwhitewell.com
Website www.innatwhitewell.com

A family had a 'wonderful' three-night stay this year at Charles Bowman's 300-year-old inn which sits in some of the finest scenery in the North of England, high above the River Hodder. They had unusual praise for Mr Bowman, the third generation of his family to be involved: 'Lancashire's answer to Hugh Grant, so amusing and charming.' The building is filled with family antiques, old paintings and prints, oriental rugs, and is decorated in a quirky style. Antique baths are a speciality. Fourteen bedrooms have an open fire. The river-facing rooms have 'gorgeous views', and all but one of the 'less appealing rooms' facing the car park have been 'very satisfactorily' refurbished this year. Log fires warm the public rooms, and the busy bar which serves 'excellent' food and is popular with locals 'has a delightful ambience'. The riverside dining room 'is a touch more formal'. Chef Jamie Cadman uses local ingredients in dishes like roast loin of Bowland lamb, with barley and carrots. 'No tea-making facilities, but room service starts at 7 am.' 'Good breakfasts: freshly squeezed orange juice, good fruit, porridge with cream and honey, full English.' The inn owns seven miles of fishing for salmon, trout, etc. (*Mrs G Wolstenholme and others*)

Bedrooms: 23, 4 (2 on ground floor) in coach house, 150 yds. *Open*: all year. *Facilities*: 2 bars, restaurant, boardroom, orangery, civil wedding licence, 5-acre garden, 7 miles fishing (ghillie available), unsuitable for &. *Background music*: none. *Location*: 6 miles NW of Clitheroe. *Smoking*: not allowed. *Children*: all ages welcomed. *Dogs*: not allowed in dining room. *Credit cards*: MasterCard, Visa. *Prices*: [2009] B&B £52.50–£165 per person, full alc £30.

WHITSTABLE Kent   Map 2:D5

Windy Ridge   *Tel* 01227-263506
Wraik Hill   *Email* scott@windyridgewhitstable.co.uk
Whitstable CT5 3BY   *Website* www.windyridgewhitstable.co.uk

'A wonderful welcome from Tessa and Tizzie, two friendly retrievers, and from Boris the cat,' was enjoyed by a visitor this year to this B&B. In a garden on a small country road, this characterful conversion of two farm cottages has panoramic views of town and sea. 'We get fantastic sunsets,' say the owners, Hugh and Lynda Scott ('excellent hosts'). An earlier guest wrote: 'The pleasure of this place is how comfortable it feels, unlike many anonymous hotels.' One of the gargoyles on the front wall is reputedly from Canterbury cathedral; there are beamed ceilings, a wood-burning stove in the 'cosy' lounge, and cast iron fireplaces. The bedrooms 'have been refurbished to a very high standard'. One has a four-poster bed, and there is a two-room family suite. 'Great value.' 'The dining room, facing the garden and estuary, is lovely.' Breakfast, 'done superbly', has healthy and vegetarian options, and meat from local butchers. No evening meal, but 'the Scotts are very good at recommending local restaurants'. Wi-Fi is available. (*B and P Orman, and others*)

Bedrooms: 8, 2 on ground floor, 1 suitable for & (wheelchair access with a carer). *Open*: all year. *Facilities*: lounge, bar, dining room, meeting/conference facilities, civil wedding licence, ½-acre garden (gazebo), unsuitable for &. *Background music*: at breakfast. *Location*: 1½ miles from centre, off A299. *Smoking*: not allowed. *Children*: not under 9. *Dogs*: allowed by prior arrangement, in 1 bedroom only. *Credit cards*: Amex, MasterCard, Visa. *Prices*: [2009] B&B £45–£55 per person, 3-night rates, Christmas/New Year packages, 1-night bookings refused weekends in season. *V*

WILMINGTON East Sussex   Map 2:E4

Crossways Hotel
Lewes Road
Wilmington
BN26 5SG

Tel 01323-482455
Fax 01323-487811
Email stay@crosswayshotel.co.uk
Website www.crosswayshotel.co.uk

'As ever, a warm, informal welcome, name and previous conversations miraculously recalled, exemplary provision for the needs of Glyndebourne aficionados.' So writes a returning visitor to this pretty house in a village in the Cuckmere valley. The owners for 22 years, David Stott and Clive James, have a loyal following (not just among opera fans). Some bedrooms have been refurbished ('getting rid, we hope, of the 1960s feel'), and more work was scheduled for late 2009. The four-course *prix-fixe* dinner menu, served in an intimate dining room, 'is far better than just an adjunct to a Glyndebourne trip; finely cut calf's liver with a gin and lime sauce the highlight; scallops and monkfish also much appreciated'. There is no guest lounge, but bedrooms contain 'every appliance imaginable: TV, clock, knick-knacks galore'. Some rooms have a sofa; one has a balcony. A 'hugely enjoyable' breakfast is served in a sunny room with a collection of cheese plates: 'some of the best eggs and bacon'; 'nice, tart fruit salad'. The large garden, with pond, rabbits and herb garden, runs down to a busy main road ('not so noisy as to prevent sleep, but no chance of pre-prandial in the garden'). (*Richard Parish*)

Bedrooms: 7, also self-catering cottage. *Open*: all year except 22 Dec–29 Jan, restaurant closed Sun/Mon evening. *Facilities*: breakfast room, restaurant, 2-acre grounds (duck pond), unsuitable for &. *Background music*: light classical/popular in restaurant. *Location*: 2 miles W of Polegate on A27. *Smoking*: not allowed. *Children*: not under 12. *Dogs*: not allowed. *Credit cards*: Amex, MasterCard, Visa. *Prices*: B&B £60–£79 per person, D,B&B £85–£99, set dinner £36.95.

Looking for a hotel for a special occasion; perhaps a romantic weekend, or a memorable meal? The Hotelfinder section (page 11) identifies hotels in 20 categories designed to match your mood and meet your special interests.

WINCHELSEA East Sussex   Map 2:E5

The Strand House
Tanyard's Lane
Winchelsea TN36 4JT

Tel 01797-226276
Fax 01797-224806
Email info@thestrandhouse.co.uk
Website www.thestrandhouse.co.uk

Before the river silted up, these two Grade II listed buildings (one
13th-century, the other Tudor) stood on the quayside at Winchelsea
harbour, below the lovely old town. They are now run as a small hotel
by owners Hugh Davie and Mary Sullivan. 'She is a wonderful
hostess,' said inspectors, 'full of energy, always friendly, around most
of the day.' In the evening she dons chef's clothing, takes the orders
and 'disappears into the kitchen' to produce 'honest, unpretentious'
meals on a short daily-changing menu. She uses local produce in her
dishes which might include salad of warm beetroot, black pudding
and Sussex goat's cheese; organic Romney Marsh lamb cutlets, pork
and herb sausage, red onion and mint sauce. Some of the bedrooms are
up steep steps and many have low beams (which might 'leave an
impression' on taller visitors). This year some rooms have been given
a new bed and shower, and flat-screen TV. 'Our delightful room had
flowery fabrics, a large inglenook fireplace, brass bedhead. Bags were
carried and the room was serviced during breakfast', which has 'all
manner of cooked dishes': 'they even make their own baked beans'.
'In the early morning we heard birds and pheasants.' (*AR, and others*)

Bedrooms: 10, 1 on ground floor. *Open*: all year. *Facilities*: reception, lounge, bar,
breakfast room, civil wedding/partnership licence, 1-acre garden, unsuitable
for &. *Background music*: jazz/big bands/crooners in public rooms. *Location*:
300 yds from centre, 2 miles SW of Rye. *Smoking*: not allowed. *Children*: not
under 5. *Dogs*: allowed by arrangement, but not in public rooms. *Credit cards*:
Amex, MasterCard, Visa. *Prices*: [2009] B&B £35–£62.50 per person, D,B&B
£62.50–£90, set dinner £29.50, special breaks, Christmas/New Year packages,
1-night bookings refused weekends Apr–Sept, Christmas/New Year.

WINCHESTER Hampshire   *See Shortlist*

We say 'Unsuitable for &' when a hotel tells us that it cannot
accommodate wheelchair-users. We do not have the resources
to inspect such facilities or to assess the even more complicated
matter of facilities for the partially disabled. We suggest that
you discuss such details with the hotel.

WINDERMERE Cumbria   Map 4: inset C2

Gilpin Lodge
Crook Road
nr Windermere LA23 3NE

Tel 015394-88818
Fax 015394-88058
Email hotel@gilpinlodge.co.uk
Website www.gilpinlodge.co.uk

🏆 *César award in 2000*

'Exceptional; a wonderful welcome from every member of staff.' Praise in 2009 for this Edwardian building (Relais & Châteaux) set amid woodland and gardens. John and Christine Cunliffe have run it as a country house hotel since 1987; they are supported by son Barney and his wife, Zoë. 'Their skill in interior design is evident.' Regular visitors appreciate the informal 'hands-on owner management' and the commitment not to hold weddings or corporate events. A drawing room opens on to the 'modern, bright bar'. The restaurant, in four rooms, is 'calm' (no muzak). Russell Plowman joined as chef in January 2009. His style is modern ('we are passionate about using local and organic ingredients'): perhaps ballottine of organic salmon, horseradish and potato mousse; loin of local venison in pancetta. Light lunches are served in the lounge. Some bedrooms have a four-poster, some a whirlpool bath. The six garden suites have a contemporary decor. 'Even the smaller rooms are comfortable.' A backpack with maps and books of walks is provided for hikers. 'Breakfast, a leisurely affair, has fruity starters, a great collection of hot dishes.' 'Expensive, but worth it.' (*David and Bridget Reed, EM Arnold, John and Jackie Tyzak*)

Bedrooms: 20, 6 in orchard wing. *Open*: all year. *Facilities*: ramps, bar, 2 lounges, 4 dining rooms, 22-acre grounds (ponds, croquet), free access to nearby country club (swimming pool, sauna, squash), golf course opposite, unsuitable for &. *Background music*: none. *Location*: on B5284, 2 miles SE of Windermere. *Smoking*: not allowed. *Children*: not under 7. *Dogs*: not allowed (kennels at nearby farm). *Credit cards*: all major cards. *Prices*: [2009] D,B&B £85–£220 per person, set dinner £52, Christmas/New Year packages, min. 2 nights weekends. *V*

Holbeck Ghyll
Holbeck Lane
Windermere LA23 1LU

Tel 015394-32375
Fax 015394-34743
Email stay@holbeckghyll.com
Website www.holbeckghyll.com

'Good food, helpful staff, lovely location and pampering make the *Holbeck Ghyll* experience. We love it,' says a returning visitor this year.

Owners David and Patricia Nicholson are 'very much in evidence' at their luxurious Lakeland hotel (Pride of Britain). Built as a hunting lodge by Lord Lonsdale in 1888, the house stands in large grounds (with streams, wildlife and tennis) which slope down to the lake. A four-bedroom house and a three-bedroom lodge are in the grounds. 'Our room in the main building was well appointed and comfortable, and had views towards the lake and the fells.' Public rooms have 'a baronial feel': stained glass, open fires, wood panelling, antiques; also free Internet access. 'Scrummy canapés in the lounge, delicious food in the restaurant.' There are two dining rooms, one oak-panelled, the other with French windows that lead on to a terrace for alfresco meals. Chef David McLaughlin has a *Michelin* star for his modern dishes, eg, ravioli of veal sweetbreads; roasted John Dory with spiced cauliflower. 'We enjoyed scallops and langoustines. All the meat dishes (chicken, duck and venison) were cooked exactly as requested.' Breakfast has a large buffet, good cooked dishes. 'Far from cheap, but worthwhile.' (*ST, M and PJ, and others*)

Bedrooms: 25, 1 suitable for &, 10 (1 with kitchenette) in lodge and houses. *Open*: all year except 3–21 Jan. *Facilities*: ramp, 2 lounges, bar, restaurant, function facilities, civil wedding licence, small spa (sauna, steam room, massage, etc), 14-acre grounds (streams, ponds, woods to lake shore, tennis, putting, croquet, jogging track). *Background music*: in 1 lounge. *Location*: 3 miles N of Windermere, off road to Ambleside. *Smoking*: not allowed. *Children*: not under 8 in restaurant. *Dogs*: not allowed in public rooms. *Credit cards*: Amex, MasterCard, Visa. *Prices*: B&B £100–£225 per person, D,B&B £125–£295, set dinner £55, Christmas/New Year packages, 1-night bookings sometimes refused Sat. *V*

See also Shortlist

WINSTER Derbyshire   Map 3:B6

The Dower House
Main Street
Winster, nr Matlock
DE4 2DH

Tel 01629-650931
Email fosterbig@aol.com
Website www.thedowerhousewinster.com

Well placed for visits to Chatsworth House, John and Marsha Biggin's 'country house B&B' is a Grade II listed building of Elizabethan origins. Recent comments: 'A most enjoyable stay; bedrooms are generously proportioned and beautifully warm.' 'A home from home.

Everything is smashing.' One room has window seats facing the main street, another a stone fireplace and views through mullioned windows of the 'lovely walled garden', which has a private gate to the churchyard. One room has an *en suite* shower room, the others have a spacious bathroom (one is along a corridor: dressing gowns can be provided). The guests' sitting room has 'squashy' sofas, 'lots of pictures', and an honesty bar. In the 'elegant' dining hall (with original beams, sash windows, part stone floor, wood fire, fresh flowers), breakfast includes home-made muesli, fruit, wholemeal and granary bread from the local baker, dry-cured bacon, 'sausages from our award-winning farm butcher' and preserves from Chatsworth's farm shop. 'Delicious, particularly the local oatcake cushioning perfectly poached eggs.' The driveway's entrance is 'rather narrow: be careful if you have a large car'. The 'cheerful' *Bowling Green* pub in the village serves 'generous, reasonable' food. Mr Biggin will advise on local walks and activities. More reports, please.

Bedrooms: 4. *Open*: all year except Christmas/New Year. *Facilities*: sitting room, bar, dining room, ¼-acre walled garden (pond), unsuitable for &. *Background music*: occasional classical, in dining room. *Location*: 3 miles W of Matlock. *Smoking*: not allowed. *Children*: not under 12. *Dogs*: not allowed. *Credit cards*: none. *Prices*: B&B £47.50–£70 per person, 1-night bookings refused Fri/Sat in season.

WOLD NEWTON East Yorkshire   Map 4:D5

The Wold Cottage
Wold Newton, nr Driffield
YO25 3HL

Tel/Fax 01262-470696
Email katrina@woldcottage.com
Website www.woldcottage.com

'The location is stunning. We could not have been made more welcome,' says a visitor in 2009 to this 'wonderful', spacious red brick Georgian farmhouse. Once a city gentleman's retreat, it stands in landscaped grounds where fruit and vegetables are grown for the table. It has views to the Yorkshire Wolds. The owners, Katrina and Derek Gray, offer 'country house accommodation'. 'Friendly, informative and helpful', they provide 'very good value'. Visitors are welcomed with tea and cake. Some of the 'spacious, well-equipped' rooms are in a converted barn. Extras include dressing gowns, hot-water bottles, fresh milk. Mrs Gray uses local produce for dinner, served by arrangement, by candlelight, communally or at separate tables. 'Like the best home cooking on dinner-party days.' The 'excellent' breakfast includes 'plenty of cereals', fresh fruit and yogurt, variations of full English or a variety of fish dishes, home-made bread and preserves. (*Yvonne Bradshaw*)

Bedrooms: 5, 2 in converted barn, 1 on ground floor. *Open*: all year. *Facilities*: lounge, dining room, 3-acre grounds (croquet) in 300-acre farmland. *Background music*: at mealtimes. *Location*: just outside village. *Smoking*: not allowed. *Children*: all ages welcomed. *Dogs*: not allowed. *Credit cards*: MasterCard, Visa. *Prices*: [2009] B&B £40–£60 per person, D,B&B £63–£83, set dinner £23.

WOLTERTON Norfolk   Map 2:A5

The Saracen's Head
Wolterton, nr Erpingham
NR11 7LZ

Tel 01263-768909
Fax 01263-768993
Email saracenshead@wolterton.freeserve.co.uk
Website www.saracenshead-norfolk.co.uk

Modelled on a Tuscan farmhouse, this country inn is 'lost in the lanes' amid fields in rural Norfolk. It is run by owner Robert Dawson-Smith with his daughter, Rachel, who also has a workshop selling retro furniture, and pictures (including her own work). Visitors like the welcome, 'polite inquiries about my family', and the 'real' bedrooms done in bold colours (red, green or blue walls, patchwork bedspreads). Three, upstairs, have a rounded dormer window. In the public areas, filled with paintings, bric-a-brac, etc, the host serves 'wonderful' dishes like wok-sizzled sirloin with anchovy and tomato; pan-fried scallops with rosemary and cream. In summer, meals are served alfresco. The restaurant is now closed all day on Monday, and on Tuesday at lunchtime 'to give us a well-earned rest'; advice is given on local alternatives. Breakfast ('especially good') includes freshly squeezed orange juice, fruit, fresh bread, good kippers. Although the inn is up for sale, the Dawson-Smiths say, 'Don't think we will be selling up in a hurry! Love it as much as ever.' More reports, please.

Bedrooms: 6. *Open*: all year except 25 Dec, evening of 26 Dec; restaurant closed Mon, Tues lunchtime. *Facilities*: lounge, 3 dining rooms, courtyard, 1-acre garden, shop, accommodation unsuitable for &. *Background music*: none. *Location*: 5 miles from Aylsham. *Smoking*: not allowed. *Children*: all ages welcomed. *Dogs*: not allowed in public areas. *Credit cards*: Amex, MasterCard, Visa. *Prices*: [2009] B&B £45 per person, D,B&B from £70, full alc £33.50, 1-night bookings usually refused weekends. *V*

WOODSTOCK Oxfordshire   *See Shortlist*

WOOKEY HOLE Somerset   Map 1:B6

Miller's at Glencot House
Glencot Lane
Wookey Hole, nr Wells
BA5 1BH

Tel 01749-677160
Fax 01749-670210
Email relax@glencothouse.co.uk
Website www.glencothouse.co.uk

At the foot of the Mendip hills, this 19th-century Jacobean-style mansion claims to have 'the most elegantly theatrical interior of any country house hotel'. It is owned by the antique dealer Martin Miller (see also *Miller's Residence*, London, Shortlist). He has filled it with exotic antiques and curiosities (paintings, prints, cartoons, stuffed birds, stags' antlers, bits of china on dressers, porcelain-headed dolls, huge Chinese vases; second-hand books are piled everywhere). Inspectors thought it 'wonderfully quirky, great fun'. In large grounds, with the River Axe running through, the house has mullioned windows, carved ceilings and panelling. Bedrooms are exuberantly furnished, some have a four-poster. 'Our quiet room had heavy, beaded curtains, a collection of teapots, neat little bathroom (but no evening turn-down).' In the *Riverview* restaurant, with candlelit tables, beamed ceiling and huge chandelier, 'dinner was fine, if not exceptional. Try for a window table.' The daily-changing menu might include smoked duck, Caesar salad; roasted Priddy Farm lamb rack. 'Breakfast had delicious croissants. Pity about the muzak, played all day in the dimly lit public rooms.' There is a tiny indoor jet stream pool, a snooker room and a cinema; in the grounds, a cricket pitch, and mirrors under trees. Local sightseeing includes the cathedral city of Wells, Wookey Hole caves, the Cheddar Gorge and Glastonbury.

Bedrooms: 15, some on ground floor. *Open*: all year. *Facilities*: 2 lounges, restaurant, small cinema, snooker room, tiny indoor pool with jet stream, 18-acre grounds (garden, river (fishing), croquet, cricket pitch). *Background music*: all day in public rooms. *Location*: 2 miles NW of Wells. *Smoking*: not allowed. *Children*: all ages welcomed. *Dogs*: not allowed in restaurant. *Credit cards*: all major cards. *Prices*: [2009] B&B £82.50–£147.50 per person, set dinner £32.50, full alc £45, 2-day half-board rates, seasonal breaks, Christmas/New Year packages, 1-night bookings sometimes refused, min. 2 nights at weekends.

Most hotels have reduced rates out of season, and offer special breaks throughout the year. It is worth checking the hotel's website for special offers and late deals. Always ask about deals when booking by telephone.

WOOLACOMBE Devon   Map 1:B4

Watersmeet   NEW
Mortehoe
Woolacombe EX34 7EB

Tel 01271-870333
Fax 01271-870890
Email info@watersmeethotel.co.uk
Website www.watersmeethotel.co.uk

On a cliff above a sandy beach, and with views over Woolacombe Bay, this traditional hotel is owned and managed by Michael and Amanda James. It returns to the *Guide* on the recommendation of a regular reporter. 'It has gone into my list of all-time favourites for the spacious rooms with sea views, the lovely restaurant and excellent service.' All but three of the bedrooms have the views; some have a balcony. 'Everything was efficient and unhurried; our room was serviced (mineral water replaced as soon as it was needed) without our noticing.' A new suite on the third floor has a bedroom and lounge, and a spa bath and a walk-in shower in its bathroom. Men are asked to wear a jacket and tie in the evening at the *Pavilion* restaurant, where many of the tables are by picture windows which look across to Lundy Island. John Prince, the chef, uses local produce for his menus, which have a 'good, varied choice', eg, wild mushroom, tarragon and cream tart; sea trout, fennel purée, prawns, almond butter. The 'reasonably priced' wine list has plenty of wines by the glass. Lunch and afternoon tea can be taken alfresco on the terrace by the pool or in the tea garden. There is good walking on the National Trust land all around. (*Robert Ribeiro*)

Bedrooms: 29, 3 on ground floor, 1 suitable for &. *Open*: all year. *Facilities*: lift, lounge, bar, function room, civil wedding licence, terrace, 3-acre gardens, heated indoor and outdoor swimming pools, sandy beach below. *Background music*: classical/romantic in restaurant. *Location*: by sea, 4 miles SW of Ilfracombe. *Smoking*: not allowed. *Children*: not under 8 in restaurant in evening (high tea at 6 pm). *Dogs*: not allowed. *Credit cards*: MasterCard, Visa. *Prices*: [2009] B&B £70–£133 per person, D,B&B £83–£146, set dinner £36, full alc £45, midweek breaks, Christmas/New Year packages, 1-night bookings sometimes refused Sat in high season.

Check the Hotelfinder section (page 11) if you are looking for a hotel for a special occasion, perhaps a memorable meal (see Gourmet and Gastropubs); a sporting weekend (see Golf, Fishing, Walking); somewhere that will welcome your children – or your dog. Our editors have selected ten hotels in each of these categories (and many more) to help you make your choice.

WORFIELD Shropshire   Map 3:C5

The Old Vicarage
Worfield
nr Bridgnorth
WV15 5JZ

Tel 01746-716497
Fax 01746-716552
Email admin@the-old-vicarage.demon.co.uk
Website www.oldvicarageworfield.com

In a 'splendid situation' in rural Shropshire, this gabled, red brick Edwardian former parsonage has a manicured lawn, and statues and seats around old elms. The owners, Sarah and David Blakstad, say they aim for a 'relaxed style'; Janet Whalley is the manager. The dress code in the light *Orangery* restaurant is smart casual (no jeans). The chef, Simon Diprose, serves a seasonally-changing menu of British dishes, eg, buttered asparagus with Parma ham; roast saddle of English lamb, carrot and rosemary purée. There is a decanter of sherry, fresh fruit, milk in a jug in the bedrooms, which vary in size. Most have antique furniture; some have a four-poster or a half-tester bed. Rooms in the coach house have a private garden; one is equipped for the disabled. There is fresh fruit at breakfast; cooked dishes include 'very good' sausages. The Blakstads, parents themselves, write: 'While we have limited facilities for children, we actively encourage them to stay.' (*AL, and others*)

Bedrooms: 14, 4 in coach house, 2 on ground floor, 2 suitable for ♿. *Open*: all year. *Facilities*: ramps, lounge, bar, restaurant, 2 private dining rooms, small conference facilities, civil wedding licence, 2-acre grounds (patio, croquet). *Background music*: 'very low' in public areas. *Location*: 2 miles NE of Bridgnorth. *Smoking*: not allowed. *Children*: all ages welcomed. *Dogs*: not allowed in public rooms. *Credit cards*: Diners, MasterCard, Visa. *Prices*: [2009] B&B £40–£95 per person, D,B&B £70–£100, set dinner £38–£45, full alc £50, special breaks. *V*

WROXHAM Norfolk   Map 2:B6

Broad House Hotel
The Avenue
Wroxham NR12 8TS

Tel/Fax 01603-783567
Email info@broadhousehotel.co.uk
Website www.broadhousehotel.co.uk

In large gardens with a private jetty on to Wroxham Broad, this beautiful Queen Anne house is owned by Philip and Caroline Search. It is liked for its 'wonderfully relaxing atmosphere', and the 'careful way in which modernisation has been done'. Bedrooms are named after members of the Trafford family, former owners of the house and one of Norfolk's largest landowning families. The Lady Betty suite, 'sumptuously decorated in shades of green and deep aubergine', has a king-size carved oak four-poster bed. The Abbott's room, in terracotta with reds and gold, has a dark cherry sleigh bed and views of the formal gardens. 'Our bathroom was excellent, large, brightly lit, smartly designed. A chocolate was left on the bed during the turn-down service.' The library has books, games, etc; French windows open on to the garden. The restaurant is bright with 'striking red walls, antique chairs and tables, contemporary cutlery and china'. Chef Andy Parle's menu is a 'celebration of Norfolk produce', perhaps Swannington pork; Gressingham duck. Service, by local staff, was 'friendly, informal'. There is a snack menu during the day. 'Breakfast had fresh juice, excellent fruit salad, good scrambled eggs.' (*P and JT*)

Bedrooms: 9. *Open*: all year, restaurant closed Sun to non-residents. *Facilities*: drawing room, library, bar, restaurant, civil wedding/function facilities, 24-acre grounds, heated swimming pool (10 by 4 metres), jetty, market garden, only restaurant suitable for &. *Background music*: classical. *Location*: 8 miles NE of Norwich (airport 5 miles). *Smoking*: not allowed. *Children*: all ages welcomed. *Dogs*: allowed in some bedrooms, not in public rooms. *Credit cards*: Amex, MasterCard, Visa. *Prices*: [2009] B&B £86–£115.50 per person, set dinner £45–£49, special breaks, Christmas/New Year packages.

YARM North Yorkshire   Map 4:C4

Judges
Kirklevington Hall
Yarm TS15 9LW

Tel 01642-789000
Fax 01642-782878
Email reservations@judgeshotel.co.uk
Website www.judgeshotel.co.uk

'The service was outstanding, the food was gorgeous and the attention to detail was brilliant,' says a reader who spent her tenth wedding anniversary in this former residence for circuit judges (Pride of Britain). The Victorian house stands in large, peaceful, wooded grounds, with stream, birds and 'well-kept landscaped gardens' (floodlit at night). Owned by the Downs family, it is liked for the 'gentle hospitality', and 'slightly old-fashioned' atmosphere. 'No mobile phones or intrusive muzak.' Tim Howard is the 'kind, supportive' manager. The 'charming' staff have 'a lovely style and sense of humour'. In the conservatory restaurant, chef John Schwarz serves modern dishes, eg, slow-poached salmon, foie gras; Yorkshire Dales venison, scallops, parsnip, chicory. Light meals can be taken during the day, in the panelled bar or the lounge, with its antiques, fire and flowers. Six of the bedrooms have been refurbished this year and given a new bathroom. All rooms have feather mattress, footbath, video recorder with tapes, CD-player, and 'a goldfish in a bowl and a request to feed it'. 'I liked the small touches (bath salts, needle and thread in a cushion, chocs and a liqueur).' 'The shower was awful but the spa bath made up for this.' Beds are turned down at night and shoes are shined. Weddings are held. (*Kara Sandys, MSB*)

Bedrooms: 21, some on ground floor. *Open*: all year. *Facilities*: ramps, lounge, bar, restaurant, private dining room, function facilities, business centre, civil wedding licence, 36-acre grounds (paths, running routes), access to local spa and sports club. *Background music*: none. *Location*: 1½ miles S of centre. *Smoking*: not allowed. *Children*: all ages welcomed. *Dogs*: only guide dogs allowed. *Credit cards*: all major cards. *Prices*: [2009] B&B £89.50–£97 per person, D,B&B £125–£132.50, set menu £27.50, full alc £54, Christmas/New Year packages. *V*

YORK North Yorkshire   Map 4:D4

Dean Court   NEW
Duncombe Place
York YO1 7EF

Tel 01904-625082
Fax 01904-620305
Email sales@deancourt-york.co.uk
Website www.deancourt-york.co.uk

'Splendidly situated', in the shadow of the famous minster, this city hotel (Best Western, managed by David Brooks) is recommended for the 'classy service' and 'attention to detail'. 'It is smoothly and effortlessly run,' say trusted reporters who enjoyed the extras: 'fruit and bathrobes in the bedroom, free Wi-Fi'. Another comment: 'The staff were helpful: the barman lent me a corkscrew, the night porter gave me his newspaper for the TV guide.' The bedrooms are decorated in contemporary style; superior rooms face the minster (its bells are silent at night). Children are welcomed: there are special menus and several family rooms; cots and extra beds can be supplied, and 'toddlers are invited to plunder our toy box'. *The Court* bistro/bar serves light meals (eg, bangers and mash) from 9.30 am until 11 pm. In the *D.C.H.* restaurant, Valerie Storer's cooking was enjoyed: her seasonal menus of modern dishes with a French influence might include gin-cured salmon; roast breast of guineafowl, dried morello cherry jus. Breakfast is 'first class'. For a £5 charge it can be delivered to the bedroom. Valet parking is available: if you are arriving by car, 'ask for directions'. (*Francine and Ian Walsh, WK*)

Bedrooms: 37, 3 suitable for &. *Open*: all year. *Facilities*: ramp, 2 lounges, bar, restaurant, bistro/bar, conference/function facilities, civil wedding licence. *Background music*: in public areas, not in restaurant at breakfast. *Location*: Central, opposite minster. *Smoking*: not allowed. *Children*: all ages welcomed. *Dogs*: not allowed. *Credit cards*: all major cards. *Prices*: B&B £42.50–£67.50 per person, D,B&B £55–£112.50, full alc £40, special breaks, Christmas/New Year packages, 1-night bookings sometimes refused.

Middlethorpe Hall & Spa

Bishopthorpe Road
York YO23 2GB

Tel 01904-641241
Fax 01904-620176
Email info@middlethorpe.com
Website www.middlethorpe.com

Now owned by the National Trust, with all profits going to the charity, this red brick William III mansion stands in large grounds on a busy road on the city outskirts, by the racecourse. It continues to be liked: 'An excellent welcome, friendly staff.' 'All was perfection.' 'Ideal for a traditional, relaxing weekend in a beautifully restored country house.' A Pride of Britain member, managed by Lionel Chatard, it has a walled garden, small lake and venerable trees; inside are antiques, period furnishings, much panelling, stucco ceilings, historic paintings. 'We drooled over the decor, fabrics, lamps, etc,' says a visitor this year. The large best bedrooms in the main house have a sitting room and gas coal fire; cheaper rooms are in converted stables and cottages. All rooms have a flat-screen TV/DVD-player and Wi-Fi connection. There is a smart casual dress code (no trainers, tracksuits or shorts) in the formal restaurant in interlinked rooms facing the 'delightful' walled garden. Nicholas Evans serves modern dishes, eg, pan-fried organic salmon fillet with creamed leeks and roast artichoke; roast Goosnargh corn-fed duck breast with fondant potatoes. Light meals are available in the 18th-century drawing room. One reader thought the cooked breakfast (charged extra) 'not up to the standard of the evening meal'. (*Michael Williamson, Zara Elliott, and others*)

Bedrooms: 29, 17 in coach house, 2 in garden, 1 suitable for &. *Open*: all year. *Facilities*: drawing room, sitting rooms, library, bar, restaurant, private dining rooms, function facilities, civil wedding licence, 20-acre grounds (walled garden, white garden, croquet, lake), spa (health and beauty facilities, heated indoor swimming pool, 13 by 6 metres). *Background music*: none. *Location*: 1½ miles S of centre, by racecourse. *Smoking*: not allowed. *Children*: not under 6. *Dogs*: not in public rooms. *Credit cards*: Amex, MasterCard, Visa. *Prices*: [2009] B&B (continental) £95–£225 per person, Yorkshire breakfast £6.95 extra, full alc £52, Christmas/New Year packages.

See also Shortlist

ZENNOR Cornwall   Map 1:D1

The Gurnard's Head   *Tel* 01736-796928
Treen, nr Zennor   *Email* enquiries@gurnardshead.co.uk
St Ives TR26 3DE   *Website* www.gurnardshead.co.uk

* *César award in 2009*

'A laid-back, right-on kind of place', this yellow-painted inn is 'one of the best pubs we have stayed in', says a regular *Guide* reader this year. Owned by brothers Charles and Edmund Inkin (see also *The Felin Fach Griffin*, Felin Fach, in Wales, *qv*), it has a 'wonderful position' on the 'last stretch of the Cornish coast that hasn't been swamped by tourism'. Andrew Wood is the 'charming' manager. The bar has old tables and chairs, rugs on stone floor, log fires, books everywhere. A snug with big sofas leads to the simply furnished, candlelit restaurant. The chef, Robin Wright, 'takes his food-sourcing seriously': local farmers deliver vegetables and herbs, fish comes from Newlyn. A reporter this year enjoyed 'the meal of the year. Fillet of roast hake with rosemary mash, pancetta and spinach with a Béarnaise sauce was an entirely successful combination of flavours and textures.' There is 'nothing fancy' in the bedrooms, which have a digital radio rather than a TV. 'Our small room was very comfortable, with a superb bed; looking out the window to see the cows on their way to milking was memorable.' The 'excellent' breakfast has rustic breads on a side table with a toaster, home-made marmalade, jam and lemon curd in large jars. (*Nigel Mackintosh, and others*)

Bedrooms: 7. *Open*: all year except 24/25 Dec, 4 days early Jan. *Facilities*: bar area, small connecting room with sofas, dining room, 1-acre garden, unsuitable for &. *Background music*: radio by breakfast table for guests' use. *Location*: 6 miles SW of St Ives, on B3306. *Smoking*: not allowed. *Children*: all ages welcomed. *Dogs*: not allowed in dining room. *Credit cards*: MasterCard, Visa. *Prices*: B&B £40–£75 per person, full alc £32.50, midweek offers, 'Sunday sleepover' rates, 1-night bookings 'occasionally' refused, particularly for guests not eating in.

SCOTLAND

This year's Scottish *César* winner, *Kilberry Inn,* on the remote Kintyre peninsula, is liked for the wonderful scenery, good food and great hospitality. This could be a template for many of the places in our Scottish chapter (some are in cities and towns), which has breadth of choice that illustrates the diversity of the accommodation available in Scotland. As in other chapters, there are simple B&Bs, welcoming guest houses, inns enjoyed by locals as well as visitors, and delightful island hotels.

Kilberry Inn, Kilberry

ABERDEEN   *See Shortlist*

ABERFELDY Perth and Kinross   Map 5:D2

Fortingall Hotel   `NEW`   *Tel* 01887-830367
Fortingall, Aberfeldy   *Email* hotel@fortingallhotel.com
PH15 2NQ   *Website* www.fortingall.com

In a small Arts and Crafts village in a 'wonderful landscape'
dominated by Glen Lyon and Loch Tay, this privately owned hotel
is managed by Roddy Jamieson, 'hands on and ubiquitous'. It is
upgraded from the Shortlist after a positive inspection report (with
some reservations). 'Our nicely proportioned bedroom had views of
the glen; good bedside lights and excellent tea/coffee-making
facilities (leaf tea and fresh milk). Housekeeping was excellent, too.
The bathroom was generous, and well equipped except for towels
that were past their best-by date.' The large lounge has 'Scottish
elements, well done in subtle colours; a welcome open log fire'. In
the 'agreeable' half-panelled dining room, the chef, Darin Campbell,
serves modern dishes: 'Our starters and puddings were fine but a
main course of slow-cooked daube of beef disappointed; Roddy
whisked the plate away and offered us a fillet steak.' A simpler menu
is served in the 'cosy' bar, 'well patronised by locals and visitors'.
Children have their own menu. Breakfast has 'standard sideboard
starters' (packets of cereal, packaged juices); 'very good toast from
home-made bread, decent butter and good marmalade; charming and
attentive service'. The village churchyard has a 5,000-year-old yew
tree, said to be the oldest in Europe.

Bedrooms: 10, 2 in annexe. *Open*: all year. *Facilities*: lounge, library, bar, dining
room, function room, wedding facilities, garden. *Background music*: in restaurant
(live harpist once a month), live fiddle music in bar Friday. *Location*: in village
7 miles W of Aberfeldy. *Smoking*: not allowed. *Children*: all ages welcomed. *Dogs*:
allowed. *Credit cards*: Diners, MasterCard, Visa. *Prices*: [2009] B&B £74–£122
per person, D,B&B £109–£157, full alc £40, special breaks, Christmas/New
Year packages.

ACHILTIBUIE Highland   *See Shortlist*

ARDUAINE Argyll and Bute   *See Shortlist*

ARISAIG Highland   *See Shortlist*

ASCOG Argyll and Bute   *See Shortlist*

AVIEMORE Highland   Map 5:C2

Corrour House   *Tel* 01479-810220
Rothiemurchus   *Fax* 01479-811500
Inverdruie   *Email* enquiries@corrourhouse.co.uk
by Aviemore PH22 1QH   *Website* www.corrourhouse.co.uk

Set in beautiful grounds, this 'delightful' bay-windowed former dower house of the Rothiemurchus estate has 'outstanding' views across to the Lairig Ghru pass and the Cairngorms. The owners, Carol and Robert Still, 'take immense trouble to make sure that guests have all they need, and to give them information about the neighbourhood', says a visitor this year. Tea and shortbread are offered on arrival. An earlier guest wrote of 'a house of real antique character, scrupulously maintained'. The public rooms are 'beautifully decorated': the lounge, where an open fire burns much of the time, has been refurbished. Bedrooms vary in size and are 'lovely' and 'chintzy'. 'The bathroom was well equipped.' An evening meal is no longer available, but there are plenty of eating places nearby. 'A very good breakfast' is taken in a 'stunning' room. You might see red squirrels, deer or even a pine marten crossing the lawn. Aviemore is ten minutes away on foot, and there is 'much good walking in the area'. (*Mary Hewson, AM*)

Bedrooms: 8. *Open*: New Year–mid-Nov. *Facilities*: lounge, cocktail bar, dining room, 4-acre gardens and woodland, unsuitable for &. *Background music*: none. *Location*: ¾ mile S of Aviemore. *Smoking*: not allowed. *Children*: all ages welcomed (under-4s stay free). *Dogs*: not allowed in public rooms or unsupervised in bedrooms. *Credit cards*: MasterCard, Visa. *Prices*: [2009] B&B £40–£55 per person, reductions for 3 or more nights, New Year package, 1-night bookings refused in season.

BALLANTRAE Ayrshire   Map 5:E1

Cosses Country House   NEW   *Tel* 01465-831363
Ballantrae   *Fax* 01465-831598
KA26 0LR   *Email* staying@cossescountryhouse.com
                      Website www.cossescountryhouse.com

Originally a shooting lodge (later a farm), this pretty, low, white building stands in flower-filled gardens and woodland in a secluded valley just outside an old fishing village. It is a Wolsey Lodge, run by its owners Robin and Susan Crosthwaite (she is the chef). 'We knew it was a great place from the moment we were greeted by Susan and her Labradors,' says a visitor this year, restoring it to the *Guide* after a period without reports. Two of the 'clean and comfortable' bedrooms are in converted byres and stables across a courtyard; each has a large bed and a single, a bath and a walk-in shower; and a sitting room with antique furniture, books, maps, etc; also tea-making facilities, home-made biscuits, fresh fruit, and flowers from the garden. A smaller room is in the main house. The hostess, who has written a book of local recipes, uses home-grown produce for her 'fantastic' four-course meals (no choice, taken communally). Typical dishes: Crailoch pheasant and chicken liver pâté; Ballantrae lobster with saffron sauce, pea risotto. A Scottish breakfast is taken in the dining room or kitchen, or on the patio in good weather. There are 'breathtaking' walks from the grounds, which have views across the sea to the Kintyre peninsula. (*Tanya Simmonds*)

Bedrooms: 3, on ground floor, 2 across courtyard. *Open*: Mar–24 Dec. *Facilities*: drawing room, dining room, games room, utility room, 12-acre grounds. *Background music*: none. *Location*: 2 miles E of Ballantrae. *Smoking*: not allowed. *Children*: not under 12 in dining room for dinner. *Dogs*: allowed by arrangement, not in public rooms. *Credit cards*: MasterCard, Visa. *Prices*: B&B £42.50–£65 per person, D,B&B £72.50–£95, special breaks.

Glenapp Castle   NEW   *Tel* 01465-831212
Ballantrae   *Fax* 01465-831000
KA26 0NZ   *Email* enquiries@glenappcastle.com
                   Website www.glenappcastle.com

Once the seat of the Earl of Inchcape, this 19th-century Scottish baronial castle was turned by Graham and Fay Cowan into a luxurious country hotel (Relais & Châteaux). 'Highly recommended as a place of peace and privacy,' says a long-standing *Guide* reader. 'The atmosphere is warm. They have furnished it beautifully with antiques lovingly collected during the restoration.' There are fine paintings, colourful rugs, intricate plasterwork; an Austrian oak-panelled entrance and staircase, floor-to-ceiling bookshelves in the parquet-floored library. The massive main drawing room feels 'cosy'. The spacious bedrooms have an open fire, there are wide beds, books, 'everything for your comfort'. The staff are 'attentive yet unobtrusive'. John Orr, the manager, is 'informed and helpful with his recommendations in the dining room'. Adam Stokes, the 'innovative and confident' chef, serves modern dishes, eg, baby artichoke tart with veal sweetbread; poached and roasted Ayrshire grouse with Morteau sausage. Guests 'can wander at will' through the large wooded grounds which have a lake, a walled garden, and a magnificent Victorian glasshouse. 'The Cowans will suggest local jaunts.' (*Dr John D Schofield*)

Bedrooms: 17, 7 on ground floor. *Open*: 3 Mar–2 Jan, except Christmas. *Facilities*: ramp, lift, drawing room, library, 2 dining rooms, wedding facilities, 36-acre gardens (tennis, croquet), fishing, golf nearby, access to spa. *Background music*: none. *Location*: 2 miles S of Ballantrae. *Smoking*: not allowed. *Children*: not under 5 in dining room after 7 pm. *Dogs*: allowed in 1 bedroom, not in public rooms. *Credit cards*: Amex, MasterCard, Visa. *Prices*: [2009] B&B £157.50–£257.50 per person, D,B&B £187.50–£287.50, set dinner £55, New Year package, website offers. *V*

BALLATER Aberdeenshire   Map 5:C3

Deeside Hotel
45 Braemar Road
Ballater AB35 5RQ

Tel 013397-55420
Fax 0871 989 5933
Email mail@deesidehotel.co.uk
Website www.deesidehotel.co.uk

Set back among trees on the road to Braemar, this Victorian village house was thought 'superb value, especially for an autumn break' this year. Owned by Gordon Waddell (the chef) and the 'unfailingly pleasant' Penella Price, it is a member of the Green Tourism Business Scheme. There are log fires in the 'small, comfortable' library, 'well supplied with books and recent magazines'. The bar has over 40 whiskies. In the restaurant, whose conservatory area overlooks the walled garden (where red squirrels may be seen), there is always a vegetarian option, though 'the emphasis is on meat – I enjoyed some particularly good pheasant'. Herbs and soft fruit are home grown; breads, seafood and meat come from local suppliers. The 'short, fairly mundane' main wine list has a 'more interesting – and expensive' supplement. A children's menu is available. Bedrooms, 'inoffensively' decorated, have generous storage space, books, toiletries and home-made shortbread. There are king-size beds and a two-room family suite with its own entrance. 'The low prices put any minor housekeeping shortcomings into context.' At breakfast, eggs are free range, and 'I enjoyed a fine Achiltibuie kipper'; marmalade is home made, but there was 'carton orange juice'. Good for walking, fishing, distilleries and Balmoral. (*Alan and Edwina Williams, Andrew Wardrop, and others*)

Bedrooms: 10, 2 on ground floor. *Open*: Mar–Oct. *Facilities*: ramp, lounge, library, bar, restaurant, 1-acre garden. *Background music*: Mozart in restaurant. *Location*: village outskirts, on road to Braemar. *Smoking*: not allowed. *Children*: all ages welcomed. *Dogs*: not allowed in upstairs bedrooms or public rooms. *Credit cards*: Diners, MasterCard, Visa. *Prices*: [2009] B&B £40–£50 per person, D,B&B £60–£75, set dinner £20, full alc £34, reductions for 3 or more nights, 1-night bookings sometimes refused Sat in season. *V*

BALLYGRANT Argyll and Bute   *See Shortlist*

BALQUHIDDER Stirling   Map 5:D2

Monachyle Mhor   *Tel* 01877-384622
Balquhidder   *Fax* 01877-384305
Lochearnhead   *Email* monachyle@mhor.net
FK19 8PQ   *Website* www.mhor.net

In a 'remote, peaceful, beautiful' setting at the end of a four-mile track skirting Loch Voil, this pale-pink converted 18th-century farmhouse is run as a restaurant-with-rooms by Tom and Dick Lewis, and their sister, Melanie. 'It is friendly, relaxed; we felt very welcome,' says a visitor in 2009. 'We were greeted by a local girl who helped us with our bags and showed us around.' Bedrooms vary in size: 'Ours was small, nicely decorated, and a good temperature on a freezing day; it had proper coffee with a miniature cafetière and fresh milk; a large bathroom.' Three luxury suites are in converted stables: two have a steam room, and there are plenty of 'audio-visual gadgets'. The 'cosy' bar has modern furniture and an open fire. Tom Lewis's 'excellent' cooking is based on local produce; vegetables and herbs from the walled garden. It is served in the conservatory dining room (views of loch and mountains). All the meat comes from the estate;

dishes might include pork with kohlrabi *choucroute* and wild mushrooms. 'Our lamb was perfectly cooked.' There are inventive vegetarian dishes and good bar meals. Breakfast has muesli, yogurts, fruit, pastries; the cooked menu includes kippers. 'Tom Lewis was in Reception as we left, making sure guests had enjoyed their stay.' (*Katie Shaw*)

Bedrooms: 14, 2 on ground floor, 8 in courtyard. *Open*: all year. *Facilities*: sitting room, bar, conservatory restaurant, wedding facilities, 2,000-acre estate (garden, *pétanque* pitch, clay-pigeon shooting), unsuitable for &. *Background music*: classical/jazz in bar/restaurant. *Location*: 11 miles NW of Callander. *Smoking*: not allowed. *Children*: all ages welcomed (under-2s free). *Dogs*: allowed in 2 bedrooms. *Credit cards*: all major cards. *Prices*: [2009] B&B £52.50–£127.50 per person, D,B&B £98.50–£173.50, set dinner £46, 1-night bookings refused Sat in season.

BLAIRGOWRIE Perth and Kinross   Map 5:D2

Kinloch House
Dunkeld Road
by Blairgowrie PH10 6SG

Tel 01250-884237
Fax 01250-884333
Email reception@kinlochhouse.com
Website www.kinlochhouse.com

In 'a fine situation' in the gentle Perthshire hills, the Allen family's early Victorian mansion (Relais & Châteaux) near Dunkeld is decorated in 'suitably' traditional style. With its oak-panelled hall, *objets d'art*, log fires ('even in August'), portrait gallery and ornate glass ceiling, it provides 'comfort and quality at a price'. Visitors this year had an 'encouraging welcome; luggage carried to our room without question'. An earlier guest commented: 'Definitely a family-run hotel; we encountered the patriarch in gardener's clothing in the walled garden and, later, his wife in Reception. Day-to-day management is by their son, Graeme.' The bedrooms have 'plenty of hanging space'; many are spacious. Some have a four-poster bed and a large Victorian bath. Most showers are hand held. There is a 'professional welcome' in the dining room where chef Andrew May serves seasonal dishes, eg, langoustine and melon; breast of mallard with rösti; plum tarte Tatin. 'Well cooked, delicious, but more vegetables would have been welcome.' All the herbs and salads are grown in the walled garden, where guests may sit. Breakfast has 'excellent kippers, good choice of juices, plentiful tea, coffee and toast'. The health centre is another attraction. Shooting and fishing can be arranged. (*Elspeth Jervie and John Gibbon, M Tannahill*)

Bedrooms: 18, 4 on ground floor. *Open*: all year except 12–29 Dec. *Facilities*: ramp, drawing room, 2 lounges, conservatory, bar, dining room, private dining room, health centre (swimming pool, 12 by 5 metres, sauna, etc), wedding facilities, 25-acre grounds (walled garden, field with Highland cattle, and horses). *Background music*: none. *Location*: 3 miles W of Blairgowrie, on A923. *Smoking*: not allowed. *Children*: no under-7s in dining room at night. *Dogs*: allowed by arrangement (dog units available). *Credit cards*: Amex, MasterCard, Visa. *Prices*: [2009] B&B £85–£155 per person, D,B&B £133–£203, set dinner £48, full alc £60, see website for offers, New Year package, 1-night bookings sometimes refused.

BOWMORE Argyll and Bute   *See Shortlist*

BRACHLA Highland   Map 5:C2

Loch Ness Lodge   NEW   *Tel* 01456-459469
Brachla   *Fax* 01456-459439
Loch Ness-side   *Email* escape@lodgeatlochness.com
IV3 8LA   *Website* www.lodgeatlochness.com

'A romantic get-away': in 'well-landscaped' grounds, this handsome white-painted lodge (recently built 'with a neat nod to the Scottish vernacular') has 'attention-grabbing' views over Loch Ness. It is run as a luxury hotel by the 'likeable' Scott Sutherland with his sister, Iona. Inspectors found much to admire in the 'near-perfect' welcome and 'creature comforts': 'The public rooms are well proportioned, in muted beige and cream (nothing to frighten the horses); good fabrics, reproduction antique furniture. Our compact but not claustrophobic ground-floor bedroom had two small but comfortable armchairs; high-quality bedlinen, a beautiful bedspread, excellent lighting. No expense had been spared in the bathroom. Housekeeping was exemplary.' In the snug (with open fire and up-to-date magazines), 'decent leaf' afternoon tea is served with sponge cake. The candlelit dining room has 'a pleasant ambience, well-spaced tables, linen cloths'. Preferences are discussed in advance for Ross Fraser's daily menu which has choice only for two main courses. 'Portions were small, and we thought the cooking OK, if uninspired.' The wine list was 'modest in size, immodest in prices'. Breakfast has a 'well-presented' sideboard buffet with freshly squeezed orange juice, good cereals, dried fruit, yogurt; cooked dishes were 'enjoyable'; toast 'alas not from home-made bread'. (*Mary McPherson, and others*)

Bedrooms: 7, 1 on ground floor suitable for &. *Open*: all year except Jan. *Facilities*: snug, drawing room, dining room, small spa, garden, fishing, shooting nearby. *Background music*: in public rooms. *Location*: 10 miles SW of Inverness. *Smoking*: not allowed. *Children*: not under 12. *Dogs*: not allowed. *Credit cards*: Amex, MasterCard, Visa. *Prices*: [2009] B&B £95–£140 per person, set dinner £45, special offers.

BRODICK North Ayrshire   Map 5:E1

Kilmichael Country House
Glen Cloy, by Brodick
Isle of Arran KA27 8BY

Tel 01770-302219
Fax 01770-302068
Email enquiries@kilmichael.com
Website www.kilmichael.com

Owners Geoffrey Botterill and Antony Butterworth are 'much in evidence, and it shows' at their 'beautifully kept hotel', said to be Arran's oldest house. Standing in wooded grounds with spectacular mountain views, it has the atmosphere of a private house, and contains 'pictures collected with care from around the world'. Some bedrooms are in the main house (one has a four-poster bed and a 'bath big enough for two'). Three are in converted stables a short, if sometimes muddy, walk away. 'Our lovely room had lots of thoughtful touches: bone china tea set, Ordnance Survey map, history of the island.' Mr Butterworth, who says he is 'the cook, not the chef', serves a daily-changing three-course menu with fine silver and crystal in the conservatory dining room. Vegetables and herbs from the *potager* feature in dishes like pear, pea and rocket soup; halibut with celery and apples. Vegetarian options are provided 'as a matter of course'. 'Gluten-free bread was baked especially for my wife.' *Kilmichael* was named country house hotel of the year in the 2009 Scottish Hotel Awards. (*EMA, DH*)

Bedrooms: 8, 3 in converted stables (20 yds), 7 on ground floor, 4 self-catering cottages. *Open*: Mar–Oct, restaurant closed midday and Tues. *Facilities*: 2 drawing rooms, dining room, 4½-acre grounds (burn). *Background music*: light classical background music during meals. *Location*: 1 mile SW of village. *Smoking*: not allowed. *Children*: not under 12. *Dogs*: not allowed in public rooms. *Credit cards*: MasterCard, Visa. *Prices*: [2009] B&B £64–£99.50 per person, dinner £42, discounts for 3–7 nights, ferry-inclusive packages, 1-night bookings sometimes refused Sat.

If you are recommending a B&B and know of a good restaurant nearby, please mention it in your report.

CARRADALE Argyll   Map 5:E1

Dunvalanree in Carradale   NEW   *Tel* 01583-431226
Port Righ, Carradale   *Email* book@dunvalanree.com
PA28 6SE   *Website* www.dunvalanree.com

On the edge of a little Kintyre fishing village, Alan and Alyson
Milstead's small hotel/restaurant above Port Righ Bay has 'breathtaking' views across Kilbrannan Sound to the Isle of Arran. 'They are
a warm and delightful couple, generous and genuine,' says the
nominator. 'The rooms are comfortable, well presented. Ours was
nicely decorated and tastefully furnished. Alan's attention to detail
was demonstrated by his instructions for the bedrooms' shower setting
in the comprehensive "about our hotel" folder (he tried them all).
Quality tea and decent coffee were to hand, as was a tin of Alyson's
delicious home-made biscuits.' A 'superb' cook, she is listed in the
Good Food Guide for her short *table d'hôte* menu, using local seafood
and produce in dishes like stargazy pie with spiced tomato sauce; roast
Ifferdale pork with apple and sage gravy. There is a short wine list
and a more extensive whisky selection. Breakfast includes organic
porridge, spiced grapefruit, eggs Benedict, and smoked haddock with
a poached egg. Carradale has a 'challenging' nine-hole golf course.
(*Jane Smith*)

Bedrooms: 5, 1 on ground floor suitable for &. *Open*: all year except Christmas.
Facilities: lounge, dining room, ½-acre garden. *Background music*: radio at
breakfast, Scottish/jazz in evening in dining room. *Location*: on edge of village
15 miles N of Campbeltown. *Smoking*: not allowed. *Children*: all ages welcomed.
Dogs: allowed in 1 bedroom only. *Credit cards*: all major cards. *Prices*: B&B
£51–£66 per person, D,B&B £71–£86, full alc £27. *V*

CASTLEBAY Western Isles   *See Shortlist*

CHIRNSIDE Borders   Map 5:E3

Chirnside Hall   *Tel* 01890-818219
Chirnside, nr Duns   *Fax* 01890-818231
TD11 3LD   *Email* reception@chirnsidehallhotel.com
                              Website www.chirnsidehallhotel.com

'The welcome was warm; we were made to feel at home.' Visitors who
arrived during a snowstorm in 2009 at the Regency mansion in the

Borders add: 'The other guests had cancelled, but we had an enjoyable stay.' Tessa Korsten, owner with her husband, Christian, 'seemed to read our minds; not once did we have to chase for assistance'. An earlier comment: 'She looked after us with great charm.' The public rooms have bold colours, rich fabrics: 'The lounge had a good fire, lots of seating, enough cushions to fill a football pitch.' The bedrooms have 'all the amenities that one expects'. 'Our south-facing room, large and warm, had dark colours, heavy drapes; a small bathroom.' Some top rooms may be 'a little dark'. There is back-ground music ('avoid the window table, the speaker sits underneath') in the handsome dining room with its big tables, upholstered chairs. Mark Wilkinson has been the chef since April 2009: we would welcome reports on his modern cooking on a daily-changing menu (perhaps shredded confit of duck leg; monkfish tail, saffron potatoes, asparagus and chive sauce). 'Breakfasts fairly traditional (haggis instead of black pudding for the full Scottish).' There are 'inspiring' views across fields to the Cheviot hills. (*Andrew McManus, and others*)

Bedrooms: 10. *Open*: all year except Mar. *Facilities*: 2 lounges, dining room, billiard room, fitness room, private dining room, library/conference room, wedding facilities, 5-acre grounds, unsuitable for ♿. *Background music*: 'easy listening'. *Location*: 1½ miles E of village, NE of Duns. *Smoking*: allowed in 2 bedrooms. *Children*: all ages welcomed. *Dogs*: not allowed in public rooms. *Credit cards*: Amex, MasterCard, Visa. *Prices*: [2009] B&B £55–£165 per person, D,B&B £80–£215, set dinner £30, short breaks.

COLONSAY Argyll and Bute　　　　Map 5:D1

The Colonsay
Isle of Colonsay
PA61 7YP

Tel 01951-200316
Fax 01951-200353
Email reception@thecolonsay.com
Website www.colonsayestate.co.uk

On an 'idyllic' Hebridean island just eight miles long, this unpretentious inn has been renovated by a group headed by the laird and his wife, Alex and Jane Howard. Visitors this year were 'well looked after' by the manager, Scott Omar, and his team. 'They picked us up from the ferry. We didn't have to check in; a table was waiting for us in the restaurant. A memorable visit.' Spacious sitting areas have log fires, deep sofas and chairs; 'lots of books and games'. 'We liked the bar, full of locals.' The bedrooms are simply furnished, 'comfortable, spotless'. 'Ours, the best, was super, with excellent bathroom.' There are harbour views from the informal restaurant. 'We had some excellent meals.' The short menu might include 'squeaky-fresh oysters from the south of the island'; spring lamb casserole; 'veg from the hotel's organic garden'. 'Breakfasts outstanding; home-baked bread, home-made jams, even possets'; cooked dishes cost extra. Packed lunches are provided: 'We were dropped off on the other side of the island so we could walk back; bicycles were found when we asked for them.' Colonsay has sandy beaches, archaeological remains, golf, tennis and fishing. (*Katherine Chater, GD, REH*)

Bedrooms: 9. *Open*: Mar–Jan, no Monday check-in. *Facilities*: conservatory lounge, log room, bar, restaurant, accommodation unsuitable for &. *Background music*: none. *Location*: 400 yds W of harbour. *Smoking*: not allowed. *Children*: all ages welcomed. *Dogs*: not allowed in bedrooms. *Credit cards*: Amex, MasterCard, Visa. *Prices*: [2009] B&B £42.50–£72.50 per person, D,B&B £24 added, full alc £25–£35, 1 free night for a 3-night stay at certain times, Christmas/New Year packages. *V*

CONTIN Highland   Map 5:C2

Coul House
Contin
IV14 9ES

Tel 01997-421487
Fax 01997-421945
Email stay@coulhousehotel.com
Website www.coulhousehotel.com

Stuart and Susannah Macpherson 'continue to improve' their Grade A listed Regency hunting lodge in large gardens outside a Highland village. Chris McLeod, the 'hard-working' manager, and his staff are 'unendingly helpful'. 'As we parked the car, he came out to welcome us,' said a returning visitor. The house has 'particularly attractive public rooms' (plaster ceilings, log fires). The stone terrace, which has 'stunning' views of the Strathconon valley, is a 'lovely place to sit with a drink'. In the high-ceilinged, octagonal dining room, with its full-height windows, Garry Kenley's contemporary Scottish cooking was thought 'good', though sometimes 'with too many ingredients' in dishes like goose breast with an oriental sweet and sour glaze, Parma ham and potato tart, turnip, sour apple purée, red cabbage jus. 'A good choice of desserts, particularly the ice creams and sorbets.' There is a separate vegetarian menu. The bedrooms, individually decorated, are 'clean, comfortable, with good pillows' (some have a four-poster). 'Our bathroom was small but had a heated towel rail and good toiletries.' Breakfast has a wide selection of cereals, bread, etc; the usual choices on the cooked menu. 'A quiet, pleasant location. Our Labrador was made very welcome; she was able to join us in the lounge after dinner.' (*ST, and others*)

Bedrooms: 21, some on ground floor. *Open*: all year except 24–26 Dec. *Facilities*: ramp, hall, lounge, bar/lounge, restaurant, conference/wedding facilities, 8-acre garden (children's play area, 9-hole pitch and putt). *Background music*: in lounge bar and restaurant. *Location*: ½ mile above village, 17 miles NW of Inverness. *Smoking*: not allowed. *Children*: all ages welcomed (under-5s stay free). *Dogs*: allowed. *Credit cards*: Amex, MasterCard, Visa. *Prices*: [2009] B&B £65–£95 per person, D,B&B £87.50–£117.50, full alc £35, special breaks, New Year package, 1-night bookings refused New Year. *V*

CRIANLARICH Perthshire   *See Shortlist*

CRINAN Argyll and Bute   Map 5:D1

Crinan Hotel
Crinan
by Lochgilphead
PA31 8SR

Tel 01546-830261
Fax 01546-830292
Email reservations@crinanhotel.com
Website www.crinanhotel.com

'Great location, quiet, good food and service.' 'Sensationally' set in a hamlet where the Crinan Canal meets the Atlantic, this white-painted building has been a hotel for 250 years. Nick and Frances Ryan (the artist Frances Macdonald, whose 'wonderful' paintings hang throughout) have owned and run it for 39 years. 'The hotel benefits from Mr Ryan's hands-on style,' says a visitor in 2009. 'The informal ambience is one of its charms.' Earlier praise: 'Luggage carried to our most agreeable bedroom: spacious, with large bed, armchairs from which to admire the view, fresh flowers, ornaments.' Some rooms have a balcony. At the top of the building, pre-dinner drinks are served in the panoramic *Gallery Bar*, and there is a new residents' observation lounge. The panelled *Mainbrace* bar provides seafood and traditional bar meals. The coffee shop serves snacks all day. In the 'well-proportioned' *Westward* restaurant, with candles, linen cloths and Lloyd Loom chairs, chef Gregor Bara (promoted from *sous-chef*) uses local produce in main courses like Aberdeen Angus fillet, braised shin, celeriac purée. One visitor wished that the menu had changed during a four-day stay, and added: 'No refreshments were offered when we arrived after a long drive.' Breakfast is 'impressive'. Children (they have their own menu) and dogs are welcomed. There is a lush 'secret garden' up the hill behind the hotel. (*ST*)

Bedrooms: 20. *Open*: all year except 20–27 Dec. *Facilities*: lift, ramps, 2 lounges, observation lounge, seafood bar, rooftop bar, public bar, restaurant, coffee shop, art gallery, treatment room (health and beauty), wedding facilities, patio, ¾-acre gardens, safe, sandy beaches nearby. *Background music*: none. *Location*: village centre, waterfront. *Smoking*: only on balconies. *Children*: all ages welcomed. *Dogs*: not allowed in restaurant. *Credit cards*: MasterCard, Visa. *Prices*: B&B £65–£105 per person, D,B&B £85–£150, set dinner £45, full alc (*Mainbrace*) £22.50, short breaks, courses, New Year package.

DORNOCH Highland   Map 5:B2

2 Quail   NEW

Castle Street
Dornoch IV25 3SN

Tel 01862-811811
Email goodhotel@2quail.com
Website www.2quail.com

'As good as ever', this restaurant-with-rooms returns to the *Guide* after a time with no reports. The Victorian house, on the main street of a town with mellow stone houses and a long sandy beach, is run without assistance by owners Michael and Kerensa Carr. He, *Ritz*-trained, is the chef ('first rate'), she ('a strong personality, cheerful, amusing') is front-of-house, also wine waiter, bartender, housekeeper and bookkeeper. 'They are delightful hosts, friendly and helpful; the food is sublime.' Residents need to book a table in the popular, book-lined restaurant, which has only 12 covers. It is 'appreciated' if they dine in once during their stay, but this is not obligatory. The three-course menu (two choices for each course) might include monkfish with an orange crust; veal with chanterelles, a creamy sherry and truffle sauce. The lounge, with its large bookcase, is small. Breakfast, served at 8.30 am, has home-made yogurts and muesli, croissants and cooked dishes. Bedrooms are 'clean, comfortable' and well pro-portioned. Housekeeping is 'exemplary'. 'We are undoubtedly the smallest golf hotel and restaurant in Scotland,' say the Carrs, keen members of Royal Dornoch. In summer 2009, Michael Carr temporarily moved to cook at the club. Prospective visitors should check the position when booking.

Bedrooms: 3. *Open*: Apr–Oct, restaurant closed midday, and Sun/Mon. *Facilities*: lounge, restaurant, unsuitable for &. *Background music*: occasional. *Location*: central. *Smoking*: not allowed. *Children*: not under 10. *Dogs*: only guide dogs allowed. *Credit cards*: Amex, MasterCard, Visa. *Prices*: [2009] B&B £35–£60 per person, set dinner £36.

See also Shortlist

DUNDEE   *See Shortlist*

DUNKELD Perth and Kinross   Map 5:D2

Kinnaird
Kinnaird Estate
by Dunkeld PH8 0LB

Tel 01796-482440
Fax 01796-482289
Email enquiry@kinnairdestate.com
Website www.kinnairdestate.com

'Stunning setting, log fires, discreet service, quality cooking.' A trusted *Guide* correspondent endorses this Victorian listed stone mansion (Relais & Châteaux) in a huge wooded sporting estate. Sumptuously furnished, it has portraits, grand piano, antiques, flowers, billiards. 'The art is worth the trip in itself.' The owner, Mrs Constance Cluett Ward, is American, and so are many guests. Her manager, Anne Schaeflein, formerly worked at *Gleneagles*. Most bedrooms are large, with a view of the valley; three are in cottages. Extras include home-made shortbread. 'Each morning a chambermaid brings tea on a tray and lights the gas log fire.' Male guests wear a jacket at dinner in the restaurant (with delicate Adam-style frescoes), where Jean-Baptiste Bady serves a three-course Franco-Scottish set dinner (main courses like guineafowl, spiced aubergine cannelloni, Madeira sauce), using home-produced or local ingredients, The newly restored smokehouse supplies some unusual items for the tasting menu. The wine list offers many half bottles. Good breakfasts have freshly squeezed juice. Guests may fish for salmon and trout, and hone their skills on a 'cast and curl up' break with the estate's ghillies. (*Robert Gower*)

Bedrooms: 12, 1 on ground floor, 3 in 2 cottages in courtyard. *Open*: all year. *Facilities*: lift, ramp, lounge, 2 studies, billiard room, restaurant, dining room, function/wedding facilities, beauty/therapy room, 7,000-acre estate (gardens, tennis, croquet, shooting, walking, birdwatching, salmon fishing on Tay, 3 trout lochs). *Background music*: gramophone in lounge. *Location*: 5 miles NW of Dunkeld. *Smoking*: not allowed. *Children*: not under 8 in main dining room. *Dogs*: not allowed in house (heated kennels available). *Credit cards*: Amex, MasterCard, Visa. *Prices*: [2009] B&B £95–£260 per person, D,B&B £140–£295, set dinner £55, special breaks, Christmas/New Year packages, 1-night bookings sometimes refused at weekends.

DUNOON Argyll and Bute   *See Shortlist*

DUNVEGAN Highland   Map 5:C1

The Three Chimneys and	*Tel* 01470-511258
The House Over-By	*Fax* 01470-511358
Colbost, Dunvegan	*Email* eatandstay@threechimneys.co.uk
Isle of Skye IV55 8ZT	*Website* www.threechimneys.co.uk

❦ *César award in 2001*

'Despite the high prices, we consider it worth every penny.' This year's praise for Eddie and Shirley Spear's award-winning restaurant-with-rooms in a beautiful and remote setting by Loch Dunvegan in north-west Skye. The two-room restaurant is in a white-painted crofter's cottage; the split-level bedrooms are in the house 'over-by' (next door), which is built in a similar style. They have a modern decor (wood, natural fabrics, soft colours, uncluttered lines); large, comfortable beds, luxurious bathrooms; nothing can be seen from the windows but the sheep, and the sea. The restaurant has candles, dark beams, stone walls, a fire in the adjoining bar. Shirley Spear is the *patronne*/director; Michael Smith, the acclaimed chef, uses local meat and fish in dishes like Broadford hot-smoked salmon and smoked haddock, quail egg mimosa; roast saddle of Highland venison, Anna potatoes, celeriac remoulade. A 'perfect' lunch was enjoyed in 2009. Breakfast, taken in a morning room in *The House Over-By*, has freshly squeezed orange juice, fruit salad, cheeses, porridge, smoked fish; toast when requested, home-made marmalade and jams; a hot dish of the day (perhaps kipper fillets or smoked haddock). There are sitting areas, books, maps, Wi-Fi access. The single-track road between *The Three Chimneys* and the sea has light traffic by day; it is quiet at night. (*Paul Rouse, Richard Macey*)

Bedrooms: 6, all on ground floor in separate building, 1 suitable for ♿. *Open*: all year except 7–28 Jan, restaurant closed midday in winter, Sun lunch all year. *Facilities*: ramps, reception/lounge area/morning/breakfast room, bar, restaurant, garden on loch. *Background music*: in lounge/morning room at mealtimes. *Location*: 4 miles W of Dunvegan on B884 to Glendale. *Smoking*: not allowed. *Children*: all ages welcomed (under-6s stay free in parents' room), no under-8s at dinner. *Dogs*: only guide dogs allowed. *Credit cards*: Amex, MasterCard, Visa. *Prices*: B&B from £137.50 per person, D,B&B from £192.50, set dinner £55, autumn/winter/spring breaks, Christmas/New Year packages, 1-night bookings refused Sat in winter.

Most hotels have reduced rates out of season, and offer breaks throughout the year.

DUROR Argyll and Bute   Map 5:D1

Bealach House
Salachan Glen, Duror
Appin PA38 4BW

Tel 01631-740298
Email enquiries@bealach-house.co.uk
Website www.bealach-house.co.uk

♜ *César award in 2009*

'We arrived at 11 pm and were welcomed as if it were 4 pm. Our room was perfect, with a carafe of whisky by the bed – just what we needed to recover.' Typical warm praise for Jim and Hilary McFadyen who, without staff, run this small guest house, the only dwelling in the 'stunning' scenery of the Salachan Glen. Up a 'challenging' one-and-a-half-mile forestry track, it is a 'handsome, well-maintained' building inside and out. There is a log-burning stove in the comfortable lounge. Bedrooms, though not large, are 'warmly furnished', and have 'thick mattress, gorgeous soft pillows and duvet'. Bathrooms have a power shower (one also has a bath). Dinner is communally served, a daily-changing menu of three courses, each with three alternatives (including vegetarian). Hilary McFadyen is a 'superb' cook. A complimentary glass or two of 'very drinkable' wine is offered (no licence; guests may bring their own). 'If it can be made on the premises it is', including the cake with your tea on arrival, the breads, chutneys, jams and ice creams. 'Eggs, bacon, sausages and black pudding' for breakfast were 'heartbreakingly delicious', and there are 'unusual cereals and two kinds of marmalade'. Golden eagles and deer have been seen nearby. (*Ann Duncan, and many others*)

Bedrooms: 3. *Open*: Feb–Nov. *Facilities*: lounge, conservatory, dining room, 8-acre grounds. unsuitable for ♿. *Background music*: none. *Location*: 2 miles S of Duror, off A828. *Smoking*: not allowed. *Children*: not under 14. *Dogs*: not allowed. *Credit cards*: MasterCard, Visa. *Prices*: B&B £40–£55 per person, set dinner £28.

EDINBANE Highland   Map 5:C1

Greshornish House
Edinbane, by Portree
Isle of Skye IV51 9PN

Tel 01470-582266
Fax 01470-582345
Email info@greshornishhouse.com
Website www.greshornishhouse.com

'Wonderful, comfortable, elegant, in beautiful grounds', this listed, white country house (18th-century with Victorian additions) faces a sea loch in a remote corner of Skye. The owners, Neil and Rosemary Colquhoun, 'create a friendly atmosphere, but are not intrusive'. 'Neil was most helpful, and introduced us to a lovely walk across the peninsula,' say visitors this year who found this a 'relaxing place to stay'. Others thought it 'slightly formal, perhaps because other guests were less chatty than elsewhere'. Two of the bedrooms have a four-poster; some rooms are spacious, some, in the eaves, have a sloping ceiling. 'Our huge room had a particularly comfortable bed.' A smaller room, also comfortable, had 'lovely toiletries and the best bath of our trip'. Log fires burn in the public rooms. The drawing room and billiard room have been refurbished this year. Mac Browning, who has been promoted to head chef, uses local produce for his traditional menus, served in the candlelit restaurant (open to non-residents), eg, Skye salmon mayonnaise; escalope of venison, redcurrant jus; 'delicious breast of duck'. A seafood lunch menu is served in summer. Children get reduced rates, high chairs, cots, etc. (*Jane and Tony Cowan, Diana Goodey, CM*)

Bedrooms: 8. *Open*: Mar–Dec, restaurant closed Mon/Tues in winter. *Facilities*: drawing room, cocktail bar, billiard room, dining room, conservatory, wedding facilities, 10-acre grounds (croquet, tennis), sea loch, only public rooms accessible for &. *Background music*: classical/Celtic on request. *Location*: 17 miles NW of Portree. *Smoking*: not allowed. *Children*: all ages welcomed. *Dogs*: not allowed in public rooms, or unaccompanied in bedrooms. *Credit cards*: Amex, MasterCard, Visa. *Prices*: [2009] B&B £60–£102.50 per person, D,B&B £90–£132.50, set dinner £38–£45, seasonal and 3-day breaks, 1-night bookings sometimes refused at weekends in high season. *V*

EDINBURGH   Map 5:D2

Ingrams   *Tel* 0131-556 8140
24 Northumberland Street   *Fax* 0131-556 4423
Edinburgh EH3 6LS   *Email* info@ingrams.co.uk
                                            Website www.ingrams.co.uk

The slopes of Edinburgh's Georgian New Town are the setting for this 'elegant' B&B in a classically elegant town house. Its handsome stone staircase is lit by an oval cupola. Run by its owners, the 'attentive' David and Theresa Ingram, it is 'comfortable and convenient', and furnished with antiques (the 'forthright and entertaining' host is also an antique dealer). His breakfasts, served round one large table in the 'beautiful, formal' dining room, 'are a highlight, especially the amazing porridge, a gourmet delight'. As well as 'perfectly cooked' traditional fare, there is fresh fruit salad with rose water, home-made muesli, and 'fine coffee'. There are two twin-bedded bedrooms, and a double which faces the garden. 'My room,' said one visitor, 'was simple, well laid out and comfortable. Housekeeping standards were impressive.' Another visitor found his room 'cramped', and subject to overhead noise. Princes Street is within easy, though mostly uphill, walking distance, and restaurants of all kinds are nearby. (*John and Kay Patterson, MS, and others*)

Bedrooms: 3. *Open*: all year except Christmas. *Facilities*: sitting room, dining room, garden. *Background music*: baroque at breakfast if required. *Location*: New Town, 5 mins' walk from centre, parking for 3 cars, bus stop nearby. *Smoking*: not allowed. *Children*: not under 15. *Dogs*: not allowed. *Credit cards*: Diners, MasterCard, Visa. *Prices*: B&B £50–£65 per person.

See also Shortlist

EDNAM Borders   Map 5:E3

Edenwater House   *Tel/Fax* 01573-224070
Ednam, nr Kelso   *Email* jeffnjax@hotmail.co.uk
TD5 7QL   *Website* www.edenwaterhouse.co.uk

'Talented and creative' Jeff and Jacqui Kelly have 'sumptuously' decorated this old stone manse by the 17th-century kirk in a peaceful hamlet near Kelso. She formerly ran a restaurant in Edinburgh, and is 'a superb cook'. An American couple, who awarded 'the highest marks', 'thoroughly enjoyed life in a Scottish country house: collections everywhere, comfortable and beautiful furniture, all making a perfect whole'. There are lovely views over the pretty garden to the Eden Water which winds through fields and across to the Cheviots. Of the 'very comfortable' bedrooms, two face the river; one has a small single room adjacent. 'After a long day's hiking we looked forward to a cocktail by the fire in the lounge, sometimes with a chat with regular visitors.' In the 'exquisite' dining room (open at weekends to non-residents), the three-course candlelit dinner (no choice but guests' preferences and dietary needs are catered for) might include Parmesan-crusted Eyemouth scallops; roast squab and breast of dove with morels. 'Delicious' breakfasts have 'just about everything one could ask for'. (*T and RV*)

Bedrooms: 4. *Open*: Feb–mid-Dec. *Facilities*: lounge, drawing room, study, dining room, wedding facilities, 1-acre grounds, unsuitable for &. *Background *music*: none. *Location*: 2 miles N of Kelso on B6461. *Smoking*: not allowed. *Children*: not under 10. *Dogs*: not allowed. *Credit cards*: MasterCard, Visa. *Prices*: [2009] B&B £40–£65 per person, set dinner £35, 2-night breaks.

ELGIN Moray   *See Shortlist*

ERISKA Argyll and Bute   Map 5:D1

Isle of Eriska   *Tel* 01631-720371
Benderloch, Eriska   *Fax* 01631-720531
by Oban PA37 1SD   *Email* office@eriska-hotel.co.uk
                               Website www.eriska-hotel.co.uk

♕ *César award in 2007*

Reached by a wrought iron vehicle bridge, this Scottish baronial mansion (Pride of Britain) stands on a 'peaceful and beautiful' 300-acre private island. 'Remains the best hotel I know,' one devotee writes. 'Expensive, but still good value. Our dog enjoyed it as much as we did.' 'Smoothly run and beautifully kept', 'more resort than hotel', it is run in a 'discreet and understated way', by brothers Beppo and Chay Buchanan-Smith. Your car is parked, cases carried by the 'unfailingly friendly, courteous', mainly young, staff. There are wellington boots by the entrance, a year-round log fire, panelled lounges, large sofas 'where sinking into the cushions and dozing is almost obligatory'. 'Immaculate' bedrooms vary from 'traditional' in the main building ('ours had sofa, decent-sized TV, huge bed, made while we breakfasted') to modern spa suites in the grounds, each with conservatory and private garden with hot tub. Robert MacPherson's six-course dinners in the newly refurbished dining room (male guests wear jacket and tie) are 'consistently good': 'home-cured ham carved from the trolley; an impressive cheeseboard; delicious desserts like chestnut parfait'. Light meals are served on a veranda. Breakfasts have 'limitless fresh orange juice'; 'wonderful haddock and kippers'. 'Morning coffee/tea and afternoon tea with cakes freely available within the tariff.' (*Roland Cassam, David EW Jervois, Joanna Russell*)

Bedrooms: 23, including 5 spa suites and 2 garden cottages, some on ground floor. *Open*: all year except Jan. *Facilities*: ramp, hall, drawing room, library, dining room, leisure centre (swimming pool (17 by 6 metres), gym, sauna, massage, beauty treatments, bar, restaurant), wedding facilities, 300-acre island (tennis, croquet, 6-hole par 22 golf course, marked walks, clay-pigeon shooting). *Background music*: none. *Location*: 12 miles N of Oban. *Smoking*: allowed in 16 bedrooms. *Children*: all ages welcomed, but no under-5s in swimming pool. *Dogs*: not allowed in public rooms or unaccompanied in bedrooms. *Credit cards*: Amex, MasterCard, Visa. *Prices*: B&B £115–£210 per person, D,B&B (*min. advance reservation 2 nights*) £150–£300, set dinner £40, off-season breaks, Christmas/New Year packages, 1-night bookings sometimes refused. *V*

FORT AUGUSTUS Highland   Map 5:C2

Lovat Arms   NEW

Fort Augustus
PH32 4DU

Tel 01320-366366
Fax 01320-366677
Email info@lovatarms-hotel.com
Website www.lovatarms-hotel.com

On the southern shore of Loch Ness, this former railway hotel has been renovated by experienced hoteliers David and Geraldine Gregory – who ran *The Torridon*, Torridon (*qv*) for ten years – and their daughter Caroline, the managing partner. 'What a good job they have made of it, mixing the traditional with the modern,' say the nominators. 'Caroline is out to make her mark and she has certainly excelled here.' A green policy is followed: a biomass woodchip burner provides heating and hot water, eco-friendly cleaning products are used, as are energy-saving lamps. 'The staff, mainly female, are attentive: we made four suggestions on a card in the room which asked how they could improve; all were attended to within hours.' Colin Clark is the chef, serving a brasserie menu (eg, battered Mallaig haddock and chips) and more formal restaurant dishes, like goat's cheese mousse, pear purée; haunch of venison, braised red cabbage. 'After a light-hearted comment about the difficulty of finding apple pie in the Highlands, we were presented with a great specially made dessert; that's service.' The Gregorys' other daughter, Rohaise, and her husband, Daniel Rose-Bristow, now own and run *The Torridon*. (*Michael and Maureen Heath*)

Bedrooms: 28, 6 in annexe, 2 suitable for &. *Open*: all year. *Facilities*: lounge, 2 bars, 4 dining rooms, 2¾-acre grounds. *Background music*: in bar. *Location*: in village SW of Inverness by A82. *Smoking*: not allowed. *Children*: all ages welcomed. *Dogs*: allowed in 1 bedroom only. *Credit cards*: Amex, MasterCard, Visa. *Prices*: [2009] B&B £40–£130 per person, D,B&B £100, set meals £26–£35, full alc £50, special breaks, Christmas/New Year packages.

Hotels do not pay to be included in the *Guide*.

FORT WILLIAM Highland   Map 5:C1

The Grange   *Tel* 01397-705516
Grange Road   *Email* info@thegrange-scotland.co.uk
Fort William PH33 6JF   *Website* www.thegrange-scotland.co.uk

'The welcome and desire to make our stay enjoyable were outstanding,' say visitors this year to Joan and John Campbell's B&B. The
white-painted Victorian Gothic house stands in a 'lovely, peaceful
garden', and has 'stunning' views over Loch Linnhe. Earlier visitors,
'after being wowed by our room, took tea and shortcake in the
beautiful lounge'. Each bedroom is different: the Garden Room ('the
most peaceful') faces the loch; west-facing Rob Roy, with colonial-
style bed, is where Jessica Lange stayed while making that film; the
Turret Room has a window seat with garden and loch views and a
Louis XV king-size bed; the Terrace Room, with a private terrace
facing the garden, has a king-size bed and Victorian slipper bath.
Visitors like the 'fresh flowers from the garden', 'the little extras:
towels tied up with a ribbon; decanter of sherry with lovely glassware'.
At breakfast (ordered the evening before), 'we enjoyed the poached
haddock, and the fresh fruit and yogurt'. 'My poached eggs arrived
with a flower; porridge came with whisky, cream, brown sugar and
honey.' (*John and Sylvia Barns, CW*)

Bedrooms: 4. *Open*: Mar–Nov. *Facilities*: lounge, breakfast room, 1-acre garden,
unsuitable for &. *Background music*: none. *Location*: edge of town. *Smoking*: not
allowed. *Children*: not under 12. *Dogs*: not allowed. *Credit cards*: MasterCard, Visa.
Prices: [2009] B&B £55–£59 per person, 1-night bookings sometimes refused.

See also Shortlist

FORTROSE Highland   *See Shortlist*

GATEHOUSE OF FLEET   *See Shortlist*
Dumfries and Galloway

Everyone who writes to the *Guide* is a potential winner of the
Report of the Year competition (page 10)

GATESIDE Fife   Map 5:D2

Edenshead Stables   *Tel/Fax* 01337-868500
Gateside, by Cupar   *Email* info@edensheadstables.com
KY14 7ST   *Website* www.edensheadstables.com

'Delightful' owners Gill and John Donald have turned derelict pink
stone stables on the edge of a village into this modern 'luxury B&B'.
Set in wooded grounds, it has fine views of the Lomond hills, and the
River Eden borders its garden. The 'air of relaxed comfort' is admired,
as is the 'good value'. 'It's a bit of an Aladdin's cave,' wrote a visitor
who 'really enjoyed' his visit. 'Far bigger inside than you'd expect.'
The 'immaculate' interior is filled with 'beautiful furnishings, lovely
paintings'. The dining room is 'elegant' and 'formal', and the large,
comfortable sitting room, leading on to a patio, contains books, maps
and local information. The bedrooms, one with a four-poster, have an
'upmarket' bathroom with an 'excellent' shower. Guests sit round one
big table for breakfast, served 7.45–8.45 am (earlier by arrangement).
It includes local kippers, Arbroath smokies, oatmeal porridge, black
pudding, home-made preserves. Dinner (three courses) can be
arranged for groups of four to six. Bring your own wine (free corkage).
There are pubs and restaurants to 'suit all pockets' nearby. The single-
storey house is suitable for physically disabled guests, but not
wheelchair-bound ones. Many golf courses are nearby. No visiting
dogs, but look out for the owners' two Hungarian vizslas, Rosa and
Zeta. (*John and Annette Kinsella, JH*)

Bedrooms: 3, all on ground floor. *Open*: March–end Nov. *Facilities*: lounge, dining
room, patio, courtyard, 3-acre grounds bordering River Eden, unsuitable
for &. *Background music*: none. *Location*: on edge of village 12 miles SE of Perth,
train to Ladybank/Cupar/Kirkcaldy. *Smoking*: not allowed. *Children*: not under
12. *Dogs*: not allowed. *Credit cards*: Amex, MasterCard, Visa. *Prices*: B&B
£40–£55 per person, set dinner £25, off-season breaks, 1-night bookings
occasionally refused weekends and July/Aug.

GIFFORD East Lothian   Map 5:D3

Eaglescairnie Mains   *Tel/Fax* 01620-810491
Gifford, nr Haddington   *Email* williams.eagles@btinternet.com
EH41 4HN   *Website* www.eaglescairnie.com

On a working farm that has won awards for its green policies, this
'impeccable' white-painted Georgian B&B is run 'on very personal
lines' by Michael and Barbara Williams. In deepest countryside, the

house is 'quiet and tranquil'. 'It makes reasonable lodging within easy reach of Edinburgh (18 miles),' said one visitor, recommending the park and ride facility. The house is 'full of character': the drawing room is 'tasteful and comfortable', with coral walls, chintz sofas, an open fire, books, board games, television. Wi-Fi is now available. The bedrooms are spacious, with matching curtains and fabrics; a tea and coffee tray, a radio, and a folder of local information; a shower over the bath in the *en suite* bathroom. In summer, breakfast is taken in a conservatory; Mrs Williams uses farm and local produce; hot dishes are cooked to order. Mr Williams runs the farm with a neighbour on ecological lines, seeking 'to unite wildlife and landscape conservation with profitable modern agriculture'. No evening meal; there are two pubs in Gifford, a mile away. 'Unlimited' golf courses are within ten miles. (*JR*)

Bedrooms: 3. *Open*: all year except Christmas week. *Facilities*: sitting room, conservatory, large garden (tennis) in 350-acre farmland, unsuitable for &. *Background music*: none. *Location*: 1 mile W of Gifford, 4 miles SE of Haddington. *Smoking*: not allowed. *Children*: all ages welcomed. *Dogs*: allowed by prior arrangement. *Credit cards*: MasterCard, Visa. *Prices*: [2009] B&B £35–£50 per person, discount for 4-night stay, 1-night bookings refused Fri and Sat in July/Aug, bank holiday weekends.

GIGHA Argyll and Bute   *See Shortlist*

GLAMIS Angus   Map 5:D2

Castleton House   *Tel* 01307-840340
by Glamis   *Fax* 01307-840506
DD8 1SJ   *Email* hotel@castletonglamis.co.uk
                          Website www.castletonglamis.co.uk

Built on the site of a medieval fortress, this Edwardian stone country house is surrounded by a dry moat. It is close to a main road, but sheltered by tall trees; there are good woodland walks from the pretty garden. Run by its owners, David and Verity Webster, it is liked for the warmth of welcome and the elegance of the bedrooms – they have antiques, good artwork, digital TV, flowers, mineral water, coffee and tea. All the bathrooms have been upgraded this year. Mrs Webster, an interior designer, styled the elegant public rooms with tasteful colour schemes; complimentary afternoon tea on arrival can be taken in front of a log fire in the drawing room. There is no dress code in either of the dining rooms, one in an attractive conservatory. Matt Dobson has joined as chef from a sister hotel, *Raemoir House*, Banchory. He cooks Scottish dishes with European influences, eg, terrine of rabbit and pigeon, date relish; baked wild sea bass, dauphinoise potatoes, braised fennel. Vegetables and herbs come from the kitchen garden; eggs from the hotel's free-range chickens (one reader enthused about the scrambled eggs at breakfast). Mrs Webster tells us that they no longer rear pigs, and that dairy farming has been given up on the farm nearby ('temporary rural smells are no more'). Children are welcomed (special menus, climbing frame, etc). (*R and TB*)

Bedrooms: 6. *Open*: all year except 2 weeks at Christmas/New Year. *Facilities*: drawing room, library/bar, conservatory/dining room, dining room, conference/wedding facilities, 10-acre grounds (stream, climbing frame, croquet, putting), only restaurant suitable for &. *Background music*: 'gentle jazz' in dining rooms and bar. *Location*: on A94 Perth–Forfar, W of Glamis. *Smoking*: not allowed. *Children*: all ages welcomed. *Dogs*: allowed. *Credit cards*: Amex, MasterCard, Visa. *Prices*: [2009] B&B £80–£95 per person, D,B&B £105–£120, full alc £45, special breaks. *V*

GLASGOW   *See Shortlist*

GLENFINNAN Highland   Map 5:C1

Glenfinnan House   *Tel/Fax* 01397-722235
Glenfinnan   *Email* availability@glenfinnanhouse.com
by Fort William PH37 4LT   *Website* www.glenfinnanhouse.com

Dramatically situated on the shores of Loch Shiel, with a view of Ben Nevis, *Glenfinnan House* gave a 'warm welcome' to a *Guide* correspondent this year. With 'a hint of small medieval French château' about it, it looks across the water to the Glenfinnan Monument where Bonnie Prince Charlie, fresh from exile in France, raised the standard at the start of the 1745 Jacobite Rebellion. Inside, its style is traditional country house, with wood panelling. Owned by Jane MacFarlane-Glasow and managed by Manja and Duncan Gibson ('we are proud to have no TV in the bedrooms,' they say), it is locally popular for celebrations of all kinds. The rooms at the front have 'superb views'; one has a four-poster. Noise may be a problem in some attic bedrooms. 'The food was excellent: fine cuisine in the restaurant.' Duncan Gibson ('we do not serve fast food') provides French-influenced Scottish dishes, eg, nage of West Coast king scallops; fillet of prime Scotch beef with herb creamed potatoes. The bar meals, also liked, are more traditionally Scottish. There is also a 'good-value' children's menu. Breakfast has croissants, home-baked bread, and unusual additions, eg, smoked local venison. Meals are accompanied by CDs of local musicians. There is Wi-Fi, and the hotel has its own rowing boat and fishing tackle. (*Margaret Ritchie, SH, MWS*)

Bedrooms: 13. *Open*: mid-Mar–end of Oct. *Facilities*: ramps, hall, drawing room, playroom, bar, restaurant, function/conference/wedding facilities, 1-acre grounds, children's playground, unsuitable for &. *Background music*: Scottish CDs, bar and restaurant. *Location*: 15 miles NW of Fort William. *Smoking*: not allowed. *Children*: all ages welcomed (under-12s accommodated free). *Dogs*: not allowed in restaurant. *Credit cards*: all major cards. *Prices*: [2009] B&B £45–£80 per person, D,B&B £75–£110, set meals £28.50–£34.50, special breaks (see website). *V*

See also Shortlist

GRANTOWN-ON-SPEY Highland   Map 5:C2

Culdearn House
Woodlands Terrace
Grantown-on-Spey PH26 3JU

Tel 01479-872106
Fax 01479-873641
Email enquiries@culdearn.com
Website www.culdearn.com

Once the country home of the Earls of Seafield, this Victorian granite house, on the edge of a picturesque Speyside market town, is run as an 'unassuming' hotel by its owners, William and Sonia Marshall. They are 'business-like, friendly', say visitors who enjoyed tea by a 'welcoming' log fire. Mrs Marshall, a 'very good cook', serves a four-course dinner in a candlelit dining room (open to non-residents), also with log fire. 'Thoughtful combinations included venison with blackberries and chocolate sauce (gorgeous); a beautiful local fillet steak; best of all, seasonal fresh vegetables were served separately; a Pavlova was delightfully soft.' Of the 'immaculate' bedrooms, 'our spacious room had a nice firm bed; the bathroom was chilly; they turned the heating on early for us'. The lounge has original wood panelling, 'lots of easy armchairs and sofas', watercolours, antique maps, a fine choice of malt whiskies. 'Breakfasts were splendid;

porridge, fruits, delicious potato scones, plenty of cooked choices; wholemeal bread with a nutty crunch.' Salmon and sea-trout fishing on the Spey, as well as private beats with ghillie service, can be arranged. Anagach Woods adjoin the garden. (*Jill and Mike Bennett*)

Bedrooms: 6, 1 on ground floor. *Open*: all year. *Facilities*: lounge, dining room, ¾-acre garden. *Background music*: pre-dinner classical in lounge. *Location*: edge of town, by Anagach Woods. *Smoking*: not allowed. *Children*: not under 10. *Dogs*: only guide dogs allowed. *Credit cards*: Diners, MasterCard, Visa. *Prices*: [2009] B&B £58–£83 per person, D,B&B £89–£110, set dinner £34, spring/autumn breaks, reduced rates for 4–7 nights, Christmas/New Year packages.

The Pines   `NEW`

Tel/Fax 01479-872092
Woodside Avenue
Email info@thepinesgrantown.co.uk
Grantown-on-Spey PH26 3JR   *Website* www.thepinesgrantown.co.uk

Beside woodland on the outskirts of the historic Speyside town, this Victorian house is run as a small hotel by Michael and Gwen Stewart, who are 'charming, helpful' owners. It is 'beautifully kept, and adorned with original paintings and *objets d'art*'. There are two 'elegantly furnished' lounges (one on the first floor), and a 'well-stocked' library which has maps and tourist information. The bedrooms vary in size and style; all have a refreshment tray, fresh flowers, and an evening turn-down service. Guests are invited to take drinks and canapés at 7 pm in the downstairs lounge. 'Mrs Stewart does all the cooking, and very good she is, too, producing a different menu each day.' The no-choice four-course meal (including cheese) is discussed at breakfast (alternatives are available). It might include rarebit of smoked haddock; Moray rump steak bourguignon, crushed new potatoes. 'Special attention was given to my wife's allergies. The best-value wine list we have seen for some time.' Breakfasts are

'unimprovable: proper butter, marmalade in a dish, freshly squeezed orange juice'; cooked dishes include pancakes with crispy bacon, maple syrup. Guests are encouraged to 'relax in the gardens' where red squirrels and capercailzie might be seen; a gate leads into 'The Wild Woods of Anagach', mixed woodland that is part of the Cairngorm national park. (*Colin Fielder, and others*)

Bedrooms: 5, 1 on ground floor. *Open*: Mar–Oct. *Facilities*: 2 lounges, library, dining room, 1-acre garden. *Background music*: none. *Location*: on outskirts of town. *Smoking*: not allowed. *Children*: not under 12. *Dogs*: not allowed in public rooms. *Credit cards*: MasterCard, Visa. *Prices*: [2009] B&B £63 per person, D,B&B £96, set dinner £33.

See also Shortlist

GRULINE Argyll and Bute   Map 5:D1

Gruline Home Farm	*Tel* 01680-300581
Gruline, Isle of Mull	*Email* boo@gruline.com
PA71 6HR	*Website* www.gruline.com

Once again, everything was found 'first class' at this 'handsome' conversion of a non-working 19th-century farmhouse and its outbuildings overlooking the foothills of Ben More on a remote peninsula. For 11 years it has been run by the 'warmly welcoming' (except to children) owners, Colin (the chef) and Angela Boocock. They tell us that they will review their plans for retirement at the end of the 2010 season: 'Many of our guests return year on year, and we feel we would be letting them down.' Access is along a long, rough drive, and arriving guests are given afternoon tea in a conservatory. The house is well decorated: good antique and modern furniture. All the bedrooms have been refurbished this year, and there are new carpets, curtains and furniture. In the 'attractive' dining room, open to non-residents, a dinner-party atmosphere is encouraged. 'Colin's cooking and presentation skills appear endless; Angela maintains her enthusiasm in her fine delivery of everything.' The four-course dinner might include pan-fried prawn tails in a ginger and cream sauce; escalope of venison in a juniper and red wine sauce. No licence (bring your own wine; no corkage charged), but you are offered complimentary sherry. Breakfast has 'outstanding' warm fruit compote, and lots of cooked dishes. (*Joan and David Marston*)

Bedrooms: 3, 1, on ground floor, 5 yds from main house. *Open*: Apr–Oct. *Facilities*: lounge, conservatory, dining room, 2½-acre garden, stream. *Background music*: light classical always. *Location*: 2½ miles from Salen village, 14 miles S of Tobermory. *Smoking*: not allowed. *Children*: not under 16. *Dogs*: allowed in annexe bedroom only. *Credit cards*: none. *Prices*: D,B&B (min. 2 nights) £100 per person, set dinner £40.

INVERGARRY Highland   Map 5:C2

Tomdoun Hotel   NEW   *Tel* 01809-511218
Invergarry   *Email* enquiries@tomdoun.com
PH35 4HS   *Website* www.tomdoun.com

Among hills and woodland overlooking the Upper Garry river, Mike Pearson's simple sporting hotel is off the single-track drovers' road to Skye. It is recommended as an 'unreconstructed hideaway with old-world charm'. There is no TV, telephone or tea-making equipment in the bedrooms. 'The interior possesses a shabby charm: there are roaring log fires, squashy sofas to lounge in after a day's walking or fishing.' Front bedrooms have views of Glengarry; simpler, cheaper rooms share a bathroom. Guests can eat in the bar (popular with locals and holidaymakers) or in the dining room, where David Errington's cooking is praised (even by visitors who would have liked more facilities in their room). 'From a choice of halibut, langoustines, roll-mop herrings and smoked salmon, each dish was beautifully presented with the perfect accompaniment, be it chopped fennel, puréed peas, velvety sauces, nut-brown crisp coatings.' Sporting pursuits include excellent fishing, and walking (from the door or to 30 Munros near at hand). (*Rosemary Logan, and others*)

Bedrooms: 10, 5 with facilities *en suite*. *Open*: all year. *Facilities*: drawing room, bar, dining room, 80-acre grounds (fishing, walking, stalking, shooting, mountain biking). *Background music*: none. *Location*: 10 miles W of Invergarry; 6 miles off A87. *Smoking*: not allowed. *Children*: all ages welcomed. *Dogs*: allowed. *Credit cards*: Diners, MasterCard, Visa. *Prices*: B&B £40–£65 per person, set meal £13.95, full alc £35, 1-night bookings refused high-season weekends. ***V***

The ***V*** sign at the end of an entry indicates that a hotel has agreed to take part in our Voucher scheme and to give *Guide* readers a 25% discount on their bed-and-breakfast rates for a one-night stay, subject to the conditions on the back of the voucher and explained in 'How to use the *Good Hotel Guide*' (page 57).

INVERNESS Highland   Map 5:C2

Trafford Bank Guest House   `NEW`   *Tel* 01463-241414
96 Fairfield Road   *Fax* 01463-241421
Inverness IV3 5II   *Email* info@traffordbankguesthouse.co.uk
                         Website www.traffordbankguesthouse.co.uk

'Lorraine Freel and Koshal Pun have taken a former bishop's house
and turned it into a superb B&B,' say regular *Guide* readers. 'The best
accommodation we have found in Inverness.' In mature gardens, the
house is a short walk from the centre. Ms Freel, an interior designer,
has furnished it with a mix of antiques and contemporary furniture
(some of which she designed herself). Free Wi-Fi is available
throughout. Most of the 'luxurious' bedrooms are large. All have a
hospitality tray, decanter of sherry, silent fridge, flat-screen television.
The Floral suite has a large, modern half-tester bed; a roll-top bath.
The Trafford suite has a king-size bed and a day bed. The Green
room is suitable for a small family. Breakfast, ordered the evening
before, 'hits the right buttons; excellent choices, served piping hot'.
(*Michael and Maureen Heath*)

Bedrooms: 5. *Open*: all year except 21 Nov–15 Dec. *Facilities*: ramps, 2 lounges,
conservatory, garden, unsuitable for &. *Background music*: none. *Location*:
10 mins' walk from centre. *Smoking*: not allowed. *Children*: all ages welcomed.
Dogs: only guide dogs allowed. *Credit cards*: MasterCard, Visa. *Prices*: [2009]
B&B £40–£90 per person. *V*

See also Shortlist

IONA Argyll and Bute   Map 5:D1

Argyll Hotel   *Tel* 01681-700334
Isle of Iona PA76 6SJ   *Fax* 01681-700510
                         Email reception@argyllhoteliona.co.uk
                         Website www.argyllhoteliona.co.uk

'A delightful hotel on a magical island,' writes a visitor in 2009 to this,
the smaller of Iona's two hotels. Part of a row of 19th-century houses in
the main village, it is a short walk from the jetty where the ferry from
Mull docks. There are 'idyllic views' over the sound from its book-filled
lounges (one with open fire) and conservatory. Owners Daniel Morgan
and Claire Bachellerie and manager Jann Simpson are ecologically

committed. They are locals, as are most of their 'delightful' staff. When possible, produce and resources are acquired locally; waste is recycled or composted. 'The good food is the centre of this hotel,' said a visitor who thought the soups 'outstanding'. Chef Peter Janicina's chatty menus use local lamb and fish, and vegetables and herbs grown in the organic kitchen garden. One guest disliked the 'inappropriate beat music at mealtimes; it percolated into some bedrooms'. Children are welcomed (early supper provided), so are dogs, 'but local crofters insist they be exercised on a lead'. Some bedrooms are small (best ones are in the main house); housekeeping 'could be better', but they have 'good storage, pleasant watercolours, paperback books and a well-planned bathroom'. (*Richard Macey, and others*)

Bedrooms: 16, 7 (cheaper) in annexe. *Open*: Mar–Oct. *Facilities*: 2 lounges, conservatory, TV/computer room, restaurant, large organic garden, unsuitable for &. *Background music*: in restaurant. *Location*: village centre. *Smoking*: not allowed. *Children*: all ages welcomed. *Dogs*: not allowed in dining room, £10 charge per stay. *Credit cards*: MasterCard, Visa. *Prices*: [2009] B&B £26–£87.50 per person, full alc £30, 1-night bookings sometimes refused.

KELSO Borders   *See Shortlist*

KILBERRY Argyll and Bute   **Map 5:D1**

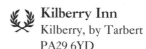
Kilberry Inn   *Tel* 01880-770223
Kilberry, by Tarbert   *Email* relax@kilberryinn.com
PA29 6YD   *Website* www.kilberryinn.com

César award: Inn of the year

'Beautifully set' on the remote Kintyre peninsula, this unpretentious small restaurant-with-rooms is liked for the 'amazing scenery, great hospitality and sublime food'. 'It has a happy atmosphere,' write inspectors in 2009. 'Accommodation is simple but much more than adequate. Service is deft, unobtrusive and highly personal.' A *Michelin Bib Gourmand*, for good cooking at moderate prices, goes to co-owner Clare Johnson ('we like to keep things simple, emphasis on seafood in summer, red meat and game in winter'), now assisted by Tom Holloway. Her partner, David Wilson, is 'on hand to provide ideas for beach walks and local whisky', and 'runs front-of-house with friendly efficiency'. Beams and bare stone walls with local artwork 'give plenty of character' to the two dining rooms (there is no lounge).

'Langoustines caught that morning; rack of blackface lamb – both a triumph. Vegetables sometimes let down a meal: not here; all were splendid.' 'Hearty' breakfasts include smoothies, scrambled eggs with smoked salmon, home-made marmalade. The 'stylish, modern' bedrooms (one more this year) in adjacent single-storey buildings are 'immaculate' and have their own small hallway, a shower, and 'melt-in-the-mouth home-made ginger biscuits'. A good base for trips to Arran, Gigha, walking, sailing, seeing otters and 'fabulous sunsets'. (*Margaret and Marc Wall, Robert and Shirley Lyne, and others*)

Bedrooms: 5, all on ground floor. *Open*: 19 March–2 Jan, Tues–Sun, weekends only Nov and Dec. *Facilities*: bar/dining room, smaller dining room, small grounds. *Background music*: in larger dining room, lunch and dinner. *Location*: 16 miles SW of Tarbert, on B8024. *Smoking*: not allowed. *Children*: no under-12s in bedrooms (any age allowed in small dining room). *Dogs*: not allowed in public rooms, 4 bedrooms. *Credit cards*: MasterCard, Visa. *Prices*: [2009] D,B&B £87.50 per person, full alc £35, winter breaks, New Year package, 1-night bookings sometimes refused weekends in summer.

KILCHRENAN Argyll and Bute   Map 5:D1

Ardanaiseig

Kilchrenan
by Taynuilt PA35 1HE

Tel 01866-833333
Fax 01866-833222
Email ardanaiseig@clara.net
Website www.ardanaiseig.com

Remotely set in large grounds on Loch Awe, this grey stone baronial mansion has been filled with antiques, bold colour schemes, tapestries and rich furnishings by its owner Bennie Gray, of Gray's Antiques Market in London. Peter Webster is the manager. 'Good service, good food,' say visitors in 2009. Many of the 'opulently furnished' bedrooms have loch views ('I saw an osprey'). One has apple-green walls, one has Chinese-style lacquered furnishings and an open-plan 'bathing room' with a central bath big enough for two. A boathouse has been converted into a 'romantic' suite with modern decor, double-height windows and a glass balustrade giving an uninterrupted view of the water. Beds are large; there are some four-posters. Open fires burn in the long drawing room, which has panelled walls painted in mottled gold, and in the more intimate library bar. In the candlelit dining room, Gary Goldie's no-choice four-course dinners use local produce in dishes like 'a wonderful scallop and courgette starter'; Aberdeen Angus Wellington with shallot purée, wild mushrooms. Breakfast ('plenty of choice') has brown toast, and honey and preserves in jars.

Guests can go in the hotel's boats to its own island. Performances of song and dance are sometimes held in a small amphitheatre in the grounds. The walled garden is said to be in need of attention. (*AB, Josie and Guy Mayers, and others*)

Bedrooms: 18, some on ground floor, 1 in boat house, 1 self-catering cottage. *Open*: 1 Feb–2 Jan. *Facilities*: drawing room, library/bar, restaurant, wedding facilities, 350-acre grounds on loch (formal garden, open-air theatre, tennis, croquet, safe bathing, fishing, boating). *Background music*: classical/jazz in restaurant. *Location*: 3 miles E of Kilchrenan, by Loch Awe. *Smoking*: not allowed. *Children*: all ages welcomed, but no under-12s at dinner. *Dogs*: not allowed in public rooms. *Credit cards*: all major cards. *Prices*: B&B £64–£212 per person, set dinner £50, spring/autumn reductions (3 nights for the price of 2), special breaks (mid-summer madness, autumn gold, etc), Christmas/New Year packages. *V*

KILDRUMMY Aberdeenshire   *See Shortlist*

KILLIECRANKIE Perth and Kinross   Map 5:D2

Killiecrankie Hotel
Killiecrankie
by Pitlochry PH16 5LG

Tel 01796-473220
Fax 01796-472451
Email enquiries@killiecrankiehotel.co.uk
Website www.killiecrankiehotel.co.uk

Owner Henrietta Fergusson 'is a real star: her warmth, humour and professionalism make this a most welcoming hotel'. Praise comes from many *Guide* readers this year for the white-painted dower house which she has extensively refurbished. Overlooking the River Garry, it stands in peaceful grounds at the entrance to the Pass of Killiecrankie, 'gateway to the Highlands'. 'The staff rushed out to help with our luggage; the atmosphere was welcoming and relaxed.' 'Our ground-floor suite was spacious and beautifully furnished; hot-water bottles at turn-down.' In the handsome, candlelit dining room, tables are well spaced; 'no muzak, thank goodness'. Chef Mark Easton's modern British cooking was found 'consistently excellent' in dishes like terrine of pork, hare and pigeon; sea bream, seared monkfish cheek and cockles, potato and onion rösti. Special diets are catered for. 'Breakfast was even better': 'freshly squeezed orange juice, porridge, very good bacon and sausages, excellent toast and world-class coffee'. There is a 'lovely garden where you can sit during the long summer evenings'. Much wildlife – roe deer, red squirrels, birds, etc – is in the grounds and beyond. Pitlochry Festival Theatre is nearby. 'Our children loved the games room.' (*Roland and Diana Fernsby, Alan and Edwina Williams, Bob and Brenda Halstead, Thomas Gibson*)

Bedrooms: 10, 2 on ground floor. *Open*: early Mar–3 Jan. *Facilities*: ramp, sitting room, bar with conservatory, dining room, breakfast conservatory, 4½-acre grounds, unsuitable for &. *Background music*: none. *Location*: hamlet 3 miles W of Pitlochry. *Smoking*: not allowed. *Children*: all ages welcomed. *Dogs*: not allowed in eating areas, some bedrooms. *Credit cards*: MasterCard, Visa. *Prices*: [2009] B&B £75–£85 per person, D,B&B £89–£119, set dinner £38, special breaks, Christmas/New Year packages, 1-night bookings sometimes refused. *V*

KINGUSSIE Highland   Map 5:C2

The Cross at Kingussie
Tweed Mill Brae, Ardbroilach Road
Kingussie PH21 1LB

Tel 01540-661166
Fax 01540-661080
Email relax@thecross.co.uk
Website www.thecross.co.uk

For first-time visitors, this restaurant-with-rooms 'exceeded expectations in all respects'. Returning guests in 2009 were equally enthusiastic: 'A brilliant place to stay.' The converted tweed mill stands in wooded grounds with abundant wildlife by the River Gynack in the Cairngorm national park. The owners, David and Katie Young, and their staff are friendly; 'seldom have we eaten better'. David Young, a former AA hotel inspector, shares the cooking with Becca Henderson, using Scottish produce 'carefully but simply' on a short menu. Typical dishes: shallot tarte Tatin, goat's cheese emulsion; wild Shetland pollack, olive and chickpea confit. Vegetarians and those with other dietary requirements should give advance warning. There is a pretty terrace where champagne is served in summer, whisky in winter. Interiors are 'light and bright'; modern Scottish art hangs on the walls. Most bedrooms are spacious, with a king-size bed; they have books, music, ample lighting, 'top-quality toiletries', tea-making facilities on request. 'Riverside rooms have nice views and are very comfortable.' Breakfast, 'the one against which I judge all others', has freshly squeezed juices, fruit, fresh-baked croissants, and a hot dish of the day, perhaps buttermilk pancakes with blueberries. *The Cross* was named restaurant-with-rooms of the year in the 2009 Scottish Hotel Awards. (*Brian Bellamy, Tony and Marlene Hall*)

Bedrooms: 8. *Open*: early Feb–mid-Dec, New Year, normally closed Sun/Mon except Easter. *Facilities*: 2 lounges, restaurant, 4-acre grounds (woodland, river (no bathing/fishing), *pétanque*), only restaurant suitable for &. *Background music*: none. *Location*: 440 yds from village centre. *Smoking*: not allowed. *Children*: no toddlers or young children. *Dogs*: not allowed. *Credit cards*: Amex, MasterCard, Visa. *Prices*: [2009] B&B £45–£125 per person, D,B&B £90–£170, set dinner £50, full alc £60–£65, special breaks, website offers, New Year package.

KIRKCOLM Dumfries and Galloway   Map 5:E1

Corsewall Lighthouse
Corsewall Point
Kirkcolm, Stranraer
DG9 0QG

Tel 01776-853220
Fax 01776-854231
Email info@lighthousehotel.co.uk
Website www.lighthousehotel.co.uk

'The perfect place to wind down', this listed working lighthouse (built in 1815) is run as a hotel by the Ward family, Gordon, Kay and Pamela. It stands on a windy promontory north of Stranraer, on Loch Ryan. 'Quite remote, and not for those who want the bright lights', it is down a roughish track ('not for the nervous'). 'Gordon and his staff were attentive,' says a visitor who booked *Corsewall* for a wedding in 2009. Some bedrooms, with shower, are in the main building (some are small). Three suites are in separate buildings (one is 'almost on the rocks'). 'Ours had an average-size bedroom and a large conservatory lounge with panoramic views.' In the restaurant (with black beams and seascapes), chef Andrew Downie's daily-changing five-course dinner menu might include Marrbury smoked duck supreme ('from our local smokehouse'); roast monkfish fillet with citrus-scented redcurrant and port wine jus. One couple found the cooking 'inconsistent: perfect salmon, sea bass overcooked; excellent chocolate fondant'. Mr Ward has put *Corsewall* on the market; he tells us he wants to retire but an early sale is not expected. Check before booking. (*Jane Eden, and others*)

Bedrooms: 10, some on ground floor, 1 suitable for &, 3 suites in grounds. *Open*: all year. *Facilities*: 2 small lounges, restaurant, function/conference facilities, wedding facilities, 20-acre grounds (golf, pony trekking, birdwatching, walking nearby). *Background music*: in hall and restaurant. *Location*: 5 miles N of Stranraer. *Smoking*: not allowed. *Children*: all ages welcomed. *Dogs*: allowed in 3 designated suites. *Credit cards*: all major cards. *Prices*: [2009] B&B £55–£120 per person, D,B&B £75–£140, set menu £32.50, full alc £45, 3-night midweek breaks, Christmas/New Year packages, 1-night bookings refused Sat in season.

KIRKCUDBRIGHT
Dumfries and Galloway   **Map 5:E2**

Gladstone House
48 High Street
Kirkcudbright DG6 4JX

Tel/Fax 01557-331734
Email hilarygladstone@aol.com
Website www.kirkcudbrightgladstone.com

'Gordon and Hilary Cowan were as welcoming as ever,' say visitors returning again in 2009 to this small guest house, an elegant, Grade II listed Georgian building in the centre of this pleasant little town (pronounced Kurcoobrie). 'A great attraction' is the fine drawing room with comfortable seating, which 'takes up most of the first floor'. Bedrooms are cosy, well furnished, with a good if 'old-fashioned' bathroom. Particularly recommended is the double room with window seats overlooking the impressive High Street and the maze of gardens running to the River Dee. Mr Cowan cooks an evening meal by arrangement, served at separate tables in a pretty room. No licence; bring your own wine. If you choose to eat out, the *Selkirk Arms*, around the corner, 'has developed a good reputation'. The breakfast 'was more than up to standard; the attractive starters table has a wide range of fresh fruit; Gordon's cooked dishes are hard to beat'. Guests may use the secluded garden which supplies flowers and fruit for the house. (*David and Joan Marston*)

Bedrooms: 3. *Open*: all year except for occasional holidays. *Facilities*: drawing room, dining room, ½-acre garden, unsuitable for &. *Background music*: none. *Location*: town centre. *Smoking*: not allowed. *Children*: normally no children under 14 ('but we are flexible'). *Dogs*: not allowed. *Credit cards*: MasterCard, Visa. *Prices*: [2009] B&B £35–£45 per person, set dinner £21, 3-night breaks or longer.

See also Shortlist

KIRKWALL Orkney   **Map 5:A3**

Lynnfield Hotel
Holm Road
Kirkwall KW15 1SU

Tel 01856-872505
Fax 01856-870038
Email office@lynnfield.co.uk
Website www.lynnfieldhotel.com

There are 'lovely views over Kirkwall and the bay' from this hotel in Orkney's capital. 'Tucked away behind a housing development', it is run by owner Malcolm Stout ('laid-back, helpful') with Lorna Reid. Their mainly local staff are 'friendly'. 'Our room was huge, with a half-tester bed, armchairs, large TV, walk-in closet, spa bath and big shower.' All the 'very comfortable' rooms have free Wi-Fi. The 'good-sized' residents' lounge has 'comfortable sofas' and 'well-stocked bookcases'. Coffee and 'home-made sweeties' are taken here after dinner. The restaurant, with its whisky theme, faces the water. Visitors this year thought it 'outstanding'. 'Fish and seafood dishes particularly delicious', eg, scallops on jewelled couscous and roast red pepper sauce. 'The varied wine list has some inexpensive bottles.' The Highland Park Distillery is adjacent; twenty of its malts are served in the small bar. From October to March a six-course 'Lynnfield Lux' gourmet dinner is held on several Friday evenings. (*Mary Hewson, David and Judy Stewart*)

Bedrooms: 10, 1 suitable for &. *Open*: all year except 25/26 Dec, 1/2 Jan. *Facilities*: residents' lounge, bar lounge, restaurant, business/small conference/ wedding facilities, small garden. *Background music*: Scottish, in restaurant. *Location*: ½ mile from centre, by Highland Park Distillery, parking. *Smoking*: not allowed. *Children*: not under 12. *Dogs*: not allowed in public rooms. *Credit cards*: MasterCard, Visa. *Prices*: B&B £45–£75 per person, full alc £40, packages throughout the year, 1-night group bookings occasionally refused. *V*

KYLESKU Highland   Map 5:B2

Kylesku Hotel
Kylesku
by Lairg IV27 4HW

Tel 01971-502231
Fax 01971-502313
Email info@kyleskuhotel.co.uk
Website www.kyleskuhotel.co.uk

'We cannot resist the charm of this place, the location, the relaxed atmosphere, the friendliness of the owners, Struan and Louise Lothian.' 'A wonderfully warm, welcoming place with excellent food.' This white-painted 17th-century former coaching inn stands on the shore where lochs Glendhu and Glencoul meet in 'breathtaking' north-west Sutherland. The young, seasonal staff are 'well trained'. Children are welcomed. There are 'magnificent views' from the 'lovely' lounge, 'cosy with wood-burning stove, squashy sofas and large library', the dining room, and the 'simple but comfortable' bedrooms. 'The bathrooms may not have been upgraded but the view from the loo more than makes up for lack of a shower.' The 'minuscule' annexe rooms, reached by a 'lethal' staircase and with shared facilities, are not liked. The busy bar has a 'cheery atmosphere', locals eating in the early evening. The same menu is served in the quieter dining room. 'The best dinner of our trip: perfect scallops and moist, tender duck.' 'Breakfast the best we had in Scotland: delicious scrambled egg and smoked salmon.' The Lothians have put the hotel on the market but an early sale is not expected. Check before booking. (*Janet and Dennis Allom, Diana Goodey, Mary and Rodney Milne-Day, and others*)

Bedrooms: 8, 1 in adjacent annexe. *Open*: 1 Mar–mid-Oct, restaurant closed Mon. *Facilities*: lounge, bar, restaurant, small garden (tables for outside eating), unsuitable for &. *Background music*: 'easy listening' all day in bar. *Location*: 10 miles S of Scourie, 30 miles north of Ullapool. *Smoking*: not allowed. *Children*: all ages welcomed. *Dogs*: not allowed in bar, restaurant. *Credit cards*: MasterCard, Visa. *Prices*: B&B [2009] £47–£60 per person, set dinner £25–£29, full alc (bar) £27, 3-night breaks.

LANARK South Lanarkshire   Map 5:E2

New Lanark Mill	*Tel* 01555-667200
Mill One, New Lanark Mills	*Fax* 01555-667222
Lanark G75 8RZ	*Email* hotel@newlanark.org
	Website www.newlanark.org

Hardly a typical *Guide* hotel: set in a steep, wooded valley below the Falls of Clyde, this restored 18th-century cotton mill (managed by Michael Ward and owned by New Lanark Trust) forms part of a World Heritage Site. Originally a manufacturing centre developed by the utopian social pioneer, Robert Owen, in the early 19th century, the complex now includes a visitor centre, shops, self-catering accommodation, a youth hostel and extensive health and fitness facilities. The mill's original Georgian windows and barrel-vaulted ceilings have been kept, and on the adjoining building there is a new roof garden with views of the 'spectacular setting'. Decor is light, simple, modern – possibly 'bland'. Most of the spacious, 'well-furnished and clean' bedrooms overlook the river. 'Nothing fancy, but comfortable. Very good staff.' There is again a new head chef this year, Fraser Meechan. His extensive set meals use ingredients from Clydesdale farms, eg, pan-fried loin of local lamb with butternut squash. Breakfast is a 'standard' buffet. The 'jolly' bar is busy with non-residents, and the village is popular for weddings and celebrations (check about this when booking). Ceilidhs and party nights are held in winter. The accessible Clyde walkway leads to the Falls of Clyde wildlife reserve. 'A useful stop-over en route to the Highlands.' (*Tony and Marlene Hall, RM, and others*)

Bedrooms: 38, 5 suitable for &. *Open*: all year. *Facilities*: lounge, bar, restaurant, heated indoor swimming pool (16 by 7 metres), free access to leisure club, function/conference/wedding facilities. *Background music*: varied, in public areas. *Location*: 1 mile S of Lanark. *Smoking*: allowed in 6 bedrooms. *Children*: all ages welcomed. *Dogs*: allowed in some bedrooms, only guide dogs in public rooms. *Credit cards*: all major cards. *Prices*: B&B [2009] £45–£59.50 per person, D,B&B £54.50–£69.50, set dinner £27.50, special breaks, Christmas/New Year packages. *V*

LARGOWARD Fife   *See Shortlist*

LOCHEPORT Western Isles   Map 5: inset A1

Langass Lodge   NEW   *Tel* 01876-580285
Locheport, Isle of North Uist   *Fax* 01876-580385
HS6 5HA   *Email* langasslodge@btconnect.com
                          Website www.langasslodge.co.uk

In an isolated setting above an ancient stone circle, this former hunting lodge has been renovated and extended as an 'elegant' modern hotel with a 'personal touch'. It is owned by Niall and Amanda Leveson Gower; they run it with John and Anne Buchanan who take charge of cooking and hospitality. The bedrooms are in the main house and in a hillside extension with 'fabulous' views over a sea loch to Skye. 'Our room was comfortable and spacious with doors opening to the garden; the bathroom was rather OTT: modern taps, basin, etc, but no handrails.' There is 'plenty of storage, a king-size bed, wooden floors with rugs'. Visitors can dine in the bar or more formally in the restaurant. John Buchanan's short menus specialise in seafood (sometimes gathered from the owners' boat and pots), eg, steamed Barra cockles; surf and turf of wild Uist venison and monkfish loin. 'Delicious food; Niall and Amanda were friendly, sometimes serving at table.' Children are 'positively encouraged': there are high chairs, a special menu, toys in the lounge. 'Perhaps an English country house rather than a North Uist feel.' (*Jane and Tony Cowan, and others*)

Bedrooms: 12, 1 suitable for &. *Open*: Mar–Jan. *Facilities*: lounge, sitting room, 2 dining rooms, wedding facilities, 24-acre grounds (birdwatching, fishing, walking). *Background music*: in bar. *Location*: 5 miles W of Lochmaddy. *Smoking*: not allowed. *Children*: all ages welcomed. *Dogs*: allowed 'everywhere'. *Credit cards*: MasterCard, Visa. *Prices*: [2009] B&B £45–£80 per person, set meals £28–£34, 1-night bookings occasionally refused.

LOCHINVER Highland   Map 5:B1

The Albannach
Baddidarroch
Lochinver IV27 4LP

Tel 01571-844407
Email info@thealbannach.co.uk
Website www.thealbannach.co.uk

Picture windows in the intimate dining room of this handsome, white-painted 19th-century house look over a deep sea loch to the dome of Suilven. It stands in a walled garden with mature trees and shrubs, high above Lochinver's working harbour. Colin Craig and Lesley Crosfield, the 'unpretentious and easy' owner/manager/chefs, gained a *Michelin* star in 2009. 'Perfect,' say visitors in 2009. An earlier comment: 'Considerate service; imaginative cooking.' There is no choice on the five-course hand-written dinner menu (preferences discussed in advance), which is based on local produce, eg, monkfish tail wrapped in air-dried ham; roast fillet of Highland beef, roast vegetable parcel, thyme mash, amontillado sauce. The fish and shellfish come from the harbour, herbs and vegetables are organically grown, bread and oatcakes are home baked. There is no bar 'but drinks can be ordered anywhere' (they might be accompanied by fresh oysters). The conservatory, the snug (wood panelled and with an old stone fireplace) and all the bedrooms, share the view. The penthouse suite up steep steps is 'large and luxurious'; the byre suite has a conservatory sitting room and a hot tub on its terrace. 'Good breakfasts.' (*JS Waters, R and TB, and others*)

Bedrooms: 5, 1 in byre with private patio. *Open*: mid-Mar–early Jan. *Facilities*: ramp, snug, conservatory, dining room, 1-acre garden, 6 acres croftland, unsuitable for &. *Background music*: none. *Location*: ½ mile from village. *Smoking*: not allowed. *Children*: not under 12. *Dogs*: not allowed. *Credit cards*: MasterCard, Visa. *Prices*: D,B&B £125–£175 per person, set dinner £50, off-season breaks, Christmas/New Year packages.

Inver Lodge
Iolaire Road
Lochinver IV27 4LU

Tel 01571-844496
Fax 01571-844395
Email stay@inverlodge.com
Website www.inverlodge.com

'We would recommend it to anyone,' says a visitor this year to Robin Vestey's modern hotel. It has a 'stunning' position on a hill above Lochinver harbour, amid the mountains of Assynt. Nicholas Gorton, the manager, and his staff 'were welcoming and more than helpful; they coped very well with a demanding guest'. There are picture windows in the public areas which, with many of the bedrooms, have 'fantastic' views. Tables are reallocated daily in the restaurant to ensure that these views are shared. The chef, Peter Cullen, serves a 'superb' six-course menu of modern dishes, eg, baby spinach and ricotta tart; home-smoked duck breast, green lentils, black pudding. The wine list is wide ranging and fairly priced; 'half bottles more than usually numerous'. The spacious bedrooms are well fitted: 'A very comfortable bed, lovely shower over the bath.' The good breakfast has a buffet table of freshly squeezed orange juice, compote, cereals, etc; porridge, croissants, toast; alternatives to the full grill include local kipper or smoked haddock, omelettes, scrambled eggs with smoked salmon. Fishing is available in two rivers and four lochs. 'We loved our stay.' (*Mrs R Porter*)

Bedrooms: 20. *Open*: 2 Apr–31 Oct. *Facilities*: 2 lounges, bar, restaurant, 1-acre garden, wedding facilities, unsuitable for &. *Background music*: none. *Location*: ½ mile above village. *Smoking*: not allowed. *Children*: not under 10 in restaurant at night. *Dogs*: not allowed in public rooms except foyer lounge. *Credit cards*: all major cards. *Prices*: [2009] B&B £100–£140 per person, D,B&B £135–£175, set dinner £35–£50, seasonal breaks. *V*

LOCHRANZA North Ayrshire   Map 5:D1

Apple Lodge   *Tel/Fax* 01770-830229
Lochranza
Isle of Arran KA27 8HJ

❦ *César award in 2000*

Returning visitors who 'cannot count how many times we have stayed' at this white-painted, grey-roofed former manse 'have already provisionally booked for 2010'. They love the homely atmosphere (handmade artefacts, family photographs, books, teddy bears) created by John and Jeannie Boyd, the owners of this small guest house. Near the sea (and the small ferry to Kintyre), it has wonderful views. 'Warm and comfortable' bedrooms have antique fireplace, embroidery, paintings, books and local information; bathrooms are 'beautifully fitted'. But Pippin, above the living room, may be subject to noise. Apple Cottage has a small sitting room and kitchen: 'French doors look on to the garden with the hills and passing red squirrels to see.' Mrs Boyd ('a first-class all-rounder') cooks a three-course, no-choice dinner menu discussed with guests beforehand ('dietary needs catered for without fuss') and served with candlelight, crystal and flowers (but not always: see below). She calls her cooking 'best of British'. Main courses come with 'a good selection of vegetables'. No licence; bring your own wine. In the surrounding countryside, deer and eagles are often sighted. A golf course is adjacent. (*Joan and David Marston*)

Bedrooms: 4, 1 on ground floor. *Open*: all year except Christmas/New Year, dining room closed midday, for dinner Tues and July/Aug. *Facilities*: lounge, dining room, ¼-acre garden, unsuitable for &. *Background music*: none. *Location*: outside village on N side of island. *Smoking*: not allowed. *Children*: not allowed. *Dogs*: not allowed. *Credit cards*: none. *Prices*: B&B £39–£55 per person, set dinner £26, usually min. 3-night booking.

LOCKERBIE
Dumfries and Galloway

See Shortlist

LYBSTER Highland

See Shortlist

MAYBOLE South Ayrshire   Map 5:E1

Ladyburn
by Maybole KA19 7SG

Tel 01655-740585
Fax 01655-740206
Email jh@ladyburn.co.uk
Website www.ladyburn.co.uk

Visitors this year 'were looked after superbly' at this 17th-century former dower house. Surrounded by woods and fields, it stands in a beautiful Ayrshire valley. 'It is our home; we invite you to share it with us,' says Jane Hepburn. It has a 'luxurious feel', with family antiques, a 'light and airy' drawing room. One bedroom has a Victorian four-poster. Families can stay in the 'Granny Flat', accessible from the main house but with its own entrance. Mrs Hepburn no longer offers supper as a matter of course, but afternoon tea is served, and late ferry arrivals can arrange for soup and sandwiches. Breakfast has home-made jams and marmalade, Aga-cooked porridge, eggs 'as you like them', a full cooked platter. There are three national rose collections in the large garden (part of Scotland's Garden Scheme), which is glorious in spring when rhododendrons, azaleas and bluebells are in bloom. *Ladyburn*'s guests may explore the grounds of the adjacent Kilkerran estate. Shooting parties, weddings and functions are catered for. Good golf at Turnberry, Prestwick and Troon nearby; salmon fishing can be arranged; racing at Ayr. Study the map before you go as *Ladyburn* is 'not easy to find'. (*WE Strachan, and others*)

Bedrooms: 5. *Open*: all year but restricted opening Oct–Mar. *Facilities*: drawing room, dining room, wedding/function facilities, 5-acre garden (croquet), unsuitable for &. *Background music*: none. *Location*: 14 miles S of Ayr. *Smoking*: not allowed. *Children*: not under 16 in main house. *Dogs*: only guide dogs allowed. *Credit cards*: MasterCard, Visa. *Prices*: [2009] B&B £55–£80 per person, dinner from £23.50.

MELROSE Borders   *See Shortlist*

MONTROSE Angus   *See Shortlist*

MUIR OF ORD Highland   Map 5:C2

The Dower House   *Tel/Fax* 01463-870090
Highfield   *Email* info@thedowerhouse.co.uk
Muir of Ord IV6 7XN   *Website* www.thedowerhouse.co.uk

🦂 *César award in 2008*

In a 'large, beautiful' wooded garden bordered by the rivers Beauly and Conon, this pretty Georgian *cottage-orné* is the family home of Robyn and Mena Aitchison. It is like a 'miniature treasure chest', say admirers: Persian rugs, Chinese vases, antiques, chintzy wallpaper, flowery fabrics, potted plants, stacked bookcases create a 'much-loved' feel. The lounge has an open fire, a baby grand piano, and a bar cupboard full of malt whiskies. The Aitchisons 'are friendly but don't interfere'; 'I felt totally pampered' is a typical comment. Guests are expected to dine in, in the 'most attractive' dining room with its 'gleaming mahogany tables'. The host is an 'excellent self-taught cook', who describes his no-choice menu (agreed in advance) as 'gutsy modern British' cooking, eg, darn of venison with peppercorn sauce. 'Magnificent puddings' include strawberries and lemon posset. 'Dietary requests speedily dealt with.' Generous breakfasts have fresh fruit salad, local honey, eggs from the owners' free-range hens. All the 'cosy' bedrooms face the garden (with monkey puzzle trees, shrubs, a large goldfish pond and a miniature orchard): they have a large bed; the suite has a sitting room. Children are welcomed.

Bedrooms: 4, all on ground floor. *Open*: all year except Christmas Day. *Facilities*: lounge, dining room, TV room with Internet access, 4½-acre grounds (small formal garden, swings, pond, tree house), unsuitable for &. *Background music*: none. *Location*: 14 miles NW of Inverness. *Smoking*: not allowed. *Children*: no under-5s at dinner (high tea at 5). *Dogs*: not allowed in public rooms. *Credit cards*: MasterCard, Visa. *Prices*: B&B £60–£85 per person, set dinner £38.

NEWTON STEWART   Map 5:E1
Dumfries and Galloway

Kirroughtree House   *Tel* 01671-402141
Newton Stewart DG8 6AN   *Fax* 01671-402425
                              Email info@kirroughtreehouse.co.uk
                              Website www.kirroughtreehouse.co.uk

César award in 2003

'It just gets better,' according to a correspondent on his fourth visit to 'this very well-run hotel' in large grounds by the Galloway Forest Park. The imposing, white, bow-windowed mansion is owned by the small McMillan group and managed by Jim Stirling, who 'takes great pride in looking after his guests'. 'The service was personal, friendly; we were met in the car park, and cases were collected.' Arriving visitors are given afternoon tea with silver service in one of the 'elegant' public rooms. Housekeeping is 'faultless' in the bedrooms; all are supplied with sherry and fruit. A 'well-furnished' second-floor room had 'marvellous views and a great bath'. Men are required to wear a jacket and tie at dinner ('dressing up adds to the occasion'). The chef, Rolf Mueller, serves modern European dishes on his 'varied' menus, eg, chicken liver and foie gras parfait; fillet of turbot and brill, turned potatoes, spring onions. 'Dietary preferences are accommodated and remembered for returning guests.' An earlier comment: 'A totally consistent standard of a style.' Breakfast is 'really good'. The 'book town' of Wigtown is nearby. (*Jeffrie Strang, and others*)

Bedrooms: 17. *Open*: mid-Feb–2 Jan. *Facilities*: lift, 2 lounges, 2 dining rooms, 8-acre grounds (gardens, tennis, croquet, pitch and putt). *Background music*: none. *Location*: 1½ miles NE of Newton Stewart. *Smoking*: not allowed. *Children*: not under 10. *Dogs*: allowed in lower ground-floor bedrooms only, not in public rooms. *Credit cards*: Amex, MasterCard, Visa. *Prices*: [2009] B&B £90–£125 per person, D,B&B £75–£160, set dinner £35, special breaks, Christmas/New Year packages, 1-night bookings sometimes refused.

NORTH BERWICK East Lothian   *See Shortlist*

OBAN Argyll and Bute   Map 5:D1

Lerags House
Lerags, by Oban
PA34 4SE

Tel 01631-563381
Email stay@leragshouse.com
Website www.leragshouse.com

A 'really lovely place, and excellent value', this handsome grey stone house stands in a mature garden by Loch Feochan. Owners Bella and Charlie Miller have run it since 2001, after coming from Australia more than 15 years ago 'for a summer'. 'We are a two-person show, offering very personal service,' she says. Hungarian vizsla dogs Libby and Rex contribute to the 'warm welcome'. Her cooking ('Scottish with Australian flair') is 'inventive and artistic, ingredients fresh, cooking perfect'; the three-course menu might include Gressingham duck braised in mulled wine and with red cabbage. No choice, but 'Bella is flexible to guests' preferences'. The wine list reflects the Millers' Australian background. Public rooms and bedrooms are comfortably furnished, each in a different pastel or neutral colour. 'Our spacious suite had lovely views. Bed one of the best ever, beautifully made, with crisp, white linen.' The breakfast menu includes waffles, kippers, porridge and 'full Scottish'. A 'delighted' couple took the whole house for their wedding. 'The setting is beautiful in all weathers, the rooms are stylish, food is delicious.' Visitors with 'limited disability' can be accommodated. (*D and KV, Sandra and Jim Haslam, and others*)

Bedrooms: 6. *Open*: Easter–Dec, except Christmas. *Facilities*: sitting room, dining room, wedding facilities, 1-acre grounds, unsuitable for &. *Background music*: in dining room. *Location*: 5 miles S of Oban, by Loch Feochan. *Smoking*: not allowed. *Children*: not under 12. *Dogs*: not allowed. *Credit cards*: MasterCard, Visa. *Prices*: [2009] D,B&B £85–£100 per person, 1-night bookings refused holiday weekends.

The Manor House
Gallanach Road
Oban PA34 4LS

Tel 01631-562087
Fax 01631-563053
Email info@manorhouseoban.com
Website www.manorhouseoban.com

'A most enjoyable experience; we are trying to think of a good reason to return.' Much praise came this year for Lesley and Margaret Crane's 'excellent' Georgian hotel on the south shore of Oban bay. 'Superb location; a room with a great view; building well managed within and without.' 'As good as ever.' On a rocky headland, half a mile from the town centre, the house was built as the principal residence of the Duke of Argyll's estate in 1780. Binoculars are provided in each of the 'tastefully and immaculately decorated' bedrooms. Most have the view; they also have Wi-Fi. 'Our small room was sparkling clean; fresh fruit, bottled water, chocolate and biscuits provided; bed soft and comfortable; shower room fittings high quality.' At dinner, 'seating is staggered, which meant service was efficient'. Chefs Patrick Freytag and Shaun Squire prepare a 'varied and interesting' five-course menu, eg, spring salad with quail's eggs; halibut with Meaux mustard butter, wilted spinach, braised fennel. The 'superb' breakfast has freshly squeezed orange juice, 'excellent scrambled eggs with smoked salmon'. The bar (a popular local) provides 'good lunches'. In fine weather, lunch and drinks are served on a panoramic terrace. Ferries leave near here for Mull, Iona and Fingal's Cave. (*CH Hay, Rosemary Lindop, David Carment, Joan and David Marston*)

Bedrooms: 11. *Open*: all year except 25/26 Dec. *Facilities*: 2 lounges, bar, restaurant, wedding facilities, 1½-acre grounds, unsuitable for &. *Background music*: 'easy listening' in bar and dining room. *Location*: ½ mile from centre. *Smoking*: not allowed. *Children*: not under 12. *Dogs*: not allowed in public rooms. *Credit cards*: Amex, MasterCard, Visa. *Prices*: [2009] B&B £54–£150 per person, D,B&B £86–£128.50, set dinner £32, alc £45, off-season breaks, New Year package.

See also Shortlist

PEAT INN Fife   Map 5:D3

The Peat Inn	*Tel* 01334-840206
Peat Inn, by Cupar	*Fax* 01334-840530
KY15 5LH	*Email* stay@thepeatinn.co.uk
	Website www.thepeatinn.co.uk

At the crossroads of a tiny village near St Andrews, this famous old coaching inn is run as a restaurant-with-rooms by owner/chef Geoffrey Smeddle and his wife, Katherine, the 'friendly' front-of-house. In three 'discreet' dining rooms (big windows, widely spaced tables), he serves local produce where possible in his 'honest, unpretentious' modern cooking (dishes like rillette of kiln-smoked salmon; roast cod, chorizo, artichokes, sage jus). Service is by 'keen young waiters'.

Pre-dinner drinks are served in a sitting room. Accommodation is in suites in the adjacent *Residence*. Seven are on two levels, with a gallery living room. These have recently been refurbished and given new carpet and curtains, and a better shower in the marble bathroom. One visitor wrote of a 'pleasant' room, with 'good bed, fine view'. The continental breakfast, delivered to the room at an agreed time, has freshly squeezed juice, boiled eggs, ham, cheeses, a basket of toast and croissants, cheese. (*DG*)

Bedrooms: 8 suites, all on ground floor in annexe. *Open*: all year except Christmas, 1–16 Jan, and Sun/Mon. *Facilities*: ramp, lounge, restaurant, 1-acre garden. *Background music*: none. *Location*: 6 miles SW of St Andrews. *Smoking*: not allowed. *Children*: all ages welcomed. *Dogs*: not allowed in public rooms. *Credit cards*: Amex, MasterCard, Visa. *Prices*: B&B £95–£145 per person, set dinner £32, tasting menu £50, full alc £52, special breaks, New Year package.

PEEBLES Borders   *See Shortlist*

PERTH Perth and Kinross   *See Shortlist*

PITLOCHRY Perth and Kinross   *See Shortlist*

PORT APPIN Argyll and Bute   Map 5:D1

The Airds Hotel   *Tel* 01631-730236
Port Appin PA38 4DF   *Fax* 01631-730535
                          Email airds@airds-hotel.com
                          Website www.airds-hotel.com

'A supremely comfortable place to stay', Shaun and Jenny McKivragan's luxury hotel (Relais & Châteaux), once a simple ferry inn, has 'fabulous views' over Loch Linnhe. Visitors this year 'enjoyed a memorable tea outside, overlooking the water'. The lounges have 'squashy, comfy seating' and landscape paintings. The conservatory at the front, where pre-dinner drinks are served, is 'light and airy'. The bedrooms have a mix of plain and floral fabrics, antiques, flat-screen TV and DVD-player: 'Lovely, if a bit dated.' 'Our smallish, well-fitted room had the loch view; a spacious bathroom.' 'Our room at the back was nicely decorated. Two built-in cupboards, gleaming bathroom with power shower, never-ending hot water.' All rooms have Wi-Fi. In the restaurant, picture windows face the loch. Award-winning chef Paul Burns serves 'excellent' modern French dishes ('with a hint of Scottish'), eg, turbot with scallops, asparagus and vermouth velouté. 'Fine, fresh ingredients beautifully arranged.' Service is by 'female staff, mainly East European, kilted at night'. Breakfasts are 'excellent' (fresh juice; home-made jams; 'very good kippers'), as are packed lunches and afternoon tea (with freshly made scones). There is a croquet lawn and a summer house. (*Tony and Marlene Hall, and others*)

Bedrooms: 11, 2 on ground floor, also self-catering cottage. *Open*: all year except 2 days a week Nov, Dec, Jan. *Facilities*: 2 lounges, conservatory, snug bar, restaurant, wedding facilities, ¾-acre garden (croquet, putting), unsuitable for &. *Background music*: none. *Location*: 25 miles N of Oban. *Smoking*: not allowed. *Children*: all ages welcomed, but no under-9s in dining room after 7.30 (high tea at 6.30). *Dogs*: allowed by prior agreement; not in public rooms. *Credit cards*: Amex, MasterCard, Visa. *Prices*: [2009] D,B&B £122.50–£370 per person, off-season breaks, Christmas/New Year packages.

PORT CHARLOTTE
Argyll and Bute
See Shortlist

PORTPATRICK
Dumfries and Galloway
Map 5:E1

Knockinaam Lodge
Portpatrick
DG9 9AD

Tel 01776-810471
Fax 01776-810435
Email reservations@knockinaamlodge.com
Website www.knockinaamlodge.com

'The great charm is the level of service; staffed by local youngsters, *Knockinaam* ran like clockwork,' say visitors in 2009 to David and Sian Ibbotson's grey stone 19th-century hunting lodge. Shielded by cliffs and wooded hills, it is 'virtually on the seashore' (with private beach); it stands at the end of a 'long, bumpy track'. 'Warm, spacious public rooms' have rich fabrics, antiques, oak panelling, open fires. Churchill met Eisenhower secretly here during World War II: you can stay in his bedroom, the largest. 'Our room (South) was comfortable, airy, with dual-aspect windows: the large bathroom and walk-in shower also looked out to sea.' In the candlelit dining room, chef Tony Pierce has a *Michelin* star for his 'beautifully created' four-course menus (dishes like white onion, leek and thyme velouté; roast cannon of Galloway lamb, pomme purée, garlic beignet, root vegetables). No choice until dessert or cheese, but vegetarians are well catered for; other diets can be accommodated. 'Early risers get to sit in the bay window and watch the sea' at breakfast, which has 'freshly pressed fruit juice'. In fine weather there are tea, drinks and barbecues on the lawn. There is a tree house for children (they are welcomed). 'The resident black Labradors will walk with anyone who gives them a pat.' (*Andrew McManus, Judi Taylor-Evans, RG*)

Bedrooms: 10. *Open*: all year. *Facilities*: 2 lounges, 1 bar, restaurant, wedding facilities, 30-acre grounds (sand/rock beach 50 yds), only restaurant suitable for &. *Background music*: classical in restaurant. *Location*: 3 miles S of Portpatrick. *Smoking*: not allowed. *Children*: no under-12s in dining room after 7 pm (high tea at 6). *Dogs*: allowed in some bedrooms (£20 per stay), not in public rooms. *Credit cards*: Amex, MasterCard, Visa. *Prices*: [2009] D,B&B £120–£285 per person, set dinner £50, reductions for 3 or more nights off-season, midweek breaks, Christmas/New Year packages, 1-night bookings sometimes refused. *V*

PORTREE Highland   Map 5:C1

Viewfield House
Portree
Isle of Skye IV51 9EU

Tel 01478-612217
Fax 01478-613517
Email info@viewfieldhouse.com
Website www.viewfieldhouse.com

  César award in 1993

Liked for its 'faded grandeur', 'Gothic' air and 'absence of hotel-type notices', this characterful guest house stands in large wooded grounds in Skye's capital. It is run by the 'affable' Hugh Macdonald, whose great-grandfather turned a modest Georgian house into this baronial pile, complete with castellated tower, in the 1880s. Its 'interesting and comfortable' public rooms contain family pictures, stags' antlers, Indian brass, and other relics of the family's colonial service; Persian rugs sit on polished wooden floors. There are new soft furnishings and upholstery in the drawing room and some bedrooms this year, and the heating has been upgraded. 'Our huge bedroom had four windows overlooking the gardens and bay. The vast bathroom had a walk-in power shower, claw-footed bath and two washstands.' There is no Reception or bar, but drinks are served more or less on request. No formal evening meal, but simple hot dishes and salads are available (home-made soups, chilli con carne, cheese platter, etc). 'Breakfast has plenty of fresh and dried fruit, Mallaig kippers, fresh juices.' There is Wi-Fi Internet access throughout, and a small office for guests' use. Children are welcomed. More reports, please.

Bedrooms: 11, 1 on ground floor suitable for ♿. *Open*: Easter–mid-Oct. *Facilities*: ramp, drawing room, morning/TV room, dining room, 20-acre grounds (croquet, swings). *Background music*: none. *Location*: S side of Portree. *Smoking*: not allowed. *Children*: all ages welcomed. *Dogs*: not allowed in public rooms except with permission of other guests (except guide dogs). *Credit cards*: MasterCard, Visa. *Prices*: B&B £50–£65 per person, full alc £30, 3- to 5-day rates, 1-night group bookings sometimes refused. *V*

See also Shortlist

ST ANDREWS Fife   *See Shortlist*

ST OLA Orkney   Map 5:A3

Foreran	*Tel* 01856-872389
St Ola	*Fax* 01856-876430
Kirkwall KW15 1SF	*Email* foveranhotel@aol.com
	Website www.foveranhotel.co.uk

'A very pleasant, relaxed, informal sort of place.' In their simple, single-storey hotel overlooking Scapa Flow, the Doull family provide 'traditional Orcadian hospitality'. There is 'a warm welcome with tea'. The well-equipped bedrooms, decorated in blond woods, vary from 'small' to 'spacious' but lack the views. 'Ours was clean and comfortable, with tea-making facilities and shortbread, just what we wanted.' 'Not posh, and without the gimmicks that many hotels provide these days.' Pre-dinner drinks are served by a fire in the lounge. In the restaurant, 'large, light and airy', with well-spaced tables and fine views, Paul Doull's 'consistently good' cooking is enjoyed by locals as well as residents. The emphasis is on the island's fine local produce: 'Memorable mutton one day, sole and monkfish another.' The list of 35 wines is 'sensible enough'. The service from 'a splendid team of youngsters' is praised. 'One waitress produced guidebooks for us without prompting.' Breakfast, served from 7.45 to 8.45 am, was 'a good buffet spread including stewed rhubarb, a welcome addition'. Orkney is a 'marvellous place' with abundant wildlife and fascinating archaeological sites. (*Richard and Catriona Smith, and others*)

Bedrooms: 8, all on ground floor. *Open*: mid-Apr–early Oct, by arrangement at other times, only restaurant Christmas/New Year, restaurant closed Sun evening end Sept–early June. *Facilities*: lounge, restaurant, wedding facilities, 12-acre grounds (private rock beach). *Background music*: Scottish, in evening, in restaurant. *Location*: 3 miles SW of Kirkwall. *Smoking*: not allowed. *Children*: all ages welcomed. *Dogs*: not allowed. *Credit cards*: MasterCard, Visa. *Prices*: B&B £49.50–£69.50 per person, D,B&B £74.50–£94.50, full alc £32, 1-night bookings sometimes refused.

SCARISTA Western Isles   *See Shortlist*

SCOURIE Highland   *See Shortlist*

SHIELDAIG Highland   Map 5:C1

Tigh an Eilean
Shieldaig, Loch Torridon
IV54 8XN

Tel 01520-755251
Fax 01520-755321
Email tighaneilean@keme.co.uk

♕ *César award in 2005*

At the water's edge of a 'gorgeous' village, this extended whitewashed hotel provides 'peace, quiet and charm'. Its owners, Chris and Cathryn Field, 'are much in evidence; a simple request is immediately dealt with', says a visitor this year. Other comments: 'It improves each time we visit.' 'Glorious views.' The dining room and many bedrooms have views across the sea to Shieldaig Island (a sanctuary for ancient pines, otters and sea eagles). Complimentary afternoon tea is available in the two 'comfortable' lounges; an honesty bar is 'a nice touch'. The bedrooms vary in size; some are small but 'decor and furnishings are beautiful'. All bathrooms are being renovated and given a 'proper shower'; most should be ready by March 2010. The dining room serves a three-course menu with choice. 'I particularly enjoyed quail and an excellent mash. Desserts were very good: fresh fruit salad with lavender ice cream, delicious Pavlova and cherry and almond clafoutis.' An informal first-floor restaurant, *The Coastal Kitchen*, has 'fantastic local seafood simply cooked' and pizzas from a wood-fired oven. Generous breakfasts have freshly squeezed juice, 'just-right scrambled eggs', smoked haddock, etc. There is free Wi-Fi . Children are well catered for, and 'our Labrador was truly welcomed – the Fields have dogs'. (*ST, Brenda and Bob Halstead, Josie and Guy Mayers*)

Bedrooms: 11. *Open*: mid-Mar–late Oct. *Facilities*: 2 lounges (1 with TV and wood-burning stove), bar/library, village bar (separate entrance), 2 restaurants, drying room, wedding facilities, small front courtyard, roof terrace, unsuitable for &. *Background music*: none. *Location*: village centre. *Smoking*: not allowed. *Children*: all ages welcomed (under-8s stay free, under-16s half price). *Dogs*: not allowed in public rooms. *Credit cards*: Amex, MasterCard, Visa. *Prices*: [2009] B&B £70 per person, D,B&B £110, bar meals, set dinner £40, full alc in *The Coastal Kitchen* £25, discounts for 3 or more nights. *V*

SKIRLING Borders   Map 5:E2

Skirling House

Skirling, by Biggar ML12 6HD

Tel 01899-860274
Fax 01899-860255
Email enquiry@skirlinghouse.com
Website www.skirlinghouse.com

◊ *César award in 2004*

'Delightful building, interesting artefacts, comfortable room and charming owners.' Returning visitors in 2009 again praise this fine Arts and Crafts house (Wolsey Lodge) on the green of a tiny village amid lovely Borders countryside. The owners, Bob and Isobel Hunter, give 'a warm welcome': 'tea and home-made cakes on the sunny patio with three friendly dogs'. Built in 1908 as the summer retreat of the art collector Sir Gibson Carmichael, *Skirling House* contains a 'stunning collection' of works of art, books, fresh flowers. The drawing room has a 16th-century carved Florentine ceiling, full-height windows, a log fire and a baby grand piano. 'Our spacious bedroom was supplied with everything we might need.' 'Bathroom the best ever, clean and beautifully equipped.' Mr Hunter cooks a 'superb' four-course no-choice menu (preferences discussed) with 'flavour-driven' dishes, perhaps rare breed pork and prune filo pies. 'Don't miss the poached pear with tarragon cream or the guanaja chocolate soufflé.' 'Good wine list' with suggested pairings and unusual bin ends. 'Breakfasts as good as you get' (fresh orange juice, French toast with caramelised apples and black pudding, home-made jams and marmalades). Children are welcomed. (*Janet and Dennis Allom, Mary Hewson, and others*)

Bedrooms: 5, plus 1 single available if let with a double, 1 on ground floor suitable for &. *Open*: Mar–Dec, closed Christmas. *Facilities*: ramps, drawing room, library, conservatory, dining room, 5-acre garden (tennis, croquet) in

100-acre estate with woodland. *Background music*: none. *Location*: 2 miles E of Biggar, by village green. *Smoking*: not allowed. *Children*: all ages welcomed. *Dogs*: allowed by arrangement, not in public rooms or unattended in bedrooms. *Credit cards*: MasterCard, Visa. *Prices*: [2009] B&B £50–£80 per person, D,B&B £80–£110, set dinner £30, 1-night bookings occasionally refused. *V*

SLEAT Highland   Map 5:C1

Toravaig House
Knock Bay, Sleat
Isle of Skye
IV44 8RE

Tel 0845-0551117
Fax 01471-833231
Email info@skyehotel.co.uk
Website www.skyehotel.co.uk

'Best service I experienced on my trip,' says a visitor this year to this handsome, white-painted 1930s building in a 'wonderful location' on the coast road, close to the Armadale ferry. It has been renovated by Anne Gracie and Kenneth Gunn; they are 'hands on, greeting guests, waiting at table'. The interior is decorated in 'strong, but not intimidating' colours, and the drawing room has a log fire and comfortable seating. Andrew Lipp is now the chef: his modern Scottish cooking (eg, sauté of Atlantic halibut and globe artichoke), served in the 'pleasing' dining room, was widely commended, though one guest found it 'fussily presented'. Rooms vary: 'Ours was small but comfortable, with a view.' 'Ours faced the car park; nicely decorated, it had effective reading lights, armchairs, good fabrics; spotless, compact bathroom.' New this year is a varied *à la carte* breakfast menu, including oatmeal porridge served with 'a wee dram', kippers and Stornoway black pudding. Kenneth Gunn was formerly captain of a cruise ship and *Toravaig* guests can take trips on his 42-foot yacht, or even get married on it, 'a most wonderful and memorable experience' for one couple this year. (*David Carment, Mrs A Watson, Andrew and Julie Appleyard*)

Bedrooms: 8. *Open*: all year. *Facilities*: lounge, dining room, wedding facilities, 2-acre grounds, unsuitable for &. *Background music*: none. *Location*: 7 miles S of Broadford. *Smoking*: not allowed. *Children*: not under 8. *Dogs*: not allowed. *Credit cards*: Diners, MasterCard, Visa. *Prices*: B&B £55–£95 per person, D,B&B £85–£130, set dinner £42.50, full alc £50, seasonal offers, midweek breaks, Christmas/New Year packages.

STRACHUR Argyll and Bute   *See Shortlist*

STRATHYRE Perth and Kinross   *See Shortlist*

STRONTIAN Highland   Map 5:C1

Kilcamb Lodge
Strontian
PH36 4HY

Tel 01967-402257
Fax 01967-402041
Email enquiries@kilcamblodge.co.uk
Website www.kilcamblodge.co.uk

In a 'lovely location', surrounded by woodland and hills on the shore of Loch Sunart, this is one of the oldest stone houses in Scotland. 'It never disappoints,' say visitors who stayed while the manager, Phillip Fleming, was in charge. When at home Sally Fox and her husband, David, are 'friendly', 'hands-on' owners; their staff are 'all excellent'. 'Beautifully furnished', the lodge has open fires, fresh flowers and 'spacious, comfortable, period lounges'. Tammo Siemers has been chef since August 2008: his cooking was thought 'good' but verging on pretentious. 'Foam featured on the menu every evening'; 'Presentation was ostentatious, most vegetables were puréed.' The best, large bedrooms have 'enormous bed, window seat and loch view'; 'quality linen and towels'. Breakfast has newly baked croissants, a good selection of cereals, free-range eggs. Dogs are welcomed: you might find some 'doggy treats' in your bedroom. Much wildlife can be seen on the nearby Ardnamurchan peninsula. There are falconry weekends and dolphin- and whale-watching trips. (*Brenda and Bob Halstead, and others*)

Bedrooms: 10. *Open*: Feb–early Jan, closed 2 days a week Feb, Nov. *Facilities*: drawing room, lounge bar, dining room, wedding facilities, 22-acre grounds (loch frontage, beach with safe bathing, fishing, boating), unsuitable for &. *Background music*: jazz/classical in bar, dining room. *Location*: edge of village.

Smoking: not allowed. *Children*: not under 10. *Dogs*: not allowed. *Credit cards*: Amex (*with surcharge*), MasterCard, Visa. *Prices*: B&B [2009] £69–£126.50 per person, D,B&B (min. 2 nights) £105 to £167.50, set dinner £48, off-season breaks, Christmas/New Year packages. *V*

SWINTON Borders   *See Shortlist*

TARBERT Western Isles   Map 5:B1

Ceol na Mara   NEW   *Tel* 01859-502464
7 Direcleit, Tarbert   *Email* midgie@madasafish.com
Isle of Harris HS3 3DP   *Website* www.ceolnamara.com

'Full marks for everything,' say trusted *Guide* correspondents nominating John and Marlene Mitchell's renovated stone house. Set above a rocky tidal loch, it has 'wonderful views from all windows'. 'They are friendly and hard-working hosts. John is a teacher but welcomes every visitor [with a drink] and serves breakfast. Our large, comfortable room appeared to have been decorated daily – not a mark or blemish anywhere; new carpets, rugs, flat-screen TV, fridge, masses of storage; a good bathroom with a shower, not a bath.' The large guest lounge is 'full of books and family treasures; you can sit outside in good weather or in the pleasant sun lounge'. Breakfast, served from 8 to 8.30 am, 'has the most generous choice ever: porridge that must be sampled, home-made breads and yogurt, a wide selection of fish and fruit'. The cooked dishes include 'Granny's pancake surprise' (haggis, pancake, bacon and herb omelette). No dinner: the Mitchells recommend eating at the *Hotel Hebrides*, which opened in 2009. *Ceol na Mara* ('music of the sea') is minutes from the ferry terminal. 'We spent three glorious days exploring the white sand beaches and archaeological remains of Harris and Lewis.' (*Janet and Dennis Allom*)

Bedrooms: 4. *Open*: all year. *Facilities*: 2 lounges, sun lounge, dining room, unsuitable for &. *Background music*: soft Highland/Celtic at breakfast. *Location*: ½ mile S of Tarbert. *Smoking*: not allowed. *Children*: all ages welcomed. *Dogs*: not allowed. *Credit cards*: all major cards (*3% surcharge*). *Prices*: B&B £30–£45 per person.

See also Shortlist

TAYNUILT Argyll and Bute   *See Shortlist*

THORNHILL   *See Shortlist*
Dumfries and Galloway

TIGHNABRUAICH Argyll and Bute   Map 5:D1

An Lochan	*Tel* 01700-811239
Shore Road	*Fax* 01700-811300
Tighnabruaich PA21 2BE	*Email* info@anlochan.co.uk
	Website www.anlochan.co.uk

'Staff were delightful,' reports a visitor this year to Roger and Bea McKie's white, bay-windowed seafront hotel. Named in Gaelic 'by the small loch', it stands across a small road from the shore in an unspoilt fishing village on the Kyles of Bute. Both restaurants and all but three of the bedrooms look across the sea to Bute. Earlier guests enjoyed complimentary tea and cake on arrival. 'Our well-appointed room had an excellent view and a spacious bathroom.' In the wooden-floored *Deck* brasserie, and the intimate and more formal *Crustacean* restaurant, chef Paul Scott's modern Scottish menu might include langoustines and scallops straight from the local waters. Puddings are 'superb'. The menu in the *Snug Bar* (popular with locals) is simpler, eg, supreme of salmon; pot-roasted chicken. Bold colours are used in the bedrooms and the 'attractive and comfortable' public rooms, which have local paintings and sculpture, books and family memorabilia. 'A good breakfast, with plenty of choice.' Golf, sailing, riding, fishing and cruises (to see porpoises, seals and dolphins) can be arranged. (*PB, and others*)

Bedrooms: 11. *Open*: all year except 2 weeks at Christmas. *Facilities*: lounge, library, bar, 2 restaurants, wedding facilities, ½-acre grounds, 100 yards from sea (shingle beach, moorings, pontoon), only restaurant and bar suitable for &. *Background music*: none. *Location*: on shore road, edge of village. *Smoking*: not allowed. *Children*: all ages welcomed (no charge for extra bed). *Dogs*: allowed by arrangement, and in some public rooms. *Credit cards*: MasterCard, Visa. *Prices*: B&B £55–£95 per person, D,B&B £85–£125, full alc £60, special rates for 2 or more nights, New Year package, 1-night bookings occasionally refused. *V*

Report forms (Freepost in UK) are at the end of the *Guide*.

TIRORAN Argyll and Bute   Map 5:D1

Tiroran House

Tiroran, Isle of Mull
PA69 6ES

Tel 01681-705232
Fax 01681-705240
Email tiroran-house@btinternet.com
Website www.tiroran.com

In large grounds on the shores of Loch Scridain, Laurence and Katie Mackay run their Victorian home on house-party lines. 'They are perfect hosts,' says an enthusiastic report. He is 'charming', 'quietly efficient, arranging drinks, introducing guests to each other before dinner', and 'a mine of local information'. She runs the kitchen, preparing 'wonderful' dinners for the candlelit dining room or vine-draped conservatory. Many ingredients for the three-course menu (three options each, order by 6 pm) come from her newly created organic kitchen garden. Aga-cooked dishes include venison and duck terrine; sea bass with red onion, herb, garlic and tomato sauce vierge. 'Starters and puddings particularly delicious.' Each bedroom is different: 'Ours, spacious, peaceful, had wonderful views; its bathroom was separated from the room by curtains only.' The front porch has a 'friendly clutter of useful things – sticks, fishing nets, binoculars, etc'. Both sitting rooms 'continue the country house theme, with comfortable chairs, books, magazines and log fire'; one has a polished wooden floor. Breakfast (full cooked is £6 extra) includes home-made muesli, breads, marmalade and preserves, and free-range eggs. Children are welcomed: under-14s have an early supper. A burn with waterfalls runs through the secluded gardens which lead to a private beach; otters, red deer and eagles can be seen. 'Mobile phones don't work well here.' (*CHH, Anthony Bradbury*)

Bedrooms: 7, 2 on ground floor, 1 in annexe. *Open*: Apr–Dec, except Christmas. *Facilities*: 2 sitting rooms, dining room, conservatory, 17½-acre grounds (burn, beach with mooring). *Background music*: traditional/'easy listening'. *Location*: N side of Loch Scridain. *Smoking*: not allowed. *Children*: all ages welcomed, usually no under-14s in dining room. *Dogs*: allowed in 2 bedrooms, not in public rooms. *Credit cards*: MasterCard, Visa. *Prices*: [2009] B&B £72.50–£81 per person, set dinner £42, New Year package, 1-night bookings sometimes refused.

TOBERMORY Argyll and Bute   *See Shortlist*

New reports help us keep the *Guide* up to date.

TORRIDON Highland   Map 5:C1

The Torridon   *Tel* 01445-791242
Torridon, by Achnasheen   *Fax* 01445-712253
IV22 2EY   *Email* info@thetorridon.com
                              Website www.thetorridon.com

In a remote setting on the shores of Loch Torridon, at the foot of Ben
Damph, this grand, turreted mansion (once a shooting lodge) is now
a 'romantic' luxury hotel (Pride of Britain). 'We felt relaxed and
pampered,' one couple wrote. Owners Rohaise and Daniel Rose-
Bristow run it with manager Robert Ince and 'friendly staff, not
over-attentive'. Original features have been retained in the 'beautiful'
public rooms, which have a 'sense of Victorian grandeur'. There are
patterned ceilings, traditional furnishings, wood panelling, big open
fireplaces, leather couches. Bedrooms are well furnished, too; some
have a king-size bed and a claw-footed freestanding bath; two have a
four-poster. 'I sat in the bath with a cup of tea, looking at the
spectacular Torridon mountains.' 'Superb housekeeping.' Chef Kevin
John Broome serves 'excellent' 'classic British' dinners on a five-
course menu using local langoustines and scallops, and home-grown
produce, in the restaurant. 'A leisurely and substantial meal.' 'First-
class breakfast': porridge with whisky, kippers, haggis, 'delicious'
raspberry jam. An activities manager can arrange archery, fishing,
kayaking, rock climbing and so on. This is a popular wedding venue.
The Torridon Inn, in former stables and sheds, provides accommodation
for 'the budget traveller'. (*AM, and others*)

Bedrooms: 19, 1, on ground floor, suitable for &, 1 suite in adjacent cottage.
Open: all year except Jan, Mon/Tues Nov–Mar. *Facilities*: ramp, lift, drawing
room, library, whisky bar, dining room, wedding facilities, 58-acre grounds
(croquet, kitchen garden, river, nature walk, loch). *Background music*: classical
at night in dining room. *Location*: On W coast, 10 miles SW of Kinlochewe.
Smoking: not allowed. *Children*: no under-10s in dining room in evening (high
tea provided). *Dogs*: allowed in cottage only. *Credit cards*: Amex, MasterCard,
Visa. *Prices*: B&B £70–£197.50 per person, D,B&B £115–£242.50, set dinner
£45, special breaks, Christmas/New Year packages.

We update the *Guide* every year. Hotels are dropped or may be
demoted to the Shortlist if there has been a change of owner
(unless reports after the change are positive), if this year's
reports are negative, or in rare cases where there has been no
feedback. A lot of hotels are omitted every year, and many new
ones are added.

ULLAPOOL Highland   Map 5:B2

The Ceilidh Place   *Tel* 01854-612103
14 West Argyle Street   *Fax* 01854-613773
Ullapool IV26 2TY   *Email* stay@theceilidhplace.com
                                     Website www.theceilidhplace.com

'A truly original combination of great hotel, buzzing coffee shop, good
restaurant, arts centre and eclectic bookshop.' A visitor returning in
2009 after five years found Jean Urquhart's unusual undertaking in a
Highland fishing village 'better than before'. From its origins as a small
café dedicated to music, *The Ceilidh Place* has grown to include a
wholefood shop and an arts centre with plays, poetry readings and
exhibitions by Scottish artists. Effie MacKenzie is the general
manager. The 'intimate' feel is liked. The simple, spacious bedrooms
have been 'smartly refurbished'. Each has a radio (no TV) and a small
library; extras include thick bathrobes, hot-water bottles. More basic
rooms in the Clubhouse across the road have bunk beds 'for those who
wish to spend less on the bed and more on the wine'. The 'very good'
guests' living room has books, games, Wi-Fi, a pantry with free tea
and coffee, and an honesty bar. Chef Scott Morrison serves 'great food
at fair prices' on his 'Scottish eclectic' menu (based on what the
fishermen catch and what is ripe in the garden). A typical dish: smoked
haddock, Parmesan and cream sauce. Vegetarian dishes are a
speciality. Ceilidhs are often held. In summer, the café serves meals
all day; in winter, food and drink are served in the parlour. 'We had
stopped visiting because our children wanted something livelier. They
loved it so much this time that they have begged us to book again for
Hogmanay.' (*Richard Macey, Josie and Guy Mayers*)

Bedrooms: 13, 10 with facilities *en suite*, plus 11 in bunkhouse across road. *Open*:
all year. *Facilities*: bar, parlour, café/bistro, restaurant, bookshop, conference/
function/wedding facilities, 2-acre garden, only public areas suitable for &.
Background music: 'eclectic' in public areas. *Location*: village centre, large car
park. *Smoking*: not allowed. *Children*: all ages welcomed. *Dogs*: not allowed in
public rooms. *Credit cards*: Amex, MasterCard, Visa. *Prices*: [2009] B&B £48–£70
per person, full alc £32.50, Christmas/New Year packages.

See also Shortlist

For good-value deals exclusively for *Guide* readers, see our
website's Special Offers section: www.goodhotelguide.com.

WALKERBURN Borders   Map 5:E2

Windlestraw Lodge   *Tel* 01896-870636
Tweed Valley   *Email* reception@windlestraw.co.uk
Galashiels Road   *Website* www.windlestraw.co.uk
Walkerburn EH43 6AA

'Off the tourist trail', above the River Tweed in the Scottish borders, this pink stone Edwardian house wins plaudits again this year. The owners Alan Reid (the chef) and his wife, Julie, 'achieve the perfect balance of friendly interest with efficiency'. The candlelit open-plan public rooms are 'romantic and elegant'; the wood-panelled dining area has 'breathtaking views'. 'Tasteful decor (*objets d'art*, family photos). Lovely open fires. Superb food.' Another regular guest enjoyed 'a shot of divine Jerusalem artichoke soup followed by veal with calf's liver – intensely flavoured and beautifully presented'. The organic rose veal, bred nearby, is new this year, and fish and shellfish are delivered to the door from Eyemouth. 'Smart, comfortable' bedrooms (all have views) have recently been redesigned and upgraded. The east-facing Willison room has a panoramic outlook over the Tweed valley. The Mackintosh master bedroom has a king-size brass bed and original bathtub. Cooked breakfast dishes include Mull Cheddar cheese omelette; scrambled eggs with smoked salmon. The Reids cater for house parties, private meetings and small weddings; they offer one-to-one cookery lessons, and can arrange golf, fishing, shooting and mountain biking. (*Patricia Burgon, and others*)

Bedrooms: 6, all on first floor. *Open*: all year except 2 days Christmas, 2 days New Year, 2 weeks Feb, 1 week June. *Facilities*: bar lounge, sun lounge, drawing room, dining room, 'exclusive use for small weddings', 1-acre grounds, unsuitable for &. *Background music*: none. *Location*: outskirts of village, 2 miles E of Innerleithen. *Smoking*: not allowed. *Children*: no under-10s at dinner (high teas 5–6 pm). *Dogs*: allowed in some bedrooms, not in public rooms. *Credit cards*: MasterCard, Visa. *Prices*: B&B £65–£95 per person, D,B&B £105–£145, set meal £45, 2-night getaway breaks. *V*

How to contact the *Guide*
By mail: From anywhere in the UK, write to Freepost PAM 2931, London W11 4BR (no stamp is needed)
From outside the UK: *Good Hotel Guide*, 50 Addison Avenue, London W11 4QP, England
By telephone or fax: 020-7602 4182
By email: editor@goodhotelguide.com
Via our website: www.goodhotelguide.com

WHITHORN Dumfries and Galloway   Map 5:E2

The Steam Packet Inn
Harbour Row
Isle of Whithorn
Newton Stewart DG8 8LL

Tel 01988-500334
Fax 01988-500627
Email steampacketinn@btconnect.com
Website www.steampacketinn.com

'An excellent, friendly place,' says a visitor in 2009. 'Good food. Good value.' On the quay of a pretty seafaring village at the southernmost tip of the Machars peninsula (the Isle of Whithorn is not actually an island), this 'delightful' inn has been owned by the Scoular family for 27 years. It is run by the 'quietly dedicated', 'ever helpful' Alastair Scoular, who promises that visitors will not be disturbed 'by TV, fruit machines or piped music' and offers, say visitors, 'good value'. The chef, Christopher Mills, uses fish from catches landed at the doorstep for his blackboard menus. These are served in the 'small, busy' bars, the 'bright, cheerful' dining room and the conservatory. 'Generous' dishes include salmon with a white wine and prawn sauce; braised Galloway lamb shank. Tea and coffee are available all day. Breakfast was 'satisfactory, particularly the marmalade, home made by Mrs Scoular senior'. Her husband is often around in the morning, chatting to guests. The best, spacious bedroom has large picture windows, seating area, modern bathroom, a big bed. Seven of the rooms are in the family's neighbouring pub, *The Queen's Arms*. Children are welcomed. The area has interesting archaeological remains, the 'book town' of Wigtown, 'wonderful coastal walks along springy turf, and some beautiful gardens'. (*Gordon Murray, MB, JB*)

Bedrooms: 14, 7 in adjacent pub. *Open*: all year except 25 Dec. *Facilities*: 2 bars, 2 restaurant areas, small garden, unsuitable for &. *Background music*: none. *Location*: village centre, 9 miles S of Wigtown. *Smoking*: allowed in 7 bedrooms. *Children*: all ages welcomed. *Dogs*: not allowed in front restaurant. *Credit cards*: MasterCard, Visa. *Prices*: [2009] B&B £30–£35 per person, full alc £20, winter and spring packages.

WALES

The *Guide*'s Welsh entries are widely scattered, from the Brecon Beacons to Cardigan Bay. This year's *César* winner, *Neuadd Lwyd*, Penmynydd, on the Isle of Anglesey, is in the north, where the Welsh language and culture is particularly celebrated. It is run in a warm, personal style; visitors are encouraged to embrace the local ways and enjoy the best of regional produce. Here, and across the nation, the quality of the cooking is a hallmark.

Neuadd Lwyd, Penmynydd

ABERAERON Ceredigion   Map 3:C2

Harbourmaster Hotel	*Tel* 01545-570755
Pen Cei, Aberaeron	*Fax* 01545-570762
SA46 0BA	*Email* info@harbour-master.com
	Website www.harbour-master.com

♕ *César award in 2005*

'Wholeheartedly endorsed' again this year, this bright blue hotel is
'superbly located' on the quay of a 'delightful' small west Wales town.
It has a 'real buzz, combining local pub with restaurant and rooms'.
The bilingual owners, Glyn and Menna Heulyn, are 'very hands on',
say fans, and their 'good, hard-working team' is 'friendly and helpful'.
The recently expanded bar is thought 'a big improvement; spacious,
with different types of seating, from comfy sofas to high bar stools'.
Meals are available here (eg, smoked haddock and cockle chowder;
steak and kidney pie). A new chef, Simon Williams, arrived in 2009:
he uses local meat and seafood for modern dishes like herb-crusted
cod, crushed potatoes. We'd welcome reports on his cooking. The
Georgian building has been 'brilliantly updated' in modern yet locally
sympathetic fashion. All bedrooms have views. 'Our lovely room was
filled with things that were a pleasure to use.' 'Ours had a squashy
sofa on which to crash out and stare at boats and the sea. It was
peaceful, while plenty of bustling went on below. Outstanding
breakfast.' The cottage two doors down, also overlooking the harbour,
and where children under five may stay, is 'well furnished and
equipped'. (*LM Mayer-Jones, Lynn Wildgoose*)

Bedrooms: 13, 2 in cottage, 1 suitable for ♿. *Open*: all year except 25 Dec.
Facilities: bar, restaurant, pebble beach (safe bathing nearby). *Background music*:
'modern, relaxed'. *Location*: central, on harbour. *Smoking*: not allowed. *Children*:
under-5s in cottage only. *Dogs*: not allowed. *Credit cards*: Diners, MasterCard,
Visa. *Prices*: [2009] B&B £55–£125 per person, D,B&B £80–£150, set lunch
£15–£18, full alc £36, special breaks, 1-night bookings refused weekends
Easter to Nov.

ABERGAVENNY Monmouthshire   *See Shortlist*

Always discuss accommodation in detail when making a
booking, and don't hesitate to ask for an upgrade on arrival if a
hotel is obviously not full. If you don't like the room you are
shown, ask for another one.

ABERSOCH Gwynedd   Map 3:B2

Porth Tocyn Hotel   *Tel* 01758-713303
Bwlch Tocyn   *Fax* 01758-713538
Abersoch LL53 7BU   *Email* bookings@porthtocyn.fsnet.co.uk
                         Website www.porth-tocyn-hotel.co.uk

♛ *César award in 1984*

'As good as ever – how can he stay so unfailingly cheerful and
welcoming?' Nick Fletcher-Brewer's 'welcoming, idiosyncratic style'
encourages visitors to 'feel immediately at home' at his family-friendly
hotel in the Lleyn peninsula. He tells us: 'My son, Richard, and his
girlfriend, Emma, have enthusiastically given the public rooms and
several bedrooms a fresh look.' Facing Cardigan Bay and the
Snowdonia mountains ('few dining rooms could have such a magnificent view'), the hotel is near some beautiful beaches. In its grounds
are a heated swimming pool, sun loungers, and 'secret corners' for
taking tea. The rambling structure of former lead miners' cottages has
'grown organically' over the years. A conservatory and many sitting
rooms provide space to relax inside ('fine old furniture, pictures,
books, interesting knick-knacks'). Some bedrooms are interconnected.
A three-generation family on a return visit enjoyed 'comfortable,
relaxed accommodation and delicious food'. Other visitors wrote of
the 'excellent, young, well-trained staff'. John Bell and Louise
Fletcher-Brewer run the kitchen (a *Good Food Guide* entry since 1957).
'Very good fish dishes.' Main courses might include pan-fried scallops
with tarragon blini; cannon of Welsh lamb with truffle omelette,
shitake mushroom spring roll. Vegetarian options are available.
(*Richard Creed, and others*)

Bedrooms: 17, some on ground floor. *Open*: week before Easter–early Nov.
Facilities: ramp, sitting rooms, children's rooms, cocktail bar, dining room,
25-acre grounds (swimming pool (10 by 6 metres, heated May–end Sept),
tennis), beach (5 mins' walk, sailing), fishing, golf, riding nearby, telephone to
discuss disabled access. *Background music*: none. *Location*: 2 miles outside
village. *Smoking*: not allowed. *Children*: no tiny children at dinner (high tea at
5.30 pm). *Dogs*: by arrangement, not allowed in public rooms. *Credit cards*:
MasterCard, Visa. *Prices*: [2009] B&B £45–£85 per person, cooked breakfast
£6, set dinner £32.50–£39, off-season breaks, walking breaks, 1-night bookings
sometimes refused. *V*

We asked hotels to quote their 2010 tariffs. Many had yet to fix
these rates as we went to press. Prices should always be
checked on booking.

ABERYSTWYTH Ceredigion   Map 3:C3

Gwesty Cymru   *Tel* 01970-612252
19 Marine Terrace   *Fax* 01970-623348
Aberystwyth SY23 2AZ   *Email* info@gwestycymru.co.uk
                              Website www.gwestycymru.co.uk

On Aberystwyth's Victorian seafront promenade, this Grade II listed
Georgian terrace house is run as a restaurant-with-rooms by owners
Huw and Beth Roberts. They have converted it 'with sympathy and
flair', say inspectors, who 'thoroughly enjoyed' their stay. 'Judicious
use has been made of Welsh materials': slate; furniture handmade
from Welsh oak; oil paintings by local artists. In the restaurant, Tim
Morris provided a 'first-class dinner at a reasonable price'. Typical
dishes ('with a Welsh twist'): seared king scallops with black pudding,
celeriac mash; cannon of Ystwyth valley lamb in an amaretti crust with
bubble and squeak. 'The staff were without exception both friendly
and efficient.' The bedrooms are 'well equipped'; those in the eaves
are 'a long climb'; some, above the kitchen, might be warm, and
bedside lighting may be 'inadequate'. No guest lounge: guests may sit
in the cellar bar, and the restaurant's sea-facing terrace provides
outdoor drinking and dining in good weather.

Bedrooms: 8, 2 on ground floor. *Open*: all year except Christmas/New Year,
restaurant closed for lunch Tues in winter. *Facilities*: bar, restaurant, terrace,
secure parking (book in advance), unsuitable for &. *Background music*: in
Reception and restaurant. *Location*: central, on seafront. *Smoking*: not allowed.
Children: 'well-behaved' children welcomed. *Dogs*: only guide dogs allowed. *Credit
cards*: MasterCard, Visa. *Prices*: [2009] B&B £42.50–£65 per person, full alc £35.

BALA Gwynedd   Map 3:B3

Bryniau Golau   `NEW`   *Tel* 01678-521782
Llangower, Bala   *Email* katrinalesaux@hotmail.co.uk
LL23 7BT   *Website* www.bryniau-golau.co.uk

On the eastern edge of Snowdonia national park, this Victorian house
has 'wonderful' views over Bala Lake to the Arenig Mountains. The
owner/managers, Katrina Le Saux and Peter Cottee, are 'welcoming,
personal and natural' hosts, writes the nominator. 'We were offered
tea and home-made cakes when we arrived.' The 'impeccably
furnished' bedrooms have 'all the facilities you need'; two have a four-
poster bed; bathrooms are 'state of the art' (with spa bath). There is
'plenty of space' for guests in the sitting room and study. 'In fine

weather, all will be tempted outside to the terrace and gardens, which have lots of little corners for relaxation. Sunsets are breathtaking.' Breakfast is served at a long table in a room with a grand piano. There is 'freshly squeezed orange juice, local sausages and bacon'. The hostess will cook a three-course dinner by arrangement (eg, Parma ham, blue cheese and pine nuts; pork steak in sage and onion butter; strawberry tart). She hopes to have a drinks licence for 2010. 'Wildlife abounds,' she writes. 'House martins nest in the eaves, bats roost on the roof, and wild black rabbits eat my roses.' There is good walking from the door. (*John Rowlands*)

Bedrooms: 3. *Open*: Mar–Dec. *Facilities*: sitting room, study, dining room, ½-acre garden, unsuitable for &. *Background music*: none. *Location*: 2 miles SE of Bala. *Smoking*: not allowed. *Children*: not under 12. *Dogs*: not allowed. *Credit cards*: MasterCard, Visa. *Prices*: [2009] B&B £40–£65 per person, dinner £25, 1-night bookings refused weekends and peak times. *V*

BARMOUTH Gwynedd   *See Shortlist*

BEAUMARIS Anglesey   Map 3:A3

Ye Olde Bulls Head
Castle Street
Beaumaris, Isle of Anglesey
LL58 8AP

Tel 01248-810329
Fax 01248-811294
Email info@bullsheadinn.co.uk
Website www.bullsheadinn.co.uk

'Another happy stay, with the signature welcome by friendly staff. One of our favourite hotels in the area.' Praise again for this former medieval staging inn for coaches to Ireland. In May 2009, the owners, Keith Rothwell and David Robertson, opened 13 new bedrooms in *The Townhouse*, a redeveloped adjacent building. Contemporary in style, each is named after a colour; they have iPod, Wi-Fi. There is a family room, and one for disabled visitors. In the old inn, with ancient beams and creaking staircases, 'smartly cosy' bedrooms are named after Dickens's characters (he once stayed here). The Lofthouse courtyard suite is 'spacious, traditional in style, relatively peaceful; the slightly dated bathroom did not detract from the overall feel'. Most of the rooms are quiet, but visitors wishing for an early night should avoid those above the bar. There is a 'luxuriously appointed' lounge. The brasserie, in converted stables, serves modern European dishes (eg, cassoulet of local seafood). In the *Loft* restaurant, the chef is now Hefin

Roberts. His set menu might include ravioli of confit duck, vegetable consommé; roast tronçon of halibut, caramelised fennel. 'The wine list is extensive; a big effort has been made in this department.' We would welcome reports on the cooking. (*Seth O Thomas, JB*)

Bedrooms: 26, 2 on ground floor, 1 in courtyard, 13 in *The Townhouse* adjacent, 1 suitable for &. *Open*: all year, except 25/26 Dec, 1 Jan, *Loft* restaurant closed lunch, Sun night. *Facilities*: lift (in *Townhouse*), lounge, bar, brasserie, restaurant, sea 200 yds, only brasserie and *Townhouse* suitable for &. *Background music*: 'chill-out', jazz in brasserie. *Location*: central. *Smoking*: not allowed. *Children*: no under-7s in restaurant or bedroom suites. *Dogs*: not allowed. *Credit cards*: Amex, MasterCard, Visa. *Prices*: B&B £50–£77.50 per person, set dinner (restaurant) £38.50.

BODUAN Gwynedd   Map 3:B2

The Old Rectory   *Tel/Fax* 01758-721519
Boduan   *Email* thepollards@theoldrectory.net
nr Pwllheli LL53 6DT   *Website* www.theoldrectory.net

Roger and Gabrielle Pollard 'obviously enjoy sharing their beautifully restored former Georgian rectory with visitors', say their guests. These 'very kind hosts' have for many years run this small, pale yellow B&B. 'An elegant, comfortable, well-loved home in a quiet location', it stands in large grounds amid the spectacular scenery of the Lleyn Peninsula. It has 'large, attractive' public rooms with antique family furniture and paintings by contemporary artists. A log fire is lit in the drawing room on cold days. 'Spacious, well-equipped' bedrooms are individually styled: 'Ours, shining clean, had tea-making facilities, complimentary sherry, and fine views over fields.' Some bathrooms have a roll-top bath. Breakfast, 'well cooked and elegantly presented',

includes porridge, compotes made from home-grown fruit, smoked salmon, home-made breads, jam and marmalade. Dinner reservations for guests can be made at local restaurants. Babies under one stay free: cots and high chairs are provided. There is good walking from the bottom of the drive. Nearby are three golf courses, Bodnant Gardens, coastal footpaths, and splendid sandy beaches. More reports, please.

Bedrooms: 3, also self-catering cottage. *Open*: all year except Christmas week. *Facilities*: drawing room, dining room, 3½-acre grounds, walking, riding, sailing, unsuitable for &. *Background music*: none. *Location*: 4 miles NW of Pwllheli. *Smoking*: not allowed. *Children*: all ages welcomed, under-1s stay free, babysitting by arrangement. *Dogs*: allowed in grounds only. *Credit cards*: none. *Prices*: [2009] B&B £45–£75 per person, 1-night bookings refused bank holidays.

BRECHFA Carmarthenshire   Map 3:D2

Tŷ Mawr   *Tel* 01267-202332
Brechfa SA32 7RA   *Email* info@wales-country-hotel.co.uk
                                  Website www.wales-country-hotel.co.uk

'A delightful, hard-working couple', Annabel Viney and Stephen Thomas, run this 16th-century farmhouse as a country hotel and restaurant. In a village on the edge of the Brechfa forest, it is a 'very relaxing place', providing 'good value'. 'They could not have been more helpful' to a wheelchair-user this year. The host is the chef, providing 'good bistro-style cooking', using seasonal ingredients from a large network of nearby suppliers. The hostess ('intelligent, responsive, helpful') 'uses a curious system which enables the guests to enjoy a different menu each day'. 'The food was a delight.' Try the coracle-caught sewin with a cucumber sauce, or griddled Welsh lamb chops on a chestnut and leek gravy. 'Breakfasts were good, too.' An inspector found both the house, with its original thick stone walls, fireplaces and beams, and the grounds attractive. And the bedrooms are liked: 'Ours was fairly plain, but very comfortable. It had two chairs (so often a double has only one). In perfect weather, we sat on the patio with our drinks, watching the river.' 'Good lighting.' The micro-brewery has been turned into a new 'superior' bedroom. Wi-Fi is available.

Bedrooms: 5, 1 on ground floor. *Open*: all year. *Facilities*: sitting room, bar, breakfast room, restaurant, 1-acre grounds, unsuitable for &. *Background music*: classical in restaurant. *Location*: village centre. *Smoking*: not allowed. *Children*: not under 12. *Dogs*: not allowed in restaurant. *Credit cards*: Amex, MasterCard, Visa. *Prices*: B&B £55–£60 per person, D,B&B £75–£80, set meals £24–£29, alc £43, seasonal breaks, Christmas/New Year packages. *V*

BRECON Powys   *See Shortlist*

BROADHAVEN Pembrokeshire   Map 3:D1

The Druidstone   *Tel* 01437-781221
nr Broadhaven   *Email* enquiries@druidstone.co.uk
Haverfordwest SA62 3NE   *Website* www.druidstone.co.uk

In a 'stunning cliff-top location' above a huge sandy beach, Rod, Jane and Angus Bell's 'family holiday centre' is 'very relaxed'. 'It feels like a real hotel, not at all corporate; full of character, and of characters,' says a returning visitor. 'Not for those who require perfection in service and decor. Our children are made to feel welcome; they have a high tea with other children around a big kitchen table.' The staff are 'lovely and helpful,' says another guest. Mrs Bell tells us: 'Rod and I are gradually retiring, though still living on site; Angus is now in charge.' Angus also runs the kitchen (with Andrew Bennett and Matt Ash): guests might be joined by locals in the bar for pub dishes like chicken and leek pie. The restaurant menu might include Brie rolls stuffed with roasted pepper; monkfish Provençal. Four bedrooms have private facilities (the others share three bathrooms); the two pent-house bedrooms each have a balcony facing St Bride's Bay. Sound insulation may not always be perfect. Self-catering cottages in the grounds include the tiny Roundhouse, an 'Eco Hut' which derives its energy from the sun. Pets are welcomed, so long as they get on with Jake, the donkey. Popular for weddings and parties. (*Melissa Midgen, and others*)

Bedrooms: 11, also 5 holiday cottages. *Open*: all year. *Facilities*: sitting room, TV room, bar (occasional live music), farmhouse kitchen, restaurant, small conference/function facilities, civil wedding licence, 22-acre grounds, sandy beach, safe bathing 200 yds, unsuitable for &. *Background music*: in bar. *Location*: 7 miles W of Haverfordwest. *Smoking*: not allowed. *Children*: all ages welcomed. *Dogs*: not allowed in restaurant. *Credit cards*: Amex, MasterCard, Visa. *Prices*: [2009] B&B £35–£80 per person, full alc £34, courses, conferences, Christmas/ New Year/midweek packages, 1-night advance bookings refused Sat.

CAERNARFON Gwynedd   *See Shortlist*

All our inspections are paid for, and carried out, anonymously.

CAPEL GARMON Conwy   Map 3:A3

Tan-y-Foel Country House
Capel Garmon
nr Betws-y-Coed LL26 0RE

Tel 01690-710507
Fax 01690-710681
Email enquiries@tyfhotel.co.uk
Website www.tyfhotel.co.uk

A new greenhouse provides fruit and vegetables for the 'exceptionally good' cooking at this 17th-century stone house in a 'wonderful' setting, high on wooded hills in the Snowdonia national park. It is popular with walkers. 'If you want a really peaceful location, this is for you,' one visitor writes. The 'highly professional' owners, Peter and Janet Pitman, and their 'charming' daughter, Kelly, run it as a guest house, without other help. Perhaps because of this, it has 'strict rules' (say inspectors): breakfast is between 8 and 9 am, dinner at 7.30 pm. 'Very comfortable' bedrooms, in muted shades, have flat-screen TV, DVD/CD-player. Some have a 'magnificent view' of the valley; one has a four-poster bed; two (one, the junior suite, is a converted hayloft) have their own external entrance. There are 'spacious, well-equipped' bathrooms. Mrs Pitman's modern dishes use organic ingredients in a daily-changing menu with two choices for each course, eg, turbot with smoked salmon open lasagne, watercress cappuccino; tandoori-style loin of Welsh mountain lamb, masala and spinach potato. 'Food cooked with passion and elegance, so good it is not to be missed.' A car is essential, the Pitmans warn. (*GH, CC, and others*)

Bedrooms: 6, 1 on ground floor. *Open*: All year except Christmas/New Year, limited availability during winter, dining room closed midday. *Facilities*: sitting room, breakfast room, dining room, 3-acre grounds, unsuitable for ♿. *Background music*: none. *Location*: 2 miles from Betws-y-Coed, 1½ miles off A470. *Smoking*: not allowed. *Children*: not under 12. *Dogs*: only guide dogs allowed. *Credit cards*: MasterCard, Visa. *Prices*: B&B £70–£100 per person, set dinner £45, midweek breaks, 1-night bookings refused weekends, bank holidays.

CARDIFF   Map 3:E4

Jolyon's
5 Bute Crescent, Cardiff Bay
Cardiff CF10 5AN

Tel 029-2048 8775
Fax 029-2045 5155
Email info@jolyons.co.uk
Website www.jolyons.co.uk

'The vibe is friendly and laid-back' at this 'slightly eccentric', small converted Georgian seamen's lodge opposite the 'wonderful' Millennium Centre, home of the Welsh National Opera. The owner,

Jolyon Joseph, is 'an extremely helpful host when there', says a visitor in 2009. There is no restaurant: breakfast is served in *Bar Cwtch* (Welsh for a 'cuddle' or a 'hug') in the basement, a popular local venue with a *tapas* menu (eg, dates wrapped in bacon; prawns in chilli and garlic) and pizzas from a wood-burning oven. The bedrooms are decorated in 'modern neutral style, with an eclectic mix of furniture'. 'Our first-floor room overlooking the piazza had a scattering of Welsh lifestyle magazines, Freeview television, a pot of sweets as well as the usual tea and coffee; the large bathroom had a spa bath.' A ground-floor room with a four-poster bed was thought less good value. All rooms have Wi-Fi. There is a small, 'basic' lounge. Breakfast has a selection of juices, fresh and dried fruit, pastries, toast: cooked dishes include scrambled eggs with bacon or smoked salmon. 'When we had to rush for a train, the manager [Charlie Dyer], who was unable to leave breakfast preparation, told us he would bill us later in the week. It is now my firm favourite for Cardiff visits.' (*Seth O Thomas, David Berry, and others*)

Bedrooms: 6, 1 on ground floor. *Open*: all year. *Facilities*: residents' lounge, bar, live music sometimes, terrace, unsuitable for &. *Background music*: 'easy listening' in bar. *Location*: Cardiff Bay waterfront, under 2 miles from centre. *Smoking*: not allowed. *Children*: not under 14. *Dogs*: not allowed. *Credit cards*: Amex, MasterCard, Visa. *Prices*: [2009] B&B £49.50–£75 per person, Christmas/New Year packages, 1-night bookings refused weekends of sporting events, etc.

See also Shortlist

CONWY   Map 3:A3

Sychnant Pass Country House
Sychnant Pass Road
Conwy LL32 8BJ

Tel 01492-596868
Fax 01824 790441
Email bre@sychnantpasscountryhouse.co.uk
Website www.sychnantpasscountryhouse.co.uk

'To say that the house is generously furnished is an understatement,' wrote an inspector of this 'handsome, well-kept' Edwardian house in the foothills of Snowdonia national park. 'Lots of furniture, a huge library of books, DVDs, etc; every wall covered to the ceiling with pictures, many of dogs and cats.' It is run 'with enthusiasm' by owners Bre (Irish) and Graham (the chef, Welsh) Carrington-Sykes, with their young son, Conor, and manager, Joanne Scott. The resident three cats and two dogs 'will be delighted to share their garden with your pets', they say. The welcome is 'genuinely warm', with complimentary tea. 'Our bedroom was well supplied (fridge, ironing board, sherry, etc), soft toys much in evidence.' Children are well catered for (swings and a swimming pool in the garden, games indoors). The bedrooms, named after TS Eliot's 'practical cats', vary greatly. Three are small, two have a private deck with hot tub, some have a balcony. 'Dinner was substantial' (traditional British: baked smoked haddock; rib-eye of beef, crunchy mustard sauce; vegetarian options available). 'Breakfast the usual buffet, with offers of full English.' The front porch has 'wonderful' views to the Vale of Conwy (this is a designated area of 'outstanding natural beauty'). The family also offer accommodation in *Pentre Mawr*, Llandyrnog (see Shortlist).

Bedrooms: 12. *Open*: all year, restaurant closed Mon off-season. *Facilities*: sitting room, study, restaurant, indoor 12-metre swimming pool, gym, civil wedding licence, terraces (hot tub, sauna, tanning room), 3-acre garden. *Background music*: blues, in restaurant. *Location*: 1½ miles SW of Conwy by A457. *Smoking*: not allowed. *Children*: all ages welcomed. *Dogs*: welcomed. *Credit cards*: MasterCard, Visa. *Prices*: [2009] B&B £47.50–£90 per person, D,B&B £77.50–£120, set meal £32.50, alc £40, special offers, Christmas/New Year packages, 1-night bookings refused Sat in peak season. *V*

CRICKHOWELL Powys   Map 3:D4

Glangrwyney Court
Glangrwyney, Crickhowell
NP8 1ES

Tel 01873-811288
Fax 01873-810317
Email info@glancourt.co.uk
Website www.glancourt.co.uk

In 'beautiful, peaceful' gardens, amid parkland on the edge of the Brecon Beacons national park, this Grade II listed three-storey Georgian house is the family home of Christina and Warwick Jackson who run it as an upmarket B&B. Reached by a cantilevered staircase of architectural significance, the spacious bedrooms are individually decorated in country house style; all face the garden with its views to the Black Mountains. They have TV, DVD and free Wi-Fi. The master suite has a steam shower; one twin room has a spa bath. Guests are encouraged to relax in the lounge and library, which have log fires in winter, comfortable seating, books and magazines, an honesty bar. An evening meal ('very good, all local produce') is available by arrangement for groups (weddings and other functions are held). The Jacksons will recommend places to eat locally, and organise taxis. The garden has secret sitting areas, tennis and croquet. More reports, please.

Bedrooms: 9, 1, on ground floor, in courtyard, also self-catering cottages. *Open*: all year. *Facilities*: sitting room, library/honesty bar, dining room, civil wedding licence, 4-acre garden (croquet, *boules*, tennis) in 33-acre parkland, river 500 yds (fishing by arrangement), unsuitable for &. *Background music*: at dinner if requested. *Location*: 2 miles SE of Crickhowell, off A40. *Smoking*: not allowed. *Children*: all ages welcomed. *Dogs*: allowed in courtyard room, cottages only. *Credit cards*: MasterCard, Visa. *Prices*: [2009] B&B £40–£62.50 per person, D,B&B £70–£92.50, set dinner £30, special breaks, off-season discounts, 1-night bookings sometimes refused weekends, bank holidays.

Gliffaes
Crickhowell
NP8 1RH

Tel 01874-730371
Fax 01874-730463
Email calls@gliffaeshotel.com
Website www.gliffaes.com

♕ *César award in 2009*

'Beautifully set' in mature parkland on a broad sweep of the River Usk, this 19th-century Italianate building is run as a smart sporting hotel by Susie and James Suter (the third generation of the family owners) with her parents, Mr and Mrs Brabner. 'Though the grey stone exterior is a little gloomy, light floods in through enormous windows,' said a reporter this year. Earlier praise: 'The comfort and peacefulness of the house, combined with the unaffected approach, made our stay memorable.' There are attractive indoor sitting areas, particularly the conservatory with its view down the valley. Most of the 'well-appointed, comfortable and homely' bedrooms are large; the best have a balcony overlooking the river. 'The view from our room made the journey worthwhile.' *Gliffaes* subscribes to the Slow Food Movement, sourcing 65 per cent of ingredients from within 75 miles. Chef Carl Cheetham's cooking is 'excellent, well presented': 'superb' Welsh lamb and venison were enjoyed this year. The hotel has a private stretch of the trout- and salmon-laden river (fishing courses arranged). The self-service breakfast has 'kippers, much to my delight'. 'Good walks from the hotel door.' 'For the brave, there is free use of a tandem.' Children are welcomed. (*Jonathan and Sandra Mundy, and others*)

Bedrooms: 23, 4 in annexe (1 on ground floor). *Open*: all year except 2–31 Jan. *Facilities*: ramp, 2 sitting rooms, conservatory, bar, dining room, civil wedding licence, 33-acre garden (tennis, croquet, fishing, ghillie available). *Background music*: jazz in bar in evenings. *Location*: 3 miles W of Crickhowell, off A40. *Smoking*: not allowed. *Children*: all ages welcomed. *Dogs*: not allowed indoors. *Credit cards*: all major cards. *Prices*: [2009] B&B £47–£113.50 per person, D,B&B £82–£148.50, set dinner £28–£35, fishing courses, website deals, Christmas/New Year packages, 1-night bookings refused weekends, bank holidays.

See also Shortlist

DALE Pembrokeshire   Map 3:D1

Allenbrook   *Tel* 01646-636254
Dale   *Fax* 01646-636954
SA62 3RN   *Email* info@allenbrook-dale.co.uk
                            Website www.allenbrook-dale.co.uk

'It would have been cheap at one-and-a-half times the price,' wrote visitors to Colonel and Mrs Webber's guest house in a village near the Pembrokeshire Coast national park. It stands in a large, rambling garden (with peacocks, bantams, guineafowl and geese), which leads down to the sea. 'The walls are cluttered with pictures and prints of horses and hounds and hunting scenes, some witty, others poignant. Our charming, large bedroom combined traditional luxury with modern comforts: fireplace, half-tester bed, comfy chairs, good lighting, flat-screen TV; bathroom almost as big, just as comfortable, with another fireplace, a large maroon-coloured bath on legs.' In the guest lounge, 'straight out of Trollope', family photographs 'create an air of intimacy', and there are Staffordshire dog statues, collections of birds' eggs, etc. 'We shared a breakfast table with a different couple each morning. The meal was made memorable by Mrs Webber's offer of a couple of boiled guineafowl eggs; we enjoyed them so much she gave us another two to take home.' Dale holds the sunshine record for mainland Britain. (*TT*)

Bedrooms: 3, 1 self-catering cottage. *Open*: Feb–Dec except Christmas/New Year. *Facilities*: 2 sitting rooms, breakfast room, large garden, walking, sailing, windsurfing. *Background music*: 'definitely not'. *Location*: 12 miles SW of Haverfordwest. *Smoking*: not allowed. *Children*: not under 12. *Dogs*: not allowed. *Credit cards*: none. *Prices*: [2009] B&B £40 per person.

> Please always send a report if you stay at a *Guide* hotel, even if it's only to endorse the existing entry.

DOLFOR Powys   Map 3:C4

The Old Vicarage   *Tel* 01686-629051
Dolfor, nr Newtown   *Email* tim@theoldvicaragedolfor.co.uk
SY16 4BN   *Website* www.theoldvicaragedolfor.co.uk

There is a 'generous feel' about this small guest house, a red brick
Victorian vicarage high in the hills of the Welsh Marches and with fine
views of the Montgomeryshire countryside. The owners, Tim and
Helen Withers, 'combine consummate professionalism with friendliness and informality', say visitors in 2009. 'The welcome was warm,
with tea, and Welsh cakes straight from the oven.' The lounge, with
log fire, is decorated in period style. There are antique tables and
candles in the dining room. Mr Withers, who was 'brought up in the
Elizabeth David tradition', serves 'wholesome, very fresh' food on a
limited-choice menu. 'Our meal was superb: smoked salmon bavarois;
Welsh Black beef; brill; marmalade sponge with the freshest home-
made custard.' Most of the ingredients, and the wines on a short list,
are organic. 'Breakfast was equally good: home-made muesli, bread
and marmalade, eggs from the happy-looking hens we passed on the
way in, everything from local suppliers.' Bedrooms have 'all modern
comforts: flat-screen TV, sherry, chocolates'. 'Everything we needed,
and a sizeable bathroom with good towels. Tea was brought in the
morning.' 'A peaceful setting. Ideal walking country near the start of
the Kerry Ridgeway.' (*Sarah and Tony Thomas, JR*)

Bedrooms: 3. *Open*: all year. *Facilities*: drawing room, dining room, 2-acre garden,
unsuitable for &. *Background music*: none. *Location*: 3 miles S of Newtown.
Smoking: not allowed. *Children*: not under 12. *Dogs*: not allowed. *Credit cards*:
MasterCard, Visa. *Prices*: B&B £47.50–£65 per person, D,B&B £75.50–£93, set
dinner £28, special breaks (walking, etc), 1-night bookings may be refused at
Christmas/New Year. *V*

DOLYDD Gwynedd   Map 3:A2

Y Goeden Eirin   *Tel* 01286-830942
Dolydd, Caernarfon   *Email* john_rowlands@tiscali.co.uk
LL54 7EF   *Website* www.ygoedeneirin.co.uk

César award in 2008

The name means 'The Plum Tree' in Welsh, and is the title of a book
of short stories by the local writer John Gwilym Jones. This homage
indicates the strong cultural interests of John and Eluned Rowlands.

Welsh art and books fill their small guest house in a hamlet on the edge of the Snowdonia national park, and guests come every August for Bryn Terfel's music festival nearby. There is much praise: 'Good value.' 'A fine welcome. It is hard to think how things could be improved.' 'Wonderfully situated.' It is very Welsh (bilingual menus) and very green (solar panels, recycling and composting policies; locally sourced organic food). The renovated farm buildings (local granite, slate, beams; decor a mixture of traditional and modern) stand amid rough pasture with views of mountains and sea. There is under-floor heating, Wi-Fi, and a Bechstein grand piano in the dining room, which is open to the public. Aga-cooked dishes, 'wholesome, with the occasional exotic touch', use local and home-grown ingredients. No choice, but prior consultation. 'Excellent' breakfasts. The 'large and bright' bedroom in the main house was liked ('glorious views, beautiful objects, large TV, good-sized bathroom'), and so was a room in the purpose-built annexe ('Arts and Crafts' feel). (*OP, and others*)

Bedrooms: 3, 2 in annexe. *Open*: all year except Christmas/New Year, dining room occasionally closed. *Facilities*: lounge, dining room (occasional live piano music), Wi-Fi access, 20-acre pastureland, unsuitable for &. *Background music*: occasionally. *Location*: 3 miles S of Caernarfon. *Smoking*: not allowed. *Children*: not under 12. *Dogs*: not allowed. *Credit cards*: none, cash or cheque payment requested on arrival. *Prices*: [2009] B&B £40–£50 per person, set dinner £28, 1-night bookings sometimes refused weekends. *V*

EGLWYSFACH Powys   Map 3:C3

Ynyshir Hall   NEW

Eglwysfach
nr Machynlleth SY20 8TA

Tel 01654-781209
Fax 01654-781366
Email ynyshir@relaischateaux.com
Website www.ynyshirhall.co.uk

'The beautiful, tranquil setting, the intimacy of the building and the friendliness of the staff mean that to visit *Ynyshir* is to be welcomed as a member of the family.' A ringing endorsement from a regular correspondent restores this small luxury hotel (Relais & Châteaux) to the *Guide*. Rob and Joan Reen sold it to the von Essen group in 2007, but she remains as manager; his striking artwork is 'much in evidence' throughout. The cooking of the chef, Shane Hughes, is 'stunning': 'Everything is good; the home-baked bread (brioche, rosemary focaccia, etc), the cheese list, a feast. We enjoyed a divine carrot soup with ginger emulsion; beautifully pink beef; pumpkin soufflé with dark chocolate was a highlight. Some excellent-value Italian wines.'

The 'beautifully appointed' bedrooms, each named after a famous artist, are done in bold colours. 'The furniture is stylish (one table in the drawing room excepted); sofas are opulent; the place is spotless. Service is exceptional; the staff went out of their way to assist an elderly visitor.' The landscaped gardens on the Dyfi estuary are surrounded by an RSPB reserve. (*Robert Gower*)

Bedrooms: 9, 2 in studio annexe, 1 on ground floor. *Open*: all year. *Facilities*: drawing room, bar lounge, breakfast room, restaurant, civil wedding licence, 14-acre gardens in 365-acre bird reserve (croquet, putting). *Background music*: light classical in bar, restaurant. *Location*: 6 miles SW of Machynlleth. *Smoking*: not allowed. *Children*: not under 9 (except for exclusive use). *Dogs*: allowed in 2 bedrooms, not in public rooms. *Credit cards*: all major cards. *Prices*: [2009] B&B £147.50–£202.50 per person, D,B&B £212.50–£267.50, tasting menu £80, full alc £80, special breaks, Christmas/New Year packages, 1-night bookings sometimes refused busy weekends, bank holidays. *V*

ERWOOD Powys   *See Shortlist*

FELIN FACH Powys   Map 3:D4

The Felin Fach Griffin   *Tel* 01874-620111
Felin Fach, nr Brecon   *Email* enquiries@felinfachgriffin.co.uk
LD3 0UB   *Website* www.felinfachgriffin.co.uk

'A relaxed but attentive place; everyone is friendly, and knowledge-able about the food.' New praise this year for this old inn on a main road between the Brecon Beacons and the Black Mountains. Its owners, brothers Charles and Edmund Inkin, also own *The Gurnard's Head*, Zennor, Cornwall (*qv*). In a restaurant noted for its 'evening buzz', the cooking of Ricardo Van Ede is 'imaginative and delicious'. He uses local produce with vegetables and herbs from the kitchen garden for his modern dishes, eg, soft-boiled egg, creamed morel mushrooms; slow-roasted pork belly, buttered savoy cabbage. 'The perfectly cooked pork cheek restored my husband's confidence in less than prime cuts.' 'Slices of fresh soda bread were already on the table; replenished on request.' More than 20 wines are available by the glass. The simple bedrooms have 'luxurious bedlinen', a Roberts radio; three have a four-poster bed. Visitors 'won over by the food' found that their bedroom 'belied our first impressions that it was cramped; there was plenty of storage, the bed was firm and comfortable; a well-designed bathroom'. Background music is sometimes played:

Edmund Inkin writes that 'the type of music (if any) depends on the customers'. Radio 4 is usually played at the 'excellent' breakfast, taken at a communal table in the old farmhouse kitchen. 'Scrambled eggs were delicious.' 'Inform the staff if you want an early start, as the approach is relaxed,' says a visitor who is 'looking for an opportunity to book again'. (*Deborah Starbuck-Edwards, Jill and Mike Bennett*)

Bedrooms: 7. *Open*: All year except 24–26 Dec, 4 days in early Jan, restaurant closed Mon midday. *Facilities*: bar area, dining room, breakfast room, private dining room, 1½-acre garden (stream, kitchen garden), only bar/dining room suitable for ♿. *Background music*: CDs/radio most of the time (*Today* programme at breakfast). *Location*: 4 miles NE of Brecon, in village on A470. *Smoking*: not allowed. *Children*: all ages welcomed. *Dogs*: not allowed in dining room. *Credit cards*: MasterCard, Visa. *Prices*: [2009] B&B £52.50–£75 per person, set meals £21.50–£27.50, full alc £42.50, special breaks, 1-night bookings occasionally refused. *V*

FISHGUARD Pembrokeshire   *See Shortlist*

HARLECH Gwynedd   Map 3:B3

Castle Cottage   NEW   *Tel* 01766-780479
Y Llech, Harlech   *Email* glyn@castlecottageharlech.co.uk
LL46 2YL   *Website* www.castlecottageharlech.co.uk

'Everything has a personal feel' at Glyn and Jacqueline Roberts's restaurant-with-rooms in two of the oldest buildings in this 'quirky, historic' town. They are 'friendly, warm' hosts: he is the chef; she runs front-of-house. The restaurant, in a converted 17th-century coaching inn is 'the centrepiece'. Pre-starters are taken in the 'cosy' bar area while dinner is ordered. Mr Roberts champions local and Welsh producers for his menu of modern dishes, eg, asparagus grilled with Carmarthen ham; duet of Welsh beef (slow-roasted ox cheek, fillet mignon). 'Well handled and full of flavour, though some portions were large. The wide wine list is well priced.' Three of the bedrooms are in the main building, the others in a converted Grade II listed stone cottage next door. All are decorated in contemporary style: 'Our spacious room was clean, modern (with atmospheric original roof beams); the bathroom had limestone tiles, a walk-in shower and a huge bath. We missed breakfast one morning, but our hostess brought us a pot of coffee for which she didn't charge.' *Castle Cottage* won the 2008/2009 *Taste of Wales* restaurant-of-the-year award. (*Seth O Thomas*)

Bedrooms: 7, 4 in annexe, 2 on ground floor. *Open*: all year except 3 weeks Nov. *Facilities*: bar/lounge, restaurant. *Background music*: in bar and dining room. *Location*: town centre. *Smoking*: not allowed. *Children*: all ages welcomed. *Dogs*: only guide dogs allowed. *Credit cards*: MasterCard, Visa. *Prices*: [2009] B&B £55–£75 per person, D,B&B £88–£108, set dinner £35, full alc £41, Christmas/New Year packages, 1-night bookings refused bank holidays. *V*

HAVERFORDWEST
Pembrokeshire

See Shortlist

HAY-ON-WYE Powys

See Shortlist

KNIGHTON Powys

Map 3:C4

Milebrook House
Milebrook
Knighton
Powys LD7 1LT

Tel 01547-528632
Fax 01547-520509
Email hotel@milebrook.kc3ltd.co.uk
Website www.milebrookhouse.co.uk

In 'very special' gardens facing the Shropshire hills and running down to the River Teme, this 18th-century house was once owned by Wilfred Thesiger and visited by Emperor Haile Selassie. It is run as a small hotel/restaurant by owners Beryl and Rodney Marsden and their family, 'lovely people in a lovely house'. 'It soothes and reassures,' said a recent visitor. 'Real log fires smoulder in lounge and bar; pleasant young staff serve the food and service the rooms.' But some guests find the noise from the nearby road a drawback. 'Beautiful art hangs on the walls', there are plenty of books in the lounge, and the bedrooms are 'homely' and comfortable. In the garden-facing restaurant, the owners' grandson, Chris Marsden, is the 'extremely competent' chef, serving a 'simply delicious' three-course *table d'hôte* menu (main courses like pan-roasted loin of venison, horseradish and white truffle mashed potato). Many vegetables are home grown. 'An excellent wine list: especially by the glass.' Otters and kingfishers are to be found in and by the river, and walkers are spoilt for choice in the surrounding Welsh Marches. A non-refundable deposit of £85 per room is required. (*AK, and others*)

Bedrooms: 10, 2 on ground floor. *Open*: all year, restaurant closed Mon lunch. *Facilities*: lounge, bar, 2 dining rooms, 3½-acre grounds on river (terraces, pond, croquet, fishing). *Background music*: none. *Location*: on A4113, 2 miles E of Knighton. *Smoking*: not allowed. *Children*: not under 8. *Dogs*: not allowed. *Credit cards*: MasterCard, Visa. *Prices*: [2009] B&B £54–£74 per person, set dinner £33.50, full alc £40, short breaks, Christmas/New Year packages, 1-night bookings refused weekends. *V*

LAMPETER Ceredigion   *See Shortlist*

LLANARMON DYFFRYN CEIRIOG Map 3:B4
Denbighshire

The Hand at Llanarmon	*Tel* 01691-600666
Llanarmon Dyffryn Ceiriog	*Fax* 01691-600262
Ceiriog Valley	*Email* reception@thehandhotel.co.uk
LL20 7LD	*Website* www.thehandhotel.co.uk

'Charming welcome, comfortable room, beautiful views,' writes a visitor in 2009. Returnees liked their 'splendidly refurbished' bathroom and the new dining room furniture, and endorsed their earlier comment: 'Owner/managers Martin and Gaynor De Luchi have strong ideas of what a hotel should be, and have achieved a well-deserved success. *The Hand* plays a valuable role in the community.' This down-to-earth, 'unpretentious' old inn stands at the head of a pretty valley beneath the Berwyn Mountains. It has three bars, an 'attractive' residents' lounge, and a large restaurant in a converted dairy, which has stone walls and a large wood-burning stove. The chef, Grant Mulholland, serves 'straightforward, hearty' fare: 'Superb roast Welsh beef; plump trout from the River Ceiriog.' Housekeeping is 'immaculate'. 'The staff, all local, are without exception friendly and helpful. Very reasonable prices.' 'Our bedroom faced the village square.' Two wheelchair-users found access 'excellent'. The 'very good' breakfast has ample cooked choice, and is served until 10 am. Tables and chairs stand on the terrace and in the garden. Many sites of interest are nearby, and 'you can step out of the front door to walk for miles in any direction and probably not see another soul'. 'No mobile phone signal here, just peace.' (*Therese Hickland, Richard and Jean Green*)

Note Not to be confused with the *Hand Hotel* at Chirk, 11 miles away.

Bedrooms: 13, 4 on ground floor, 1 suitable for &. *Open*: all year, accommodation closed at Christmas. *Facilities*: ramp, lounge, bar, restaurant, games/TV room (pool, darts), civil wedding licence, terrace, ¾-acre grounds. *Background music*:

none. *Location*: 10 miles W of Oswestry. *Smoking*: not allowed. *Children*: all ages welcomed. *Dogs*: not allowed in some bedrooms, public rooms except bar. *Credit cards*: MasterCard, Visa. *Prices*: [2009] B&B £42.50–£70 per person, D,B&B £60–£87.50, set dinner £17.50, full alc £30, special breaks, New Year package. *V*

See also Shortlist

LLANDEGLA Clwyd   *See Shortlist*

LLANDEILO Carmarthenshire   *See Shortlist*

LLANDOVERY Carmarthenshire   Map 3:D3

The New White Lion   *Tel* 01550-720685
43 Stone Street, Llandovery   *Email* info@newwhitelion.co.uk
SA20 0BZ   *Website* www.newwhitelion.co.uk

'A warm welcome, including tea and cakes,' was accorded by owner/managers, Gerald and Sylvia Pritchard, to a photographer visiting in 2009. These 'natural hosts' (an earlier comment) run their 'stylish' guest house, a Grade II listed former pub, in a side street in a small town near Brecon. They promise to provide 'local historical insight as well as comfort'. Both are locals: he was born on the premises. 'I felt I could have asked them for anything.' The ambience is sophisticated, but 'personal touches make it homely'. There are chandeliers, fine fabrics, smart wallpaper; comfortable sofas, an open fire and honesty bar in the spacious lounge. The pub's old benches are now in the dining room. The bedrooms, 'influenced by Welsh folklore', have wide-screen TV and antiques. 'Mine was small but comfortably furnished; lovely fluffy towels and power shower in a tiny but cleverly designed bathroom.' 'The bed provided a wonderful night's sleep.' A large ground-floor room has a walk-in wet room, and there is a family room. Chef Peter Devlin serves pre-booked dinners on a short menu. 'Fantastic food, truly home made: lemon-roast chicken with perfect vegetables.' 'Good raw materials; service brisk and friendly.' Some wines are local. Breakfast ('also great') includes local organic sausages and bacon. (*Jim Grover, JR*)

Bedrooms: 6, 1 on ground floor. *Open*: all year except Christmas. *Facilities*: lounge, dining room. *Background music*: none. *Location*: town centre, 17 miles W of Brecon. *Smoking*: not allowed. *Children*: all ages welcomed (cot, early supper available). *Dogs*: not allowed. *Credit cards*: MasterCard, Visa. *Prices*: [2009] B&B £50–£80 per person, D,B&B £75–£100, set dinner £25, alc £31.50, New Year package.

LLANDRILLO Denbighshire   Map 3:B4

Tyddyn Llan
Llandrillo
nr Corwen LL21 0ST

Tel 01490-440264
Fax 01490-440414
Email enquiries@tyddynllan.co.uk
Website www.tyddynllan.co.uk

❦ *César award in 2006*

This 'elegant Georgian house in manicured grounds', former shooting lodge of the dukes of Westminster, is run as a restaurant-with-rooms by chef/proprietor Bryan Webb and his wife, Susan. He 'continues to produce what must be as good as any food you will find in Wales', writes a fan, while she remains 'the ultimate hostess'. In the vale of Edeyrnion, facing the Berwyn Mountains, the house has 'spacious and comfortable public rooms'. The lounges have 'elegant drapes, soft lighting'; one has a piano. The bedrooms are 'thoughtfully furnished'. 'Mine was good sized, with sofa, writing table and a selection of glossy magazines.' 'Nicely framed paintings, bathroom with beautifully tiled floor and large walk-in shower.' Some rooms have 'views across stunning scenery in two directions'; all have flat-screen TV and DVD-player. 'A fantastic dinner, served at just the right pace, at well-spaced tables.' Dishes include buffalo mozzarella with dandelion, chicory, walnuts and Parmesan; rack of lamb with spiced aubergine purée. The wine list is wide-ranging. 'Great breakfast': fruit compote, freshly segmented pink grapefruit; delicious porridge; undyed smoked haddock; 'perfect poached eggs'. (*Jim Grover, Gordon Hands*)

Bedrooms: 13, 1 on ground floor. *Open*: all year, restaurant closed midday Mon–Thurs. *Facilities*: ramp, 2 lounges, bar, 2 dining rooms, civil wedding licence, 3-acre grounds (fishing, riding, golf), sailing, walking nearby. *Background music*: none. *Location*: 5 miles SW of Corwen. *Smoking*: not allowed. *Children*: all ages welcomed (£20 a night). *Dogs*: not allowed in public rooms, allowed in some bedrooms (£5 a night). *Credit cards*: MasterCard, Visa. *Prices*: [2009] B&B £45–£130 per person, D,B&B £95–£150, set dinner £45–£65, full alc £58, special offers, gourmet dinners, Christmas/New Year house parties. *V*

LLANDUDNO Conwy   Map 3:A3

Bodysgallen Hall and Spa   *Tel* 01492-584466
Llandudno LL30 1RS   *Fax* 01492-582519
                                      Email info@bodysgallen.com
                                      Website www.bodysgallen.com

♧ *César award in 1988*

'A really lovely place. First-class seating in three beautiful panelled
lounges. I couldn't fault the bedroom.' A long-time *Guide* correspondent praises this Grade I listed, 17th-century mansion (Pride of Britain).
'Beautifully situated' outside Llandudno, it stands in a large park with
a knot garden, follies, and views of Snowdonia and Conwy Castle. Now
owned by the National Trust, it is still run by Historic House Hotels and
managed by Matthew Johnson. It offers 'great old-fashioned luxury'.
'The staff are smiling and polite.' There are ancestral portraits, antiques,
splendid fireplaces and stone mullioned windows, log fires, and a 'well-
equipped' spa (guests have unlimited access); also Wi-Fi. Best
bedrooms are 'large and elegant', traditionally furnished; some have a
four-poster. The cottage suites suit families, provided children are over
six (and under-eights may not use the swimming pool). The chef,
Gareth Jones, serves modern dishes, eg, scallops and sliced truffle. The
afternoon teas are admired. (*Zara Elliott, AB, RM*)

Bedrooms: 31, 16 in cottages, 1 suitable for ♿. *Open*: all year, restaurant closed
Sun lunch, all day Mon. *Facilities*: hall, drawing room, library, bar, dining room,
bistro, conference centre, civil wedding licence, 220-acre park (gardens, tennis,
croquet), spa (16-metre swimming pool, gym, sauna, 5 treatment rooms), riding,
shooting, fishing, sandy beaches nearby. *Background music*: in bistro. *Location*:
2 miles S of Llandudno. *Smoking*: not allowed. *Children*: no children under 6 in
hotel, under 8 in spa. *Dogs*: not allowed. *Credit cards*: Amex, MasterCard, Visa.
Prices: [2009] B&B £82.50–£197.50 per person, D,B&B £115–£242.50, set
dinner £39–£45, full alc £49, special breaks, Christmas/New Year packages,
1-night bookings sometimes refused.

St Tudno Hotel   *Tel* 01492-874411
The Promenade   *Fax* 01492-860407
Llandudno LL30 2LP   *Email* sttudnohotel@btinternet.com
                                      Website www.st-tudno.co.uk

♧ *César award in 1987*

'Excellent: food, service and accommodation all first rate.' This 'small,
friendly' hotel on the promenade of this popular seaside resort

continues to attract praise from *Guide* readers. 'One of our favourites. High standards of service are maintained even in the quieter periods,' say returning visitors. The owner, Martin Bland, 'is often about, and makes a point of talking to his guests'. His staff are 'well trained, helpful and professional'. Once frequented by Alice Liddell who inspired Lewis Carroll (it has an Alice in Wonderland suite), the Grade II listed building is opposite the Victorian pier and gardens, and the beach. Public rooms have patterned wallpaper, swagged drapery, potted plants. *The Terrace* restaurant is Italianate (murals of Lake Como, stone fountains, tented ceiling, and chandeliers). Ian Watson has returned as chef: his 'classic modern British' dishes (eg, asparagus and winter truffle soup; slow-roasted shoulder of Welsh lamb with minted red wine jus) are 'excellent, imaginative'. 'Good wines at reasonable prices.' Bedrooms have colourful wallpaper and furnishings. 'Our small second-floor room had sea view; comfortable bed; delicious shortbread and fresh milk with the tea tray.' A rear room was 'cramped', with a poor outlook. There is a 'lovely little' indoor swimming pool. Car parking space is limited. (*Keith Robinson, Stephen and Pauline Glover, Richard Creed, and others*)

Bedrooms: 18. *Open*: all year. *Facilities*: lift, sitting room, coffee lounge, lounge bar, restaurant, patio, civil wedding licence, indoor heated swimming pool (8 by 4 metres), 'secret garden', unsuitable for &. *Background music*: none. *Location*: central, on promenade opposite pier, secure car park, garaging. *Smoking*: not allowed. *Children*: all ages welcomed. *Dogs*: allowed by arrangement (£10 per night), but not in public rooms or left unattended in bedrooms. *Credit cards*: all major cards. *Prices*: B&B £45–£155 per person, D,B&B £75–£185, set lunch £18–£22, set dinner £30, full alc £40, special breaks, Christmas/New Year packages. *V*

See also Shortlist

LLANDWROG Gwynedd   Map 3:A2

Rhiwafallen   *Tel* 01286-830172
Llandwrog, nr Caernarfon   *Email* ktandrobjohn@aol.com
LL54 5SW   *Website* www.rhiwafallen.co.uk

Large windows give distant views of sea (spectacular sunsets) over the
beautiful Lleyn Peninsula at Rob and Kate John's restaurant-with-
rooms. She is the 'cheerful front-of-house', he the chef. These
'excellent hosts' are 'very helpful, suggesting local excursions, etc'.
They 'do almost everything themselves', and create a 'welcoming
atmosphere'. The 'characterful' Welsh farmhouse 'with the feel of a
London town house inside' stands well back from a main road ('traffic
noise should not be a problem'). The spacious lounge is 'stylish',
furnished with an emphasis on natural materials, slate, wood, subdued
colours. In the small conservatory dining room, 'crammed with tables',
the 'honest country cooking' is admired: 'First class, without
pretension. Lovely starter of vine leaves stuffed with Parmesan, with
a piquant dipping sauce.' Main courses might include seared best end
of lamb, mutton hotpot, pickled red cabbage. 'Wonderful date and
walnut pudding.' But there are some mutters about 'London prices',
and not everyone can manage the three courses every night. At breakfast, juices are freshly squeezed, and cooked dishes include 'fabulous
home-made black pudding'. Afternoon tea is included in the price.
The 'extremely comfortable', contemporary bedrooms have oak
flooring, goose-feather duvet, Egyptian cotton bedlinen, 'sleek *en suite*
bathroom'. 'Our room, with sitting area, opened on to a terrace facing
the garden.' (*JR, Susanna Loveridge, D Baxter, Clare Whitehurst, and others*)

Bedrooms: 5, 1 on ground floor. *Open*: all year, except 25/26 Dec, 1 Jan, restaurant
closed Sun night/Mon. *Facilities*: ramps, lounge, restaurant, 2-acre garden.
Background music: modern 'chill-out'. *Location*: 6 miles S of Caernarfon. *Smoking*:
not allowed. *Children*: not under 12 (must have own room; standard rates). *Dogs*:
not allowed. *Credit cards*: Amex, MasterCard, Visa. *Prices*: [2009] B&B £50–£90
per person, D,B&B £85–£110 per person, set dinner £35, special breaks.

LLANDYRNOG Denbighshire   *See Shortlist*

'Set meal' indicates a fixed-price meal, with ample, limited or
no choice. 'Full alc' is the hotel's estimated price per person of
a three-course *à la carte* meal, with a half bottle of house wine.
'Alc' is the price of an *à la carte* meal excluding the cost of wine.

LLANGAMMARCH WELLS Powys   Map 3:D3

The Lake   *Tel* 01591-620202
Llangammarch Wells   *Fax* 01591-620457
LD4 4BS   *Email* info@lakecountryhouse.co.uk
                    Website www.lakecountryhouse.co.uk

César award in 1992

Built as a hunting lodge, this mock-Tudor Edwardian hotel in 'beautiful' grounds by the River Irfon is endorsed by *Guide* readers again in 2009. 'Excellent by any standards,' is one comment. Owner Jean-Pierre Mifsud circulates among guests during dinner; his staff are 'helpful, courteous'. The lounges are richly furnished, with paintings, log fires; one has a grand piano. The dress code in the formal dining room is smart casual (no jeans). Chef Sean Cullingford serves a modern menu, perhaps pressing of Raglan ham and foie gras; fillet of sea bass, scallop and tomato nage. Vegetarians have their own menu with equal choice. One visitor commented on the coldness of the red wine served straight from the cellar. Twelve suites in a new wing are 'tastefully done'; a room for wheelchair-users has been 'thoughtfully designed'. Bedrooms in the main house are being upgraded. The Badger suite has been given a 1920s theme based on a black lacquered screen found in the hotel's attic. Breakfast has 'everything you would expect'. The Kingfisher spa has a 'good-sized' swimming pool, health and beauty treatments. There are black swans on the lake which has 'been restocked with trout; unfortunately an otter has been spotted'. Good golfing, fishing and other open-air pursuits are nearby. (*Dr Mike Irving, John and Jackie Tyzack*)

Bedrooms: 30, 12 suites in adjacent lodge, 7 on ground floor, 1 suitable for &. *Open*: all year. *Facilities*: ramps, 3 lounges, billiard room, restaurant, spa (20-metre swimming pool, sauna, gym), civil wedding licence, 50-acre grounds (lake, fishing, river, tennis, croquet, 9-hole par 3 golf course, clay-pigeon shooting, archery). *Background music*: none. *Location*: 8 miles SW of Builth Wells. *Smoking*: not allowed. *Children*: no under-8s in spa, or in dining room after 7 pm (high tea provided). *Dogs*: allowed in some bedrooms (£8 a day), only guide dogs in public rooms. *Credit cards*: all major cards. *Prices*: B&B £92.50–£175 per person, D,B&B (min. 2 nights) £117.50–£200, set meals £38.50, full alc £55, Christmas/New Year packages. *V*

LLANGOLLEN Denbighshire   *See Shortlist*

LLANRWST Conwy
See Shortlist

LLANWRTYD WELLS Powys
Map 3:D3

Carlton Riverside
Irfon Crescent
Llanwrtyd Wells LD5 4ST

Tel 01591-610248
Email info@carltonriverside.co.uk
Website www.carltonriverside.co.uk

César award in 1998

'What a lovely place. The food was extraordinarily good.' The 'delightful' Mary Ann Gilchrist, and her 'affable' husband, Alan, run their unpretentious, 'very pleasant' restaurant-with-rooms in a building near the River Irfon in this old spa town. They live 175 yards away, but can be reached by intercom when not on the spot. 'Our room was small and a touch noisy, but it had all we needed, and did not break the bank,' says a visitor this year. An earlier comment: 'The accommodation was spacious, well equipped, beautifully decorated.' The building, window and door frames painted blue, 'is hard to miss'. Its interior is 'tasteful in brown and cream'. The L-shaped lounge (with bar and library) is comfortable if 'a little small', and well lit (large windows). In the 'simple but elegant' dining room, the best tables face the river. The food 'was, as ever, innovative, delicious; recommended wines a superb complement' (the list has more than 80 wines and many half bottles). Mrs Gilchrist, 'passionate about cooking', serves main courses like grilled cod with spring onion mash, stir-fried pak choi. There are two fixed-price menus, one with limited choice, and 'very good' vegetarian options (discuss these in advance). Breakfast, 'a joy', has fresh orange juice, 'very good scrambled eggs'. (*John Moy, and others*)

Bedrooms: 5. *Open*: all year except 10–28 Dec, restaurant closed Sun, bistro open Fri/Sat/Sun. *Facilities*: reception, bar/lounge, restaurant, bar/bistro, unsuitable for ♿. *Background music*: classical piano in bar. *Location*: town centre, no private parking. *Smoking*: not allowed. *Children*: all ages welcomed. *Dogs*: not allowed in public rooms. *Credit cards*: MasterCard, Visa. *Prices*: [2009] B&B £32.50–£50 per person, D,B&B £49.50–£105, set meals £17.50–£22.50, full alc £46, gourmet breaks, New Year package, 1-night bookings occasionally refused. *V*

See also Shortlist

MUMBLES Swansea   *See Shortlist*

NANT GWYNANT Gwynedd   Map 3:A3

Pen-y-Gwryd Hotel
Nant Gwynant
LL55 4NT

Tel 01286-870211
Website www.pyg.co.uk

🏆 *César award in 1995*

Popular with walkers and more serious climbers, this eccentric old inn below Snowdonia has been run on house-party lines by the same family since 1947. The third generation, brothers Rupert and Nicolas, have taken over the day-to-day running from their parents, Brian and Jane Pullee. 'They have maintained the heart-warming traditions started by their grandfather,' says a visitor this year. The three bars are the 'social hub for locals, passing travellers and hotel guests'; the front lawn is now a beer garden, 'popular in the late afternoon with thirsty walkers returning from the hills'. Guests are summoned to meals by a gong; everyone eats at the same time. The tables in the restaurant have flower arrangements, 'spotless, old-fashioned table-cloths', silver cutlery, 'napkins in napkin rings'. The long-serving chef, Lena Jensen, assisted by a young local, Elwyn Edwards, produces traditional dishes, perhaps cream cheese and garlic soup; French trim rack of Welsh lamb. There are 'scrumptious' packed lunches. Breakfast (served from 8.30) includes porridge and kippers. The bedrooms are simply furnished (no locks on the doors), only five have facilities *en suite*, but 'there is an inexhaustible supply of hot water'. 'The absence of TV, radio and canned music is bliss.' Children are warmly welcomed: any child under 13 who climbs Snowdon becomes a member of the Snowdon Club, receiving a lapel pin. (*JW*)

Bedrooms: 16, 1 on ground floor. *Open*: all year except Nov–Feb, but open New Year, weekends Jan, Feb. *Facilities*: lounge, bar, games room, dining room, chapel, 2-acre grounds (natural unheated 60-metre swimming pool, sauna), unsuitable for ♿. *Background music*: none. *Location*: between Beddgelert and Capel Curig. *Smoking*: not allowed. *Children*: all ages welcomed. *Dogs*: allowed. *Credit cards*: MasterCard, Visa. *Prices*: [2009] B&B £40–£50 per person, set dinner £22–£28, 3-night rates, 1-night bookings often refused weekends.

> Smaller hotels, especially in remote areas, may close at short notice off-season. Check before travelling that a hotel is open.

NEWPORT Pembrokeshire   Map 3:D1

Cnapan
East Street, Newport
nr Fishguard SA42 0SY

Tel 01239-820575
Fax 01239-820878
Email enquiry@cnapan.co.uk
Website www.cnapan.co.uk

'The warmth with which *Cnapan* is run is self-evident, and the staff seemed to really enjoy being there.' This 'superb' pink-painted restaurant-with-rooms stands on the fairly quiet main street of this seaside town in the Pembrokeshire national park (the larger Newport is in Gwent). The owners, Michael and Judith Cooper and Eluned Lloyd, are 'thorough and thoughtful'. 'Every afternoon we were offered tea with Welsh scones in the comfortable little drawing room, log-burning stove lit for us.' The listed Georgian house is crammed with family treasures, books and games; a crowded Welsh dresser stands in the hall. 'Dinner in the restaurant, with slightly old-fashioned feel, consisted of the freshest sea bass ever.' Puddings are a speciality and there is a fine selection of Welsh cheeses. 'Vegetables especially good, locally sourced, seasonal and organic; service brisk, attentive, everyone showed kindness.' The small bedrooms have pine furniture, bright colours, tea/coffee-making facilities (a jug of fresh milk left in the fridge for early-morning tea). 'Shower room a miracle of compactness; a shared bathroom available for wallowers.' The family room has an adjoining bunk-bedroom. Huge breakfasts include home-made marmalade, free-range eggs, and kippers. (*AK, BS*)

Bedrooms: 5. *Open*: 20 Mar–30 Nov, restaurant closed midday, Tues evening. *Facilities*: lounge, bar, restaurant, small garden, unsuitable for &. *Background music*: jazz/world music some evenings. *Location*: town centre. *Smoking*: not allowed. *Children*: all ages welcomed (£9 for B&B in family room). *Dogs*: only guide dogs allowed. *Credit cards*: MasterCard, Visa. *Prices*: [2009] B&B £40–£50 per person, D,B&B £68, full alc £40, 1-night bookings sometimes refused Sat and in season.

Llys Meddyg   NEW
East Street, Newport
Nr Fishguard SA42 0SY

Tel 01239-820008
Email contact@llysmeddyg.com
Website www.llysmeddyg.com

'A welcoming place with outstanding food', this Georgian town house was a coaching inn, then a doctor's house (the name translates as Doctor's Court). It is run as a restaurant-with-rooms by owners Ed and

Lou Sykes; Scott Davies is the chef. The 'smartly done-up' building has a guest sitting room, a 'spacious' dining room, and an 'atmospheric' cellar bar. Paintings by contemporary Welsh artists are displayed throughout (and are for sale). 'The service from young Welsh-speaking girls was cheerful and efficient. We enjoyed mini-crabcakes with our aperitifs,' said one visitor. 'The food really makes the place,' wrote another guest. The fish and meat are locally sourced: 'Delicious sewin, halibut, coconut shrimp and rock oysters.' Herbs and vegetables come from a 'secret' garden at the back. The cooking is 'inventive but not over-elaborate': the menu might include deep-fried local sprats; Welsh Black beef hash, poached Pantyderi egg. Each of the two larger bedrooms has a separate dressing room. 'Our room had a very comfortable bed, and a sofa; a modish bathroom.' Breakfast includes fruit pancakes. There is a tented garden room for summer eating. (*David Birnie, John Rowlands*)

Bedrooms: 8, 1 on ground floor. *Open*: all year, restaurant closed Sun/Mon Oct–June. *Facilities*: bar, restaurant, sitting room, civil wedding licence in 2010, garden. *Background music*: in bar and restaurant. *Location*: central. *Smoking*: not allowed. *Children*: all ages welcomed. *Dogs*: in bedrooms and cellar bar 'when appropriate'. *Credit cards*: MasterCard, Visa. *Prices*: B&B £50–£75 per person, D,B&B £75–£95, full alc £37, off-season midweek offers on website, 1-night bookings refused Sat high season. *V*

NEWTOWN Powys   *See Shortlist*

PENARTH Cardiff   *See Shortlist*

PENMAENPOOL Gwynedd   Map 3:B3

Penmaenuchaf Hall   *Tel* 01341-422129
Penmaenpool, nr Dolgellau   *Fax* 01341-422787
LL40 1YB   *Email* relax@penhall.co.uk
                                     Website www.penhall.co.uk

Built in imposing Victorian style in the 1860s, this cotton magnate's house stands amid 'strikingly beautiful' woodland and landscaped gardens. It is within Snowdonia national park, in a fine position overlooking the Mawddach estuary. 'All staff were friendly and efficient,' said inspectors. 'It is a spacious, dependably comfortable place.' Some bedrooms have a four-poster bed, some a sitting area with sofa. The panelled drawing room has leather sofas and a log fire. The 'handsome' conservatory restaurant, *Llygad yr Haul* ('eye of the sun'), has a 'smart ambience: well-dressed candlelit tables, oak panelling, slate floor, Gothic windows and Snowdonia views'. Chefs Justin Pilkington and Tim Reeve serve 'contemporary Welsh' food, eg, seared scallops trio of Welsh purées; roasted Bala pheasant, crisp bacon. Herbs, salads and vegetables are home grown. 'Wine is a passion of ours,' write the 'hands-on' owners, Lorraine Fielding and Mark Watson: their list has won awards, and they run a wine club. 'Though the price of dinner was on the high side, wines were very reasonably priced.'

Bedrooms: 14. *Open*: all year. *Facilities*: ramps, reception hall, drawing room, morning room, library, bar, breakfast room, restaurant, conference room, civil wedding licence, 21-acre grounds (gardens, lake, woodland), unsuitable for &. *Background music*: classical/light jazz in bar and restaurant. *Location*: 2 miles W of Dolgellau. *Smoking*: not allowed. *Children*: babes in arms and over-6s welcome. *Dogs*: allowed by arrangement in 1 bedroom and hall. *Credit cards*: Diners, MasterCard, Visa. *Prices*: [2009] B&B £75–£145 per person, set dinner £40, special breaks, Christmas/New Year packages, 1-night bookings refused Christmas/New Year. *V*

How to contact the *Guide*
By mail: From anywhere in the UK, write to Freepost PAM 2931, London W11 4BR (no stamp is needed)
From outside the UK: *Good Hotel Guide*, 50 Addison Avenue, London W11 4QP, England
By telephone or fax: 020-7602 4182
By email: editor@goodhotelguide.com
Via our website: www.goodhotelguide.com

PENMYNYDD Anglesey   Map 3:A3

 Neuadd Lwyd   *Tel/Fax* 01248-715005
Penmynydd,   *Email* post@neuaddlwyd.co.uk
nr Llanfairpwllgwyngyll   *Website* www.neuaddlwyd.co.uk
Isle of Anglesey LL61 5BX

César award: Welsh country house of the year

'We could not have been better looked after,' say visitors this year to
this 'loved and immaculate', early Victorian rectory. It stands amid
farmland in a 'beautiful location' with spectacular views of the
mountains of Snowdonia national park. The 'wonderful' Welsh-
speaking hosts, Susannah and Peter Woods, who are 'enthusiastic
about Anglesey', are proud of the Welsh atmosphere. Susannah
Woods, who trained at *Ballymaloe* cookery school in Ireland, uses local
ingredients for her 'excellent' four-course dinner (served at 'well-laid'
tables). Typical dishes: spelt risotto of leeks and Cemaes Bay crab;
fillet of Welsh Black beef, gratin dauphinoise, shallot and thyme
purée. The well-chosen wines are 'good value'. There are lots of
pictures, chandeliers, Victorian details, in the 'extremely comfortable'
lounge. Binoculars are provided in its bay window so guests can
admire the views. The bedrooms are 'well appointed, clean and
stylish'. They have a flat-screen TV/DVD/CD-player. One room has
a white-painted cast iron bedstead and furniture, the original black-
slate fireplace. Bathrooms, 'tastefully done', have slipper bath, painted
floor and expensive soap. The 'first-class' breakfast includes fresh fruit
juice of the day, home-made compotes and cereals, local honeys;
cooked dishes include 'creamy' scrambled eggs, Welsh rarebit with
Bragdy Orme beer. (*Angela Thomason, and others*)

Bedrooms: 4. *Open*: 22 Jan–30 Nov, closed Sun/Mon/Tues except bank holidays.
Facilities: drawing room, lounge, dining room, 6-acre grounds, only dining room
suitable for &. *Background music*: in evening 'if requested'. *Location*: 3 miles W
of Menai Bridge, train to Bangor. *Smoking*: not allowed. *Children*: not under 16.
Dogs: only guide dogs allowed. *Credit cards*: MasterCard, Visa. *Prices*: [2009]
B&B £70–£170 per person, D,B&B £90–£190, set dinner £39, see website for
mid-week rates.

When you make a booking you enter into a contract with a
hotel. Most hotels explain their cancellation policies, which
vary widely, in a letter of confirmation. You may lose your
deposit or be charged at the full rate for the room if you cancel
at short notice. A travel insurance policy can provide protection.

PENTREFOELAS Denbighshire   Map 3:A3

Hafod Elwy Hall   *Tel* 01690-770345
Hiraethog, nr Pentrefoelas   *Fax* 01690-770266
LL16 5SP   *Email* enquiries@hafodelwyhall.co.uk
                      Website www.hafodelwyhall.co.uk

'Far from anywhere', on a working farm on 'the bare mountains of
Denbighshire', stands Roger and Wendy Charles-Warner's
'characterful house with an Edwardian feel'; 'a great place'. 'The
welcome is personal, natural, unforced.' The 'very green' owners have
won awards for sustainability. There are wood-burning stoves in the
bay-windowed lounge and the red-walled dining room. 'Lots of odd
knick-knackery.' Original features include slate floors, bread oven,
archways, old wells. Two bedrooms have a four-poster (one has a big
cast iron bath and a thunderbox loo in its bathroom). One room is let
with an adjacent small single room. All lamb, pork and beef comes
from the farm; 'eggs from our own hens, nothing bought in'. Vegetables and fruit are organically grown. 'The cooking is country style,
authentic. Delicious sucking pig.' No liquor licence; bring your own.
'Stylish bedrooms with everything one could wish for.' Normally up
to six people are catered for, but there is 'scope for flexibility'. 'Very
isolated; should be a magnet for those tired of city life, who want
lovely home-grown, home-cooked food, peace and quiet, nice hosts.'
A non-refundable deposit of 20% is required to ensure a booking. Not
easy to find: 'Not on most satnavs.' (*JR*)

Bedrooms: 3, 1 on ground floor suitable for &. *Open*: all year. *Facilities*: 2 lounges,
sun room, dining room, 60-acre grounds (private fishing). *Background music*:
none. *Location*: 12 miles SE of Betws-y-Coed, 11 miles SW of Denbigh,
6½ miles N of Pentrefoelas off A543. *Smoking*: not allowed. *Children*: normally
not under 16. *Dogs*: allowed in sun room and lounge 'if dry and clean and no
other guest objects', not in bedrooms. *Credit cards*: MasterCard, Visa. *Prices*:
B&B £35–£70 per person, set dinner £18, Christmas/New Year packages,
1-night bookings refused weekends, bank holidays.

PONTDOLGOCH Powys   *See Shortlist*

If you dislike piped music, why not join Pipedown, the
campaign for freedom from piped music? 1 The Row,
Berwick St James, Salisbury SP3 4TP. *Tel* 01722-690622,
www.pipedown.info.

PORTHKERRY Cardiff   Map 3:E3

Egerton Grey   *Tel* 01446-711666
Porthkerry, nr Cardiff   *Fax* 01446-711690
CF62 3BZ   *Email* info@egertongrey.co.uk
                             Website www.egertongrey.co.uk

A wealth of fine antiques, porcelain and paintings fills this handsome grey stone Victorian rectory in the wooded Vale of Glamorgan. 'Charming and old-fashioned', and with 'high standards', it has views through a viaduct to the Bristol Channel. Recent praise: 'The welcome from staff and proprietors was superb. Good dinners, an extensive wine cellar.' The terraced gardens are bordered by mature woodland, creating an air of tranquillity. Cardiff airport is two miles away but the hotel stands in its own valley, and few guests have been bothered by this. Inspectors described how Richard Morgan-Price, co-owner with Huw Thomas, 'though coping with a busy restaurant, came to carry our bags and lead us to our room'. Most bedrooms are spacious, and they have colourful wallpaper and fabrics, thick carpet, antique or repro furniture. There are 'interesting objects' and squashy sofas in the lounges. Dinner (modern British cooking by Andrew Lawrence) is served by candlelight in the panelled former billiard room. Main courses might include pan-roasted rump of Breconshire lamb; baked fillet of Gower sea bass; there are vegetarian options. Breakfast has 'a nice choice of well-cooked classics'. Children are welcomed. Small weddings and functions are held. (*RB, and others*)

Bedrooms: 9. *Open*: all year. *Facilities*: 2 lounges, drawing room, library, conservatory, bar, restaurant, private dining room, function facilities, civil wedding licence, 7-acre garden (croquet), rock beach 400 yds, only restaurant suitable for &. *Background music*: light classical. *Location*: 9 miles SW of Cardiff. *Smoking*: not allowed. *Children*: all ages welcomed. *Dogs*: allowed in bedrooms and some public rooms. *Credit cards*: Amex, MasterCard, Visa. *Prices*: B&B £70–£120 per person, set dinner £25, full alc £38, special breaks, Christmas/New Year packages, 1-night bookings occasionally refused at weekends. *V*

Readers' contributions, written on the forms at the back of the book or sent by email, are the lifeblood of the *Good Hotel Guide*. Our readers play a crucial role by reporting on existing entries as well as recommending new discoveries. Everyone who writes to the *Guide* is a potential winner of the Report of the Year competition (page 10) in which a dozen correspondents each year win a copy of the *Guide* and an invitation to our annual launch party in October.

PORTMEIRION Gwynedd   Map 3:B3

Portmeirion Hotel   *Tel* 01766-770000
Portmeirion LL48 6ER   *Fax* 01766-770300
                    Email enquiries@portmeirion-village.com
                    Website www.portmeirion-village.com

Sir Clough Williams-Ellis's eccentric resort, 'a home for fallen
buildings', as he called it, still enchants visitors on the wooded hillside
of a Snowdonia peninsula. 'Can there be a more beautiful setting?' is
a recent comment. The bedrooms are in buildings throughout the
village: some in a Victorian hotel; others in *Castell Deudraeth* and in
various eclectically designed cottages and villas. The hotel was
destroyed by fire in 1981 and faithfully restored to Williams-Ellis's
original design, with a carved Italian Renaissance fireplace, and a
staircase with an elegant balustrade. *Castell Deudraeth* is an 1850s
baronial folly (mock-Tudor towers and ramparts), which was opened
in 2001 as a hotel with contemporary bedrooms. Village rooms, each
'unique', should be chosen carefully as some are in the busier parts of
the village (residents may be visible to the 'curious eyes of day
visitors'). Guests can eat in the hotel's restaurant (lovely estuary views)
or *Castell Deudraeth*'s gastropub (grills, oysters, local seafood). 'An
efficient minibus service links the buildings.' Manager Robin
Llywelyn, grandson of Clough Williams-Ellis, leads a 'long-established staff' who 'without exception make one most welcome'.
Weddings are often held, and 'there is a lot of climbing to get
anywhere on the estate'. (*PF, BP*)

Bedrooms: 14 in hotel, some on ground floor, 1 suitable for &, 11 in *Castell
Deudraeth*, 28 in village. *Open*: all year except 4–22 Jan. *Facilities*: hall, lift,
3 lounges, bar, restaurant (harpist sometimes), brasserie in *Castell*, children's
supper room, function room, beauty salon, civil wedding licence, 170-acre
grounds (garden), heated swimming pool (8 by 15 metres, May–Sept).
Background music: none. *Location*: edge of Snowdonia national park, 2 miles
from Porthmadog, free minibus from Minffordd station. *Smoking*: not allowed.
Children: all ages welcomed. *Dogs*: not allowed. *Credit cards*: all major cards.
Prices: [2009] B&B £85–£150 per person, D,B&B £110–£175, full alc £40,
special offers on website, Christmas/New Year packages.

Small hotels will often try to persuade you to stay for two nights
at the weekend. We ask all the hotels in the *Guide* whether they
ever refuse a one-night booking, and indicate those that won't
take them. It is worth asking about this, especially off-season or
when booking late.

PWLLHELI Gwynedd   Map 3:B2

Plas Bodegroes   *Tel* 01758-612363
Nefyn Road   *Fax* 01758-701247
Pwllheli LL53 5TH   *Email* gunna@bodegroes.co.uk
                          Website www.bodegroes.co.uk

❧ *César award in 1992*

'It pulls off a difficult trick by balancing the warmth of small scale and access to fresh local produce with the professionalism and high standard of a first-rate, busy city restaurant.' 'A most enjoyable three nights.' Praise this year for Chris Chown and his wife, Gunna, at their restaurant-with-rooms in a white, Georgian manor house. The setting is 'idyllic', up an avenue of beech trees in lovely wooded grounds. 'Gunna provides a friendly, professional service from the clockwork pre-dining sequence' ('delicious pre-starters' in the bar). The 'gorgeous' L-shaped dining room has 'delightful illuminated display cabinets', polished wood floor, modern Welsh paintings, 'perfect lighting'. Chris Chown's 'classically based' use of local ingredients, in dishes like chargrilled rib-eye of Welsh Black beef with braised cheek ('one the best cuts of beef I have ever tasted'), is much admired. The wine list, 'one of the best in Wales', has a wide selection of half bottles. Meal service can be leisurely. The 'attractively furnished' bedrooms have Scandinavian-style decor, flat-screen TV and Wi-Fi. Guests are advised that two smaller attic rooms are best for a one-night stay. Two rooms are in a cottage, facing a tranquil courtyard garden. (*Seth O Thomas, Brian Pullee, Jacqueline and Philip Speakman*)

Bedrooms: 11, 2 in courtyard annexe. *Open*: Mar–mid-Nov, closed Sun and Mon except bank holidays. *Facilities*: lounge, bar, breakfast room, restaurant, 5-acre grounds, unsuitable for ♿. *Background music*: in restaurant. *Location*: 1 mile W of Pwllheli. *Smoking*: not allowed. *Children*: all ages welcomed. *Dogs*: not allowed in public rooms, 1 bedroom. *Credit cards*: MasterCard, Visa. *Prices*: [2009] B&B £55–£87.50 per person, D,B&B £97.50–£130, set dinner £42.50, full alc £55, midweek breaks, 1-night bookings refused bank holidays.

Check the Hotelfinder section (page 11) if you are looking for a hotel for a special occasion, perhaps a memorable meal (see Gourmet and Gastropubs); a sporting weekend (see Golf, Fishing, Walking); somewhere that will welcome your children – or your dog. Our editors have selected ten hotels in each of these categories (and many more) to help you make your choice.

REYNOLDSTON Swansea   Map 3:E2

Fairyhill   *Tel* 01792-390139
Reynoldston, Gower   *Fax* 01792-391358
nr Swansea SA3 1BS   *Email* postbox@fairyhill.net
                                      Website www.fairyhill.net

Fairyhill's large grounds have manicured lawns with sculptures, woodland, a trout stream and a lake with wild ducks. And this small, creeper-covered, 18th-century mansion is near the magnificent beaches of the Gower coast. Andrew Hetherington, front-of-house, owns it with Paul Davies (chef with James Hamilton). Service ('first class,' one couple wrote) is by young men in black. All bedrooms (a few are a bit small) have flat-screen TV/DVD/CD-player and free Wi-Fi. 'Our spacious room had a large bathroom; fruit bowl replenished daily; housekeeping immaculate.' 'Ours was lovely; dinner was superb.' Imaginative dishes in modern Welsh style include slow-braised Welsh Black ox cheek with crispy bacon, root vegetables and mash. There's a strong commitment to local and organic produce. Breakfast has 'a comprehensive buffet and the usual cooked offerings'. Jam, biscuits and bread are home made; a walled garden and orchard provide vegetables, herbs and fruit. Holistic treatments can be arranged. Some visitors find the muzak played in the public areas 'ghastly'. (*R and CS, HB*)

Bedrooms: 8. *Open*: all year except 24–26 Dec, first three weeks in Jan, restaurant closed 26 Dec. *Facilities*: lounge, bar, 3 dining rooms, meeting room, spa treatment room, 24-acre grounds (croquet, woodland, stream, lake), beaches (water sports 3 miles), unsuitable for &. *Background music*: jazz/classical/pop in lounge, bar, dining room at mealtimes. *Location*: 11 miles W of Swansea, M4 exit 47 to Gowerton. *Smoking*: not allowed. *Children*: not under 8. *Dogs*: allowed in bedrooms and grounds only. *Credit cards*: MasterCard, Visa. *Prices*: [2009] B&B £87.50–£137.50 per person, D,B&B £122.50–£182.50, set dinner £35–£45, special breaks, 1-night bookings sometimes refused Sat.

RUTHIN Denbighshire   *See Shortlist*

ST DAVID'S Pembrokeshire   *See Shortlist*

Make sure that the hotel has included VAT in the prices which it quotes.

SKENFRITH Monmouthshire   Map 3:D4

The Bell at Skenfrith
Skenfrith NP7 8UH

Tel 01600-750235
Fax 01600-750525
Email enquiries@skenfrith.co.uk
Website www.skenfrith.co.uk

By an old stone bridge across the River Monnow, Janet and William Hutchings's 17th-century coaching inn has a 'wonderfully quiet', 'very beautiful' setting, deep in the Welsh Marches. 'We were made most welcome, and very much enjoyed our stay,' says a visitor this year. There are flagstone floors, an inglenook fireplace, and 'simple yet sophisticated' bedrooms. One visitor, who had booked a single room, was delighted, on a quiet weekend, to be upgraded to a 'magnificent suite, with huge, stylish bathroom, very comfortable bed, large sofa'. Another guest enjoyed the 'idyllic' experience of lying in the bath and 'watching ewes with their lambs on a green hillside'. All bedrooms have DVD/CD-player and free Internet access. The kitchen garden was granted full organic status in 2009, reinforcing a commitment to local and organic produce by providing vegetables, herbs, soft fruits and salads. The restaurant serves elaborate modern British dishes like a trio of Talgarth beef (braised blade, oxtail faggot, seared sirloin) with spiced red wine sauce and horseradish foam. There is a 'splendid', wide-ranging wine list. Children are welcomed: they have their own organic menu, and electronic listening devices are available. (*Brian Pullee, and others*)

Bedrooms: 11. *Open*: all year except last week Jan, first week Feb, also Tues Nov–Easter (not Christmas fortnight). *Facilities*: large open sitting area, restaurant, private dining room, bar, 1-acre grounds (river opposite, quad biking, archery, go-carting, clay-pigeon shooting, fishing nearby), only restaurant suitable for &. *Background music*: none. *Location*: 9 miles W of Ross-on-Wye. *Smoking*: not allowed. *Children*: all ages welcomed, no under-8s in restaurant in the evening. *Dogs*: not allowed in restaurant or unattended in bedrooms. *Credit cards*: MasterCard, Visa. *Prices*: [2009] B&B £55–£120 per person, full alc £35, midweek breaks, Christmas package, 1-night bookings refused Saturday nights. *V*

SWANSEA   *See Shortlist*

If you are recommending a B&B and know of a good restaurant nearby, please mention it in your report.

TALSARNAU Gwynedd   Map 3:B3

Maes-y-Neuadd   *Tel* 01766-780200
Talsarnau LL47 6YA   *Fax* 01766-780211
                                         Email maes@neuadd.com
                                         Website www.neuadd.com

❦ *César award in 2003*

'Well located in this lovely area; friendly service, very good food,'
writes a visitor in 2009. In immaculate grounds with spectacular views
over Snowdonia, this 14th-century 'mansion in the meadow', owned
by Peter and Lynn Jackson and Peter Payne, is liked for its peaceful
setting and its staff, 'who really care about their guests'. The bedrooms
vary in size and style; refurbishment is continuing. Some are 'inviting,
cosy', but some annexe rooms may be 'functional, but small and dark'.
'I like being presented with a letter on arrival detailing the staff one
is likely to encounter; also the complimentary bottle of sloe gin in the
room.' Some guests are uncomfortable with a 'sense of officialdom'
('too many rules'), including a £10 charge for amending a booking.
'Good-sized, bright' sitting areas have oak beams, antique and modern
furniture, inglenook fireplace. In the elegant dining room, with well-
spaced tables, Peter Jackson uses vegetables, herbs and fruit from the
kitchen gardens, and local meat for his daily-changing menus which
might include warm game rillette with candied aubergine; roast loin
of pork with pork confit cake, rosemary-scented potatoes. The 'well-
chosen' wine list has a 'good range of prices'. Children have their own
menu. (*Jim Grover, GH, and others*)

Bedrooms: 15, 4 in coach house, 3 on ground floor. *Open*: all year. *Facilities*: lift,
ramps, lounge, bar, conservatory, family dining room, main dining room,
business facilities, civil wedding licence, terrace, 85-acre grounds (croquet,
helipad). *Background music*: some traditional music in the restaurant. *Location*:
3 miles NE of Harlech off B4573. *Smoking*: not allowed. *Children*: all ages
welcomed but no under-8s in main dining room at night. *Dogs*: allowed in
2 coach house bedrooms only, must be on a leash in grounds. *Credit cards*:
MasterCard, Visa. *Prices*: [2009] B&B £49.50–£100, D,B&B £79–£135, set
dinner £35–£39, full alc 48, 2/3-night breaks, special offers, Christmas/New
Year packages, 1-night bookings refused bank holidays. *V*

TALYLLYN Gwynedd   *See Shortlist*

For details of the Voucher scheme see page 57.

TREMADOG Gwynedd   Map 3:B3

Plas Tan-Yr-Allt   *Tel* 01766-514545
Tremadog, nr Porthmadog   *Email* info@tanyrallt.co.uk
LL49 9RG   *Website* www.tanyrallt.co.uk

🏆 *César award in 2008*

'A wonderful experience, more reminiscent of a house party than a
hotel; a clear reflection of the engaging, easy-going personalities of
the owners.' Praise this year for Michael Bewick and Nick Golding
(the chef) at their 'exquisite and tranquil' Grade II listed house which
overlooks the Glaslyn estuary. 'The interior verges between country
house and Boho chic; it is packed with character (as well as a parrot).'
'Theatrical touches' include comedy cushions, and a loo done like a
library. Each bedroom is different: Shelley's Theatre has 'a wonderful
four-poster and a spacious Victorian-themed bathroom'. Madocks has
a domed ceiling, white paintwork, huge modern chandelier, metal-
framed bed, 'wonderful sea views'. Guests dine together at 8.15 off a
set menu, at a 'fabulous' oak and slate table. 'We were impressed by
the quality of the locally sourced food and the light touch of the
cooking. On our second night there were just two of us, and by
candlelight we were served crab caught that morning, a deftly cooked
partridge, and passion fruit tart in the shape of a heart with ice cream.
A most romantic meal.' Breakfast, 'another social affair', was 'a quality
concoction of fresh fruits, cereals and hot dishes, served in the light-
filled dining room'. A new ground-floor suite was due to open in 2009.
(*Seth O Thomas, and others*)

Bedrooms: 7. *Open*: all year except Christmas, Feb, Mon/Tues Oct–Mar.
Facilities: drawing room, library, dining room, 47-acre grounds, unsuitable
for ♿. *Background music*: none. *Location*: 1 mile N of Porthmadog, guests
collected by car. *Smoking*: not allowed. *Children*: not under 16. *Dogs*: not allowed.
Credit cards: Amex, MasterCard, Visa. *Prices*: [2009] B&B £60–£140 per person,
D,B&B £98.50–£178.50, set dinner £38.50, New Year package, 1-night
bookings refused bank holidays and peak weekends.

We update the *Guide* every year. Hotels are dropped or may be
demoted to the Shortlist if there has been a change of owner
(unless reports after the change are positive), if this year's
reports are negative, or in rare cases where there has been no
feedback. A lot of hotels are omitted every year, and many new
ones are added.

WHITEBROOK Monmouthshire   Map 3:D4

The Crown at Whitebrook   *Tel* 01600-860254
Whitebrook, nr Monmouth   *Fax* 01600-860607
NP25 4TX   *Email* info@crownatwhitebrook.co.uk
Website www.crownatwhitebrook.co.uk

This 'really special place' was found by a reader through the *Guide* in
2009, when snow closed the main roads. She was 'reluctant to leave'
when the weather improved. Earlier, an inspector reported that
'residents are no less important than guests at table' at this restaurant-
with-rooms. Surrounded by woods in the Wye valley, the former
17th-century drovers' inn, managed by David Hennigan, is in a small
village near Monmouth. The chef, James Sommerin, has a *Michelin* star
for his 'elaborate, flavoursome' cooking. He sources local produce for
dishes like terrine of pork cheek and foie gras with chorizo and fig;
seared turbot, confit belly pork, cèpe, sage and onion. A vegetarian
visitor enjoyed a 'relaxing meal, because they understood the details of
vegetarian cooking. Portions were of a comfortable size, leaving room
for the little extras served between courses, and the delicious bread.'
The bedrooms, in a modern extension, have a contemporary feel: 'Our
executive room was well furnished: large bed, dressing table, writing
desk, bookcase, ample wardrobe; decanter of sherry. The spotless
bathroom had a double-ended bath, a walk-in shower. It was peaceful,
with views over the garden.' The 'welcoming' lounge/bar has leather
sofas. Breakfast is 'sumptuous'. (*Jeanette Bloor, and others*)

Bedrooms: 8. *Open*: all year except Christmas/New Year, restaurant closed Sun
night. *Facilities*: ramp, lounge/bar, restaurant, business facilities, 2-acre garden,
River Wye 2 miles (fishing), only restaurant suitable for &. *Background music*:
varied. *Location*: 6 miles S of Monmouth. *Smoking*: not allowed. *Children*: not
under 12. *Dogs*: only guide dogs allowed. *Credit cards*: MasterCard, Visa. *Prices*:
B&B £57.50–£100 per person, set meals £45–£70, full alc £55, special breaks,
1-night bookings refused bank holidays.

CHANNEL ISLANDS

The hotels most loved by *Guide* readers on these islands close to the Normandy coast are in out-of-the-way locations. One is an idiosyncratic little place on car-free Sark, another, on the tiny island of Herm which continues to operate after a change of ownership. This is the shortest chapter in the *Guide* and we would welcome new nominations, and reports on the hotels selected for our Shortlist, as well as on the full entries.

St Brelade's Bay Hotel, St Brelade

BRAYE Alderney   *See Shortlist*

HERM   Map 1: inset D6

The White House   *Tel* 01481-722159
Herm, via Guernsey GY1 3HR   *Fax* 01481-710066
                                      Email sion@herm-island.com
                                      Website www.herm-island.com

♥ *César award in 1987*

There have been significant changes at this beautiful, tiny island since
Herm's lease was bought in September 2008 by Starboard Settlement.
A new Guernsey company, controlled by John and Julia Singer, was
set up to run the island. They wish to be 'hands off', and have
promoted Jonathan Watson, the manager of Herm's only hotel, to a
new position of hospitality director of the island. Sion Dobson Jones,
formerly of the *Portmeirion Hotel* (*qv*), now manages the hotel, and
Kevin Hyde is the chef. Visitors who have known *The White House* for
many years reported 'with relief' in 2009 that 'it was functioning just
as before, with friendly young staff from around the world, though the
personal touch was missing: we never got to speak to the manager.
The building looked newly decorated; our room was spacious and
comfortable, but there is no longer a turn-down service. No TV in the
hotel or telephone in the bedrooms – guests come to get away from
them. The meals were beautifully presented; desserts outstanding,
starters and main dishes had more emphasis on presentation than
taste.' The menu might include beef fillet with smoked savoy
cabbage; baked breast of duck with black cherry sauce. A jacket and
tie are expected of male guests at dinner. Neighbouring islands are
visible from a series of interconnecting lounges, which have board
games, free self-help tea and coffee, and 'sofas and chairs arranged to
encourage guests to chat'; an 'ample light lunch' is available here.
Children are welcomed (high teas and baby-listening); 'muzak is still
mercifully absent from the hotel, and transistor radios are not allowed
on the beaches, so the whole island has an air of peace'. Car-free Herm
has cliffs, pastel-coloured cottages, a little harbour, three shops, an inn
and a 10th-century chapel. Hotel guests are met at the boat; their
luggage is transported by tractor. (*Nigel and Jennifer Jee*)

Bedrooms: 40, 18 in cottages, some on ground floor. *Open*: 26 Mar–3 Oct.
Facilities: 3 lounges, 2 bars, 2 restaurants, conference room, 1-acre garden

(tennis, croquet, 7-metre solar-heated swimming pool), beach 200 yds, Herm unsuitable for ♿. *Background music*: none. *Location*: by harbour, air/sea to Guernsey, then ferry from Guernsey (20 mins). *Smoking*: not allowed. *Children*: all ages welcomed, no under-9s in restaurant at night (high teas provided). *Dogs*: only guide dogs allowed. *Credit cards*: MasterCard, Visa. *Prices*: [2009] D,B&B £80–£130 per person, set dinner £25, see website for special offers.

KINGS MILLS Guernsey   *See Shortlist*

ST BRELADE Jersey   Map 1: inset E6

The Atlantic Hotel   *Tel* 01534-744101
Le Mont de la Pulente   *Fax* 01534-744102
St Brelade JE3 8HE   *Email* info@theatlantichotel.com
                                        Website www.theatlantichotel.com

Visitors returning after four years to this modern hotel found it 'as lovely as ever'. Owned by Patrick Burke, with Jason Adams as manager, it has 'fabulous views' over the five-mile beach of St Ouen's Bay. The 'beautiful' bedrooms have full-length, sliding windows and a terrace or a Juliet balcony. Many overlook the swimming pool; standard rooms face the neighbouring La Moye golf course. Spacious studios and suites are in a garden wing. Luxurious public areas have antique terracotta flagstones, wrought iron staircase, rich carpeting, urns, fountains, antiques, specially designed furniture. 'Even the corridors are beautiful.' In the *Ocean* restaurant, head chef Mark Jordan 'fully justified' his *Michelin* star with meals of 'consistently high quality over a week'. He uses local ingredients whenever possible for his seasonal *carte* and daily-changing set menus, eg, smoked salmon pavé, Jersey royals; pot-roast chicken, sweetcorn mash, truffle bubbles. Breakfast is 'perfectly OK, but a slight let-down after dinner; fresh bread would have been welcome'. Guests have free access to a leisure centre. The *Atlantic* is popular with families in summer: there are nursery menus and board games for families. The airport is close by: 'We did not notice any aircraft noise.' (*Tony and Marlene Hall*)

Bedrooms: 50, some on ground floor. *Open*: Feb–Dec. *Facilities*: lift, lounge, library, cocktail bar, restaurant, private dining room, fitness centre (swimming pool, sauna), wedding facilities, garden (tennis, indoor and outdoor heated swimming pools, 10 by 5 metres), golf club and beach ½ mile, unsuitable for ♿. *Background music*: in restaurant in evening. *Location*: 5 miles W of St Helier. *Smoking*: not allowed. *Children*: all ages welcomed. *Dogs*: not allowed. *Credit cards*: all major cards. *Prices*: [2009] B&B £75–£225 per person, D,B&B £125–£275, set meal £50, full alc £75, special breaks, off-season rates, Christmas/New Year packages.

St Brelade's Bay Hotel
St Brelade JE3 8EF

Tel 01534-746141
Fax 01534-747278
Email info@stbreladesbayhotel.com
Website www.stbreladesbayhotel.com

For five generations, the Colley family has run this 'large, glamorous hotel' that 'seems to cater for everyone'. The long, white modern building faces Jersey's loveliest bay: the 'beautiful beach' is across a road. Elegant public rooms have parquet floors, panelled ceilings, chandeliers, oriental rugs and a 'wonderful collection of paintings'. Loungers stand on lawns near the freshwater swimming pools. In summer, alfresco lunches are served, and 'afternoon tea is brought while you laze in the shade'. Bedrooms are spacious; there are some two-bedroom penthouse suites; front rooms have 'fantastic' views (most have a balcony); there are communicating family rooms. A visitor this year, on a three-generation visit, appreciated the 'always courteous' staff, headed by manager Margriet Barnes, and the 'excellent facilities for children: playroom, TV room, two small pools and slides, etc, in a small garden area away from adults'. Cots, high chairs and high tea are provided. 'Some chambermaids were willing to babysit, although baby-listening is available.' Chef Franz Hacker is commended for his 'amazing' and 'never repetitive' dinners, with dishes like veal tournedos with cider apple jus. The English breakfast is 'superb'. No jeans, T-shirts or trainers in the dining room and mobile phones are 'not welcome' in public areas. (*Jean Taylor, JJW*)

Bedrooms: 85. *Open*: 4 Apr–3 Nov. *Facilities*: lift, ramps, lounge, cocktail bar (evening entertainment, singers, disco, magician, etc, daily except Sun), restaurant (pianist 3 nights a week), toddlers' room, games room, snooker room, sun veranda, 7-acre grounds (outdoor restaurant, 2 heated swimming pools (25 by 10 metres, 1 for children) with bar and grill, sauna, mini-gym, tennis, croquet, putting, *boules*, children's play area), beach across road, golf nearby. *Background music*: none. *Location*: 5 miles W of St Helier. *Smoking*: allowed on terrace and balcony only. *Children*: all ages welcomed. *Dogs*: not allowed. *Credit cards*: all major cards. *Prices*: [2009] B&B £70–£262 per person, D,B&B £30 added, set dinner £35, full alc £45, weekend breaks.

ST HELIER Jersey   *See Shortlist*

ST MARTIN Guernsey   *See Shortlist*

ST PETER PORT Guernsey   *See Shortlist*

ST SAVIOUR Guernsey   *See Shortlist*

ST SAVIOUR Jersey   Map 1: inset E6

Longueville Manor   *Tel* 01534-725501
Longueville Road   *Fax* 01534-731613
St Saviour JE2 7WF   *Email* info@longuevillemanor.com
                                     Website www.longuevillemanor.com

Inland from St Helier, in wide grounds by a lovely wooded valley, this extended 13th-century manor house is Jersey's most sumptuous hotel (Relais & Châteaux). It is run by Malcolm Lewis (the third-generation owner) and his wife, Patricia; her brother-in-law, Pedro Bento, is the manager. Although the building has a smart decor (swagged curtains, antiques, original paintings), it has an unstuffy air: the family dogs and cats can be seen in the reception rooms. The spacious bedrooms are traditionally decorated; they have fresh flowers, bowls of fruit, home-made shortbread; a soft-toy dog on each bed. Each of the ground-floor rooms has a private patio. Dinner is served in a large, light room or in the oak-panelled Great Hall. The cooking of executive head chef Andrew Baird 'revolves around fresh local produce' (vegetables from the walled kitchen garden) in dishes like croustillant of local crab, brown soufflé, Bloody Mary granité; assiette of pork, ragout of vegetables, pancetta emulsion. The 'relaxed' breakfast has a generous buffet, an extensive choice of cooked dishes. Light meals can be taken by the swimming pool in the grounds, which have a croquet lawn and a lake with black swans. More reports, please.

Bedrooms: 31, 8 on ground floor, 2 in cottage. *Open*: all year. *Facilities*: lift, ramp, 2 lounges, cocktail bar, 2 dining rooms, function/conference/wedding facilities, 15-acre grounds (croquet, tennis, heated swimming pool, woodland), sea 1 mile. *Background music*: none. *Location*: 1½ miles E of St Helier by A3. *Smoking*: allowed in 5 bedrooms. *Children*: all ages welcomed. *Dogs*: not allowed in public rooms. *Credit cards*: all major cards. *Prices*: [2009] B&B £105–£272.50 per person, D,B&B £160–£327.50, set dinner £47.50–£55, full alc £80, special breaks, Christmas/New Year packages.

SARK   Map 1: inset E6

La Sablonnerie
Little Sark
Sark, via Guernsey GY9 0SD

Tel 01481-832061
Fax 01481-832408
Email lasablonnerie@cwgsy.net
Website www.lasablonnerie.com

'A force of nature', Elizabeth Perrée, owner of this 'idiosyncratic' little hotel/restaurant on the quiet southern corner of this car-free island, is 'around most of the time, and on friendly terms with her guests'. 'She and her staff always addressed us by name,' say inspectors in 2009. The cooking of chef Colin Day is 'a great strength'. His daily-changing *table d'hôte* is served by solicitous young waiters in the small dining room (formal place settings, elegant white china, no muzak). 'Delicious quail's egg on asparagus; lovely crab soup; freshly caught sea bass with a mussel cream sauce; delicious desserts, eg, chocolate parfait with poached pears.' The bedrooms vary greatly; most are in small buildings in the garden. 'Ours was quite basic: only one bedside light; no extras; heating by an electric heater. Comfortable bed with sheets and blankets; the night was beautifully quiet.' Some spacious rooms are in cottages. There is a 'lovely, large' room above the bar, but it might be noisy at times. Breakfast has cereals and stewed fruit; 'so-so' toast and jams; 'perfect' scrambled eggs. *La Sablonnerie* has many fans. 'As wonderful as ever,' one wrote. 'The glories are the lovely, large garden with benches for alfresco drinks and eating in summer, and the walks from the door.' Guests are brought by horse-drawn open cart, 'romantic on a sunny day, less so when it is pouring with rain'. (*John Barnes, and others*)

Bedrooms: 22, also accommodation in nearby cottages. *Open*: Easter–Oct. *Facilities*: 3 lounges, 2 bars, restaurant, wedding facilities, 1-acre garden (tea garden/bar, croquet), Sark unsuitable for &. *Background music*: classical/piano in bar. *Location*: S part of island, boat from Guernsey (hotel will meet). *Smoking*: allowed in some bedrooms. *Children*: all ages welcomed. *Dogs*: allowed at hotel's discretion, but not in public rooms. *Credit cards*: MasterCard, Visa. *Prices*: B&B £40–£85 per person, D,B&B £59.50–£115, set meal £25.80, full alc £39.50 (*excluding 10% service charge*).

See also Shortlist

There is no VAT in the Channel Islands.

IRELAND

Hospitality is second nature in Ireland, which may explain why some of the *Guide*'s favourite hotels and guest houses can be found in this chapter. The great majority of hotels in Ireland remain in private ownership with hands-on management. This year's *César* award goes to a splendid example, *Rosleague Manor*, Letterfrack, where Mark Foyle has taken over the day-to-day running from his father, Edmund. A visitor this year said that guests are made to feel special, which is exactly how it should be.

Rosleague Manor, Letterfrack

BAGENALSTOWN Co. Carlow   Map 6:D6

Lorum Old Rectory	*Tel* 00 353 59-977 5282
Kilgreaney, Bagenalstown	*Fax* 00 353 59-977 5455
	Email bobbie@lorum.com
	Website www.lorum.com

In the rolling land at the foot of Mount Leinster, this granite mid-Victorian former rectory is run by its owner, the 'delightful' Bobbie Smith, who prides herself on providing a 'family atmosphere'. A member of Euro-Toques, dedicated to using local and organic produce, she serves an imaginative six-course dinner (with sorbet and cheese). 'I plan what I am going to cook and discuss it with the people staying,' she says. Typical dishes: broccoli and horseradish with lime soup; roast pork stuffed with prunes and apricots. Dinner is served communally around a large mahogany table in the red dining room. Tea and home-baked scones, and after-dinner port, may be taken by a log fire in the drawing room with its books, family photographs and memorabilia. The spacious, high-ceilinged bedrooms have 'perfect proportions', and are decorated with 'an eye for colour'; some have a four-poster; all have good views. 'Our room was pretty and comfortable; shower, no bath.' One bedroom has a separate bathroom. The 'wonderful', leisurely breakfast includes fresh orange juice, a good full Irish, home-baked breads, much fruit. Nearby are the gardens at Kilfane, Woodstock and Altamont. More reports, please.

Bedrooms: 4. *Open*: Mar–Nov. *Facilities*: drawing room, study, dining room, 1-acre garden (croquet), unsuitable for &. *Background music*: none. *Location*: 4 miles S of Bagenalstown on R705 to Borris. *Smoking*: not allowed. *Children*: welcomed by arrangement. *Dogs*: allowed by arrangement. *Credit cards*: Amex, MasterCard, Visa. *Prices*: B&B €75–€100 per person, D,B&B €123–€128, set dinner €48, 10% discount for stays of more than 2 nights.

BALLINROBE Co. Mayo   *See Shortlist*

Check the Hotelfinder section (page 11) if you are looking for a hotel for a special occasion, perhaps a memorable meal (see Gourmet and Gastropubs); a sporting weekend (see Golf, Fishing, Walking); somewhere that will welcome your children – or your dog. Our editors have selected ten hotels in each of these categories (and many more) to help you make your choice.

BALLYCASTLE Co. Mayo   Map 6:B4

Stella Maris   *Tel* 00 353 96-43322
Ballycastle   *Fax* 00 353 96-43965
                          Email info@stellamarisireland.com
                          Website www.stellamarisireland.com

Facing the sea on the wild coast of north Mayo (the least populated
county in Ireland), this 19th-century coastguard station has been
turned into a hotel by Frances Kelly, a local, and her American
husband, Terence McSweeney. 'Wonderful, friendly hosts', they
create a 'relaxed atmosphere'. 'The welcome, on first-name terms, is
warm. They are attentive to guests throughout,' is one recent
comment. 'Redecoration of the public and private rooms is of the
highest standard.' Mr McSweeney is a sportswriter and keen golfer: he
works for the US PGA in Florida during the winter. There are golfing
books aplenty in the 100-foot-long conservatory that runs the length
of the building. 'Each bedroom is named after a golf course, and there
is excellent golfing available nearby.' Some rooms are small, but most
have a sea view. Frances Kelly ('her cooking is a real bonus') serves an
inventive cuisine using 'local, organic artisan produce', eg, teriyake-
seasoned beef, caramelised fennel; breast of Mayo chicken with
herbed cheese pocket, wild rice and pine nut pilaf. There is a 'brief
but carefully chosen wine list'. Breakfast has fresh grapefruit, home-
made preserves, 'the usual cooked things attractively presented'. (*SS*)

Bedrooms: 11, 1, on ground floor, suitable for &. *Open*: May–Sept, restaurant
closed to non-residents on Mon. *Facilities*: ramps, lounge, bar, restaurant,
conservatory, 2-acre grounds (golf), sea/freshwater fishing, sandy beach nearby.
Background music: in public rooms. *Location*: 2 miles W of Ballycastle. *Smoking*:
not allowed. *Children*: all ages welcomed (limited availability). *Dogs*: not allowed
in house. *Credit cards*: Diners, MasterCard, Visa. *Prices*: [2009] B&B €100–€185
per person, full alc €57.

BALLYLICKEY Co. Cork   Map 6:D4

Seaview House   *Tel* 00 353 27-50073
Ballylickey, Bantry Bay   *Fax* 00 353 27-51555
                          Email info@seaviewhousehotel.com
                          Website www.seaviewhousehotel.com

'We love staying at *Seaview*.' 'Excellent value for money. The hotel
runs like clockwork.' Set back from the road above Bantry Bay, this
extended, white, bay-windowed Victorian building is run under the

'sharp eye' of its owner, Kathleen O'Sullivan. 'Nothing passes her by: the gardens and house are maintained to a high standard.' Earlier praise, from a guest who stayed for a week with three generations of his family: 'Miss O'Sullivan and her staff could not have been kinder. My young granddaughters were given delicious high teas, and made to feel special.' The library has mahogany bookcases; the lounge has an open fire. There is 'a lively mix of guests': they gather in the bar for drinks before dinner. No music ('absolute bliss') here or in the restaurant with its conservatory extension. Chef Eleanor O'Donovan's four-course dinner menu, priced according to number of courses taken, has wide choice (so does breakfast). Typical dishes: cheese tartlet with crispy bacon; roast sirloin of beef with horseradish sauce. All meat and fish is sourced locally. This year some bedrooms have been refurbished. Those in the new wing have under-floor heating in the bathroom; sea 'glimpses' from the top-floor rooms. 'A serene environment.' (*Patrick and Patricia Palmer, D and GC*)

Bedrooms: 25, 2, on ground floor, suitable for &. *Open*: mid-Mar–mid-Nov. *Facilities*: bar, library, 2 lounges, restaurant/conservatory, 3-acre grounds on waterfront (fishing, boating), riding, golf nearby. *Background music*: none. *Location*: 3 miles N of Bantry. *Smoking*: allowed in 5 bedrooms. *Children*: all ages welcomed, special menus and babysitting available. *Dogs*: not allowed in public rooms. *Credit cards*: Amex, MasterCard, Visa. *Prices*: B&B €70–€120 per person, D,B&B €95–€130, set dinner €35–€45, special breaks. *V*

BALLYMENA Co. Antrim   Map 6:B6

Marlagh Lodge	*Tel* 028-2563 1505
71 Moorfields Road	*Fax* 028-2564 1590
Ballymena	*Email* info@marlaghlodge.com
BT42 3BU	*Website* www.marlaghlodge.com

'Wonderful quirky Victorian furniture everywhere which suits the building.' A recent visitor felt 'very well looked after' at this listed Victorian dower house. It has been restored with 'a natural sense of design' by owners Robert and Rachel Thompson. 'You won't find satellite TV or DVD-player in our bedrooms,' they say, 'each room has its own bookcase instead.' There are feather duvets and fine bedlinen. The Blue Room has a king-size cast iron four-poster bed, and a roll-top bath in its bathroom. The Chintz Room, in aquamarine and cream, has a spacious shower room. The Print Room, 'populated by cherubs', has brass beds; bathroom ('more cherubs') across a landing. Guests may play the piano in the study (the Thompsons are keen musicians). Rachel Thompson's 'inventive' five-course dinners use local produce in dishes like warm smoked bacon and avocado salad with Cashel blue cheese dressing; roast duck with red wine and cherry sauce. Breakfasts, 'lavish and over-tempting', have 'excellent home-made bread', 'Tummy Warmer' (porridge with Bushmills whiskey), Ulster fry, scrambled eggs with smoked salmon. The house is just off a busy road 'but quiet at night'. Children are welcomed. Ballymena ('middle town') is between Belfast and the nine glens of Antrim. (*CG*)

Bedrooms: 3. *Open*: all year except Christmas/New Year, dining room closed Sun night. *Facilities*: drawing room, dining room, ½-acre garden, unsuitable for ♿. *Background music*: classical/jazz during dinner. *Location*: 1½ miles E of Ballymena. *Smoking*: not allowed. *Children*: all ages welcomed. *Dogs*: not allowed. *Credit cards*: MasterCard, Visa. *Prices*: B&B £45 per person, D,B&B £77.50, 10% discount for 3 nights or more. *V*

BALLYVAUGHAN Co. Clare   Map 6:C4

Gregans Castle   *Tel* 00 353 65-707 7005
Ballyvaughan   *Fax* 00 353 65-707 7111
                                   Email stay@gregans.ie
                                   Website www.gregans.ie

Open turf fires burn in the elegant public rooms of this Georgian house, once the country home of a local family. Set in large grounds on a hill above Galway Bay, it has views of the 'magical' limestone landscapes of the Burren. The welcome is warm from the owner, Simon Haden, and his wife, Frederieke McMurray. There are paintings, and photographs of local characters in the bar; flowers, books and magazines in the lounge; in the porch, wellington boots for visitors' use. The chef, Mickael Viljanen, serves inventive modern dishes using local, seasonal, organic produce, eg, venison loin with pumpkin, confit turnip, fondant potato, pear; rabbit saddle with ventrèche ham, *boudin noir*, barley milk. Vegetarians are catered for. The wine list is 'excellent'. Light lunches and afternoon teas are served in the bar. Small children are fed at 6 pm. Recent visitors were pleased to be upgraded to a large ground-floor suite with four-poster bed, small sitting room, radio, CD-player; no television ('a bonus'), but free Wi-Fi. 'Everything was perfect.' Breakfast has large buffet and a wide choice of cooked dishes. Guided walks of the Burren, and day-trips to the Aran Islands can be arranged. (*DR*)

Bedrooms: 20, some on ground floor. *Open*: 12 Feb–30 Nov. *Facilities*: hall, lounge/library, bar, dining room, 15-acre grounds (ornamental pool, croquet), wedding facilities, safe sandy beach 4½ miles, golf, riding, hill walking nearby. *Background music*: light jazz in bar. *Location*: 3½ miles SW of Ballyvaughan. *Smoking*: not allowed. *Children*: no under-6s in dining room at night. *Dogs*: allowed in 2 bedrooms, not in public rooms. *Credit cards*: Amex, MasterCard, Visa. *Prices*: [2009] B&B €97.50–€305 per person, set dinner €50–€65, special breaks on website, 1-night bookings sometimes refused bank holiday weekends.

BANGOR Co. Down   Map 6:B6

Cairn Bay Lodge   NEW
278 Seacliff Road
Ballyholme, Bangor
BT20 5HS

Tel 028-9146 7636
Fax 028-9145 7728
Email info@cairnbaylodge.com
Website www.cairnbaylodge.com

'Excellent, a relaxing break,' writes a visitor this year to the white, pebble-dashed home of Chris and Jenny Mullen and their young daughters, Poppy and Daisy. It has a 'fantastic position' on Ballyholme Bay. 'After trying the noisy hotels in the town centre, I was pleased to find this tranquil B&B. The attentive hosts do not intrude on your privacy.' Other visitors enjoyed the 'friendly welcome' and their 'good-sized room with a view over the bay'. The bedrooms have an 'imaginative tea tray; cake left outside'. The lounge also has bay views. The 'exceptional' breakfast, served in an oak-panelled room, is 'the highlight: home-made wheaten bread, fruit juices; in addition to the usual fry-up, we enjoyed a smoked salmon omelette (duck eggs) with soda bread, and, *pièce de résistance*, Irish goat's cheese with mushrooms and tomatoes'. The off-street parking is appreciated, too.

Jenny Mullen, a beauty therapist, gives treatments in her salon. (*Graham Smith, Sheelagh Dunk, Dermot K Stewart*)

Bedrooms: 5. *Open*: all year except 2–30 Jan. *Facilities*: 2 lounges, dining room, beauty salon, small shop, ½-acre garden, unsuitable for &. *Background music*: in dining room during breakfast. *Location*: ¼ mile E of centre. *Smoking*: not allowed. *Children*: all ages welcomed. *Dogs*: not allowed. *Credit cards*: MasterCard, Visa. *Prices*: [2009] B&B £37.50–£50 per person, special breaks, 1-night bookings sometimes refused. *V*

BELFAST   Map 6:B6

Ravenhill House
690 Ravenhill Road
Belfast BT6 0BZ

Tel 028-9020 7444
Fax 028-9028 2590
Email info@ravenhillhouse.com
Website www.ravenhillhouse.com

'Breakfast is the most important meal of the day,' say Roger and Olive Nicholson, the owners and 'most helpful hosts' of this detached Victorian house in a leafy suburb. Guests at their 'well-run, friendly' B&B choose the evening before from an impressive morning selection: home-made bread, muesli, granola and fruit compote, organic porridge, Ardglass kippers and a full Ulster fry. It is convenient for the city, having good bus links on the busy road ('I was not disturbed by traffic'). 'My small single bedroom was clean, well equipped and well lit; comfortable bed, with good pillows and sheets, blankets not a duvet; a clean bathroom with a good shower; just enough storage space.' 'Good value for money.' Free Wi-Fi connection; maps and other information are provided. Many eating places are nearby. More reports, please.

Bedrooms: 5. *Open*: all year except Christmas/New Year, 2 weeks in July. *Facilities*: sitting room, dining room, unsuitable for &. *Background music*: occasional, with radio at breakfast. *Location*: 2 miles S of centre. *Smoking*: not allowed. *Children*: all ages welcomed. *Dogs*: not allowed. *Credit cards*: MasterCard, Visa (*3% surcharge*). *Prices*: [2009] B&B £35–£50 per person, 1-night bookings refused at weekends.

See also Shortlist

BLARNEY Co. Cork   *See Shortlist*

BUSHMILLS Co. Antrim   *See Shortlist*

CAPPOQUIN Co. Waterford   Map 6:D5

Richmond House
Cappoquin

Tel 00 353 58-54278
Fax 00 353 58-54988
Email info@richmondhouse.net
Website www.richmondhouse.net

In 'well-tended grounds' in the Blackwater valley, this 'charming' Georgian house has a 'pleasantly old-fashioned feel'. 'Excellent in every way', it is decorated with hunting and fishing trophies. 'Appropriate antique furniture, flowers, chintz furnishings and flowery wallpaper that reminded me of my grandmother go hand in hand with mod cons, efficiency and comfort,' says a report in 2009. It is 'brilliantly' run by owners Paul and Claire Deevy. He is the award-winning chef in this 'popular dining venue'; she the hostess 'who oversees operations with charm and efficiency'. 'His parents are on hand, too; it is all very homely, though professional.' 'The staff, mostly local, many long serving, are helpful.' 'Our spacious second-floor room had a large bed, plenty of storage. The bathroom had good plumbing and toiletries. Housekeeping is meticulous.' The cooking 'majors on local meat and fish, all of quality. On busier nights a separate vegetarian menu was offered.' Dishes include chicken liver pâté, duck terrine; monkfish with basil mash and beurre blanc. 'The imaginative, reasonably priced wine list has a good selection of half bottles.' 'Breakfasts in June included fresh strawberries and raspberries. Scones were sometimes straight from the oven. Cooked dishes carefully done, toast and coffee better than average.' One visitor found the background music 'a little intrusive'. (*Eithne Scallan, Andrew Wardrop, and others*)

Bedrooms: 9. *Open*: mid-Jan–mid-Dec, restaurant closed Sun/Mon except July and Aug. *Facilities*: lounge, restaurant, 12-acre grounds, fishing, golf, pony trekking nearby, unsuitable for &. *Background music*: 'easy listening' in restaurant. *Location*: ½ mile E of Cappoquin on N72. *Smoking*: not allowed. *Children*: all ages welcomed. *Dogs*: not allowed. *Credit cards*: MasterCard, Visa. *Prices*: [2009] B&B €75–€120 per person, set dinner €35 (early bird), €58, special breaks. *V*

Deadlines: nominations for the 2011 edition of this volume should reach us no later than 15 May 2010. Latest date for comments on existing entries: 1 June 2010.

CARAGH LAKE Co. Kerry   Map 6:D4

Carrig Country House   *Tel* 00 353 66-976 9100
Caragh Lake   *Fax* 00 353 66-976 9166
Killorglin   *Email* info@carrighouse.com
                              Website www.carrighouse.com

A former hunting lodge, this attractive yellow 1850s building has a
'sublime setting' by a lake facing the MacGillycuddy Reeks. It is
owned and managed by Mary and Frank Slattery, who greet their
visitors warmly. In the evening, drinks are served with canapés in a
handsome drawing room with an open fire; the Slatterys take orders for
dinner. In the restaurant (open to non-residents), the chef, John Luke,
cooks an extensive seasonal menu of Irish/continental dishes,
eg, potted pork coppa, grain mustard, bulgar wheat; Kerry beef
bourguignon, roasted pearl onions, basmati rice. A pianist sometimes
accompanies the meal, or there might be background music. The
bedrooms 'have everything you need', and views of lake or woodland
(ground-floor rooms have a patio). In the large grounds are camellias
and azaleas, 950 species of trees, rare flowers and shrubs; also marked
walks, a stream and waterfalls. Outdoor activities of all kinds are
available in the area, and the Slatterys offer an 'exclusive massage and
beauty treatment'. More reports, please.

Bedrooms: 17, some on ground floor. *Open*: 5 Mar–end Nov, lunch not served.
Facilities: 2 lounges, snug, library, TV room, dining room (occasional pianist),
wedding facilities, 4-acre garden on lake (croquet, private jetty, boat, fishing,
walks), 10 golf courses locally. *Background music*: classical in lounge and
restaurant. *Location*: 22 miles W of Killarney. *Smoking*: allowed in 4 bedrooms.
Children: not under 8 (except infants under 12 months). *Dogs*: only guide dogs
allowed. *Credit cards*: Diners, MasterCard, Visa. *Prices*: [2009] B&B €75–€175
per person, set dinner €39.50, special breaks. *V*

CARRIGBYRNE Co. Wexford   Map 6:D6

Cedar Lodge   *Tel* 00 353 51-428386
Carrigbyrne, Newbawn   *Fax* 00 353 51-428222
                           Email info@cedarlodgehotel.ie
                           Website www.cedarlodgehotel.ie

A short drive from the ferry port at Rosslare, this low, white, modern
hotel has long been popular with visitors heading towards the south
and west. It stands in award-winning gardens below the slopes of
Carrigbyrne forest ('lovely walks'). A regular visitor commends the

'happy, homely atmosphere' created by owners Tom and Ailish Martin. The 'comfortable and well-equipped' bedrooms 'are quiet; you don't hear the traffic from the main road'. Mr Martin is a 'charming and ebullient' host, who 'has an eye for detail'; his staff are 'courteous and well trained'. In the dining room with its exposed brick walls and large copper-canopied log fire, Mrs Martin serves 'excellent' traditional dishes, eg, quail's egg salad; sirloin steak, black peppercorn sauce. (*JFR*)

Bedrooms: 28, some on ground floor. *Open*: 1 Feb–20 Dec. *Facilities*: ramp, lounge, lounge/bar, restaurant, wedding facilities, 1½-acre garden. *Background music*: varied in bar and restaurant. *Location*: on N25, 14 miles W of Wexford. *Smoking*: not allowed. *Children*: all ages welcomed. *Dogs*: allowed by arrangement. *Credit cards*: all major cards. *Prices*: B&B €80–€110 per person, set dinner €55.

CASHEL BAY Co. Galway   Map 6:C4

Cashel House
Cashel Bay

Tel 00 353 95-31001
Fax 00 353 95-31077
Email res@cashel-house-hotel.com
Website www.cashel-house-hotel.com

♥ *César award in 2008*

In 'rambling gardens, full of surprises', this 19th-century manor house, 'very much a home', has been run for more than 40 years by the McEvilly family. Kay McEvilly 'seems never to be off-duty', said a returning visitor. 'If she is not in the dining room, she's gardening.' To combine her passions, she has introduced two-night gardening courses hosted by a leading Irish plantsman, Ciaran Burke. The house, 'cleverly extended' to side and rear, has an 'appropriate country house decor, antiques in the hall and the welcoming lounge', leather seating in the big bar. Bedrooms vary in size; not all face the sea. 'Our corner room had big bed, neat sitting area, traditional furnishings, heavy drapes, a little faded.' Ray Doorley assists Mrs McEvilly in the restaurant with its conservatory extension. The five-course menus of Arturo Amit and Arturo Tillo have a wide choice, including locally caught fish, eg, monkfish with saffron and coriander. One couple encountered linguistic problems with foreign staff. Breakfast has a big buffet with porridge, croissants, fresh fruits; three types of fish (a supplement is charged for smoked salmon); leaf tea, 'super bread', home-made preserves. More reports, please.

Bedrooms: 30. *Open*: all year. *Facilities*: ramps, 2 lounges, bar, library, dining room/conservatory, wedding facilities, 50-acre grounds (tennis, riding, small private beach). *Background music*: none. *Location*: 42 miles NW of Galway. *Smoking*: allowed in 8 bedrooms. *Children*: all ages welcomed. *Dogs*: not allowed in public rooms. *Credit cards*: Amex, MasterCard, Visa. *Prices*: (*12½% service charge added*) B&B €105–€190 per person, D,B&B €155–€240, set dinner €60, winter breaks, Christmas/New Year packages. *V*

CASTLEBALDWIN Co. Sligo   *See Shortlist*

CASTLEHILL Co. Mayo   Map 6:B4

Enniscoe House
Castlehill, Ballina

Tel 00 353 96-31112
Fax 00 353 96-31773
Email mail@enniscoe.com
Website www.enniscoe.com

Once described as the last great house in the mountainous scenery of north Mayo, this 'well-maintained' Georgian building is now a small private hotel. The owner, Susan Kellett (the thirteenth generation of her family to have lived on the estate), runs it with her 'quiet-spoken, humorous' son, Donald John ('everybody calls me DJ'). They tell us that this year the old window frames have been replaced: 'No more rattles, and all clean glass.' The massive front door opens on to a high-ceilinged hall with family portraits and fishing trophies. A huge elliptical staircase leads to the bedrooms; three face Lough Conn, where guests may sail and fish. 'Our spacious room had high canopy bed, dressing table, wardrobe; small bathroom.' Two bedrooms (one with a connected smaller room) have a working open fire. Pre-dinner drinks are taken in one of two vast sitting rooms: it has 'cosy corners', and big sofas round a roaring fire. Dinner is served by DJ in an attractive room with well-spaced wooden tables. His mother cooks in 'good country style'. Two choices (except soup) for each of the five courses: dishes like kidneys and rice with sherry sauce; baked cod with red lentils and smoked bacon. Breakfast has a silver dish of porridge on the sideboard; a basket of breads and toast; 'super bacon and sausages'. The estate has a heritage centre and a walled garden with a tea room.

Bedrooms: 6, plus self-catering units behind house. *Open*: Apr–Oct, groups only at New Year. *Facilities*: 2 sitting rooms, dining room, 150-acre estate (garden, tea room, farm, heritage centre, conference centre, forge, fishing), unsuitable for &.

Background music: none. *Location*: On R315, 2 miles S of Crossmolina. *Smoking*: not allowed. *Children*: all ages welcomed. *Dogs*: not allowed in public rooms. *Credit cards*: MasterCard, Visa. *Prices*: B&B €98–€130 per person, D,B&B €146–€178, set dinner €50, 10% discount for 3 nights or more, New Year package, 1-night bookings refused bank holiday Sat. *V*

CASTLELYONS Co. Cork   Map 6:D5

Ballyvolane House   *Tel* 00 353 25-36349
Castlelyons, Fermoy   *Fax* 00 353 25-36781
                                         Email info@ballyvolanehouse.ie
                                         Website www.ballyvolanehouse.ie

❧ *César award in 2009*

In north Cork farming country, this fine Georgian house is run in a 'relaxed, modern' style by Justin and Jenny Green. These 'generous, hospitable' hosts 'welcome guests to their family home on first-name terms, and foster a house-party atmosphere' (said inspectors). 'Justin gave us an informal greeting, showing us round before carrying our bags to our room. This had big sash windows overlooking the garden, lovely old furniture, an enormous bed, bottled water, home-made blackcurrant juice; in the large bathroom a claw-footed bath and a stag's head.' Guests help themselves to drinks from an honesty bar before the four-course no-choice dinner ('we'll think of a plan B if you don't like something'), taken at 8 pm around a huge mahogany table with silver candelabras. A reporter this year found the food cooked by Teena Mahon 'hearty and dazzlingly fresh (the potatoes had been dug up that afternoon)'. Typical dishes: goat's cheese and avocado salad; roast rib of McGrath's beef, rosemary and garlic potatoes. Breakfast, 'unrushed' and served until noon, has freshly squeezed juice, poached fruits and cereals from the sideboard; 'good cooked dishes'. *Ballyvolane House* has 'glorious' grounds, with woodland and three trout lakes, and it owns six miles of fishing on the River Blackwater. Children are warmly welcomed.

Bedrooms: 6. *Open*: 4 Jan–23 Dec. *Facilities*: hall, drawing room, honesty bar, dining room, 15-acre grounds (garden, croquet, 3 trout lakes), unsuitable for &. *Background music*: none. *Location*: 22 miles NE of Cork. *Smoking*: not allowed. *Children*: all ages welcomed. *Dogs*: not allowed in bedrooms (outhouse provided). *Credit cards*: Amex, MasterCard, Visa. *Prices*: B&B €95–€115 per person, set dinner €60, fishing school, monthly supper club, special breaks. *V*

CLIFDEN Co. Galway   Map 6:C4

The Quay House   *Tel* 00 353 95-21369
Beach Road   *Fax* 00 353 95-21608
Clifden   *Email* thequay@iol.ie
                                  Website www.thequayhouse.com

❦ *César award in 2003*

'An absolutely splendid breakfast menu; I have never before seen
such choice.' It was enjoyed at this former harbourmaster's house
which overlooks the estuary below this interesting little town on the
western Connemara coast. The 'welcoming and chatty' owners, Paddy
and Julia Foyle, run their B&B with 'easy informality'. 'They were
there to greet us each evening on return from exploring; on our last
night we were invited into their kitchen for drinks and conversation,'
one visitor wrote. 'They make you feel as if you have known them all
their lives. He helped us change a punctured tyre in the rain.' The
house is 'amusingly eccentric': 'We had the quirky Mirror Room, a
good size, especially the bathroom.' There are gilt-framed family
portraits, Irish paintings and antiques, Napoleonic mementos, and a
peat fire at night in the cosy drawing room. The bedrooms in the main
house have garden or bay view; most are spacious, though ones at the
top are small. The newest section contains studios with a balcony
overlooking the water. The Foyles have a licence, and sell a good
selection of wines. The town has 'great pubs and shops; we enjoyed
our meal at *Foyle's* (yes, a relation)'. (*Stuart Smith, and others*)

Bedrooms: 14, 2, on ground floor, 1 suitable for &, 7 studios (6 with kitchenette)
in annexe. *Open*: Mid-Mar–end Oct. *Facilities*: 2 sitting rooms, breakfast
conservatory, ½-acre garden, fishing, sailing, golf, riding nearby. *Background
music*: none. *Location*: harbour, 8 mins' walk from centre. *Smoking*: not allowed.
Children: all ages welcomed. *Dogs*: not allowed. *Credit cards*: MasterCard, Visa.
Prices: B&B €70–€90 per person, special breaks, 1-night bookings refused bank
holiday Sat.

CLONES Co. Monaghan   *See Shortlist*

The more reports we receive, the more accurate the *Guide*
becomes. Please don't hesitate to write again about an old
favourite, even if only to endorse the entry. New reports help
us keep the *Guide* up to date.

CONG Co. Mayo   Map 6:C4

Ballywarren House   *Tel/Fax* 00 353 9495-46989
Cross, Cong   *Email* ballywarrenhouse@gmail.com
                                     Website www.ballywarrenhouse.com

'Delightful stay; splendid hosts, very good food.' Praise for David
and Diane Skelton's creeper-covered replica Georgian home in
farming country between Lough Corrib and Lough Mask. There are
open peat fires, an oak staircase, and books and magazines in the
sitting room where tea with home-baked cake is taken. 'There is no
such thing as fast food at *Ballywarren House*,' says Mrs Skelton, who
posts her four- to five-course daily-changing *table d'hôte* menu on a
blackboard, discussing likes and dislikes in advance. She cooks
French/Irish dishes in her Aga, using local free-range and organic
produce. The short wine list is entirely French. The Skeltons
sometimes join guests for after-dinner drinks. There are 'pleasing
little touches' in the 'well-equipped and comfortable' bedrooms. A
room with a four-poster bed had 'good white linen; the huge bath
was deep and double-ended, and there was a pile of lovely thick
towels'. Breakfast has a 'brilliant buffet spread', a choice of six
cooked dishes, home-made bread, jams and marmalades; eggs come
from the hens which roam the grounds. Good fishing nearby; 'we
have our own ghillie'. (*JC*)

Bedrooms: 3. *Open*: all year. *Facilities*: reception hall, 2 sitting rooms, dining
room, 1-acre garden in 6-acre grounds (lake, fishing nearby), unsuitable for &.
Background music: none. *Location*: 2 miles E of Cong. *Smoking*: not allowed.
Children: not under 14, except babies. *Dogs*: not allowed in house. *Credit cards*:
Amex, MasterCard, Visa. *Prices*: B&B €68–€136 per person, set dinner €42.

See also Shortlist

CRAIGAVON Co. Armagh   *See Shortlist*

DERRY Co. Londonderry   *See Shortlist*

DINGLE Co. Kerry   *See Shortlist*

DONEGAL Co. Donegal   *See Shortlist*

DUBLIN   Map 6:C6

Aberdeen Lodge   *Tel* 00 353 1-283 8155
53–55 Park Avenue,   *Fax* 00 353 1-283 7877
Ballsbridge, Dublin 4   *Email* aberdeen@iol.ie
                        Website www.halpinsprivatehotels.com

'They could not have been kinder or more helpful when we arrived
after an early flight; though it was mid-morning, they made us a
wonderful breakfast with a smile.' One of this year's comments on Pat
Halpin's small hotel at the southern end of Ballsbridge: it has good bus
and rail connections to the city centre, and its own car park. 'If you
enjoy home comforts, this is the place,' said another visitor. It is
managed by Ann Keane; the 'lovely staff, mostly young Polish girls',
were generally praised this year (a dissenter wrote of a communication
problem). There is free Wi-Fi Internet access in the rooms, but neither
clock nor radio. Breakfast is taken in the 'attractive' dining room (now
with floor-to-ceiling windows overlooking the 'superb gardens'). It has
a table with fruit, yogurt, cereals, freshly squeezed orange juice, and a
'tasty, cooked selection', eg, scrambled eggs with smoked salmon. The
piped music annoys some visitors. A limited drawing room/room-
service menu is available; there is good dining at Sandymount village
ten minutes' walk away (*Browne's* and *Mario's* are recommended). The
family owns three other hotels in Dublin, and one in Kilkee, County
Clare. (*Angela Thomason, John Armstrong, and others*)

Bedrooms: 17. *Open*: all year. *Facilities*: ramps, drawing room, dining room,
½-acre garden, beach nearby. *Background music*: classical. *Location*: S of city,
close to DART station. *Smoking*: not allowed. *Children*: all ages welcomed. *Dogs*:
not allowed. *Credit cards*: all major cards. *Prices*: B&B €69.50–€170 per person,
set meals €25–€35, special offers, Christmas/New Year packages. ***V***

See also Shortlist

The terms printed in the *Guide* are only an indication of the size
of the bill to be expected at the end of your stay. It is wise to
check the tariffs when booking.

DUNFANAGHY Co. Donegal   Map 6:A5

The Mill   *Tel/Fax* 00 353 74-913 6985
Figart   *Email* themillrestaurant@oceanfree.net
Dunfanaghy   *Website* www.themillrestaurant.com

'Honest and unpretentious', this informal restaurant-with-rooms is a
modest, white, late 19th-century former flax mill, outside a small
coastal village. It is run by owners Derek and Susan Alcorn: he is the
chef, she the 'hard-working' front-of-house, in the former home of her
grandfather, Frank Egginton, a watercolour artist whose work is
displayed in the public rooms. 'Nothing exceptional, just decent
value,' said an inspector in 2009. The bedrooms are simple: 'Ours was
large, comfortable, with a proper TV, coffee/tea-making facilities; an
adequate bathroom. Housekeeping was immaculate.' The hostess
takes dinner orders over drinks in an 'atmospheric' drawing room with
open fire, or a conservatory which faces a lake (both are spacious).
Tables must be booked ahead for the two-tier restaurant, which is
often busy. Seafood is a speciality on the seasonally changing menus.
'We enjoyed a starter of pastry layers with wild mushroom, asparagus
and Cashel Blue cheese dressing; fine hake; and a chocolate pudding
fit for a chocoholic. A lamb shank dish was disappointing.' Breakfast,
'in a narrow window' between 9 and 9.30 am, has a comprehensive
range of cooked dishes and a buffet which includes 'particularly nice
Guinness bread', carrageen moss, and stewed rhubarb. Guests are
asked not to check in between 1 and 4 pm.

Bedrooms: 6. *Open*: mid-Mar–mid-Dec, weekends only off-season, restaurant
closed Mon. *Facilities*: sitting room, conservatory, restaurant, 1-acre grounds
(lake, beach ½ mile), only restaurant suitable for &. *Background music*: in lounge
and restaurant. *Location*: at Figart, ½ mile W of Dunfanaghy. *Smoking*: not
allowed. *Children*: all ages welcomed. *Dogs*: not allowed. *Credit cards*: Amex,
MasterCard, Visa. *Prices*: [2009] B&B €50–€70 per person, set dinner €43.50.

DUNGARVAN Co. Waterford   Map 6:D5

The Tannery Restaurant   *Tel* 00 353 58-45420
& Townhouse   *Fax* 00 353 58-45814
10 Quay Street   *Email* info@tannery.ie
Dungarvan   *Website* www.tannery.ie

'More a restaurant than a hotel', celebrity chef Paul Flynn's venture
in this small seaside town is endorsed by a *Guide* reporter this year.
'The cooking is excellent, the accommodation is cool and stylish, very

21st-century, if a little impersonal.' The two-level dining room is in a converted leather warehouse; the bedrooms are in *The Tannery Townhouse*, in nearby Church Street. 'Check-in at the restaurant was friendly; we were taken over to our room, and given clear instructions about the use of the key, parking, etc.' The beds are large, the shower rooms 'spacious'. Mr Flynn can be seen through glass as he cooks: his modern menu might include prawn broth, coco beans and prawn cocktail; braised rabbit and bacon, savoy cabbage. 'Expensive, but an Early Bird menu is good value.' Breakfast is a DIY affair in the bedroom: 'Fresh milk in the fridge, self-serve porridge in a packet, good coffee in a cafetière; a delicious lemon cake was delivered in a bag hung on the door; no sign of the promised croissants.' Children (and dogs) are welcomed. (*John Rowlands*)

Bedrooms: 7. *Open*: all year except 2 weeks end Jan, 1 week Sept, restaurant closed Sun/Mon. *Facilities*: restaurant, private dining room, unsuitable for &. *Background music*: 'appropriate' CDs. *Location*: town centre. *Smoking*: not allowed in restaurant. *Children*: all ages welcomed. *Dogs*: not allowed. *Credit cards*: all major cards. *Prices*: [2009] B&B €60–€80 per person, early bird menu €30, full alc €110.

See also Shortlist

DUNKINEELY Co. Donegal   Map 6:B5

Castle Murray House	*Tel* 00 353 74-973 7022
St John's Point	*Fax* 00 353 74-973 7330
Dunkineely	*Email* info@castlemurray.com
	Website www.castlemurray.com

In a fine location on the Donegal coast, overlooking the ruins of McSwyne's Castle, this small hotel/restaurant was a 'wonderful discovery' for a visitor this year. Owned by Marguerite Howley, and managed by Jorg Demmerer, it provided 'excellent accommodation, high-quality food and service, warm and helpful reception'. Dinner orders are taken in a seating area facing the sea; not surprisingly the accent of chef Remy Dupuy's menu is on fish caught locally, eg, tartlette of crab and spinach; seared Donegal scallops with ratatouille ravioli, coconut curry jus. On fine evenings, visitors seated at a window table can enjoy the 'splendid sunset'; background music is played. Most of the bedrooms (on the first and second floors) have sea views;

there is no lift, but assistance is offered with luggage. There is freshly squeezed orange juice at the 'very good' breakfast; also fresh fruit salad, 'proper' coffee, preserves and butter; a 'substantial fry'. 'Very good value.' (*Russell Birch, and others*)

Bedrooms: 10. *Open*: all year except Christmas, Jan. *Facilities*: lounge, bar, restaurant, wedding facilities, ¼-acre garden, unsuitable for &. *Background music*: jazz. *Location*: 1 mile SW of village. *Smoking*: not allowed. *Children*: all ages welcomed. *Dogs*: allowed. *Credit cards*: MasterCard, Visa. *Prices*: B&B €35–€65 per person, D,B&B €80–€116, set dinner €51–€67, New Year package.

ENNISCORTHY Co. Wexford   Map 6:D6

Ballinkeele House   NEW   *Tel* 00 353 91-38105
Ballymurn   *Fax* 00 353 91-38468
Enniscorthy   *Email* john@ballinkeele.ie
                                            Website www.ballinkeele.ie

'We are not a hotel; this is our historic family home,' say John and Margaret Maher, the fifth generation to live in this late Regency manor house. It stands on a working farm in a large park with lakes ('at the last count three'), ponds and woods; the walled gardens are being restored. It has a pillared portico entrance, 'superb' public rooms, 'well-appointed' bedrooms. 'But the real charm of the place lies with the family who look after you,' says a returning visitor ('my 11th stay'), restoring *Ballinkeele* to the *Guide*. Swiss guests enjoyed 'special hospitality in a beautifully maintained building'. The spacious hall has two Corinthian columns, a decorated ceiling and large fireplace. Much of the furniture is original, as are many of the paintings and prints on the walls. John Maher serves pre-dinner drinks in the drawing room; dinner is taken communally by candlelight in the rich- red dining room. Margaret Maher is a member of Euro-Toques, a group which promotes the use of naturally produced ingredients; her no-choice menu might include feta salad; chicken with herb sauce. Vegetables are home grown. 'All the bedrooms have their individual character, some with four-poster. Very comfortable beds.' Breakfast, also taken communally, is 'good fun; a great opportunity to meet other people who appreciate staying in a house of style and character'. (*Peter Tilley, J Hausmann, and others*)

Bedrooms: 5. *Open*: Feb–Nov. *Facilities*: 2 drawing rooms, dining room, 3-acre gardens in 350-acre estate, lake, pond, unsuitable for &. *Background music*: none. *Location*: 6 miles SE of Enniscorthy. *Smoking*: not allowed. *Children*: all ages welcomed. *Dogs*: not allowed. *Credit cards*: MasterCard, Visa. *Prices*: [2009] B&B €80–€90 per person, D,B&B €108–€138, set dinner €48.

Salville House

Salville
Enniscorthy

Tel/Fax 00 353 92-35252
Email info@salvillehouse.com
Website www.salvillehouse.com

Regular visitors to this Victorian country house like the 'home from home' feel and 'ambience of warmth, both literal and metaphysical'. Owner Gordon Parker, who runs it with his wife, Jane, is 'evidently passionate about food'. Three of the bedrooms (Pink, Yellow, Blue) are in the main house, and have splendid views over the Slaney River valley and the Blackstairs Mountains. Most rooms are spacious. 'Pink is well done, though its bathroom reminds me of my schooldays.' 'Our lovely, bright room had large bed, good bathroom.' There is free Wi-Fi throughout. The 'excellent' dinners must be booked the evening before: likes and dislikes are taken into account for a four-course no-choice menu served at 8 pm and using local meat and fish and organic ingredients from the garden. 'Fillet of beef a highlight; puddings irresistible.' Bring your own wine; no corkage charge. Early suppers are provided for guests attending the Wexford opera festival. Breakfast has fresh orange juice, fruit compote, toasted oats and honey; full Irish or smoked haddock with rösti and poached egg. The grass tennis court in the garden is 'definitely not Wimbledon standard', the Parkers tell us. (*RR, S and PW*)

Bedrooms: 5, 2 in apartment at rear. *Open*: all year except Christmas. *Facilities*: drawing room, dining room, 2-acre grounds ('rough' tennis, badminton, croquet), golf nearby, beach, bird sanctuary 10 miles, unsuitable for &. *Background music*: none. *Location*: 2 miles S of town. *Smoking*: not allowed. *Children*: all ages welcomed. *Dogs*: allowed by arrangement, but not in public rooms, bedrooms. *Credit cards*: none. *Prices*: B&B €55–€65 per person, D,B&B €95–€105, set dinner €40, New Year package.

GALWAY Co. Galway   *See Shortlist*

How to contact the *Guide*
By mail: From anywhere in the UK, write to Freepost PAM 2931, London W11 4BR (no stamp is needed)
From outside the UK: *Good Hotel Guide*, 50 Addison Avenue, London W11 4QP, England
By telephone or fax: 020-7602 4182
By email: editor@goodhotelguide.com
Via our website: www.goodhotelguide.com

GLIN Co. Limerick   Map 6:D4

Glin Castle   *Tel* 00 353 68-34173
Glin   *Fax* 00 353 68-34364
                                                       Email knight@iol.ie
                                                       Website www.glincastle.com

'More historic house than hotel', this Georgian Gothic castle, beautifully set on the Shannon estuary, is the country seat (and family home)
of Desmond FitzGerald, the 29th Knight of Glin. The Knight (his
formal title) and his 'peerless' manager, Bob Duff, create a 'relaxed
and friendly atmosphere'. In 2009, they reverted to receiving only
groups. Mr Duff assures us: 'We battened down the hatches for one
year only, keeping on key staff; we will be reopening as normal in
2010.' 'The elegant rooms are adorned with FitzGerald portraits and
the furniture and *objets d'art* which they have assembled over the
years; the castle is decorated in pitch-perfect taste.' Some of the family
treasures were sold at auction in 2009 to raise funds to maintain the
castle. The drawing room has an Adam-influenced plaster ceiling;
huge windows face the garden. The Knight sometimes joins visitors
for the 'excellent' dinner cooked by Eddie Baguio. 'The food is
elegant and unpretentious; locally sourced meat, salmon from the
Shannon which the castle faces, organic fruit and vegetables from the
garden.' The bedrooms have four-poster bed, *chaise longue*, porcelain
plates and Irish prints on walls, river or garden views. 'Ours had a
huge, hard bed, with heavenly linen sheets; enormous bathroom with
bath large enough for a cow.' The background music, even at
breakfast, is not to all tastes. (*JH, and others*)

Bedrooms: 15. *Open*: 1 Apr–31 Oct. *Facilities*: hall, drawing room, sitting room,
library, dining room, 500-acre estate (10-acre garden, tennis, croquet, tea/craft
shop, parkland, dairy farm, clay-pigeon shooting), on Shannon estuary boating
(fishing), golf nearby, unsuitable for &. *Background music*: classical, dining room.
Location: edge of village, 32 miles W of Limerick. *Smoking*: not allowed. *Children*:
not under 10. *Dogs*: not allowed. *Credit cards*: all major cards. *Prices*: [2009] B&B
€155–€250 per person, set dinner €60, off-season rates, house parties.

We update the *Guide* every year. Hotels are dropped or may be
demoted to the Shortlist if there has been a change of owner
(unless reports after the change are positive), if this year's
reports are negative, or in rare cases where there has been no
feedback. A lot of hotels are omitted every year, and many new
ones are added.

GOREY Co. Wexford   Map 6:D6

Marlfield House   *Tel* 00 353 53-942 1124
Courtown Road   *Fax* 00 353 53-942 1572
Gorey   *Email* info@marlfieldhouse.ie
                             Website www.marlfieldhouse.com

'Antiques and pictures abound, contributing to the elegant charms of this handsome Regency house.' The former home of the Earls of Courtown, owned by Ray and Mary Bowe, is run as a luxury hotel (Relais & Châteaux) by their daughters, Margaret and Laura. It has a grand marble hall, a lounge with open fire, spectacular flower displays. 'After a warm greeting we were shown to a large ground-floor room with a welcoming coal-effect gas fire and French windows opening on to the lovely grounds. Fruit and a bucket of ice were thoughtful extras.' Earlier praise: 'Faultless; wonderful care and attention from the family.' In the 'glorious' flower-filled dining room (with frescoes and a large domed conservatory), Conor MacCann is now the chef; he serves classic dishes with French and Mediterranean influences, eg, haddock and crab fishcakes, sauce gribiche; grilled rib-eye of Wexford beef, confit potato, slow-roasted tomato, red wine sauce. 'Exquisitely presented and a challenge to the appetite.' Home-grown herbs, fruit and vegetables are gathered daily. Meat and fish are sourced locally. Breakfast is a 'superb buffet'. In the wooded grounds are a lake with ducks, geese and swans, and a wildfowl reserve. Nearby are sandy beaches and golf. (*P and RB*)

Bedrooms: 19, 8 on ground floor. *Open*: Mar–Dec. *Facilities*: reception hall, drawing room, library/bar, restaurant with conservatory, function/conference facilities, wedding facilities, 36-acre grounds (gardens, tennis, croquet, wild fowl reserve, lake), sea (sandy beaches, safe bathing 2 miles), fishing, golf, horse riding nearby. *Background music*: classical in library. *Location*: 1 mile E of Gorey. *Smoking*: not allowed. *Children*: no under-8s at dinner, high tea provided, babysitting available. *Dogs*: not allowed in public rooms. *Credit cards*: all major cards. *Prices*: B&B €90–€280 per person, D,B&B €157–€350, set dinner €68, special breaks, Christmas package, 1-night bookings sometimes refused Sat. *V* (not Sat)

The *V* sign at the end of an entry indicates that a hotel has agreed to take part in our Voucher scheme and to give *Guide* readers a 25% discount on their bed-and-breakfast rates for a one-night stay, subject to the conditions on the back of the voucher and explained in 'How to use the *Good Hotel Guide*' (page 57).

HOLYWOOD Co. Down   Map 6:B6

Rayanne House   *Tel/Fax* 028-9042 5859
60 Demesne Road   *Email* rayannehouse@hotmail.com
Holywood BT18 9EX   *Website* www.rayannehouse.com

With its rooms revamped and modernised (there is Wi-Fi access
throughout), Conor and Bernadette McClelland's guest house offers
'high standards of comfort and food', and an ambience of
'cheerful luxury'. The 'lovely' Victorian building, above this
attractive small town, has wide landings, sweeping stairs, display
cabinets, bookshelves; 'a wonderful Art Deco theme'. There are
spectacular views: many rooms look over the town and across the
Belfast Lough to the Antrim hills. A ground-floor room is equipped
for disabled visitors. Conor McClelland has won awards for the
breakfast, which must be ordered the evening before. It has an array
of interesting dishes in addition to the traditional items, eg, chilled
creamed porridge with raspberry purée; toasted potato bread with
melted Irish Cheddar, bacon and chutney. He also serves meals 'of
the highest standard', by arrangement, for a minimum of ten
people. The cuisine is modern, using local high-quality seasonal
ingredients in dishes like cream of celeriac, shrimp and Pernod
soup; grilled filet mignon with oxtail and Guinness sauce. More
reports, please.

Bedrooms: 11, 1, on ground floor, suitable for &. *Open*: all year. *Facilities*:
2 lounges, dining room, wedding/conference facilities, 1-acre grounds.
Background music: contemporary/classical/jazz. *Location*: ½ mile from town
centre, 6 miles E of Belfast. *Smoking*: not allowed. *Children*: all ages welcomed.
Dogs: not allowed. *Credit cards*: MasterCard, Visa. *Prices*: B&B £55–£95 per
person, set dinner £48, full alc £40–£60.

KENMARE Co. Kerry   Map 6:D4

Shelburne Lodge   *Tel* 00 353 64-41013
Cork Road   *Fax* 00 353 64-42135
Kenmare   *Email* shelburnekenmare@eircom.net
                                       Website www.shelburnelodge.com

'*Shelburne Lodge* continues to operate at a very high standard,' reports
a visitor this year, returning to Tom and Maura Foley's handsome
18th-century farmhouse just outside the town. 'As usual, we had a
warm welcome from the family, and a very comfortable bed.' The
oldest house in the area, it has large grounds with lawns, a grass tennis

court, a small orchard and a pretty herb garden. It is filled with antiques and modern art; there are log fires; striking colours on the landing. Visitors are 'treated to tea and delicious home-made cake' in one of the elegant sitting rooms. The spacious bedrooms are traditionally furnished. Two (one big enough for a family) are in a coach house, which has a separate lounge. Tom Foley is in charge of the breakfast, served in a spacious room: 'The best ever; a choice of fresh fish each day, plus smoked salmon, full cooked, etc; delicious fruit salads.' Kenmare, a 'short, flat' walk away, has plenty of eating places. *Packies* (owned by the Foleys) and *Mulcahy's* are both recommended. For lighter daytime meals, Maura Foley's sister runs the *Purple Heather* bistro. (*Esler Crawford, RL*)

Bedrooms: 9, 2 in coach house. *Open*: mid-Mar–mid-Oct. *Facilities*: drawing room, library, lounge in annexe, breakfast room, 3-acre garden (tennis), golf adjacent, unsuitable for &. *Background music*: none. *Location*: on R569 to Cork, ⅓ mile E of centre. *Smoking*: not allowed. *Children*: all ages welcomed. *Dogs*: not allowed. *Credit cards*: MasterCard, Visa. *Prices*: B&B €50–€87.50 per person.

Virginia's Guesthouse

36 Henry Street
Kenmare

Tel 00 353 64-41021
Fax 00 353 64-42415
Email virginias@eircom.net
Website www.virginias-kenmare.com

'We were welcomed with such engaging charm that we knew we were going to enjoy our stay.' Praise this year for Neil and Noreen Harrington's unpretentious guest house on the first and second floors above the popular *Mulcahy's* restaurant on the 'busy main street of this colourful little town'. They are 'helpful, charming' hosts; guests can serve themselves coffee, tea and biscuits in the lounge. 'The bedrooms and bathrooms are bright and spotless, the furnishings cheerful, homely. Traffic noise might be intrusive for front rooms, but I slept well thanks to the earplugs thoughtfully provided.' No meals, but 'you don't have to walk far for a very good dinner' at *Mulcahy's* and other 'lively' pubs. Breakfast is ordered the evening before (when a time is agreed). 'Everything seemed to be home made and organic, from the porridge, breads and preserves, to the interesting and delicious cooked dishes, involving eggs, bacon, mushrooms, cheese and rhubarb. Mr Harrington was delighted to give us whatever information we could wish for, crucially the best route for exploring the Ring of Kerry without competing with the convoys of tourist coaches.' (*Trevor Lockwood*)

Bedrooms: 8. *Open*: all year except 24/25 Dec. *Facilities*: library, breakfast room, unsuitable for &. *Background music*: classical in breakfast room. *Location*: central. *Smoking*: not allowed. *Children*: not under 12. *Dogs*: not allowed. *Credit cards*: MasterCard, Visa. *Prices*: B&B €30–€70 per person, 3-night off-season breaks, 1-night bookings refused New Year, bank holidays.

See also Shortlist

KILCONNELL Co. Galway   Map 6:C5

Ballinderry Park   *Tel/Fax* 00 353 90-968 6796
Kilconnell   *Email* george@ballinderrypark.com
nr Ballinasloe   *Website* www.ballinderrypark.com

Restored, 'with taste and imagination' from ruin, by George and Susie Gossip, this 'charming yellow Georgian building, beautifully proportioned' stands in 'glorious isolation' east of Galway. 'A fine stopping place for any aficionado of the Irish country house,' said a returning visitor. The panelled drawing room ('cosy on a chilly evening, with a roaring log fire') has a Kilkenny marble chimneypiece, prints, old porcelain, and an honesty bar 'disguised as a cupboard'. The blue-walled dining room has 17th-century oak and 18th-century mahogany furniture. Mr Gossip is the host, 'tending to everyone's whim'. His four-course set dinners are taken by candlelight, with 'proper' silver. 'An excellent cook', he has lectured on cooking game at the famous cookery school at *Ballymaloe House*, Shanagarry (*qv*). 'We do not go in for portion control,' he writes, 'nor the anonymity of piped music. Our guests dine at one table and talk to one another.' Local produce, organic when possible, is used: 'No menu or choice; preferences discussed when booking.' The bedrooms, on two floors, are painted in strong colours and furnished with antiques; each has an external lobby opening on to a landing. 'We rarely charge a single supplement,' Mr Gossip tells us. 'Good ingredients' are used at breakfast. (*EC*)

Bedrooms: 4. *Open*: 1 April–30 Sept, closed Christmas, groups only at New Year (other times by arrangement). *Facilities*: hall, drawing room, dining room, 40-acre grounds, fishing, horse riding nearby, unsuitable for &. *Background music*: none. *Location*: 7 miles W of Ballinasloe. *Smoking*: not allowed. *Children*: all ages welcomed. *Dogs*: 'allowed if well behaved, must sleep in enclosed lobby outside bedroom'. *Credit cards*: MasterCard, Visa. *Prices*: B&B €80–€100 per person, set dinner €55.

KILLARNEY Co. Kerry   *See Shortlist*

KILMALLOCK Co. Limerick   Map 6:D5

Flemingstown House
Kilmallock

Tel 00 353 63-98093
Fax 00 353 63-98546
Email info@flemingstown.com
Website www.flemingstown.com

♧ *César award in 2005*

The Sheedy family have owned this 18th-century building for five generations. Today Imelda Sheedy-King is 'the heart and soul of the place', the 'perfect hostess, attending to every detail'. Her 'flawless' guest house is 'comfortable rather than luxurious', with a 'cosy lounge with mostly 19th-century pieces'. The bedrooms are spacious; some have a king-size bed and 'superb' views across fields to the Ballyhoura Mountains. 'Our well-lit room had a cheerful air, a crystal chandelier.' There is a self-catering lodge in the grounds. Dinner, in a room with big stained-glass windows, is highly recommended, but 'give plenty of notice that you wish to dine, and bring your own wine'. Mrs Sheedy-King's five-course menu features traditional dishes using local produce (eg, beef consommé; sea trout on a tomato compote); her sister's own Cheddar cheese might be offered. If she is not cooking, there is a 'good restaurant and pub with food' nearby. Breakfast has home-made breads, cheeses, jams and cakes; fresh juices and a range of cooked dishes including pancakes with banana and grapes. Visitors can explore the farm and watch the cows being milked. (*GRS, PH*)

Bedrooms: 5, 1 self-catering lodge. *Open*: Mar–Oct. *Facilities*: lounge, dining room, 1-acre garden in 100-acre farm (golf, riding, fishing, cycling nearby), unsuitable for &. *Background music*: 'easy listening' in dining room. *Location*: on R512, 2 miles SE of Kilmallock. *Smoking*: not allowed. *Children*: not under 10. *Dogs*: not allowed in house. *Credit cards*: MasterCard, Visa. *Prices*: B&B €60–€70 per person, set dinner €45, special rates for stays of more than 1 night.

KINSALE Co. Cork   *See Shortlist*

LAHINCH Co. Clare   *See Shortlist*

LETTERFRACK Co. Galway   Map 6:C4

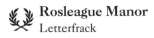 **Rosleague Manor**   *Tel* 00 353 95-41101
Letterfrack   *Fax* 00 353 95-41168
                                          Email info@rosleague.com
                                          Website www.rosleague.com

César award: Irish hotel of the year

Looking out across 'exquisite' gardens to sea and mountains on Connemara's Atlantic coast, this Georgian manor house is owned by Edmund Foyle and managed by his son, Mark. 'They make us feel not merely welcome, but a bit special,' is a comment this year from a visitor who has been returning for 30 years. 'Mark goes from strength to strength, a personable and hands-on manager who involves himself in all aspects of the hotel.' The elegant lounges have log and turf fires, paintings, antiques and *objets d'art*. A conservatory and bar opening on to a landscaped internal courtyard is a 'delightful venue for a pre-dinner drink'. In the 'beautiful' dining room, Pascal Marinot serves 'short uncomplicated menus using high-quality ingredients': dishes like Cleggan Bay crabmeat with garden herb mayonnaise; grilled sea bass with black olive tapenade. 'We enjoyed the freshest fish, though we would have liked a wider range of vegetables. Fish is also a highlight of the breakfasts (mackerel, plaice, bass), which also have freshly squeezed juice, plenty of fruit, home-baked scones and brown bread.' 'Our large first-floor room overlooked the bay; it was nicely decorated in blue and yellow; adequate storage space; huge

Victorian roll-top bath.' (*Andrew Wardrop, Ann Walden, David Berry, and others*)

Bedrooms: 20, 2 on ground floor. *Open*: Mar–mid-Dec. *Facilities*: 2 drawing rooms, conservatory/bar, dining room, wedding facilities, 30-acre grounds (tennis), unsuitable for &. *Background music*: none. *Location*: 7 miles NE of Clifden. *Smoking*: not allowed. *Children*: all ages welcomed. *Dogs*: only 'well-behaved dogs' allowed in public rooms, with own bedding in bedrooms. *Credit cards*: Amex, MasterCard, Visa. *Prices*: [2009] B&B €80–€140 per person, set dinner €48, 1-night bookings refused bank holidays. *V*

LISDOONVARNA Co. Clare   Map 6:C4

Sheedy's
Lisdoonvarna

Tel 00 353 65-707 4026
Fax 00 353 65-707 4555
Email info@sheedys.com
Website www.sheedys.com

In neat grounds in a town on the edge of the Burren (a limestone landscape rich in unusual plant life and historic sites), this yellow building has been owned by John Sheedy's family since the 18th century. He and his wife, Martina, run 'a very friendly but efficient ship', say recent visitors. 'It fully lived up to its outstanding reputation.' Bedrooms, in the main house and a modern extension, are 'well cared for'. 'Ours was spacious, cool, decorated in excellent taste.' Martina Sheedy is the 'hands-on, charming' manageress. Her husband is 'an accomplished cook', using fresh local ingredients for his modern dishes, eg, confit of duck leg, celeriac salad, pickled plums; baked fillet of hake, orzo pasta with crab, red pepper sauce. There's 'wonderful, delicious' food in the bar, too. Breakfast, served at table, has 'real' juice, home-made preserves, good teas, unusual cooked dishes. The Aran Islands and the Cliffs of Moher are nearby. (*GLD*)

Bedrooms: 11, some on ground floor, 1 suitable for &. *Open*: Apr–Sept. *Facilities*: ramp, sitting room/library, sun lounge, bar, restaurant, ½-acre garden (rose garden). *Background music*: jazz at dinner. *Location*: 20 miles SW of Galway. *Smoking*: not allowed. *Children*: all ages welcomed. *Dogs*: not allowed. *Credit cards*: Amex, MasterCard, Visa. *Prices*: [2009] B&B €65–€90 per person, D,B&B €100–€120, full alc €72, special breaks, 1-night bookings refused Sept weekends.

LONGFORD Co. Longford   *See Shortlist*

MILLSTREET Co. Waterford   Map 6:D5

The Castle Country House   NEW   *Tel* 00 353 58-68049
Millstreet   *Fax* 00 353 58-68099
Cappagh   *Email* castlefm@iol.ie
                        Website www.castlecountryhouse.com

A 'memorable visit' by a reader this year restores to the *Guide* Joan and
Emmett Nugent's unusual farmhouse after a time without reports.
'Joan and her family made us feel truly at home, arranging our daily
excursions and providing tea and basketfuls of delicious scones at
every encounter.' Guests are 'invited to experience a slice of life' on
this large working dairy farm (they may lend a hand with the milking).
Accommodation is in a restored wing of an older (16th-century)
fortified tower house built to protect livestock. The gardens run down
to the River Finisk which has good fishing (rods provided, and they
will cook your catch). 'Our beautifully decorated bedroom overlooked
rolling countryside.' Mrs Nugent cooks 'delicious farm-fresh food'
(perhaps cream of vegetable soup; roast beef with Yorkshire pudding,
home-made horseradish cream). Meals are taken in the original castle
dining room with its five-foot-thick walls. Breakfast has a selection of
fruit, cereals and cheeses; cooked dishes might include French toast
with bacon and maple syrup; organic eggs. There are three villages
called Millstreet in this part of Ireland; this is the one closest to the
estuary town of Dungarvan. (*Beverly Williams*)

Bedrooms: 5. *Open*: Mar–Nov. *Facilities*: sitting room, dining room, 2-acre garden
on 170-acre farm, unsuitable for &. *Background music*: classical in dining room.
Location: 10 miles NW of Dungarvan towards Cappoquin. *Smoking*: not allowed.
Children: all ages welcomed. *Dogs*: not allowed in house. *Credit cards*: MasterCard,
Visa. *Prices*: B&B €45–€55 per person, dinner €30–€35, 3-night breaks.

MOUNTRATH Co. Laois   Map 6:C5

Roundwood House   *Tel* 00 353 57-873 2120
Mountrath   *Fax* 00 353 57-873 2711
                              Email roundwood@eircom.net
                          Website www.roundwoodhouse.com

❧ *César award in 1990*

Amid 'shimmering trees and meadows, bluebells and blackberries',
this handsome Palladian villa was built in the 18th century, though
the oldest part dates back to 1650. It is run in relaxed style by

Rosemarie and Frank Kennan, who have long been restoring the house, which they bought from the Irish Georgian Society. 'The perfect home from home,' wrote a visitor who first stayed here 20 years ago. 'They made us as welcome as ever. The decor may be "battered", but it would not be the same if it became smart.' The Kennans, 'gracious and unaffected' hosts, sometimes join guests for drinks after dinner when 'good company and conversation abound'. The two-storey main hall has creaking floorboards, an eclectic collection of books, furniture and ornaments. The first-floor Blue Bedroom, large and high-ceilinged, is 'very comfortable'. Mrs Kennan's cooking is widely praised: her no-choice menus are based on 'what is available in the market', perhaps smoked mackerel in choux pastry with horseradish mayonnaise; medallions of lamb, port and redcurrant sauce. Children are welcomed (there is a 'wet-day' nursery with toys). A coach house, forge and cottage have been turned into self-catering units. (*RR*)

Bedrooms: 10, 4 in garden annexe. *Open*: all year except Christmas. *Facilities*: drawing room, study/library, dining room, playroom, table tennis room, 20-acre grounds (garden, woodland), golf, walking, river fishing nearby, unsuitable for ♿. *Background music*: none. *Location*: 3 miles N of village. *Smoking*: allowed in 4 bedrooms. *Children*: all ages welcomed. *Dogs*: not allowed indoors. *Credit cards*: all major cards. *Prices*: B&B €60–€80 per person, set dinner €50, special breaks. *V*

MULTYFARNHAM Co. Westmeath   Map 6:C5

Mornington House
Multyfarnham

Tel 00 353 44-937 2191
Fax 00 353 44-937 2338
Email stay@mornington.ie
Website www.mornington.ie

Built on the site of an ancient castle, this substantial old Anglo-Irish house has been owned by one family since 1858. Its present incumbents, Warwick and Anne O'Hara ('wonderful, welcoming hosts, great conversationalists'), entertain guests on a house-party basis, with meals served around one large table. 'Grand yet homely', it stands in grounds with ancient trees, near the fish-filled Lough Derravaragh. Much of the furniture is original; there are family portraits, strong colours on walls, oriental rugs. Visitors help themselves to drinks in the 'pleasant, light' drawing room where a turf or log fire burns in cold weather. Mrs O'Hara's country house cooking, using vegetables, fruit and herbs from the walled garden, is much admired. Vegetarians are 'particularly welcome', but should give advance notice. Mr O'Hara cooks the 'very good' breakfast: fresh orange juice; 'superb home-made muesli and brown bread; a full Irish fry'; linen napkins. Bedrooms are 'a bit idiosyncratic'. 'Ours was large, quiet, with plenty of light.' More reports, please.

Bedrooms: 4. *Open*: Apr–Oct. *Facilities*: drawing room, dining room, 2-acre garden, 50-acre grounds (croquet, bicycle hire), unsuitable for &. *Background music*: none. *Location*: 9 miles NW of Mullingar. *Smoking*: not allowed. *Children*: all ages welcomed. *Dogs*: not allowed in house. *Credit cards*: all major cards. *Prices*: B&B €75 per person, D,B&B €120, set dinner €45, 3-night breaks.

NEWPORT Co. Mayo   Map 6:B4

Newport House   *Tel* 00 353 98-41222
Newport   *Fax* 00 353 98-41613
                                      Email info@newporthouse.ie
                                      Website www.newporthouse.ie

Popular with fisherfolk in pursuit of salmon, this creeper-covered Georgian mansion holds rights on the River Newport ('all our fish are wild'). Liked for its 'unstuffy' atmosphere, it is run 'like a large private home' by owners Thelma and Kieran Thompson and manageress Catherine Flynn. Many of the 'helpful' staff are local: 'The receptionists are particularly friendly,' said a visitor this year. 'It feels as every country house hotel should but rarely does,' said an earlier guest. It has a grand staircase with lantern and dome, fires in the public rooms with their fine plasterwork and chandeliers. Some rooms are in self-contained units, good for a family. The rooms in two houses in a courtyard are popular with dog owners and 'angling guests'. A ghillie is generally available; a picnic lunch can be provided; there is a drying room, and freezing or smoking of the catch can be arranged. 'A handsome nine-pounder was on view in the hall while we were there.' In the formal dining room, chef John Gavin's 'sophisticated' menus might include chicken liver parfait, home-made gooseberry chutney; charcoal-grilled veal steak, brandy and wholegrain mustard sauce. Breakfast, with freshly squeezed orange juice, 'was our best in Ireland: incomparable eggs Benedict'. (*Michael Wace*)

Bedrooms: 16, 5 in courtyard, 4 on ground floor. *Open*: mid-Mar–end Oct. *Facilities*: sitting room, bar, dining room, restaurant, billiard/TV room, table-tennis room, 15-acre grounds (walled garden, private fishing on River

Newport), golf, riding, walking, shooting nearby, unsuitable for &. *Background music*: none. *Location*: in village 7 miles N of Westport. *Smoking*: allowed in 8 bedrooms. *Children*: all ages welcomed. *Dogs*: allowed in 1 courtyard bedroom, not in public rooms. *Credit cards*: Amex, MasterCard, Visa. *Prices*: B&B €114–€194 per person, D,B&B €176–€226, set dinner €68, full alc €63. *V*

OUGHTERARD Co. Galway   Map 6:C4

Currarevagh House
Oughterard

Tel 00 353 91-552312
Fax 00 353 91-552731
Email rooms@currarevagh.com
Website www.currarevagh.com

César award in 1992

The Hodgson family are 'as attentive as one could wish' at their early Victorian manor house in beautiful parkland and woodland on Lough Corrib in Connemara. Henry Hodgson has retired ('though he still takes pleasure in greeting guests old and new'); June Hodgson continues to assist her son, Henry, in running the front-of-house; his wife, Lucy, is the chef. Any changes in the handover to the second generation are 'imperceptible', says an annual visitor. 'The atmosphere and satisfaction quotient remain very high scoring.' There are fresh flowers and hot-water bottles, blankets and sheets, in the bedrooms, many of which have 'wonderful views'. The lavish afternoon tea served in the drawing room includes sandwiches, home-made scones and cakes. At dinner, the cooking has 'shifted in a happy direction, with stronger, more "southern" flavours', in dishes like baked parsley mussels with Parmesan and mustard; poached loin of Connemara lamb, basil mousse, Puy lentils. Henry Hodgson cooks breakfast, an 'Edwardian' buffet: 'I have seldom met better: a good ham to carve, salmon fillets, kedgeree, porridge, and all the usual hot items carefully monitored and replaced when they become cool.' There is much to do in the area, but fishing is a major draw. *Currarevagh* has its own boats and ghillies on Lough Corrib. (*Michael Wace, RP*)

Bedrooms: 13. *Open*: 20 Mar–mid-Oct. *Facilities*: sitting room/hall, drawing room, library/bar with TV, dining room, 180-acre grounds (lake, fishing, ghillies available, boating, swimming, tennis, croquet), golf, riding nearby, unsuitable for &. *Background music*: none. *Location*: 4 miles NW of Oughterard. *Smoking*: none. *Children*: all ages welcomed. *Dogs*: allowed in all areas. *Credit cards*: MasterCard, Visa. *Prices*: B&B €80–€105 per person, D,B&B €120–€140, set dinner €49. *V*

RAMELTON Co. Donegal   Map 6:B5

Frewin   *Tel/Fax* 00 353 74-915 1246
Rectory Road   *Email* frewin.ramelton@gmail.com
Ramelton   *Website* www.frewinhouse.com

Regina and Thomas Coyle are 'warmly welcoming', say visitors to their Victorian former rectory. It stands in mature wooded grounds outside a Georgian port at the mouth of the River Lennon. The building (which has been described as a 'country house in miniature') has been renovated with care, retaining period features: stained glass, the elegant Victorian staircase, a fine library. There are open fires, bright colours and potted plants. 'Small and stylish, peaceful and relaxing,' is a typical comment. The largest bedroom, on a corner at the front, has views to both sides, and its own sitting room (with bookcases). Mrs Coyle will serve a 'simple but satisfactory' dinner by arrangement; 'reasonable' restaurants are within walking distance. Breakfast, taken communally around a large table, has home-made muesli, fresh fruit salad; warm home-baked bread, freshly squeezed orange juice; a full fry-up. (*EC, and others*)

Bedrooms: 4, self-catering cottage for 2 in grounds. *Open*: 1 Jan–20 Dec. *Facilities*: sitting room, library, dining room, 2-acre garden, golf, horse riding, beaches nearby, unsuitable for ♿. *Background music*: none. *Location*: outskirts of town. *Smoking*: not allowed. *Children*: 'not suitable for young children'. *Dogs*: not allowed. *Credit cards*: MasterCard, Visa. *Prices*: [2009] B&B €65–€100 per person, set dinner €50. *V*

RATHMULLAN Co. Donegal   Map 6:B5

Rathmullan House   *Tel* 00 353 74-915 8188
Rathmullan   *Fax* 00 353 74-915 8200
                 Email info@rathmullanhouse.com
             Website www.rathmullanhouse.com

'It would be hard to find a more comforting or cosseting place,' says a regular visitor this year to the Wheeler family's informal country hotel. A handsome, white 1800s mansion, it is a few minutes' walk from the village in 'superb', well-maintained gardens which lead to a long sandy beach on Lough Swilly (an inlet of the sea). The family are 'very much in evidence'; 'the staff, some foreign, some long-standing locals, are polite, friendly, efficient'; 'attentive not over-attentive'. 'Sound management,' adds a wheelchair-user, who felt well cared for. There are spacious public rooms, high ceilings, chandeliers, antiques, marble fireplaces, log fires, oil paintings, lots of books. Bedrooms vary: older ones are 'classic country house', some with 'beautiful views of the gardens and Lough Swilly beyond', some with a balcony. Ten newer rooms are spacious, and have restful colours and under-floor heating. Families are welcomed, and one bedroom has a 'room' for a dog. Ian Orr is head chef in *The Weeping Elm*, a conservatory-style dining room with a tented ceiling. He serves 'excellent', imaginative dishes, eg, roast boneless quail with quail Scotch egg, celeriac purée; Greencastle hake with Lissadell clams, spinach and fennel. The breakfasts 'have long been renowned'. There's a large indoor swimming pool and a resident masseuse. (*Esler Crawford, Richard W Bowden*)

Bedrooms: 32, some on ground floor, 2 suitable for &. *Open*: 11 Feb–7 Jan except Christmas, midweek Nov, Dec. *Facilities*: ramps, 4 sitting rooms, library, TV room, cellar bar/bistro, restaurant, 15-metre indoor swimming pool (steam room), small conference centre, wedding facilities, 7-acre grounds (tennis, croquet), direct access to sandy beach (safe bathing), boating, golf, riding, hill walking nearby. *Background music*: none. *Location*: ½ mile N of village. *Smoking*: not allowed. *Children*: all ages welcomed. *Dogs*: allowed in 1 dog-friendly bedroom, but not in public rooms. *Credit cards*: Amex, MasterCard, Visa. *Prices*: B&B €80–€135 per person, D,B&B €125–€180, set dinner €45–€55, full alc €75, special breaks, New Year package, 1-night bookings refused at weekends, bank holidays.

See also Shortlist

RIVERSTOWN Co. Sligo   Map 6:B5

Coopershill   *Tel* 00 353 71-916 5108
Riverstown   *Fax* 00 353 71-916 5466
                                   Email ohara@coopershill.com
                                   Website www.coopershill.com

& *César award in 1987*

Simon O'Hara is the seventh generation of his family to live at this large estate with its extensive woodland (with wild deer) and sizeable farm. It has long been liked by readers for the 'old-fashioned hospitality' and warm welcome provided by the 'engaging' family. The public rooms of the magnificent Palladian mansion, with their 14-foot ceilings, contain original 18th-century furniture, family portraits, stags' heads. 'Unlike some of its Irish peers', the house is in 'pristine' condition. The chef, Christina McCauley, who trained at *Ballymaloe House*, Shanagarry (*qv*), cooks country house dishes like tomato, basil and goat's cheese tart; venison medallions with juniper cream sauce. 'We can boast that the distance from farm to plate for 75% of the ingredients is about 200 metres,' the family say. Bedrooms retain their original dimensions; many have a four-poster bed, some have a freestanding Victorian bath. One room has its bathroom down the corridor (bathrobes and slippers provided). Dinner, a leisurely candlelit affair starting some time around 8.30 pm, is taken at separate tables in the elegant dining room, with family silver and glass. The 'fine breakfast' has fresh orange juice, leaf tea with a strainer, 'superior porridge'. Fishing is available on the River Arrow. Children are welcomed.

Bedrooms: 8. *Open*: Apr–Oct, off-season house parties by arrangement. *Facilities*: 2 halls, drawing room, TV room, dining room, snooker room, 500-acre estate (garden, tennis, croquet, woods, farmland, river with trout fishing), unsuitable for &. *Background music*: none. *Location*: 11 miles SE of Sligo. *Smoking*: not allowed. *Children*: all ages welcomed. *Dogs*: not allowed in house (accommodation in stables). *Credit cards*: all major cards. *Prices*: B&B €109–€171 per person, D,B&B €166–€228, set dinner €59, discounts for 3 or more nights. *V*

ROSSLARE Co. Wexford   Map 6:D6

Churchtown House
Tagoat
Rosslare

Tel 00 353 53-913 2555
Fax 00 353 53-913 2577
Email info@churchtownhouse.com
Website www.churchtownhouse.com

In large grounds in a hamlet south of Rosslare, this handsome white Georgian house has long been liked by readers for the warmth of the welcome from the 'open and approachable' owners, Austin and Patricia Cody, and for the beautiful location. The public areas have original Irish paintings, attractive modern *objets d'art*. Guests gather for sherry before dinner, perhaps in front of an open fire in the sitting room. Ingredients for the four-course no-choice meal (served at separate tables) are locally sourced when possible: dishes like leek and potato soup; chicken risotto, ginger and honey sauce. Children are catered for. The bedrooms have a thick carpet and traditional fabrics; there are big, comfortable beds; a ground-floor bedroom had 'ample storage, good lighting; a fierce shower'. Breakfast has yogurt, prunes, various egg dishes. It can be provided early for guests catching a dawn ferry to Fishguard. The medieval walled town of Wexford is nearby; early suppers are provided for residents attending its opera festival. More reports, please.

Bedrooms: 12, 5 on ground floor. *Open*: mid-Mar–31 Oct, dinner served Tues–Sat, supper on Sun and Mon. *Facilities*: 2 lounges, 2 dining rooms, private dining room, 8-acre grounds (golf, fishing, riding), beaches nearby, unsuitable for &. *Background music*: none. *Location*: on R736, 2½ miles S of Rosslare. *Smoking*: not allowed. *Children*: all ages welcomed. *Dogs*: not allowed in house. *Credit cards*: MasterCard, Visa. *Prices*: B&B €50–€95 per person, set dinner €35, website offers, 2- to 3-night breaks.

SCHULL Co. Cork   Map 6:D4

Rock Cottage
Barnatonicane
Schull

Tel/Fax 00 353 28-35538
Email rockcottage@eircom.net
Website www.rockcottage.ie

♥ *César award in 2004*

'A much-loved house with a warm atmosphere', Barbara Klötzer's 'truly beautiful' slate-sided Georgian hunting lodge stands in large grounds among grassy hillocks, one of which has 'stunning' views of Dunmanus Bay. 'She sees that you are thoroughly welcome and well looked after,' one visitor wrote. 'After walking and exploring, we would come back to crash out and read or snooze in the garden.' The 'sunny and uncluttered' building has fine furnishings, flowers, and an eclectic collection of paintings, prints and ornaments. Two bedrooms are 'spacious and airy, with a sitting area'. 'Ours was comfortable, decorated in simple, bright Tyrolean style. Ms Klötzer is an accomplished cook; breakfasts and dinners were all fabulous imaginatively put together.' Her three-course menu, based on fresh local produce (lamb, fish and shellfish), has no choice. 'Let me know your preferences, otherwise it is a surprise,' she says. 'No licence, bring your own drink.' Breakfast (ordered the night before) includes 'freshly squeezed orange and lemon juice, home-baked bread, lavish fruit platter with Greek yogurt, blissfully soft scrambled eggs', or continental. Two new donkeys have 'joined the crew' of animals which roam on the working farm next door. (*David Berry, JH*)

Bedrooms: 3, also 1 self-catering cottage. *Open*: all year (advance notice essential for Sun night). *Facilities*: lounge, dining room, 17-acre grounds, unsuitable for &. *Background music*: when guests want it. *Location*: 8 miles NW of Schull. *Smoking*: not allowed. *Children*: not under 10. *Dogs*: only disability dogs allowed. *Credit cards*: MasterCard, Visa. *Prices*: B&B €70–€100 per person, set dinner €50, 1-night bookings refused in winter.

SHANAGARRY Co. Cork   Map 6:D5

Ballymaloe House   *Tel* 00 353 21-465 2531
Shanagarry   *Fax* 00 353 21-465 2021
                                        Email res@ballymaloe.ie
                                        Website www.ballymaloe.ie

César award in 1984

Now well into its fifth decade, *Ballymaloe* 'maintains the standards by which it transformed Irish cooking'. Myrtle Allen, who opened her renowned hotel/restaurant in 1964, still oversees the cooking. The ivy-covered Georgian mansion is filled with original paintings and books and has the 'atmosphere of a cultured private home'. It stands in large grounds on a farm which supplies the kitchen. Daughter-in-law Hazel is manager; another daughter-in-law, Darina, the cookery writer, runs the nearby cookery school, with its famous *potager*. At the heart of the enterprise is the 'fantastic, faultless food'. Jason Fahey, head chef, serves country house meals in a series of small dining rooms: tart of Wexford wild mushrooms with tarragon beurre blanc; braised East Cork ox cheeks with wild watercress might appear on the menu. 'No piped music, just the sound of people talking and laughing.' Bedrooms in the main house are the largest; some open on to the garden through French windows. Some rooms are in a Norman keep. Some rooms may be a bit cramped. Breakfast includes fresh juices, porridge, 'very good marmalade and kippers'. In the grounds are sculptures, ponds with duck and geese, a swimming pool, a play area for children (who are warmly welcomed).

Bedrooms: 30, 8 in adjacent building, 4 on ground floor, 5 self-catering cottages. *Open*: all year except 24–26 Dec, 2 weeks mid-Jan. *Facilities*: drawing room (live traditional music weekly), 2 small sitting rooms, conservatory, 7 dining rooms, conference facilities, 6-acre gardens, 400-acre grounds (farm, gardens, tennis, swimming pool (10 by 4 metres, heated in summer), 8-hole golf course, croquet, children's play area, craft shop), cookery school nearby, sea 3 miles (sand and rock beaches). *Background music*: none. *Location*: on L35 Ballycotton road, 20 miles E of Cork. *Smoking*: not allowed. *Children*: all ages welcomed. *Dogs*: allowed in courtyard rooms, not in house. *Credit cards*: all major cards. *Prices*: B&B €110–€195 per person, D,B&B €185–€270, set dinner €75, special breaks, New Year package. *V*

Looking for a hotel for a special occasion; perhaps a romantic weekend, or a memorable meal? The Hotelfinder section (page 11) identifies hotels in 20 categories designed to match your mood and meet your special interests.

STRAFFAN Co. Kildare   Map 6:C6

Barberstown Castle
Straffan

Tel 00 353 1-628 8157
Fax 00 353 1-627 7027
Email info@barberstowncastle.ie
Website www.barberstowncastle.ie

In extensive grounds, this large hotel is purpose-built around a 13th-century castle keep linked to a whitewashed Elizabethan house and a refurbished Victorian extension. Dublin city centre and airport are both 30 minutes' drive away. Richard Millea is the manager. 'We were looked after very well by friendly staff of various nationalities,' said one visitor. 'Our surprisingly large bedroom was nicely decorated and well equipped.' Furnished with antiques, the rooms are named after people who have lived in the castle over the years. There are log fires in the public areas. In the restaurant, in the castle keep, head chef Bertrand Malabat serves French/Irish dishes 'of gourmet standard', eg, organic smoked salmon, coriander crab salad; roast guineafowl supreme, bacon and red wine jus. Lighter meals and afternoon tea are available in the *Tea Room*, which has a terrace facing the attractive landscaped gardens. 'A limited amount of noise from the nearby road, but not enough to disturb unduly.' Free Wi-Fi is available. (*JH*)

Bedrooms: 58, 21 on ground floor, 3 suitable for &. *Open*: Feb–Dec, except Christmas. *Facilities*: ramps, lift, bar, 2 lounges, restaurant, tea room, terrace, banqueting/conference/wedding facilities, business centre, 20-acre grounds (walking, archery, clay-pigeon shooting), fishing, golf, horse riding nearby. *Background music*: classical in tea room and restaurant. *Location*: village 12 miles W of Dublin. *Smoking*: not allowed. *Children*: all ages welcomed. *Dogs*: not allowed. *Credit cards*: Amex, MasterCard, Visa. *Prices*: B&B €125–€160 per person, D,B&B €149–189, set dinner €65, special breaks, New Year package. *V*

STRANGFORD Co. Down   *See Shortlist*

THURLES Co. Tipperary   *See Shortlist*

WATERFORD Co. Waterford   *See Shortlist*

WESTPORT Co. Mayo   *See Shortlist*

SHORTLIST

This Shortlist fulfils two purposes: to suggest accommodation in towns and cities that have no main entry or only a limited selection; and to test places that might well qualify for a full entry in future editions of the *Guide*. Because our selection of hotels for main entries is based on quality and character rather than on location, we have a limited choice in some towns and cities (in some cases no hotels at all). Rather than lower our standards to fill these gaps in our maps, we suggest here establishments which we believe will provide reasonable accommodation. Some are more business-oriented than the places that we include in the main section. The Shortlist also includes new nominations that we have not yet checked, new openings on which as yet we have no reports, and places which have had a full entry in the past but have no recent reports or mixed reviews, or have recently changed hands. We welcome readers' comments on all the shortlisted entries. Those which do not also have a full entry in the *Guide* are indicated on the map by a triangle.

LONDON   Map 2:D4

Apex City of London, 1 Seething Lane, EC3N 4AX. *Tel* 0845-365 0000, www.apexhotel.co.uk. In side street near Tower of London: hi-tech, large, contemporary hotel (stainless steel, marble, grainy wood). Managed by Yousif Al-Wagga. Panoramic views. *Addendum* restaurant and gastro bar; background music; business facilities; gym; sauna. Garden. Wi-Fi. Free local telephone calls. Children welcomed. 179 bedrooms: £64.50–£122.50. Breakfast £15. Dinner £19.50. (Underground: Tower Hill)

base2stay, 25 Courtfield Gardens, SW5 0PG. *Tel* 0845-262 8000, www.base2stay.com. In pillared, white stucco town house, no-frills hotel with smart, modern rooms, each with mini-kitchen; state-of-the-art equipment. Managed by Mr Khalil. Reception, lobby (background music). 67 bedrooms (some on ground floor, some with bunk beds): £81–£199. (Underground: Earls Court, Gloucester Road)

B+B Belgravia, 64–66 Ebury Street, SW1W 9QD. *Tel* 020-7259 8570, www.bb-belgravia.com. Elegant Georgian town house (part of B+B Collection Ltd: see also Weymouth). Contemporary interior. Lounge (fireplace; complimentary tea/coffee, DVD/book library). Open-plan kitchen/breakfast room: organic breakfasts. Free Wi-Fi and bicycles. No background music. Small garden. 17 bedrooms (2 family; 1 suitable for &). B&B £60–£99 per person. (Underground: Victoria)

The Berkeley, Wilton Place, SW1X 7RL. *Tel* 020-7235 6000, www.the-berkeley.co.uk. Overlooking Hyde Park: large, luxury designer hotel managed by Klaus Kabelitz. 'Phenomenally well-trained staff make it a personal, comforting place for a relaxing stay.' *The Caramel Room* (afternoon tea), *The Blue Bar*, 2 restaurants: *Marcus Wareing at The Berkeley* (2 *Michelin* stars), *Boxwood Café*; health club and spa; rooftop swimming pool (spectacular views over Knightsbridge); meeting rooms; private dining room. 214 bedrooms: £259–£1,850. Breakfast £25. (Underground: Hyde Park Corner, Knightsbridge)

The Bingham, 61–63 Petersham Road, Richmond, TW10 6UT. *Tel* 020-8940 0902, www.thebingham.co.uk. Sophisticated riverside hotel in 2 Georgian town houses, owned by Ruth and Samantha Trinder. Contemporary decor. Cocktail bar ('a delightful, relaxing space'), restaurant (large windows; river views), terrace (alfresco dining). Background music. Function facilities. Civil wedding licence. Landscaped gardens. Children welcomed. 15 bedrooms. B&B £75–£152.50 per person. Dinner £47. (Underground: Richmond, 10 mins' walk)

City Inn Westminster, 30 John Islip Street, SW1P 4DD. *Tel* 020-7630 1000, www.cityinn.com. 'Admirable' large, contemporary hotel (City Inn group) by Tate Britain, managed by Simon Morpuss. Lounge (ruby-red decor; background music); modern art; *City* café; gym. Wi-Fi. Function facilities. 460 bedrooms. B&B from £115 per person. (Underground: Pimlico)

County Hall Premier Inn, Belvedere Road, SE1 7PB. *Tel* 0870-238 3300, www.premierinn.com. Well-located, budget hotel (Whitbread-owned) in old County Hall building beside London Eye, across river from Houses of Parliament. Managed by Nuno Sacramento. Lobby, bar, restaurant; lift. Background music. Children welcomed. 314 uniform bedrooms (some suitable for &): £125–£135. Breakfast £7.95. Dinner £25. (Underground: Waterloo)

Covent Garden Hotel, 10 Monmouth Street, WC2H 9HB. *Tel* 020-7806 1000, www.coventgardenhotel.co.uk. In theatreland: suitably splendid luxury (Firmdale) hotel, managed by Helle Jensen. Drawing room, library, refurbished bar and restaurant, *Brasserie Max*; meeting rooms; screening room; gym; beauty treatments. No background music. Wi-Fi. Granite bathrooms. 58 bedrooms (CD/DVD-player, flat-screen TV; 1 suite has 'largest four-poster bed in London'): £235–£1,150. Breakfast £19.50. Dinner from £19.95. (Underground: Covent Garden)

Dorset Square Hotel, 39 Dorset Square, NW1 6QN. *Tel* 020-7723 7874, www.dorsetsquare.co.uk. Facing garden square (site of Thomas Lord's first cricket ground): Regency residence (grand country house interior). Owned by Luxury Hotel Partners, managed by Nicholas Chek Makjian. Dorset country produce in *The Potting Shed* restaurant. Lounge, bar. Live jazz Fri night. 37 bedrooms: £240–£350. Breakfast £13.50–£15.75. (Underground: Marylebone)

The Draycott, 26 Cadogan Gardens, SW3 2RP. *Tel* 020-7730 6466, www.draycotthotel.com. 'Cosy home-from-home', owned by Adrian Gardiner, managed by John Hanna, in 3 Edwardian buildings, between Knightsbridge and Chelsea. 2 drawing rooms, breakfast room. No background music. Afternoon tea at 4 pm, champagne at 6 pm, hot chocolate at bedtime. 1-acre garden. Wi-Fi. Children welcomed. 35 bedrooms (*excluding VAT*): £130–£385. Breakfast £16.95–£21.95. (Underground: Sloane Square)

Dukes Hotel, 35 St James's Place, SW1A 1NY. *Tel* 020-7491 4840, www.dukeshotel.com. Recently restyled (contemporary look): exclusive hotel, in quiet courtyard. Part of Gordon Campbell Gray's group (see also *One Aldwych*, main entry); David Silver is manager. Drawing room, bar, restaurant (classic British dishes); 24-hour room service; health club; courtyard garden. No background music. Up-to-date technology. Wi-Fi. 90 bedrooms: £255–£1,110. Breakfast from £15. (Underground: Green Park)

Fox & Anchor, 115 Charterhouse Street, EC1M 6AA. *Tel* 020-7250 1300, www.foxandanchor.com. By Smithfield: renovated pub with 'buzzy feel', retaining Victorian heritage, and with 'chic, tasteful' rooms. An offshoot of Malmaison hotels (the London *Malmaison* (*qv*) is next door); managed by Scott Malaugh. Dining room, 3 snugs, 'cosy, evocative of times past', oyster bar; real ales. Background music. Some late-night/early-morning street noise. 6 bedrooms: £95–£250. Breakfast £8.95. (Underground: Barbican)

Haymarket Hotel, 1 Suffolk Place, SW1Y 4BP. *Tel* 020-7470 4000, www.haymarkethotel.com. Bold, contemporary interior, in 3 John Nash-designed buildings near Theatre Royal. Part of Firmdale group, managed by Lisa Brooklyn. Lift, drawing room, library, bar, *Brumus* restaurant; background music. Indoor swimming pool, gym. 50 bedrooms: £250–£3,000. Breakfast £18.50. (Underground: Green Park, Piccadilly)

High Road House, 162 Chiswick High Road, W4Y 1PR. *Tel* 020-8742 1717, www.highroadhouse.co.uk. Hotel/private members' club (Soho House group), managed by Mark Jones. Retro-modern style. Bar, brasserie (some outdoor seating); games room (red leather sofas, pool table, football table, board games); 'Playground' (plasma screens, DVDs, Wi-Fi). Background music. 14 (small, minimalist) bedrooms: £145–£165. English breakfast £9.50. (Underground: Turnham Green)

Hotel 55, 55 Hanger Lane, W5 13HL. *Tel* 020-8991 4450, www.hotel55-london.com. In Ealing: former hostel, turned into 'luxury budget' hotel with cool, contemporary style. Bar, restaurant (Japanese: *Momo*); background music. Original art. Wi-Fi. Children welcomed. Parking. 30 mins from Heathrow; Piccadilly line to central London. 25 bedrooms (2 suitable for &). B&B (continental) £65–£125 per person. (Underground: North Ealing) *V*

The Hoxton, 81 Great Eastern Street, EC2A 3HU. *Tel* 020-7750 1000, www.hoxtonhotels.com. Buzzy hotel owned by Sinclair Beecham (co-founder of Pret A Manger); managed by David Taylor. Radical preferential early booking system, inexpensive phone calls, Wi-Fi. Huge lobby, sitting area, bar, brasserie *Hoxton Grille*; background music; business facilities; lift; shop. Courtyard. Children welcomed. Use of local leisure centre (£5). 205 bedrooms. B&B

(Pret Lite breakfast) £29.36–£194.77 per person. Full breakfast £8.75. (Underground: Old Street)

Indigo, 16 London Street, W2A 1HL. *Tel* 020-706 4444, www. hippaddington.com. Hip hotel (London Town Hotels). Wood floors, vibrant colours, huge photographic murals of interesting local architecture. 3 mins' walk from station and Heathrow Express. Fitness studio; terrace. Wi-Fi. Background music. 64 bedrooms: £125–£225. Breakfast £6.95–£8.95. (Underground: Paddington)

Kensington House, 15–16 Prince of Wales Terrace, W8 5PQ. *Tel* 020-7937 2345, www.kenhouse.com. 19th-century stucco-fronted town house in quiet road near Kensington Gardens. Managed by Antonio Sola. Crisp, contemporary interior; cosy atmosphere. Informal dining in *Tiger Bar*; 24-hour room service. No background music. Wi-Fi. 41 (mainly small) bedrooms. B&B (continental) £90–£230 per person. (Underground: High St Kensington)

Knightsbridge Hotel, 10 Beaufort Gardens, SW3 1PT. *Tel* 020-7584 6300, www.knightsbridgehotel.com. Understated contemporary decor, modern British art, in peaceful, tree-lined cul-de-sac near shops. Managed by Gisele Clark for Firmdale group. Drawing room, library, bar. Room service. No background music. Wi-Fi. Granite and oak bathrooms. 44 bedrooms: £170–£297.50. Breakfast £17.50. (Underground: Knightsbridge)

Knightsbridge Green Hotel, 159 Knightsbridge, SW1X 7PD. *Tel* 020-7584 6274, www.thekghotel.co.uk. B&B, decorated in plain, contemporary style, near South Kensington museums and Knightsbridge shops. Managed by Ann Gronager. Reception (background music), lounge; business centre. Lift. Wi-Fi. Children welcomed. 28 bedrooms (some suitable for &): £100–£250. Room-service breakfast (continental) £12.50. (Underground: Knightsbridge) *V*

Lord Milner, 111 Ebury Street, SW1 9QU. *Tel* 020-7881 9880, www.lordmilner.com. Small town house B&B with contemporary interior, owned by Anton and Amber Engelbrecht. Traditional furnishing; marble bathrooms. Convenient for Victoria rail and coach stations. Lift, reception (fireside seating). Background music ('soft hits'). Wi-Fi. 11 bedrooms: £115–£255. Breakfast £11.99–£13.99. (Underground: Victoria).

The Main House, 6 Colville Road, Notting Hill, W11 2BP. *Tel* 020-7221 9691, www.themainhouse.co.uk. Caroline Main's stylish, small, Victorian town house in tranquil location off Portobello Road. Spacious rooms (period features, antique furnishings). No background music. Guests may borrow bicycles and DVDs. Roof terrace. Wi-Fi. Children welcomed. 4 bedrooms: £120–£130. No breakfast, but tea, coffee brought to room; special rates at nearby deli. (Underground: Notting Hill Gate)

Malmaison, Charterhouse Square, EC1M 6AH. *Tel* 020-7012 3700, www.malmaison.com. Chic conversion of nurses' hostel, on quiet Clerkenwell square. Managed by Anthony Thwaites. Subterranean bar, brasserie (informal dining in vaults, cosy corners, plump silk and velvet cushions); background music; gym. Dogs welcomed (£10 charge). 97 bedrooms (lilac, dove and earth tones): £235–£575. Breakfast £14.95–£17.95. (Underground: Farringdon, Barbican)

Mandeville Hotel, Mandeville Place, W1U 2BE. *Tel* 020-7935 5599, www.mandeville.co.uk. Large, glitzy hotel in Marylebone (Summit Hotels & Resorts), managed by Alexander Watenphul. *de Vigne* bar, *de Ville* restaurant (theatrical decor; organic produce; Gunter Geiger is chef); function facilities; background music. 142 bedrooms (6 suitable for ♿): £289–£880. Breakfast £17.25–£22.50. Dinner £75. (Underground: Bond Street)

Miller's Residence, 111A Westbourne Grove, W2 4UW. *Tel* 020-7243 1024, www.millershotel.com. 'So much to captivate the eye – like being let into an exclusive, secret haunt.' Packed with antiques and curios: 3-storey guest house owned by Martin Miller (of *Miller's Antiques* guides; see also *Glencot House*, Wookey Hole, main entry). Managed by his daughter, Cara. 'Very helpful, friendly service.' Large candlelit drawing room/breakfast room ('good continental breakfast'); bar (complimentary drinks 5 pm–11 pm); background jazz/classical music; complimentary tea/coffee all day; guests may bring their own food and drink. Children welcomed. 8 bedrooms, named after British poets (DVD-player; iPod dock; Wi-Fi). B&B (*excluding VAT*) £75–£115 per person. (Underground: Notting Hill Gate, Bayswater, Queensway)

Montagu Place, 2 Montagu Place, W1N 2ER. *Tel* 020-7467 2777, www.montagu-place.co.uk. In quiet location near Baker Street: intimate hotel in 2 Grade II listed Georgian town houses. Dimitrios Neofitidis is manager. Dark woods, textured fabrics, earth tones, mirrors. Lounge, bar, breakfast room. No background music. Wi-Fi. 16 bedrooms: £200–£260. Continental buffet breakfast from £10. (Underground: Marylebone, Baker Street)

The Montague on the Gardens, 15 Montague Street, WC1B 5BJ. *Tel* 020-7637 1001, www.montaguehotel.com. Elegant, large hotel (Red Carnation group), managed by Dirk Crokaert: white stucco Georgian town house near British Museum. Bar, *Blue Door* bistro (modern British food from chef Martin Halls); conservatory (afternoon tea); background music; terrace (wood deck, alfresco dining: barbecues; spit-roasts). Rear private garden with statuary. 24-hour room service. Function facilities. Civil wedding licence. Family-friendly, pet-friendly. 100 rooms (*excluding VAT*): £145–£355. Breakfast £14.50–£16.50. (Underground: Tottenham Court Road, Holborn, Russell Square)

Number Sixteen, 16 Sumner Place, SW7 3EG. *Tel* 020-7589 5232, www.numbersixteenhotel.co.uk. White stucco mid-Victorian terraced building (Firmdale group), managed by Alison Huxley, in quiet street. Stylish modern decor. Lift, 2 drawing rooms, conservatory. No background music. Courtyard garden: fountain. 'Great location: neighbourhood feel.' 42 bedrooms: £120–£270. Breakfast £17.50. (Underground: South Kensington)

The Pelham, 15 Cromwell Place, SW7 2LA. *Tel* 020-7589 8288, www.pelhamhotel.co.uk. White Victorian terraced hotel with balconies and stripy awnings. Smart interior; modern and antique furniture; wood panelling; open fires. Managed by Ian Dick. 'Helpful staff; good food.' Drawing room ('immaculate, chic'), library, bar, bistro/bar, 3 private dining/meeting rooms, gym. No background music. Wi-Fi. 52 bedrooms: £207–£706. Breakfast £14.95–£17.95. (Underground: South Kensington)

Portobello Gold, 95–97 Portobello Road, W11 2QB. *Tel* 020-7460 4910, www.portobellogold.com. Idiosyncratic restaurant-with-rooms owned by Michael Bell, on street famed for Saturday market. Monthly photographic/art exhibitions in Gold Gallery. Live music. Steve Edwards is manager. Bar, conservatory restaurant with sliding roof (much foliage; lively atmosphere); Internet café; function facilities. Lots of stairs. 6 bedrooms (plus apartment): with continental breakfast £70–£170. (Underground: Notting Hill Gate)

Royal Park Hotel, 3 Westbourne Terrace, W2 3UL. *Tel* 020-7479 6600, www.theroyalpark.com. N of Hyde Park: elegant conversion of 3 Grade II listed Georgian town houses (part of Franklyn Hotels and Resorts), managed by Gareth Rowlands. Antiques; plain-painted walls in Regency colours. Four-poster and half-tester beds. Drawing room. Background music. Small room-service menu. 48 bedrooms: £171–£303. (Underground: Paddington)

San Domenico House, 29–31 Draycott Place, SW1X 0HJ. *Tel* 020-7581 5757, www.sandomenicohouse.com. Marisa Melpignano's sumptuously furnished hotel in red brick Chelsea house; staffed by Italians. Lobby, lounge (background music), breakfast room;

extensive room service; fitness/massage rooms; roof terrace; meeting facilities. 16 bedrooms (*excluding VAT*): £235–£360. Breakfast £14–£18. (Underground: Sloane Square)

The Sanctuary House, 33 Tothill Street, SW1H 9LA. *Tel* 020-7799 4044, www.fullershotels.com. Near Houses of Parliament: good-value B&B (Fuller's Hotels) with refurbished rooms above traditional ale and pie house (where breakfast is served). Managed by Sol Yepes. 34 bedrooms. B&B £92.50–£185 per person. (Underground: St James's Park)

Savoro, 206 High Street, Hadley Green, Barnet, EN5 5SZ. *Tel* 020-8449.9888, www.savoro.co.uk. Light-filled restaurant-with-rooms, in whitewashed former inn, boathouse, bakery/traditional tea shop. 'Very relaxed; top-class food.' Owned by Jack Antoni, managed by Dino Paphiti. Chef Robert Brown concentrates on fish and seasonal produce on modern menus. Dining room (background music). Function facilities. Wi-Fi. 9 bedrooms (plainly decorated in browns and creams; some with four-poster bed). B&B £37.50–£70 per person. Dinner £23.95 (3 courses). *V*

Searcy's Roof Garden Rooms, 30 Pavilion Road, SW1X 0HJ. *Tel* 020-7584 4921, www.30pavilionroad.co.uk. Quaint, friendly B&B in Georgian town house, in small Knightsbridge street. Managed by Neringa Zutautaite. No public rooms. No background music. Large roof garden. Function facilities. Free Wi-Fi. 10 bedrooms. B&B (continental) £60–£120 per person. (Underground: Sloane Square)

The Soho Hotel, 4 Richmond Mews, off Dean Street, W1D 3DH. *Tel* 020-7559 3000, www.sohohotel.com. Glamorous contemporary hotel (Firmdale group), managed by Carrie Wicks. Spacious rooms; luxurious bathrooms; modern art. Lift. Drawing room, library, *Refuel* bar/restaurant (Robin Read is chef); background music; 4 private dining rooms; gym; 2 screening rooms. 91 bedrooms (some suitable for &): £280–£2,750. Breakfast £18.50. (Underground: Leicester Square)

The Stafford, 16–18 St James's Place, SW1A 1NJ. *Tel* 020-7493 0111, www.thestaffordhotel.co.uk. Formed from 3 town houses: large sophisticated hotel in quiet backwater off St James's St, managed by Stuart Procter. Lounge, American bar (food served), restaurant; lift. Courtyard. No background music. Children welcomed. Access to nearby fitness studio. Function facilities. Civil wedding licence. Parking (charge). 105 bedrooms (11 in Carriage House; 26 in mews; 1 suitable for &) (*excluding VAT*): £312–£1,450. Breakfast £25. (Underground: Green Park)

Threadneedles, 5 Threadneedle Street, EC2R 8AY. *Tel* 020-7657 8080, www.theetoncollection.com. Opulent conversion of 1856 banking hall near Bank of England, managed for Eton Collection by Julian Payne. Original stained-glass dome towers over reception lounge (background music). Contemporary artwork. Bar, *Bonds* restaurant (closed weekends; Barry Tonks is chef); 3 meeting rooms; conference facilities. 69 bedrooms (some suitable for &): £145–£545. Breakfast £19. (Underground: Bank)

Tophams, 24–32 Ebury Street, SW1W 0LU. *Tel* 020-7730 3813, www.tophamshotel.com. Luxury B&B spread over 5 handsome stucco-fronted houses, enlarged and rejuvenated in contemporary style in £4 million refurbishment. Managed by Paul Fizia, formerly of *Knightsbridge Green Hotel* (*qv*). Bar, breakfast room; lift; concierge service; small business centre. No background music. Wi-Fi. 'We enjoyed our stay; will go back.' 48 bedrooms: £225–£375 per person. Breakfast £14.95. (Underground: Victoria)

ENGLAND

ABINGDON Oxfordshire   Map 2:C2
B&B Rafters, Abingdon Road, Marcham, OX13 6NU. *Tel* 01865-391298, www.bnb-rafters.co.uk. Sigrid and Arne Grawert's B&B in half-timbered house in village 3 miles W of Abingdon, 8 miles S of Oxford. Award-winning breakfast (organic ingredients; whisky porridge speciality; vegetarians catered for). Contemporary design; massage chair, waterbed. Lounge, breakfast room (no background music); garden. Parking. 4 bedrooms. B&B £39.50–£47 per person.

BAMPTON Devon   Map 1:C5
The Bark House, Oakfordbridge, EX16 9HZ. *Tel* 01398-351236, www.barkhouse.co.uk. 'Delightful' wisteria-covered cottage guest house now run by Melanie McKnight and Martin French. By busy road, overlooking Exe valley; 9 miles N of Tiverton. 'A most friendly welcome; excellent tea on arrival; delicious dinner and breakfast.' Lounge, dining room (occasional background music). Garden. Dogs welcomed. Parking. 6 bedrooms. B&B £38–£64 per person; D,B&B £68–£94. *V*

BATH Somerset   Map 2:D1
Aquae Sulis, 174–176 Newbridge Road, BA1 3LE. *Tel* 01225-420061, www.aquaesulishotel.co.uk. Peaceful, traditionally furnished

Edwardian guest house run by owners David and Jane Carnegie. Short bus trip from abbey (or 30-min riverside stroll); Park & Ride close by. 2 lounges (1 computer room); background music. Wi-Fi. Children welcomed. ½-acre garden. Parking. 14 bedrooms (some family). B&B £32.50–£89 per person.

The Ayrlington, 24–25 Pulteney Road, BA2 4EZ. *Tel* 01225-425495, www.ayrlington.com. Near centre, B&B in Simon and Mee-Ling Roper's elegant, listed Victorian house. Oriental antiques; some four-poster beds; sustainable environment policy. Bar, breakfast room; background music. Wi-Fi. Award-winning walled garden; views over city. Parking. Spa breaks. 14 bedrooms. B&B £40–£97.50 per person (2-night min. stay at weekends).

Dorian House, 1 Upper Oldfield Park, BA2 3JX. *Tel* 01225-426336, www.dorianhouse.co.uk. 'Unexpectedly eccentric' B&B in characterful Victorian stone house (recently refurbished), 10 mins' downhill walk to centre. Owned by cellist Tim Hugh and wife, Kathryn; managed by Peter Lund. Lounge (open fire), breakfast room/music library; classical background music. Good views over city. Wi-Fi. Garden. Parking. 11 bedrooms (named after musicians; 1 on ground floor; some have four-poster). B&B £32.50–£97.50 per person.

Dukes Hotel, Great Pulteney Road, BA2 4DN. *Tel* 01225-787960, www.dukesbath.co.uk. Flower-bedecked Grade I Palladian-style town house (lots of stairs). Elegant interior, contemporary comforts. Owned by Alan Brookes and Michael Bokenham, managed by Tina Paradise. Lounge, bar, *Cavendish* restaurant (chef Fran Snell uses local produce; background music). Patio garden. 17 bedrooms (1 on ground floor). B&B £49.50–£116 per person; D,B&B £62.50–£151.

Harington's Hotel, 8–10 Queen Street, BA1 1HE. *Tel* 01225-461728, www.haringtonshotel.co.uk. Group of 17th-century houses, now contemporary hotel, in quiet cobbled street near abbey; owned by Melissa and Peter O'Sullivan. Lounge, bar, restaurant (background music). Patio. Reserved parking nearby. Wi-Fi. 13 bedrooms (free Sky movies and sports), 2 self-catering apartments. B&B £44–£150 per person. Dinner £34.

Paradise House, 86–88 Holloway, BA2 4PX. *Tel* 01225-317723, www.paradise-house.co.uk. Panoramic city views from listed Georgian house with Victorian extension, owned by David and Annie Lanz, managed by Nicci and Russell Clarke. 7 mins' walk (steep hill) from centre. Drawing room, breakfast room. Classical background music. Wi-Fi. 11 bedrooms (4 on ground floor, 2 in annexe in ½-acre landscaped walled garden). B&B £32.50–£115 per person.

BATHFORD Somerset   Map 2:D1

Eagle House, Church Street, BA1 7RS. *Tel* 01225-859946, www. eaglehouse.co.uk. In peaceful surroundings, 3 miles outside Bath (regular buses): B&B in listed Georgian mansion, home of John and Rosamund Napier. Drawing room, breakfast room. No background music. 2-acre grounds: croquet lawn, grass tennis court, tree house, sandpit. Wi-Fi. Children welcomed; dogs (by arrangement; resident dog and cat). 8 bedrooms (2 in garden cottage). B&B (continental) £36–£68 per person. Cooked breakfast £5.50. *V*

BELFORD Northumberland   Map 4:A3

Waren House, Waren Mill, NE70 7EE. *Tel* 01668-214581, www.warenhousehotel.co.uk. Anita and Peter Laverack's Georgian house in wooded grounds above natural bird sanctuary of Budle Bay; views of Holy Island. Drawing room, dining room, library. No background music. Wi-Fi. 6-acre garden; secure parking. Dogs welcomed. 13 bedrooms (1 suitable for &). B&B £60–£110 per person; D,B&B £117.50–£184.

BIRMINGHAM West Midlands   Map 2:B2

Simpsons, 20 Highfield Road, Edgbaston, B15 3DU. *Tel* 0121-454 3434, www.simpsonsrestaurant.co.uk. Andreas Antona's restaurant-with-rooms in Georgian mansion, 1 mile from centre. *Michelin* star for classic French cooking. Themed bedrooms: French, Oriental, Venetian, Colonial. Dining areas; private dining room (no background music); terrace (alfresco dining); garden. Cookery school. 4 bedrooms. B&B (continental) £80–£112.50 per person. Dinner £32.50 (3 courses).

BLACKBURN Lancashire   Map 4:D3

The Millstone at Mellor, Church Lane, Mellor, BB2 7JR. *Tel* 01254-813333, www.millstonehotel.co.uk. 'Friendly pub with excellent food.' 3 miles NW of Blackburn, in attractive village in Ribble valley: stone-built former coaching inn retaining quaint style. Owned by Shire Hotels, run by chef/*patron* Anson Bolton. Residents' lounge (log fire), bar, *Millers* restaurant (emphasis on Lancashire produce). No background music. Parking. 23 bedrooms (6 in courtyard; 1 suitable for &). B&B £49.50–£109 per person; D,B&B £65.50–£131.

BLACKPOOL Lancashire   Map 4:D2

Four Seasons, 60 Reads Avenue, FY1 4DE. *Tel* 01253-752171, www.fourseasonsblackpool.co.uk. Marcus and Bea Sewell's friendly

B&B in peaceful surroundings, 5 mins' walk to centre. Breakfast room (local ingredients). No background music. Children welcomed. Wi-Fi. 4 quirkily colourful suites with seasonal theme. B&B £60–£95 per person.

Number One St Lukes, 1 St Lukes Road, South Shore, FY4 2EL. *Tel* 01253-343901, www.numberoneblackpool.com. Small, stylish B&B in detached house on quiet corner, a short walk from Pleasure Beach. Proprietors Mark and Claire Smith also own *Number One South Beach* on promenade (see below). State-of-the-art gadgetry. No background music. Large garden. Ample parking. 3 bedrooms. B&B £60–£75 per person

Number One South Beach, 4 Harrowside West, FY4 1NW. *Tel* 01253-343900, www.numberonesouthbeach.com. Claire and Mark Smith (proprietors of *Number One St Lukes*, above) joined forces with Janet and Graham Oxley to create this high-tech, low-carbon-footprint boutique hotel, with sea views over South Beach Promenade. Lounge, bar, restaurant; background music; pool table; meeting/conference facilities. Lift. Parking. 14 bedrooms (some with four-poster; disabled facilities). B&B £60–£140 per person.

Raffles Hotel & Tea Room, 73–77 Hornby Road, FY1 4QJ. *Tel* 01253-294713, www.raffleshotelblackpool.co.uk. Small, flower-fronted, bay-windowed hotel run by owners Ian Balmforth (chef) and Graham Poole. 5 mins from Winter Gardens, shops, promenade. Lounge, bar, traditional English tea room (closed Mon); classical background music. Parking. Children welcomed. 17 bedrooms, plus 3 apartment suites. B&B £33–£38 per person.

BLOCKLEY Gloucestershire   Map 3:D6
Lower Brook House, Lower Street, GL56 9DS. *Tel* 01386-700286, www.lowerbrookhouse.co.uk. Julian and Anna (the cook) Ebbutt's Cotswold stone house (Grade II listed) in cottage garden with brook and dovecote. Views of village and surrounding countryside. Lounge, restaurant (candlelit dinners). 'Breakfasts something to get out of bed for, set you up for the day.' No background music. 6 bedrooms. B&B £50–£92.50 per person.

BONCHURCH Isle of Wight   Map 2:E2
Winterbourne Country House, Bonchurch Village Road, PO38 1RQ. *Tel* 01983-852535, www.winterbournehouse.co.uk. In tranquil sea-facing gardens 2 miles E of Ventnor: traditionally furnished B&B owned by Michael Sharrock, house where Dickens

wrote *David Copperfield*. Andrew Eccott and Andy Harper are the managers. 2 lounges, breakfast room, snug; classical background music. Garden: swimming pool, terrace, stream, private path to small beach. 7 bedrooms. B&B £55–£95 per person.

BOSCASTLE Cornwall   Map 1:C3

Trerosewill Farmhouse, Paradise, PL35 0BL. *Tel* 01840-250545, www.trerosewill.co.uk. Steve and Cheryl Nicholls's B&B has a gold award in Green Tourism Business Scheme. 40-acre farmland, coastal views. Home-made and local produce. Packed lunches available. 2 lounges, conservatory dining room; DVD/video library. No background music. 1-acre garden; summer house; hot tub. 8 bedrooms (2 suites). B&B £33.50–£45 per person.

BOURNEMOUTH Dorset   Map 2:E2

Urban Beach, 23 Argyll Road, BH5 1EB. *Tel* 01202-301509, www.urbanbeachhotel.co.uk. Buzzy, contemporary hotel in Victorian building close to Boscombe beach, 1 mile from centre. Run by 'laid-back' owner Mark Cribb, with manager James Fowler. Bar, bistro (local produce, home-made bread); background music. Wi-Fi. DVD library; wellies, umbrellas. Complimentary use of local gym. 12 bedrooms. B&B £60–£170 per person. Dinner from £25.

BOVEY TRACEY Devon   Map 1:D4

The Edgemoor, Haytor Road, Lowerdown Cross, TQ13 9LE. *Tel* 01626-832466, www.edgemoor.co.uk. Large Victorian house, former school, now country house hotel with contemporary rooms, owned by Simon and Heather Crow and Morten Hansen. On edge of Dartmoor. 15 mins' walk from village. Bar, *Fireside* bistro, restaurant (seasonal menus; background music). Wi-Fi. Large selection of wines (some locally produced); 20 whiskies. Garden (alfresco dining). Civil wedding licence. Conference facilities. Child-friendly. Dogs welcomed. Parking. 15 miles SW of Exeter. 16 bedrooms. B&B from £47.50 per person. Dinner £32.

BOWNESS-ON-WINDERMERE   Map 4: inset C2
Cumbria

Lindeth Howe, Lindeth Drive, Longtail Hill, LA23 3JF. *Tel* 015394-45759, www.lindeth-howe.co.uk. 1 mile S of town: imposing country house overlooking lake (owned by Potter family 1902–1913: Beatrix wrote tales of Timmy Tiptoes and Pigland Bland here). Managed by

Alison Magee Barker. Recently refurbished ground floor. Lounge, library, bar, restaurant (Marc Guibert is chef). Background music. Sun terrace; leisure centre (swimming pool, sauna, fitness room). 6-acre garden. 34 bedrooms (some on ground floor). B&B £45–£175 per person; D,B&B £65–£215. *V*

BRADFORD-ON-AVON Wiltshire   Map 2:D1

Woolley Grange, Woolley Green, BA15 1TX. *Tel* 01225-864705, www.woolleygrangehotel.co.uk. Luxury family-oriented hotel (von Essen group; managed by Clare Hammond). Jacobean stone manor house in 14-acre grounds on edge of town. 2 lounges, TV room, bar, restaurant, conservatory. No background music. Children's nursery, games room; outdoor heated swimming pool, badminton, croquet, trampoline, play area; cycling, riding, golf, tennis, fishing, hot-air ballooning nearby. Ornamental garden, kitchen garden, herb garden, orchard. Function facilities. Dogs welcomed. 26 bedrooms (7 in *Stone Cottage*, 2 in *Coach House*, 3 in *Pavilion*; some suitable for &). B&B £65–£230 per person; D,B&B £100–£265.

BRIDPORT Dorset   Map 1:C6

The Bull Hotel, 34 East Street, DT6 3LF. *Tel* 01308-422878, www.thebullhotel.co.uk. Richard and Nikki Cooper's informal gastropub-with-rooms in Grade II listed coaching inn. Modern English dishes from chef Marc Montgomery. 'Food good; popular with locals.' 2 bars (background music), restaurant; ballroom; private dining room; courtyard. Children welcomed. 14 eclectically styled bedrooms. B&B £35–£90 per person. Dinner from £36.

BRIGHTON East Sussex   Map 2:E4

Fivehotel, 5 New Steine, BN2 1PB. *Tel* 01273-686547, www.fivehotel.com. On a Kemp Town Regency square, Caroline and Simon Heath's contemporary B&B in period town house. 1 minute from sea; close to The Lanes. 'Lovely room. We watched the sun sparkle on the water, the yachts race in the bay.' 2 public rooms; roof terrace. Communal breakfast (local, organic ingredients; no background music). Free Wi-Fi. 10 bedrooms (some with sea views). B&B £40–£80 per person.

Hotel du Vin, Brighton, 2–6 Ship Street, BN1 1AD. *Tel* 01273-718588, www.hotelduvin.com. Lively atmosphere at Brighton outpost of small chain: original features retained in collection of Gothic revival and mock-Tudor buildings between The Lanes and seafront. 'Food and wine excellent. Room good, if unusual – twin bathtubs in bay window with sea view.' Lounge/bar, bistro. 'Easy listening' background music. Children welcomed. 37 bedrooms (6 in courtyard; 2 on ground floor). B&B £85–£180 per person. Breakfast £9.95–£13.50. Dinner from £35.

Grey's, 11 Charlotte Street, BN2 1AG. *Tel* 01273-603197, www.greyshotel.co.uk. Between town centre and marina, 1 min from beach, contemporary B&B run by owner Terry Sessions in Kemp Town Georgian house. Cosy; decorated in muted tones. Breakfast room (vegetarian full English breakfast available). No background music. 9 bedrooms. B&B £49–£55 per person.

Hotel Una, 55–56 Regency Square, BN1 2FF. *Tel* 01273-820464, www.hotel-una.co.uk. On Regency square with views of West Pier, hotel with unpretentious balance of old and new (wood, dark leather furniture, lots of art). Owned by Zoran Mericevic and Jelena Popic, 'funky' bar (background music), breakfast room; treatment room, conference facilities. Lift. 19 bedrooms (named after rivers; sauna, whirlpool in 2 suites). B&B £57.50–£95 per person.

BROCKENHURST Hampshire   Map 2:E2

Thatched Cottage, 16 Brookley Road, SO42 7RR. *Tel* 01590-623090, www.thatched-cottage.co.uk. Matysik family's restaurant-with-rooms in cosy 400-year-old timber-framed thatched cottage in New Forest national park. Dainty decor; 'indulgent' afternoon teas. Lounge, dining room. No background music. Garden. Dogs welcomed. 5 bedrooms. B&B £60–£150 per person. Dinner £40.

BUCKLAND Gloucestershire   Map 3:D6

Buckland Manor, Buckland, nr Broadway, WR12 7LY. *Tel* 01386-852626, www.bucklandmanor.com. 'Well-maintained', ancient manor house in isolated village. 'Lovely gardens.' Owned by von Essen hotels, managed by Nigel Power. 'Cooking to the highest standard' by chef Matt Hodgkins. 2 lounges; dining room. No background music. 10-acre grounds (stream, waterfalls); croquet lawn, tennis. 13 bedrooms (no room key; 1 on ground floor). B&B £142.50–£235 per person. Dinner £40–£50.

BUDE Cornwall   Map 1:C3

Bangors Organic, Poundstock, EX23 0DP. *Tel* 01288-361297, www.bangorsorganic.co.uk. On unspoiled north Cornish coast 5 miles S of town, Gill and Neil Faiers's organically run 'B&B & Restaurant'.

Carbon-neutral home-grown produce; solar-heated water, green electricity, wood fires. Background music 'when requested'. Eclectic decor. Holistic treatments. No smoking in grounds. Widemouth Bay beach nearby. 5-acre garden and farmland. 4 contemporary bedrooms (2 suites in coach house; 1 suitable for &). B&B £55–£80 per person; D,B&B £75–£100.

BUNGAY Suffolk   Map 2:B6

Earsham Park Farm, Old Railway Road, Earsham, NR35 2AQ. *Tel* 01986-892180, www.earsham-parkfarm.co.uk. Bobbie and Simon Watchorn's Victorian farmhouse on 600-acre working farm (arable crops, free-range pig herd), with sweeping views over Waveney valley. 3 miles W of town, up ½-mile drive off A143. Traditionally furnished; informal. Lounge, dining room. No background music. Garden. Child-friendly; dogs, horses welcomed. 3 bedrooms. B&B £37.50–£67 per person.

BURFORD Oxfordshire   Map 3:D6

The Highway Inn, 117 High Street, OX18 4RG. *Tel* 01993-823661, www.thehighwayInn.co.uk. In centre: 15th-century inn, restored in traditional style by friendly owners Scott and Tally Nelson. Beams, stone walls. Bar, restaurant; courtyard (alfresco dining). Modern British food. Occasional background music. Children welcomed. 9 bedrooms. B&B £42.50–£75 per person.

BURY ST EDMUNDS Suffolk   Map 2:B5

The Angel Hotel, Angel Hill, IP33 1LT. *Tel* 01284-714000, www.theangel.co.uk. On Georgian square opposite cathedral, historic ivy-covered coaching inn with modern additions. Popular with locals; run by Gough family for over 2 decades. Contemporary design and wall art. Lounge (log fire), bar, restaurant (Simon Barker serves modern Mediterranean food); background music. Function facilities. Child-friendly. Dogs welcomed. 76 bedrooms. B&B £55–£110 per person. Dinner £40. *V*

Ounce House, Northgate Street, IP33 1HP. *Tel* 01284-761779, www. ouncehouse.co.uk. Spacious Victorian merchant's house run by owners Simon and Jenny Pott. Homely atmosphere: chintzy drawing room (photographs, knick-knacks; honesty bar), snug/bar/library. Communal breakfast. No background music. Parking. 5 bedrooms (the quietest 2 face ¾-acre walled garden). B&B £60–£95 per person. Dinner £30–£40.

Ravenwood Hall, Rougham, IP30 9JA. *Tel* 01359-270345, www. ravenwoodhall.co.uk. Historic home (Tudor origins; inglenook fireplaces) of Craig Jarvis, in 7-acre grounds (garden, croquet, outdoor heated swimming pool, woodland). Yvonne Howland manages. Child-friendly, pet-friendly. Ramps, lounge, bar (informal meals); background jazz/classical music; restaurant, garden dining room; Edwardian pavilion for conferences/weddings (civil licence). Off A14 (some traffic noise), 3 miles SE of Bury. 14 bedrooms (7 in mews, some on ground floor). B&B £76.50–£132.50 per person. Dinner from £32. *V*

BUXTON Derbyshire   Map 3:A6

Grendon, Bishops Lane, SK17 6UN. *Tel* 01298-78831, www. grendonguesthouse.co.uk. Hilary and Colin Parker's welcoming guest house with spacious rooms. On quiet country lane, ¾ mile W of town. Lounge, breakfast room (home-made bread and muesli); terrace. No background music. 1-acre garden overlooking golf course. Parking. Wi-Fi. 5 bedrooms. B&B £30–£65 per person.

Hartington Hall, Hall Bank, SK17 0AT, *Tel* 0845-371 9740, www. yha.org.uk/hartington. On edge of Dovedale, YHA-owned hostel in 1611 manor house (mullioned windows, oak panelling; log fires) in large grounds. Spread over 3 buildings (main house, coach house, barn, plus The Roost bridal suite); managed by William Greenwood. Lounge, bar, restaurant (traditional English, local ingredients); background music; games room, self-catering kitchen, drying room, meeting rooms; beer garden; adventure playground; pet area (pygmy goats, chickens; wildlife pond); ½-acre garden. Civil wedding licence. 35 bedrooms (19 en suite, 1 suitable for &). B&B £16.50–£34.50; D,B&B £29–£48 per person. *V*

CAMBER East Sussex   Map 2:E5

The Place at the beach, Camber Sands, New Lydd Road, nr Rye, TN31 7RB. *Tel* 01797-225057, www.theplaceatthebeach.co.uk. A new 'driftwood' theme and name change at this red-roofed, white, single-storey building, opposite dunes of famous sandy beach, 3 miles SE of Rye. Now owned by Harry Cragoe; managed by Tudor Hopkins. Seaside decor; brasserie (seasonal produce; background jazz/classical music); conference facilities. Terrace; decked area. Children welcomed. 18 bedrooms (all on ground floor). B&B £42.50–£77.50 per person; D,B&B £69–£97.50.

CAMBRIDGE Cambridgeshire   Map 2:B4

Hotel Felix, Whitehouse Lane, Huntingdon Road, CB3 0LX. *Tel* 01223-277977, www.hotelfelix.co.uk. Late Victorian, yellow brick mansion, with slick, contemporary interior, on edge of city. Business hotel, managed by Shara Ross. Small lounge, bar, *Graffiti* restaurant (modern Mediterranean cooking from Nick Parker; background music); function facilities. 4-acre garden, terrace. Parking. 52 bedrooms (4 suitable for &). B&B (continental) £97.50–£150 per person; D,B&B from £99. Cooked breakfast £7.50. Dinner from £30.

Hotel du Vin Cambridge, 15–19 Trumpington Street, CB2 1QA. *Tel* 01223-227330, www.hotelduvin.com. Interesting conversion of old (Grade II listed) university building (exposed brickwork, reconditioned fireplaces, original bread oven, vaulted cellar). Managed by Denis Frucot. 21st-century comfort. Library, bar, bistro (open-style kitchen, under Jonathan Dean); terrace. Background music ('easy listening'). Wi-Fi. Children welcomed. 41 bedrooms (each named after a wine producer; 1 suitable for &): £145–£380. Breakfast £9.95–£13.50. Dinner from £45.

CAMPSEA ASHE Suffolk   Map 2:C6

The Old Rectory, Station Road, IP13 0PU. *Tel* 01728-746524, www.theoldrectorysuffolk.com. 'We had a really good stay, and all the other guests seemed happy.' In rural location, 8 miles NE of Woodbridge, Sally Ball's Georgian rectory in 'wonderful', tranquil gardens. Modern interior (log fires, four-poster beds, cast iron baths); traditional, mainly organic food. Sitting room, dining room, conservatory; terrace. No background music. 'Very family-friendly.' 7 bedrooms (1 on ground floor; dogs allowed in 2 garden rooms: resident Labrador, Hector). B&B £42.50–£70; D,B&B £70–£97.50.

CANTERBURY Kent   Map 2:D5

Ebury Hotel, 65–67 New Dover Road, CT1 3DX. *Tel* 01227-768433, www.ebury-hotel.co.uk. Close to cathedral and centre, Henry Mason's 'splendid' Victorian house (*c.* 1840) with original features. 'Spacious bedrooms; friendly staff; very good food.' 2 lounges, restaurant (French cuisine from Jean-Pierre Cabrol); indoor swimming pool. Background music. Wi-Fi. 2-acre grounds: 1-acre garden. Charlie the labradoodle ('promoted' to reception manager) has his own web page. 15 bedrooms; self-catering cottages. B&B £42.50–£60 per person; D,B&B £65–£75.

Magnolia House, 36 St Dunstan's Terrace, CT2 8AX. *Tel* 01227-765121, www.magnoliahousecanterbury.co.uk. In residential street ½ mile from centre, Isobelle Leggett's late Georgian guest house. Dinner by arrangement (no alcohol licence but BYO; complimentary soft drinks). Sitting room, dining room (background music). Walled garden. Parking. No children under 12. 7 bedrooms (some four-poster beds). Wi-Fi. B&B £27.50–£72.50 per person. Dinner £35. *V*

CASTLE COMBE Wiltshire   Map 2:D1
The Castle Inn, SN14 7HN. *Tel* 01249-783030, www.castle-inn.info. In one of England's prettiest villages, 'olde-world inn cobbled together from several dwellings' (some 12th-century). Fireside nooks, low beams, cosy seating. 2 lounges, bar, dining room, breakfast room; small courtyard garden. Chef Jamie Gemell cooks traditional dishes; Jo Worsley is manager. Background music. 11 bedrooms. B&B £55–£87.50 per person. Dinner from £50.

CHARMOUTH Dorset   Map 1:C6
The Abbots House, The Street, DT6 6QF. *Tel* 01297 560339, www.abbotshouse.co.uk. In centre, Sheila and Nick Gilbey's restaurant-with-rooms in house with medieval origins (short walk to beach; 4 miles E of Lyme Regis). State-of-the-art fittings, flat-screen TV in bathrooms, sophisticated sound systems; oak-panelled walls, ornate beamed ceilings, ancient flagstones. Dining room (local produce, fusion cooking), lounge and garden room. Background music. 4 bedrooms. B&B £60–£80 per person. Dinner £24–£28.

CHELTENHAM Gloucestershire   Map 3:D5
The Big Sleep, Wellington Street, GL50 1XZ. *Tel* 01242-696999, www.thebigsleephotel.com. Minimalist budget accommodation (sister hotels in Eastbourne and Cardiff (*qqv*), in centre, in unobtrusive former Inland Revenue building. Managed by Scott Thorley. Lobby with seating (background music); breakfast room. Function facilities. Wi-Fi. Parking. Children welcomed. 60 bedrooms (2 family; some suitable for &). B&B (continental) £55–£80 per person.
The Cheltenham Townhouse, 12–14 Pittville Lawn, GL52 2BD. *Tel* 01242-221922, www.cheltenhamtownhouse.com. 10 mins' walk from Pittville Pump Rooms, Adam and Jayne Lillywhite's contemporary B&B in Regency building. 'Good location; comfortable, quiet.' Lift. Lounge (honesty bar), breakfast room (background

music); sun deck. Wi-Fi. Children welcomed. Parking. 22 bedrooms. B&B £32.50–£60 per person.

Hotel du Vin Cheltenham, Parabola Road, GL50 3AQ. *Tel* 01242-588450, www.hotelduvin.com. Contemporary conversion of Georgian house in fashionable Montpellier district, managed by Tom Ross. Spacious public areas around showpiece spiral staircase. Bar, bistro; function facilities; alfresco dining. No background music. Wi-Fi. Spa, beauty treatment rooms. Children welcomed. 49 bedrooms: £145–£285. Breakfast £9.95–£13.50. Dinner from £40.

Thirty Two, 32 Imperial Square, GL50 1QZ. *Tel* 01242-771110, www.thirtytwoltd.com. Overlooking Imperial Gardens in listed Regency terrace: B&B with sophisticated contemporary interior (showcase for designer-owners Jonathan Sellwood and Jonathan Parkin). Drawing room, breakfast room (soft background music). Shop stocking lighting, furniture, accessories, scents, fragrances. 4 bedrooms. B&B £82.50–£170 per person.

CHESTER Cheshire   Map 3:A4

The Chester Grosvenor, Eastgate, CH1 1LT. *Tel* 01244-324024, www.chestergrosvenor.co.uk. 'Unashamedly luxurious' hotel owned by Duke of Westminster, managed by Ross Grieve. Near Roman walls and cathedral. Timbered facade (Grade II listed), elegant interior (doormen, marble lobby, chandeliers, grand staircase). Lounge, brasserie, *The Chester Grosvenor* restaurant (Simon Radley is chef; *Michelin* star). Background music. Function facilities. Spa (crystal steam room, herb sauna, themed shower, ice fountain, salt grotto, footbaths, relaxation areas). 80 bedrooms and suites (*excluding VAT*): £205–£855. Breakfast £20. Dinner £35–£59.

CHICHESTER West Sussex   Map 2:E3

The Ship, North Street, PO19 1NH. *Tel* 01243-77800, www.theshiphotel.net. Within old city walls (5 mins' walk from theatre), Georgian building (Grade II listed), revamped in modern style. Privately owned, managed by Mark Thomas. Circular Adam staircase. Lift, bar, 2-tier brasserie (*The Place Bar & Grill*: Paul Jones is chef) with conservatory (light oak floor, tub seating); conference facilities. Background music. Wi-Fi. Parking. 36 bedrooms (on 3 floors; some family). B&B £47.50–£87.50 per person; D,B&B £65–£105.

CHIDDINGFOLD Surrey   Map 2:D3
The Swan Inn, The Green, Petworth Road, GU8 4TY. *Tel* 01428-682073, www.theswaninn.biz. Gastropub in converted 15th-century inn, on main road of leafy village N of Petworth on A283. Now owned by Cygnet Hotels. Bar, restaurant (traditional/modern British cooking by Darren Tidd); background music. Wi-Fi throughout. Large terraced garden. Easy parking. Children welcomed. 11 bedrooms (front ones hear traffic). B&B £40–£75 per person; D,B&B £62.50–£100.

CHIPPING CAMPDEN Gloucestershire   Map 3:D6
Cotswold House, The Square, Heath Street, GL55 6AN. *Tel* 01386-840330, www.cotswoldhouse.com. Understated luxury and up-to-the minute features at town house hotel in 1½-acre garden, managed by Duncan Fraser. Lounge (background music), bar, *Hick's* brasserie, *Juliana's* restaurant (local, 'artisan' food from chef Steve Love). Terrace. Children welcomed. 28 bedrooms (some in garden cottages). B&B £65–£325 per person; D,B&B £105–£365.

CHRISTCHURCH Dorset   Map 2:E2
Captain's Club Hotel, Wick Ferry, Wick Lane, Mudeford, BH23 1HU. *Tel* 01202-475111, www.thecaptainsclub.com. On River Stour at Christchurch Quay (panoramic river views): style-conscious contemporary hotel (chic metal and glass construction) owned by Robert Wilson and Timothy Lloyd. Lounge, bar, *Tides* restaurant; terrace (Andrew Gault is chef; alfresco dining); function facilities. Background music. Spa (pool, sauna; treatments). Lift. Children welcomed. 29 'superbly appointed' bedrooms (12 apartments; some suitable for &). B&B £74.50–£99.50 per person; D,B&B £99.50–£129.50. *V*

Waterford Lodge, 87 Bure Lane, Friars Cliff, Mudeford, BH23 4DN. *Tel* 01425-282100, www.bw-waterfordlodge.co.uk. 'Everything a small hotel should be': Hooper family's enterprise (Best Western), '4 mins' stroll from natural coastline', 2 miles SE of Christchurch. Lounge, bar (light meals; background music), garden-facing restaurant; patio; conference facilities; civil wedding licence. Wi-Fi. Parking. 18 bedrooms (3 on ground floor). B&B £60–£95 per person. Dinner £24.95–£28.50.

COLCHESTER Essex   Map 2:C5

Prested Hall, Feering, CO5 9EE. *Tel* 01376-573300, www.prested.
co.uk. Country hotel, restored and extended (15th-century origins),
with 2 real tennis courts. Part-moated, in 75-acre parkland. Managed
by Alan Brazier. Reception room, drawing room/library, restaurant,
bistro, private dining. Background music. Leisure suite (indoor pool,
sauna, steam room; flotation tank planned; treatments; gym); 3 tennis
courts. Wi-Fi. Function facilities in *The Orangery*. 16 bedrooms
(6 serviced apartments). B&B £57.50–£95 per person; D,B&B
£77.50–£115. *V*

COOKHAM DEAN Berkshire   Map 2:D3

The Inn on the Green, The Old Cricket Common, SL6 9NZ. *Tel*
01628-482638, www.theinnonthegreen.com. Stylish restaurant-with-
rooms in 1-acre grounds, 3 miles NW of Maidenhead. Owned by Mark
Fuller and Andy Taylor; José Asyuso manages. Lounge/bar, 3 dining
rooms (*Lamp Room, The Stublie, Conservatory*); cooking by Polish chef
Leszek Patoka; background music; alfresco summer dining in
Mediterranean-style courtyard. Hot tub. Parking. Function facilities.
Civil wedding licence. 9 bedrooms (2 off courtyard; 3 in coach house).
B&B (continental) £42.50–£75 per person. Dinner £35.

CROSBY RAVENSWORTH Cumbria   Map 4: inset C2

Crake Trees Manor, nr Penrith, CA10 3JG. *Tel* 01931 715205,
www.craketreesmanor.co.uk. In Eden valley, Ruth and Mike Tuer's
remote guest house in converted 18th-century barn on modern
working farm. Galleried hall with wood fire and library, dining area.
Background radio. 'Epitomizes the true meaning of laid-back, no
nonsense, few frills, genuine, homely hospitality.' Farmhouse supper;
generous Aga-cooked breakfast; vegetarians catered for. Garden.
4 bedrooms (1 on ground floor); plus 1-bedroom self-catering cottage.
B&B £43–£45 per person. Dinner £20.

DARLINGTON Co. Durham   Map 4:C4

Headlam Hall, nr Gainford, DL2 3HA. *Tel* 01325-730238,
www.headlamhall.co.uk. Robinson family's traditionally furnished
17th-century country house in rural location in lower Teesdale hamlet.
Stone walls, huge fireplaces, Jacobean hall. 4 lounges, drawing room,
bar, restaurant (classical background music). Spa (pool, sauna, gym,
treatment rooms; lift). Terraces. 4-acre walled garden: lake,
ornamental canal; tennis, 9-hole golf course, croquet. 40 bedrooms

(15 in mews or coach house; 7 in spa; 2 suitable for &). B&B
£57.50–£95 per person; D,B&B £79–£82.

DARTMOUTH Devon   Map 1:D4

Browns, 27–29 Victoria Road, TQ6 9RT. *Tel* 01803-832572,
www.brownshoteldartmouth.co.uk. Informal town-centre hotel with
contemporary decor in earthy tones, owned by Clare and James
Brown. Lounge, bar, restaurant (Mediterranean-inspired dishes from
chef Robin Tozer). Background music. 10 bedrooms. B&B £60–£85
per person. Dinner £22.

Dart Marina, Sandquay Road, TQ6 9PH. *Tel* 01803-832580,
www.dartmarina.com. On waterfront overlooking marina, stylish spa
hotel 'that keeps getting better and better'. Owned by Richard Seton;
Christopher Jones is manager. 'Staff one of its major strengths, helpful,
friendly.' Contemporary decor. Lounge bar. *River* restaurant
('consistently good' cooking by chef Mark Streeter; terrace: alfresco
dining), *Wildfire* bistro; background music. Lift. Spa (pool, gym,
treatments). Parking. Pebble beach. Children welcomed. 49 bedrooms
('very comfortable'; all with river view, some with balcony or French
window; 1 suitable for &). B&B £65–£97.50 per person; D,B&B
£85–£120.

DEDHAM Essex   Map 2:C5

Maison Talbooth, Stratford Road, CO7 6HN. *Tel* 01206-322367,
www.milsomhotels.com. Milsom family's Victorian mansion (major
refurbishment in 2008), managed by Daniel Courtney. In tranquil
Constable country: spectacular views over Stour valley. Ramp. Large
drawing room, *Garden Room* (breakfasts, light lunches). Guests may
eat at the family's restaurant, *Le Talbooth*, and hotel/brasserie, *milsom's*,
both nearby. No background music. 4-acre grounds: heated swimming
pool complex (sun terrace, hot tub); tennis court; beauty treatment
rooms. Children welcomed. 12 poetically themed bedrooms. B&B
(continental) from £95 per person; D,B&B from £140. *V*

DERBY Derbyshire   Map 2:A2

Cathedral Quarter, 16 St Mary's Close, DE1 3JR. *Tel* 01332-546080,
www.cathedralquarterhotel.com. Former council offices, bank vault
and police station: Grade II-listed building now transformed into
contemporary hotel (Finesse Collection), managed by Jessica
MacDonald. Interesting features retained. Lounge, bar *Sixteen*,
Opulence restaurant (modern British food; chef Dean Crews); small

conference facilities; *Clink* spa. Background music. Wi-Fi. 38 bedrooms (some with cathedral views). B&B £60–£110 per person. Dinner from £40.

DODDISCOMBSLEIGH Devon   Map 1:C4
The Nobody Inn, nr Exeter, EX6 7PS. *Tel* 01647-252394, www.nobodyinn.co.uk. Hidden amid hills and fields, 6 miles SW of Exeter: 16th-century inn run by owner Sue Burdge. Characterful features retained (inglenook fireplaces, beams, antiques). 2 bars, restaurant (chef Andy Hopkins provides English cuisine using local produce). Extensive whisky and wine list. No background music. 5 recently refurbished bedrooms (all with DVD-player). Small cottage garden, patio. B&B £30–£95 per person. Dinner £30–£42.

DONCASTER South Yorkshire   Map 4:E4
Mount Pleasant, Great North Road, DN11 0HW. *Tel* 01302-868696, www.mountpleasant.co.uk. Handy for airport and racecourse: Best Western member with mix of modern and country house interior, in 100-acre grounds. Managed by Richard Tyas. 4 lounges, 3 bars. *Garden* restaurant. Background music. Wi-Fi. *therapié* health and wellness centre; function facilities; civil wedding licence. Parking. 56 bedrooms (some on ground floor) plus 8 self-catering cottages. B&B £45–£70 per person; D,B&B £80–£102.50.

DORCHESTER Dorset   Map 1:D6
The King's Arms, 30 High Street, DT1 1HF. *Tel* 01305-265353, www.kingsarmsdorchester.com. 'Exceeded our expectations.' Porticoed Georgian coaching inn (built 1720, now Best Western member) in centre, owned by chef/proprietor Simon Monsai. Country house interior (four-poster beds); smart, modern bathrooms. Bar, 'superb' restaurant ('easy listening' background music; food from local producers). Function facilities. Civil wedding licence. Wi-Fi. Parking. 37 bedrooms. B&B £52.50–£85 per person. Dinner £45.

DOVER Kent   Map 2:D5
Loddington House, 14 East Cliff, CT16 1LX. *Tel* 01304-201947, www.loddingtonhousehotel.co.uk. Mother and son Kathy and Robert Cupper's seafront Regency Grade II listed guest house. 'Dinner superb. High standard of cleanliness.' Some traffic noise. Harbour views; convenient for terminals; 10 mins' walk from centre. Lounge (balcony with sea view), dining room (evening meal by arrangement,

£25). No background music. Small garden. 6 bedrooms (4 *en suite*; rear ones quietest). B&B £32.50–£55 per person.

The White Cliffs Hotel, High Street, St Margaret's-at-Cliffe, CT15 6AT. *Tel* 01304-852229, www.thewhitecliffs.com. Chef/proprietor Gavin Oakley's 'very comfortable, quietly efficient' traditional, white weather-board inn with sophisticated, modern interior. In pretty village 10 mins' drive from port. Lounge, *Bay* restaurant ('easy listening' background music); terrace; walled garden; 'micro spa' treatments; conference facilities; civil wedding licence. Wi-Fi. Parking. Children and dogs welcomed. 'Excellent breakfast.' 16 bedrooms (7 rooms, 2 apartments in mews cottages). B&B (continental) £49.50–£94 per person; D,B&B £74.50–£119. Cooked breakfast £5.

DULVERTON Somerset   Map 1:B5

Three Acres Country House, Brushford, TA22 9AR. *Tel* 01398-323730, www.threeacrescountryhouse.co.uk. Julie and Edward Christian's peaceful hideaway in 2-acre mature grounds on edge of Exmoor, 2 miles S of village. Children welcomed. Sitting room with open fire, bar, dining/breakfast room (light meals by arrangement); sun terrace. Locally sourced/home-made food. No background music. Wi-Fi. Picnic hampers; country pursuits arranged. 6 bedrooms (1 on ground floor). B&B £45–£75 per person. *V*

DURHAM Co. Durham   Map 4:B4

The Fallen Angel, 39 Old Elvet, DH1 3HN. *Tel* 0191-384 1037, www.fallenangelhotel.com. Unusual themed rooms (Russian Bride, Edwardian Express, The Cruise) in John Marshall's Grade II listed Georgian townhouse in centre. Views of cathedral and castle from front, university's cricket pitch and River Wear from rear. Restaurant (seasonal produce used by chef Stuart West). Background music. Children welcomed. 10 bedrooms (plus 3 garden apartments). B&B £75–£150 per person; D,B&B from £100. Dinner from £25. *V*

Grafton House, 40 South Street, DH1 4QP. *Tel* 0191-375 6790, www.grafton-house.co.uk. In 'charming' cobbled street in conservation area on S side of river, Mary Parker's plush, 'friendly' hotel in 19th-century building. 'Spectacular' views of castle and cathedral. Snug, dining room; 'easy listening' background music; courtyard. Function facilities. Limited parking; valet service available. 9 bedrooms (1 on ground floor; 3 best ones face cathedral). B&B £75–£125 per person. Dinner £25.

EASTBOURNE East Sussex   Map 2:E4

The Big Sleep, King Edwards Parade, BN21 4EB. *Tel* 01323-722676, www.thebigsleep.com. Zany budget hotel on beachfront corner, opened July 2008 (part owned by Cosmo Fry and John Malkovich; other hotels in Cheltenham and Cardiff, also shortlisted). Colourful decor. Canteen-like dining. Lounge, bar (background music); ping-pong. 50 bedrooms. B&B (continental) £35–£60 per person.

Grand Hotel, King Edwards Parade, BN21 4EQ. *Tel* 01323-412345, www.grandeastbourne.com. 'The spaciousness of the immaculate public rooms takes one's breath away.' Traditional 5-star, 19th-century seafront 'white palace' (Elite Hotels), managed by Jonathan Webley. 'Service first class; you feel that staff are there just to make your holiday perfect.' Live band at weekend; monthly teatime Palm Court quartet. Children welcomed (playroom, carers, high teas). 3 lounges, bar, *Mirabelle* and *Garden* restaurants (both with pianist; 'food very good'); conference/function facilities; health spa; heated indoor and outdoor swimming pools; 2-acre garden: putting, etc. Parking. 152 bedrooms (many with sea view). B&B £95–£267.50 per person; D,B&B £126–£295. *V*

Ocklynge Manor, Mill Road, BN21 2PG. *Tel* 01323-734121, www.ocklyngemanor.co.uk. Fairy-pink mansion (on site of monastery of the Knights of the Order of St John of Jerusalem; former home of illustrator Mabel Lucy Atwell), 1 mile from seafront. Owner Wendy Dugdill provides comfortable accommodation and organic breakfasts (home-made bread and marmalade). Sitting room. No background music. Walled garden (remains of 18th-century gazebo and grotto). Parking. Wi-Fi. DVD-players. 3 bedrooms. B&B £40–£80 per person.

EXETER Devon   Map 1:C5

Moorstone, Bridford, EX6 7HS. *Tel* 01647- 252071, www.moorstone. net. Late 18th-century house, on edge of Dartmoor national park, painted white, with colourful, contemporary interior. Chic renovation by ex-chefs John Willig and Serge Bouchet. Home-made bread; classic English cooking with continental twist. Lounge, dining room. Background music. Parking. 9 miles SW of Exeter (adjacent to *Bridford Inn*). 3 bedrooms. B&B £30–£55 per person. Dinner (BYO wine) £16–£19.

FALMOUTH Cornwall   Map 1:E2

Green Lawns, Western Terrace, TR11 4QJ. *Tel* 01326-312734, www.greenlawnshotel.com. In style of small French château, ivy-clad hotel in subtropical gardens, managed by Wendy Symons. Views across Falmouth Bay; ¼ mile from centre. Traditional decor. Lounge, bar, *Garras* restaurant (background music); leisure/ conference/function facilities (indoor swimming pool, sauna, whirlpool). Award-winning garden; patio area. 39 bedrooms (11 on ground floor). B&B £45–£120 per person; D,B&B (min. 3 nights) £60–£145.

FOLKESTONE Kent   Map 2:E5

The Relish, 4 Augusta Gardens, CT20 2RR. *Tel* 01303-850952, www.hotelrelish.co.uk. Sarah and Chris van Dyke's B&B in grand 1850s merchant's house in West End, ¼ mile from centre. Managed by Amanda Smith. Contemporary interior; unlimited coffee/tea with cake; complimentary daily glass of wine or beer. Lounge, breakfast room (Radio 2 played). DVD library. Wi-Fi. Small terrace. Families welcomed. Direct access to private 4-acre Augusta Gardens. Parking. 10 bedrooms. B&B £45–£130 per person.

FOWEY Cornwall   Map 1:D3

Fowey Hall, Hanson Drive, PL23 1ET. *Tel* 01726-833866, www.foweyhallhotel.co.uk. 'Relaxed', family-friendly hotel (von Essen Luxury Family group), managed by Darryl Reburn. Victorian mansion, high above port ('terrific location'; estuary views), said to be inspiration for Toad Hall (*The Wind in the Willows*). 'The rooms are great (we had interconnecting ones).' Large drawing room, library, billiard/meeting room, 2 restaurants (*Palm Court*, *Hansons*). Background music. Extensive function facilities; civil wedding licence. Walled garden in 5-acre grounds; croquet, badminton. Crèche, children's games room; indoor swimming pool; *Aquae Sulis* spa. 36 bedrooms (8 in annexe, 6 on ground floor; 2 suitable for ठ). B&B £70–£282.50 per person; D,B&B £82.50–£295.

GATWICK West Sussex   Map 2:D4

Langshott Manor, Langshott, RH6 9LN. *Tel* 01293-786680, www.alexanderhotels.co.uk. Luxury hotel in classic timber-framed Tudor house (*c.* 1580; ancient moat). 10 mins' drive from airport. Managed by Sakis Dinas. 2 lounges, bar, *Mulberry* restaurant (Phil Dixon is chef; background music); conference facilities; civil wedding licence. Peaceful, 2-acre landscaped gardens. 22 bedrooms (7 in mews; 8 across garden). B&B £75–£160 per person; D,B&B £125–£185. ***V***

GOLANT-BY-FOWEY Cornwall   Map 1:D3

The Cormorant, Golant, PL23 1LL. *Tel* 01726-833426, www.cormoranthotel.co.uk. 3 miles N of Fowey, Mary Tozer's clean-lined hotel/restaurant in tranquil setting on hillside overlooking River Fowey. Vertiginous views. Sitting room, bar, 'charming' dining room; 'subdued easy listening' music; garden terraces 'perfect for fine-weather breakfasts'; indoor swimming pool, hot tub. Wi-Fi. Parking. 14 bedrooms (all with river views; most with balcony). B&B £60–£130 per person; D,B&B £90–£160.

GORING-ON-THAMES Oxfordshire   Map 2:D3

The Miller of Mansfield, High Street, RG8 9AW. *Tel* 01491-872829, www.millerofmansfield.com. Old creeper-covered red brick village coaching inn managed by Nicolas Jahandie, overlooking Goring Gap. Modern interior; colourful bedrooms. Commitment to organic, local produce: modern British/European dishes. Lounge, 2 bars, restaurant; terraced courtyard garden. Background music. Function facilities. 13 bedrooms. B&B £65–£117.50 per person; D,B&B £95–£147.50.

GRANGE-OVER-SANDS Cumbria   Map 4: inset C2

Clare House, Park Road, LA11 7HQ. *Tel* 015395-33026, www.clarehousehotel.co.uk. Overlooking bay, imposing 19th-century house where Read family celebrate 40 years as hoteliers. 'As good as ever. Super breakfast.' 2 lounges, dining room. No background music. ¾-acre grounds. Parking. 18 bedrooms. Mile-long promenade at bottom of garden (bowling greens, tennis courts, putting green; easy access to Ornamental Gardens). 18 bedrooms. B&B £52 per person; D,B&B £85.

GRASMERE Cumbria   Map 4: inset C2

Moss Grove, LA22 9SW. *Tel* 015394-35251, www.mossgrove.com. Environmentally friendly B&B in 'very pretty' Lakeland village 4 miles from Ambleside. Run by owner Susan Lowe 'without loss of style or luxury'. Natural materials (wood, glass); local or Fairtrade produce; recycling and pollution policy. Lounge, kitchen. Latest gadgetry; Wi-Fi. No background music. 'Lovely room; reasonable value; clientele varied but young-at-heart.' 11 bedrooms (2 on ground floor). B&B (Mediterranean-style organic buffet) £55–£125 per person.

GREAT BIRCHAM Norfolk   Map 2:A5

The King's Head, Lynn Road, PE31 6RJ. *Tel* 01485-578265, www.the-kings-head-bircham.co.uk. Grade II listed 19th-century coach house, with stylish modern interior, in tranquil location 8 miles from Brancaster Beach; Sandringham close by. Managed by Jackie Galloway; Ashley Miles is chef. Drawing room, bar, restaurant; courtyard (alfresco dining in summer); background music; conference facilities. Child-friendly. Dogs welcomed. 12 bedrooms. B&B £55–£125 per person; D,B&B £70–£140.

GREAT LANGDALE Cumbria   Map 4: inset C2
Old Dungeon Ghyll, Great Langdale, LA22 9JY. *Tel* 015394-37272, www.odg.co.uk. Extended 300-year-old mountain hotel at head of Great Langdale valley, 3 miles from village. Owned by National Trust; run by 'welcoming' Jane and Neil Walmsley. Lounge, residents' bar, public *Hikers' Bar* (old cow stalls); live music occasionally; no background music; dining room, drying room. 1-acre garden. Fell walkers, climbers, cyclists. Child-friendly. Dogs welcomed. 13 bedrooms (5 with shared facilities). B&B £50–£55 per person; D,B&B £72.50–£77.50.

GREAT TEW Oxfordshire   Map 3:D6
The Falkland Arms, OX7 4DB. *Tel* 01608-683653, www.falklandarms.org.uk. Traditional Cotswold inn (16th-century) opposite village green. Managed by Paula and James Meredith. Roaring fires; impressive mug and jug collection; local ales, English country wines, real cider; clay pipes and snuff. Bar, small dining room (booking advisable). No background music. Garden. 5 characterful bedrooms up old stone spiral staircase. B&B £42.50–£57.50 per person. Dinner £45.

HALIFAX West Yorkshire   Map 4:D3
Shibden Mill Inn, Shibden Mill Fold, HX3 7UL. *Tel* 01422-365840, www.shibdenmillinn.com. In valley 3 miles from town, Simon and Caitlin Heaton's renovated 17th-century country inn. Glen Pearson is manager. Oak beams, rafters, traditional furnishing. Bar, restaurant (candlelit dining). Background music. Children welcomed. Patio garden. Parking. 11 bedrooms. B&B £45–£71.50 per person. Dinner £29.95. *V*

HARMONDSWORTH Middlesex   Map 2:D3
Harmondsworth Hall, Summerhouse Lane, Harmondsworth Village, UB7 0BG. *Tel* 020-8759 1824, www.harmondsworthhall.com. In peaceful village 7 mins from Heathrow (not on flight path): Elaine

Burke's flower-bedecked B&B in large 17th-century Grade II listed building. Grand entrance hall (stained glass), carved staircase, wood panelling. Breakfast room (espresso coffee machine, water cooler; radio played). Conference facilities. Room-service snacks until 9 pm. Wi-Fi. Secure car park for long stays (charge). Transport links to London from West Drayton and Heathrow. 12 bedrooms. B&B £40–£70 per person.

HARROGATE North Yorkshire   Map 4:D4
The Bijou, 17 Ripon Road, HG1 2JL. *Tel* 01423-567974, www. thebijou.co.uk. Stephen and Gill Watson's B&B in Victorian villa in fashionable Duchy Estate area, close to all amenities. Sleek decor, mellow colours. Lounge. Background music. Wi-Fi. Small garden. Parking. 10 bedrooms (1 on ground floor; 2 in coach house). B&B £40–£95 per person.

HAWORTH West Yorkshire   Map 4:D3
Ashmount Country House, Mytholmes Lane, BD22 8EZ. *Tel* 01535-645726, www.ashmounthaworth.co.uk. Near Brontë Parsonage, stone-built guest house 'with hotel standards', owned by Ray and Gill Capeling. Former home of Dr Amos Ingham, physician to the Brontë sisters. Traditional decor, modern comforts (hot tubs, whirlpool baths, music, 'mood lighting'). 'Pure luxury and indulgence!' Lounge, 2 dining rooms. Soft background music. Mature ¾-acre garden; open views; ample private parking; Yorkshire breakfasts. Picnics available. Wi-Fi. Function facilities. 10 bedrooms (2 on ground floor). B&B £37.50–£92.50 per person.

HAY-ON-WYE Herefordshire   Map 3:D4
Tinto House, 13 Broad Street, HR3 5DB. *Tel* 01497-821556, www.tinto-house.co.uk. B&B in Georgian town house with large garden running down to River Wye. Run by John (an artist) and Karen Clare (who runs *Sage Femme* across the road, selling antique French textiles and vintage clothing). Oak staircase; paintings, books; wooden sculptures. Dining room; library. No background music. 1-acre garden. Children welcomed. 4 bedrooms. B&B £37.50–£60 per person.

HELMSLEY North Yorkshire   Map 4:C4
No54, 54 Bondgate, YO62 5EZ. *Tel* 01439-771533, www.no54.co.uk. Near market place, 'good hostess' Lizzie Would's town house B&B. Crisp white linen, limed wood furniture, York stone floors, open fires.

Torches, hot-water bottles provided. Dining/sitting room. No background music. Garden. North Yorkshire Moors national park nearby. Dinner by arrangement; picnics available. Breakfast includes muffins, kedgeree. 4 bright, simple bedrooms (3 double around peaceful sunny courtyard, 1 single in house). B&B £40–£55 per person. Dinner £28–£35.

HENLEY-ON-THAMES Oxfordshire   Map 2:D3

Hotel du Vin Henley-on-Thames, New Street, YO62 5EZ. *Tel* 01491-848400, www.hotelduvin.com. 'Perhaps the best of the chain': in centre, 50 yds from river: converted Georgian brewery (formerly Brakspear's). Managed by Steven Hodgkinson; 'friendly, efficient staff'; 'lovely, spacious room'. Bar (background music), snug, busy bistro; courtyard (alfresco dining). Wi-Fi. Function facilities. Civil wedding licence. Children welcomed. Valet parking. 43 bedrooms (2 suitable for &; some on 2 levels; 1 has balcony with outdoor tub): £145–£295. Breakfast £9.95–£13.50. Dinner £40.

HEREFORD Herefordshire   Map 3:D4

Castle House, Castle Street, HR1 2NW. *Tel* 01432-356321, www.castlehse.co.uk. 'It ticks all the boxes.' 'Delightful' luxury hotel in centre, sensitively converted from 2 Grade II listed town houses; garden beside old castle moat. Owned by David Watkins; managed by Michelle Marriott-Lodge. 'Dinner delicious. Breakfast similarly impressive and enjoyable.' Lounge, *Bertie's* bar, restaurant; light jazz/classical background music. Lift. Garden, terrace. Parking. 15 bedrooms (1 on ground floor, suitable for &). B&B £92.50–£125 per person; D,B&B £117.50–£145. *V*

HEXHAM Northumberland   Map 4:B3

The Hermitage, Swinburne, NE48 4DG. *Tel* 01434-681248, *email* katie.stewart@themeet.co.uk. Katie and Simon Stewart's B&B: family home with 'true country house atmosphere'. Approached through grand arch and up long drive. 7 miles N of Hexham and Corbridge. Drawing rooms, breakfast room. No background music. 4-acre grounds: terrace, tennis. 3 bedrooms. B&B £40–£50 per person.

HOARWITHY Herefordshire   Map 3:D4

Aspen House, HR2 6QP. *Tel* 01432-840353, www.aspenhouse.net. In Wye valley village, Sally Dean and Rob Elliott's environmentally friendly B&B in pink 18th-century farmhouse. Lounge. No background music. Dinner for 4 or more by arrangement. 'Slow' food: organic produce, home-made bread. Small garden. 4 bedrooms. B&B £37–£45 per person.

HOLKHAM Norfolk   Map 2:A5

The Victoria at Holkham, Park Road, NR23 1RG. *Tel* 01328-711008, www.victoriaatholkham.co.uk. 'Perfect for exploring north Norfolk coast; close to one of its most beautiful, isolated beaches.' On Earl of Leicester's Holkham estate, refurbished pub, now managed by Ian and Lisa Clark. 'Curious, comfortable' decor (ornate Indian furniture, vibrant colours). Lounge area, 3 bars, restaurant (Roger Hickman is the chef); background music. 3-acre grounds: children's play area, barbecue. 10 bedrooms (1 suitable for &) plus accommodation in 3 'follies'. B&B £60–£140 per person. Dinner £15.50–£18.50.

HOLMFIRTH West Yorkshire   Map 4:E3

Sunnybank, 78 Upperthong Lane, HD9 3BQ. *Tel* 01484-684857, www.sunnybankguesthouse.co.uk. Run with 'impressive attention to detail' by Peter and Anne White: B&B in Victorian gentleman's hillside residence; views over Holme valley. 'Delicious' breakfasts' in oak-panelled dining room (roaring fire in winter; no background music). 'Just the place for a quiet, relaxing weekend.' Wi-Fi. 2-acre wooded garden. ¼ mile from centre. 5 bedrooms (2 on ground floor). B&B £32.50–£45 per person.

HOPE Derbyshire   Map 3:A6

Losehill House, Edale Road, S33 6RF. *Tel* 01433-621219, www.losehillhouse.co.uk. Secluded spa hotel on side of Losehill, owned by Paul and Kathryn Roden. Panoramic views over Hope valley. Solid, white-painted house with comfortable, modern furnishing. Drawing room, bar, restaurant; lift. Background music (evenings). 1-acre garden; terrace. Indoor swimming pool; hot tub; treatment rooms. Function/conference facilities. Civil wedding licence. Footpath access to Peak District national park. 21 bedrooms (4 with external entrance). B&B £67.50–£120 per person; D,B&B £92.50–£145. *V*

HUDDERSFIELD West Yorkshire   Map 4:E3

Three Acres Inn & Restaurant, Roydhouse, Shelley, HD8 8LR. *Tel* 01484-602606, www.3acres.com. Smart old roadside drovers' inn (busy morning traffic) in Pennine countryside, 5 miles SE of centre. Owned by Neil Truelove and Brian Orme: at its heart is modern British regional food from chef Jason Littlewood. 'The place is packed.' *Seafood Bar*, 2 dining rooms; background music. Small function/private dining facilities. Terraced garden; decked dining terrace. Children welcomed. 20 bedrooms (1 suitable for ♿; 6 in adjacent cottages). B&B £60–£125 per person. Dinner from £37.95.

HULL East Yorkshire   Map 4:D5

Willerby Manor, Well Lane, Willerby, HU10 6ER. *Tel* 01482-652616, www.bw-willerbymanor.co.uk. Edwardian mansion (Best Western hotel) in rural setting, 4 miles W of centre. Run by owner Alexandra Townend. *Figs* bar/brasserie (alfresco dining), *Icon* restaurant ('food a bit complicated'). Background jazz. Health club (swimming pool, gym, etc), crèche; wedding/extensive business/function facilities. 3-acre garden. Parking. 63 bedrooms (1 suitable for ♿). B&B £65–£98 per person; D,B&B £85–£118.

HUNGERFORD Berkshire   Map 2:D2

The Bear, 41 Charnham Street, RG17 0EL. *Tel* 01488-682512, www.thebearhotelhungerford.co.uk. In town, ancient roadside inn, stylishly made over in contemporary style. 'Comfortable, attractive. Perfect service and food when the East European staff are on duty.' 2 lounges, bar. Background music. Function facilities. Civil wedding licence. Large courtyard with umbrellas, tables, chairs. Peaceful riverside garden. 41 bedrooms (some on ground floor). B&B £42.50–£95 per person.

ILMINGTON Warwickshire   Map 3:D6

The Howard Arms, Lower Green, nr Stratford-upon-Avon, CV36 4LT. *Tel* 01608-682226, www.howardarms.com. On village green, flower-bedecked, mellow stone 400-year-old country inn, managed by Quentin Creese. Inglenook fireplace; blackboard menu (food from local suppliers; Bob Stratta is chef). Snug, dining room ('easy listening' background music); patio/garden. Wi-Fi. Parking. Children welcomed. 8 attractive modern bedrooms (5 in annexe). B&B £57.50–£70 per person.

IPSWICH Suffolk   Map 2:C5

Salthouse Harbour Hotel, 1 Neptune Quay, IP4 1AS. *Tel* 01473-226789, www.salthouseharbour.co.uk. 'Splendid view over quay.' On waterfront, large, contemporary warehouse conversion (exposed brick-work, industrial pillars), owned by Robert Gough. Spacious bedrooms; modern art. Lounge, brasserie (seafood and Mediterranean 'all-day' dishes; background music). Lift. Courtyard. Child-friendly. Dogs welcomed. 70 bedrooms (some with balcony). B&B £80–£150 per person. Dinner £40. *V*

IRONBRIDGE Shropshire   Map 2:A1
The Library House, Severn Bank, TF8 7AN. *Tel* 01952-432299, www.libraryhouse.com. Small guest house in old village library (Georgian, Grade II listed), sensitively furnished by owner Liz Steel. Sitting room, dining room. No background music. Wi-Fi. Quiet courtyard garden overlooking River Severn. Parking. Restaurants nearby. 3 bedrooms (each named after a literary figure; 1 with private terrace). B&B £32.50–£75 per person.

KINGHAM Oxfordshire   Map 3:D6
The Kingham Plough, The Green, nr Chipping Norton, OX7 6YD. *Tel* 01608-658327, www.thekinghamplough.co.uk. 'First and foremost a dining pub: outstanding food at reasonable prices' (*Michelin Bib Gourmand* in 2009). In pretty village, old pub opposite green, given a modern make-over by Miles Lampson and his wife, Emily Watkins (the chef). Shabby-chic decor: stripped wood, wooden tables and chairs, vaulted roof, original beams, sisal flooring, large candles. 4 miles SW of Chipping Norton. Bar, restaurant (background music), terrace, garden. Wi-Fi. Child-friendly, dogs welcomed (annexe only; £10). 7 bedrooms (3 in annexe). B&B £42.50–£55 per person, Dinner £45. *V*

KING'S LYNN Norfolk   Map 2:A4
Bank House, King's Staithe Square, PE30 1RD. *Tel* 01553-660492, www.thebankhouse.co.uk. In historic Grade II listed Georgian town house on quay, new enterprise, opened autumn 2008, by Anthony and Jeannette Goodrich (owners of *The Rose & Crown*, Snettisham, see main entry). Ed Lewis is chef. Brasserie, wine bar, coffee shop; smart bedrooms above. No background music. Wi-Fi. Children welcomed. 11 bedrooms. B&B £40–£60 per person. Dinner £35. *V*
Congham Hall, Lynn Road, Grimston, PE32 1AH. *Tel* 01485-600250, www.conghamhallhotel.co.uk. In 'exceptionally peaceful' setting, Georgian country house (von Essen hotels), managed by Julie Woodhouse. On 30-acre estate (famous herb garden – over 700

varieties), 6 miles E of King's Lynn. Front rooms face walled garden and cricket pitch; lawns and parkland at rear. Lounge, *Orangery* restaurant; terrace. No background music. Clay-pigeon shooting. 14 bedrooms. B&B £82.50–£125 per person. Dinner £41–£48.

KINGSBRIDGE Devon   Map 1:D4

Buckland-Tout-Saints, Goveton, TQ7 2DS. *Tel* 01548-853055, www.tout-saints.co.uk. William and Mary manor house in 'glorious' rural setting, 2½ miles NE of Kingsbridge. Part of Sir Peter Rigby's Eden Hotel Collection; Matthew Gibbs is manager. Wood-panelled public rooms, open fires. Lounge, bar, 2 dining rooms; light jazz/classical background music; function facilities; civil wedding licence. 4½-acre garden and woodland. Children welcomed. 16 bedrooms (traditional or contemporary decor). B&B £60–£140 per person; D,B&B £95–£175. *V*

Thurlestone Hotel, Thurlestone, TQ7 3NN. *Tel* 01548-560382, www.thurlestone.co.uk. Grose family's large white, 'almost Art Deco' hotel in subtropical gardens (bay views; coastal walks, sandy beaches close by), 4 miles SW of Kingsbridge. Family-friendly. 'Comfortable, homely; cheerful staff.' Lounges, bar, *Margaret Amelia* restaurant; alfresco *Rock Pool* eating area (teas, lunches, snacks, dinners), terrace (alfresco dining); *The Village Inn* 16th-century pub; leisure complex/beauty spa (indoor and outdoor heated swimming pools, tennis, squash, badminton). No background music. Function facilities. Civil wedding licence. 19-acre gardens. 9-hole golf course adjacent. 64 bedrooms (some with balcony, sea views). B&B £92–£186 per person; D,B&B £104–£204.

KIRKBY LONSDALE Cumbria   Map 4: inset C2

Sun Inn, 6 Market Street, LA6 2AU. *Tel* 015242-71965, www.sun-inn.info. 17th-century inn (white-painted walls hung with flower baskets), in centre of market town. Run by owners Lucy and Mark Fuller with manager Steven Turner; Sam Carter is chef. Bar (background music), restaurant. Flagstone and wood floors, panelling, exposed stonework, roaring fires, contemporary furniture. Children welcomed; dog-friendly. 11 bedrooms. B&B £45–£75 per person. Dinner £30.

KIRTLINGTON Oxfordshire   Map 2:C2

The Dashwood, South Green, Heyford Road, OX5 3HJ. *Tel* 01869-352707, www.thedashwood.co.uk. Family-owned restaurant-with-rooms in Grade II listed old pub with contemporary interior. Managed by Christopher Lidgitt; Emma Berriman is chef. Natural materials (brick, wood, stone) offset by splashes of colour and artwork. Bar, restaurant; patio. Background music. Wi-Fi. Children welcomed. 12 bedrooms (7 in converted barn; 1 suitable for &). B&B £57.50–£80 per person; D,B&B £80–£97.50. *V*

KNUTSFORD Cheshire   Map 4:E3

Belle Epoque, 60 King Street, WA16 6DT. *Tel* 01565-633060, www.thebelleepoque.com. In commuter town near Manchester, restaurant-with-rooms in listed Art Nouveau building. Run by Mooney family owners for over 3 decades. Original Venetian glass floor, marble-pillared alcoves, statuary, lavish drapes, tall glass vases, cosy recesses. Bar, restaurant. Background jazz. Mediterranean roof garden. Function facilities. 7 bedrooms. B&B £95 per person. Dinner £40.

Longview, 51 and 55 Manchester Road, WA16 0LX. *Tel* 01565-632119, www.longviewhotel.com. Traditionally furnished former Victorian merchant's home, run by Greek owner Lulu Ahooie. Just off town centre, looking across busy road to heath. Cellar bar, *Stuffed Olive* restaurant (Mediterranean cuisine/'British standbys'); 'easy listening' background music. Children welcomed. 32 bedrooms (13 in annexe; 1 suitable for &; suites have lounge and private garden). B&B £53–£89 per person; D,B&B £64.95–£91.95.

LAVENHAM Suffolk   Map 2:C5

The Swan, High Street, CO10 9QA. *Tel* 01787-247477, www.theswanatlavenham.co.uk. Characterful hotel/restaurant owned by Tim Rowan-Robinson and Guy Heald, in 3 timber-framed houses (15th-century). Lounge, 2 bars, galleried dining room (chef David Ryan uses local produce; home-made bread and ice cream; classical background music; live piano Sat). Garden (alfresco dining); business facilities. Children welcomed. 45 bedrooms (some beamed, some with four-poster bed), named after local villages. B&B £80–£140 per person; D,B&B £100–£160.

LEEDS West Yorkshire   Map 4:D4

42 The Calls, 42 The Calls, LS2 7EW. *Tel* 0113-244 0099, www.42thecalls.co.uk. Converted 18th-century grain mill overlooking River Aire (fishing rods supplied). Part of Eton Collection, managed by Belinda Dawson. Industrial girders, beamed ceilings, exposed

brickwork, contemporary art. Lounge, bar, breakfast room (radio played at breakfast); lift; conference facilities. Lively, independently owned *Brasserie 44* next door. Children welcomed. 41 bedrooms (1 suitable for &): from £52.50 per person. Breakfast £11.95–£14.75.
Woodlands, Gelderd Road, Gildersome, LS27 7LY. *Tel* 0113-238 1488, www.tomahawkhotels.co.uk. In landscaped grounds, 4 miles S of centre, contemporary hotel (originally residence of textile mill owner) owned by Rob Foulston and Tom Horsforth (Tomahawk Hotel group). Craig Squelch is manager; Robert Corless is chef. Lounge, bar, 3 dining rooms; conservatory; patio. Background music throughout (modern and classical). 4-acre garden in 50-acre grounds. Function facilities. Civil wedding licence. Children welcomed. 22 bedrooms, named after unusual fabrics (some on ground floor). B&B £69.50–£124.50 per person. Dinner £18.95–£42. *V*

LEWES East Sussex   Map 2:E4
Berkeley House, 2 Albion Street, BN7 2ND. *Tel* 01273-476057, www.berkeleyhouselewes.co.uk. Roy Patten and Steve Johnson's friendly town-centre B&B in late Georgian town house (*c*. 1820). Residents' lounge with material relating to Glyndebourne (help given with taxis, etc); roof terrace with views of South Downs. Copious breakfast. 3 bedrooms on 2nd and 3rd floors (no lift): 1 might hear traffic. B&B £37.50–£70 per person. *V*
The Shelleys, 135 High Street, BN7 1XS. *Tel* 01273-472361, www.the-shelleys.co.uk. 16th-century manor house in centre, once owned by poet's family; elegantly upgraded by owner Shelton Fernando. 'A hotel we look forward to returning to.' Interior is a 'rabbit warren of corridors, steps and doors'. Lounge, bar, restaurant, terrace, garden; function facilities; civil wedding licence. Background music. Parking adjacent. Children welcomed. 19 bedrooms. B&B £65–£150 per person; D,B&B £90–£180.

LINCOLN Lincolnshire   Map 4:E5
The Old Bakery, 26–28 Burton Road, LN1 3LB. *Tel* 01522-576057, www.theold-bakery.co.uk. Behind castle, restaurant-with-rooms owned by Alan Ritson with daughter Tracey, and son-in-law Ivano de Serio (chef). Original features retained (brick walls, stone floors, bread ovens). 'Impressive' restaurant in glassed-in garden room (alfresco dining in warm weather). Modern English cooking with Italian twist; home-made bread, ice cream and pasta. 'Interesting, experimental menu; huge cheese list.' Background music. Cookery courses. In quiet

street, but some noise at night. 4 simple bedrooms (2 *en suite*; 2 with private bathroom). B&B £53–£63 per person. Dinner £38.

LITTLE SHELFORD Cambridgeshire   Map 2:C4

Purlins, 12 High Street, CB22 5ES. *Tel* 01223-842643, *email* dgallh@ndirect.co.uk. David and Olga Hindley's 'welcoming' B&B in Arts and Crafts-style home (built 1978), in village on River Cam, 4½ miles S of Cambridge. Conservatory, vaulted dining room, gallery. No background music. Beautiful gardens; 2-acre mature woodland, meadow, lawn, orchard; wildlife (foxes, deer). Closed Nov–Mar. 3 bedrooms. B&B £39–£56 per person.

LIVERPOOL Merseyside   Map 4:E2

Hard Days Night, Central Buildings, North John Street, L2 6RR. *Tel* 0151-236 1964. www.harddaysnighthotel.com. Large Beatles-themed hotel in Grade II listed building in old merchant quarter (noisy location at night). Managed by Michael Dewey. Artwork and photographs devoted to the Fab Four throughout. Contemporary decor; state-of-the-art gadgetry. Lounge, *Bar Four*, *Blake's* restaurant; art gallery. Background music. 110 bedrooms: £85–£295. Breakfast £12.50. Dinner £40.

Malmaison, 7 William Jessop Way, Princes Dock, L3 1QZ. *Tel* 0151-229 5000, www.malmaison.com. On waterfront, in regenerated area of city: ultra-stylish, 11-storey, purpose-built hotel managed by Mark James. Minimalist decor (exposed brickwork, air-conditioning ducts, industrial metal staircase). Lounge, *Plum* bar, brasserie; gymtonic; background music; function facilities. 24-hour room service. 130 bedrooms (some suitable for &; wet-room showers; circular baths): £75–£250. Breakfast £11.95–£13.95. Dinner from £35.

LOOE Cornwall   Map 1:D3

Barclay House, St Martins Road, PL13 1LP. *Tel* 01503-262929, www.barclayhouse.co.uk. Malcolm Brooks's white painted hotel in 6-acre garden and woodland: spectacular views. 10 mins' walk from town centre and harbour. 'A treat; welcoming staff.' Sitting room, bar, restaurant (background jazz; chef Benjamin Palmer uses local produce); gym, sauna, outdoor heated swimming pool; terrace. Children welcomed. 11 bedrooms (1 on ground floor). Also 8 self-catering cottages. B&B £55–£85 per person. Dinner £35. *V*

Fieldhead Hotel, Portuan Road, Hannafore, PL13 2DR. *Tel* 01503-262689, www.fieldheadhotel.co.uk. In elevated position (views across

Looe Bay), Julian Peck's traditional hotel (built 1896 as private home). 15 mins' walk from centre. Lounge with huge bow window, bar, *Horizons* restaurant; 'gentle' classical background music. 'Loved it. Great food; excellent buffet at breakfast; excellent dinner.' Wi-Fi. 1½-acre award-winning garden, veranda, terrace (views, parasols), heated outdoor swimming pool. Parking. Children welcomed. 16 bedrooms (most with sea view, 3 with balcony). B&B £40–£75 per person; D,B&B £66–£88.

LOWESTOFT Suffolk   Map 2:B6

Ivy House, Ivy Lane, off Beccles Road, Oulton Broad, NR33 8HY. *Tel* 01502-501353, www.ivyhousecountryhotel.co.uk. On southern shores of Oulton Broad: converted farm owned by Caroline Coe. 'Beautifully appointed; wonderful value for money.' 2 sitting rooms, conservatory, *The Crooked Barn* restaurant (in 18th-century thatched, beamed barn; head chef Martin Whitelock); background music. Function/conference facilities; courtyard. Lovely 4-acre garden (2 lily ponds, summer house), surrounded by 50-acre meadows. 20 annexe bedrooms (1 suitable for &). B&B £67.50–£125 per person. Dinner £27.50.

LUDLOW Shropshire   Map 3:C4

The Bringewood, Burrington, SY8 2HT. *Tel* 01568-770033, www.thebringewood.co.uk. Just outside Ludlow (5 mins' drive), modern rustic renovation of Victorian farm building in 250-acre grounds, owned by Neil and Stephen Cocum. Peaceful: 'wonderful countryside; great views'. Lounge (exposed beams), bar (open log fire); *Oaktree* restaurant (home-made country cuisine); patio (alfresco dining); conference/business facilities; civil wedding licence. Background music. 12 bedrooms. B&B £42.50–£85 per person; D,B&B £72.50–£135.

Dinham Hall, by the castle, SY8 1EJ. *Tel* 01584-876464, www. dinhamhall.co.uk. 'Lovely views from our bedroom over gardens and roofs of Ludlow and out to the hills beyond.' Mellow stone building in market square, once used by boarders of Ludlow grammar school. Now owned by Mr and Mrs Choblet of *Overton Grange* (*qv*), managed by Ian Hazeldine. Good cooking from chef Wayne Vickarage. Country house decor, recently refurbished. Sitting room, library, bar, restaurant (light background jazz). 1-acre walled garden. Function facilities. Civil wedding licence. Parking. 13 bedrooms (2 in cottage). B&B £95–£120 per person; D,B&B £87.50–£160.

The Feathers, Bull Ring, SY8 1AA. *Tel* 01584-875261, www.feathersatludlow.co.uk. Landmark Ludlow building with ornate, timber-framed facade (Jacobean, Grade I listed), managed by Ian Taylor. Oak panelling, huge fireplaces, plaster ceilings. Lounge, bar (tea, coffee, light meals), restaurant ('attentive service'). No background music. Conference facilities. Civil wedding licence. Parking (spaces limited). 'A good 2-night break.' 40 bedrooms (2 family; some in adjoining buildings; 4 four-posters). B&B £47.50–£105 per person; D,B&B £67.50–£85.

Fishmore Hall, Fishmore Road, SY8 3DP. *Tel* 01584-875148, www.fishmorehall.co.uk. Symmetrical, white Regency house (former school), now 'very comfortable' hotel with pared-down interior. Overlooking Ludlow, and with panoramic views over countryside. Managed by owner Laura Penman. 'Delightful colours, efficient lighting, plenty of cupboard space, comfortable seating.' Lift, bar, sitting room, restaurant (background music). Wi-Fi. Garden; terrace. Function facilities. Civil wedding licence. 15 bedrooms (1 suitable for &). B&B £70–£125 per person; D,B&B £115–£170.

Overton Grange, Old Hereford Road, SY8 4AD. *Tel* 01584-873500, www.overtongrangehotel.com. In rural location, 1½ miles S of town, country house hotel in Edwardian manor, owned by Mr and Mrs Choblet. 'Stunning bedroom, with views to match. The bathroom was new; we were delighted to find a power shower.' Lounge, library, breakfast room, restaurant. Background music (light jazz/classical). Swimming pool planned for late 2009. 2½-acre garden. 14 bedrooms. B&B £47.50–£120 per person; D,B&B £87.50–£160.

LYME REGIS Dorset   Map 1:C6

Alexandra Hotel, Pound Street, DT7 3HZ. *Tel* 01297-442010, www.hotelalexandra.co.uk. Long-established 'hotel of character' in 'excellent' situation overlooking lawns, sea and harbour, above The Cobb and Lyme Bay. Run by one family for over 25 years; Kathryn Richards now in charge. Refurbishment almost complete: 'Everything looking beautiful.' 3 sitting rooms, cocktail bar, conservatory (light lunches: 'delicious'), restaurant (under Ian Grant: 'very good, with excellent service'). Packed lunches available. Aromatherapy treatments. Background music (light jazz). 1-acre garden with viewing deck. Children welcomed. Parking. 24 bedrooms. B&B £57.50–£90 per person; D,B&B £87.50–£120.

LYNMOUTH Devon   Map 1:B4

Shelley's, 8 Watersmeet Road, EX35 6EP. *Tel* 01598-753219, www.shelleyshotel.co.uk. Overlooking harbour, with views over Lynmouth Bay, Jane Becker and Richard Briden's B&B in 18th-century house in centre (Shelley honeymooned here in summer 1812). Lounge, bar, conservatory breakfast room. No background music. 11 bedrooms (1 on ground floor). B&B £35–£68 per person.

LYNTON Devon   Map 1:B4

Victoria Lodge, Lee Road, EX35 6BS. *Tel* 01598-753203, www.victorialodge.co.uk. In village within Exmoor national park: Jacqueline Holding's guest house. Cascades of flowers outside; decorated inside in keeping with Victorian origins: drapes, prints, photographs, antiques, tiled fireplaces. Lounge, reading room, dining room. No background music. Terrace; water garden. Packed lunches by arrangement. Parking (steep steps). 8 bedrooms. B&B £35–£70 per person.

LYTHAM Lancashire   Map 4:D2

Clifton Arms, West Beach, FY58 5QJ. *Tel* 01253-739898, www.cliftonarms-lytham.com. 'A lovely, welcoming hotel' (Fairhaven group); historic beachfront town house overlooking Lytham green and seafront. Managed by Victoria Tipper. *Churchills* bar/lounge (brasserie menu), library/TV room, *West Beach* restaurant (classical background music; chef, James Rodgers); conference/banqueting facilities. 'Splendid breakfasts.' Lift. Small garden. Parking. 48 bedrooms. B&B £62.50–£130 per person. Dinner £29.50.

The Rooms, 35 Church Road, FY8 5LL. *Tel* 01253-736000, www.theroomslytham.co.uk. Sophisticated B&B near memorial gardens, run with personal touch by owners Andy and Jackie Baker. State-of-the-art equipment, quirkily designed bathrooms, locally sourced food at breakfast (home-made smoothies; champagne breakfasts at weekends). Dining room (background radio). Walled garden. Wi-Fi; iPod docking stations. 5 bedrooms. B&B £47.50–£125.

MANCHESTER   Map 4:E3

Bewley's Hotel, Outwood Lane, Manchester Airport, M90 4HL. *Tel* 0161-498 0333, www.bewleyshotels.com. Airport hotel (Moran group), managed by Alison Diggle. 10 mins' walk to Terminals 1 and 3; 24-hour shuttle service. 20 mins' drive from city. Large, modern, triple glazed. Sitting area, bar, brasserie. Wi-Fi; business facilities. No background music. Parking. 226 bedrooms (some suitable for &): £69–£124. Breakfast £8.95.

City Inn, 1 Piccadilly Place, 1 Auburn Street, M1 3DG. *Tel* 0161-242 1000, www.cityinn.com/manchester. Contemporary, purpose-built chain hotel (City Inn group) near station, managed by Faye Kelly. State-of-the-art fittings: floor-to-ceiling opening windows; iMac system in every bedroom; mist-free mirrors; walk-in power showers, etc. Exhibitions (open 24 hours) by local artists. *Piccadilly* lounge, *City* café. Background music. Wi-Fi. Fitness suite. Meeting rooms. 285 bedrooms (14 suitable for &). B&B from £46 per person.

Eleven Didsbury Park, 11 Didsbury Park, Didsbury Village, M20 5LH. *Tel* 0161-448 7711, www.elevendidsburypark.com. In 'convenient, yet peaceful' location (conservation area), an easy walk from Didsbury green, 20-min bus ride from centre, 10 mins from airport. Victorian town house converted by Eamonn and Sally O'Loughlin into smart, 'very nice' small hotel with 'helpful staff'. Managed by Andrew Hughes. 2 lounge/bars (background music all day), veranda. Conference facilities. Large walled garden. Parking. 19 bedrooms (1, on ground floor, suitable for &): £140–£260. Breakfast £12.50–£14.50.

Malmaison, 1–3 Piccadilly, M1 3AQ. *Tel* 0161-278 1000, www. malmaison.com. Imposing former cotton spinners' warehouse by station, managed by Graham Bradford. Buzzy atmosphere; dramatic red and black decor; lots of cushions in bedrooms; dimly lit public areas. Bar, brasserie; background music; gym. Conference facilities. Child-friendly. Dogs welcomed. 167 bedrooms: £160–£325. Breakfast ('impressive range and quality of buffet items') £11.95–£13.95. Dinner from £25.

Old Trafford Lodge, Lancashire County Cricket Club, Talbot Road, Old Trafford, M16 0PX. *Tel* 0161-874 3333, www. oldtraffordlodgehotel.co.uk. Beside Lancashire's test match ground, purpose-built hotel, managed by Claire Jones. Photographs of cricketing heroes; pictures of bats, balls, stumps, etc; free match tickets. Lounge, bar (sandwiches available); lift. No background music. Wi-Fi. Parking. 68 bedrooms (36 have balcony overlooking pitch; others face car park). B&B (continental) £32–£69 per person.

MATLOCK Derbyshire   Map 3:A6

The Red House Country Hotel, Old Road, Darley Dale, DE4 2ER. *Tel* 01629-734854, www.theredhousecountryhotel.co.uk. 'A great favourite. Excellent location for touring the Peak District.' Next to carriage museum (carriage driving), David and Kate Gardiner's hotel on edge of village (on quiet road off A6). Views over Derwent valley. 2 sitting rooms, candlelit restaurant: Alan Perkins is chef ('excellent; interesting flavour combinations'). Complimentary home-made tea and cake. 'Simply the best' breakfasts. No background music. Wi-Fi. ¾-acre lawned garden. Parking. 10 bedrooms (2 four-poster; 3, on ground floor in coach house, suitable for &). B&B £45–£83 per person; D,B&B £61–£110.

MIDHURST West Sussex   Map 2:E3
Park House, Bepton, GU29 0JB. *Tel* 01730-819000, www.parkhouse hotel.com. In 'heaven-sent setting' 2½ miles SW of Midhurst, small country hotel in imposing Victorian house at foot of South Downs. Owned by O'Brien family for over 60 years; managed by James (the chef) and Rebecca Coonon. Lounge, bar, dining room, conservatory; terrace. No background music. Spa: indoor pool, sauna, treatment rooms. 9-acre grounds: heated swimming pool, tennis, croquet, pitch-and-putt golf. Conference/function facilities. Child-friendly. Dogs welcomed. 21 bedrooms (some in 2 cottages; 1 on ground floor). B&B £77.50–£265 per person; D,B&B from £85.

MILDEN Suffolk   Map 2:C5
Milden Hall, nr Lavenham, CO10 9NY. *Tel* 01787-247235, www.thehall-milden.co.uk. Eco-conscious B&B in listed 'Georgian-ised' 16th-century hall farmhouse, on 500-acre arable land. Down quiet drive, 3 miles SE of Lavenham. Owned by keen conservationists and historians, Juliet and Christopher Hawkins. Hall/sitting/breakfast room. Farm produce. No background music. 3-acre garden. Children welcomed. Tennis court; bicycles; outdoor nature activities. 3 bedrooms (plus simple self-catering in Tudor barn). B&B £32.50–£90 per person.

MILLOM Cumbria   Map 4: inset C2
Broadgate House, Broadgate, Thwaites, LA18 5JY. *Tel* 01229-716295, www.broadgate-house.co.uk. Overlooking Dudden Estuary, within Lake District national park: white Georgian house (built 1819), owned by Lewthwaite family for almost 200 years; run by Diana Lewthwaite. Drawing room, cosy sitting room (wood-burning stove), dining room, breakfast room. Country house decor. No background music. Walled garden, croquet lawn, terraces. Dogs welcomed. 4 bed-rooms. B&B £40–£45 per person. Dinner £18.50.

MORETON-IN-MARSH Gloucestershire   Map 3:D6

The Manor House Hotel, High Street, GL56 0LJ. *Tel* 01608-650501, www.cotswold-inns-hotels.co.uk. Contemporary styling (£2 million renovation project after 2007 floods) in 16th-century building. Part of small Cotswold Inns & Hotels group; popular drop-in/meeting place, managed by Simon Stanbrook. Bedrooms traditionally furnished; some four-poster beds. Lounge, library, bar, *The Beagle* brasserie, *Mulberry* restaurant; terrace; garden (300-year-old mulberry tree; water features). Background music. Conference facilities. Civil wedding licence. 35 bedrooms. B&B £71–£161.50 per person. Dinner £37.50.

MORPETH Northumberland   Map 4:B4

Eshott Hall, NE65 9EP. *Tel* 01670-787777, www.eshott.com. Home of Sanderson family for 6 generations: wisteria-clad, symmetrical 17th-century building on 500-acre estate (farm, walled garden, arboretum, formal gardens), ½-hour drive NW of Newcastle. 'Luxurious accommodation' (no telephone or TV). Panelling, ornate plasterwork, stained glass. Drawing room, dining room (private-party atmosphere, communal meals), library, ballroom. No background music. Tennis court. Weddings (civil licence), house parties, small conferences a speciality. 7 bedrooms. B&B £64–£79 per person. Dinner £33.

MUCH WENLOCK Shropshire   Map 3:C5

The Raven, Barrow Street, TF13 6EN. *Tel* 01952-727251, www.ravenhotel.com. White-fronted 17th-century coaching inn, 12 miles SE of Shrewsbury. 'Central yet quiet.' Traditional interior; some four-poster beds. Managed by 'very helpful' Kirk Heywood; 'warm welcome'. Bar, 2 dining rooms ('way-above-average cooking') in original 15th-century almshouses (alfresco meals in summer); classical background music. Courtyard: small herb garden. Parking. 15 bedrooms (some across courtyard). B&B £42.50–£65 per person; D,B&B £72.50–£95.

NEWBURY Berkshire   Map 2:D2

Carnarvon Arms, Winchester Rd, Burghclere, RG20 9LE. *Tel* 01635-278222, www.carnarvonarms.com. Renovated coaching inn (Grade II listed), retaining traditional style, with rooms (some small) above. Seating in nooks and crannies; leather sofas; dining room with vaulted ceiling. Background music. Modern British cuisine from chef Justin Brown. Function facilities. Wi-Fi. Parking. 23 bedrooms. B&B

(continental) £45–£80 per person. Cooked breakfast £5.95. Dinner from £30.

NEWBY BRIDGE Cumbria   Map 4: inset C2

Lakeside Hotel, LA12 8AT. *Tel* 01539-530001, www.lakesidehotel. co.uk. 'Runs like clockwork': large, luxury hotel managed by Clive Wilson, in former coaching inn (17th-century origins) on SW shore of Lake Windermere. Lounge, bar, *Lakeview* restaurant. Chef Richard Booth sources 'good local produce' for 'brilliant brasserie dishes'. Conservatory. Background music (live pianist some evenings). Landscaped gardens. Health/leisure spa: pool, with shallow, 'beach-style' family area, etched glass panels of surrounding scenery; steam room, sauna; gym; treatment rooms. Civil wedding licence. Children welcomed. 75 bedrooms. B&B £99.50–£199.50 per person. Dinner £35–£45.

NEWCASTLE UPON TYNE Tyne and Wear   Map 4:B4

Malmaison, The Quayside, NE1 3DX. *Tel* 0191-245 5000, www. malmaison.com. Near Millennium Bridge: former warehouse converted in lavish contemporary style (plush fabrics, strong colours, modern furniture); quirky touches. Managed by Lizzy Kelk. 2 lounges, café, bar, brasserie (dimly lit); background music. Lift. Spa (holistic/beauty treatments). 122 bedrooms (most with river views; 4 suitable for &), £160–£350. Breakfast £11.95–£13.95. Dinner from £25.

The Townhouse, 1 West Avenue, Gosforth, NE3 4ES. *Tel* 0191-285 6812, www.thetownhousehotel.co.uk. Elegant Victorian town house hotel, opened in late 2008 by Cathy Knox and Sheila Armstrong, in leafy Gosforth suburbs, 2 miles N of centre. Contemporary/classical mix; theatrical bathrooms. Breakfast room, café (open until 7 pm; room service). Background music. Wi-Fi; iPod docking station. Children welcomed. 10 bedrooms. B&B £37.50–£62.50 per person.

NEWLANDS Cumbria   Map 4: inset C2

Swinside Lodge, Grange Road, CA12 5UE. *Tel* 01768-772948, www.swinsidelodge-hotel.co.uk. Georgian Lakeland property in 'beautiful location – quiet, surrounded by wooded fields and hills', owned by Mike and Kath Bilton since October 2008. 5 mins' walk from jetty on Derwentwater, 2 miles SW of Keswick. 2 lounges, dining room (chef Clive Imber has stayed on; background music). ½-acre garden. 7 bedrooms. B&B £62–£78 per person; D,B&B £82–£98.

NEWMARKET Suffolk   Map 2:B4

Bedford Lodge, Bury Road, CB8 7BX. *Tel* 01638-663175, www.bedfordlodgehotel.co.uk. Smart hotel in Georgian hunting lodge near racecourse, an easy walk from town. Managed by Noel Byrne. Lounge, *Roxanna* bar, *Orangery* restaurant (Paul Owens is chef; background music); extensive function/conference facilities. Civil wedding licence. *The Edge* fitness centre (indoor swimming pool, gym, beauty salon); 24-hour room service. Civil wedding licence. 3-acre secluded garden. 55 bedrooms (1 suitable for &). B&B from £47.50 per person; D,B&B from £85. Dinner £47. *V*

NEWQUAY Cornwall   Map 1:D2

The Headland Hotel, Fistral Beach, TR7 1EW. *Tel* 01637-872211, www.headlandhotel.co.uk. Owners John and Carolyn Armstrong ensure 'good food, and a friendly atmosphere' at their imposing, 'beautifully located' Victorian edifice by Fistral beach ('UK's surfing capital'). 'Magnificent' coastal views on all sides. Contemporary/ traditional decor. 'Wonderful communal areas.' Lounges, bar, *Sand Brasserie*; *Terrace Restaurant* (alfresco dining); no background music; conference/event facilities; snooker; table tennis; 10-acre grounds. 2 heated swimming pools (indoor and outdoor), sauna; croquet; 3 tennis courts; 9-hole golf approach course and putting green. Families welcomed (bunk beds, baby-listening, entertainments, etc). Civil wedding licence. 104 bedrooms. B&B £47.50–£175 per person. Dinner £25. *V*

NORWICH Norfolk   Map 2:B5

Annesley House, 6 Newmarket Road, NR2 2LA. *Tel* 01603-624553, www.bw-annesleyhouse.co.uk. In 2 Grade II listed Georgian houses: (Best Western) hotel managed by Shellie Miller, in conservation area, ½ mile from centre. Bar/lounge, conservatory restaurant (local pro- duce; views over water gardens and koi pond; background music); conference/function facilities. Wi-Fi. 3-acre grounds. Parking. 26 bed- rooms (some face main road). B&B £44–£62 per person; D,B&B £79.50–£87.

Norfolk Mead, Church Loke, Coltishall, NR12 7DN. *Tel* 01603- 737531, www.norfolkmead.co.uk. Georgian merchant's house on edge of Norfolk Broads, 7 miles NE of Norwich: 'near-perfect location'. 'Magnificent' 8-acre grounds: 'rolling lawns down to River Bure'. Owned by Jill and Don Fleming; managed by Sharon Hardy. 'Delighted with this find. We were treated like house guests; staff and owners impressive.' Lounge, bar, restaurant (local produce; traditional Sunday lunches; 'excellent food, breakfast up there with the best'); background music; conference facilities. Walled garden, unheated swimming pool; fishing lake; off-river mooring. Civil wedding licence. Children welcomed. 13 bedrooms (2 beamed ones in cottage suite; some with four-poster). B&B £55–£95 per person; D,B&B £80–£125. *V*

St Giles House, 41–45 St Giles Street, NR2 1JR. *Tel* 01603-275180, www.stgileshousehotel.co.uk. Landmark building (former Telephone House, built 1906), in centre. Baroque facade, Georgian and modern additions, Art Deco interior. Lounge, bar, restaurant; terrace; background music; function facilities; beauty treatments. Civil wedding licence. Wi-Fi. Parking. 24 bedrooms (2 suitable for &). B&B £60–£110 per person; DB&B £95–£140. *V*

NOTTINGHAM Nottinghamshire   Map 2:A3

Lace Market Hotel, 29–31 High Pavement, NG1 1HE. *Tel* 0115-852 3232, www.lacemarkethotel.co.uk. Modern hotel (Finesse Collection) in 4 Georgian and Victorian town houses (1 a former lace factory), facing 14th-century church of St Mary the Virgin. Managed by Susanne Williams. Lounge, *Saint* cocktail bar, *Merchants* restaurant, *Cock & Hoop* gastropub (Tom Earle is chef). Background music. Lift. Function facilities. Civil wedding licence. Free access to nearby health club. 42 bedrooms: £89–£144.50. Breakfast £9.95–£13.95. Dinner £22.50–£40.

Restaurant Sat Bains, Lenton Lane, NG7 2SA. *Tel* 0115-986 6566, www.restaurantsatbains.com. Bustling, award-winning restaurant on outskirts of city, run by eponymous chef/*patron* and wife Amanda. Lounge, bar, restaurant (dinner only, closed Sun/Mon), Tasting Room, conservatory; courtyard. Background music. 8 sleek bedrooms. B&B £45–£132.50 per person. Dinner £55–£150.

OTLEY West Yorkshire   Map 4:D3

Chevin Country Park Hotel, Yorkgate, LS21 3NU. *Tel* 01943-467818, www.crerarhotels.com. 'Convenient for exploring the Yorkshire dales.' In 44 acres of peaceful woodland grounds (3 fishing lakes: roach, carp): spa hotel (Crerar Hotels). Largest log building in England. Conservatory lounge, bar, restaurant; background music. 'Staff friendly, helpful.' Indoor swimming pool, sauna; gym; tennis. Civil wedding licence. 49 bedrooms (19 in main house; 30 in pine lodges; some on ground floor). B&B £40–£120 per person; D,B&B £19.95 added. *V*

OTTERBURN Northumberland   Map 4:B3

Otterburn Tower, NE19 1NS. *Tel* 01830-520620, www.
otterburntower.com. Fortified country house on ancient site (founded
1086 by cousin of William the Conqueror), 30 mins' drive from
Newcastle. On 32-acre estate; fronted by terraced lawns amid woodland. Managed by owner John Goodfellow ('knowledgeable, helpful');
John Calton is chef. Florentine marble fireplace. 2 drawing rooms, bar,
breakfast room, *Oak Room* restaurant (farm produce; outdoor eating);
classical background music; function facilities; lake; private stretch of
River Rede (fishing). Civil wedding licence. Children welcomed. 'The
Northumbrian cooked breakfast is a first-class fry-up.' 18 bedrooms
(1 suitable for &). B&B £45–£95 per person, D,B&B £65–£115.

OXFORD Oxfordshire   Map 2:C2

Burlington House, 374 Banbury Road, OX2 7PP. *Tel* 01865-513513,
www.burlington-house.co.uk. In leafy Summertown, 1½ miles from
centre (frequent bus service): B&B in handsome Victorian house on
busy road. Modern decor, original fireplaces. Sitting room, breakfast room.
Wi-Fi. No background music. Small rear oriental garden. Parking.
12 bedrooms (3 on ground floor). B&B £42.50–£65 per person.

The Randolph, Beaumont Street, OX1 2LN. *Tel* 0844 8799132,
www.macdonaldhotels.co.uk/randolph. Oxford institution (Victorian
Gothic) by Ashmolean Museum, now part of Macdonald group;
managed by Michael Grange. Drawing room (pianist on Sat), *Morse*
bar, restaurant (Tom Birks is chef; classical background music); lift;
cellar spa (vaulted ceilings, Italian tiling, candlelight; thermal suite,
hydrotherapy bath, relaxation room). Conference facilities. Civil
wedding licence. Child-friendly. Dogs welcomed. 151 bedrooms
(1 suitable for &). B&B £79.50–£270 per person; D,B&B £110–£290.
Dinner £29.50–£34.

PENRITH Cumbria   Map 4: inset C2

The George, Devonshire Street, CA11 7SU. *Tel* 01768-862696,
www.georgehotelpenrith.co.uk. Traditional hotel in centre; 300-year-
old coaching inn. Part of Grange family's small Lakeland group;
managed by Wayne Bartholomew. Lake Ullswater 4 miles. Lounges
(background music at night), *Oak* bar, candlelit *Devonshire* restaurant
(ornate ceiling; Phillip Cooke is chef); function/conference facilities;
civil wedding licence. Parking. Children welcomed. 35 bedrooms.
B&B £56–£149 per person; D,B&B £76–£167.

Westmorland Hotel, nr Orton, CA10 3SB. *Tel* 01539-624351, www.westmorlandhotel.com. 'What a pity more motorway service areas do not contain accommodation like this!' Surrounded by open fell, secluded modern hotel just off M6 (Tebay Motorway Services, Junction 38), managed by Jeff Brimble. Bryan Parsons is chef. Contemporary design blended with traditional materials. Lounge, bar (log fires), split-level dining room; background music. Wi-Fi. Function facilities. Civil wedding licence. Children welcomed. 'Totally recommendable as a stopover or as a base for touring that side of the lakes.' 50 bedrooms. B&B £41–£60 per person; D,B&B £52–£80. *V*

PLYMOUTH Devon   Map 1:D4

Bowling Green Hotel, 9–10 Osborne Place, Lockyer St, The Hoe, PL1 2PU. *Tel* 01752-209090, www.bowlingreenhotel.co.uk. B&B run by owner Tom Roberts in Georgian house facing 'Drake's bowling green'. 5 mins' walk from Barbican; views across Plymouth Hoe. Lounge, TV room, breakfast room, conservatory. Business facilities. No background music. Wi-Fi. Parking. 12 bedrooms. B&B £34–£47 per person.

POOLE Dorset   Map 2:E1

Hotel du Vin Poole, Thames Street, BH15 1JN. *Tel* 01202-685666, www.hotelduvin.com. Georgian town house (1779) in quiet cul-de-sac near church and quay. Managed by Emma Lloyd. Bar (traditional pub), bistro; courtyard (alfresco dining); function facilities. Classic European cuisine by chef Darren Rockett. No background music. Parking. 38 bedrooms: £170–£350. Breakfast £11.95–£13.95. Dinner from £25.

RAMSGATE Kent   Map 2:D6

The Royal Harbour Hotel, Nelson Crescent, CT11 9JF. *Tel* 01843-591514, www.royalharbourhotel.co.uk. Waterfront B&B hotel in 2 adjoining Georgian Grade II listed town houses. Run by owner James Thomas. Views over harbour, yacht marina and English Channel. Elegant interior. 2 lounges, snug; log fires, breakfast room. No background music. Lots of books. Complimentary evening snacks. 20-seat cinema in basement. Walled herb garden. Wi-Fi. Children welcomed. Parking. 19 bedrooms (1 on ground floor; some with balcony). B&B £49.50–£109.50 per person.

ROCK Cornwall   Map 1:D2

St Enodoc, nr Wadebridge, PL27 6LA. *Tel* 01208-863394, www.enodoc-hotel.co.uk. In 'super position' (views across Camel estuary), family-friendly hotel. Managed by Kate Simms; new head chef, Ben Harmer. 2 lounges, library, bar/restaurant (classical background music); playroom; games room; sauna, heated outdoor swimming pool. Terrace; ½-acre garden. Bright, colourful decor; 'exceptional bathrooms'. Sandy beach nearby. 20 bedrooms. B&B £65–£200 per person; D,B&B £90–£345. Dinner £45.

ROSS-ON-WYE Herefordshire   Map 3:D5

The Hill House, Howle Hill, HR9 5ST. *Tel* 01989-562033, www.thehowlinghillhouse.com. High above Forest of Dean (views of Black Mountains): Duncan and Alex Stayton's 17th-century house in 4-acre woodlands. One-off, quirky style (ghosts promised); eco-friendly. Organic local produce (home-grown vegetables; free-range hens, ducks, pigs); Aga-cooked, vegetarian-friendly breakfasts; packed lunch/evening meal by arrangement. Wood-burning stoves. Morning room, lounge, bar (background music morning Radio 4), restaurant; hot tub; sauna (charge); cinema (DVD film library). Garden. 5 bedrooms. B&B £25–£35 per person. Supper £15.

Pencraig Court, Pencraig, HR9 6HR. *Tel* 01989-770306, www.pencraig-court.co.uk. Overlooking River Wye, managed by 'hospitable' owners Malcolm and Liz Dobson: yellow-painted Georgian country house, traditionally furnished. 4 miles SW of town. 3½-acre garden (croquet) and woodlands; lovely views. 2 lounges, dining room (classical background music; garden produce). Dogs welcomed (by arrangement). 11 bedrooms (1 family). B&B £44.50–£75 per person; D,B&B £64.50–£95. *V*

ROTHBURY Northumberland   Map 4:A3

Orchard House, High Street, NE65 7TL. *Tel* 01669-620684, www.orchardhouserothbury.com. Graham ('all affability') and Lisa Stobbart's Georgian town house in village on edge of Northumberland national park. 'Good base for walking and outdoor pursuits.' 'Emphasis on quality and luxury.' Scrambled egg with smoked salmon on toasted brioche 'too good for breakfast'. Drawing room, breakfast room; garden. No background music. Children welcomed. 6 bedrooms. B&B £49–£87.50 per person.

RYE East Sussex   **Map 2:E5**
White Vine House, 24 High Street, TN31 7LA. *Tel* 01797-224748,
www.whitevinehouse.co.uk. Javed Khan's cosy B&B, managed by
Kim Raymond, in Georgian town house. Lounge (oak-panelled; log
fire in winter), dining room, *Vine* restaurant (Stefan Enache cooks fresh
pasta, hand-made pizzas, gourmet burgers), café. Background music.
Organic toiletries. Small civil wedding facilities. Wi-Fi; iPod docking
stations. Children welcomed. 7 bedrooms. B&B £55–£85 per person.
Dinner £35.

ST ALBANS Hertfordshire   **Map 2:C3**
St Michael's Manor, Fishpool Street, AL3 4RY. *Tel* 01727-864444,
www.stmichaelsmanor.com. Imposing building in oldest part of city,
beneath cathedral. Owned and run by Newling Ward family for over
40 years; Paul Crossey is manager. Bedroom styles vary (period in old
building; modern-classical in later wing). 2 lounges, bar, restaurant,
conservatory; classical background music; private dining room. Eric
Maboti provides a modern menu. Civil wedding licence. 5-acre
gardens: croquet, lake. 30 bedrooms (8 in garden wing; 1 suitable
for &). B&B £72.50–£172.50 per person. Dinner £15.50–£45.

ST IVES Cornwall   **Map 1:D1**
Blue Hayes, Trelyon Avenue, TR26 2AD. *Tel* 01736-797129,
www.bluehayes.co.uk. Small luxury hotel in 1920s house owned by
Malcolm Herring. On Porthminster Point, overlooking bay and
harbour. Small garden: gate leading to South West Coast Path.
2 lounges, bar, dining room; terrace (panoramic views). No background music. Small function facilities. Civil wedding licence.
Parking. Open Mar–Oct. 6 bedrooms (some with balcony, roof terrace
or patio). B&B £75–£105 per person. Supper £12–£16.
The Garrack, Burthallan Lane, TR26 3AA. *Tel* 01736-796199,
www.garrack.com. Overlooking Porthmeor beach, a short, steep walk
from centre: creeper-clad building, run for over 40 years by Kilby
family owners. 'Excellent value.' Lounge, restaurant (sea/garden
views; Cornish produce; extensive wine list; background music);
leisure centre (gym, sauna, indoor swimming pool). 2-acre garden: sun
terrace. Parking. 18 bedrooms (2 suitable for &). B&B £47–£97 per
person; D,B&B £63–£119.
The Porthminster Hotel, The Terrace, TR26 2BN. *Tel* 01736-
795221. Victorian building in subtropical gardens overlooking bay and

Godrevy Lighthouse; ½ mile from centre. Direct access to beach; impressive sea views. Owned by Harbour Hotels, managed by Ben Young. Lift. Lounge, bar, cocktail bar, restaurant (modern European fare; fish and seafood); background jazz; function/business facilities; civil wedding licence. Wi-Fi. Heated indoor and outdoor swimming pools, tennis. 42 bedrooms (some family). B&B £60–£150 per person; D,B&B £75–£165. *V*

Primrose Valley Hotel, Primrose Valley, TR26 2ED. *Tel* 01736-794939, www.primroseonline.co.uk. Reached down steep hill above Porthminster Beach: Edwardian seaside villa with striking modern interior. Wooden floors, leather sofas, bright stair carpets. Owned by Sue and Andrew Biss and Rose Clegg. Emphasis on sustainability. Bar (low lighting; light Cornish platters); breakfast room; patio; background music. Treatments. Beaches and town close by. Closed Jan. 9 bedrooms (some with sea views). B&B £50–£117.50 per person.

ST LEONARDS-ON-SEA East Sussex   Map 2:E4

Hastings House, 9 Warrior Square, TN37 6BA. *Tel* 01424-422709, www.hastingshouse.co.uk. Seng and Elisabeth Loy spent 2 years transforming this white stuccoed house on historic garden square near sea into an imaginatively styled luxury B&B. Indulgent bathrooms. 'The *en suite* room was amazing. Warm welcome. Fantastic breakfast.' Lounge with bar, dining room. Background music. Civil wedding licence applied for. Decked terrace. Children welcomed. 8 bedrooms. B&B £49.50–£70 per person. *V*

SALISBURY Wiltshire   Map 2:D2

Leena's, 50 Castle Road, SP1 3RL. *Tel* 01722-335419. Good-value, welcoming B&B, long run by Leena and Malcolm Street. Edwardian house on busy Amesbury road (double glazing). 15 mins' riverside walk from centre. Lounge, breakfast room. No background music. Children welcomed. Garden. Parking. 6 bedrooms (1 on ground floor). B&B £32.50–£41 per person.

Spire House, 84 Exeter Street, SP1 2SE. *Tel* 01722-339213, www.salisbury-bedandbreakfast.com. In centre, close to cathedral, shops, etc: Lois and John Faulkner's B&B in 18th-century Grade II listed town house. Healthy option breakfasts available. No background music. Walled garden. Parking opposite. 4 bedrooms. B&B £35–£65 per person.

SANDWICH Kent   Map 2:D5

The Bell Hotel, The Quay, CT13 9EF. *Tel* 01304-613388, www.
bellhotelsandwich.co.uk. 19th-century listed building overlooking
quay. 'Ideal position for golf and beach life.' Recently refurbished:
'classy', unfussy decor. Owned by Matt Collins (manager) and Matthew
Wolfman. 'Friendly, helpful staff.' Lounge, club room, new restaurant,
The Old Dining Room, opened Mar 2009: 'simple and delicious' cooking
by Stephen Piddock. Background music. Conservatory, sun terrace.
Wi-Fi. Civil wedding licence. Limited parking. 34 bedrooms. B&B
£52.50–£105 per person; D,B&B £79.50–£132. *V*

SAXMUNDHAM Suffolk   Map 2:B6

The Bell Hotel, 31 High Street, IP17 1AF. *Tel* 01728-602331,
www.bellhotel-saxmundham.co.uk. Near station: Georgian coaching
inn (Grade II listed) run by chef/proprietor Andrew Blackburn. Real
ales; log fires in winter. 'Comfortable; good value.' Lounge, bar,
restaurant. No background music. Small back courtyard. Function
facilities. 10 bedrooms. B&B (continental) £40–£45 per person. Full
breakfast £5.95. Dinner £18.50.

SCARBOROUGH North Yorkshire   Map 4:C5

Phoenix Court, 8/9 Rutland Terrace, YO12 7JB. *Tel* 01723-501150,
www.hotel-phoenix.co.uk. On headland overlooking North Bay:
Alison and Bryan Edwards' recently renovated guest house, created
from 2 Victorian terrace houses. 10-min walk from centre. Lounge,
bar area, dining room (background music). Packed lunches; drying
facilities for walkers. Local and Fairtrade produce at breakfast.
Children welcomed. Parking. 15 bedrooms (9 with sea views, 1 on
ground floor). B&B £26–£36 per person. *V*

SHEFFIELD South Yorkshire   Map 4:E4

The Leopold, Leopold Street, S1 2JG. *Tel* 0114-252 4000, www.
leopoldhotel.co.uk. Large hotel in quirkily converted old school
building in revitalised Leopold Square area. Owned by Irish PREM
group, managed by George Arizmendi. Sombre colours, school
memorabilia (old photos, ranks of coat pegs). Bar, restaurant (Daniel
Self is chef), terrace; 24-hour room service. Background music.
Conference/function facilities. Civil wedding licence. 90 bedrooms
(6 suitable for &): £75–£123. Breakfast £7.50–£10.95. B&B rates at
weekend: £34.50 per person.

SHREWSBURY Shropshire   Map 3:B4

Chatford House, Bayston Hill, Chatford, SY3 0AY. *Tel* 01743-718301, www.chatfordhouse.co.uk. Homely B&B in Grade II listed farmhouse in hamlet 5 miles S of town, run by owners Christine and Rupert Farmer. Views of The Wrekin. Home-made cake and damson gin. Local ingredients used for Aga-cooked breakfast. Sitting room, dining room (piano CDs). Country garden. Children welcomed. No credit cards. 3 bedrooms. B&B £30–£45 per person.

SIDLESHAM West Sussex   Map 2:E3

The Crab & Lobster, Mill Lane, PO20 7NB. *Tel* 01243-641233, www.crab-lobster.co.uk. In area of outstanding natural beauty, on banks of Pagham Harbour nature reserve (marshland): remote 350-year old inn (part of The Sussex Pub Company), renovated with spare, modern interior. Food based on local produce; emphasis on fish and seafood. Bar, restaurant (background music); terrace; garden. 6 bedrooms (2 in adjoining cottage; deluxe ones with binoculars/telescope). B&B £65–£100 per person. Dinner £35.

SIDMOUTH Devon   Map 1:C5

Hotel Riviera, The Esplanade, EX10 8AY. *Tel* 01395-515201, www.hotelriviera.co.uk. Seafront hotel with handsome Regency facade and 'continental air', overlooking Lyme Bay. Traditionally run by Wharton family for over 3 decades; 'long-serving, courteous staff'. Lounge, bar (live pianist), restaurant; ballroom; terrace. Lift. Chef Matthew Weaver places emphasis on seafood. Children welcomed. 26 bedrooms. B&B £52–£88.50 per person; D,B&B £60–£96.50.
Victoria Hotel, The Esplanade, EX10 8RY. *Tel* 01395-512651, www.victoriahotel.co.uk. Large, majestic hotel (Brend group), in 5-acre grounds on hill at W end of esplanade (views across bay). Managed by Matthew Raistrick; David Gardener is chef; long-serving staff. 'We came away satisfied: excellent value for money.' Lounges, restaurant; background music; Wi-Fi; lift; snooker; gym; outdoor/indoor swimming pool, whirlpool, sauna, solarium; tennis, putting. Families welcomed. 61 bedrooms (some with sea views and balcony): £145–£340. Breakfast from £17.50. Dinner from £37.

SKIPTON North Yorkshire   Map 4:D3

The Lister Arms, Malham, 22 The Lane, BD23 4DB. *Tel* 01729-830330, www.listerarms.co.uk. In southern dales, 'very popular' 17th-century village-centre pub (Shire Hotels) serving traditional fare;

modern rooms above. Managed by Nick and Brigitte Frankgate; Terry Quinn is chef: 'Dishes inventive; hearty breakfasts.' Bar, dining room. Background music. Good walking, climbing nearby. Child-friendly. Dogs welcomed. 9 bedrooms. B&B £40–£45 per person. Dinner £26.

SOUTHAMPTON Hampshire   Map 2:E2

White Star Tavern and Dining Rooms, 28 Oxford Street, SO14 3DJ. *Tel* 02380-821990, www.whitestartavern.co.uk. Former seafarers' hotel made shipshape. Now stylish bar and restaurant (renamed after famous shipping line), with contemporary, well-equipped rooms (some small) above. Managed by Oliver Weeks; Jim Haywood is chef. Tongue and groove panelling, mosaic-tiled bathrooms; spacious showers. Lounge, bar restaurant (background music); roof terrace. Wi-Fi. 13 bedrooms, plus one 3-bedroom serviced apartment: £89–£159. Breakfast £3–£8. Dinner £30. *V*

SOUTHPORT Merseyside   Map 4:E2

The Vincent, 98 Lord Street, PR8 1JR. *Tel* 01704-883800, www.thevincenthotel.com. On fashionable boulevard: contemporary 'lifestyle' hotel, opened 2008. Bar, *V* café/sushi bar; *Warehouse* brasserie; background music; spa; gym; beauty treatments. Wi-Fi. Function facilities. Civil wedding licence. Valet parking. 'Enthusiastic, helpful staff.' Children welcomed. 60 'very stylish', modern bedrooms (some suitable for &) on 6 floors; state-of-the-art technology. B&B £72.50–£170 per person. Dinner from £12.95.

SOUTHWOLD Suffolk   Map 2:B6

The Swan, Market Place, IP18 6EG. *Tel* 01502-722186, www.adnamshotels.co.uk. 'Pleasantly old-fashioned' hotel in 300-year-old building on market square, managed for Adnams by Jade Arnold. 'Friendly, helpful staff.' Traditional decor. Lift. 2 lounges, bar, restaurant ('good cuisine' from Rory Whelan); function facilities. No background music. Parking. Beach 200 yds. 42 bedrooms (1 suitable for &; 16 refurbished ones in garden: dogs allowed). B&B £65–£90 per person; D,B&B £85–£115.

SPALDING Lincolnshire   Map 2:A4

St Nicholas House, Main Road, Deeping St Nicholas, PE11 3HA. *Tel* 01775-630484, www.stnicholashouse.co.uk. 'Charming' farmhouse (1812) on E side of village, 2 miles SW of Spalding. Elegantly decorated in period style; 'bold, unusual colours give the place a modern twist'. 2 bars, drawing room, dining room, *Hollies* restaurant; occasional background music; garden. 10 bedrooms (5 in house, 5, more contemporary, with wet room, in barns). B&B £50–£95 per person; D,B&B £70–£115.

STANSTED Essex   Map 2:C4

Oak Lodge, Jacks Lane, Smiths Green, Takeley, CM22 6NT. *Tel* 01279-871667, www.oaklodgebb.com. In tranquil village setting, 2 miles SE of airport: B&B in Tudor-style 16th-century house, run by 'welcoming' owners Jan and Ron Griffiths. Lounge, breakfast room. Wi-Fi. No background music. 2-acre garden. Parking (moderate long-term rates). 4 bedrooms. B&B £30–£50 per person. Dinner (by arrangement) £19.

STOKE CANON Devon   Map 1:C5

Barton Cross Hotel, Huxham, EX5 4EJ. *Tel* 01392-841245, www.thebartoncrosshotel.co.uk. Brian Hamilton's 'very quiet, peaceful' hotel, converted from 3 thatched 14th-century cottages. 4 miles N of Exeter, off A396. Full of character: low beams, gallery, inglenook fireplaces. Lounge, bar, candlelit restaurant (English with French flavour). No background music. 'Accommodation and food both very good. Excellent breakfast. I gave the porridge 11/10.' 2-acre garden. Parking. 9 bedrooms (2 on ground floor). B&B £49–£90 per person; D,B&B £79–£105.

STRATFORD-UPON-AVON Warwickshire   Map 3:D6

White Sails, 85 Evesham Rd, CV37 9BE. *Tel* 01789-264326, www.white-sails.co.uk. Former nursing home, rejuvenated by Roy and Janet Emerson into upmarket B&B, 15 mins' walk from centre. Tasteful decor (creams, whites, colourful touches). Lounge, dining room. Garden. No background music. Wi-Fi. 4 bedrooms. B&B £47.50–£57.50 per person.

SWAY Hampshire   Map 2:E2

The Nurse's Cottage, Station Road, nr Lymington, SO41 6BA. *Tel* 01590-683402, www.nursescottage.co.uk. Restaurant-with-rooms in small house, once the home of successive district nurses. 'Hands-on' owner/manager Tony Barnfield. 'Den' (computer, ironing, books, CDs, DVDs, videos), conservatory restaurant; shop selling local goods. Background music. Wi-Fi. 5 bedrooms (some on ground floor; good accessibility). D,B&B £90–£105 per person.

SWINDON Wiltshire   Map 2:C2

Chiseldon House Hotel, New Road, Chiseldon, SN4 0NE.
Tel 01793-741010, www.chiseldonhousehotel.co.uk. 'In a very quiet,
pleasant location', 5 miles SE of Swindon, convenient for M4 Junction
15: wisteria-covered, Italianate style, Grade II listed country house.
Owned by John Sweeney, it 'gets on with the job of providing a good
night's lodging unobtrusively and well'. Lounge, bar, *Orangerie*
restaurant (Robert Harwood is chef); mellow background jazz; terrace;
extensive gardens. Civil wedding licence. Conference facilities.
Children welcomed (some restrictions in restaurant). 21 bedrooms.
£55–£90 per person. Dinner from £19.95.

The Landmark Hotel, Station Road, Chiseldon, SN4 0PW.
Tel 01793-740149, www.landmarkhotel.com. In centre of Chiseldon:
light, modern hotel bedecked with flowery hanging baskets. Run by
Trevor Mitchell (owner) and Paul Heal (manager). Lounge/bar area,
restaurant (background music); courtyard; small function facilities. Wi-
Fi. 16 bedrooms (5 with balcony; 5 with courtyard garden access).
B&B £42.50–£50 per person.

TALLAND-BY-LOOE Cornwall   Map 1:D3

Talland Bay Hotel, PL13 2JB. *Tel* 01503-272667, www.
tallandbayhotel.co.uk. 'Splendidly located', in 2½-acre subtropical
gardens, high above bay, 2½ miles SW of Looe. Run by owner/
managers Mary and George Granville. 'Beautiful setting and views.'
Lounge, bar, *Terrace* restaurant (modern cooking by chef Steven
Buick; booking essential). No background music. Country house
decor. Outdoor pool (heated May–Sept), badminton, putting, croquet.
5 mins' walk to beach. Child-friendly. Dogs welcomed. Closed Jan.
23 bedrooms (3 in cottages, 2 in walled garden, 1 near car park). B&B
£47.50–£97.50 per person; D,B&B £72.50–£122.50. ***V***

THIRSK North Yorkshire   Map 4:C4

Oswalds, Front Street, Sowerby, YO7 1JF. *Tel* 01845-523655,
www.oswaldsrestaurantwithrooms.co.uk. Restaurant-with-rooms with
quaint interior, on quiet tree-lined street, a short walk from racecourse.
North Yorkshire national park and Yorkshire dales nearby. Owned by
David Hawkins's IDH group, managed by Mark Dempsey. John Paul
is chef. Lounge, bar, restaurant; background music; function facilities.
Wi-Fi. Parking. Children welcomed. 16 bedrooms (3 in stable block,
5 in old farmhouse; 1 suitable for &). B&B £35–£100 per person;
D,B&B £47.50–£115.

THORPE ST ANDREW Norfolk   Map 2:B5
The Old Rectory, 103 Yarmouth Road, NR7 0HF. *Tel* 01603-700772, www.oldrectorynorwich.com. Home of Sally and Chris Entwistle, son James, and Birman cats Rolo and Milli: creeper-clad Georgian rectory (Grade II listed) overlooking River Yare, 2½ miles from Norwich. Drawing room, dining room, conservatory; terrace. Background music. Wi-Fi. Meeting/function facilities. 1-acre garden: unheated swimming pool. 8 bedrooms (3 in coach house; all have bathrobes, LCD TV, CD-player). B&B £65–£95 per person. Dinner £26–£30.

TISBURY Wiltshire   Map 2:D1
The Compasses Inn, Lower Chicksgrove, SP3 6NB. *Tel* 01722-714318, www.thecompassesinn.com. In rural setting off A30, halfway between Salisbury and Shaftesbury: Alan and Susie Stoneham's quaint 14th-century pub (thatched roof, stone-paved path; views; some low ceilings). Separate entrance to plain, light bedrooms. Bar, dining room. Pub grub cooked by Dave Cousin. Garden. No background music. 5 bedrooms (plus 2-bedroom cottage). B&B £42.50–£65 per person. Dinner from £25.

TOTNES Devon   Map 1:D4
Royal Seven Stars, The Plains, TQ9 5DD. *Tel* 01803-862125, www.royalsevenstars.co.uk. Imposing, white 17th-century coaching inn in centre. Recently refurbished in contemporary style by owners Nigel and Anne Way; managed by Margaret Stone. Environment-friendly policy. Local watering hole; light meals available all day. Lounge, 2 bars (background music; log fires in winter); *TQ9* restaurant; alfresco dining; terrace; balcony. Wi-Fi. Business facilities. Civil wedding licence. Children welcomed. Parking. 21 bedrooms (quietest at back). B&B £54.50–£110 per person. Dinner £25.

TUNBRIDGE WELLS Kent   Map 2:D4
Hotel du Vin Tunbridge Wells, 13 Crescent Road, TN1 2LY. *Tel* 01892-526455, www.hotelduvin.com. 'Stylish, reasonably priced, informal.' Chain hotel (Marylebone Warwick Balfour) in 18th-century Grade II listed sandstone mansion with views over Calverley Park. Managed by Robert Morris. Bars, lively bistro; function facilities. No background music. Wi-Fi. 1-acre garden; terrace; *boules*. 'Service, in both Reception and restaurant, was friendly; generally pretty efficient.' Child-friendly. Dogs welcomed. 34 bedrooms: £140–£230. Breakfast £9.95–£13.50. Dinner from £25.

Smart and Simple, 54–57 London Road, TN1 1DS. *Tel* 0845-402 5744, www.smartandsimple.co.uk. Good-value hotel in convenient location near centre. Owned by William Inglis. Views over 'secret' garden (lots of steps down) or town common. Bar, restaurant (*tapas* dishes), conservatory; 3 meeting rooms; small gym (£5 fee). Wi-Fi. Background music. Civil wedding licence. Small car park. 40 bedrooms (some suitable for &), plainly furnished with stylish touches. B&B (continental) £32.50–£85 per person.

TWO BRIDGES Devon   Map 1:D4

Prince Hall Hotel, Dartmoor, PL20 6SA. *Tel* 01822-890403, www.princehall.co.uk. 'A lovely place; wonderful setting.' Cream-painted country house (built 1787) in middle of Dartmoor; panoramic views over West Dart valley. Recently refurbished in traditional style; run by 'delightful' proprietors Fi and Chris Daly. 2 sitting rooms, bar, 'light and airy' dining room (seasonal menus); classical background music in early evening. Dog-friendly. 8 bedrooms. B&B £60–£90 per person; D,B&B £75–£110.

ULLSWATER Cumbria   Map 4: inset C2

The Inn on the Lake, Glenridding, CA11 0PE. *Tel* 017684-82444, www.lakedistricthotels.net. In 15-acre grounds leading to shore, at rugged end of Lake Ullswater ('superb location'): large, traditional, 3-star hotel (Lake District group), managed by Gary Wilson. Lounge, 2 bars, *Lake View* restaurant ('fabulous views'), terrace; background music; conference/function facilities; civil wedding licence. Pitch and putt, croquet, bowls. Children welcomed. 47 bedrooms. B&B £72–£116 per person; D,B&B £97–£140.

UPPINGHAM Rutland   Map 2:B3

The Lake Isle, 16 High St East, LE15 9PZ. *Tel* 01572-822951, www.lakeisle.co.uk. Hotel/restaurant on High Street, in Grade II listed building owned and recently refurbished by Richard and Janine Burton. 'Excellent food; good portions.' Bar, restaurant; background music. Wi-Fi. Courtyard. Limited parking. Child-friendly. Dogs welcomed. 12 bedrooms. B&B £37.50–£65 per person. Dinner from £35.

VENTNOR Isle of Wight   Map 2:E2

The Hambrough, Hambrough Road, PO38 1SQ. *Tel* 01983-856333, www.thehambrough.com. High above harbour (spectacular views), at

S end of Ventnor Bay: *Michelin*-starred restaurant-with-rooms run by chef/*patron* Robert Thompson. Lounge, bar; terrace on 3 levels; background music. Parking. 7 sleek bedrooms (some with balcony). B&B £65–£120 per person; D,B&B £110–£165.

The Royal Hotel, Belgrave Road, PO38 1JJ. *Tel* 01983-852186, www.royalhoteliow.co.uk. Large, elegant, old-fashioned seaside hotel (used by Queen Victoria as annexe to Osborne House). Owned by William Bailey; managed by Jennie McKee. 'Personal, friendly service.' 2 lounges, bar with terrace, restaurant ('high-quality' modern British food); conservatory; resident pianist during peak season weekends; function rooms; civil wedding licence. 2-acre landscaped gardens: heated swimming pool, children's play area. Sandy beach nearby (hilly walk). Parking. 54 bedrooms (some recently refurbished, some suitable for &). B&B £85–£138 per person; D,B&B £141–£174. *V*

WARWICK Warwickshire   Map 3:C6
Northleigh House, Five Ways Road, Hatton, CV35 7HZ. *Tel* 01926-484203, www.northleigh.co.uk. In countryside 4 miles N of Warwick: Viv and Fred Morgan's white-painted B&B, simply decorated. Sitting room (log fire), dining room. Organic breakfasts. No background music. Wi-Fi. 1-acre garden. 7 bedrooms (1 suitable for &). B&B £35–£50 per person. Family-style evening meal by arrangement £7.

WEM Shropshire   Map 3:B5
Old Rectory Hotel, Lowe Hill Road, SY4 5UA. *Tel* 01939-233233, www.oldrectorywem.co.uk. Keith and Kathy Hanmer's handsome Georgian house on edge of Shropshire town, managed by their daughter, Selina Cuss. Refurbished in traditional style. Bar, lounge, *Orangery* (light snacks), restaurant (high ceiling, sash windows; background music); terrace; small function facilities; civil wedding licence. 3½-acre lawns and walled garden. 14 bedrooms. B&B £45–£90 per person. Dinner from £21.95 (3 courses).

Soulton Hall, nr Wem, SY4 5RS. *Tel* 01939-232786, www.soultonhall.co.uk. Ann and John Ashton's 'excellent' hotel: historic country house (Tudor origins, Grade II* listed; owned by the family since 1556). 2 miles E of Wem. 'Very personal service. Food amazing.' Wood panelling; stone carvings; moated castle mound. Lounge, bar/study, dining room (background music; traditional English and Welsh dishes); function facilities; civil wedding licence. Terrace; courtyard. 500-acre estate: large walled garden; 50 acres woodland; river and brook frontage; working farm. 8 bedrooms (some on ground floor; 2 in coach house, 2 in lodge). B&B £56–£80 per person; D,B&B £80–£100.

WESTON-SUPER-MARE Somerset   Map 1:B6

Beachlands, 17 Uphill Road North, BS23 4NG. *Tel* 01934-621401, www.beachlandshotel.com. Traditional hotel, overlooking sand dunes (beach 300 yds) and 18-hole golf course. Owned by Charles and Beverly Porter. 'Informative, efficient front-of-house.' 2 lounges, bar, restaurant; background music. 10-metre indoor swimming pool, sauna; function/business facilities. Wi-Fi. Garden. Parking. Children welcomed. 21 bedrooms (some on ground floor). B&B £61.62–£100 per person. Dinner £21.50.

Church House, 27 Kewstoke Road, Kewstoke, BS22 9YD. *Tel* 01934-633185, www.churchhousekewstoke.co.uk. Jane and Tony Chapman's 'immaculate' B&B, in peaceful setting by Norman church. Georgian house with Norman origins (former residence of vicar of Kewstoke); plainly elegant inside. Free-range food at breakfast; eggs from own hens). 1½ miles from Weston-super-Mare; sea views to Wales. Lounge, conservatory. No background music. Garden. Wi-Fi. 5 bedrooms. B&B £40–£65 per person. *V*

WEYMOUTH Dorset   Map 2:E1

B+B Weymouth, 68 The Esplanade, DT4 7AA. *Tel* 01305-761190, www.bb-weymouth.com. On promenade: Grade II listed Georgian building: sister hotel of *B+B Belgravia* (see London Shortlist). Contemporary accommodation at affordable rates. 10 mins' walk from station, town centre, ports. Lounge (sea views; complimentary tea/coffee; computer), breakfast room. No background music. Wi-Fi. Free bicycles. 23 bedrooms (plus 3-bed apartment). B&B £42.50–£89 per person.

WHITBY North Yorkshire   Map 4:C5

Bagdale Hall, 1 Bagdale, YO21 1QL. *Tel* 01947-602958, www.bagdale.co.uk. Steeped in character: central hotel in 3 historic buildings, owned by John Cattaneo, managed by Michael Fagg. Lounge, bar, restaurant. No background music. Children welcomed. 6 bedrooms in *The Hall* (Tudor manor house: mullioned windows, beamed ceilings, carved wooden over-mantles; four-poster beds). 8 bedrooms in *No 4* (Georgian town house). 12 bedrooms in *The Lodge* (detached Georgian mansion with modern furnishings). 1 room suitable for &. B&B £30–£75 per person. Dinner £20–£35.

Dunsley Hall, Dunsley, YO21 3TL. *Tel* 01947-893437, www. dunsleyhall.com. Traditional hotel run by owner Bill Ward in Victorian mansion built for shipping magnate. In hamlet 3 miles NW of Whitby. Oak panelling, stained-glass window with seafaring scene, inglenook fireplace, four-posters. Lounge, *Pyman's* bar (background music), restaurant. Function facilities; civil wedding licence. 4-acre landscaped gardens: putting, croquet, tennis; hotel's working farm nearby; sea 1 mile. Parking. 26 bedrooms (8 in new wing; 1 suitable for &). B&B £65–£120 per person; D,B&B £87.50–£107. *V*

WINCHESTER Hampshire   Map 2:D2

Lainston House, Sparsholt, SO21 2LT. *Tel* 01962-776088, www. lainstonhouse.com. 2½ miles NW of city by B3049: luxury hotel (Exclusive Hotels collection) with environmental policy. 17th-century building in 'superb' 63-acre grounds (12th-century chapel ruin; dovecote; sundial garden). Managed by Cliff Hasler. Wood panelling; four-poster beds; smart bathrooms; elegant, traditional style. Drawing room, *Cedar* bar, *Avenue* restaurant (award-winning chef, Andy MacKenzie); terrace (alfresco dining); gym; tennis; croquet; function facilities; civil wedding licence. No background music. Children welcomed. Fishing (River Test), shooting packages. 50 bedrooms (4 in courtyard or stables; some suitable for &): £62.50–£285. Breakfast £15–£20.

Hotel du Vin Winchester, 14 Southgate Street, SO23 9EF. *Tel* 01962-841414, www.hotelduvin.com. The first Hotel du Vin, now part of Marylebone Warwick Balfour group (also owners of Malmaison hotels). Grade II listed Queen Anne house near cathedral, managed by Mark Jones. Drawing room (stuffed animal head over fireplace), champagne bar, lively bistro; terrace. Civil wedding licence. No background music. 24 bedrooms (4 quietest ones in walled garden): £165–£225. Breakfast £9.95–£13.50. Dinner from £25.

The Wykeham Arms, 75 Kingsgate Street, SO23 9PE. *Tel* 01962 853834, www.fullershotels.com. In oldest part of city, between college and cathedral: 250-year-old inn. Owned by Fuller's brewery; managed by Dennis and Ann Evans. Old curving doors open directly on to bar; series of eating places radiates off; tables are old college desks. Contemporary cooking. 7 bedrooms above the pub (some are small, some may hear noise), 7 in annexe across street. B&B £47.50–£75 per person. Dinner from £17.95.

WINDERMERE Cumbria   Map 4: inset C2

Cedar Manor, Ambleside Road, LA23 1AX. *Tel* 015394-43192, www. cedarmanor.co.uk. 'A great bolt hole.' On outskirts: Caroline and Jonathan Kaye's hotel dominated by 200-year-old cedar tree. Built 1854 as private country retreat. Lounge, dining room (light background music during meals). Walled garden. 'Good, proper food, ideal for guests who have been walking all day.' Children welcomed. 11 bedrooms (2, noisier, in coach house). B&B £31.50–£75 per person; D,B&B £44–£100. *V*

1 Park Road, 1 Park Road, LA23 2AW. *Tel* 015394-42107, www. 1parkroad.com. 'A great base for exploring the lakes': Mary and Philip Burton's small guest house in residential area 2 mins' walk from centre. Lounge (grand piano), dining room (locally sourced food). Background music ('a key point of life here') at dinner, sometimes at breakfast. Picnic hamper/rucksack available. Wi-Fi. Children welcomed. Parking. 6 bedrooms. B&B £40–£55 per person; D,B&B £65–£80.

WOODSTOCK Oxfordshire   Map 2:C2

The Feathers, Market Street, OX20 1SX. *Tel* 01993-812291, www.feathers.co.uk. Smart hotel, managed by Luc Morel: former 17th-century coaching inn near Blenheim Palace. 'Impeccable service; delicious food; breakfast a delight.' 'A rabbit warren', lots of steps. Antiques, paintings, log fires. Drawing room, study, bar, restaurant, bistro (background jazz); function facilities; beauty treatments; pretty garden/patio (alfresco dining). 20 individual, 'comfy' bedrooms (1 suite has private steam room). B&B £47.50–£162.50 per person; D,B&B £87.50–£202.50.

YORK North Yorkshire   Map 4:D4

Bar Convent, 17 Blossom Street, YO24 1AQ. *Tel* 01904-643238, www.bar-convent.org.uk. Simple accommodation in England's oldest active convent (sisters of the Congregation of Jesus) in Georgian building (Grade I listed) near Micklegate. Managed by Joanne Dodd. Communal self-catering facilities, sitting area on each floor. Lounges, games room; licensed café; meeting rooms, museum, shop, 18th-century domed chapel (weddings); function facilities. Lift to 1st/part of 2nd floor. No background music. Garden. 18 bedrooms (some suitable for &; beds upgraded this year). B&B (continental) £32–£37.50 per person. Full English breakfast £3.50.

The Bloomsbury, 127 Clifton, YO30 6BL. *Tel* 01904-634031, www. bloomsburyhotel.co.uk. Dawn and Paul Fielding's 'welcoming' guest house: Victorian building in leafy area, 12 mins' walk from minster. Dining room: vegetarian/special diets catered for. No background music. Wi-Fi. Flowery courtyard. Parking. 9 bedrooms. B&B £30–£65 per person.

Hotel du Vin York, 89 The Mount, YO24 1AX. *Tel* 01904-557350, www.hotelduvin.com. Just outside city walls: 19th-century Grade II listed building (former orphanage). Atmospheric, dark decor; lots of wood, candles; freestanding baths. Bar (large selection of malts), bistro (Nico Cecchella is chef); courtyard (alfresco dining); background music; function facilities; 3-acre grounds. Limited parking. 44 bedrooms (some suitable for &): £165–£395. Breakfast £9.95–£13.50. Dinner from £25.

SCOTLAND

ABERDEEN   Map 5:C3
The Marcliffe Hotel and Spa, North Deeside Road, Pitfodels, AB15 9YA. *Tel* 01224-861000, www.marcliffe.com. Large, luxury country house in lower Dee valley, 20 mins' drive from airport/centre. Owned by Stewart Spence, managed by John Davidson. Lift. Drawing room, lounge, snooker room, bar, conservatory restaurant; terrace (alfresco meals); Mike Stoddard is chef. 24-hour room service. No background music. Spa (treatments); gym. Wedding/function facilities. 8-acre wooded grounds: putting. 42 bedrooms (1 suitable for &; complimentary soft drinks and snacks). B&B £75–£225 per person; D,B&B £122.50–£142.50.

ACHILTIBUIE Highland   Map 5:B1
Summer Isles Hotel, IV26 2YG. *Tel* 01854-622282, www. summerisleshotel.com. In 'beautiful, remote location', overlooking Atlantic Ocean, 'croft-style' hotel/restaurant now owned by Terry and Irina Mackay; Duncan Evans appointed manager in 2009. Chef Chris Firth-Bernard (*Michelin* star for his 5-course menus) remains from previous regime. Lounge, bar; garden. Dogs welcomed. 3 bedrooms in main house; log cabin sleeps 4; stone croft sleeps 2; cottage sleeps 4. B&B £70–£130 per person. Dinner £54.

ARDUAINE Argyll and Bute   Map 5:D1
Loch Melfort Hotel, by Oban, PA34 4XG. *Tel* 01852-200233, www.lochmelfort.co.uk. On Asknish Bay ('superb' views of islands of

Jura, Shuna and Scarba): Victorian country hotel with new, 'hands-on' owners Calum and Rachel Ross. Sitting room, library, bar, *Arduaine* restaurant (locally caught seafood), bistro. No background music. 17-acre gardens (part-owned by National Trust). 25 bedrooms (all with balcony or terrace and sea views; 20 in annexe; 10 have wheelchair access). B&B £49–£104 per person; D,B&B £69–£129. *V*

ARISAIG Highland   Map 5:C1

Cnoc-Na-Faíre, Back of Keppoch, PH39 4NS. *Tel* 01687-450249, www.cnoc-na-faire.co.uk. Simple, small hotel with lively atmosphere and 'gorgeous views', 1 mile from village, on Road to the Isles. Run by owners Jenny and David Sharpe. Lounge/bar/café (Internet; light lunches, suppers; views over sea to Skye), restaurant (Scottish theme); background music; wedding facilities (marquee); house parties. Complimentary dram before retiring. Substantial breakfast (can be in bed). Children welcomed; dogs by arrangement (£5 charge for charity). Parking; bicycle storage. 6 bedrooms (plaid fabrics; Wi-Fi, no telephone). B&B £45–£65 per person. Dinner £25–£30.

ASCOG Argyll and Bute   Map 5:D1

Balmory Hall, PA20 9LL. *Tel* 01700-500669, www.balmoryhall.com. On Isle of Bute, overlooking Ascog Bay (seal colony): elegant B&B in secluded Victorian mansion (Grade A listed), run by owners Tony and Beryl Harrison. Country house decor; house-party atmosphere. Lounge, dining room. No background music. No stiletto heels. 6-acre grounds (deer, owls, hawks). 5 mins' walk to beach (seal colony). 3 bedrooms (plus self-catering lodge). B&B £55–£85 per person.

BALLYGRANT Argyll and Bute   Map 5:D1

Kilmeny Country House, Isle of Islay, PA45 7QW. *Tel* 01496-840668, www.kilmeny.co.uk. Traditional, white-painted 19th-century house on working farm, in elevated position ½ mile S of village: 'spectacular views' over countryside and moorland. Owner Margaret Rozga offers 'wonderful' dinners (Tues and Fri only), enormous breakfasts. 'Warm welcome, with complimentary tea and cakes.' No background music. Sitting room, sun room; garden. 5 bedrooms (1 with separate entrance). B&B £60–£70 per person. Dinner £35.

BOWMORE Argyll and Bute   Map 5:D1

Harbour Inn and Restaurant, The Square, Isle of Islay, PA43 7JR. *Tel* 01496-810330, www.harbour-inn.com. Whitewashed old inn by harbour of village on E side of Loch Indaal, managed by owners Neil and Carol Scott. Light, fresh decor. Conservatory lounge, *Schooner* bar, restaurant (seasonal specialities; 'mellow' background music). Wi-Fi. Small garden. 11 bedrooms (some in neighbouring *Inn Over-by*). B&B £57.50–£72.50 per person.

CASTLEBAY Western Isles   Map 5: inset A1

Castlebay Hotel, Isle of Barra, HS9 5XD. *Tel* 01871-810223, www. castlebayhotel.com. Overlooking Kisimul Castle, harbour and island of Vatersay: Terry MacKay's small hotel, managed by John Campbell, on southernmost of the Western Isles. 'Easy access from Oban.' Lounge, bar, restaurant (fish/seafood specialities); conservatory/ sun porch; background music. ¼-acre garden. Children welcomed. Lively pub next door. 15 bedrooms (1 suitable for &). B&B £38.50–£71 per person; D,B&B £15 added. ***V***

The Craigard Hotel, Isle of Barra, HS9 5XD. *Tel* 01871-810200, www.craigardhotel.co.uk. Helpful owner Julian Capewell's small, white hotel on hillside above town: 'breathtaking views' of bay and southern islands. Lounge, 2 bars (pool table), restaurant (local seafood specialities: cockles, scallops, line-caught fish-of-the-day); terrace (panoramic views). Beach airport 6 miles away; town and ferry terminal close by. Parking. 7 bedrooms. B&B from £40 per person.

CRIANLARICH Perthshire   Map 5:D2

West Highland Lodge, FK20 8RU. *Tel* 01838-300283, www. westhighlandlodge.com. In elevated position (views E to Ben More, Stob Binnein and surrounding countryside): 'superb' B&B in low-built, white Victorian lodge in Loch Lomond and Trossachs national park, 'We were made most welcome' by hosts, Paul and Jen Lilly. 6-acre garden. Free pick-up service from Crianlarich and Tyndrum. B&B from £30 per person. Dinner £15.

DORNOCH Highland   Map 5:B2

Dornoch Castle Hotel, Castle Street, IV25 3SD. *Tel* 01862-810216, www.dornochcastle.com. Opposite cathedral: 15th-century castle with modern extension. Colin Thompson is manager. Bar, restaurant (Scottish cooking by Brian Sangster; background music); walled garden. 'Cosy', traditional decor; some four-poster beds. 21 bedrooms (some in garden wing). B&B £42.50–£117 per person; D,B&B £67.50–£142.

DUNDEE   Map 5:D3

Apex City Quay Hotel & Spa, 1 West Victoria Dock Road, DD1 3JP. *Tel* 01382-202404, www.apexhotels.co.uk. In city quay development ('stunning' views over River Tay): 5-storey modern dockside hotel, unprepossessing outside; stylishly contemporary within. *Metro* bar/brasserie, *Alchemy* restaurant; *Yu* spa: gym, sauna, hot tubs, treatments; conference/events centre; background music throughout. Wi-Fi; complimentary newspaper. Children welcomed. 152 bedrooms: £45–£120 per person. Breakfast £10. Dinner £19.95.

Duntrune House, Duntrune, DD4 0PJ. *Tel* 01382-350239, www.duntrunehouse.co.uk. Family history enthusiasts Barrie and Olwyn Jack's B&B in lovingly restored stately home (1826). Part of Green Business Tourism Scheme. In 8-acre grounds and woodland, 5 miles NE of city; views over River Tay. Sitting room, breakfast room. Dinner by arrangement. No background music. Wi-Fi. Parking. Children welcomed. Closed Nov–Mar. 4 bedrooms (1 on ground floor; all with garden view). B&B £35–£50 per person; D,B&B £55–£70.

DUNOON Argyll and Bute   Map 5:D1

Hunters Quay Hotel, Marine Parade, PA23 8HJ. *Tel* 01369-707070, www.huntersquayhotel.co.uk. On Cowal Peninsula: Graham and Christine Togwell's stately, listed seafront Victorian villa. 'Huge' lounge, restaurant (Scottish cooking). 'Excellent dinner; massive breakfast.' No background music. Garden, mature woodland. Wi-Fi. Wedding/conference facilities. 10 bedrooms (some with panoramic views of River Clyde). B&B £49–£85 per person; D,B&B from £73.50.

EDINBURGH   Map 5:D2

Acer Lodge, 425 Queensferry Road, EH4 7NB. *Tel* 0131-336 2554, www.acerlodge.co.uk. Gillian and Terry Poore's homely B&B in suburban house 3 miles W of centre ('wonderful bus service: 15 mins to Princes Street'); ample parking. No background music. Wi-Fi. Children welcomed. 5 bedrooms (some on ground floor). B&B £25–£45 per person.

Apex City Hotel, 61 Grassmarket, EH1 2JF. *Tel* 0131-243 3456, www.apexhotels.co.uk. Large, contemporary hotel in Old Town (castle/city skyline views). *Agua* bar, restaurant (seafood); background music; conference facilities. Spa at *Apex International* hotel next door (ozone pool, sauna, gym). Parking. 119 bedrooms: £42.50–£185 per person. Breakfast £10. Dinner £19.95.

Glenora Guest House, 14 Rosebery Crescent, EH12 5JY. *Tel* 0845-180 0045, www.glenorahotel.co.uk. Victorian town house in quiet Haymarket district, refurbished in understated modern style. Wendy Phillips is manager. Reception, breakfast room. Eco-friendly; organic produce used. No background music. Wi-Fi. 11 bedrooms. B&B £35–£75 per person.

The Howard, 34 Great King Street, EH3 6QH. *Tel* 0131-557 3500, www.thehoward.com. Discreet luxury hotel (Town House Collection) in 3 Georgian houses on cobbled New Town street. Managed by Fiona McIlroy. Dedicated butler, chauffeur service. Drawing room, intimate *Atholl* restaurant (background music; traditional Scottish fare; William Poncelet is chef); room-service meals. Parking. 18 bedrooms. B&B £82.50–£142.50 per person; D,B&B £112.50–£177.50.

Malmaison, 1 Tower Place, Leith, EH6 7DB. *Tel* 0131-468 5000, www.malmaison.com. 10 mins' drive from centre, overlooking Leith harbour, on cobbled street: boldly converted 19th-century seamen's mission, managed by William Verhoeven. Stylish, colourful interior. Café/bar (lots of mirrors), brasserie ('home-grown and local' food); terrace (alfresco dining); meeting/function facilities; fitness room; background music. Wi-Fi. Free parking. 100 bedrooms: £49.50–£179. Breakfast £11.95–£13.95.

Prestonfield, Priestfield Road, EH16 5UT. *Tel* 0131-225 7800, www.prestonfield.com. In Royal Holyrood Park by Arthur's Seat. Restaurateur James Thomson's flamboyantly decadent hotel (17th-century mansion), managed by Alan McGuiggan. Sumptuous decor; state-of-the-art equipment. Complimentary champagne on arrival. 2 drawing rooms, 2 bars, *Rhubarb* restaurant; 4 private dining rooms; background music; Wi-Fi; lift; function facilities; terrace; 'Gothic' tea house; 20-acre garden/parkland surrounded by golf course; croquet, putting; bicycles. Dogs welcomed. (See also *The Witchery by the Castle*, next page.) Parking. 23 bedrooms (1 suitable for &). B&B £112.50–£175 per person. Dinner £60.

Six Mary's Place, Raeburn Place, EH4 1JH. *Tel* 0131-332 8965, www.sixmarysplace.co.uk. 'Super' guest house. In Stockbridge area, 10 mins' walk from centre: tastefully modernised Georgian building (1829), managed by Muriel Campbell. 'Rooms of enormous comfort and quietness; reasonably priced; convenient location.' Lounge, conservatory (vegetarian breakfasts); meeting room; awards for green tourism. 'Helpful atmosphere.' Lounge. Garden. No background music. Wi-Fi. 8 bedrooms. B&B £49–£70 per person. *V*

Tigerlily, 125 George Street, EH2 4JN. *Tel* 0131-225 5005, www.tigerlilyedinburgh.co.uk. In 'fantastic location' (shops, restaurants nearby), buzzy hotel in Georgian house, managed by David Hall. Glamorous, ultra-modern design; gadgetry. 2 bars (opulent *Lulu* bar: booths, revolving glitter balls, beaded curtains; and club below, crowded at weekends), restaurant (background music). Wi-Fi. 33 bedrooms. B&B £97.50–£225 per person.

Windmill House, 21 Coltbridge Gardens, EH12 6AQ. *Tel* 0131-346 0024, *email* windmillhouse@btinternet.com. Four-square Georgian house (Wolsey Lodge B&B), in rural hilltop setting overlooking Water of Leith. Handsomely furnished by Michael and Vivien Scott (interior designer). 'We felt like family guests.' Drawing room, dining room, terrace, garden. No background music. 2-acre grounds: waterfall, weir, ducks, swans, 17th-century windmill. 3 bedrooms. B&B £55–£75 per person.

The Witchery by the Castle, Castlehill, EH1 2NF. *Tel* 0131-225 5613, www.thewitchery.com. By castle gates: atmospheric restaurant-with-suites in 2 adjacent 16th-century buildings at top of Royal Mile. Owned by restaurateur James Thomson (see *Prestonfield*, previous page), managed by Steve Hall. Gothic style: ornate red and gold paintwork; decadent drapery; sybaritic bathrooms. 2 restaurants (Douglas Roberts uses Scottish produce; background music); terrace. 7 suites (in 2 buildings): £295 (includes continental breakfast, bottle of champagne).

ELGIN Moray   Map 5:C2
Mansion House Hotel & Country Club, The Haugh, IV30 1AW. *Tel* 01343-548811, www.mansionhousehotel.co.uk. A short walk to centre: 19th-century baronial mansion in large grounds, on banks of River Lossie. Owned by David Baker; managed by Lynn Macdonald. Country house interior; four-poster beds. Piano lounge, snooker room, bar, restaurant, bistro. Background music. Leisure club (indoor swimming pool, sauna, steam room; treatments; gym); snooker; function/business facilities. Parking. 23 bedrooms (some interconnecting). B&B £74.50–£96 per person; D,B&B £97–£118.50. ***V***

FORT WILLIAM Highland   Map 5:C1
Huntingtower Lodge, Druimarbin, PH33 6RP. *Tel* 01397-700079, www.huntingtowerlodge.com. Chris and Jackie Clifford's low-built, eco-friendly lodge, 2 miles SW of Fort William, with panoramic views of Loch Linnhe (sightings of seabirds, porpoise, otter and seal), Stronchreggan hamlet on the far shore, and Ardgour hills. Light,

contemporary interior; some low sloping walls in bedrooms. 'Extremely well-appointed rooms, beautiful environment.' Lounge (CD/DVD library); drying facilities; garaging for bicycles. No background music. Home-baked biscuits, cakes and bread. 4-acre woodland: wild-flower garden, waterfall, roe deer, red squirrel, pine marten. Wi-Fi. Complimentary transport into town by arrangement. 4 bedrooms. B&B £45–£130 per person.

Inverlochy Castle, Torlundy, PH33 6SN. *Tel* 01397-702177, www.inverlochycastlehotel.com. 'Almost perfect; worth every penny.' Baronial pile (built 1863) in foothills of Ben Nevis, 4 miles N of Fort William. Managed by Calum Milne; Philip Carnegie is executive chef. 'Dinner elaborate; breakfast excellent, plenty of choice.' Lavishly embellished interior: Great Hall (Venetian chandeliers, frescoed ceiling), drawing room, dining rooms (live classical music at night), billiard room; terrace; weddings, conferences, etc. 500-acre grounds: tennis, loch, fishing. Children welcomed; dogs by arrangement. 17 bedrooms. B&B £122.50–£320 per person. Dinner £64.

FORTROSE Highland   Map 5:C2

The Anderson, Union Street, by Inverness, IV10 8TD. *Tel* 01381-620236, www.theanderson.co.uk. On cathedral square: 1840s building now award-winning restaurant-with-rooms, run by American owners Jim and Anne Anderson (she cooks). Public bar (real ales), *Whisky* bar (*tapas* menu; over 200 single malts), dining room (Scottish fare). Cosy atmosphere; wood-burning stove; quirky touches. Background music. Wi-Fi. Beer garden. Parking. Sandy beach 1¼ miles. 9 bedrooms (redecorated in 2008). B&B £40–£49 per person. Dinner £35.

GATEHOUSE OF FLEET   Map 5:E2
Dumfries and Galloway

The Bank of Fleet, 47 High Street, DG7 2HR. Tel 01557-814302, www.bankoffleet.co.uk. On edge of Galloway Forest Park: small budget hotel run by chef/manager Ian Hogg. Extensive choice of food; simple decor. Bar/restaurant (inglenook fireplace) overlooking walled garden (alfresco eating); small function facilities; background music. 6 bedrooms. B&B £32.50–£65 per person. Dinner £20.

GIGHA Argyll and Bute   Map 5:D1

Gigha Hotel, Isle of Gigha, PA41 7AA. *Tel* 01583 505254, www.gigha.org.uk. White hotel by ferry terminal on community-owned island off Mull of Kintyre (views over Ardminish Bay). Owned by island Trust;

managed by Colin Johnston. Lounge, bar (occasional background music), restaurant (Scottish fare: prawns, clams, lobsters, lamb, beef, Gigha cheese; Libby Donaldson is chef). Garden (alfresco eating). Wedding/function facilities. Log fires in winter. 13 simple, spacious bedrooms. B&B £48 per person. Dinner £25–£30.

GLASGOW   Map 5:D2
Malmaison, 278 West George Street, G2 4LL. *Tel* 0141-572 1000, www.malmaison.com. Converted Greek Orthodox church in financial district. Managed by Scott McKie. Notable Art Nouveau iron sculpted central staircase; huge vaulted ceilings. Bold colours, stripes; prints and black-and-white photographs. Lift. Bar, lounge, brasserie; background music. Dogs welcomed. 72 bedrooms: £160–£210. Breakfast £13.95. Dinner £23–£30.

GLENFINNAN Highland   Map 5:C1
The Prince's House, by Fort William, PH37 4LT. *Tel* 01397-722246, www.glenfinnan.co.uk. Traditional coaching inn (1658) in rural village, 17 miles W of Fort William: useful stopover for Glenfinnan Viaduct and monument/Mallaig ferries. Run by chef/proprietor Kieron Kelly ('exciting menu; outstanding crème brûlée with cherries') and his 'welcoming' wife, Ina. Lounge, bar, restaurant; classical background music. 'Breakfast excellent, very generous.' Closed Jan–Mar. 9 bedrooms. B&B £42.50–£65 per person. D,B&B £72.50–£95. ***V***

GRANTOWN-ON-SPEY Highland   Map 5:C2
Ravenscourt House, Seafield Avenue, PH26 3JG. *Tel* 01479-872286, www.ravenscourthouse.co.uk. Edwardian stone-built country house (former Church of Scotland manse) in quiet location on edge of Cairngorms national park. Run by owners Andrew and Sheena Williamson and son Mark. Traditional decor. 2 lounges, conservatory restaurant (classical background music). Over 50 malt whiskies. Small garden. 8 bedrooms. B&B £30–£90 per person; D,B&B from £50.

INVERNESS Highland   Map 5:C2
Culloden House, IV2 7BZ. *Tel* 01463-790461, www.cullodenhouse. co.uk. 'Near faultless accommodation; great food; relaxed, comfortable style.' Palladian country house, managed by mother and son, Pat and Steven Davies, in 40-acre parkland. Grand interior: Adam plasterwork, chandeliers. Scottish specialities from chef Michael Simpson. Lounge,

dining room (classical background music); wedding/corporate facilities. 25 lavish, traditionally furnished bedrooms. B&B £125–£187.50 per person. Dinner from £28.

Dunain Park, IV3 8JN. *Tel* 01463-230512, www.dunainparkhotel. co.uk. Secluded 19th-century Italianate country mansion 2 miles from centre. Part of Classic British Hotels organisation; managed by Suzy Rankin. Elegant Scottish country house decor with modern slant. 2 lounges, restaurant (modern Scottish cuisine); terrace (alfresco dining); drying room. No background music. 6-acre grounds: 2 walled gardens, woodland, croquet, badminton. 15 bedrooms (4 in garden cottages). B&B £45–£130 per person. Dinner £45.

Glenmoriston Hotel, 20 Ness Bank, IV2 4SF. *Tel* 01463-223777, www.glenmoristontownhouse.com. 'Brilliantly situated for walk into centre': Barry Larsen's riverside hotel. Lounge, piano bar. *Contrast* brasserie (river views; alfresco dining in summer), *Abstract* restaurant; function facilities. Wi-Fi. Garden. 30 smart, 'well-equipped, comfortable' bedrooms (1 suitable for ♿) in 2 separate buildings. B&B £47.50–£95 per person; D,B&B £60–£132.

KELSO Borders   Map 5:E3

The Cross Keys, 36–37 The Square, TD5 7HL. *Tel* 01573-223303, www.cross-keys-hotel.co.uk. 'Delightful owners and staff. Straightforward, well-prepared food.' Former coaching inn (built 1769) on cobbled town square. Run by Becattelli family since 1981. Lift. Lounge, *No. 36* bar, restaurant (Scottish and international dishes); contemporary background music. Conference facilities. Child-friendly. Dogs welcomed. 26 bedrooms. B&B £35–£52 per person; D,B&B £46–£67. *V*

KILDRUMMY Aberdeenshire   Map 5:C3

Kildrummy Castle Hotel, by Alford, AB33 8RA. *Tel* 01975-571288, www.kildrummycastlehotel.co.uk. 35 miles W of Aberdeen, by ruins of 13th-century castle and Kildrummy Castle gardens, gabled, castellated house with fine interior: ornate panelled walls and ceilings, carved oak staircase. Owned by Jayne and Frans Faber (in charge of the kitchen, he is Dutch). 'Good choice in his menus'; exotic touches. Drawing room, library, bar, restaurant. Gardens ('in fine condition'). Small wedding/function facilities. Child-friendly. Dogs welcomed. Private trout/salmon fishing on Rover Don, 2 miles. 16 bedrooms. B&B £69.50–£90 per person. Dinner £33.50.

KIRKCUDBRIGHT Dumfries and Galloway   Map 5:E2
The Marks, DG6 4XR. *Tel* 01557-330854, www.marksfarm.co.uk.
Sheila Watson and Chris Caygill's B&B in 16th-century dower
house cradled by Galloway hills, 4 miles E of town. Drawing
room, study, breakfast room. No background music. Rambling
gardens (woods, loch, walks, stabling; on national cycle route 7). By
working farm with sheep, dairy herd, worms (for organic waste
management, fishing, composting). 3 bedrooms. B&B £30–£35 per
person. D,B&B £55.

LARGOWARD Fife   Map 5:D3
The Inn at Lathones, KY9 1JE. *Tel* 01334-840494, www.theinn.
co.uk. Cluster of modern buildings around 400-year-old single-storey
coaching inn, in hamlet 5 miles W of St Andrews. Owned by Nick
White; Morag Peattie manages. Lounge, bar, restaurant; background
music; live gigs; music memorabilia on walls. Chef Richard
Brockenbury serves modern European dishes. Function facilities.
Child-friendly. Dogs welcomed. 21 'nice' bedrooms. B&B £45–
£122.50 per person. Dinner £35. *V*

LOCKERBIE Dumfries and Galloway   Map 5:E2
The Dryfesdale, Dryfebridge, DG11 2SF. *Tel* 01576-202427,
www.dryfesdalehotel.co.uk. Useful staging post near border, 1 mile
from centre, near M74 exit 17: Best Western hotel in former
manse, managed by owner Glenn Wright. Lounge, *Malt* bar,
Kirkhill restaurant; conference/function facilities; background music.
5-acre grounds. Child-friendly; pets welcomed. 28 bedrooms (some
patio rooms suitable for &). B&B £55–£75 per person; D,B&B
£77.50–£170.

LYBSTER Highland   Map 5:B3
The Portland Arms, KW3 6BS. *Tel* 01593-721721, www.
portlandarms.co.uk. 'Welcoming entrance hall; good atmosphere.'
Old coaching inn (1850s) on outskirts of fishing village, 12 miles
SW of Wick; ½ mile from sea. Convenient stop-over for Orkney
ferry. Pedro Matra-Grano is the new owner/manager. Large lounge,
library, bistro/bar, restaurant ('straightforward, home-cooked food');
wedding/function facilities. No background music. Small front garden.
22 bedrooms. B&B £43–£110 per person.

MELROSE Borders   Map 5:E3

Burts, Market Square, TD6 9PL. *Tel* 01896-822285, www.burtshotel.co.uk. Owned by Henderson family for over 35 years: listed 18th-century building (black-and-white facade; window boxes) on square. 2 lounges, bar (over 90 malt whiskies), restaurant (head chef Trevor Williams serves modern British dishes; 'the best roast fillet of pork I have tasted'); classical background music. ½-acre garden. Parking. 20 bedrooms. B&B from £70 per person; D,B&B from £95.

The Townhouse, Market Square, TD6 9PQ. *Tel* 01896-822645, www.thetownhousemelrose.co.uk. 'Thoroughly recommended': smartly renovated building (white-painted exterior), in town square, opposite Henderson family's other hotel, *Burt's* (above). 'Very efficient; great attention to detail.' Brasserie, restaurant (Scottish fusion food); conservatory; background music; patio; wedding/function facilities. 11 bedrooms. B&B £62–£100 per person. Dinner £25–£31.50.

MONTROSE Angus   Map 5:D3

Links Hotel, Mid Links, DD10 8RL. *Tel* 01674-671000, www.linkshotel.com. Grand Edwardian town house (Best Western member, managed by Kasper Ninteman), on historic Mid Links, within walking distance of 3-mile sandy beach. Fine entrance hall; imposing staircase; stained-glass windows. Bar, *Koffiehuis* bistro, restaurant (open-view kitchen: Frank Rivault cooks Scottish and French dishes of 'outstanding quality'); background music; folk, jazz and classical evenings; function facilities. Wi-Fi. 25 bedrooms. B&B from £39.50 per person; D,B&B from £62.

NORTH BERWICK East Lothian   Map 5:D3

The Glebe House, 4 Law Road, EH39 4PL. *Tel* 01620-892608, www.glebehouse-nb.co.uk. Overlooking seaside town: Gwen and Jake Scott's B&B in listed, elegantly proportioned, Georgian manse (1780). 2 mins' walk to beach and centre. Sitting room, dining room. 2-acre secluded garden. Parking. 3 bedrooms. B&B £25 per person.

OBAN Argyll and Bute   Map 5:D1

dun na mara, Benderloch, PA37 1RT. *Tel* 01631-720233, www.dunnamara.com. By the sea: Mark and Suzanne McPhillips's guest house, a 'gorgeous retreat'. Elegantly decorated Edwardian building with white-painted exterior, on edge of village 8 miles N of Oban (views to Mull). 'Amazing! Contemporary, chic, comfortable.' Sitting room, dining room ('delicious breakfast'). No background music. Wi-Fi. Informal gardens leading to private beach. 7 bedrooms (1st floor, no lift). B&B £47.50–£70 per person.

PEEBLES Borders   Map 5:E2
Cringletie House, off Edinburgh Road, EH45 8PL. *Tel* 01721-725750, www.cringletie.com. Luxury hotel, 2 miles N of town, owned by Jacob and Johanna van Houdt, managed by Jeremy Osborne. Turreted, pink stone Victorian baronial mansion on 28-acre wooded estate. Lift. Lounge, library, bar, dining room (spectacular painted ceiling; Craig Gibb is chef); background music. Wi-Fi. Walled garden; outdoor chess; *pétanque*. Child-friendly. Dogs welcomed. 12 bedrooms (1 suitable for &.). B&B £87.50–£185 per person; D,B&B £125–£160. *V*

Park Hotel, Innerleithen Road, EH45 8BA. *Tel* 01721-720451, www.parkpeebles.co.uk. A short walk from town: gabled, white building (McMillan Hotels), with views of Peeblesshire hills. Managed by Jo Williamson; Jenny Thomson is chef. Lift. Lounge, bar (background music), restaurant. Garden: putting. Access to sports/health facilities at large sister hotel, *Peebles Hydro* (700 yds): swimming pool, sauna, tennis, etc. 24 bedrooms. B&B £38.50–£84 per person; D,B&B £46–£99.

PERTH Perth and Kinross   Map 5:D2
The Parklands, 2 St Leonard's Banks, PH2 8EB. *Tel* 01738-622451, www.theparklandshotel.com. On edge of South Inch Park (views across River Tay to Kinnoull Hill), 5 mins' stroll into town: well-equipped hotel run by owners Scott and Penny Edwards. Lounge, bar, *Acanthus* restaurant, *Number 1 The Bank* bistro; function facilities; light background music. Wi-Fi. Terrace. Garden leading to park. Dogs welcomed. 15 bedrooms. B&B £49.50 per person; D,B&B £59.50–£149. *V*

Sunbank House, 50 Dundee Road, PH2 7BA. *Tel* 01738-624882, www.sunbankhouse.com. By River Tay, Remigio (chef) and Georgina Zane's Victorian house in landscaped gardens, 2 miles E of centre. Traditionally furnished. Italian-influenced dishes using Scottish produce. Lounge/bar, restaurant (light classical background music). Wi-Fi. 9 bedrooms (some on ground floor). B&B £35–£79 per person. Dinner £27.50.

PITLOCHRY Perth and Kinross   Map 5:D2

Craigatin House & Courtyard, 165 Atholl Road, PH16 5QL. *Tel* 01796-472478, www.craigatinhouse.co.uk. 'Lovely' B&B in Martin and Andrea Anderson's 1820s house in secluded wooded grounds, 5 mins' walk from town. Dining room; conservatory. Background music. Terrace; courtyard; garden. 'Courteous owners and staff. Well appointed. Interesting breakfast menu. Good value.' 13 bedrooms (6 in courtyard; 1 suitable for &). B&B £32.50–£50 per person. *V*

Green Park, Clunie Bridge Road, PH16 5JY. *Tel* 01796-473248, www.thegreenpark.co.uk. 'Our favourite hotel in the Highlands.' In 'superb position' on Loch Faskally (putting, fishing, boat hire): traditional country hotel, on N edge of town. The McMenemie family owners 'are everywhere, putting problems right before they happen'. 3 lounges, library, bar, restaurant. 'Food consistently excellent.' Popular with older visitors. No background music. Child-friendly. Dogs welcomed. 3-acre garden. 51 bedrooms. B&B £58–£70 per person; D,B&B £70–£95. *V*

Pine Trees, Strathview Terrace, PH16 5QR. *Tel* 01796-472121, www.pinetreeshotel.co.uk. Above town: Kerr family's classically furnished Victorian mansion in 'well-kept' 7-acre grounds. Lounge, bar, *Garden* restaurant (Scottish fare). 'Good food; speedy, efficient service; sensible wine list.' Background music. 20 bedrooms. B&B £47–£67 per person; D,B&B £67–£87.

PORT CHARLOTTE Argyll and Bute   Map 5:D1

Port Charlotte Hotel, Main Street, Isle of Islay, PA48 7TU. *Tel* 01496-850360, www.portcharlottehotel.co.uk. In 'lovely' position on waterfront (sandy beach) of pretty conservation village, Grahame and Isabelle Allison's small hotel. Lounge (polished floors, oriental rugs), live traditional music in bar, restaurant (booking advisable). 9 of the 10 bedrooms have sea views. B&B £75–£95 per person. Dinner £35.

PORTREE Highland   Map 5:C1

Cuillin Hills Hotel, Isle of Skye, IV51 9QU. *Tel* 01478-612003, www.cuillinhills-hotel-skye.co.uk. Secluded in 15-acre wooded grounds overlooking Portree Bay: 'old-style' hotel. Gabled, white-walled former Victorian hunting lodge owned by small Wickman group, managed by Peter Sim. Lounge, bar ('good food, well served'), restaurant (seasonal cooking from Robert MacAskill); background music. 26 bedrooms (some on ground floor; 7 in annexe). B&B £100–£300 per person. Dinner £35.

ST ANDREWS Fife   Map 5:D3

Rufflets, Strathkinness Low Road, KY16 9TX. *Tel* 01334-472594, www.rufflets.co.uk. Turreted, white, baronial-style mansion (built in 1920s for Dundee jute baron), in award-winning gardens just outside 'home of golf'. Owned by Ann Murray-Smith; managed by Stephen Owen. Mix of traditional with chic contemporary design. Drawing room, music room, bar, *Terrace* restaurant (chef Mark Nixon: modern Scottish cooking; local, seasonal produce); background music; wedding/function facilities; 10-acre grounds. Children welcomed. 24 bedrooms (3 in *Gatehouse*; 2 in *Lodge*; 1 suitable for &). B&B £50–£120 per person; D,B&B £85–£155.

SCARISTA Western Isles   Map 5:B1

Scarista House, Isle of Harris, HS3 3HX. *Tel* 01859-550238, www.scaristahouse.com. In remote position (views over the Atlantic): handsome white Georgian manse, 15 miles SW of Tarbert. Managed by Tim and Patricia Martin (co-owners with Neil King). Drawing room, library (open fires), dining room (home-cooked food). No background music. 1-acre garden: trampoline. 3-mile sandy beach nearby. Children welcomed. 5 bedrooms (2 self-catering units adjacent). B&B £87.50–£99.50 per person. Dinner £49.50.

SCOURIE Highland   Map 5:B2

Eddrachilles Hotel, Badcall Bay, IV27 4TH. *Tel* 01971-502080, www.eddrachilles.com. 'Wonderful location'; 'spectacular views'. 2 miles S of village, in area of outstanding natural beauty: white-painted old manse above bay, owned by Isabelle and Richard Flannery. 'A gastronomic delight in a wild area.' Stone walls, flagstone floors. Reception, conservatory, bar (125 single malt whiskies), restaurant (French/Scottish food, local produce where possible, seafood; extensive wine list); classical background music. Children welcomed. Wi-Fi. 4-acre garden; 60-acre grounds. 11 bedrooms. B&B £45–£48 per person; D,B&B £62–£65.

Scourie Hotel, IV27 4SX. *Tel* 01971-502396, www.scourie-hotel.co.uk. Above Scourie Bay: Patrick and Judy Price's fishing hotel (old coaching inn). 2 lounges, 2 bars, *table d'hôte* restaurant. No background music; no TV; radios on request. 7-acre grounds leading to sea (5 mins' walk to sandy beach); 36 fishing beats exclusive to guests, plus 3 beats on lochs Stack and More (sea trout and salmon). 20 bedrooms (bay or mountain views; 2 family rooms in garden). B&B £33–£37 per person; D,B&B £53–£58.

STRACHUR Argyll and Bute   Map 5:D1

The Creggans Inn, PA27 8BX. *Tel* 01369-860279, www.creggans-inn.co.uk. In 'fantastic location', Archie and Gill MacLellan's informal inn on shores of Loch Fyne. 2 lounges, bar (background music), 2 restaurants ('food excellent'): Gordon Smillie is chef. 2-acre garden. 'Hands-on owners; we felt well looked after.' Children welcomed. 14 bedrooms. B&B £59–£90 per person; D,B&B £80–£120. *V*

STRATHYRE Perth and Kinross   Map 5:D2

Creagan House, FK18 8ND. *Tel* 01877-384638, www.creaganhouse. co.uk. 'Outstanding' restaurant with 'comfortable, well-appointed bedrooms' in Gordon and Cherry Gunn's quietly situated, renovated 17th-century farmhouse. He is the award-winning chef, she the 'caring' front-of-house. Baronial dining hall (grand fireplace; antiques). 'Breakfast coffee particularly good; toast made from home-baked bread; home-made marmalade.' Lounge, restaurant; private dining room. No background music. Landscaped gardens. ¼ mile N of village. 5 bedrooms (1 on ground floor). B&B £60–£90 per person; D,B&B £89.50–£119.50. *V*

SWINTON Borders   Map 5:E3

The Wheatsheaf at Swinton, Main Street, TD11 3JJ. *Tel* 01890-860257, www.wheatsheaf-swinton.co.uk. Opposite village green: Chris and Jan Winson's old stone-built country roadside inn. 10 miles SW of Berwick-upon-Tweed. Seasonal, locally sourced food cooked by Scott MacIntyre. 2 lounges, 2 dining rooms; background music; conservatory; small garden. Children welcomed. 10 spruce, simply furnished bedrooms (1 suitable for ♿). B&B £39–£95 per person; D,B&B £69–£125. *V*

TARBERT Western Isles   Map 5:B1

Hotel Hebrides, Pier Road, Isle of Harris, HS3 3DG. *Tel* 01859-502364, www.hotelhebrides.com. By pier, Angus and Chirsty Macleod's hotel given muted, contemporary look. Loch and harbour views. *Pierhouse* restaurant (Richard Agnew and his partner, Lisa Healy, use seasonal, local ingredients). Wi-Fi. Conference facilities. Children welcomed. 21 bedrooms. B&B £55–£60 per person. Dinner from £25.

TAYNUILT Argyll and Bute   Map 5:D1

Roineabhal Country House, Kilchrenan, PA35 1HD. *Tel* 01866-833207, www.roineabhal.com. Smart, small country guest house near Loch Awe: family home of Roger and Maria Soep. Lounge, dining room (4-course dinners; booking advisable; background music at night); covered veranda. 2-acre garden. Afternoon teas. Child-friendly; pets welcomed. 18 miles E of Oban. 3 bedrooms (1 on ground floor). B&B £45–£60 per person. Dinner £40.

THORNHILL Dumfries and Galloway   Map 5:E2
Trigony House, Closeburn, DG3 5EZ. *Tel* 01848-331211, www.countryhousehotelscotland.com. Former shooting lodge for Closeburn Castle, 1 mile S of Thornhill, now informal country hotel run by owners, mother and son Jan and Adam (the chef) Moore. 'Friendly, relaxed atmosphere.' Lounge, bar (background music), dining room (organic rustic cuisine). 'Excellent food; welcoming staff.' Wood-burning stoves. 4-acre grounds: walled garden. Wi-Fi. Dog-friendly (resident Labrador). Children welcomed. Country activities organised. 10 plain, light bedrooms (1 on ground floor). B&B £45–£95 per person; D,B&B £70–£120. *V*

TOBERMORY Argyll and Bute   Map 5:D1
The Tobermory Hotel, Main Street, PA75 6NT. *Tel* 01688-302091, www.thetobermoryhotel.com. On Isle of Mull: 'perfectly situated', popular waterfront hotel on bay: converted row of colourful fishermen's cottages, owned and managed by Ian and Andi Stevens; Helen Swinbanks is chef. Simple accommodation. 2 lounges, bar, *Water's Edge* restaurant; drying facilities. Background music. 'Food and service good.' Packed lunches available. Child-friendly. Dogs welcomed. 'Fantastic views.' Landscape photography workshops. 16 'cottagey' bedrooms (most with sea view; 1 suitable for &). B&B £38–£61 per person; D,B&B £61.50–£92.50. *V*

ULLAPOOL Highland   Map 5:B2
Riverview, 2 Castle Terrace, IV26 2XD. *Tel* 01854-612019, www.riverviewullapool.co.uk. In village: Nadine Farquhar's B&B. 'Clean, quiet; perfect location; great breakfast.' Open-plan lounge/dining area with views. Flexible breakfast time. Evening meal by arrangement. No background music. Free Wi-Fi; DVD library. Complimentary use of leisure centre. 'Nadine makes you feel at home.' 3 modern bedrooms (creams, browns; white linen). B&B £28–£35 per person. *V*
The Sheiling, Garve Road, IV26 2SX. *Tel* 01854-612947, www.thesheilingullapool.co.uk. By shore of Loch Broom: 'value-for-money' B&B, Iain and Lesley MacDonald's modern, white, low-roofed home, 5 mins' walk from town. Light, contemporary interior. Lounge (log

fire), breakfast room (Scottish fare). Background radio. Sauna; drying room. 1-acre garden; patio; loch and mountain views; fishing permits. 6 bedrooms. B&B £33–£45 per person.

WALES

ABERGAVENNY Monmouthshire   Map 3:D4
The Angel Hotel, 15 Cross Street, NP7 5EN. *Tel* 01873-857121, www.angelhotelabergavenny.com. Lively social hub in centre: old coaching inn managed by owners William and Charlotte Griffiths. Sitting room, *Foxhunter* bar, restaurant (Mark Turton is chef); occasional 'easy listening' background music; function facilities; civil wedding licence. Wi-Fi. Courtyard. Children welcomed. 34 bedrooms (2 in *The Mews* annexe, 2 in *The Lodge* 2 mins' walk). B&B £42.50–£100 per person. Dinner £35.

BARMOUTH Gwynedd   Map 3:B3
Llwyndu Farmhouse Hotel, Llanaber, LL42 1RR. *Tel* 01341-280144, www.llwyndu-farmhouse.co.uk. Peter (who cooks: 'bang up to date', using local produce) and Paula Thompson's hotel/restaurant: white-painted, Grade II-listed farmhouse and surrounding buildings (1585–early 1600s), overlooking Cardigan Bay. 2 miles N of town. 'Sympathetically restored', quirky interior: beams, inglenook fireplaces, sloping ceilings, four-poster beds. Lounge, restaurant (occasional soft classical background music); 3-acre garden. Child-friendly. 7 bedrooms (4 in converted granary; dogs welcomed). B&B £47–£50 per person. Dinner £28 (3 courses).

BRECON Powys   Map 3:D3
Cantre Selyf, 5 Lion Street, LD3 7AU. *Tel* 01874-622904, www.cantreselyf.co.uk. Homely B&B run by owners Helen and Nigel Roberts. 17th-century sandstone town house (Grade II* listed) near St Mary's church. Lounge, dining room (traditional Welsh/continental breakfast; local organic produce). 1-acre walled garden. No background music. Parking. 3 bedrooms (beamed ceilings, Georgian fireplaces, cast iron beds). B&B £35–£80 per person.

CAERNARFON Gwynedd   Map 3:A2
Plas Dinas Country House, Bontnewydd, LL54 7YF. *Tel* 01286-830214, www.plasdinas.co.uk. Grade II listed gentleman's residence with extensive Victorian additions, former country home of

Armstrong-Jones family, managed by 'amiable, witty' owners Andy and Julian Banner-Price. Handsomely refurbished (traditional/contemporary mix; antiques and royal memorabilia). Drawing room, dining room (closed Sun/Mon; background music). Wi-Fi. Small function facilities; civil wedding licence. 15-acre wooded grounds. No children under 12. Dogs welcomed (£10 charge). 10 bedrooms (1 suitable for &). B&B £54.50–£199 per person. Dinner £25–£30. *V*

CARDIFF   Map 3:E4
The Big Sleep, Bute Terrace, CF10 2FE. *Tel* 02920-636363, www.thebigsleephotel.com. In converted 1960s block (former British Gas office building): budget B&B hotel, ½ mile from station. Owned by Cosmo Fry with consortium including John Malkovich; managed by Claire Musa. Retro/minimalist decor (much Formica). Good views over city from top floors. Lift. Residents' bar, breakfast room; background music; conference room. Wi-Fi. Limited parking. 81 bedrooms (some family; some suitable for &). B&B (continental) £29–£99 per person.

CRICKHOWELL Powys   Map 3:D4
The Manor, Brecon Road, NP8 1SE. *Tel* 01873-810212, www.manorhotel.co.uk. 'Smashing' views over valley and River Usk. In Brecon Beacons national park, ¼ mile from town: white-painted 18th-century manor house, owned by Glyn and Jess Bridgeman and Sean Gerrard, managed by Roger Francis. Lounge, bar, bistro (locally reared, organic meat, mainly from family farm, 7 miles away); background music; leisure suite (indoor swimming pool, sauna, steam room, whirlpool, gym); conference facilities; civil wedding licence. 22 bedrooms. B&B £37.50–£80 per person; D,B&B £67.50–£110.

ERWOOD Powys   Map 3:D4
Trericket Mill, LD2 3TQ. *Tel* 01982-560312, www.trericket.co.uk. Converted corn mill (Grade II listed) 9 miles SE of Builth Wells, overlooking River Wye. Run as guest house by welcoming owners Nicky and Alistair Legge. Interesting interior (grain bins, gear wheels, chutes, shafts). Environmentally considerate, 'cosy, not luxurious'. 2 lounges (wood-burning stove; lots of games), dining room ('delicious' vegetarian cooking; vegans catered for; BYO wine). No background music. 3 simple bedrooms in *Veggie Guest House* plus 3 basic rooms in bunkhouse; also riverside campsite. B&B £30–£36.50 per person; D,B&B £48–£54.50.

FISHGUARD Pembrokeshire   Map 3:D1

The Manor Town House, 11 Main Street, SA65 9HG. *Tel* 01348-873260, www.manortownhouse.com. Georgian Grade II listed town house near market square, recently taken over by Helen and Chris Sheldon (his mother runs *Ynyshir Hall*, Eglwysfach, see main entry). 'Spectacular views' from garden and 4 bedrooms. Complimentary tea and home-made cake on arrival. 2 lounges, breakfast room (local, free-range produce; classical background music); walled garden (terrace). Children welcomed. A gate at the bottom of the garden leads to the Coast Path. Nearest parking 150 yards; safe sea bathing 2 miles. 6 bedrooms. B&B £37.50–£45 per person.

HAVERFORDWEST Pembrokeshire   Map 3:D1

Crug-Glas, Abereiddy, Solva, SA62 6XX. *Tel* 01348-831302, www.crug-glas.co.uk. On 600-acre mixed working farm, 1½ miles inland from Pembrokeshire coast: Perkin and Janet Evans's elegantly furnished family home (heirlooms). 2 drawing rooms (videos, books), bar; small restaurant (classical background music). 1-acre garden. 7 bedrooms (2 suites in converted coach house). B&B £50–£65 per person. Dinner £25.

College Guest House, 93 Hill Street, St Thomas Green, SA61 1QL. *Tel* 01437-763710, www.collegeguesthouse.com. Close to centre: Georgian town house B&B (Grade II listed; former college for Baptist ministers), run by owners Colin Larby and Pauline Good. Lounge (tea/coffee available all day), dining room (Welsh breakfast); background music. Wi-Fi. Parking. Small garden. Swimming pool 100 yds; beach 6 miles. 8 bedrooms (some family). B&B £34–£56 per person.

HAY-ON-WYE Powys   Map 3:D4

The Old Black Lion, Lion Street, HR3 5AD. *Tel* 01497-820841, www.oldblacklion.co.uk. 400-year-old coaching inn near Lion Gate, 3 mins' walk from centre: popular eaterie, owned by Dolan Leighton, managed by her daughter, Julie Davies. Bar (oak timbers, scrubbed pine tables, comfy armchairs), restaurant (Peter Bridges is the long-serving chef). No background music. Garden. 10 quirky bedrooms (beams, uneven floors, low ceilings; 1 with gallery). B&B £45–£57.50 per person; D,B&B £70–£82.50.

LAMPETER Ceredigion   Map 3:D3

Tŷ Mawr Mansion, Cilcennin, SA48 8DB. *Tel* 01570-470033, www.tymawrmansion.co.uk. Peaceful retreat, 4 miles E of Aberaeron:

Grade II-listed country house, elegantly restored by owner/managers Catherine and Martin McAlpine. Ramps, 3 lounges, library, restaurant (chef Jeremy Jones uses Welsh produce, mainly from garden/within 10-mile radius; 'easy listening' background music); 30-seat cinema. Wi-Fi. 12-acre mature grounds. 9 bedrooms (1 suite on ground floor in annexe). B&B £80–£160 per person. Dinner £24.95.

LLANARMON DYFFRYN CEIRIOG   Map 3:B4
Denbighshire
The West Arms, LL20 7LD. *Tel* 01691-600665, www.thewestarms. co.uk. By River Ceiriog: 16th-century building in hamlet 7 miles SW of Llangollen. Owned by 'charming hosts' Lee and Sian Finch and Grant Williams (the chef). 'Beautifully cooked' food. 'Scrambled eggs at breakfast deserve special mention.' Inglenook fireplaces, original beams. Lounge, 2 bars (meal service), restaurant (traditional Welsh fare with modern twist); 'mellow' background music; conservatory; conference/function facilities. 1-acre garden facing Berwyn Mountains. Children welcomed. 15 bedrooms (1 suitable for &). B&B £43.50–£112.50 per person; D,B&B £70–£144.

LLANDEGLA Clwyd   Map 3:B4
Bodidris Hall, LL11 3AL. *Tel* 01978-790434, www.bodidrishall.com. In 'glorious countryside': 650-year-old creeper-covered stately home, refurbished by owners David and Stephanie Booth. 2 miles from village. Approached by mile-long drive through 6,500-acre estate with lake. Mullioned windows, oak beams, priest hole, chapel, duelling stair. Lounge, library, 'baronial' restaurant ('excellent food': head chef Brian Eccles); classical background music. Conference facilities; shoots. Civil wedding licence. Complimentary use of spa at sister hotel, *The Wild Pheasant*, Llangollen. 9 bedrooms. B&B £49.95–£89.95 per person; D,B&B £105–£117.50.

LLANDEILO Carmarthenshire   Map 3:D3
Fronlas, 7 Thomas Street, SA19 6LB. *Tel* 01558-824733, www.fronlas.com. Sleek B&B in Edwardian town house, run on ecological lines, 'without skimping on luxury', by owners Eva and Owain Huw. Rural location, 5 mins' walk from centre. Lounge, dining room (organic breakfasts; background music). Garden. Children welcomed. 3 bedrooms (all with views over Tywi valley to Brecon Beacons). B&B £40–£100 per person.

LLANDUDNO Conwy   Map 3:A3

The Lighthouse, Marine Drive, Great Orme's Head, LL30 2XD. *Tel* 01492-876819, www.lighthouse-llandudno.co.uk. Fiona Kilpatrick's unique B&B: clifftop lighthouse, built in castle style in 1862. 2 miles from centre, in Great Orme country park. Keeper's Hall with pitch pine panelling and gallery. Welsh breakfast in Victorian dining room: visitors can look down 100-metre vertical drop. No background music. 3 bedrooms, all with lounge or sitting area (Lamp Room has panoramic views). B&B £75–£95 per person.

Osborne House, The Promenade, 17 North Parade, LL30 2LP. *Tel* 01492- 860330, www.osbornehouse.co.uk. 'Very personal' seafront hotel with sumptuous decoration, owned by Elyse and Michael (the chef) Waddy with Len and Elizabeth Maddocks. 'Very nice staff; excellent food.' Lounge, bar, café/grill (chandeliers, candles, drapes, portraits; brasserie-style cooking); background music. Wi-Fi. 6 suites (sea views; gas fire). Parking. Use of pool and spa at *Empire Hotel* close by. B&B £72.50–£100 per person. Dinner from £21. ***V***

LLANDYRNOG Denbighshire   Map 3:A4

Pentre Mawr, LL16 4LA. *Tel* 01824-790732, www.pentremawr countryhouse.co.uk. Carrington-Sykes family's home for 400 years, offering country house accommodation, and luxury canvas lodges in grounds (oak floor, bathroom with freestanding bath and shower, super-king-size leather bed, hot tub). Graham and Bre Carrington-Sykes also run *Sychnant Pass House*, Conwy (main entry). 2 sitting rooms, restaurant (background music). Walled garden; heated swimming pool; 200 acres of meadow, park, woodland. 10 bedrooms (each named after 1 of TS Eliot's 'Practical Cats'; 3, opened in 2009, in 'canvas lodges'). B&B £47.50–£75 per person; D,B&B £80–£105.

LLANGOLLEN Denbighshire   Map 3:B4

Gales, 18 Bridge Street, LL20 8PF. *Tel* 01978-860089, www. galesofllangollen.co.uk. Owned for over 30 years by Gale family: 'Hotel, Food and Wine Bar' in 18th-century town house 20 yds off main street. Reception in wine shop cellar. Chunky wood furniture, carved bedheads, beams. Popular wine bar (background music); conference facilities; gift shop. Wi-Fi. Small patio area; car park. Children welcomed. 15 bedrooms (8 above wine bar; others in older building; 1 suitable for &). B&B (continental) £35–£65 per person. Cooked breakfast £5. Dinner £30. ***V***

LLANRWST Conwy   Map 3:A3

Meadowsweet, Station Road, LL26 0DS. *Tel* 01492-642111, www.wales-snowdonia-hotel.co.uk. Mary and Nelson Haerr's large, yellow-painted hotel (views of open countryside) in small market town on edge of Snowdonia national park. Lounge, bar, *Lle Hari* restaurant (traditional Welsh food); background music. Hearty breakfast. Courtyard. Wi-Fi. Children welcomed. 10 bedrooms. B&B £40–£100 per person. Dinner £28.

LLANWRTYD WELLS Powys   Map 3:D3

Lasswade Country House, Station Road, LD5 4RW. *Tel* 01591-610515, www.lasswadehotel.co.uk. In foothills of Cambrian Mountains, with 'breathtaking' views: peaceful, 'unassuming' Edwardian house on outskirts of UK's smallest town. Managed with green emphasis by owners, Roger and Emma Stevens. Traditionally furnished. Drawing room, library, restaurant; conservatory/function room. No background music. Garden: kennels. Children welcomed. Parking. 8 bedrooms. B&B £37.50–£55 per person; D,B&B £69.50–£87. ***V***

MUMBLES Swansea   Map 3:E3

Patricks with Rooms, 638 Mumbles Road, SA3 4EA. *Tel* 01792-360199, www.patrickswithrooms.com. On bay (beautiful views), 5 miles SW of Swansea: restaurant-with-rooms owned and managed by Catherine and Patrick (the chef) Walsh, and Sally (Catherine's sister) and Dean Fuller. Contemporary interior. Lounge/bar, restaurant; background music; gym; greenhouse for herbs. Children welcomed. Sea 200 yds. 16 sea-facing bedrooms (all different). B&B £55–£150 per person. Dinner £30 (3 courses).

NEWTOWN Powys   Map 3:C4

The Forest Country Guest House, Gilfach Lane, Kerry SY16 4DW. *Tel* 01686-621821, www.bedandbreakfastnewtown.co.uk. In Vale of Kerry: secluded, white-painted Victorian house, home of Paul and Michelle Martin, their 2 children and assorted pets. 3 miles SE of Newtown (train and bus stations). Drawing room, dining room; kitchenette; games room. No background music. Wi-Fi. 4-acre garden; play area; tennis. Child-friendly; dogs welcomed (kennels); stabling available. 5 bedrooms (plus 3 holiday cottages in outbuildings). B&B £35–£45 per person.

PENARTH Cardiff   Map 3:E4
Holm House, Marine Parade, CF64 3BG. *Tel* 029-2070 1572, www.holmhouse.com. Glamorous spa hotel in 1920s mansion behind esplanade (views over Bristol Channel). 15 mins' drive from Cardiff. Sophisticated decor (foil wallpaper, wooden floors, freestanding copper baths) created by owners Susan Sessions (also manager) and Margaret Hewlett. Lounge/bar, restaurant (new chef, Chris Lelliott); background jazz; spa: indoor 7.5-metre hydrotherapy pool; ¾-acre garden. 12 bedrooms (2 on courtyard; 1 suitable for &). B&B £82.50–£177.50 per person; D,B&B £100–£202.50. *V*

PONTDOLGOCH Powys   Map 3:C3
The Talkhouse, Caersws, SY17 5JE. *Tel* 01686-688919, www.talkhouse.co.uk. Low, whitewashed roadside coaching inn, 5 miles S of Newtown. Owners Stephen (the chef, 'superlative food') and Jacqueline Garratt 'could not have been more welcoming'. Lounge, bar (beams, log fires), 2 dining rooms ('easy listening' background music). Garden. 3 'cosy' bedrooms. B&B £62.50–£70 per person. Dinner £27–£35.

RUTHIN Denbighshire   Map 3:A4
Manorhaus, Well Street, LL15 1AH. *Tel* 01824-704830, www.manorhaus.com. In Grade II listed Georgian building off main square: boutique hotel/art gallery owned by Christopher Frost and Gavin Harris. Interior designed in collaboration with contemporary Welsh artists whose work is displayed. Lounge, bar, *à la carte* restaurant, library; 'easy listening' background music; cinema; fitness room, sauna, steam room; seminar/meeting facilities. Children welcomed. Parking nearby. 8 bedrooms. B&B £50–£75 per person; D,B&B £77.50–£97.50.
The Wynnstay Arms, Well Street, LL15 1AN. *Tel* 01824-703147, www.wynnstayarms.com. Historic, half-timbered coaching inn (1549) in centre, owned by Kelvin Clayton (manager), Jason Jones (chef) and their wives. Contemporary comforts within. Lounge, bar, *Fusions* brasserie (home-made and local food); background music. Children welcomed. Parking. 6 bedrooms. B&B (continental) £32.50–£55 per person; D,B&B £49.50–£72.50. *V*

ST DAVID'S Pembrokeshire   Map 3:D1
Old Cross Hotel, Cross Square, SA62 6SP. *Tel* 01437-720387, www.oldcrosshotel.co.uk. Traditional stone-built hotel in centre,

owned by Alex and Julie Babis, managed by Janet Davies. 2 lounges, bar (popular with locals; TV for sports events; background radio), restaurant. Garden: alfresco meals in summer. Child-friendly. Dogs welcomed. Parking. 16 bedrooms. B&B £35–£65 per person; D,B&B £57.50–£87.50.

SWANSEA   Map 3:E3
Morgans, Somerset Place, SA1 1RR. *Tel* 01792-484848, www. morganshotel.co.uk. Imaginatively modernised hotel in converted Regency Port Authority building (Grade II* listed) in centre. Owned by Martin and Louisa Morgan; managed by Christine Owen. Bar, restaurant (emphasis on Welsh produce); background music; lift; fitness room; exclusive events/function facilities; civil wedding licence. Courtyard. Parking. 41 bedrooms (21, cheaper, in *Morgans Townhouse* opposite). 'Daring double showers.' B&B £42.50–£170 per person. Dinner £25.

TALYLLYN Gwynedd   Map 3:B3
Tynycornel, Tywyn, LL36 9AJ. *Tel* 01654-782282, www.tynycornel. co.uk. 'Stunning views; service and food excellent.' Traditional hotel, managed by Mair Jones, beside 222-acre Talyllyn Lake, popular with anglers. Both owned by Milmar Leisure Ltd. Lounge (lake views), bar, restaurant (local produce; background music). Packed lunch available. Civil wedding licence. 22 bedrooms (9 in annexe). B&B £40–£65 per person; D,B&B £65–£90. *V*

CHANNEL ISLANDS

BRAYE Alderney   Map 1: inset D6
Braye Beach Hotel, Braye Street, GY9 3XT. *Tel* 01481-824300, www.brayebeach.com. Stylishly modernised beachfront hotel converted from old pirates' warehouses, 15 mins' walk from Alderney's main town, St Anne. Owned by Derek Coate; Scott Chance is manager/chef. 'High standards without pretension.' Lounge, bar, restaurant (local and French produce); decked terrace; private cinema; Wi-Fi; background music. Special-interest breaks. 27 bedrooms (some with balcony, sea views). B&B £60–£120 per person; D,B&B £25 added.

KINGS MILLS Guernsey   Map 1: inset D5
Fleur du Jardin, Grand Moulins, Castel, GY4 7JT. *Tel* 01481-257996, www.fleurdujardin.com. Pub/restaurant-with-rooms, revitalised by Ian

and Amanda Walker (owners of *Bella Luce*, St Martin, below). Bleached wood walls; sandstone bathrooms; wet rooms. 10 mins' bus ride to town; 10 mins' walk to beach. Bar, restaurant (David Hayden is chef); background music; health suite (beauty treatments, relaxation rooms). Garden: heated swimming pool, terrace. Children welcomed. 15 bedrooms (2 garden suites). B&B £46–£103 per person. Dinner from £20.

ST HELIER Jersey   Map 1: inset E6

The Club Hotel & Spa, Green Street, JE2 4UH. *Tel* 01534-876500, www.theclubjersey.com. Contemporary, understatedly luxurious spa hotel; convenient location in town. Managed by Tim Phillips. Library, *Club* café, adjacent *Bohemia* restaurant (*Michelin* star); background music ('fairly muted'). Wi-Fi. Spa: saltwater pool, sauna, hydrotherapy bench, treatments. Beaches nearby. Parking. 46 bedrooms (suites have sitting room and balustrade). B&B (continental) £107.50–£222.50 per person. Dinner £49.50.

ST MARTIN Guernsey   Map 1: inset E5

Bella Luce Hotel, La Fosse, GY4 6EB. *Tel* 01481-238764, www.bellalucehotel.com. Manor house (11th-century origins), in scenic area 2 miles SW of St Peter Port, given recent makeover by owners Ian and Amanda Walker (see *Fleur du Jardin*, above). Bar, restaurant; background music; wedding/function facilities. Wi-Fi. Garden (alfresco dining); swimming pool (heated in summer). Rock beach 5 mins' walk. 31 bedrooms (some family, 1 suitable for &). B&B £62–£116 per person; D,B&B £22 added.

ST PETER PORT Guernsey   Map 1: inset E5

The Clubhouse @ La Collinette, St Jacques, GU1 1UT. *Tel* 01481-710331, www.lacollinette.com. Hotel and self-catering accommodation near seafront and centre, run for nearly 50 years by Chambers family owners. Bar, restaurant; background music; DVD library; conference facilities. Garden; heated swimming pool. Children welcomed: children's pool; play area. 30 bedrooms (plus self-catering cottages and apartments): B&B £50–£95 per person. Dinner from £20.

La Frégate, Les Cotils, GY1 1UT. *Tel* 01481-724624, www.lafregatehotel.com. Contemporary interior in 18th-century manor house high above town (views over St Peter Port harbour and neighbouring islands), 2 mins' walk from centre. Managed by Chris Sharp; Neil Maginnis is chef. Lounge, bar, restaurant; terrace; function facilities. No background music. Small, secluded garden. Children welcomed. 22 bedrooms (all with sea views; some with balcony). B&B £80.50–£350 per person. Dinner £30.

ST SAVIOUR Guernsey   Map 1: inset E5
The Farmhouse, Bas Courtils, GY7 9YF. *Tel* 01481-264181, www.thefarmhouse.gg. David and Julie Nussbaumer's country hotel: former farmhouse (part 15th-century). Sophisticated modern interior; luxurious bathrooms. Ankur Biswas cooks 'fantastic' local fresh seafood; Alan Sillett is manager. Bar, restaurant ('easy listening' background music; live music at weekends); courtyard; wedding/conference facilities. Wi-Fi. Large garden; heated swimming pool. Children welcomed. 14 bedrooms. B&B £60–£125 per person. Dinner £28.

SARK Guernsey   Map 1: inset E6
Hotel Petit Champ, via Guernsey, GY9 0SF. *Tel* 01481-832046, www.hotelpetitchamp.co.uk. On west coast headland facing Guernsey (spectacular views, sunsets): low, late Victorian granite building, now owned by John Donnelly. Allan Reid is new chef. 3 sun lounges, library, TV room, bar, restaurant (background music). 15 mins' walk from village. 1-acre garden; solar-heated swimming pool, putting, croquet. Closed Nov–late Apr. 10 bedrooms. B&B £47–£62.50 per person; D,B&B £64.25–£79.75. Dinner £21.50. *V*

IRELAND

BALLINROBE Co. Mayo   Map 6:C5
JJ Gannons Hotel, Main Street. *Tel* 00 353 94-954 1008, www.jjgannons.com. Jay and Niki Gannon (3rd generation) run this central bar/restaurant-with-accommodation. Traditional building (1838) with stylishly refurbished interior: leather seating, wood floors, colourful decor. Lounge, bar, *Red Room* restaurant (views across Lough Mask to Tourmakeady Mountains; herbs, vegetables, fruits from kitchen garden, seasonal, local produce; Cian Mulholland is chef). 'Food straightforward, but fresh and interesting.' Background music. Business facilities. Golf nearby. 10 bedrooms (some suitable for &). €52.50–€150 per person. Dinner €35–€40.

BELFAST   Map 6:B6
Culloden Estate & Spa, Bangor Road, Holywood, BT18 0EX. *Tel* 028-9042 1066, www.hastingshotels.com. Luxury hotel overlooking

Belfast Lough, 6 miles E of city. Former bishop's palace (baronial architecture; modern extension). Owned by Hastings Hotels group; managed by Kem Akkari. Lift. Lounges, *Culloden Mitre* restaurant; background music; spa/health club (indoor swimming pool, whirlpool, steam room, fitness suite); wedding/conference facilities; medieval banquets; after-funeral gatherings. 12-acre grounds: *Cultra Inn*. Children welcomed. 105 bedrooms. B&B £50–£120 per person. Dinner £40.

Malmaison, 34–38 Victoria Street, BT1 3GH. *Tel* 028-9022 0200, www.malmaison-belfast.com. Near River Lagan in cathedral quarter (edge of centre): 'stylish', contemporary conversion of 2 red brick seed warehouses (1860s). Managed by Helen Caters. Iron pillars, beams, gargoyles; sombre tones and lighting. Lounge, bar, brasserie ('surprisingly good food'); background music; gymtonic; small business centre. Wi-Fi. 64 bedrooms: £120–£320. Breakfast £12.95–£13.95.

The Merchant Hotel, 35–39 Waring Street, BT1 2DY. *Tel* 028-9023 4888, www.themerchanthotel.com. Opulent hotel in cathedral quarter: former headquarters of Ulster Bank. Owned by Bill Wolsey; managed by Adrian McLaughlin. Extravagant Victorian Italianate interiors; distinctive striped carpets. Lifts. 2 bars. *The Cloth Ear* (informal eating), *The Great Room* restaurant (stained-glass domed ceiling; Roland Graham is chef); *Ollie's* club; background music; wedding/function facilities. Bentley car for hire. Children welcomed. 26 bedrooms (2 suitable for &). B&B from £110 per person; D,B&B from £160.

Old Inn, Main Street, Crawfordsburn, Co. Down, BT19 1JH. *Tel* 028-9185 3255, www.theoldinn.com. Rice family's old coaching inn (1640), in village 10 miles E of city, on edge of wooded country park that sweeps down to sea. Old-world charm: part-thatched, beamed ceilings, wood-panelled walls. Gallery lounge, *Parlour* bar, conservatory-style *1614* restaurant (Alex Taylor is chef); background music; Wi-Fi. Wedding/function facilities. Small garden. 30 bedrooms (plus garden cottage; 1 suitable for &). B&B (buffet) £57.50–£160 per person.

BLARNEY Co. Cork   Map 6:D5

The Muskerry Arms. *Tel* 00 353 21-438 5200, www.muskerryarms.com. Characterful, yellow-painted, timber-panelled public house-with-rooms in village centre, owned by Nell O'Connor and sons. Wood flooring; soft colour scheme. Lounge, bar (live music; lively *craic*; sporting events on 8 plasma TV screens), *Tavern* restaurant.

Wi-Fi. Parking. 11 bedrooms (some in *Lodge*, reached by walkway).
B&B €33–€49 per person. Dinner from €32.

BUSHMILLS Co. Antrim   Map 6:A6
Bushmills Inn, 9 Dunluce Road, BT57 8QG. *Tel* 028-2073 3000,
www.bushmillsinn.com. On River Bush: old coaching inn and mill
house joined together, recently enlarged by owners Alan and Zoë
Dunlop. Traditional last stop for visitors to Giant's Causeway. Old
parts atmospheric, maze-like; new rooms have mezzanine. Peat fires,
wooden booths. Drawing room, 'secret' library, gallery, loft, 2 bars
(1 lit by gaslight), restaurant in 4 sections; 'Garden Room'; new Irish
cooking; classical background music; courtyard; conference facilities.
3-acre garden. Parking. 41 bedrooms (some on ground floor; spacious
ones in *Mill House*; smaller ones in inn). B&B £69–£118 per person.
Dinner £25–£30.

CASTLEBALDWIN Co. Sligo   Map 6:B5
Cromleach Lodge, via Boyle. *Tel* 00 353 71-916 5155, www.
cromleach.com. Moira and Christy Tighe's purpose-built, recently
enlarged hotel on low hillside above Lough Arrow; 3 miles E of town.
'Fantastic views.' Lounge, *Nuada's* bar, *Moira's* restaurant; classical
background music; spa (sauna, steam room, outdoor whirlpool);
wedding/function facilities. 30-acre grounds: forest walks; private
access to Lough Arrow: fishing, boating, surfing; walking, hill climbing.
Dogs welcomed (dog-grooming parlour). 46 bedrooms. D,B&B €100-
€240 per person.

CLONES Co. Monaghan   Map 6:B6
Hilton Park, Scothouse. *Tel* 00 353 47-56007, www.hiltonpark.ie.
Ancestral home of Madden family (since 1734): imposing Italianate
mansion run in house-party style by Lucy and Johnny with younger
generation, Fred (chef) and Joanna. Imposing interior; antiques.
2 drawing rooms, TV room, breakfast room, dining room (home-grown
herbs, salads, fruit and vegetables). No background music. 4 miles S
of town, on wooded estate: 600-acre landscaped park and gardens with
lakes, 18-hole golf course. Residential art courses. 6 bedrooms. B&B
€125–€150 per person. Dinner (by arrangement) €55. *V*

CONG Co. Mayo   Map 6:C4
Lisloughrey Lodge, The Quay. *Tel* 00 353 94-954 5400, www.
lisloughrey.ie. Overlooking quay (panoramic views of Lake Corrib):

imposing white house in grounds of Ashley Castle. 'Designed in latest boutique style: purple everywhere; *objets d'art* in lobby; digital technology throughout.' *Malt* bar and brasserie, *Salt* restaurant (locally sourced, modern Irish food from chef Wade Murphy); background music. 'Fine nooks and crannies to hide away.' Vault with pool table; Wii games room; private screening room. Beauty treatments. Wedding/function facilities. Wi-Fi. Children welcomed (playroom). 51 bedrooms (in courtyard, linked to main house). B&B €68–€125 per person. Dinner €69.

CRAIGAVON Co. Armagh   Map 6:B6

Newforge House, Magheralin, 58 Newforge Road, *Tel* 028-9261 1255, www.newforgehouse.com. Georgian country house (*c.* 1785) on edge of village, handed down over 6 generations, now owned by John and Louise Mathers. 'Accommodation, hospitality and food of a high order.' 'We enjoyed all that we tried: magnificent fillet of local beef; delectable scrambled eggs'. Muted colour scheme, antiques, log fires. Drawing room, dining room; mature gardens with 40-acre surrounding grassland. Wedding/events facilities. 6 bedrooms. B&B £55–£105. Dinner £32.50 (3 courses; Tues–Sat).

DERRY Co. Londonderry   Map 6:B6

Serendipity House, 26 Marlborough Street, Bogside, BT48 9AY. *Tel* 028-7126 4229, www.serendipityrooms.co.uk. On hill overlooking city walls: cosy, good-value B&B run by friendly owners, Paul and Stephen Lyttle. Original modern art. Lounge, dining room (background music at breakfast); sun deck (panoramic views). Wi-Fi. 5 bedrooms. B&B £30–£60 per person. Dinner from £10.

DINGLE Co. Kerry   Map 6:D4

Milltown House. *Tel* 00 353 66-915 1372, www.milltownhousedingle. com. White, 19th-century gabled house overlooking harbour, on peninsula 3 km W of town. Run as B&B by owners Mark and Anne Kerry and daughter Tara. Lounge, conservatory/breakfast room (light meals available). No background music. 1½-acre garden. Golf driving range, pitch and putt behind house. Parking. 10 bedrooms (some with views of garden or sea). B&B €65–€85 per person.

DONEGAL Co. Donegal   Map 6:B5

Harvey's Point. *Tel* 00 353 74-972 2208, www.harveyspoint.com. Luxury hotel in secluded position on Lough Eske. Run for over

20 years by Gysling family owners with Deirdre McGlone. Elegant dining: gourmet food from chef Paul Montgomery. Lounge, bar, restaurant; ballroom; resident pianist; Irish/classical background music; wedding/conference facilities; beauty treatments. 2-acre garden. 70 bedrooms (some in courtyard). B&B €79–€320 per person. Dinner €59.

DUBLIN   Map 6:C6

Leixlip House, Captain's Hill, Leixlip, Co. Kildare. *Tel* 00 353 1-624 2268, www.leixliphouse.com. Traditionally furnished extended Georgian house overlooking village. Managed by Christian Schmelter. 8 miles NW of Dublin (20 mins by motorway to centre/airport). High ceilings, huge windows, antiques. Lounge, bar (background music), *Bradaun* restaurant (modern Irish cuisine); wedding/function facilities. Wi-Fi. Golf packages. Parking. 19 bedrooms (4 in coach house). B&B €55–€180 per person. Dinner €30 (3 courses).

Merrion Hall, 54–56 Merrion Road, Dublin 4. *Tel* 00 353 1-668 1426, www.halpinsprivatehotels.com. 'Delightful': Pat Halpin's extensively refurbished, creeper-covered Edwardian hotel (see also *Aberdeen Lodge*, main entry), in Ballsbridge, S of centre (DART link). 2 drawing rooms, dining room/conservatory (local and international dishes: 'delicious'); background music; function facilities. Free Wi-Fi. Courtyard, small garden. Parking. 28 bedrooms (2 suitable for &). B&B €74.50–€129 per person. *V*

Waterloo House 8–10 Waterloo Road, Dublin 4. *Tel* 00 353 1-660 1888, www.waterloohouse.ie. Managed by owner Evelyn Corcoran: 'inviting' B&B: 2 Georgian buildings in peaceful Ballsbridge avenue. Lift; ramp. Lounge (classical background music); conservatory. Wi-Fi. Garden. Parking. Irish breakfast includes 'catch of the day'. 17 bedrooms (some suitable for &). B&B €65–€99 per person.

DUNGARVAN Co. Waterford   Map 6:D5

Powersfield House, Ballinamuck West. *Tel* 00 353 58-45594, www.powersfield.com. Eunice Power's (award-winning chef) guest house/cookery school: symmetrical white neo-Georgian house on little peninsula, 1 mile outside Dungarvan. Simply decorated. Background CDs/radio if wanted. Wi-Fi. Garden. Children welcomed. Jams, marmalades, chutneys for sale. Fly fishing on Blackwater River nearby. 6 bedrooms (1 suitable for &). B&B €40–€70 per person. Dinner (by arrangement) €27.50–€35.

GALWAY Co. Galway   Map 6:C5

The g, Wellpark. *Tel* 00 353 91-865200, www.theg.ie. 'A most enjoyable stay.' Spectacularly designed by milliner Philip Treacy: large luxury hotel overlooking Lough Atalia. Edward Holdings manages; Damien O'Riordan is chef. Vibrant jewel colours (pink, cerise, purple; swirling black-and-white striped carpets); glamorous furnishings; arresting black marble lobby. Lift. 4 lounges, champagne-drinking area, *Riva* restaurant (traditional Irish cuisine); 'funky' background music; spa (indoor swimming pool); wedding/function facilities; 'secret' bamboo garden. Children welcomed. 101 rooms. B&B €75–€180 per person. Dinner €60.

KENMARE Co. Kerry   Map 6:D4

Sheen Falls Lodge. *Tel* 00 353 64-41600, www.sheenfallslodge.ie. Former summer residence of Marquis of Lansdowne, now luxury hotel (Relais & Châteaux). 2 miles SE of town (off N71). Extended manor house overlooking waterfall, in 300-acre mature woodlands. Owned by Bent Hoyer; managed by Alan Campbell. Lift. Lounge, sun lounge, library, 2 bars, *Oscar's* bistro, *La Cascade* restaurant; background music; billiard room; terrace; health club (swimming pool, whirlpool, sauna, treatments); tennis. 66 bedrooms. B&B €110–€235; D,B&B from €170.

KILLARNEY Co. Kerry   Map 6:D4

Dunloe Castle, Beaufort. *Tel* 00 353 64-71350, www.dunloecastle hotel.com. 5 miles SW of town: large, modern 5-star hotel, owned by Liebherr family, facing ruins of medieval keep (views of Gap of Dunloe and River Laune: salmon fishing). Managed by Jason Clifford; Franz Josef Osterloh is chef. Lounge, bar, *Oak Room* restaurant; background music/live pianist; indoor swimming pool; wedding/ function facilities. Children welcomed. 64-acre parkland: 20-acre subtropical garden; café, heated swimming pool, sauna, steam room, fitness room, treatment rooms; 2 indoor tennis courts; putting; horse riding. Children welcomed: playground, evening movie show, Wii room. 102 bedrooms. B&B €105–€300 per person; D,B&B from €160. Closed Nov to end Apr. *V*

KINSALE Co. Cork   Map 6:D5

The Old Presbytery, 43 Cork Street. *Tel* 00 353 21-477 2027, www. oldpres.com. Philip and Noreen McEvoy's 200-year-old rambling red-doored house, once home of priests at nearby church of St John the

Baptist. 'A rabbit warren; all ups and downs.' Sitting room ('Victorian in every detail'), dining room; patio; classical/Irish background music. 9 bedrooms (including 3 self-catering suites). B&B €50–€100 per person.

LAHINCH Co. Clare   Map 6:C4

Moy House. *Tel* 00 353 65-708 2800, www.moyhouse.com. Flat, white, tower-topped building (18th-century), converted 'with panache' by owner Antoin O'Looney. Managed by Brid O'Meara. 1 km S of town. Drawing room (honesty bar), library, dining room (Daniel O'Brien is chef; classical/contemporary background music). Popular with golfers (Lahinch has championship course). Children welcomed. 15-acre grounds; access to beach. 9 bedrooms. B&B €92.50–€180 per person. Dinner €55.

LONGFORD Co. Longford   Map 6:C5

Viewmount House, Dublin Road. *Tel* 00 353 43-41919, www. viewmounthouse.com. Adjoining Longford golf course: handsome Georgian house in 3¾-acre segmented gardens: courtyard; Japanese garden (waterways, hill, tunnel, path); upper patio and pond; orchard; herbaceous border; knot garden, etc. Striking colour schemes inside. Owners Beryl and James Kearney recently converted stables to create new *VM* restaurant (beams, wood floor, exposed brickwork, contemporary art; 'easy-listening' background music). Chef Gary O'Hanlon cooks local organic food. Sitting room, reception room, library. Wedding facilities. 13 bedrooms (7 in modern extension; some on ground floor; garden views). B&B €65–€95 per person; D,B&B €115. *V*

RATHMULLAN Co. Donegal   Map 6:B5

Fort Royal. *Tel* 00 353 74-915 8100, www.fortroyalhotel.ie. Rambling white house ½ mile N of village, in 'magnificent grounds' (views over Lough Swilly). Now country guest house run by owner/chef Tim Fletcher. 2 lounges, bar, dining room. No background music. 18-acre gardens and lawns (1 leading down to beach); tennis, pitch-and-putt golf. 11 bedrooms (plus 3 self-catering cottages). B&B €65–€75 per person. Dinner €45 (3 courses).

STRANGFORD Co. Down   Map 6:B6

The Cuan, 6–10 The Square, BT30 7ND. *Tel* 028-4488 1222, www.thecuan.com. A good stopover (ferries to Portaferry): green-painted, flower-decorated building on square in conservation village on S tip of Strangford Lough. Run as licensed guest house by owners Peter and Caroline McErlean. Modern bedrooms. Bar, restaurant (food served all day; seafood specialities); background music; function/conference facilities. Children welcomed. 9 bedrooms. B&B £37.50–£55 per person; D,B&B £53–£70.

THURLES Co. Tipperary   Map 6:C5

Inch House, Inch. *Tel* 00 353 504-51348, www.inchhouse.ie. Egan family's Georgian mansion, run as 'country house and restaurant'. On R498, 4 miles W of Thurles. Period details, tall stained-glass window, antiques. Drawing room, bar, restaurant (Michael Galvin is chef; Irish background music); chapel; conference/function facilities. 2-acre garden on 250-acre farm. Golf, riding, fishing nearby. 5 bedrooms. B&B €65–€75 per person. Dinner €60.

WATERFORD Co. Waterford   Map 6:D5

Foxmount Country House, Passage East Road. *Tel* 00 353 51-874308, www.foxmountcountryhouse.com. On working dairy farm: B&B in David and Margaret Kent's creeper-covered 17th-century house. Traditionally furnished. Drawing room. Garden, herb garden; tennis, table tennis; safe, sandy beaches/golf courses nearby. 3 miles from city. BYO drink. Children welcomed. 4 bedrooms. B&B €55–€65 per person.

WESTPORT Co. Mayo   Map 6:C4

Clew Bay Hotel, James St. *Tel* 00 353 98-28088, www.clewbayhotel.com. Backing onto Carrowbeg river: Darren Madden and Maria Ruddy's cream-painted hotel in town centre. Stylish, contemporary interior. Lounge, bar (lively music), *Madden's* bistro, *Riverside* restaurant ('easy listening' background music; Bart Chicack is chef). Beauty treatments. Wi-Fi. Complimentary access to Westport Leisure Park next door (25-metre swimming pool, sauna, steam room, plunge pool, fitness suite). Children welcomed. 54 bedrooms. B&B €50–€120 per person. Dinner €35.

Alphabetical list of hotels

(S) indicates a Shortlist entry

Hafod Elwy Hall Pentrefoelas 410

Hambleton Hall Hambleton 167

Hambrough Ventnor (S) 520

Hand at Llanarmon Llanarmon Dyffryn Ceiriog 397

Harbour Inn and Restaurant Bowmore (S) 526

Harbourmaster Aberaeron 380

Hard Days Night Liverpool (S) 499

Harington's Bath (S) 471

Harmondsworth Hall Harmondsworth (S) 490

Hart's Nottingham 236

Hartington Hall Buxton (S) 478

Hartwell Hs Aylesbury 81

Harvey's Point Donegal (S) 553

Hastings Hs St Leonards-on-Sea (S) 513

Haymarket London (S) 465

Hazel Bank Rosthwaite 261

Hazelwood Hs Loddiswell 201

Hazlitt's London 64

Headlam Hall Darlington (S) 483

Headland Newquay (S) 507

Heasley Hs North Molton 232

Hebrides Tarbert (S) 539

Heddon's Gate Martinhoe 213

Hell Bay Bryher 116

Henley Bigbury-on-Sea 95

Hermitage Hexham (S) 492

High Road Hs London (S) 465

Highway Inn Burford (S) 477

Hill Hs Ross-on-Wye (S) 511

Hilton Park Clones (S) 552

Hipping Hall Cowan Bridge 136

Hob Green Markington 212

Hodgkinson's Matlock Bath 215

Holbeck Ghyll Windermere 305

Holm Hs Penarth (S) 547

Hope Street Liverpool 200

Horn of Plenty Gulworthy 165

Horse and Groom Bourton-on-the-Hill 102

Howard Edinburgh (S) 529

Howard Arms Ilmington (S) 494

Howard's Hs Teffont Evias 287

Howtown Ullswater 294

Hoxton London (S) 465

Hunters Quay Dunoon (S) 528

Huntingtower Lodge Fort William (S) 530

Ilsington Country Hs Ilsington 183

Inch Hs Thurles (S) 557

Indigo London (S) 466

Ingrams Edinburgh 334

Inn on the Green Cookham Dean (S) 483

Inn on the Lake Ullswater (S) 520

Inn at Lathones Largoward (S) 534

Inn at Whitewell Whitewell 301

Inver Lodge Lochinver 356

Inverlochy Castle Fort William (S) 531

Island Tresco 292

Isle of Eriska Eriska 336

Ivy Hs Lowestoft (S) 500

Jeake's Hs Rye 265

Jesmond Dene Hs Newcastle upon Tyne 230

JJ Gannons Ballinrobe (S) 550

Jolyon's Cardiff 387

JSW Petersfield 246

Judges Yarm 312

Kennard Bath 87

Kensington Hs London (S) 466

Kilberry Inn Kilberry 347

Kilcamb Lodge Strontian 370

[2010]

To: *The Good Hotel Guide*, Freepost PAM 2931, London W11 4BR

NOTE: No stamps needed in UK, but letters posted outside the UK should be addressed to 50 Addison Avenue, London W11 4QP, England, and stamped normally. Unless asked not to, we shall assume that we may publish your name. If you would like more report forms please tick ☐

Name of Hotel_____

Address _____

_____

Date of most recent visit   Duration of visit
☐ New recommendation   ☐ Comment on existing entry
Report:

Please continue overleaf

I am not connected directly or indirectly with the management or proprietors

Signed _____

Name (CAPITALS PLEASE)

Address _____

_____

Email address _____

[2010]

To: *The Good Hotel Guide*, Freepost PAM 2931, London W11 4BR

NOTE: No stamps needed in UK, but letters posted outside the UK should be addressed to 50 Addison Avenue, London W11 4QP, England, and stamped normally. Unless asked not to, we shall assume that we may publish your name. If you would like more report forms please tick ☐

Name of Hotel_____

Address _____

_____

Date of most recent visit   Duration of visit

☐ New recommendation   ☐ Comment on existing entry

Report:

Please continue overleaf

I am not connected directly or indirectly with the management or proprietors

Signed _____

Name (CAPITALS PLEASE)

Address _____

_____

Email address _____

[2010]

To: *The Good Hotel Guide*, Freepost PAM 2931, London W11 4BR

NOTE: No stamps needed in UK, but letters posted outside the UK should be addressed to 50 Addison Avenue, London W11 4QP, England, and stamped normally. Unless asked not to, we shall assume that we may publish your name. If you would like more report forms please tick ☐

Name of Hotel_____

Address _____

_____

Date of most recent visit   Duration of visit
☐ New recommendation   ☐ Comment on existing entry
Report:

Please continue overleaf

I am not connected directly or indirectly with the management or proprietors

Signed _____

Name (CAPITALS PLEASE)

Address _____

_____

Email address _____

British Isles maps

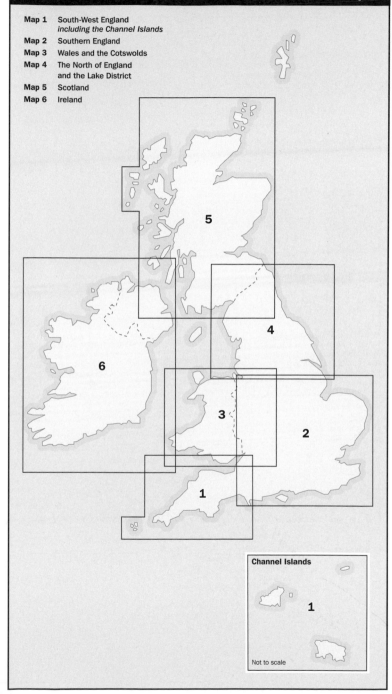

5

4

6

3

2

1

Channel Islands

1

Not to scale

1 South-West England

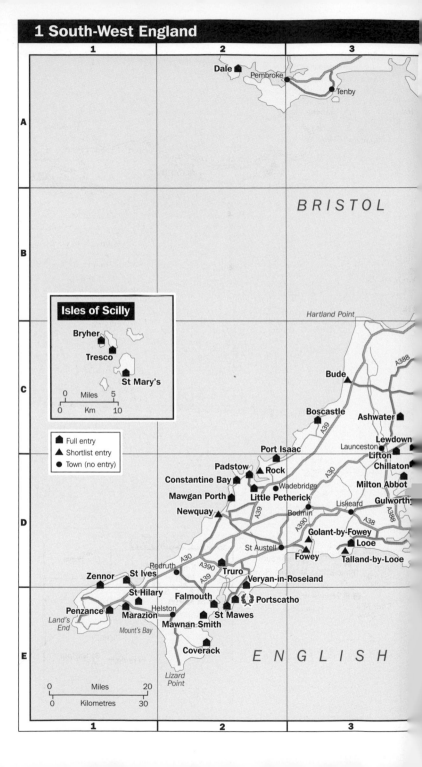

| | **1** | **2** | **3** |

A

Dale
Pembroke
Tenby

B

BRISTOL

Isles of Scilly

Bryher
Tresco
St Mary's

0   Miles   5
0   Km   10

C

Hartland Point

Bude

Boscastle

Ashwater

Lewdown
Launceston
Lifton
Chillaton

A388

A39

Port Isaac

■ Full entry
▲ Shortlist entry
● Town (no entry)

Padstow ▲ Rock
Constantine Bay
Mawgan Porth
Newquay ▲
Little Petherick
Wadebridge

A30

Milton Abbot

Liskeard
Gulworth

A390
A39
Bodmin

A38
A388

Golant-by-Fowey
Looe
Fowey
Talland-by-Looe

St Austell

D

Redruth
A30
A390
A39
Truro

Zennor   St Ives
St Hilary
Veryan-in-Roseland

Falmouth
Portscatho

Penzance
Marazion
Helston
St Mawes

Land's End
Mount's Bay
Mawnan Smith

Coverack

ENGLISH

E

0   Miles   20
0   Kilometres   30

Lizard Point

| | **1** | **2** | **3** |

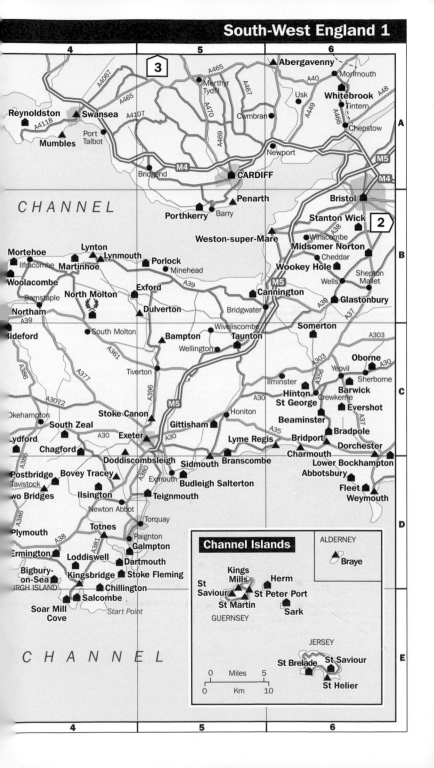

4 **5** **6**

3

A465 A465 Abergavenny A40 Monmouth

Merthyr A467 Usk A48
Tydfil A470

Reynoldston Swansea A449 Whitebrook
A4118 A4107 Cwmbran Tintern
Mumbles Port A469 A466 Chepstow
Talbot Newport

Bridgend M4 M5

CARDIFF M5
M4

A

CHANNEL Penarth Bristol

Porthkerry Barry Stanton Wick 2

Weston-super-Mare Winscombe

Mortehoe Lynton Midsomer Norton
Ilfracombe Lynmouth Porlock Cheddar
Woolacombe Martinhoe Minehead Wookey Hole Shepton
Barnstaple North Molton Exford A39 Wells Mallet
Northam Dulverton Cannington Glastonbury
Bideford South Molton Bridgwater A39 A37

B

A386 Bampton Wiveliscombe Somerton
A361 Taunton A303
Okehampton A3072 Tiverton Wellington Ilminster Oborne A30
South Zeal A396 M5 Honiton Yeovil Sherborne
Lydford Stoke Canon A30 Hinton Crewkerne Barwick
Chagford Exeter Gittisham St George Evershot
Doddiscombsleigh A35 Beaminster A37
Postbridge Bovey Tracey Sidmouth Lyme Regis Bradpole
Tavistock Exmouth Branscombe Bridport Dorchester
wo Bridges Ilsington Budleigh Salterton Charmouth
Plymouth Teignmouth Lower Bockhampton
Newton Abbot Abbotsbury
Torquay Fleet
Totnes Paignton Weymouth

C

D

Ermington Galmpton
Bigbury- Loddiswell Dartmouth
on-Sea Kingsbridge Stoke Fleming
JRGH ISLAND Chillington
Salcombe
Soar Mill Start Point
Cove

CHANNEL

E

Channel Islands

ALDERNEY

Braye

Kings
Mills Herm
St St Peter Port
Saviour St Martin
Sark
GUERNSEY

JERSEY

St Brelade St Saviour
St Helier

0 Miles 5

0 Km 10

4 **5** **6**

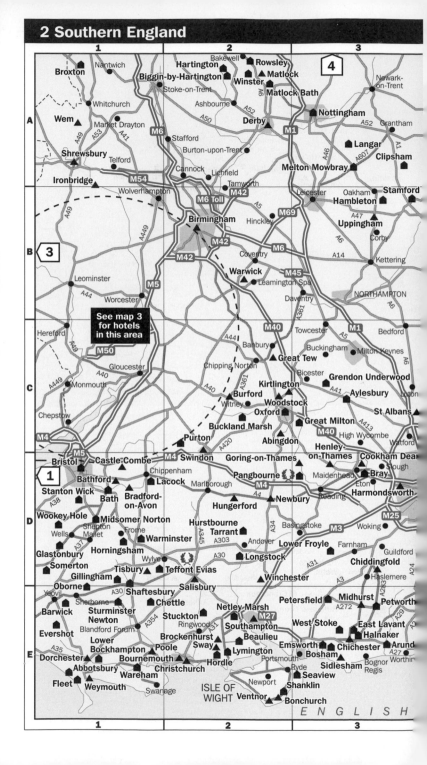

4

Broxton
Nantwich
Whitchurch
Wem
Market Drayton
Shrewsbury
Telford
Ironbridge
M54
Wolverhampton

Hartington
Bakewell
Rowsley
Biggin-by-Hartington
Winster
Matlock
Stoke-on-Trent
Matlock Bath
Ashbourne
A52
Derby
M1
Nottingham
Newark-on-Trent
A52
Grantham
Langar
Clipsham
Burton-upon-Trent
Melton Mowbray
A607
Cannock
Lichfield
Tamworth
Stamford
Leicester
Oakham
Hambleton
M6 Toll
A5
M69
Uppingham
Birmingham
Hinckley
Corby
M42
Coventry
M6
Kettering
M42
Warwick
Leamington Spa
A14
Stafford

A
B
C
D
E

3
Leominster
M5
Worcester
See map 3 for hotels in this area
Daventry
NORTHAMPTON
A6

Hereford
M50
Gloucester
A40
Chipping Norton
A44
Banbury
Great Tew
Towcester
A5
Buckingham
Bedford
Milton Keynes
A6
Monmouth
A449
Burford
Kirtlington
Bicester
Grendon Underwood
Chepstow
Witney
Woodstock
A41
Aylesbury
Luton
M4
Oxford
Great Milton
St Albans
M5
Buckland Marsh
Abingdon
M40
High Wycombe
Watford
Purton
A420
Henley-on-Thames
Castle Combe
M4
Swindon
Goring-on-Thames
Cookham Dean
Bristol
Pangbourne
Bray
Slough
Bathford
Chippenham
Maidenhead
Harmondsworth
Stanton Wick
Lacock
Marlborough
M4
Eton
Bath
Bradford-on-Avon
Newbury
Reading
M25
Wookey Hole
A38
Hungerford
A4
Basingstoke
Woking
Shepton Mallet
Frome
Midsomer Norton
Hurstbourne Tarrant
M3
Wells
Warminster
A345
A34
Glastonbury
Horningsham
Andover
Lower Froyle
Farnham
Guildford
Somerton
Wylye
A303
Longstock
A31
A24
Gillingham
Tisbury
Teffont Evias
A30
Chiddingfold
Oborne
Shaftesbury
Winchester
A3
Haslemere
Yeovil
Sherborne
Chettle
Salisbury
Petersfield
Midhurst
Petworth
Barwick
Sturminster Newton
A354
Stuckton
Netley Marsh
West Stoke
East Lavant
Evershot
Blandford Forum
Ringwood
M27
Southampton
Halnaker
Chichester
Arund
Lower Bockhampton
Poole
Brockenhurst
Beaulieu
Emsworth
Bosham
Dorchester
Abbotsbury
Wareham
Christchurch
Sway
Lymington
Hordle
Portsmouth
Sidlesham
Bognor Regis
Worthi
Fleet
Weymouth
Swanage
Ryde
Seaview
A27
Newport
ISLE OF WIGHT
Ventnor
Shanklin
Bonchurch
E N G L I S H

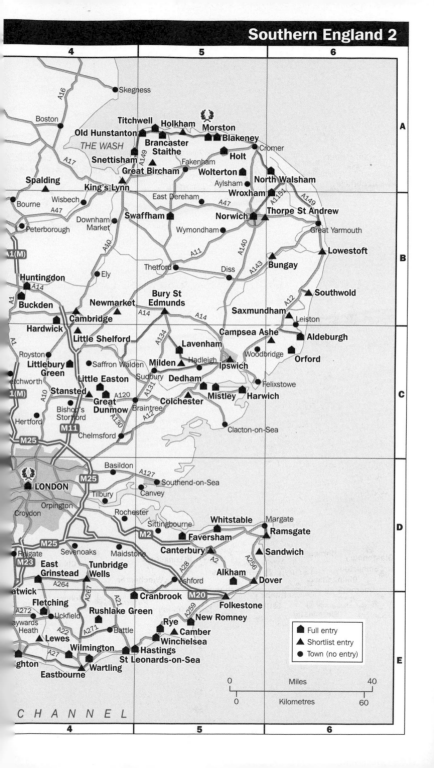

4   **5**   **6**

A16

Skegness

Boston

Titchwell Holkham Morston
Old Hunstanton   Blakeney
A17 *THE WASH* Brancaster
Staithe   Cromer
Snettisham Fakenham Holt
Great Bircham Wolterton
Spalding North Walsham
Wisbech Aylsham
King's Lynn Wroxham
Bourne
A47 East Dereham
Peterborough Downham A47
Market Swaffham Norwich Thorpe St Andrew
A10 Great Yarmouth
Huntingdon Wymondham
A14 Ely A11 A140 A143 Lowestoft
Buckden Thetford Diss Bungay
A1
Newmarket Bury St Southwold
Edmunds A14 A12
Cambridge A14 Saxmundham
Hardwick Leiston
Little Shelford Campsea Ashe
Royston A134 Lavenham Aldeburgh
Littlebury Saffron Walden Milden Hadleigh Woodbridge
Green Sudbury Ipswich Orford
Little Easton Dedham
Stansted Mistley Harwich
A120 Great Braintree Colchester Felixstowe
Bishop's Dunmow A12
Hertford Stortford A130
M11 Chelmsford Clacton-on-Sea

M25

Basildon A127
LONDON Southend-on-Sea
Orpington M25 Tilbury Canvey
Croydon Rochester
Reigate Sevenoaks Maidstone Whitstable Margate
M25 M2 Faversham Ramsgate
M23 East Tunbridge Canterbury Sandwich
Grinstead Wells A2 A256
Gatwick A264 A28 Alkham
Fletching A267 Ashford Dover
A272 Uckfield Rushlake Green A259 Folkestone
Haywards A22 Cranbrook M20
Heath A271 Battle New Romney
Lewes Rye
Wilmington A27 Camber
Brighton Hastings Winchelsea
Wartling St Leonards-on-Sea
Eastbourne

C H A N N E L

4   **5**   **6**

A B C D E

Full entry
Shortlist entry
Town (no entry)

0 Miles 40
0 Kilometres 60

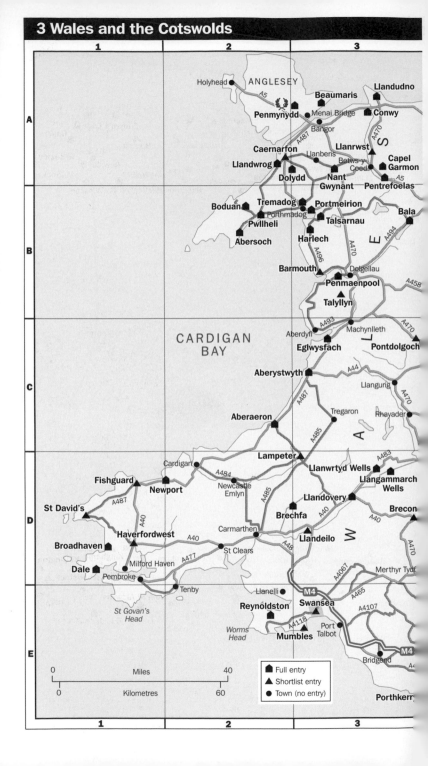

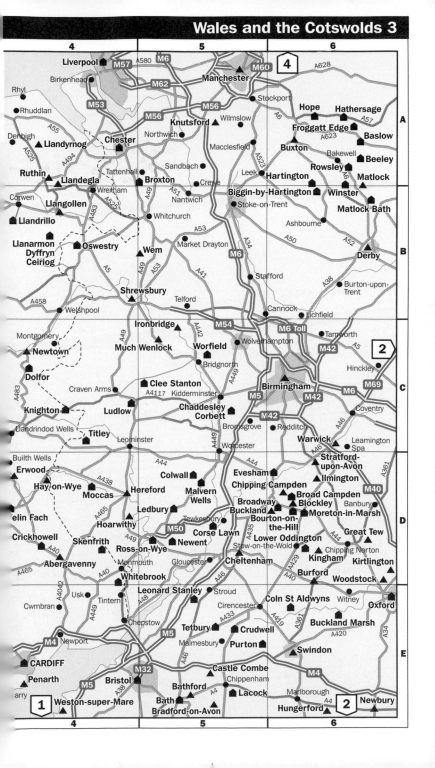

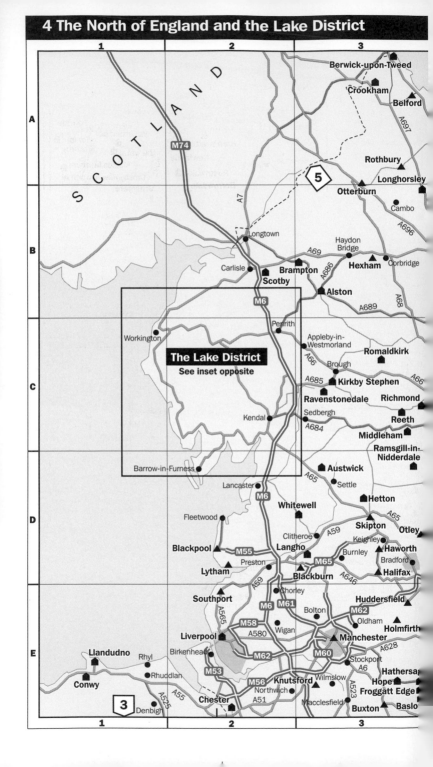

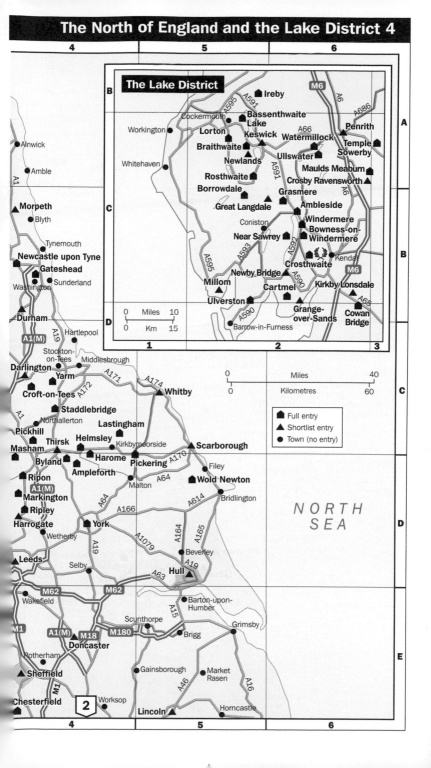

The Lake District

Ireby
Cockermouth
Bassenthwaite Lake
Lorton
Keswick
Watermillock
Workington
Braithwaite
Ullswater
Penrith
Temple Sowerby
Whitehaven
Newlands
Maulds Meaburn
Rosthwaite
Crosby Ravensworth
Borrowdale
Grasmere
Great Langdale
Ambleside
Coniston
Windermere
Bowness-on-Windermere
Near Sawrey
Kendal
Crosthwaite
Newby Bridge
Millom
Cartmel
Kirkby Lonsdale
Ulverston
Grange-over-Sands
Cowan Bridge
Barrow-in-Furness

0 Miles 10
0 Km 15

Alnwick
Amble
Morpeth
Blyth
Tynemouth
Newcastle upon Tyne
Gateshead
Washington
Sunderland
Durham
Hartlepool
Stockton-on-Tees
Middlesbrough
Darlington
Yarm
Croft-on-Tees
Whitby
Staddlebridge
Northallerton
Lastingham
Pickhill
Helmsley
Masham
Thirsk
Kirkbymoorside
Scarborough
Byland
Harome
Pickering
Filey
Ampleforth
Malton
Wold Newton
Ripon
Bridlington
Markington
Ripley
York
Harrogate
Wetherby
Beverley
Leeds
Selby
Hull
Wakefield
Barton-upon-Humber
Scunthorpe
Grimsby
Doncaster
Brigg
Rotherham
Sheffield
Gainsborough
Market Rasen
Chesterfield
Worksop
Lincoln
Horncastle

NORTH SEA

0 Miles 40
0 Kilometres 60

Full entry
Shortlist entry
Town (no entry)

5 Scotland

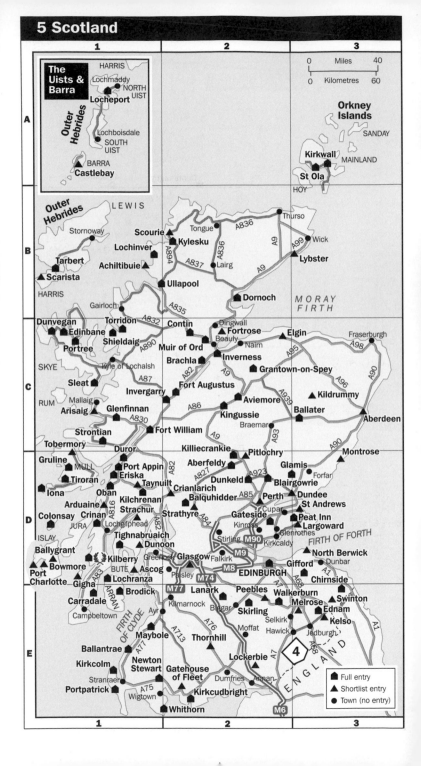

The Uists & Barra

HARRIS
Lochmaddy
NORTH UIST
Locheport
Outer Hebrides
Lochboisdale
SOUTH UIST
BARRA
Castlebay

Orkney Islands
SANDAY
Kirkwall
MAINLAND
St Ola
HOY

0   Miles   40
0   Kilometres   60

Outer Hebrides
L E W I S
Stornoway
Scourie   Tongue   A836   Thurso
Tarbert   **Kylesku**   A836   A9   Wick
Lochinver   A894   A837   Lairg   A99
Achiltibuie   **Lybster**
Scarista
HARRIS   **Ullapool**   A9
Dornoch
Gairloch   A835   M O R A Y   F I R T H

Dunvegan   Torridon   A832   Contin   Dingwall   Elgin   Fraserburgh
Edinbane   Shieldaig   A890   **Fortrose**   Beauly   Nairn   A95   A98
Portree   Muir of Ord   Inverness   A90
SKYE   Kyle of Lochalsh   **Brachla**   A82   **Grantown-on-Spey**   A96
Sleat   A87   **Fort Augustus**   A9   **Kildrummy**
RUM   Mallaig   **Invergarry**   A86   Aviemore   A939   Ballater   Aberdeen
Arisaig   Glenfinnan   A830   Kingussie   A93
Strontian   **Fort William**   Braemar   A90
Tobermory   Duror   A9   Montrose
Gruline   MULL   Killiecrankie   Pitlochry   Glamis
Tiroran   Port Appin   Aberfeldy   A827   Forfar
Eriska   A82   Dunkeld   A923   Blairgowrie
Iona   Taynuilt   Crianlarich   A85   Perth   Dundee
Arduaine   Oban   Kilchrenan   Balquhidder   Gateside   St Andrews
Colonsay   Strachur   A816   Strathyre   A84   Kinross   Peat Inn
Crinan   Lochgilphead   A82   Stirling   M90   Largoward
JURA   Tighnabruaich   Glenrothes   FIRTH OF FORTH
ISLAY   Dunoon   Kirkcaldy
Ballygrant   Kilberry   Greenock   Glasgow   Falkirk   North Berwick
Bowmore   BUTE   Ascog   Paisley   M9   Dunbar
Port Charlotte   Lochranza   M8   EDINBURGH   Gifford
Gigha   ARRAN   Brodick   M77   Lanark   Peebles   Chirnside
Carradale   Ayr   Kilmarnock   M74   Walkerburn   Swinton
Campbeltown   Biggar   Skirling   Melrose   Ednam
FIRTH OF CLYDE   Selkirk   Kelso
Maybole   A713   A76   Moffat   Hawick   Jedburgh   A1
Ballantrae   A77   Thornhill   **4**   A68
Kirkcolm   Newton Stewart   Lockerbie   A7   ENGLAND
Stranraer   A75   Gatehouse of Fleet   Dumfries   Annan
Portpatrick   Wigtown   Kirkcudbright   M6
Whithorn

Legend:
- Full entry (square)
- Shortlist entry (triangle)
- Town (no entry) (circle)

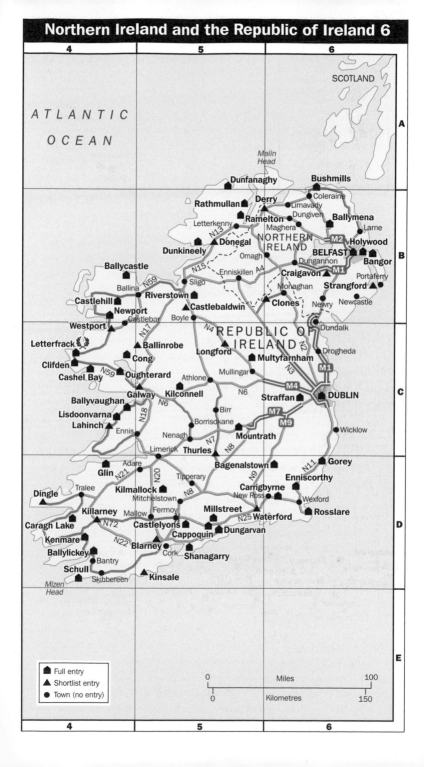

Northern Ireland and the Republic of Ireland 6

SCOTLAND

ATLANTIC OCEAN

Malin Head

Dunfanaghy **Bushmills**

Rathmullan **Derry** Coleraine

Limavady

Letterkenny **Ramelton** Dungiven **Ballymena**

Maghera Larne

Donegal NORTHERN **Holywood**

Dunkineely IRELAND **BELFAST** **Bangor**

Omagh Dungannon

Ballycastle **N15** Enniskillen A4 **Craigavon** Portaferry

Sligo Monaghan **Strangford**

Ballina **Riverstown** Newry Newcastle

Castlehill **Castlebaldwin** **Clones**

Newport Boyle

Castlebar **N4** **REPUBLIC OF** Dundalk

Westport **IRELAND** **N2**

Letterfrack **Ballinrobe** **Longford** Drogheda

Clifden **Cong** **Multyfarnham** **M1**

Athlone Mullingar **N3**

Cashel Bay **Oughterard**

Galway **Kilconnell** **M4** **DUBLIN**

Ballyvaughan N6 Birr **Straffan**

Lisdoonvarna Borrisokane **M7**

Lahinch Ennis **M9**

Nenagh **Mountrath** Wicklow

Limerick **Thurles** N8

Glin Adare **Bagenalstown** **Gorey**

N21 Tipperary **N11**

Kilmallock N9 **Enniscorthy**

Dingle Tralee Mitchelstown **Carrigbyrne**

Killarney Mallow Fermoy New Ross Wexford

Caragh Lake N72 **Castlelyons** **Millstreet** **Rosslare**

Kenmare **Cappoquin** **Waterford** **N25**

Ballylickey N22 **Blarney** **Dungarvan**

Bantry Cork **Shanagarry**

Schull Skibbereen **Kinsale**

Mizen Head

Full entry Shortlist entry Town (no entry)

0 Miles 100

0 Kilometres 150

The truly independent guide

This is the leading independent guide to hotels in Great Britain and Ireland. Hotels cannot buy their entry as they do in most rival guides. No money changes hands, and the editors and inspectors do not accept free hospitality on their anonymous visits to hotels. The only vested interest is that of the reader seeking impartial advice to find a good hotel.

Our hotels are as independent as we are. Most are small, family owned and family run. They are places of character where the owners and their staff spend time looking after their guests, rather than reporting to an area manager. We look for a warm welcome, with flexible service.

Diversity is the key to our selection. Grand country houses are listed alongside simple B&Bs. Some of our favourite places may not have the full range of hotel-type facilities. We include a few chain hotels, especially in the larger cities: each one will have met our criteria of high standards of service.

Our website works in tandem with the printed *Guide*. It carries the entries for many, but not all, of our selected hotels (unlike the printed *Guide*, hotels pay a small fee for inclusion on the website). It has pictures for each entry, and a comprehensive search engine.

Our readers play a crucial role by reporting on existing entries as well as recommending new discoveries. The editors make a balanced judgment based on these reports, backed where necessary by an anonymous inspection. Reader reports, written on the forms at the back of the book or sent by email, bring our entries to life, and give the *Guide* a unique 'word-of-mouth' quality. Many correspondents join our Readers' Club (see page 10).

Annual updates give the *Guide* an added edge. A significant number of hotels are omitted every year and many new ones are added. We drop a hotel or demote it to the Shortlist if there has been a change of owner unless reports after the change are positive, if this year's reports are negative, or in rare cases where there has been no feedback.